# Fort Benton
## WORLD'S INNERMOST PORT

by Joel Overholser

# Fort Benton
## WORLD'S INNERMOST PORT

by Joel Overholser

*Joel Raymond and Beulah Fuller Overholser
came from Iowa in 1913
to homestead in Chouteau County
and spent the final years of their lives
in Fort Benton.*

*They came to love Fort Benton and
its rich and varied history,
as has their son.*

Copyright © 1987 by River & Plains Society

Second Printing 2000

All rights reserved, including the right to reproduce this book or parts thereof, in any form, except for the inclusion of brief quotations in a review.

Library of Congress Number 87-90710

ISBN 0-937959-27-8

Cover design by DD Dowden

Published by: River & Plains Society
Box 262, Fort Benton, MT 59442

This book is a collection of Mr. Joel Overholser's notes accumulated over his years of research and published as such.

Rettig Publishing, Inc./Mountaineer Printing
Big Sandy, Montana 59520

# Introduction

This is the story of Fort Benton to the 1889 statehood period, when the most isolated transportation center in the west lost its one time importance. On the northwestern frontier, Fort Benton had occupied a position similar to that of Santa Fe in the southwest and Denver in the Central Rockies, all of vast importance to their areas during the influx of whites.

"World's Innermost Port" is indicative both of the distance from salt water and of the difficulties the "Mountain Steamboats" had in running the 2385 miles of a dangerous and tricky Missouri River to deliver the supplies that contributed vastly to building Montana, the final frontier of the contiguous 48 states.

St. Louis rivermen called them "Mountain Steamboats," reckoning it about 3000 miles to within eyeshot of the Rockies, although government engineers later measured across the meanders and came up with 2385. Add over 1100 miles from salt water to St. Louis—the Amazon is navigable by powered craft somewhat further today, but those miles were unused during the period covered, confirming "Innermost."

"Birthplace of Montana" has been claimed by Bentonites for more than 60 years, we believe this account confirms the claim.

The steamboat Yellowstone opened the Missouri to the Montana line in 1832; it was not until 1859 that the Chippewa ran out of fuel 14 river miles below Fort Benton, next year with the Key West the boat arrived at the "Innermost Port." Two years later the Montana gold rush exploded, and down the Missouri went about three fourths of the $100 million (200 tons) of gold produced through 1869.

Most of the pioneer Northwestern Plains trails hinged on Fort Benton, the Mullan (Military) road connecting heads of navigation on Missouri and Columbia-Snake the most striking. Another, the overland trail from Minnesota, was originally in part a wagon route opened by American Fur from Fort Union. Supply trails also ran south to rich southern Montana diggings, and later into the Yellowstone valley. In those pioneer days, virtually all trails ran to or from Fort Benton.

The head of navigation was also an international port, Alberta and portions of adjoining provinces were for more than a decade even more dependent on supplies off the steamboats, so the Whoop Up Trail to the whisky forts and the route to later Fort Walsh were heavily traveled even before arrival of the North West Mounted Police in 1874. After Hudson's Bay Co. sold its land and legal rights to the new Dominion of Canada in 1869, first adventurers, then legitimate merchants from Fort Benton all but drove HBC north to the Arctic Ocean, and it required arrival of the Canadian Pacific in 1883 to loosen the trade ties.

In the same year, the Northern Pacific ended Fort Benton's grip on the trade of central Montana. As to the place's pivotal position, at the time five locally owned stage lines ran out of Fort Benton.

Over the years of navigation to Fort Benton, 1860-90, Missouri River steamboats brought more than 160,000 tons of freight into Montana, took down about 35,000 tons, and transported far more than the 40,000 passengers shown in the commerce table. All but a fraction went through Fort Benton. Down cargoes included 750,000 buffalo robes, half that many wolf skins, valuable furs, and at least 120 tons of gold (more likely 150 tons) worth more than $1 billion at today's prices, as well as heavy shipments of silver ore concentrates, even some copper sent to a smelter in Swansea, Wala, as well as horses and cattle and millions of pounds of wool.

Fort Benton was the only one of dozens of fur trading posts to become a permanent Montana community, the oldest continuously occupied white settlement in Montana (Stevensville, dating its history from the 1841 St. Mary's Mission, will find a few weeks gap between departure of the priests and start of Fort Owen.)

First half of this book chronologically follows the pre-history and fur trade of the Fort Benton area, and of the steamboats to the end of their usefulness. Related articles are included here, on gold shipments, early Yellowstone River navigation, the Cow Island Trail to the major low water freight drop at the island, freighting, stages, and pony express and nonpowered craft. The second part covers the businesses, institutions, community, minorities, Indians, the army role, agriculture, Canadian connections, Fort Benton's founder and the city's legends. These are not in time scale.

This book is the result of more than 50 years of gradual accumulation of historical material, an effort speeded after retirement as editor of the River Press in 1981.

For many readers, most sources will be fairly evident. From the first issue of the Monana Post in August 1864 at Virginia City, through Helena's Radiator and Herald to 1875, then Fort Benton's Benton Record and River Press, newspapers have been heavily utilized as sources.

The period of the local area fur trade in 1860 relies almost completely on James H. Bradley in the Montana Historical Society Contributions, plus the Lewis & Clark Journals, David Wishart and John Sunder, and the Maximilian and Fr. Point journals.

Sources are as evident for the early years of steamboat navigation, from the fall of 1864 newspapers are chief sources, especially for steamboat arrivals. Other sources are normally identified in the text.

Freighting relies on numerous sources, most interesting the Alexander Toponce reminiscences and those of Mike Connelly. Early stage and express notes are chiefly from Madsen, the Wells Fargo history room and Walter Burke recollections of the start of the stage line to Billings. The fiasco of the Northern Overland Mail came from the papers, as did much on nonpowered craft.

# Acknowledgments

*O*ver the years, hundreds of persons have sought information, usually concerning ancestry, from the River Press. Many might be surprised to learn they contributed more to local history than they received in help.

Historians are special, the writer has found, with almost as many interests and approaches as their numbers. One attribute nearly all share, they are generous with help on any reasonable plea, from a vital bit to a massive contribution.

Anyone interested in history who ever asked help of Anne McDonnell at the Montana Historical Society in the 1930s and 1940s has reason to remember her with gratitude; her footnoting of the Fort Benton and Fort Sarpy Journals is an absolute basic to an understanding of the Montana fur posts. From Mrs. McDonnell to Dave Walter, the writer owes very much to MHS librarians.

Hugh Dempsey of the Glenbow Museum in Calgary has generously supplied a helping hand in efforts to reconstruct the time when Canada's North West Territories were emerging from the fur trade period. Canadian historians, busily reconstructing an as yet murky past, have been welcome visitors, appreciative of what might be found in Fort Benton, and returning information in generous measure. Far beyond a century after, the across the border ties with Fort Benton persist.

A vast area in early Montana history would still be in limbo, had it not been for the inquiring mind of Lt. James H. Bradley, stationed at Fort Benton and Fort Shaw until his death at the Big Hole in August 1877. Fortunately his youthful widow preserved the resulting manuscripts and a major portion of the early history of Fort Benton.

Especially valuable and thoroughly thumbed were the works of four authors: Merrill Burlingame's "Montana Frontier" for a balanced overlook of the early Montana scene, John Sunder on the complicated events of the fur and robe trade along the Missouri, William Lass for the background to the steamboats in the Fort Benton trade, and of course Paul Sharp for one of the finest regional histories, which thoroughly explains the Fort Benton traffic into Canada.

Dr. E.B. Trail of Berger, Missouri, from 1935 guided the writer in learning the role of the Mountain Steamboats, and was a generous donor of valued pictures, river lore, history and background over many years. It was the writer's pleasure to show Dr. Trail the Fort Benton levee one summer evening—he felt he trod holy ground, his daughter wrote after his death.

James R. Gilmore, descendant of steamboating Coulson captains, and T. T. Anderson of steamboat pilots and maternally from Wm. Waddell of the great freighting company, contributed useful data, as did several other descendants of old time rivermen.

There are many more. Some, and apologies to those overlooked, John Lepley of Fort Benton, Dave Walter of MHS, Jack Holterman of West Glacier, LeRoy Anderson of Chinook, Dorothy Ege of Great Falls, J. C. Foster of Sequim, WA, Howard Gerard of Bellingham, WA, James E. Murphy of Kalispell, Warren McGee of Livingston, Maynard Stephens of Ronan. And not least, Georgia Fooks of Lethbridge, Margaret Kennedy and Frank Tester of Calgary.

Because so much of early Montana history involves Fort Benton, the contributions of the River Press deserve mention. One of the owners, Wm. A. Johnstone, educator, one time acting head of Montana State University, a Fort Benton native and grandson of W. K. Harber of the River Press 1884-1922, writes: "It is a memorial to those who have been at the River Press in over 100 years and who have done so much to preserve the history and inform the public of the rich heritage." The writer knows, at the Press he was involved in special historical sections of the paper in 1926, 1937, 1946, 1960, 1976, and 1980. One in particular, on return from overseas early in 1946 his immediate assignment was to prepare a 16 page historical addition. In none of these was the usual advertising solicitation made, although a few local firms insisted that related advertising be included.

# Table of Contents

| | |
|---:|:---|
| v | Introduction |
| vii | Acknowledgements |
| ix | Table of Contents |
| 1 | Opening Blackfeet Trade |
| 19 | One Fur Post Survives |
| 33 | World's Innermost Port |
| 45 | Golden Years on Missouri |
| 75 | Across "The Medicine Line" |
| 93 | Tough Town Comes of Age |
| 115 | Decline of an Inland Port |
| 131 | Final River Echoes |
| 143 | Lines and Combines |
| 145 | The Golden Highway |
| 153 | On the Yellowstone |
| 157 | Cow Island Trail |
| 163 | On Dusty, Muddy Trails |
| 189 | Stages Weren't Pullmans |
| 195 | Montana's Pony Express |
| 197 | Keelboats and Mackinaws |
| 202 | Map |
| 203 | Pictures |
| 225 | A Reluctant Civic Body |
| 229 | Fort Benton Businesses |
| 261 | Life and Services |
| 279 | Cooperation Was Keynote |
| 287 | Minorities Share Story |
| 299 | The Original Montanans |
| 321 | Grass Replaces Gold |
| 339 | The Military Presence |
| 345 | Firewater On Frontier |
| 355 | Canadian Connections |
| 371 | Peacemaker Culbertson |
| 379 | Fort Benton Legends |
| 393 | Bibliography |
| 395 | Index |

# Opening Blackfeet Trade
## From Canada, By Land

Many Americans probably believe that the portentous Lewis and Clark Expedition of 1804-1806 was first across the continent, at least north of Mexico. Not so.

The British presence began in northeast America in 1668, with the first post on Hudson's Bay, north of French settlement along the St. Lawrence. In 1670 Charles II awarded a royal charter to "The Governor and Company of Adventurers of England Trading into Hudson's Bay." So began the enduring concern later known largely by initials HBC, stated by the impious to mean "Here Before Christ." Their traders for decades fought off sporadic raids by French, survived, and began to push inland, but somewhat complacently in view of the charter which in effect gave them the wild lands west of Hudson's Bay.

HBC outlasted the rival French, expunged from the mainland by the treaty which ended the, in America, French and Indian War. The French ceded Louisiana to Spain as a means of placing the vast territory west of the Mississippi in the hands of a friendlier power. (Napoleon at the height of his power forced a secret retrocession, a direct consequence of which became the Lewis and Clark Expedition.

Hudson's Bay Co. was not left unchallenged after 1763, however. Independent fur traders with a strong leavening of Scots teamed with French woodsmen in following the by then known paths via the Great Lakes into the interior. By 1787 the great North West Company had come into being. Nor' Westers out of Montreal were incredible travelers. By 1789 the company had a post on Lake Athabaska called Fort Chipewyan. A look at the map shows this to be about 550 air line miles north and slightly east of Fort Benton. From Fort Chipewyan, in the spring of 1789, Alexander Mackenzie, one of the world's great geographers, sought the Pacific Ocean and legendary Northwest Passage, down the Slave River to Great Slave Lake, thence down a broad river flowing north that now bears his name. But to Mackenzie's disappointment, it was the frozen northern ocean.

His bosses in Montreal were not too impressed. In 1793 Mackenzie tried again, up Peace River and over the Rockies, down what were later McGregor and Fraser rivers to a point where he had to portage again to cross the Coastal Range, then down the Bella Coola to the sea. At the river's mouth he proudly scrawled in vermilion and grease, "Alexander Mackenzie, from Canada by land, the 22nd of July 1793." (The intrepid voyageur meant the Province of Canada, the name for a part of the eastern settlements.)

That journey set the stage for legitimate British claims to what became the Oregon Territory.

### Americans Move Westward

The new United States had already staked a claim to that area of the Northwest. May 12, 1792, Robert Gray, commanding the ship Columbia out of Boston, entered the mouth of the great river of the west, a year, 2 months and 10 days before Mackenzie's arrival on the west coast. Gray named the river after his ship and by discovery established a legitimate claim to the land drained by it. After another war, and British-American bickering for four decades, the two discoveries became the basis for the compromise settlement that divided the Northwest along the 49th parallel, save for Vancouver Island, a sop which enterprising Canadians had earned for Britain.

## Ceremony of Three Flags

French and Spaniards, who had each controlled vast Louisiana, from St. Louis had been working their way along westward rivers in a lucrative but dangerous fur trade for years before Napoleon sold Louisiana to the fledgling United States in 1803.

Meriwether Lewis, William Clark and their Corps of Discovery arrived in the St. Louis area in late fall of 1803, spending the winter on the eastern shore pending formal transfer of the new lands which doubled the size of the nation.

Formal transfer of Upper Louisiana was on March 9, 1804. At the time the Spanish officials were still in nominal control. So the Spanish flag was raised, then lowered, and in recognition of French sovereignty that nation's flag was raised, then lowered, and finally the flag of the United States raised—all with appropriate ceremonies.

Almost casually, on May 14, 1804, the Lewis & Clark expedition left on their epic trip. President Thomas Jefferson's charge to Meriwether Lewis had included, "Explore the Missouri River and such principal streams of it as...may offer the most direct and practicable water communications across this contingent, for the purposes of commerce." (American ships, as evidenced by Gray's 1792 discovery, were already eyeing the rich trade of the Orient.) The water communications charge was to be realized, with Fort Benton as a pivotal point, but only after more than half a century.

The party made its way by keelboat and pirogue to the Mandan villages in present North Dakota. This portion of the trip covered a part of the Missouri fairly well known to Indian traders out of the St.Louis area. In fact, their journals note the presence of a number of traders, from both Louisiana and Canada. Their winter among the Mandans, where they had arrived late in October, was spent in gathering all the information possible about the further reaches of the Missouri River, from Indians and the scattering of whites and part bloods.

It was there that they engaged the services of Toussaint Charbonneau as an interpreter, who would be accompanied by a youthful wife, Sacagawea of the Shoshones, who had been kidnapped at an early age. Her knowledge of edible roots and later of the country of her tribe would prove valuable to the expedition.

February 11, 1805, Sacagawea gave birth to Jean Baptiste, nicknamed by the party "Pomp." The mother would earn a place in American folklore, the son have a strange and useful life. The father, whose role is often derided in tales of the great expedition, was age 46 at his joining, and he survived a trip which taxed the powers of much younger men. He lived to a ripe old age on the frontier, further evidence of superior powers of survival.

April 7, 1805, the Captains sent down a small party in a boat loaded with specimens, reports and dispatches, receipt of which greatly pleased the president later, and the main party headed into the unknown. They reached the mouth of the Yellowstone, barely inside of later North Dakota, on April 26. In later Montana, they found game in abundance as they made their toilsome way up the Missouri, and of white (grizzly) bears more than plenty. May 20 the expedition passed the mouth of a river they named the Muscle Shell, a misspelling that continued for 60 odd years, and began passing rapids and landmarks which in later years became familiar indeed to steamboatmen.

The Judith (named for Julia Hancock, whom Clark later married) was reached

May 29. Two days later Lewis wrote of the White Rocks, "elegant ranges of lofty freestone buildings, having their parapets well stocked with statuary...as we passed on it seemed as if those scenes of visionary enchantment would never have an end." (This area remains the longest almost unaltered reach of the Missouri.)

To this point the larger rivers flowing into the Missouri were no surprise—their Indian informants had described and approximately located the larger rivers. But June 3rd the Corps of Discovery halted at the mouth of a large river (which Lewis soon named Maria's, the apostrophe later dropped). At the date and season the Marias was obviously in flood stage, and muddy, while the other had a clearer volume. The first river was one which none of their informants in the Mandan villages had mentioned. Which was the way west? Until June 11 they camped near the later site of Fort Piegan, while Lewis headed a small party going up the Marias, Clark one up the Missouri. (Clark, Sgt. Patrick Gass, Reuben and Joseph Fields, George Shannon and York apparently camped on the Fort Benton bottom the evening of June 4, 1805, the first white visitors.) Peter Cruzette, their competent boatman, and others of the party believed the Marias the true westward course, due primarily to its muddy state. The captains felt otherwise, the men cheerfully agreeing they would follow whichever river their superiors chose. Caches of excess equipment and supplies were made, and Lewis headed a small advance party which discovered the Great Falls of the Missouri, a sought for landmark, on June 13, the same day the main party passed the later site of Fort Benton.

The captains had correctly made their most important decision. However, it can be argued that the decision worked to the disadvantage of the expedition. Had they chosen to follow the Marias they would almost certainly have discovered Marias Pass, found far easier going than through the tangle of mountains to the south and changed some threads of history.

The Corps of Discovery spent far more time working its way past the awesome series of falls which marked the limit of possible continuous navigation, almost a month of toil, before the westward course was again taken. Progress was speedier from there and July 19, 1805, the expedition had reached a point below future Helena, of which Lewis wrote, "I called it the gate to the Rocky Mountains." It may be that the explorer felt confidence in achieving Jefferson's goal of practicable water communications across the continent.

It was not to be that simple. The party found the course of Missouri southerly, made their way down to the Three Forks, reached July 27th. The captains named these for President Jefferson, Secretary of State James Madison and Secretary of Treasury Albert Gallatin. The party spent time exploring that great basin and searching for Sacajawea's tribe, from whom they hoped to secure horses, working their way up the Beaverhead, and finally making contact with the Shoshones August 13th. With horses and guides, the Corps of Discovery made its toilsome way through the jumbled mountains and on to the Snake and Columbia rivers. November 8, 1805, Lewis wrote, "Great joy in camp, we are in view of the ocean, this great Pacific ocean which we have long been so anxious to see."

On their return trip in 1806 the expedition divided at Traveler's Rest in the Bitter Root valley on July 3. Clark and party of 22 headed up the Bitter Root and on to the Three Forks. On July 13, 1806, after digging up canoes cached the previous year, William Clark detailed Sgt. John Ordway and ten men, including John Colter, to take the canoes down the Missouri to a rendezvous with Captain Lewis. The rest of the Clark party headed for the Yellowstone headwaters. They followed this river out of Montana, Clark leaving his name, the sole physical memento of the explorers, on a great rocky outcrop he named Pomp's Pillar for the young pet of the party. There were few adventures, except those great horse thieves, the Crows, in two nocturnal visits stripped the Clark party of its horses—first but far from the last remounts Crows lifted from Americans.

Meriwether Lewis took nine men, heading up the Blackfoot, across the Dearborn and down the Sun to the Great Falls to check and replenish from caches made the previous July. Lewis had wanted another look at the Marias, divided his small party, six to follow the Missouri to a reunion at the mouth of the Marias. With George Drouillard, Joseph and Reuben Fields, he headed northward on horseback into Blackfeet country, the Journal noting their bad reputation. The whites followed the Marias and Cut Bank creek to Two Medicine creek where on July 26 they encountered a small party of Piegans, one of the Blackfeet tribes. After considerable sign "talk" the two parties camped together.

With a bit of carelessness by the whites the next morning, the Indians pretty skillfully took possession of their guns. In the ensuing fracas, Reuben Fields stabbed and killed one of the thieves, Lewis drew his pistol and shot another to save the horses. For the first, but far from the last time, white men raced for their lives heading out of Blackfeet country.

(Elliott Coues, interpreting the expedition journals, in the 1893 edition postulated that the party skirted the Teton for miles, crossed near the later Valleux bull train crossing of the Teton and traveled 20 miles further by moonlight, so in the early morning hours after the fight slept near the later site of Fort Benton on July 27th.)

The Lewis party rejoined the main group and the Ordway party near later Fort Benton and went on to the old camp at the Marias. There was little of major importance on the return trip to St. Louis, the reunion with the Clark party being August 12th above the Mandan villages. At the latter point John Colter was permitted to leave the party to return with two trappers to the mountains.

There, too, the captains settled with Touissant Charbonneau for service as an interpreter and purchase from him of a horse and lodge. Charbonneau was to survive on the wild frontier for many years, taking a final squaw to wife in 1839 at age 80. He was dead by mid-1843.

Sacagawea, the weight of evidence seems to indicate, died at old Fort Manuel in later South Dakota December 20, 1812, "the best woman at the fort." One might like to believe other accounts and Shoshone traditions which place her death as April 9, 1884, on the Wind River Reservation in Wyoming, and that on an occasion or two the only feminine member of the expedition visited Fort Benton. Baptiste, her son, had an education sponsored by William Clark. In 1823 he attracted the attention of a visiting German prince, spent six years in Germany. Baptiste returned to the west in 1829 and had a long and useful career among Mountain Men as a respected interpreter and guide. Best evidence indicates his death near Danner, Oregon, in 1866, on his way back to Montana.

The Corps of Discovery returned to St. Louis September 23, 1806, to a roaring welcome from inhabitants. Their leaders, indeed the entire party, became national heroes of an expedition which has become the national epic. Meriwether Lewis was named governor of Louisiana Territory in 1809, but died later that year on the Natchez Trace in Tennessee, on a trip to Washington, D. C., perhaps a suicide, more probably murdered. William Clark was governor of Missouri Territory 1813-20. Then he was superintendent of Indian affairs, highly respected by red men and white, to his death in 1838.

## The Terrible Blackfeet and Incredible John Colter
John Colter, who left the Lewis and Clark expedition near the Mandan villages,

must be regarded as the prototype of what came to be termed the Mountain Man. The death of two Piegans at the hands of the Lewis party certainly began the emnity, if cause were needed, of the Blackfeet; the exploits of Colter in the next four years certainly solidified that hostility. To later Mountain Men the tribe became "Bug's Boys" or a bit more politely the "Terrible Blackfeet." They earned either title. In 1832 George Catlin, the famed naturalist, met a free trapper at Fort Union who had tried trapping Blackfeet country seven times, losing furs, horses and equipment five of those and who felt lucky to still have his hair.

John Colter had been across to the Pacific, giving him considerable seniority over Joseph Dickson and Forrest Hancock, coming up the Missouri from the Mandan villages. There was doubtless considerable palaver and Colter approached the captains for permission to leave the expedition and return with the two up the river to trap. Colter had earned the chance, both Lewis and Clark felt, so off he went, back up the Missouri and into American folklore. Where the three spent the winter has not been determined, but Colter at least went far into Big Horn headwaters. They probably trapped, for Clark mentions the two would furnish Colter traps, making the project advantageous to him. Luck may have been bad, the partnership had broken up, for the next record of Colter finds him canoeing down the Missouri when he met the expedition of Manuel Lisa at the mouth of the Platte River in June 1807.

By that time Colter, from his travels in the region, knew more about the area than any other white man. Lisa had been headed for the headwaters of the Missouri, and perhaps Colter suggested the area of the Big Horn river, before or after being persuaded to for the third time go back up river. Presence of three Lewis and Clark veterans, George Drouillard, John Potts and Peter Wiser, perhaps helped convince Colter.

At the mouth of the Big Horn on the Yellowstone Manuel Lisa's party built a stockaded post a few weeks later, the first white man's structure erected in what became Montana. Shortly after completion in October 1807, Lisa gave Colter a solitary mission, to contact the Crow tribe, for this was their territory and they were potential customers for the white man's trade goods. He was also instructed to make friendly contact with the Blackfeet—a portion of his mission that turned out to be a flat failure.

With a pack of 30 pounds, guns and ammunition, the pack undoubtedly including some gifts for tribesmen, Colter traveled about 500 miles. His 1810 report to William Clark in St. Louis indicates a route toward the south and west, to Jackson Hole and into later Yellowstone Park. His stories of paint pots, gushing hot springs and other wonders were credited by Clark, but brought a derisive designation of "Colter's Hell" from more staid citizens. The summer of 1808 he was again sent out as emissary to tribesmen, was in company of a large party of Flatheads and Crows when near the Three Forks the band was attacked by Blackfeet. Colter was wounded in the attack, which was beaten off, but the presence of a white man spelled "enemy" to the Blackfeet. After repairing his wounded leg, Colter struck out alone for the post on the Big Horn.

Number two misadventure with the Blackfeet in late 1808—loner John Colter took along a companion, John Potts, off to the Jefferson to tap the rich beaver crop. There the two were surprised by a band of Blackfeet and ordered ashore from their canoe. Potts, undoubtedly fearing torture, fired on the band and, Colter recounted, "was made a riddle of." Colter landed as ordered, first dropping his traps overboard, was stripped of clothes and weapons. With a Blackfeet idea of sport, Colter was then given a fairly decent head start and informed his scalp was the prize of the race. He won a six mile race to a bend in the Jefferson, with a sudden stop seized the lance of the nearest pursuer and killed the latter, hid under some driftwood in the river until his enemies tired of looking. The 300 mile trip to Fort Manuel Lisa was made in 11 days on roots, bark of trees and perhaps a raw rabbit or two killed with a rock. It took weeks to recuperate from near starvation and hundreds of cactus spines in his feet.

Those traps left on the Jefferson were valuable indeed, so Colter returned that winter to retrieve them. He was surprised by Blackfeet at a night camp, escaped the ambush, leaving Blackfeet undoubtedly chagrined at three failures in a row for the white hunter's scalp. An easy trip back to Lisa's post, Colter undoubtedly felt, with gun and ammunition, flint and steel for a fire.

Singles and duos weren't making any headway in Blackfeet country; the next effort was in force. In March 1810 Lisa sent Andrew Henry and Pierre Menard and thirty-two men, including George Drouillard of the Lewis and Clark party to Three Forks to fort up and trap the beaver. John Colter of course was guide— he certainly knew the way in, even if he'd always been too concerned about his hairdo to see where he was going on the way out. It didn't work. The Blackfeet started picking the trappers off as prize trophies, among perhaps twenty George Drouillard, who by the evidence of the fight drew his share of blood. Colter, too, ran into yet another ambush, as usual escaped, but on returning to the Three Forks post slammed his cap on the ground and called out loud and clear, "If God will only forgive me this time I'll leave this country day after tomorrow." He made good on his vow around April 10, 1810. He and two companions took off for the fort on the Big Horn. Quite naturally, they ran into another Blackfeet ambush. Of course Colter, and mates, got away, the former taking the most wanted Blackfeet trophy with him back to St. Louis. A year or so later some diarist noted seeing Colter making preparations for a long hunting trip west, but not toward Blackfeet country. He settled down on a farm in Missouri for a couple of years. He died in November 1813 in Missouri, apparently of jaundice, more likely of sheer boredom. His estate at auction brought a total of $124.45. But no record shows another who so frustrated the "Terrible Blackfeet." And few to rival his adventures.

Mountain Men out of St. Louis quickly followed the Missouri route and pioneered others into the Rockies. Meanwhile Hudson's Bay and North West men ranged south into what is now U. S. soil, including small posts in present Montana. Finnan McDonald in 1808 built Kootenai Post on that river and next year David Thompson Salish House on Clark Fork, both for North West Company. Two or three others followed.

Astorians of John Jacob Astor's American Fur Co. came in contact in the Oregon country with the venturesome men from the North. The competition went into abeyance during the War of 1812 with British and Canadians in ascendancy until peace in 1815. In these confrontations, the Blackfeet were a sort of buffer, hostile to the American trappers, tolerant toward the traders from the north. The boundary line of 1818 was in 1846 extended along the 49th parallel, save for a compromise that gave the British Vancouver Island, and the 1844 campaign slogan "54-40 or Fight" went into permanent discard with peaceful division of the Oregon country.

From 1811 to 1822 Mountain Men seemed to have skirted the territory the Blackfeet claimed, but in 1823 a reorganized Missouri Fur Co., which Manuel Lisa had helped start, sent a party led by Robert Jones and Michael Immell west in the spring toward Three Forks. The party of tough trappers had Blackfeet trouble, the two leaders, five others dead and four wounded. Next year Andrew Henry of Rocky Mountain Fur built a post on the Yellowstone, in 1823 sent a party of trappers up the Missouri—score four men killed, the beaver still undisturbed. Furthermore, the Blackfeet started hanging around fur posts on the Yellowstone after horses and scalps until the traders moved into the heart of Crow country.

For the next decade the story was unchanged; small bands of white trappers wiped out, larger groups harrassed until they gave up. By 1837 Alfred Jacob Miller, western artist, estimated that 40 to 50 beaver hunters lost their hair annually to Blackfeet warriors. The latter had worthy opposition, Miller believed more warriors died. Whites were inclined to blame British traders to the north, who traded for the peltries which were booty for the victors.

### An Act of Royalty

American Fur Co., finding the concern afforded able competition along the Missouri, in 1827 absorbed the Columbia Fur Co., and along with it the services of a guiding spirit, Kenneth McKenzie. The new segment was labelled simply the Upper Missouri Outfit or UMO. McKenzie's main goal was to end the Blackfeet hostility and secure their trade. A first step was the building of Fort Floyd in 1828, almost immediately renamed Fort Union, which was to become a focal point in the fur trade on the Missouri, and pivotal in the early years of steamboating on the Upper Missouri. Fort Union was in present North Dakota, barely across the later boundary.

McKenzie was regarded as one of the ablest traders on the river, and he also ruled affairs in an autocratic manner, soon acquiring the title "King of the Upper Missouri," in part for the mode in which he lived. In the fall of 1830 he sent Jacob Berger (in French probably Jacques Bercier) and Dacoteau, Morceau and one other up the river into Blackfeet country. Berger was an interpreter, later a trader, and spoke Blackfeet from service with Canadian traders to the north. He proved an able emissary. Accounts vary as to his party's contact with Piegans, all involve an American flag displayed when they met the Indians on Badger Creek, near the site of the Lewis fight in 1806. Curious, the Piegans talked instead of attacking. The Berger party spent the winter with the Indians, next year Berger led a group to Fort Union to talk with McKenzie. It was not without adventure, the Indians grew suspicious and Berger had to reassure them time after time that a welcome and presents were awaiting them at Fort Union.

The intransigent Blackfeet by this time were probably aware of certain costs of their semi-isolation—neighboring tribes, enemies naturally, were better armed, had iron and other tools and luxuries offered by the fur traders. Part of the Blackfeet nation of course had traded at Hudson Bay or North West posts to the north, but for the southerly bands it was a long and arduous journey. So the Piegans were willing to listen, and doubtless some chief in nodding agreement at McKenzie's proposals also added what Catlin later heard from a chief of the tribe, "Traders yes, trappers never!"

### The First Blackfeet Post

With a working, if dangerous, agreement reached, Kenneth McKenzie dispatched James Kipp and 44 men with a keelboat loaded with trade goods up the Missouri in late spring of 1831. Kipp selected a spot at the confluence of Marias and Missouri to build the first Blackfeet Post. (At least two archaeologists believe that the site of this fort is in the present river bed of the Marias.)

Probably indicating Blackfeet interest in the coming trade, almost as work got under way, here came a large party of Piegans to trade. It took all Kipp's persuasive powers to get the band to leave until the whites had their trading post up, but they finally did, for a period of 75 days. They were back on schedule, and surprised to find a complete post with high palisades—the factor probably didn't need to crack the whip to keep his employes occupied in the grace period.

Kipp described the establishment of Fort Piegan to Lt. James H. Bradley, perhaps during his 1876 visit to Fort Benton from Missouri. Arrival at the site was probably in mid-summer. The post was 110 feet square with three large log buildings, for quarters, warehouse and trading room. The gate was protected by an enclosure 25 feet square, the palisades standing 25 feet high, the interior commanded by loopholes for cannon and small arms from the main fort. The whites were prepared.

At the first, he told Bradley, the Piegans, 500 lodges, were not inclined to trade. Kipp felt Hudson Bay traders to the north had been working on Blackfeet prejudice against the Americans. Familiar with British trade prices, he offered them much higher rates for their furs, capping it with an offer of a grand treat.

It would never do to open trade with the Blackfeet nation in picayune manner. Kipp had converted a barrel of alcohol into 200 gallons of what Hudson Bay men termed "Blackfoot Rum," the Americans "Injun Whiskey." Northern Montana's first grand opening could have been one of the grandest, or at least most spectacular. Kipp indicates it was a three day spree.

Trade was excellent, that staple of the Rocky Mountains, beaver, about 6500 pelts, making the venture a success. Not all the tribes of the Blackfeet nation were reconciled to the traders. (Siksika or Blackfeet proper, Kainah or Bloods, Pikuni or Piegan, and non-related but associated Gros Ventres.) The Bloods, least reconciled in years to come, put Fort Piegan under siege for about two weeks. Kipp gave orders to his garrison not to return fire. Ultimately he loaded a four pound cannon with grapeshot, the discharge sending a large cottonwood crashing in ruin, and the Bloods called it off. Two chiefs came in to parley, telling Kipp that Hudson Bay people had persuaded them to attack the post, doubtless confirming long held opinions of American Fur factors near the border. Kipp reminded the chiefs that the fort hadn't returned fire. Later the Bloods brought in more furs, and about 3,000 buffalo robes.

The robe trade was a weak spot in Hudson Bay's trading—with the long river and portage route to the Great Lakes the Canadian traders couldn't handle the heavy robes. For the traders along the Missouri it was simply a matter of pressing, baling and building mackinaws. In later years Fort Benton firms would benefit tremendously from this weakness in the Canadian transportation system.

In the spring of 1832 Kipp loaded the impressive returns (about $46,000 worth) on the keelboat. So many of his men insisted on leaving (fur company employes were usually signed for one, two or more years) that he decided to abandon Fort Piegan. Three or four employes who had taken women from the Blackfeet wintered with the tribe. The post was burned by wandering tribesmen shortly after, evidence indicates.

The Blackfeet meant that "Trappers never!" The year 1832 was the one in which Jim Bridger is suspected of having tolled W. H. Vanderburgh and party into Blackfeet ambush near Three Forks, the leader and a trapper killed and Eagle Rib later at Fort Union proudly showed Catlin Vanderburgh's pistols and assorted scalps of white trappers. At about the same time Andrew Drips lost one man and had several wounded. As a token of appreciation for Jim Bridger's effort in removing one of the pesky trapping brigades, a few days after Vanderburgh's death a tribesman parked an arrowhead in Old Gabe's carcass. Marcus Whitman carved it out a few years later on the Oregon Trail.

## Second Blackfeet Post

Isadore Sandoval, one of the more trusted employes, was one of the handful remaining among the Blackfeet, with some supplies, including tobacco and ammunition, to convince the tribesmen that trade was not being abandoned. It was probably well that they did.

It took two efforts to found the second trading post. David D. Mitchell, then a clerk, later a partner in American Fur, was sent from Fort Union with 60 men and a large keelboat loaded with trade goods in early July 1832. Just below the mouth of Milk River a bad storm hit at night, the boat was blown down river by a high wind and three miles below camp hit a snag and sank quickly, one, perhaps two, of the engages aboard were drowned, also one Piegan. Mitchell sent Jack Ram and Jean Latress back to Fort Union, 150 miles, the men making it in two long days and nights. Meanwhile the others built a barricade fort for protection during their enforced stay. Kenneth McKenzie quickly dispatched another boat with supplies. On its arrival at Milk River, Mitchell sent a small pack train to the Marias by way of convincing the Blackfeet the white traders were on their way back.

Fort McKenzie, the new post, was about 200 feet square, according to Alexander Culbertson's account to Lt. Bradley. It was located about six miles above the mouth of Marias and of burned Fort Piegan on a medium sized bottom. When re-located for a Montana Pioneer convention at Fort Benton in 1926, mounds of burned wood, beads and other artifacts of the fur trade were to be found. Eventually, and largely due to the annoyance of pot hunters, the site was ploughed up in recent years.

There were two bastions, with upper stories projecting about two feet to provide a field of fire in case of attack. Part of the back was framed with heavy timbers at intervals, the remainder a strong palisade. The protection several times proved its worth to inhabitants of a tiny white island in a vast expanse largely peopled by hostile tribesmen.

In the spring of 1833 Mitchell and party took down the fur and robe returns, the latter only two thirds of Fort Piegan's 3000, due to missing a long period of customary spring trade.

On his return in the summer of 1833 David Mitchell brought with him on the keelboat Flora from Fort Union not only young Alexander Culbertson, to become the premier trader on the Upper Missouri, but also Prince Maximilian of Wied, Swiss artist Karl Bodmer, and David Dreidoppel, hunter and handy man. Maximilian, somewhat curiously, was one of Europe's outstanding scientists, and provides a lengthy view of the plains Indian at the apex of an almost untouched hunting and horse culture. Bodmer was the first artist to visit what became Montana.

In addition to Mitchell, Culbertson and three Europeans, 48 others accompanied the Flora, and on arrival would increase the number of whites from 27 to nearly 80, enough for bare comfort among thousands of Bloods, Blackfeet, Piegans and Gros Ventres. Maximilian wrote, "They are always dangerous to white men...it was said that in the year 1832, they shot 58 whites, and a couple of years before that time, above 80."

Arrival of the party August 9 was welcomed by 800 braves in close order and with fire of musketry. Plains Indians were always sticklers for pomp and a common complaint was the lack of similar show on the part of the whites. Still, Mitchell opened trading with ceremony and a salute from the tiny cannon of the fort, with proper gifts for the chiefs and noted warriors. In one instance, the trader made a point, equipping Ninoch-Kiaiu (Bear Chief) with a fancy red and green uniform trimmed with silver lace, and when other chiefs made known their jealousy told them Bear Chief had always faithfully traded with American Fur.

Two years before James Kipp had opened the first Blackfeet Post at the Marias with a grand drunk lasting three days on a 35 gallon barrel of alcohol transmuted into 200 gallons of trade whisky. There is distressing evidence in the Maximilian papers that the Blackfeet had thoroughly succumbed to one of the white vices, virtually all the trade he mentions is for liquor. Rather surprisingly, Maximilian wrote that Indians who had drunk too much "became exceedingly affectionate, shaking hands without end and even embracing and kissing us heartily." In later years there seemed no end to drunken, murderous brawls among Indians in their cups. There was on occasion the same at Fort McKenzie. A drunken Blood shot and killed a young man named Martin, claiming afterward it was accidental. Mitchell, although Blackfeet and Piegan chiefs urged white vengeance, chose to regard the killing as an unfortunate accident.

Liquor quite evidently was a curse for the Indians, Maximilian noted "Very sedate men offer, in a exchange for a little whisky, things that they would not part with for any price yesterday." Also, Indian women "knowing they profit nothing, tan the skins only half way and badly." Wives and daughters were also offered the whites in exchange.

In a long discussion between Mitchell and Maximilian August 24, the prince queried abuse of selling liquor to Indians. Mitchell saw Fort McKenzie as a special case, if liquor were not available, the Blackfeet would simply turn to the English (Hudson's Bay Co.) where the red men could get all they wanted; the trader also said that American Fur traded no liquor in Mandan and Minnataree country down river. There were U. S. laws, Mitchell told the prince, but Indian agents chose to overlook the traffic. Accounts by Canadians bear out in large part Mitchell's view of the traffic north of the boundary.

One event chronicled was the August 26 marriage of Alexander Culbertson to an Indian woman. "According to the local custom, he had paid to the value of 100 dollars for her...she was of the family of the White Buffalo." This was his first wife, not the better known Natawista. The couple had a short honeymoon, the most notable event of the Maximilian visit occurred on August 28.

At daybreak Doucette woke the Europeans, in French saying "get up, we have a battle." Maximilian heard gunfire and getting out saw whites firing from roofs and the prairie covered with Indians. Eight or twenty lodges under Lame Bull of the Blackfeet had been attacked by about 600 Assiniboines and Crees, the Piegans blocking their escape route by piling saddles and gear in the entrance.

While Mitchell and Berger were admitting fugitives, a hostile appeared at the gate brandishing bow and arrows and exclaimed, "White man, make room, I will shoot those enemies." Learning the attack was not on the fort Mitchell ordered the whites to stop shooting. Later, deeming it good policy, Mitchell, Culbertson and others of the traders rode with the Blackfeet, as reinforcements began arriving from the main camp eight or ten miles distant. Maximilian wrote these were "in their finest apparel, with all kinds of ornaments and arms."

The German prince totaled dead of Blackfeet, nearly all in that first attack, as 14—7 men, 5 women and 2 children. Assiniboines later admitted to 3 dead, about 20 wounded. The raiders were pressed hard north to the Marias River before the battle ended. Later Blackfeet were complaining that they were given nothing to drink although they were tired from "fighting for the whites." Bodmer's painting of the battle at the gate of Fort McKenzie is one of few based on actual presence of a white artist.

Ill feeling between Piegans and Bloods erupted after this, when a Piegan, nephew of a chief, was killed by Bloods. Then the Siksika, Blackfeet proper, menaced the whites in the fort. Maximilian, "The press of the savage Siksika was very violent," in pushing into the fort.

Maximilian makes few references to the trade in buffalo robes, soon to be a mainstay of the Blackfeet post, and the Achilles heel of Canadian traders, who could accept only a limited number. Students of Indian life have theorized that the keelboats and mackinaws of traders on the Missouri increased the practice of polygamy among the tribes—the more wives, the more tanned robes to trade for white men's wares.

Maximilian's account provides an interesting look at trading with the Blackfeet in those early years, emphasizing the introductory ceremonials, important to the Indians, who stressed formality. Whites, including Isaac Stevens at Fort Benton in 1853, were admonished for not "dressing like chiefs." Such a reception August 10, 1833, opened with hoisting of the flag and firing of two small cannon, after which the Blackfeet advanced on the fort, singing and firing their guns. Chiefs and small numbers of principal warriors were admitted to the trade room, bringing customary presents. Reciprocity was an understood portion of the opening of trade; Maximilian mentions David Mitchell's sour reception of the uniform a principal chief had acquired from the British traders in the north. Understandable, the writer valued a replacement at $150—a year's salary for a common voyageur, but a recognized part of trade costs.

Maximilian had intended to pass the winter in the Rocky Mountains, but in part because of ill feeling between Bloods and Piegans, and due to a shortage of horses and lack of an interpreter, gave up the plan. Instead, his party returned by Mackinaw to Fort Clark to winter.

Mitchell took the fur and robe returns down to Fort Union in spring of 1834. He also left American Fur for a time, rejoined in 1836 until 1839. Culbertson, then about 26, was in charge of Fort McKenzie. Early in June the post was put under a rather friendly siege by a large party of Crows under Rotten Belly, the tribe objecting in this manner to the Americans trading with and arming their Blackfeet enemies. Not a shot was fired until food ran out, the last dog was eaten, along with parfleche skins, boiled for what nutriment these possessed. Finally, Culbertson warned of the power of the white's cannon; Crows scoffed until the artillery sent a cannon ball trundling through their camp. Leaving, Chief Rotten Belly and small war party ran into a dozen Gros Ventres near the Goosebill and the chief was killed. He was one of the Crow nation's most noted warriors. Tribal fights nearby, even in sight of McKenzie were pretty common through the next few years but the whites were seldom bothered although dozens of Indians were slain in the area.

### Letter To Alexander Culbertson

A May 5, 1835, unsigned letter to Alexander Culbertson, written at Fort Union, provides advice to the new bourgeois at Fort McKenzie that James Kipp had arrived with the preceding season's trade. This could only have been authorized by Kenneth McKenzie, doubtless unsigned to prevent it being used as evidence later in any federal steps to revoke the American Fur license to trade in event of liquor trading charges.

The writer called attention to the federal law and added: "I send you two barrels of alcohol and six of wine. Make the most of it and do not sell a single drop of it to the men."

Culbertson would receive the most valuable trading stock yet sent into Montana to be, "a very valuable outfit is selected for you amounting at St. Louis prices $11,200 and upwards without any charge for commission or transportation." One lack, "In the article of white beads we are sadly deficient."

The falling price of beaver in the 1830s had already affected trade patterns: "The company is desirous to push the robe trade in order to attach the various nations in your District to the Missouri." The change benefited the Americans at the expense of Hudson's Bay traders to the north, as mackinaws on the Missouri and by this time steamboats to Fort Union made shipping the bulky, heavy buffalo robes easier; HBC could not trade in robes to any great extent, for want of cargo space on their canoe-portage route east.

The writer had more on this: "As the beaver trade for the last three years has been regularly declining....it appears to me that our sheet anchor will be the robe trade and by encouraging the Blood, Blackfeet and others to make robes, articles which they now obtain as luxuries will become necessaries and they will be compelled to remain on the Missouri in order to procure them."

Culbertson was also advised to "renew" his fort; there seems evidence that Fort McKenzie was reconstructed or strengthened on its 1832 site. And the letter writer expressed "a high opinion of his integrity and bravery" in engaging Alexander Harvey for another year.

Returns from Fort McKenzie hadn't topped two or three thousand the first few years, in 1836 robe traffic shot up to 8,000. Little beaver was coming in, the dam builders apparently depleted by Indian trappers—Mountain Men were still occasionally trying the Missouri headwaters in strong brigades—Jim Bridger as guide seemed to have a knack for finding Blackfeet more plentiful than beaver. Low, low beaver prices a couple of years later ended these efforts.

Alexander Harvey, who had entered American Fur service in 1831, was pretty shortly at Fort McKenzie, where his energy and resourcefulness made him a potentially valued employe. He understudied for Culbertson in such important tasks as taking the returns down river. He was completely fearless, with a terrible temper—and is one strong nominee for the toughest man who ever came up the Missouri.

Harvey was in charge of returns to Union in 1837. That was the year that smallpox was brought to the upper Missouri by germs in a stolen blanket—off the St. Peter, one of the annual steamboats to Fort Union. Harvey loaded his keelboat and was off quickly, trying to miss the disease, but soon had three cases aboard. Wisely, he stopped the trip at the mouth of the Judith and sent a messenger to Culbertson at McKenzie. The latter sent six men down in canoes to help Harvey—four were drowned just above the Judith, the creation of a name well known on the river, Drowned Man's Rapids—a mistranslation. Rather oddly, the only white to die of the disease later was Antoine Dauphin—Dauphin's Rapids, worst on the river, named for him, rather derisively, by his friends.

Culbertson warned the impatient Blackfeet of the disease, and its deadliness—the tribesmen, hale and healthy, scoffed, insisted on trading, and eventually the whites gave in. After there were no Blackfeet coming to trade. At the fort, despite Culbertson's attempts to inoculate, there were 27 deaths, including Dauphin, the others squaws, so the attempt may have saved white lives. In October with Sandoval, Culbertson made a trip to the Three Forks. At one Blackfeet village only two old women, both nearly dead, still lived. The carnage wrought among the Blackfeet he estimated at two thirds of the nation, perhaps 6000.

Next year the survivors traded robes salvaged from the dead, about 10,000 at McKenzie and the biggest for any year yet. Strangely, Culbertson told Bradley, although no precautions were taken by traders, there was no outbreak of the killer back in the States.

It was in 1839 that Alexander Culbertson was made a partner in American Fur. This was the key to substantial fortunes for those years, eventually his share reached $300,000. American Fur kept two thirds of the profits—by then chiefly Pierre Chouteau Jr. The other third went in half and full shares to trusted employes, a tremendous incentive.

Harvey, often left in charge while his superior had business at Fort Union, first demonstrated a steak of ruthless cruelty when a Blood chief, Big Road, attacked Culbertson, who turned the Indian over to Harvey. A few moments later Big Road was dead. It was for such deeds, and quarrels with fellow engages, that Harvey was discharged on their complaints in the latter part of 1839. He made a winter trip, alone, down the Missouri to St. Louis to confront Chouteau, and the latter, impressed by such resolute daring, rehired him.

Back up the Missouri next spring, Alexander Harvey hunted up the men who had complained, beat them savagely. Isadore Sandoval, he simply shot through the head in the store room at Fort Union. Life could be pretty desperate at a frontier trading post. This was the year that Andrew Potts, young Scot trader at Fort McKenzie, was shot through the trading wicket by an Indian who claimed to have taken Potts for another. "One Eye" was killed by his own people. Potts left an infant son, Jerry, later to become virtually a patron saint of the North West Mounted Police in Alberta.

Fort McKenzie's years were numbered. Culbertson was transferred against his wishes to Fort Laramie on the Platte in 1843 with Francis A. Chardon his successor. In preceding years the robe trade from McKenzie had reached 20,000 robes and dropped back due to fluctuations in Indian hunting success, but was still the greatest producer of wealth of any post in the Missouri valley. Chardon may have been an alcoholic, or just weak, but in either case Alexander Harvey was the dominant figure at the fort, with a couple more pretty gruesome killings of Indians to his discredit.

Culbertson, interviewed many years later by Bradley, gives an early 1842 date for the demise of Fort McKenzie, with 21 Indians killed by discharge of a cannon. A tricky memory can some times slip. Best version seems to be that of George Weippert, long time resident, who has the correct year of 1844 verified by other sources.

The massacre followed an almost casual occurrence, for anyone with understanding of Indian nature. A war party of Blackfeet came by Fort McKenzie on their way against the Crows, and demanded double the customary few rounds of ammunition and a feast for good luck. On being refused the extras, the party petulantly drove off some of the cattle at the fort and killed one or two. In pursuit, Tom Reese, Negro employe, was shot and killed. Loss of an employe was bad, worse, the slain cattle would be charged against Chardon and Harvey.

Weippert reported Chardon habitually too drunk to take control, but Harvey was perfectly willing. A cannon was loaded with a heavy charge and to the muzzle with all kinds of missiles and apparently February 19, 1844, a party of peaceful traders appeared at McKenzie. When clustered in the trading gate, the cannon was discharged. Culbertson says 21, Weippert 4 dead with 17 others wounded, and Harvey rushing out with an axe to brain any survivors.*

* Indian Agent Edwin A. C. Hatch 1857 report: Private journal of (unnamed) man now dead: "Feb. 19, 1844. Fight with the north Blackfeet, in which fight we killed six and wounded several others. Took two children prisoners. The fruits of our victory were four scalps, twenty-two horses, three hundred and forty robes, and guns, bows and arrows."

Aftermath, of course, was a sensible abandonment of Fort McKenzie. Occupants understandably felt the Blackfeet reaction would be vigorous and dangerous to all whites around. Quickly and quite secretly Chardon sent a detachment down the Missouri to a point on the north bank opposite the influx of the Judith River. According to the Bradley manuscript, the new post was completed in about six weeks, after which Chardon and Harvey loaded merchandise and other movables into boats and dropped away down the Missouri, leaving Fort McKenzie in flames.

### Fort Francis A. Chardon

The new post was named for the bourgeois, Chardon, is often referred to as Fort F. A. C. Apparently the move was made about April 1, 1844. A potential clue to date of abandonment of Fort McKenzie lies in the charge later filed by Alexander Harvey with the Superintendent of Indian Affairs that F. A. Chardon had sold liquor to Indians from May 1, 1843, to March 31, 1844. At any rate in early April, possibly by the 5th, the whites were, undoubtedly to their great relief, behind distant and hopefully safer walls. But available sources indicate the Blackfeet conducted a campaign of deliberate harassment of inhabitants of Fort Chardon, killing cattle belonging to the post and stealing or killing horses, and lacking data, presumably any employes careless enough to be caught outside its walls. Evidence indicates some trade at the fort, not much, and perhaps that with other tribes. In any event, as the U. S. Army later found, the area around the mouth of the Judith was about as isolated as any point along the Missouri could be. Transient war parties were evidently sole inhabitants.

At any rate, 1844 was a miserable year for American Fur and its employes on the Upper Missouri. Returns may have been 40% of the previous year, less than a fourth the 1840 and 1841 robe trade. Alexander Culbertson, who had been transferred to Fort Laramie on the Platte against his wishes and strong recommendations, was contacted as quickly as possible after word of the end of Fort McKenzie reached St. Louis. His account was that he met Pierre Chouteau in New York, in effect was told to write his own ticket if he succeeded in repairing the damage. He went back up the Missouri in summer 1845. As the keelboat with trade supplies neared the Judith Alexander Harvey came down to meet it. On boarding, Harvey was met by Malcolm Clark and Jim Lee; at least one source adds Jacob Berger to the list. At any rate, the men worked Harvey over with a hatchet, rifle and pistol butts, all but killing him. Harvey apparently made his own way back to Fort Chardon, would admit only Culbertson, who of course fired him. Better than his tough winter trip, Harvey was given a canoe, and went down the Missouri swearing vengeance on American Fur and all its underlings. The site was relocated in 1981 from scanty sub-surface remnants.

### Another Site For The Blackfeet Post

Culbertson quickly decided that the mouth of the Judith was no place for a trading post, went on up the Missouri, beyond old forts Piegan and McKenzie to the head of the first rapids above later Fort Benton. There on what came to be called Cotton Bottom, for a short lived trading post of Fox & Livingston of the previous year, and on the south side of the Missouri, was built, again in secrecy, what came to be called Fort Lewis, after the explorer. Culbertson first proposed to name it for Honore Picotte, member of American Fur, adding to a profusion of titles. Approximate dates of construction, between September 1, 1845, and the end of the year. From sketches made by Father Nicolas Point, an eye witness to its final days, Fort Lewis was a strong well built post with high palisades and bastions. Dimensions were about 150 feet square, bastions about 18 feet, two stories.

Through a Blackfoot emissary Culbertson contacted the nation after completion, calling for a peace council. That, Culbertson told Bradley, was a complete success. After he told the party of about fifty of steps taken against the perpetrators of the Fort McKenzie massacre, head chief Big Swan replied in part, "the ground had been made good again by Major Culbertson's return, and the Blackfeet must not be the first to stain it with blood."

American Fur could be well satisfied with Culbertson's feat as peacemaker. Robe returns from the furthest post more than tripled to around 17,000, plus a substantial trade in furs. It was a busy spring and summer. As fall began Fort Lewis had interesting visitors, recounted from Father Nicholas Point's Journal.

With Fr. Pierre Jean DeSmet, he arrived at Fort Lewis September 24, 1846. The more famed missionary had made a 1845-46 trip into Canada as far as Fort Edmonton to contact the Blackfeet, in summer 1846 had gone to the mouth of the Judith to make peace between Blackfeet and Flatheads, now had a trip to make to St. Louis and would go down with fall returns and news and orders. Fr. Point was invited to spend the winter at the fort. Next day the fall supply boat arrived, a cause for rejoicing among 60 plus inhabitants. On the 17th 33 persons were baptized and for the first time there was a Mass in Fort Lewis. Fr. DeSmet left next day in a thunderstorm. In the next few days 21 more children were baptized, eight or nine couples legitimately married. It might be noted that many at the fort were Catholic, though on the frontier religious ties were less binding. Over the years at the fur posts in the Fort Benton area numerous children were baptized, possibly some the same day their parents were married by the Father.

Father Point's published Journal, "Wilderness Kingdom," includes numerous sketches which bring to life the characters and work at a trading post in a remote area. Malcolm Clarke and Culbertson of course, but also Michel and Baptiste Champagne, Augustin Hamell who chanced a one man trading post below on the Missouri and Jacob Berger, the man who first made the Blackfeet post possible with his mission from Fort Union. There is also an enchanting sketch of two little half bloods, Marie and Josette Champagne. These men who took Indian wives were on a distant, dangerous frontier, but it might astonish a reader to discover how many, including illiterate laborers, managed an education via St. Louis convent school, for their children.

Fr. Point wrote that common employes were paid from $150 to $280 annually, not counting food and lodging, fare that of the country and often scanty or of poor quality. Carpenters, blacksmiths, other craftsmen and hunters were better paid and better fed. In addition to a better salary, clerks, chief interpreter and traders ate at the captain's table.

The missionary left Fort Lewis on March 19, 1847, the date of its removal to what became Fort Benton, by what he termed a barge—sketches indicate it to be a keelboat. What had happened was the Blackfeet had complained to Culbertson that the location on the South bank of the Missouri was too difficult for them to reach, especially in fall and spring due to floating ice that prevented crossing. Fort Benton residents have always accepted the Culbertson date of 1846—it seems most likely that a crew of men from up river began work that fall or early winter. At any rate, unlike its predecessors, Fort Lewis escaped the torch.

A passing note, one of Fr. Point's sketches shows a small structure he termed Fort Fox & Livingston, on the east bank at or near Shonkin Creek. Fort Campbell (first) is better located, slightly below the Cracon du Nez and also on the opposite bank from Fort Benton. The Fox & Livingstone post was moved in 1844 to the site where Culbertson built the first Fort Lewis the next year.

When Alexander Culbertson took the annual returns down river in May 1848, it climaxed one of the most prosperous seasons the Blackfeet post had ever had; everything that could be spared, including bedding, had been bartered "for the incessant flow of peltries." In the fall of 1848 three outposts were established. Augustin Hamell was in charge of the one at Willow Rounds on the Marias; a vicinity with a long future history of trading. Malcolm Clarke was in charge of another about 30 miles further up the Marias, and Michael Champaigne on the Milk River. The practice continued into the 1850s of tiny trading posts convenient to Indian camps.

### Alexander Harvey's Vengeance

Alexander Culbertson's reminiscences include a passing reference to the fate of Fort Chardon, that in taking robe and fur returns down (in the spring of 1846) one of his actions was burning of this post, an act for which Harvey never forgave him. That word forgive wasn't in Alexander Harvey's vocabulary. Making his way to St. Louis after being fired in 1845 Harvey charged Malcolm Clarke, James Lee and Jacob Berger with an attempt to murder him. That charge was quashed as occurring far beyond the jurisdiction of any court, but his complaint about the sale of liquor to Indians (of which Harvey undoubtedly had done his share) had American Fur mighty careful about handling of intoxicants at their posts—Fr. Point mentions the prohibition in his 1846-47 account. It required time, and friendly intervention of Senator Thomas Hart Benton to save the trading license.

More to the point in getting even with American Fur, with Charles Primeau, Anthony Bouis and Joseph Picotte he formed Harvey, Primeau & Co., the "& Co." being Robert Campbell, St. Louis business man who never seemed averse to lighting a taper under friends and business associates. (So much for business, but it does seem a bit ironic that the Harvey, Primeau robe and fur returns, at least for 1852, would be marketed by Campbell through Pierre Chouteau's company—the latter taking 50% for services rendered. In view of the bitter rivalry on the Fort Benton bottom, knowledge of that arrangement probably rankled Harvey.)

Nobody could ever fault Alexander Harvey for want of courage, aggressiveness or resourcefulness. With the financial backing he came up the Missouri in July 1846, a thundercloud of opposition with 45 men aboard the Clermont No. 2. The boat reached a point near Fort Union, where Harvey unloaded supplies and put his crew to work building mackinaws for the trip into Blackfeet country. He built log Fort Campbell a short distance below later Fort Benton on the opposite bank and when Culbertson moved Fort Lewis next spring Harvey, too, moved his trading post, probably as an irritant—to a point about a half mile above what became Fort Benton. Furthermore, he rebuilt his fort of sun dried adobe bricks, a substance abundant on the bottom, in 1847-48. (Culbertson, willing to take lessons from a rival, two years later started a decade long rebuilding of the same adobe, but was not quite willing to credit Harvey, always claimed he learned how in the Laramie country.)

Fort Campbell surprisingly did a good business, about a half that of Fort Benton, even bettering the ratio a year or two. (Only answer to why, in view of his record at McKenzie, seems to have been that his tigerish ferocity strangely appealed to the Blackfeet, themselves scarcely mollycoddles.) One unattributed tale of Fort Campbell: Mountain Chief, one of the great and grim Piegan warriors, climbed atop one of the adobe buildings one day to boast of his prowess and of the white scalps he had taken. Harvey heard and acted, climbing up to knock Mountain Chief off the roof with a club. No report on later friendship, but it may well have been so.

(John Sunder's excellent book on the "Fur Trade of the Upper Missouri" is principal source of Harvey's toughness.) In 1847 to replenish supplies Harvey found a challenge in a keelboat trip from Fort Bouis in South Dakota when November ice clogged the Missouri and the party finally switched to horses and made it to Campbell with some supplies. Then Harvey and two or three others set out for St. Louis through deep snow. Assiniboines set them afoot near Fort Union before their luck changed to just a "cold and hard" trip. His 1848 trip was anti-climatic, the Bertrand got 50 miles above the Yellowstone before the switch to keelboat. Succeeding years were easy until 1850 when Harvey and five men set out for St. Louis in early spring in a small boat. In South Dakota the boat swamped, only Harvey and another got to shore. They found a piece of steel to build a fire to warm by, then a bit of coffee in a packet washed ashore. At St. Louis in May the two announced a fine trade for Harvey, Primeau, at least 6,000 robes and probably more.

Alexander Harvey's driving energy kept Fort Campbell alive through the poor robe years of 1851-52, but time was running out for Harvey. On another of his annual trips down for supplies, he died at Fort William, just below Fort Union, in July 1854. His final letter on his deathbed to Robert Campbell concluded, "I die in peace and friendship with the world." He was 47. The Missouri Republican obituary called him "a man of stainless honesty, inflexible courage, and invincible energy." With at least two phrases even his many enemies would have agreed.

The opposition company continued to operate Fort Campbell as J. Picotte & Co. In 1857 Frost, Todd & Co. became the backers, Picotte continuing with the concern in an advisory capacity and with Malcolm Clarke in charge of the fort so long operated by his old enemy. Todd, Frost sent the steamboat Twilight to the vicinity of the Yellowstone mouth in 1857-58 with supplies, in 1859 sent the Florence, which ended its trip in later North Dakota. Probably a contributing reason for final withdrawal of the opposition was the successful voyage of the Chippewa to Fort McKenzie bottom for American Fur in 1859. However, the major reason was loss of the financial backing of Robert Campbell. Although Fort Campbell had what seems an excellent trade in robes over its years, as early as 1852 Honore Picotte of American Fur was suggesting the opposition was on its last legs. That could well have been because while Campbell was making a profit, returns to actual operators were scanty, indicated by that sale of robes via Chouteau.

The Fort Benton Journal of 1854-56 contains a number of references to the "opposition". Some of the later ones are entertaining:

May 30, 1855: This evening two men came from the other fort to ours to see if we would hire them, they being dissatified above,—told them to come back tomorrow.

May 31, 1855: The two men came down today and hired for each Twenty dollars per Month.—Recd. two notes from opposition, one of which was very insulting.

April 13, 1856: Mr. Picotte of the opposition left with his "Returns" in three Boats—gave him a passing Salute from our Cannon being we suppose the first time an opposition Bourgeois had such an honor paid him by this Fort, but both houses have been on the most amicable terms this winter both having done a most satisfactory business.

The writer was probably Andrew Dawson, and recipient of the salute was Joseph Picotte. In early spring Fort Benton had virtually run out of trade goods, Dawson wrote that there would be more than 14,000 robes to send down—Fort Campbell's trade can be estimated at about 8,000.

American Fur took over abandoned Fort Campbell in 1860, it was used with their consent by Catholic missionaries for a time. During the gold rush years the fort doubtless sheltered hundreds of miners waiting for passage as well as newly arrived hopefuls. Its location can be calculated very closely from old sketches, but all surface traces have disappeared, beads can still be found, so an archaeologist would have little trouble locating the spot. The bricks have crumbled into the topsoil or perhaps went to fill nearby gullies in the long ago.

# $O_{ne}$ $F_{ur}$ $P_{ost}$ $S_{urvives}$

## American Fur's Last Blackfoot Post

*D*ate of the beginning of what was to be the only Montana fur post to survive into modern days may be in doubt, but not the date of regular occupancy, due to Fr. Point's Journal and his date of March 19, 1847, the day the final structures and other portable materials were rafted down the Missouri a relatively short distance to become a part of a new trading post. It was located, as Blackfeet requested, on the north side of the river. For a short time, it seems, the post was termed Fort Clay, but this soon reverted to Fort Lewis.

Alexander Culbertson thus became the founder of the oldest continuously inhabited place in Montana, for while St. Mary's Mission in the Bitter Root valley was founded in 1841 and occupied by missionaries and Indians for most of a decade, it was abandoned and vacant when sold for $250 to John Owen for a trading post in November 1850. Probably each spot has a claim to "first."

Culbertson told Lt. Bradley that rebuilding of Fort Lewis was largely completed in about a month, furs and robes from the previous winter sent down river and the fort itself open for trade, although in view of around 16,500 robes traded for the previous winter the storerooms were probably all but empty. Harvey at Campbell would add about 3500 to that total. In St. Louis reports were of unprecedented success in trading.

It was the trade season of 1847-48 that rang the bells of tills. At Fort Benton the stock of goods was completely exhausted and bedding, wearing apparel, anything that could possibly be spared from the fort went across the counter to Indian customers. Fort Benton sent down more than 20,000 buffalo robes, thousands of smoked tongues and a considerable quantity of other furs. The opposition fort shared in the trading boom, more than 5100 robes—apparently Blackfeet memories were dimming in regard to Harvey and the cannon.

Returns from the Indian trade kept growing, the reported robe trade from two forts 25,000 in 1848 and 26,000 next year—a drop off following in 1850 but still well past 20,000.

It was on Christmas night in 1850, following completion of the first adobe building, that Culbertson held a traditional feast—for all hands at Fort Lewis and at the height of the festivities stilled the fiddles for an announcement that engages were now working in Fort Benton. It was named in honor of Senator Thomas Hart Benton of Missouri, good friend of the American Fur Co. Actually, the name had been used in St. Louis headquarters for about two years, but this made it official. (Fort Benton Journal in May-June 1856 mentions work on and completion of "bastion" (or blockhouse), which is not clear.)

The year 1851 was doubtless one that Alexander Culbertson remembered to the end of his years. He and Honore Picotte went down to meet the annual steamer, waiting for its arrival at St. Joseph. Aboard the St. Ange, when 500 miles above the Missouri town, cholera, the plague of the Overland Trail and of steamboats, broke out. Deaths occurred almost daily until 30 had died. The high country, and probably purer water, or more likely the fact that all susceptible to the disease had contracted it, ended the outbreak. Culbertson's success as a peacemaker with the until then implacable Blackfeet had apparently not gone unnoticed. On his way overland to Fort Pierre Culbertson was met by a messenger with a letter from the Indian affairs superintendent, asking him to make up and bring a delegation of Northern Plains tribesmen to a great peace council below Fort Laramie in September. Another participant was Fr. DeSmet. To wind up an eventful year, Culbertson and five men took a wagon from Fort Union to Fort Benton, a trip requiring about a month to December 1st. This was so far as known, the first wheeled vehicle over a distance on the northern Montana plains. The route was used by overland expeditions from Minnesota in the 1860s, and much of the route the 1851 party took is now highways 2 and 89—the present route from the Dakota line through Havre, thence to Fort Benton.

Robe trade continued strong through the first three years of the decade, about 70,000 robes in three years.

### Isaac Stevens Puts Fort Benton in Spotlight

Then an isolated though wealthy trading post in the Upper Missouri wilderness, in 1853 Fort Benton was to assume importance in the projects of planners in the nation's capital. Isaac Ingalls Stevens, Mexican War officer and at the time head of the coastal survey, was named governor of the newly created Territory of Washington. This included present Western Montana and Idaho, the remainder of Montana at the time Indian country, soon to be included in Nebraska Territory.

One time Montana governor Joseph Dixon once wrote: "The Northwest owes more to Isaac I. Stevens than to any one other man who had to do with its development." Stevens was to owe considerable to Fort Benton personnel.

He was given further instructions which would implement Jefferson's 1803 charge to Meriwether Lewis to find "the most direct and practicable water route across this continent." His second mission was to explore and survey a route for a possible northern railroad route from the Mississippi to the Pacific Coast, to explore the great river systems of the Missouri and Columbia, arrange for peace treaties with the Indian tribes of the area, before assuming his duties as governor. It was a mission strikingly similar to that of Lewis and Clark, although the country by then was far better known. Officials probably thought the appropriation of $40,000 ample. It was to be at Fort Benton that Stevens threw the limits over the walls and decided on his own responsibility, to assume necessary added costs to make the mission successful.

Isaac Stevens arranged an expedition which on the whole worked like clockwork. A western division was under Capt. George B. McClellan, of Civil War note, to work out of Puget Sound to explore the Cascade Mountain passes and meet an eastern party. This latter, which was the main Stevens responsibility, was a three pronged matter. One, under Lt. A. J. Donelson, with Lt. John Mullan and Wm. M. Graham, went up the Missouri on the steamboat Robert Campbell with instructions to establish a supply depot at Fort Union and await Stevens and the main body coming by way of St. Paul. Another under Lt. Rufus Saxton, was to organize a party in the Columbia valley to move eastward into the Bitter Root to establish a depot with rations and supplies. Those in charge of the two parties were encouraged to make exploratory trips to add to knowledge of the country.

The main body left St. Paul June 6, 1853, in three groups including supply train of wagons, with a number of civilian specialists such as doctor and naturalist Dr. George Suckley, artist John Mix Stanley, topographer John Lambert—the complete list indicates care in planning. They reached Fort Union overland on August 1st.

Stevens had Alexander Culbertson named as special agent to the Blackfeet, and had probably by then determined that post would be his headquarters for preliminaries to a treaty with the Blackfeet. Not surprisingly, in view of their warlike history, this nation was a special case, in neither eastern or western superintendencies.

Culbertson reported to Stevens that the three tribes of Blackfeet were about equal in numbers, overall total around 1200 lodges, at eight to a lodge 9600 in all, and listed the allied Gros Ventres as another 400 lodges, roughly defined the territory of each. The Piegans, closest to the trading post, ranged along the Missouri on both sides as far as the Musselshell and some times to Milk River. "The entire country of the Blackfeet is perhaps the best buffaloe country in the N. W. Territory—indeed there is seldom a season of scarcity." And, "Of all the western Indians these appear to be the most warlike—indeed with the young men war seems to be their principal occupation and amusement....They shoot well, ride well; are wary, energetic and savage."

Stevens in his overall report printed in 1860, makes note of the cooperation of both fur trading companies at Fort Union—Harvey, Primeau operated nearby Fort William. An incident while at Fort Union, Stanley greatly pleased and astounded Indians by making daguerreotypes of their chiefs, probably to them more magical than Catlin's portraits had been.

The expedition left Union August 9 and 10, in three parties, with Alexander Culbertson and wife Natawista accompanying them. Both, the report testified, were of tremendous help in arrangements for a council with the Blackfeet and other tribes. The route of course was that pioneered in November 1851 by Culbertson when he took a wagon to Fort Benton. The party Stevens headed was followed by a party of 20 Bloods and 40 Piegans "on most pleasant terms," Stevens wrote. Warlike disagreements between Gros Ventres and Blackfeet, former allies, had erupted. When Stevens met with a party of Gros Ventres August 23 near the crossing of Milk River, he made a gift distribution, about a ton in all, to persuade them to attend the planned council at Fort Benton.

Arrival at Fort Benton, except for scattered exploratory groups, was September 1. Isaac Stevens had a busy three weeks, interviewing Blackfeet and voyageurs about mountain passes and the projected council planned for Fort Benton in 1854—actually not held until the following year. Members of the expedition, in in ensuing months, incidentally reached both ends of the Marias pass, although it was not followed through the mountains. "Discovery" by John F. Stevens in 1889 resulted in routing of the Great Northern through one of the easiest crossings of the Rockies. But the pass was well described to Isaac Stevens by Little Dog, Piegan chief. For his own railroad survey, he seems to have settled on the later general course of the Great Northern to Fort Benton, thence to Sun and Dearborn, with a crossing and tunnel at Cadotte's Pass. Augustin Hamell described the route to him—it would be familiar indeed to men of his expedition.

Photographer Stanley took, on September 4, daguerreotypes of Blackfeet. "They were delighted and astonished to see their likenesses produced by the direct action of the sun. They worship the sun, and they considered that Mr. Stanley was inspired by their divinity, and he thus became in their eyes a great medicine man." These were probably the first photographs ever taken in present Montana (Fort Union being just inside Dakota). None is known to have survived, Blackfeet legend indicating they were buried with Indian owners. John M. Stanley regrettably made no scenic pictures, at least none survive, but did make a well known sketch of the Fort Benton bottom showing the two forts and other sketches of the area.

September 11, two days out of Fort Benton on his way to Cypress Hills, Stevens was overtaken by Baptiste Champaigne with the important message that Lts. Grover and Saxton had met in the Bitter Root, so he broke off the trip. The depot had been successfully established—near John Owen's trading post, the former St. Mary's Mission. There the Flatheads had a considerable village, and an early Indian effort in agriculture, with cattle, raising wheat, potatoes and poultry. Saxton, 17 men and guide, reached Fort Benton the 12th. Stevens soon decided to send Saxton, discharged soldiers and other men down the Missouri and was rather surprised that several wanted to see the adventure through to its finish; on receipt of Dr. Suckley's o.k. permission was given.

Small groups had been sent out in various directions from the fort, to contact tribesmen and add to knowledge of the area. The report included some data on the Indian travois, lodge poles made into a sort of sled for goods, including tanned robes for lodges, from 300 to 500 pounds transported by each horse 20 miles a day. Dogs could drag about 40 pounds on a similar structure.

On September 21, in a large room in the fort, Isaac Stevens held a council with about 30 chiefs and warriors of the three tribes of Blackfeet—Piegans, Bloods and Blackfeet. Augustin Hamell, "an intelligent voyageur, who had been in the country many years," was interpreter. Stevens was impressed with their costumes, "elegantly decorated with bead-work...made by their women...some must have been occupied many months." He noted the Indian attitude on his own attire to which he was not able to give the same attention, "We dress up to receive you, and why do you not wear the dress of a chief?" His talk was of the warring tribes, resultant loss of the best men of the tribe, urging inter-tribal peace, and also with the white men.

Due to the lateness of the season, Isaac Stevens had decided not to take his wagons across the mountains, using pack animals instead. On September 22 the other members saw Lt. Saxton and party depart down river by mackinaw. With them went Alexander Culbertson, who had been requested by Stevens to go to Washington to meet with authorities in regard to the decision made to continue surveys and exploration, although the $40,000 appropriation was exhausted. Culbertson was also to stress the importance of the Blackfeet council and proposed peace council.

James Doty, meteorologist among other duties as secretary, was to remain at Fort Benton through the winter in charge of the supply depot, including those wagons. Lt. Donelson had been sent ahead with the main party, Stevens left Fort Benton later the 22nd, reaching Sun river on the first night and over Cadotte's pass the 24th—with the crossing assuming authority as governor of Washington Territory. Near Fort Owen he held a council with the Flatheads, long fearful of the warlike Blackfeet, went on westward and reached Fort Vancouver November 15, 1853.

There were a number of significant loose ends from the departed expedition—Cantonment Stevens in the Bitter Root, James Doty's mission, Lt. Cuvier Grover, who had explored areas of the Missouri at least to the Judith and returned to Fort Benton to stay until January 2, 1854, and that of Lt. John Mullan. Doty took the first meteorological readings in Montana and the Bitter Root depot would be important to Lt. Mullan.

Mullan was sent to contact the Flathead Indians believed to be on the Musselshell but found 70 miles south of that stream on their fall hunt. He had also been assigned the mission of exploring, as were other members, for a possible railroad. It was probably during the stay at Fort Benton that both the young, eager lieutenant and the expedition head came up with the idea that first came a wagon road, to connect the two major navigable streams of the Northwest, the Missouri and Columbia.

Mullan made a significant addition to the record when at Cantonment Stevens he learned of a pass leading directly to Fort Benton and left March 2, 1854, via Hell Gate valley, the Little Blackfoot and Missouri to Fort Benton. He returned with a loaded wagon drawn by four mules to the Sun, Dearborn, Little Prickly Pear, an easy wagon road of 124 measured miles. From there some fallen timber had to be cleared but Mullan's party arrived in the Bitter Root with mules fat on spring grass, 14 days from Fort Benton, the first wagon over the northern Rockies in Montana. The feat may have been a factor in a later event, Congress soon appropriating $30,000 for survey of a military road from old Fort Walla Walla (not the later city of the name) on the Columbia system to Fort Benton on the Missouri. Mullan's explorations covered about a thousand miles in less than a year, including a tentative selection of the route later followed. He reported to Governor Stevens at Olympia late in 1854, and left for Washington, D. C., early in 1855, bearing letters from Stevens to the War Department and resolutions by the legislature that Mullan be surveyor and builder of the route of some 624 miles. Although the War Department favored the road, officials felt the appropriation was too little, and Indian uprisings in western Washington delayed the start.

James Doty made quite a trip in May 1854, to the Great Falls and the base of the Rockies, thence up across branches of the Marias and to the area of the St. Mary's River. He saw Chief Mountain, noted a broad lodge trail leading into the mountains. Stevens felt certain this was the route to Marias pass and regretted that Doty did not continue and find where it issued to the west side. A. W. Tinkham the previous fall had gone into the Flathead lake area and noted similar indications of an approach to a pass.

Alexander Culbertson reached St. Louis without difficulty in the fall of 1853, continued to Washington where he spent the entire winter of 1853-54 lobbying for the appropriation for Stevens' treaty, meeting many of the nation's leaders, including President Franklin Pierce. Eventually the bill appropriating $80,000 for concluding a treaty with the Blackfeet and associated tribes became a law. He returned to Fort Union by steamboat.

The September 28, 1854, Fort Benton Journal records his arrival with his wife and three men "much to the delight of all in the fort." Andrew Dawson was in charge, and post men were busy making adobe bricks, "1290 dobbies today" as reconstruction of Fort Benton was continuing. Also, they were busy getting in wood and equipping trading expeditions by wagon to the various tribes, one in charge of Louis Rivet to the Gros Ventres on Milk River. The day after his arrival, Culbertson provided all employes at the fort with a seemingly customary feast and in the evening a ball "at which two only of the number made a sorry display of their reasons." Dour Scot Dawson was probably delighted to record the pair having noteworthy hangovers next day. Fall weather was decent enough that small parties were coming and going to secure logs for building from the Highwoods. Trading, largely at a distance with good returns in robes continued into December, Culbertsons leaving for Fort Union the day after Christmas overland. The year went out with cold weather. Robe trade at Fort Benton for 1854 seems to have been 18,000, with 5,000 at Fort Campbell—actually for the preceding winter.

### The Great Council at the Judith

Despite cold weather until a late January chinook Fort Benton trading post was doing a rushing business, but the opposition was having some troubles due to the death of guiding spirit Alexander Harvey the previous July. Plans were already afoot in far away places for the great peace council Isaac Stevens had planned on his 1853 visit to Fort Benton. Probably it was Alexander Rose whose entries in the Fort Benton Journal suggest scepticism, antagonism and doubt in regard to the railroad surveys; one entry, a bit out of context as to a railroad, "which will never be" in the writer's opinion. Rose was storekeeper at Fort Benton, and in charge of the post when both Culbertson and Dawson were away.

Isaac Stevens started for Fort Benton in mid-May from Olympia, arrived July 26 ahead of his train with one man, probably James Doty. The fort welcomed him properly, with a cannon shot and flag. The Missouri, high in early spring, had lost that stage when Commissioner Cumming delayed delivery of annuities to the waiting steamboats. As a result keelboats bearing presents for the Indians attending the great council were sadly delayed in their voyage from Fort Union. An attendance of thousands from the various tribes had been anticipated, but the lengthy delay caused many to drift away in pique at unfulfilled promises by the white men. Stevens of course sent messengers with invitations to the council. He was also a bit outraged at appointment of another man as senior commissioner.

Henry Kennerly in later years recalled the council. He was a clerk in the Washington, D. C., Indian office when Col. Alfred Cumming, designated by President Pierce to head the council, invited Kennerly to go along as one of the clerks. They left via the American Fur steamboat St. Mary from St. Louis June 6, 1855, a slow trip due to the need to cut wood for the boat. Omaha, Kennerly noted, was a village of about 100, about the size of Fort Benton at the time. St. Mary reached Fort Union July 7, and the Indian presents and supplies for the fort transferred to three mackinaws, each drawn by about 30 voyageurs, all in charge of Andrew Dawson of Fort Benton.

At the same time, Alfred Cumming, Alexander Culbertson, and Alfred J. Vaughn, new Indian agent, Little Dog, chief of the Piegans, and others started overland for Fort Benton. Kennerly recalled it as one of the most enjoyable trips he had ever made. The commissioner's 350 pounds went by "ambulance" or light wagon with a top. Arrival at Fort Benton was in late July. Kennerly was one of the messengers, he with Baptiste Champagne, an old timer, were to contact the three tribes of Blackfeet, up to Sweet Grass Hills and Cypress Mountains. One of the chiefs he contacted in Canada was Lame Bull of the Piegans, for whom the Blackfeet later named the treaty.

On his return there was word from the keelboats that they could not possibly reach Fort Benton before early October. So it was reluctantly decided to halt the boats at the mouth of the Judith and hold the council there. Couriers went out again with the new site. The mackinaws were even slower than that word, but finally arrived. Kennerly recalled the council lasted six or seven days with several thousand Indians attending—other reports estimate 2500, about a fourth the number hoped for. Actual signing, "touching the pen," was October 17, 1855.

The young Kennerly was impressed with Indian oratory, especially that of Little Dog and Bear Chief, both urging peace and observance of the treaty. Then came the high spot for the Indians, the distribution of presents: Blankets, cloth, calico, sugar, coffee, beans, dried apples. Recipients knew little about preparation of foods given, and their trail was marked by strewn flour, beans, rice, hominy—saving the sacks for wearing apparel. Both commissioners made haste to depart, Cumming down the Missouri, Stevens for Washington Territory, and the great council was over. Kennerly went back to the States, but returned the following year in employ of American Fur.

One overlooked hero of this council to Isaac Stevens was his express rider, W. H. Pearson, who kept the governor in touch with events of the coastal area. On one occasion in August Pearson rode from the Bitter Root to Olympia and back to Fort Benton, about 1750 miles, in 28 days. Despite his squabbles with Cumming, Stevens was well satisfied with council and treaty, "beyond our most sanguine expectations." He left Fort Benton October 31, despite advices of an Indian war in the eastern part of present Washington, going overland westward, with no problems en route.

The Journal duly chronicled arrival of the white visitors; there is a gap between October 4 and 18 (the signing of the treaty was October 16, 17 with the oratory Kennerly mentions). October 21, "Several Indians came from treaty today laden with presents and highly pleased." American Fur bears the onus for delay of the Indian goods, quite possibly unjustly—their trade goods were likewise delayed. Some small amounts came in two wagons from the Judith October 19, the previous day J. F. Wray overland from Fort Union with six wagons of goods. It was not until November 5 that the Fort Benton Journal reported, "At long last our boats came in sight but were unable to cross the ford...this is the longest trip on record—112 days from Fort Union which includes 11 days detention in building a boat and 14 days at the Judith."

### Lt. John Mullan Builds His Road

Isaac Stevens is generally credited with the idea of a military road from Fort Benton westward across the mountains during his three weeks at Fort Benton in 1853, the man he assigned to further the project was Lt. John Mullan, who certainly proved an exceptional choice, although work was to be delayed and completion required about a decade. Mullan's explorations, and his feat of taking a wagon from Fort Benton to the Bitter Root brought the initial appropriation of $30,000, regarded as far too little by army officials. In addition an Indian war in the Spokane area intervened, and Mullan was assigned to other posts during the interval.

The 624 mile route he eventually opened to travel was intended for military use primarily, but almost from its beginnings was called the Mullan Road. In connecting the heads of navigation on Columbia and Missouri the builder opened the first route across the continent appreciably faster than the Oregon and California trails. It could also be said to represent a fulfillment of Jefferson's instructions to Meriwether Lewis to find "the most practicable water communications route across this continent." Historians have duly noted its significance, short lived in view of completion of the railroad at Promontory Point, Utah, in 1869. The military road from Fort Benton to Fort Walla Walla, Washington, in 1978 was designated a National Historic Civil Engineering Landmark by the American Society of Civil Engineers and in August a plaque was installed on the statue of Mullan on the levee at Fort Benton.

March 15, 1858, Lt. John Mullan was given the special assignment to commence work on the military road from the Washington side and reported at Fort Dalles two months later. Before the start, however, one Colonel Steptoe was licked by Indians near Rosalia, and in the aftermath another year was lost.

March 18, 1859, and by then a first lieutenant, Mullan was placed in charge again, with another $100,000 appropriation added. With a considerable party organized, actual work began on June 25, 1859. Start was from old Fort Walla Walla, present Wallula, and at first was easy, across rolling prairie, with of course some cuts to cross gullies, washes and streams, and by August 18, the Mullan party was 199 miles on its way. That was at Coeur d'Alene Mission, and in his camp John Mullan received twin barreled good tidings: First, the Chippewa had arrived at Fort Benton with 24,000 rations for the work force (actually 12 miles below Benton); second, the steamer Colonel Wright had butted its way up the Snake River to the mouth of the Tucannon. So Mullan's road would connect two heads of navigation in actuality instead of in theory. Prairie changed to forest and from mid-August the workmen were cutting their way through trees, sometimes near jungle of fallen timber; but that provided plenty of material for building numerous bridges, large and small. By December 4 they had gotten to just inside present Montana. The party wintered there, 15 miles from the Clark's Fork, at Cantonment Jordan near present St. Regis.

Mullan made a trip to Fort Benton in March of 1860, returning to his party with about half of the 24,000 rations left by the Chippewa the year before. The road builders worked their way up Clark's Fork to Hell Gate (near present Missoula) by June 28. There Mullan learned that Major Blake and 300 men were at Fort Benton, via American Fur steamers Key West and Chippewa, reinforcements for the west side. The remainder of the route was hastily roughed out—over the Rockies at Mullan Pass, just north of the present highway via McDonald pass, down the Prickly Pear, via Medicine Rock and Bird Tail divide to the Dearborn, thence easy going to Fort Benton by August 1. There the weary Mullan party rested up for four days. Then the Blake party left for the coast, Mullan with a small party working ahead of the soldiers to improve the roughest spots. The soldiers reached Walla Walla in 57 days, representing a saving of time and steamship fares via Cape Horn of about $30,000. This was apparently the only major use of the military road by any large party of soldiers, but thousands of miners and other immigrants used portions during the Idaho and Montana gold stampedes.

Mullan and men worked on the road, improving and repairing, for the years 1861-62. This was after another $100,000 appropriation and a trip to Washington, D. C., then back to Walla Walla. Part was relocating the northernmost part of the route in the Coeur d'Alene region, to the north end of that lake, about 30 miles of timber cutting and all that entailed. In summer 1862 Mullan regarded his work as ended, and at Fort Benton discharged a number of his men.

It probably never occurred, but one can speculate on an interesting meeting of road builder Mullan, and James L. Fisk, who on September 5, 1862, arrived with a wagon train of 130 persons overland from Minnesota via the 1851 Culbertson trail. Both routes were much used in the next few years. Mullan was promoted to captain on August 11, 1862. He returned east, completed a comprehensive report on the road, then resigned his commission. In view of his Virginia birth, it appears likely divided allegiance was one cause.

Mullan reported: "The road involved 120 miles of timber cutting 25 feet broad and 30 measured miles of excavation, 15 to 20 feet wide, the remainder was either through an open timbered country or open rolling prairie." He could have added that his party built hundreds of bridges, large and small, numbers of ferry boats—one of these left at Sun River and in use during the Montana gold stampede. The road, without upkeep, soon fell into disrepair, Montana newspapers in the late 1860s plugging for another appropriation to keep the route to the west coast open. In the gold rush thousands of mules were used as pack animals to bring goods from the west via this route, the traffic slowing after about 1865 from the newspaper items.

Fort Benton was a supply center throughout construction, for the parties on the east side of the great mountain ranges. John Strachan, one of the Mullan crew, in 1860, recalled "Fort Benton has everything...a bakery, blacksmith, carpenter and cooper shops, trade offices for buying, others for selling and retail shops. Goods are sold at enormous prices...sugar is sold at $1 and up a pound and everything else in proportion. Business amounts to about $160,000 a year, with buffalo robes the staple of trade."

In addition to the official report, Capt. Mullan wrote a guide book for immigrants, a suggested 47 days from Fort Walla Walla, quite evidently written for ox drawn vehicles as most daily distances are around 15 miles. However, save for the pack mules, virtually all the traffic of 20,000 persons was from Fort Benton west. The route ran via 28 Mile Springs, Benton Lake, Sun River and up (2 days), Bird Tail Rock, Dearborn, over Medicine Rock, Little Prickly Pear, Mullan Pass, Little Blackfoot, Deer Lodge River, Gold Creek (14 days this far); rest of the way out of Montana via present Drummond, Bonner, Missoula and De Borgia—29 days in all to Idaho line and 18 across northern Idaho and eastern Washington. Much of the route is that of today's highways.

## Final Years of Fur Post Fort Benton

A sideline, but still an extensive operation at Fort Benton in the years after the Stevens expedition was the making of sundried adobe bricks and reconstruction of the buildings within the stockade. The Fort Benton Journal from September 1854 to November 1856 includes many comments on the number of "dobbies" made. Another occupation was old hat, logs secured for mackinaws from the Highwoods and firewood cut locally from Teton and Marias valleys. The old American Fur trail to the Highwoods, using the old Indian ford across the Missouri, thus was probably the first Montana trail to have an appreciable travel, the general route still exists today in roads south.

Main occupation of course was trading, and the Journal entries indicate that wagon outfits with trade goods were sent in season to Blackfeet camps in the area. Those mentioned in the Journal as so trading included Louis Rivet, Antoine Bercier, Hugh Monroe, James Bird, Baptiste and Michel Champaigne. Mutual trust between white and red had apparently developed from long association, the trading trips to Indian camps were pretty much routine by the mid-1850s.

An additional business prop was the Indian annuities, on which American Fur until 1862 had a monopoly. Fort Benton in essence was the Blackfeet agency from the time of the Judith Council of 1855.

Scarcity of game in winter on occasion meant short rations. A February 1855 item included the comment: "No loafing in these times there being nothing for whites or Indians to eat." Next day a couple of wagons loaded with traded meat was "Most acceptable in these times of starvation." Later that month a buffalo was killed back of the fort and "thus the famishing thousands about the fort got a bite." The spring brought some Indians with robes in relatively small quantities, 420 robes noteworthy despite "A slow tedious trade." April also brought seasonal chores, completion of new mackinaws and pressing into packs of ten the robes traded during the winter, 250 packs a good day's work. That May of 1855 started with the loading of two boats, the trade at Fort Benton about 11,000 robes in all, the down river shipment leaving May 3. Later in the summer arrival of Isaac Stevens for his big Indian council of course disrupted routine proceedings.

That Stevens council, as noted before, was delayed because of slow progress of the keelboats from Fort Union loaded with white presents to red brothers, and the council eventually transferred to the mouth of the Judith and held in mid-October. It was not until November 5th that the trade goods arrived at Fort Benton, 112 days out of Fort Union, including 11 days to build a boat and 14 at the council grounds. The lateness indicated that charges American Fur employes deliberately held up arrival of Indian annuities were not founded in fact—the

Blackfeet got their presents before doing their fall trading at the fort anyway.

Malcolm Clarke, second in command to Culbertson at Fort Benton 1850-53, and for a time one of the shareholders in American Fur, was "in opposition" in the 1854 and 1855 seasons, the latter year arriving with 13 carts of goods to trade on the Teton. He apparently maintained good relations with successor Andrew Dawson, visited the fort several times and was an overnight guest on occasion. Clarke sold out his stock on the Teton by the end of February 1856. Later he was in charge at Fort Campbell after Frost & Todd took over from Picotte & Co. In 1860 American Fur took over Fort Campbell—at one time loaning it to Catholic missionaries.

Visiting Blackfeet during the off season occasionally stirred Andrew Dawson's orderly Scot mind to a sense of outrage. They hung around the post waiting for meal time, begged for whisky and tobacco, their war parties demanded a customary few rounds of ammunition. Hence the Journal contains comments such as the "fort is full of loafers." Dawson could occasionally find a cheering note, in July 1856 workmen completed the "Doughboy Work of the Bastion," the carpenters put in the upper floor and roof of the corner, perhaps of the blockhouse which survives. Work of conversion to adobe ended about 1860 with a second bastion and some adobe walls. Dawson's disposition doubtless grew more sour after the night in 1858 when he fell through a trap door into the basement, injuries causing leg use impairment and eventually his replacement by Isaac G. Baker in 1864.

Beginning of work on the military road from the west by John Mullan in 1859 brought the first white trade, aside from occasional visits by John Owen in the Bitter Root, the Stuart brothers from present Deer Lodge and other isolated settlers. An event of 1859, of course, was arrival of the steamboat Chippewa at the site of Fort Brule (McKenzie).

The Mullan Road was roughed out next year, two steamboats brought a number of emigrants and 300 soldiers bound west, and the fur post was no longer one of the most isolated spots in the United States. In 1861 part of the freight on the ill fated Chippewa was consigned to yet another point, the Higgins and Worden store at Hell Gate, near later Missoula. A year later, with the first important gold discovery at Bannack, suddenly the supply of small white settlements had become a major item in the trade of Fort Benton. There were alternate routes, over the Mullan Trail, or north from Salt Lake City or from the Overland Trail from Fort Hall, but these were costlier due to the long distances of wagon freighting.

The Civil War from 1861 had been a factor, but 1862 Union forces were gradually getting control of the Mississippi and hence of the Missouri River. Pierre Chouteau Jr. and his associates in American Fur, were suspected of Confederate sympathies, although in trading on the Upper Missouri this scarcely mattered. What did was that no steamboats managed to reach Fort Benton in 1863. Next year Charles Chouteau, assuming a hand in his father's business, sent the second Yellowstone, which reached only Cow Island, 120 miles below Fort Benton.

Remodeled, the Yellowstone reached Fort Benton in 1865, bringing Charles Chouteau, and I. G. Baker, who had assumed charge of Fort Benton fur post the year before. Chouteau had come to turn over the last family trading post to a syndicate, operating as North West Fur. Their six years in Fort Benton were spent as a general store, primarily supplying the incoming white miners, with some Indian trade through outposts.

The company, according to John Sunder's "Fur Trade," was incorporated as Northwestern Fur Co., but the shortened form was generally used, and not to be confused with the old Canadian North West Co. Northwestern was organized by James B. Hubbell and Alpheus F. Hawley, later included James A. Smith and C. Francis Bates, and the purchase of the Chouteau interests was made in 1864. Hubbell and Hawley accompanied Charles Chouteau on the Yellowstone in 1865.

They may have left I. G. Baker in charge, as a June 1866 Montana Post reported Hubbell, J. S. Smith and David F. Pease in Montana to take over. Employes in 1867 included D. K. Broadwater as chief clerk, next year John Riplinger was one of the managers. That year North West Fur received an Interior Department permit to trade with Indians on Teton River near present Choteau, Riplinger apparently in charge of this post, as Canadians locate a Riplinger Trail northward, which differs from the later Whoop Up Trail on the southern portion.

North West Fur can be presumed to have had an excellent business for several years. In 1869 the Helena Herald reported the company had sold its other posts to Durfee & Peck, retaining Fort Benton—late in November 1871 Durfee & Peck bought Fort Benton. F. H. Eastman was apparently the last manager of the post, and his wife Sarah was one of the earliest white women in Fort Benton.

In the years of the Indian trade, what might be considered as a typical inventory for the post is dated May 4, 1851. This includes dozens of items of blankets, shawls, cloth and wearing apparel, valued at $1200. There were around 500 pounds plus 41 bushels of beads, a hundred guns—more than half of these the well known North West trade gun, almost 1200 butcher and scalping knives (a Blackfeet wasn't particular about what he used to collect hair), a substantial number of kettles—tin, iron and brass, almost 5000 pounds of tobacco, 1400 pounds of coffee, a ton of lead and musket balls, 2500 pounds of sugar which Indians loved, and many miscellaneous items. Value of the inventory was about $7150. This was at the tag end of a trading season before arrival of new stock. With other items such as tools for workmen, the Fort Benton total of $8300 was about $2500 below that of Fort Union, supply and storage center.

The profit in the business can be seen by a financial statement of 1856, which would cover the previous year. The Pierre Chouteau & Co. sales amounted to just under $150,000. From sale of these furs and robes the company declared a dividend of $60,000, Chouteau & Co. retaining $40,000; traders shares of the remainder included $5,000 each to Alexander Culbertson and James Kipp, $2500 each to Andrew Dawson and three others. At the time the company operated three posts. The trader shares must be judged against a time when $10-$15 a month was deemed more than fair pay for a laborer, and a skilled workman might get $1 a day. For the year 1856 the robe and fur trade on the Upper Missouri was just about average, if anything 20% below a five year average.

## MISSOURI COMMERCE 1831-1858 FUR TRADE
### By Keelboat and Mackinaw

Note: Buffalo robes are figured at 25 pounds per robe. Numbers are estimated from Alexander Culbertson's figures plus for years of opposition, about half as much for Fort Campbell trade. Building mackinaws an important task to send returns down the Missouri. These boats could be almost any size, Charles Chouteau in 1859 mentions use of two, capacity of each 45 tons. Up tonnages of trade goods may have been slightly higher. Down is second column, number of robes third.

|      | Up  | Down | Robes |                            |
|------|-----|------|-------|----------------------------|
| 1831— | 10  | —    | —     | Fort Piegan                |
| 1832— | 10  | 43   | 3000  | Fort Piegan burnt          |
| 1833— | 10  | 32   | 2000  | Fort McKenzie built        |
| 1834— | 10  | 28   | 2000  |                            |
| 1835— | 10  | 40   | 3000  |                            |
| 1836— | 15  | 102  | 8000  |                            |
| 1837— | 15  | 89   | 7000  | smallpox year              |
| 1838— | 20  | 127  | 10000 |                            |
| 1839— | 20  | 127  | 10000 |                            |
| 1840— | 25  | 255  | 20000 | may have been greater      |
| 1841— | 25  | 288  | 21000 | Culbertson built 5 mackinaws |
| 1842— | 20  | 140  | 11000 |                            |
| 1843— | 20  | 180  | 12000 | May have been 2000 more    |
| 1844— | 10  | 150  | 12500 | Fort McKenzie burned       |
| 1845— | 15  | 62   | 5000  | Fort Chardon               |
| 1846— | 20  | 220  | 17000 | Fort Lewis (above Benton)  |
| 1847— | 25  | 315  | 20000 | Fort Lewis (at Benton) Fort Campbell just above |
| 1848— | 25  | 350  | 25000 | 1000s of buffalo tongues   |
| 1849— | 25  | 330  | 26000 |                            |
| 1850— | 20  | 263  | 21000 | May have been more robes   |
| 1851— | 25  | 325  | 26000 |                            |
| 1852— | 20  | 287  | 23000 |                            |
| 1853— | 25  | 300  | 24000 | Big trade, perhaps more    |
| 1854— | 20  | 287  | 23000 |                            |
| 1855— | 30  | 188  | 15000 | Judith treaty, annuities   |
| 1856— | 30  | 275  | 22000 |                            |
| 1857— | 30  | 381  | 27000 |                            |
| 1858— | 30  | 288  | 23000 |                            |
|      | **555** | **5472** | **418500** |              |

### LOCATION OF AREA FUR POSTS

FORT PIEGAN, 1831-32: Archaeologists say in channel of Marias, north side.

FORT McKENZIE, 1832-44: In cultivated field on Lundy bottom of Missouri, west side, 14 river miles below Fort Benton.

FORT FOX & LIVINGSTON of Union Fur, 1843: East bank of Missouri below Shonkin Creek indicated in Fr. Point sketch.

FORT COTTON, 1844-45: East bank of Missouri, second bottom above Fort Benton.

FORT LEWIS, 1845-47: On or near site of Fort Cotton; also was called Fort Henry, Fort Honore and Fort Picotte for an American Fur member.

FORT CAMPBELL, 1846-47: East bank of Missouri in Evans Bend, about 9 river miles below Fort Benton.

FORT CAMPBELL II, 1847-59: At historic sign on River Street, two blocks above new bridge.

FORT BENTON, 1846 to date: Built winter 1846-7, occupied as Fort Clay, then Fort Lewis from March 1847, named Fort Benton for the Missouri senator Christmas night 1850.

FORT LaBARGE, 1862-66: About 200 yards above Fort Campbell II.

FORT FRANCIS A. CHARDON, 1844-46: North side of Missouri at the mouth of the Judith, just west of later ferry approach.

## MISSOURI STEAMBOAT COMMERCE TO MONTANA 1859-1890
(Figures are estimated on best available data to give Missouri River totals)

Figures include freight to Fort Benton area, to Cow Island and other points, tonnages up and down, passengers up and down (often mere guesses). Under Cow Island 1874 are included 11 cargoes, 2400 tons dropped at Carroll and 1875 9 Carroll cargoes of 1315 tons. Part of Carroll freight eventually moved via Fort Benton. On various occasions hundreds of soldiers were moved, in 1881 2400 Sioux. Peak tonnage years coincided with killing off of buffalo in 1881-82, meaning tons of supplies from boats. Hide shipments from points below Fort Benton not included in these years, but robes, silver ore and in final years wool were major part of down freight. In 1881, D. Maratta of the Coulson Line reported Bismarck had received 160,000 buffalo hides that summer, from Montana steamboats, an indication of the slaughter.

Montana gold production amounted to perhaps as much as 225 tons prior to 1870—at $17 per Troy ounce a ton (avoirdupois) is very close to half a million dollars. One official estimated five-sixths went down the Missouri River. The writer using this, estimates about 175 tons—of which about 50 tons may have gone in small boats. Data inconclusive, partly due to secrecy of owners. Certainly a boat reported to have carried $35,000 in gold was reporting only that in its safe, if there were a 100 passengers the total gold aboard would have been many times the total given, which often reflected an approximate freight bill collected.

| | FB Vic. | Cow I. | Other | Up Tons | Down | Pass Up | Down | Robes |
|---|---|---|---|---|---|---|---|---|
| 1859— | 1 | - | 1 | 160 | 225 | - | - | 18,000 |
| 1860— | 2 | - | 1 | 500 | 250 | 350 | 25 | 20,000 |
| 1861— | - | - | 2 | 250 | 225 | 50 | 25 | 18,000 |
| 1862— | 4 | - | 1 | 1300 | 200 | 600 | 50 | 15,000 |
| 1863— | - | 1 | 3 | 1250 | 300 | 500 | 200 | 30,000 |
| 1864— | 5 | 1 | 2 | 1660 | 250 | 650 | 400 | 20,000 |
| 1865— | 13 | 2 | 4 | 3700 | 365 | 1850 | 800 | 29,000 |
| 1866— | 32 | 4 | 9 | 8944 | 350 | 2000 | 1000 | 15,000 |
| 1867— | 42 | 8 | 8 | 9219 | 600 | 2200 | 2600 | 15,000 |
| 1868— | 37 | 9 | 1 | 5716 | 350 | 1200 | 800 | 15,000 |
| 1869— | 42 | 6 | 6 | 6575 | 400 | 700 | 800 | 15,000 |
| 1870— | 8 | - | - | 1600 | 250 | 230 | 200 | 20,000 |
| 1871— | 6 | 4 | 1 | 2150 | 850 | 200 | 300 | 30,000 |
| 1872— | 13 | - | - | 2950 | 850 | 400 | 200 | 40,000 |

| | FB | Vic. | Cow I. | Other | Up Tons | Down | Pass Up | Down | Robes |
|---|---|---|---|---|---|---|---|---|---|
| 1873— | 7 | - | | 1 | 1750 | 600 | 360 | 160 | 40,000 |
| 1874— | 7 | 12 | | - | 4100 | 1250 | 400 | 500 | 30,000 |
| 1875— | 11 | 12 | | - | 4600 | 2690 | 300 | 250 | 75,000 |
| 1876— | 17 | 6 | | - | 4700 | 2300 | 425 | 460 | 75,000 |
| 1877— | 25 | 8 | | - | 6150 | 2100 | 1060 | 350 | 50,000 |
| 1878— | 54 | 11 | | - | 10,180 | 1833 | 1625 | 750 | 75,000 |
| 1879— | 42 | 9 | | - | 10,711 | 1900 | 1650 | 800 | 30,000 |
| 1880— | 46 | 1 | | 1 | 13,000 | 2500 | 1800 | 700 | 20,000 |
| 1881— | 35 | 12 | | - | 17,420 | 4200 | 1300 | 2800 | 30,000 |
| 1882— | 51 | 4 | | - | 12,898 | 3000 | 2350 | 1350 | 20,000 |
| 1883— | 31 | 2 | | - | 11,000 | 1650 | 965 | 400 | 12,000 |
| 1884— | 16 | 1 | | - | 4200 | 1500 | 450 | 150 | 3,000 |
| 1885— | 15 | 3 | | - | 4800 | 1000 | 200 | 150 | |
| 1886— | 13 | 4 | | - | 3745 | 950 | 300 | 100 | |
| 1887— | 33 | - | | - | 6550 | 1200 | 200 | 100 | |
| 1888— | 4 | 1 | | 1 | 600 | 200 | 30 | 10 | |
| 1889— | 3 | - | | - | 400 | 150 | 20 | 10 | |
| 1890— | 1 | - | | - | 300 | 150 | 15 | 5 | |
| | 616 | 121 | | 42 | 163,078 | 34,638 | 24,380 | 16,445 | 760,000 |

Tonnage totals of upbound boats reflect as far as possible, Montana tonnage via the Missouri River. Virtually all freight to Fort Union (Buford) went into Montana.

# World's Innermost Port

Some will quibble about the title, as large craft now travel further up the great Amazon, but in the heyday of the Mountain Steamboats Fort Benton was, indeed, the world's innermost port, the furthest by water from ocean or sea, in active use as a port for powered craft.

Robert Fulton is popularly regarded as inventor of the steamboat, although John Fitch as early as 1790 operated for a short time a powered boat between Philadelphia and Trenton. But it was the voyages of the Clermont on the Hudson River in 1807 which popularized the new mode of transportation.

Steamboats arrived on waters west of the Appalachians quickly. In October 1811 the New Orleans left Pittsburgh on a 2,000 mile maiden trip to New Orleans, arriving in January 1812. By that time, keelboats had been in use by Missouri traders for some years. Distances and routes, as they are to this day, were major problems in the west.

Until the Civil War, the steamboats were the only solution for cheaply moving large tonnages of freight in this area. From the Mississippi and Ohio, water routes expanded rapidly, each river providing its own problems, and a surprising number were made navigable to some extent. From these necessary variances came a rapid evolution of the steamboat.

The first operation on the Missouri was by the Independence, a tiny 98 tonner, which entered the river in mid-May 1819 and went up to Franklin and Chariton, a couple of hundred miles. The same year several boats were employed by Major S. H. Long, in support of an army campaign. The most successful was the imaginatively designed Western Engineer, a government boat, which reached Council Bluffs. (From contemporary reports, this boat was designed to impress Indians, and from these accounts Cornelius M. Ismert of Kansas City in 1948 made a sketch of the Western Engineer with a serpent's head belching smoke from the firebox near the front; paddle wheel concealed at the stern by a tail, apparently throwing a spume of water.)

Council Bluffs was about 660 miles from the mouth of the Missouri, no small distance for the first year of navigation. It was to be a dozen years before there was trade enough to impel further navigation above Omaha and Council Bluffs.

The Missouri, for all its occasional appearance in spring high water, is a shallow, turbulent stream for much of its course. The final 170-mile navigable stretch from Cow Island to Fort Benton was called the "rocky river" by steamboatmen—below to the mouth the "sandy river." In the lower stretch the channel shifted with the seasonal floods, not the least of navigational problems. Boatmen reckoned the distance from mouth to Fort Benton as about 3,000 miles, following the meanders. Army engineers, measuring a straight line course, later came up with 2285.

### The Yellowstone

The fur trade, with various partnerships struggling with American Fur of John Jacob Astor for the proceeds, was virtually the only business on the Upper Missouri for years. Supplies were taken up river by keelboats, built on the lines of a small steamboat and carrying ten tons or so. Motive power was varied, sail favored if wind permitted, poling by the crew "walking the boat up," or cordelle by a lengthy cable, men on shore pulling the boat up, exhausting and dangerous. It took a season to get beads, tobacco, alcohol and other supplies to barter for furs up to the outposts. Manuel Lisa, the Spanish trader who had put up the first white man's structure (Fort Manuel Lisa among other names) near the mouth of the Big Horn on the Yellowstone in 1807, bettered that season record. In 1811, chasing Wilson Hunt's Astorians, Lisa's keelboat crew left 19 days behind, caught Hunt's party near the Big Bend of the Missouri in present South Dakota on May 29. That was 1200 miles in 61 days, more than 18 miles a day and a record no sensible keelboater ever tried to best. Helping Lisa, without doubt, was that his party caught a remarkable, shifting wind—the party hoisted the keelboat sail and the wind followed Lisa around the 75 miles of the Great Bend.

Kenneth McKenzie, one of the ablest fur traders on the upper river, began his career with Columbia Fur Co. in 1822. Five years later American Fur bought the company and acquired McKenzie's services as well. Aware of the difficulties and time involved in transport by keelboat, McKenzie soon proposed that American Fur try a steamboat. In the summer of 1830 Pierre Chouteau, Jr., passed the proposal on to company headquarters in New York City. There was opposition of course, but the plan was approved.

The prophetically named Yellowstone was built in the winter of 1830-31, in the spring made its maiden trip down the Ohio, first of all the Mountain Steamboats. The Yellowstone was 130 feet long, 19 feet wide and drew six feet of water with 75 tons of cargo. That draught would be drastically lessened on later boats, but steamboating was in a state of flux at the time.

The Yellowstone made its trip to St. Louis with no trouble, on April 10, 1831—leaving there ten days later up the Missouri. A short distance above the Niobrara low water stopped the boat. Pierre Chouteau, aboard, sent to Fort Tecumseh for lighters to take off part of the cargo. The Yellowstone arrived June 19 at Fort Tecumseh, unloaded Indian goods, took down furs and 10,000 pounds of smoked buffalo tongues, a delicacy for eastern markets long transported in quantity. The steamboat, in spite of a shorter trip than hoped for, was regarded as a success by the company.

The next year the start was earlier, the Yellowstone leaving St. Louis March 26, and benefiting by the highest stage of water in years, reached Fort Tecumseh with no trouble. At that time the place was renamed Fort Pierre. Fort Union was attained on June 17, 1832, a date of importance in steamboating history. George Catlin, famed for Indian portraits, was a passenger. The voyage might be said to have ripped the veil of distance from a quarter of the nation.

The Yellowstone's down cargo was several hundred packs (10 each) of buffalo robes. Some of these may have come from a new outpost on American Fur's farflung fur empire, Fort Piegan, built in 1831 by James Kipp at the mouth of the Marias. Piegan's trade the previous winter had included 6450 beaver pelts and 3,000 buffalo robes, which would have weighed about 43 tons and transported to Fort Union by keelboat and mackinaw. After the single season, Piegan was abandoned, burned by tribesmen, and in fall 1832 rebuilt as Fort McKenzie a few miles up the Missouri.

Success of the Yellowstone's second trip brought the addition of another American Fur steamboat, Assinaboine, in 1833, which made a trip to Fort Union while the other boat ran into trouble. This was an epidemic of cholera, deadly in those years along the rivers. Half the crew of the Yellowstone had died by the time the boat reached the mouth of Kansas River, so Captain Bennett went back for more crew members. Terrified Missourians ordered the steamboat to leave their waters, pilot and most sub-officers were dead, and young Joseph LaBarge in charge. He fired up, and acted as pilot, engineer and all to move the Yellowstone to the Kansas shore—a start on a distinguished career on the Missouri River.

### Helping Hand For Texas

That was the end of the Yellowstone as a Mountain Steamboat, but her later services were startling, in a different area of the nation. The boat, having as noted too much draught for the Upper Missouri, worked in the sugar trade out of New Orleans for the next two years. In February 1836 the Yellowstone steamed into Texas waters, probably with arms and volunteers, right in the midst of the Texan War of Independence, arriving at San Felipe on the Brazos February 27, 1836. She went to Galveston in April, conveyed the Texan government from Galveston to Houston, returning with General Sam Houston aboard. Some time in May 1836, General Houston took the captured Mexican president and general, Santa Anna, aboard the Yellowstone to Galveston, where Santa Anna was imprisoned. In August the steamboat carried munitions from Galveston to Columbia for the new Republic of Texas. In December the boat was the funeral carriage for Stephen Austin, father and founder of the new nation, from Columbia on the Brazos to Peach Point for burial with a nation's honors. The Yellowstone sank in Buffalo Bayou on a trip from Galveston to Houston in 1840.

It might well be claimed of the Yellowstone that it was instrumental in saving Oregon Territory for the United States and played an important role in the war which after another war resulted in Texas becoming a part of our nation.

### Steamboats in the Fur Trade

Steamboats played an increasing role in the fur and robe trade of the Missouri River after the 1832 trip of the Yellowstone. One facet was the growing trade in buffalo robes, which had an effect on the history of the Northwest. Hudson's Bay Company, dominant across the border after merger with North West Co., had a long water and portage haul to eastern markets and could not handle the heavy robes with much success. Result was the robe trade tended to go to American traders who could. There was the additional impact on Indian minds of the "fire boats" as indicating the strength of the Americans.

The Assinaboine went on the river in 1833 and two years later became the first steamboat to go an appreciable distance into later Montana, reaching Poplar River that season. Its destruction by fire near Heart River in 1835 along with many robes and furs brought an American Fur Co. policy of chartering steamboats in place of owning them.

By that year Fort McKenzie, between later Fort Benton and the mouth of the Marias, was trading for a gradually increasing number of buffalo robes. Robes were packed and bound by tens (an estimated 250 pounds per pack, so 8 packs or 80 robes was about a ton). Transport down the Missouri, save for the available annual keelboat, was by mackinaw. These were flat bottomed boats built of sawn planks, about 40 to 50 feet long and 10 to 12 wide, meaning a major job at trading posts was lumbering, sawing and carpentry. (Fort Benton was always to have a better supply of artisans than of materials with which to build.) Motive power was principally the river current. While such one way boats could go all the way to St. Louis with their valuable cargoes, more often from about 1840 robes and furs were transferred to steamboats at or below Fort Union. Cargoes also included smoked tongues and tallow.

There may have been a year's hiatus in steamboating to the Yellowstone, at least one South Dakota historian found no record of any boat in 1836. Next year smallpox came to the Indians in the form of blankets aboard the St. Peters infected with smallpox, with tragic results. Trade in robes and furs of course dwindled after the great epidemic. Some of the steamboats coming to Fort Union in the next few years, Platte, Antelope, Malta, Trapper, Nimrod and General Brooke, the latter in 1845 and 1846.

By that time there was opposition in the Fort Benton area, Fr. Point's 1847 sketches indicates by Fox & Livingston, also known as Union Fur, rather short lived. More determined was that of Alexander Harvey, doing business as Harvey, Primeau & Co., and backed by Robert Campbell of St. Louis. Harvey had been fired in 1845 for his part in an attack on a trading party at Fort McKenzie in February 1844 that resulted in destruction of the post. Harvey came back up river in 1846, bringing the steamboat Clermont No. 2 to a few miles above the mouth of the Yellowstone, and below where Fort Benton would soon be located built Fort Campbell in the vicinity of Evan's Bend. Next year Harvey's supplies were brought up on the Tamerlane. Meanwhile, the American Fur post had been moved back up from the Judith and Alexander Culbertson built Fort Lewis in late 1845 on the site of a Fort Cotton a short distance above later Fort Benton. This Fort Cotton was operated by Fox & Livingston (Union Fur) in 1844-45 and bought out by American Fur early in 1845. This location for American Fur was on the opposite side of the river and inconvenient for Indians. In the winter of 1846-47 Culbertson made preparations to move, completing the transfer March 19, 1847, to what was renamed Fort Benton in 1850. (Harvey, too, moved Fort Campbell up and across the Missouri to a point about half a mile above the American Fur post.)

Incursions of opposition steamboats may have provided a nudge to the fiercely competitive American Fur, for in 1850 the company sent the El Paso above Fort Union. June 20 one of those aboard prepared a marker for a new head of navigation about 8 miles above the mouth of Milk River. Probably at this point freight for Fort Benton was unloaded, as mentioned in a journal by Thaddeus Culbertson, a passenger.

By that year steamboats for the upper Missouri were getting better adapted to the river, the St. Ange managed something like four trips to Union in the 1850s. In 1851 under John LaBarge, the St. Ange reached the mouth of Poplar River in spite of low water, unloaded goods for Fort Benton there. Probably as a direct consequence, Alexander Culbertson took a wagon and five men from Fort Union November 1st and reached Fort Benton around the first of December. The route he followed, judging by the better documented Isaac Stevens expedition of 1853, is largely perpetuated in US2 from the North Dakota line to Havre.

The Stevens expedition had several objectives. He was going west to assume governorship of Washington Territory, was to make preliminary surveys for a possible northern railroad, and also to lay the groundwork for peace councils with the Indian tribes. The fairly large party spent three weeks in Fort Benton, messengers contacting the tribesmen for a council at the post at a future date. One accomplishment was preliminary planning for a military road which would connect heads of navigation on the Missouri and Snake-Columbia system—those heads of navigation not being attained until 1860!

In 1855 Stevens and party returned to Fort Benton from the Northwest. Gifts promised those attending were carried to Fort Union on the spring trip of the steamboat St. Mary, from there to be taken to Fort Benton by small boats at 13 3/4c per pound, about three times the rate to Union. As things turned out, the toilsome boat trip from Union was slow, the council ultimately held at the mouth of the Judith River. Charges were voiced later that American Fur had deliberately slowed arrival of the treaty goods to benefit their own trade. However, the Fort Benton Journal of the period shows that trade goods for the post at Fort Benton did not arrive until after the mid-October council and it appears that delays in delivery of annuities to St. Louis by Commissioner Cumming were responsible.

In 1856 Captain John LaBarge brought the St. Mary to the mouth of Milk River in late July to land the goods consigned to Fort Benton and the Blackfeet annuities in charge of Edwin A. C. Hatch, Indian agent, and furthest use to then of the Missouri for cargo. In 1857 in a final effort by the opposition, the Twilight landed goods for Fort Campbell at Poplar River, as well as annuities in care of the new Blackfeet agent, Alfred J. Vaughan. In 1858 with the Spread Eagle, John LaBarge turned back 50 miles below Milk River.

### Voyage of the Chippewa

First of the "Mountain Steamboats," as St. Louis termed them, to actually reach the Fort Benton area, where for years most of the Montana freight was destined, was the Chippewa. By the 1850s steamboats built for western rivers had long since lost the deep draft common in the experimental years. The Missouri, by reason of its great length of potentially navigable waters, posed special problems.

The Chippewa was built at Belle Vernon, Pennsylvania, in 1857, 160 feet long and 30 wide, with three boilers and two engines, and was a sternwheeler, as ultimately the case with most Mountain Steamboats. Its rating was 175 tons, but actual capacity according to Charles Chouteau, by 1859 in charge of American Fur field operations, was about 350 tons.

The company that year held two interesting government contracts, for transportation of annuities for the Indian department, to Fort Union, Fort Sarpy (on the Yellowstone) and Fort Benton, and secondly for the transportation of Major W. F. Raynolds' military reconnaisance group. For the freight, the rate was $2.50 per 100 pounds from St. Louis to Fort Union, and $7.25 per 100 pounds from Union to Fort Benton. Small wonder that Chouteau in November reported to John Floyd, Secretary of War.

In company with the Spread Eagle, a bigger boat, the Chippewa left St. Louis May 28, 1859, the heavily laden steamboats picking up the Raynolds party at St. Joseph June 4 and landing them June 18 at Fort Pierre, whence the military proceeded overland for the Yellowstone.

The Chippewa and Spread Eagle had little trouble, save a daily stop to secure firewood, to Fort Union July 1st, where most of the cargo was discharged. There by agreement Chouteau bought the Chippewa, for the rest of the smaller boat's mission was regarded as challenging and dangerous. John LaBarge, captain of the Spread Eagle, who had two previous trips to the Milk River vicinity on his record, was to handle the Chippewa.

Reported Chouteau later to Floyd: "After transferring 160 tons of freight to the Chippewa, so as to increase her draft of 31 inches, I engaged a crew of 95 men composed chiefly of old voyageurs, so as to insure my overcoming all the difficulties represented to exist, and had two mackinaw boats of 45 tons capacity each, lashed to her sides to serve as lighters in case of need."

The boat left July 3rd, "fully a month after the water commenced receding." The travelers had all the anticipated difficulties. July 5, "Met with considerable delays, caused by the shifting of the channel. Tore out the stern post of one of the barges, which obliged us to lay up at Wolf Point the balance of the day to repair damages." Next day the Chippewa reached the previous high of navigation, "El Paso Point," and lost 24 hours in bettering the mark due to shallowness of the river. July 7th "was spent in lightening and sparring over the Many Sand Bars both above and below the 'Big Dry Fork'." Chouteau was finding those mackinaws useful.

July 8th the party was cheered by an evening stop at Round Butte, half way to Fort Benton, but snags and sawyers were more than the "annoying" Chouteau noted. Next day the boat ran 80 miles, great abundance and variety of game all the way. July 11 was spent hunting an elusive channel, but LaBarge got his command past another landmark, Chouteau spelled it "Muscilshell." Here they hit the division soon emphasized by rivermen, the "rocky river" which exists the rest of the way to Fort Benton.

July 11 the Chippewa passed "large and beautiful" islands with naturally a succession of shoals and rapids, next day found wood scarce and rapids numerous, and the barges came into use at four different rapids.

July 13 and 14, "Two whole days were occupied in crossing Dauphin's Rapids, which is by far the most formidable and dangerous encountered on the river, and until cleared of the many boulders which are all loose, will ever be a serious barrier to Steam Boat Navigation." Charles Chouteau would not be the last to so observe.

July 15 they maneuvered up a succession of rapids, reaching the mouth of the Judith River at 2 p. m., finding with satisfaction an abundance of wood. One of the barges was abandoned this day as a drag on the Chippewa, the second the next day. The result, July 16th was the best day's run of the trip, and they camped a few miles below the Marias at Spanish Island.

July 17, "We reached the mouth of Maria river at 8 o'clock a. m. and Old Fort Mackenzie at 1 o'clock p. m. Here our stock of fuel gave totally out, and without a possibility of replenishing it except by retracing our steps a considerable distance." The river was falling, so the Chippewa discharged its 160 tons of freight on the bottom. In the afternoon Chouteau visited Fort Benton and next day went down by skiff to sound the river, finding not less than three and a half feet of water. So he left instructions to have a large amount of cordwood cut for next season, and the Chippewa turned down stream at 2 p. m. July 19.

July 20, "In descending Dauphin's Rapids, we struck the rocks with great force, breaking many of our bottom timbers, and Burds Rapids came very nearly disabling us entirely." After presumable repairs, and much trouble from sand bars and high wind, the Chippewa reached Fort Union the morning of July 26th.

Despite the damage to the boat, Charles Chouteau triumphantly reported to the Secretary of War: "By my present experience I have arrived at the conclusion that with suitable boats and the removal of boulders here and there obstructing the channel and forming the rapids, that the navigation of the Upper Missouri can be made just as safe and easy as the Upper Mississippi or Ohio rivers, and I have no hesitation in affirming that the trip from Saint Louis to Fort Benton can be easily accomplished within thirty-five days." Charles Chouteau was a prophet, although it was never "easy." The fastest trips to Fort Benton were right in range of that 35 days.

And the way was open for "suitable boats."

1859 summary:

July 17, Chippewa to Fort McKenzie, 160 tons freight up, 225 tons down (by mackinaw in spring, time was lacking for transport of any great amount of freight the 12 miles to McKenzie. Spread Eagle probably took Fort Benton robes down from Union, unloading 40,000 robes—about 500 tons—at St. Louis Aug. 16.)

July 1, Spread Eagle to Fort Union, estimated tonnage 300. Some of Spread Eagle cargo may have been sent by keelboat or wagon to Benton, perhaps supplies for John Mullan's road building party.

## 1860—First Steamboats to Fort Benton

Navigation opened early on the Missouri at St. Louis in the spring of 1860, but the Chouteaus were more interested in careful preparations. They had added a boat, the Key West, apparently about the same size as the Chippewa, for it was reported in St. Louis papers as drawing only 33 inches of water with a 180 ton load. Then there was the much larger Spread Eagle, under John LaBarge, while Bob Wright was captain of the new boat and Bill Humphreys of the Chippewa.

This was to be an historic trip, heralding a new route to the Oregon country appreciably faster than the long used Oregon Trail. For Lt. John Mullan had opened a military road from old Fort Walla Walla at the head of navigation on the Snake River, and Fort Benton on the Missouri. Further, the company had contracted to carry 300 officers and men, plus "a due allowance of laundresses" to the head of navigation on the Missouri. There the miniature army would march west over Mullan's new road.

St. Louis gave the expedition a rousing sendoff; for one thing, it was one of the largest fleets yet to leave for the Upper Missouri, on departure May 3. Early going was slow, the small armada meeting the usual snow runoff rise near the Nebraska border. Thereafter there were few problems. Supplies and annuities were unloaded June 15 at Fort Union, and all three steamboats headed on up the Missouri. At the mouth of Milk River the Spread Eagle transferred its cargo to the other two, which probably were crammed with freight plus swarming soldiers.

Then, wrote a participant in the military movement, Martin D. Hardin, quoted in John Sunder's "Fur Trade," Charles Chouteau invited officers and guests aboard the empty Spread Eagle, and gave John LaBarge a go-ahead to set a new Missouri record for sidewheel steamers. LaBarge went 15 miles above El Paso Point on the joy ride before turning back. He then took over the Key West, Wright took the Spread Eagle down, and Chippewa and Key West headed for another record. It was July 2 that the boats, crammed with freight, passengers and annuities tied up at Fort Benton—a great day in the eventful history of the place. The troops waited there until early August for Lt. Mullan to join them as guide.

1860 summary:

July 2, Key West, est. 250 tons; Chippewa same, to Fort Benton.

June 22-23, Spread Eagle, to Milk River, estimate 300 tons to Fort Union, some transshipped on Benton boats.

Estimate 250 tons robes down on Chippewa, Key West, also on these boats estimate 350 passengers up, 25 down.

## Chippewa Blows Up

By 1860, Fort Benton had become the outstanding upriver outfitting point for the military and civilians alike in the Montana Rockies, wrote John Sunder in his excellent research on the "Fur Trade On The Upper Missouri," but the small, although growing colony of whites in the Bitter Root, Deer Lodge and Missoula areas were to be bitterly disappointed in their 1861 visits to Fort Benton.

American Fur relied on the proven Chippewa and Spread Eagle, which left April 25 and May 1 from St. Louis for the upper river. The boats met near Sioux City and went on to Fort Union, arriving June 15. The Spread Eagle unloaded its cargo, the passengers went aboard the Chippewa, and the Spread Eagle took down thousands of buffalo robes, about 18,000 from Fort Benton, and made it down to St. Louis in a record nine days from the Yellowstone.

The heavily loaded and overcrowded Chippewa reached what after was called Disaster Bend below Poplar River around supper time June 23, when fire broke out in the cargo hold near a large quantity of gunpowder. Accounts of the cause of the fire vary slightly, but likeliest seems to be that a deck hand went into the hold with a lighted candle to syphon off a bit from a keg of alcohol. The candle tipped or was dropped, the alcohol caught fire and there was chaos within minutes. One deckhand was badly burned, probably the man intent on replenishing his intoxicants. The Chippewa was beached while passengers and crew scrambled to safety on the bank. Then the steamboat was cut loose, drifted down a mile and lodged, burned an hour and blew up from the possibly three tons, most likely much less, of gun powder. William Cary, artist passenger, indicated 300 kegs. (Powder kegs found in the wreck of the Bertrand, sunk 1865, contained 10 pounds.)

Indians from a nearby Crow village found the explosion manna from heaven, passengers salvaged useful items as well. Then the whites were taken down to Fort Union to await a wagon train—Andrew Dawson had been sent posthaste to Fort Benton for wagons and oxen, returned in six weeks with 20 vehicles, and in a long slow trip carried perhaps 50 tons of supplies to the temporary non-head of navigation, along with the passengers bound for the Idaho mines or Oregon, who doubtless hoofed it most of the way.

The Crows continued their salvage, but their joyful efforts were interrupted by a war party of Sioux and it took a bit of fighting to establish their salvage priorities.

Lost in the explosion a few miles below Poplar Creek were about 57 tons of Blackfeet annuities, and a $7,000 stock of merchandise consigned to Frank Worden, newly set up in business at Hell Gate near present Missoula.

The Chippewa carried perhaps 250 tons, part from the Spread Eagle, on her trip which ended so abruptly, an estimate in view of the fast voyage of her companion boat.

Summary for 1861:
Chippewa........250 tons on final trip, 175 to Fort Union
Spread Eagle.....250 tons, 225 tons down
Approximately 50 to 100 tons of freight moved to Fort Benton by wagon then and later, estimated 50 passengers up, 25 down.

## 1862, A Fading Monopoly

High water and determined opposition to the near monopoly American Fur had exercised in Montana waters, in 1862 brought the heaviest freight tonnage yet to Fort Benton. Other factors entered into the spurt in steamboating to the world's innermost port, completion of the military road of John Mullan to the head of navigation on the Snake-Columbia, and a gold rush to gold placers in Idaho spurred the effort. The Civil War was in full and bloody swing, the Union armies gaining major successes toward the control of the Mississippi and hence the western territories.

John LaBarge, who had brought the first American Fur boats to the new heads of navigation in 1859 and 1860, joined his brother Joseph LaBarge and three others in the new opposition, titled LaBarge, Harkness & Co., a concern with a hectic future.

John LaBarge took the Shreveport out of St. Louis April 30 armed with a couple of small cannon (the Sioux, in ferment in Minnesota that year, were moving westward), a large cargo and 75 cabin and a number of deck passengers, and reached the Yellowstone by June 2. Water was high and the Shreveport went on. Joseph LaBarge in the larger sidewheel Emilie LaBarge, left May 14, his boat loaded with gold seekers and 400 tons of Fort Benton freight. Their trip was easy except for severe wind storms.

American Fur sent the Key West and Spread Eagle, leaving St. Louis ahead of the Emilie. June 5, above Fort Berthold, about half way between present Bismarck and the Yellowstone, the Emilie passed the Key West. Next day, partner James Harkness recorded in a diary, "The Spread Eagle is just alongside of us, and we are having a race, (probably) the first ever run on the upper Missouri. She passed us and then we passed her, when she ran into us, breaking our guards and doing other damage. There was a great deal of angry talk." (More than talk, LaBarge threatened to shoot Bob Bailey, Spread Eagle pilot, if his boat didn't give way, and passengers on both grabbed their guns, although apparently no shots were fired. Bailey had his license suspended, Joseph LaBarge interceded in his behalf.)

That was the last the opposition boats saw of each other en route. Emilie reached the Yellowstone June 8, still six days behind her companion Shreveport, ahead of the others.

The Missouri was still rising, the current so fast as to hamper progress, at one point tar was burned after 15 minutes in which the boat didn't gain an inch on the torrent. The Emilie passed the Judith River and overtook the Shreveport June 15 at Drowned Man's rapids, also having trouble with the current. The Emilie had a fairly easy passage, then dropped a line to the companion boat.

Harkness had a word about the White Rocks area, "The bluffs are magnificent beyond description. The sandstone is washed into every shape imaginable."

Both boats arrived at Fort Benton June 17, the Shreveport on a line from the Emilie, over the bar just below the bottom. The larger boat made a point of a brief stop at the American Fur post, providing its residents a good look at the first sidewheel steamboat to ever reach Fort Benton. Then both moved up past old Fort Campbell, by then owned by American Fur, and a couple of hundred yards above moored and unloaded about 600 tons of freight on open prairie. There were also about 400 passengers, most bound for gold fields in Idaho but numbers perhaps lingering around Gold Creek long enough to join the late July rush to Bannack. Steamboat fare was then around $100 for cabin passage—it was higher in later years of the gold rush.

Supplies of the LaBarge boats included the first sawmill imported to Montana; a useful item in erection of Fort LaBarge near the present water plant. Construction included a warehouse, no palisade, making the fort buildings the first built in the open on the Fort Benton bottom. When the property was sold at sheriff's sale later, it included some 11 tiny cabins, among other items, and a sawmill.

The American Fur boats reached the Yellowstone June 8 or 9, where Charles Chouteau decided the sidewheel Spread Eagle this year could make the trip to Fort Benton—a welcome decision, for the company had claimed to be able to sell wagons, animals and supplies to goldseekers when they arrived at Fort Benton. These and the freight of the opposition were probably the first sizable amounts of such equipment in the area. Four men of the Spread Eagle crew were drowned near the Judith on the trip to Fort Benton.

There was to be further enhancement of 1862 freight. The Emilie, leaving June 19, went down to St. Louis and brought another cargo up to Sioux City for the Shreveport. The latter boat reached the Milk River; its return to St. Louis included $70,000 or $80,000 gold (Sioux City Register Sept. 13 reported $100,000) and 1650 buffalo robes. The gold probably came from the area around Gold Creek near

Deer Lodge, or from the Idaho mines via the Mullan Road, the time element would indicate it couldn't be from Bannack. At any rate, it was a small cargo compared with those to go down in later years of the 1860s.

Before the Shreveport left Fort Benton, a party made an excursion to the Great Falls. Among members were Fr. DeSmet, the famed missionary, who had made the trip on the Spread Eagle, Mrs. John LaBarge, and Margaret, daughter of James Harkness, and Natawista Culbertson; the first two ladies were believed to be the first white women to ever view the falls.

Summary for 1862:
June 17, Emilie LaBarge, 400 tons; Shreveport, 200 tons.
June 20, Key West, 200 tons; Spread Eagle, 300 tons.
Total about 1100 tons and 600 passengers, 50 down.
August, Shreveport to Milk River, 200 tons.
Overall around 1300 tons up, 200 down, and a small amount of gold.

### 1863, Year of Frustration

Frustration was the keynote along the Missouri for the year 1863. An army campaign against the Sioux centered on the Dakota Territory, and Gen. Alfred Sully attempted to use steamboats to supply his troops. Four boats were chartered in St. Louis and none were apparently fit for the upper Missouri, although the Florence and West Wind show up in the Yankton area records. Sully's campaign included impressment of the Shreveport and Alone, with an impact on the growing demand for supplies in later Montana, at the time Idaho Territory, following the previous summer's rush to Bannack and the great strike on Alder Gulch in late May 1863.

LaBarge & Harkness had underbid American Fur to win the contract for movement of Indian annuities, a success that was to turn sour in view of later events.

The Shreveport was lengthened 20 feet, draft lightened and new engines installed, and John LaBarge took her up river April 20 with about 80 passengers and 100 tons of freight—for an extended drought made 1863 one of the lowest water years ever.

This year rivermen at St. Louis began looking with eager eyes at the profits to be made in the Mountain Steamboat trade. John J. Roe that spring advertised "Ho for the Yellowstone and the gold mines of Idaho" and announced that he would send two steamboats to Fort Benton. In 1862 there had been 13 departures from St. Louis to the Upper Missouri, including Fort Benton, and in view of high water probably all headed here made it. In 1863 the number for the upper river reached 18 without a single arrival, although daring freighters delivered several hundred tons of Missouri River freight to Fort Benton and on to the mining camps of Bannack and Virginia City.

The Shreveport received freight from the Robert Campbell and reached Snake Point (near Cow Island). There June 20 John LaBarge unloaded 250 tons of freight and 135 passengers, and sent word to Fort Benton for mackinaws to take the cargo to the Judith River, whence it was to be freighted to Bannack. Robert Lemon, in charge of Fort LaBarge here, ultimately contracted with King & Gillette, pioneer Montana freighters, to transport the goods at a ruinous 25c per pound. The consignees, John Roe and son-in-law Nick Wall, ultimately sued for their expense, proved to a federal court the responsibility of LaBarge & Harkness to deliver at Bannack, and took over LaBarge & Harkness oxen—the start of Montana's great Diamond R Transportation Co. Later Fort LaBarge itself was sold to satisfy further Roe claims.

After unloading, the Shreveport went back down to rendezvous with its sister steamboat. The Robert Campbell under Joseph LaBarge was having adventures to turn a steamboat captain's hair white. In an awful trip through Dakota the boat was fired on by Sioux at almost every wooding place or where the channel ran close to shore—the low stage of water increasing the Indians' targets of opportunity tremendously.

The big Robert Campbell had carried 650 tons of freight out of St. Louis, dropping 150 tons at Sioux City, another 200 tons at Fort Randall. With the contract for annuities, the Campbell had been delayed about three weeks pending arrival of the goods, another costly setback. The two boats met near Heart River. About half way between Forts Berthold and Union at Tobacco Gardens Landing the two boats had a tough fight with Sioux. When a yawl was sent in to parley before any shooting, Sioux shot and killed three crewmen outright, another wounded but with three others escaped. Returning fire with a cannon and small arms, the whites later estimated they had killed 18 hostiles and wounded 30 more.

At the mouth of the Yellowstone the channel was only two feet deep, so the Shreveport made five short trips to transfer and store the cargo of the Robert Campbell at Fort Union. The original plan of the smaller boat moving the goods to Fort LaBarge had to be abandoned. The storage, as with nearly every operation of the LaBarges that year, would prove costly, too.

American Fur steamers Nellie Rogers and Alone had quite similar 1863 trips, the two leaving St. Louis May 9 on low water, likewise full of passengers and freight for the mines. They were fired on numerous times, but without a full scale attack such as that on the LaBarge boats. The Nellie Rogers made it to Milk River, while the Alone left its freight at Fort Charles, a few miles above Poplar River. Goods from the two boats were partially transported to Bannack by Joseph A. Slade's train despite two full scale Indian attacks, an "almost incredible" feat. This trip, and the King & Gillette and Roe & Wall freighting efforts, opened the wagon trails for the hard, low water years still to come along the Missouri in Montana. (The 80 passengers on the Nellie Rogers left at Milk River were attacked by a war party of several hundred Sioux, but intervention of Fr. DeSmet, recognized by the chief, saved their lives.)

Despite one of the worst years in Mountain Steamboating history, freight reaching Montana points largely got through, and probably Dakota historians have found that some freight from boats that failed in that area got through the next year.

Summary 1863:
June 20, Shreveport to Snake Point, 250 tons, 85 passengers.
July, Nellie Rogers to Milk River, 250 tons, 80 passengers.
July, Alone to Fort Charles, 250 tons.
July 8, Robert Campbell to Yellowstone, 500 tons.
Estimated 500 passengers up, 200 down, cabin fare $125, 1250 tons freight up, 300 down, likely considerable gold by mackinaw via Missouri and Yellowstone.

# Golden Years on Missouri

## A Measure of Success in a Season of Confusion

The steamboating season of 1864 dawned in St. Louis with a realization by rivermen of tremendous profits to be made in the "Mountain" trade, as well as the perils from hostile Indians, chiefly Sioux, now harried into the hinterland of Dakota Territory. Boiler plate sheathing for pilot houses had come into fashion earlier due to Confederate guerillas along the Mississippi and Missouri, now had become a standard for the Upper Missouri as well.

But profits of a cargo to Fort Benton could be easily understood by the freight rates of 10c, 12c, even 15c—a 200 ton cargo at the lowest rate added up to $40,000, double the cost of an average small packet. Loss of a boat after delivery, even with a wage scale three to four times that on the Ohio, including pilots from $700 a month up, left the owner with the possibility of a profit far beyond the value of a snagged steamboat. In addition, $7,500 could be added from 50 passengers at $150 each. A down cargo of gold, furs and robes could become a substantial bonus. Even more likely a full passenger list of miners with weighty pokes. The potential profits made the prospect glowing.

What was to become Montana May 26, 1864, had produced approximately $8,000,000 worth of placer gold in 1863 at Bannack and Virginia City, and other finds were seemingly being made weekly. That value of gold is about 16 tons at 1864 prices. Joseph LaBarge had taken down perhaps $100,000 in gold in 1862, more went down the next year by mackinaws via the Missouri and Yellowstone, some by stage to Salt Lake City and private transport (and considerable intercepted by Henry Plummer's road agents.) The Vigilante cleanup in the winter of 1863-64 made the trails safer, but only relatively so. By far the safest was by steamboat. Gold possessors were understandably reluctant to report its presence until in a safe place, so estimation of transportation of Montana gold is hit and miss, only one positive note for 1864. At the peak of gold production a government report estimated 5/6ths went down the Missouri. That for the years ending with 1869 would be 175 to 200 tons, at an estimate 125 tons by steamboat, the remainder in smaller craft. Later news accounts tend to back up the figure.

A complicating factor of the 1864 steamboating season was the campaign waged by General Sully in the lower Yellowstone area involving the use of several steamboats. The military was unfamiliar with the uses and limitations of the boats, so the packets had only a qualified success. It did add to steamboat activity in the Fort Union area.

LaBarge, Harkness & Co. had broken in 1863 under the stress of errors and mismanagement, but the triumphant American Fur, by now under direction of Charles Chouteau, was in trouble as well. The owners were suspected of Confederate sympathies and faced potential loss of government freight contracts and loss of their Indian trading license as well. Nevertheless, Chouteau readied the new Yellowstone with its master, William Massie, to become one of the great pilots of the Upper Missouri. Other St. Louis steamboat owners were entering the field, too.

The March 15, 1864, St. Louis Republican carried for one company: (first paragraph identical on the five notices for boats)

"FOR THE GOLD FIELDS OF IDAHO, Virginia City, Bannock City and the Stinking Water Valley Gold Regions.—St. Louis and Fort Benton Freight and Passenger Packet Co.—For Fort Benton and the Great Falls of the Missouri." Then followed: "The entirely new light draught steamer Benton, T. W. Rea, master" to leave March 19; the "new, light draught and fast passenger steamer Welcome, Thomas Townsend, master" to leave April 2; the "new, light draught and excellent steamer Florence, Lawrence Ohlman, master" to leave April 16; the "exceedingly light draught and fast running steamer Marcella, Fitzgerald, master" to leave April 9; the "steamer Fanny Ogden, John P. Keiser, master" to leave April 12. Only the Benton made it to her namesake city, Welcome and Fanny Ogden got above Fort Union, Marcella was impressed by Sully.

In all around 30 steamboats left St. Louis for the Upper Missouri, not all for Fort Benton, Sully had a small fleet, but considering another season of very low water, a surprising number of boats so bound made it to Montana waters. Rivermen were learning something about the Missouri, although still not building boats especially for its problems.

The Benton must have left St. Louis on or about the date advertised, generally a matter of extreme flexibility, reaching Fort Union on May 31, and bringing its cargo here in good time on June 10. It unloaded and dropped back down to Milk River. Meanwhile a sister ship, Fanny Ogden, took Crow and Assiniboine annuities up from Union June 10, along with other freight. As the Benton made another arrival at Fort Benton June 27, from the Milk River, it undoubtedly brought in the other cargo off the Fanny Ogden and perhaps some of its own.

The year 1864 was one in which Fort Benton began a tentative expansion beyond Indian trading posts. Except for the unpalisaded cluster of Fort LaBarge, Clement Corneille (Cornoyer) had built the first log building outside the posts in either 1862 or 1863, now Vincent Mercure and Joseph Laurion were building a 36x90 log structure for Matthew Carroll and George Steell, first regular business although the Indian trade was their major interest. Because of the Mullan Road, overland expeditions of Thomas Holmes and James L. Fisk in 1862, and Fisk again in 1863 had arrived at Fort Benton from Minnesota, making their way on to the mines after replenishing supplies from the trading post. Dr. William Dibbs, with Fisk in 1862, described the place: "The fort is on a nice level prairie—a square building, something like Ft. Union—inside there is the same dirt, half breeds, and their children—dogs, pigs & bugs."

William Gladstone, former Hudson Bay carpenter, was an eye witness to Fort Benton's 4th of July: "There were 1500 men in Benton at that time and I saw such desperate characters as the James brothers among them...With feelings of mutual hate, inflamed by bad whiskey, the men of the North and South were only too eager to come to blows. It was hell upon earth for a time." Most were Southerners, as Union forces gained control of Missouri, Confederates were often paroled on condition they go up the Missouri—one result was discovery of Confederate Gulch gold, later that year. Fort Benton would see it shipped by the ton. John Buchanan, founder of the first Montana newspaper, Montana Post, was along a few days later: "As to this Fort...we...say to strangers, the less you have to do with it the better."

On July 9 the steamboat Benton was a few miles short with another cargo, this one presumably from the Welcome, which reached Fort Union June 17 and went up to Milk River. Information is lacking on provision for guarding such freight, probably the boats met, but in 1865 a small palisaded freight drop was built near Milk River, very useful in protecting supplies from the natives in low water years. For the Benton, these 1864 transshipments of freight from other boats provided a rehearsal for an amazing voyage the next season.

His company was ruined, Joseph LaBarge estimated losses at $100,000, but his steamboating career was far from over. Despite financial difficulties, LaBarge raised money to buy the brand new $40,000 Effie Deans, two times or more the usual price for Mountain packets. He left St. Louis March 22, 1864, with 49 passengers and 160 tons of cargo. The Effie Deans could have carried far more tonnage, but LaBarge was leaving space to pick up Indian annuities that the company had stored with American Fur at Fort Union the year before. The agent refused to deliver same without payment of an extortionate storage fee and surrender of receipts before delivery of goods. LaBarge suspected the American Fur had traded the annuities to Indians, a suspicion often voiced along the river. So no goods and a rather leisurely trip to the Marias on July 9. The river must have been low indeed for both the Deans and Benton to forego a trip on to Benton. So LaBarge turned the Deans over to his brother John and returned to St. Louis by way of Virginia City where he sold his cargo, and returned with about $100,000 in gold dust. No handbag full, that meant about 400 pounds.

However, another boat gave Fort Benton its last sight of a steamboat in 1864, one that extended through winter and spring of 1865. Over on the Upper Mississippi in the spring rivermen of what the Montana Post article of Aug. 27, 1864, termed the LaCrosse Line had heard the clarion call of profits. Owners got their hands on two small steamboats, the Chippewa Falls with Abe Hutchinson master and Cutter with Frank Moore, and termed their venture the Idaho Steam Packet Co. in April (no Montana until May 26).

The two boats went down to St. Louis and left for the Upper Missouri crammed with 300 tons of freight and about 250 passengers. The pair must have been pretty good boats, they passed the big Yellowstone below Yankton. By then passengers were voicing loud complaints about accomodations and grub. (The Yellowstone's passengers later would have louder complaints.) But the Idaho Steam Packet fares were in for more discomfort. May 19 General Sully impressed the Chippewa Falls, freight and passengers were shoe-horned into the Cutter, which staggered on up river. Amazingly, the Cutter reached Fort Benton on July 14, a slow trip from Fort Union, attained June 18, so some of the freight probably was moved to Milk River and may have comprised, for a price, part of one of the Benton's trips. Captain Hutchinson of the Chippewa Falls later claimed his boat was the first ever to navigate the Yellowstone, up 40 or 50 miles, then a second trip up 90 miles, for military operations. The Fort Union steamboat arrival list kept by Charles Larpenteur shows the Chippewa Falls went up August 2 and returned August 13, so the claim seems to be correct. Captain Moore was to figure in early Montana territorial politics and a tragic Indian fight before leaving Montana with the Cutter.

Other boats around Fort Union for Sully in the 1864 campaign all arrived July 25 as a fleet included the Chippewa Falls, Belle of Peoria and General Grant. A fourth, Island City, loaded with corn and forage for cavalry horses, snagged and sank eight miles below Union. A fifth, the trailing Alone, which had reached Milk River in 1863 for American Fur, came in behind, went up the Yellowstone at least as far as did Chippewa Falls. Four other steamboats under government charter failed to reach the Yellowstone.

Largest cargo, which arrived at Benton via ox teams and pack animals, was aboard the Yellowstone on a well documented trip to Cow Island. The boat reached Fort Union June 13 and Cow Island June 21, with at least 80 passengers and 400 tons of freight. In addition, there were 50 soldiers to Fort Union.

John Buchanan, who founded the Montana Post, made his trip to the gold fields on the Yellowstone, thence to Virginia City and printed an account in the Post's first issues, August 27 and September 3, 1864. The boat left St. Louis April 11, with assurances of Charles Chouteau and Captain Bill Massie that it positively would reach Fort Benton. The Yellowstone was passed by the Welcome in Missouri, by the Cutter and Chippewa Falls below Yankton May 18, bringing passenger comments about its slowness. A smallpox outbreak which caused at least two deaths among deck passengers added apprehension. Complaints were loud when passengers were notified June 20 that the Yellowstone would go no farther than Cow Island. Wrote Buchanan, "Mr. Chouteau, with French state and smooth dissimulation, informed them (passengers) that he had plenty of teams at the Fort, and in seven days the passengers and freight should be at the fort. All of which was false, for from this day we lay on the island 14 days." Buchanan didn't like Massie either, "He had long before rendered himself odious to all on board, by his overbearing and tyrannical disposition. On the most trivial pretext, he would swear and rave."

July 4 along came Joseph LaBarge and the Effie Deans; with light cargo, the boat took on the stranded passengers. John Buchanan saw one thing he liked: "July 7th, came to what is known as the Deserted City. This is the most remarkable phenomenon on the continent—far grander than the Catacombs of Egypt. Here are towers, minarets and castles of rock, towering 100 feet high, whilst regular walls, some parallel and at angles, which are as even and regular, as if laid by the hand of the most skilled workman. July 8, got to the mouth of the Marias, here we met the teams promised 18 days before."

William Gladstone, who came to Fort Benton from Canada in the spring of 1864, had a workman's view of cargo of the Yellowstone. In late June or early July a messenger came to the fort with orders to take back a "scow" as Gladstone termed it, to take the cargo ashore at Cow Island. As carpenter, he built the craft in four days and accompanied the vessel down. He mentioned meeting the Benton, which arrived at the Marias July 9, with I. G. Baker aboard to take charge of Fort Benton and relieve Andrew Dawson. The Gladstone party found the Yellowstone cargo ashore, in charge of 15 men.

Part of the 400 tons, he reported, was Indian annuities, also on the island "200 barrels of whisky and we found it to be much better than we had been drinking." Gladstone mended boxes and crates that had been damaged, and in a couple of weeks the men had laid out a road of sorts up Cow Creek toward Benton. Soon along came 16 "large prairie schooners, drawn by oxen," loaded and dispatched with baggage of passengers who had been transferred to the steamer Benton. (Another source mentions the Effie Deans, so the two boats probably shared in moving the passengers.) Mention of the road out of the Cow Island bottom provides a starting date for that invaluable adjunct to steamboating to Fort Benton.

After the work party got the wagons loaded and away on their trip to Benton, along came a large pack train of 100 mules. Gladstone said each animal was loaded with 300 pounds. "Mr. Baker sent down wagons as fast as he could get them and we were kept busy loading them."

The 200 barrels of whisky had their own particular Odyssey. "Two teams belonging to the Mormons at Salt Lake City pulled into camp and we received orders to send the whisky to Benton." (Presumably an extra precaution, the ways and wiles of teamsters with such freight notorious on the frontier; Mormon precepts preclude use of alcoholic beverages.) The crew was also expected to distribute the Indian goods at Cow Island and understandably the owners didn't want the whisky around when several thousand Indians arrived. The Mormons took their load and pulled out of Cow Island bottom. About a week and 75 miles later, which would be around the south of the Bear Paws, a war party of Blackfeet whooped down on the tiny train. With only four men to guard the treasure, the whites quite sensibly broached a cask in honor of their guests. The Blackfeet, with all the firewater any warrior could want, passed out with bright dreams of what they would do to whisky and whites when they awoke. However, the Mormons broke camp and got clean away.

Annuity distribution time at Cow Island was pandemonium, Gladstone reported, two weeks of it for 700 lodges of Gros Ventres, but there were 50 well armed whites and no threats. Soon after the final wagon train came along and after two and a half months the party hit the trail for Fort Benton. The new road up Cow Creek was far from complete, one wagon went over the bluff, killing its eight oxen in a 300 foot drop. Gladstone repaired the wagon and rest of the trip was without incident.

He had left the head of navigation with one building aside from Forts Benton, Campbell and LaBarge, returned to find a large store (Carroll & Steell, who had evidently been doing a forwarding and commission business from one of the forts), six saloons and a blacksmith shop. That was the start of the town of Fort Benton in the summer of 1864.

Summary 1864:

To Fort Benton and Marias

| | | | |
|---|---|---|---|
| June 10 | Benton | 200 tons | |
| June 27 | Benton | 150 | |
| July 17 | Cutter | 200 | 250 pass. |
| July 9 | Effie Deans, Marias | 160 | 49 |
| July 9 | Benton, Marias | 150 | |
| | | 860 tons | |
| June 20 | Yellowstone, Cow I. | 400 | 80 |
| June 15 | Fanny Ogden, Milk r. | 200 | |
| June 21 | Welcome, Milk river | 200 | 71 |
| | | 1660 | |

Estimate 250 tons down, 650 passengers up, 400 down.

To Fort Union June 25, Belle of Peoria 200 tons, Chippewa Falls 150, General Grant 150, Alone in June 150. Island City snagged 8 miles below June 25, Chippewa Falls and Alone up Yellowstone 50 or more miles for Sully, carrying about 100 tons to Glendive Creek.

### 1865—The Longest Voyage

The third low water year in a row on the upper river, 1865 was marked by the sale of the American Fur posts on the Upper Missouri to James Hubbell and Alpheus Hawley, soon in business at Fort Benton as North West Fur Co. Then there was the first effort to end Fort Benton's reign as head of navigation, which culminated in death for ten men at the site of Ophir (present Loma). Unremitting Sioux hostility continued, and if that wasn't enough, whites at Benton touched off a hit and run Blackfeet war—the growing village was flexing its muscles.

News of the rich gold strikes around Prickly Pear, and a developing one at Confederate Gulch in the Little Belts northeast of present Townsend were to help add up to an estimated $18,000,000 in gold washed out of Montana placers during 1865.

That is about 36 tons—most of which went down the Missouri. There were more people, primarily male, clustered around the scenes of the big strikes than at the time lived in what became later metropolitan areas of the west. Diamond City at Confederate Gulch, at a peak had 5,000 or more people, and the Virginia City area at its peak had earlier reached an estimated 10,000 in a string of camps along the gulches there. So goods of any kind were in demand, with ample gold to pay for same—and a double bonus, tremendous profits even in greenbacks, gold dust was worth half again as much or even double.

Naturally, even after the dismal showing of 1864, St. Louis rivermen were ready to give the Mountain business another whirl. Freight rates and passenger fares warranted presumed orders to steamboat masters, "forget she's got a bottom, run her through." And how they tried—some 39 of them!

Probably the best example of Mountain Steamboating in 1865 was the Benton. A new boat on the river in 1864, Master Tom Rea had been the success story of that season, delivering the Benton's cargo to the Fort Benton levee, returning three weeks later with that of another steamboat, then still a third time to the Marias to complete the trip of yet another boat.

This year of 1865 the Benton was to understudy a packet with an even speedier set of heels, the Deer Lodge, a boat which could quite reasonably claim to be the greatest of the long run packets. The Benton should not be confused with the later Benton which made the Block P famous on the upper river. The first Benton, a small sternwheeler, was built at Pittsburgh in 1863, made maiden trip down the Ohio in spring 1864, then clear to Fort Benton—a common enough occurrence when steamboats later were designed for the Mountain trade. In 1865 William Howard was captain, Jim Gunsollis the chief pilot, and he hired Carrol J. Atkins as second pilot at $200 a month. Atkins in 1863 left his St. Charles, Missouri, ferry to go to the Mountains on the Robert Campbell, without pay, to learn the river and earn an Upper Missouri pilot's license. Next year he had enough adventures with guerillas in Missouri to do him a lifetime. Shortly before the March 11, 1865, departure of the Benton, Carrol Atkins and Laura Beal of St. Charles were married, and the trip to the Mountains was their honeymoon. Undoubtedly the bride stayed home thereafter.

For the Benton had an awful trip—low water in Missouri, lower in Dakota, where Santee Sioux May 19 provided a baptism of fire for bride and groom. The steamboat reached Fort Union May 27, thereafter was a busy boat indeed. Before her return to St. Louis the Benton had logged, in 169 days, 10,000 of the toughest river miles a Mountain Steamboat had ever run. And the closest she came to Fort Benton may have been Round Butte, 125 miles below the Musselshell. Working in conjunction with the General Grant, the boats were relaying the freight up the Missouri for the Deer Lodge to bring into Fort Benton and earn the cheers of hungry and thirsty miners. In all, the Benton made trips upbound past Fort Union five times that year (and the Grant as many), according to Charles Larpenteur's Fort Union record.

### Tragic End of Metropolis At Ophir

Plans made in 1864 for a river port at the confluence of Marias and Missouri had been activated after a legislative charter granted February 2, 1865, to a group of men prominent in the mining camps. Through a company which had first issued stock in March 1864, a townsite to be known as Ophir was to be built at the site in the spring of 1865. Other charters had been issued for North and East Ophir, a Missouri River Portage & Railroad Company, and others—stockholders were covering all potentials for profit—townsite establishment was long a favorite path to wealth, or sudden poverty in the west.

Frank Moore, captain of the steamboat Cutter, which had wintered at the mouth of the Marias, fit right in with the ambitious plans. He too had spent the winter, met the promoters and joined in the plans. Field manager for building the new townsite was N. W. Burris, who hired a crew of men, chiefly as woodcutters, with the Cutter to haul materials for Ophir. Burris laid out 400 lots and expected the crew to cut enough cottonwoods for 300 cabins. By late May several cabins had been erected. For freighters headed for Fort Benton to meet the first steamers, the Montana Post had a suggestive line, "The grass around Ophir is now very good."

There were two causes suggested for the tragedy which followed. Hiram Upham in an August 1, 1865, letter reported second hand that "two old mountaineers" (later identified as Henry Bostwick and Joseph Spearson) were sitting in front of the Blackfeet agency in Fort Benton when a group of Indians began boasting of the white scalps they had taken. The two cut loose with their firearms, killed four and threw the bodies in the Missouri a few steps away. Some warriors escaped and went for reinforcements. In the other version, advanced in June in the Montana Post, during the previous winter Charley Carson and two other trappers had their horses stolen by three Bloods along the Missouri, followed their trail and killed all three. Evidence seemed to favor the second incident as the cause; the Fort Benton killings occurring too shortly before the Ophir tragedy.

At any rate, on May 25th, a party of ten men went up the Marias to cut more logs for the Ophir townsite. The wooding party was surrounded by a large party of Bloods under leadership of Calf Shirt, and all ten killed. (In this century a marker inscribed with the names of the men slain was erected at the site, later moved to the highway near Loma. The dead men: Franklin Friend, George W. Friend, Abraham Lotts, John Alley, John Andrews, N. W. Burris, Frank Angevine, Henry Martin, Henry Lyons, James Berry.)

The tragedy ended the plans for Ophir, and Frank Moore and his Cutter soon headed down the Missouri and out of its history, but probably with a fair down trip.

### First Steamboat Arrival

First steamboat arrival of 1865 at Fort Benton was the American Fur's steamer Yellowstone on May 28, but not without the usual adventures. The boat had been refitted, lengthened and draught lightened, perhaps a sequence to the harsh words of passengers the previous season. She left St. Louis under command of James Mahood on March 20, getting what early rise there was. Charles Chouteau and the new owners of the trading post at Fort Benton were aboard. There was the almost routine sniping by hostile Sioux. At old Fort Sully (present Pierre) passengers first heard the news of Lincoln's assassination, and when the Yellowstone reached Fort Rice, Col. Charles Dimon met the boat and placed the whole party under arrest for "jubilating over" Lincoln's death. Dimon then threatened to have Chouteau shot for his assumed Confederate sympathies. Although actions of the company during the Civil War provided no positive evidence of such, the suspicions probably influenced revocation of the Chouteau company's license for Indian trading. Intervention by Northerners Hubbell and Hawley resulted in Dimon's giving up on his firing squad. As Dimon's command was of ex-Confederate soldiers who to escape prison camp had taken a loyalty oath on provision service would be on the frontiers, one might wonder about their willingness to carry out any firing squad service. Westerners knew these troops as "Galvanized Yankees."

(The Deer Lodge May 30 brought 10 of those soldiers under Lt. Cyrus Hutchins to control trade with Indians from Fort Benton to Fort Union, the westernmost point reached by a "Galvanized" Yank.)

At Fort Benton Chouteau notified I. G. Baker of the change of ownership to North West Fur and supervised unloading of about 250 tons of freight, last his company would bring to Montana. Then the Yellowstone loaded 29,000 buffalo robes and assorted furs, plus the first large shipment of gold to be noted, $258,000 by one source, $400,000 by another—the smaller would be about 1,000 pounds.

If the Yellowstone was at Fort Benton three days, those aboard would have witnessed the May 30 arrival of the speedy Deer Lodge. On its first of three arrivals that season at Fort Benton the Deer Lodge had been strangely slow, ten days required from Fort Union. A July 29 Montana Post article gives the probable reason for the slow time: "At Milk River, the steamboat companies have erected a stockade fort, with log bastions, mounting three guns, which sweep the faces exposed to attack. The Fort is divided into three compartments, which are owned by the proprietors of different lines of boats, and are called, respectively, Fort Jacobs, Fort Copeland (actually Copelin) and Fort Keiser." A July 25 item said that a few days previously 125 wagons left Fort Benton for the Effie Deans and Copelin line, also that the Benton had been running from Fort Benton (although no arrivals by the boat were reported here by any other source located), and the General Grant and Deer Lodge to Cow Island. Most probably, roles of Benton and Deer Lodge were confused by the informant. There was tremendous movement of freight from Milk River that season. Hiram Upham, in a letter written at Fort Benton, mentions a July 31st caravan of 250 wagons leaving for Milk River, each drawn by four to eight yoke of oxen, making "a big show." (In later years, two and three wagon hitches came into pretty general use in Montana.)

Considerable amounts of freight were also coming to the Fort Benton area by steamboats. The Deer Lodge brought in the cargoes of the Benton and General Grant in June, dates undetermined. Late in June also the Effie Deans discharged its cargo at the mouth of the Marias, the St. John brought another load to the same point on June 15th. The St. John, too, had been under fire. Its mate, George Merrick, was killed by hostiles near Fort Rice. There is also a note that on this trip the boat became one of the year's treasure ships, taking down $200,000 in gold and 1,000 buffalo robes.

The arrival of boats at the Marias was pre-arranged, even though by arrival time Bloods had killed (on May 25) a party of whites cutting logs for the Ophir settlement at the Marias. The small steamboat Cutter had been associated with the Ophir project and had wintered at the Marias. About June 18 the Cutter took off down river, presumably with passengers and probably gold, as Captain Frank Moore had become well known in Virginia City and other gold camps by that time.

According to one arrival list Captain Bill Massie brought the Twilight to the Marias on June 29. In the St. Louis Republican in 1899 he recalled it a trifle differently. "At the Marias we caught up with the Kate Kearney, Sam Gaty, Fannie Ogden, Effie Deans, Lillie Martin and one or two others." All boats named were on the upper river that year and all went at least to Milk River, where a palisaded freight drop had been built for safer storage. Massie said the Twilight made it to Fort Benton, with many passengers from the other boats, but when his boat reached the shoals the passengers had to get off and walk to the head of that stretch of low water.

If Massie's recollection is correct, it increases by several hundred tons the freight delivered to the Fort Benton area, but lessening the large amount of overland freighting from the Milk River drop. While the Marias was an unloading point for some freight in future summers, 1865 was undoubtedly its biggest year as a river port.

Captain Massie had another interesting recollection of the frustrating season. At the Yellowstone, he said, the Twilight was met by a large party of men coming down in mackinaws, and there were many touching scenes as wives and children who were passengers on the boat met their husbands and fathers. Also there were single men meeting their fiancees, bringing a minister down river with them, who that evening married 16 couples in brief ceremonies aboard the Twilight. (A couple of years later, a visitor at Fort Benton sent a message to the Helena Herald suggesting that a Helena minister make a trip to Fort Benton to further Cupid's business, in view of the number of single men meeting the boats here.)

Arrival of the Twilight was the final one to the Fort Benton area in 1865. On July 21st the Deer Lodge made it to Dauphin's Rapids with its fourth cargo.

The Larpenteur Fort Union listing of boats bound up from the mouth of the Yellowstone includes the Lillie Martin, Roanoke, David Watts, Hattie May, Sam Gaty, Prairie State, Converse, Kate Kearney, Fanny Ogden and Big Horn bringing cargoes bound for Montana mines, a long dreary trip for hundreds of freighters from the Milk River freight drop. Busiest of all were the Benton and General Grant. The later boat had three crewmen killed by Indians in Dakota—the 1865 trips were costly in blood.

Summary 1865: To Fort Benton:

| Date | Steamboat | tons | Notes |
|---|---|---|---|
| May 28 | Yellowstone | 250 | $400,000 gold down, 50 soldiers up |
| May 30 | Deer Lodge | 200 | Fast long run packet |
| June | Deer Lodge | 150 | |
| June | Deer Lodge | 150 | |
| June 15 | Cutter | | Left down, wintered in area |
| June 29 | Twilight | 200 | Brought up pass. of other boats |
| | | 950 | |

To Marias: (1700 tons)

| | | | |
|---|---|---|---|
| June 25 | Effie Deans | 200 | |
| June | Lillie Martin | 200 | These boats reported at Marias |
| June | Fannie Ogden | 200 | by Wm. Massie of Twilight |
| June | Kate Kearney | 250 | |
| June | Sam Gaty | 200 | |
| June | Roanoke | 200 | |
| June | David Watts | 250 | |
| July 1 | St. John | 200 | $200,000 gold down |

To Dauphin's Rapids:

| | | | |
|---|---|---|---|
| July 21 | Deer Lodge | 150 | |
| July 29 | General Grant | 150 | |

To Milk River or above:

| | | | |
|---|---|---|---|
| June | Hattie May | 350 | 12 miles above Milk to Fort Copelin |
| July | Hattie May | - | Total 2 trips up from Union |
| July | Prairie State | 150 | In two trips up |
| July | Converse | 250 | Also in two trips |
| | | 3700 | Est. 365 tons down, 1850 pass. up, 800 down |

Aug. 17 Big Horn to Fort Union from below to take down soldiers. Marcella and G. W. Graham mentioned as coming in July 1 Montana Post, probably did not reach Montana waters. Fort Union list shows five trips of steamboat Benton up from Union or below, and similar total by General Grant, moving cargoes other boats.

## Golden Highway of 1866

If the first three years of Montana's gold rush had been frustrating for rivermen, in 1866 everything fell into place, top freight prices, many passengers, and above all, high water. While Alder Gulch (Virginia City, Nevada, etc.) was past its peak, the great finds around Prickly Pear and Confederate Gulch were if anything increasing in volume. Only the hostile Sioux and Blackfeet were to be reckoned with. In the war with the Sioux, Red Cloud and his warriors were besieging the forts along the Bozeman Trail, the hostiles acting as a lightning rod, inadvertently aiding the influx of whites by way of the safer steamboats.

Returns from the mines made the Missouri a golden highway indeed in 1866. Estimates of the "treasure" carried on the steamboats total up into the millions, depending on which source is credited. That could be gold reported to or handled by boat clerks, the next year the Helena Herald reported of one boat, $100,000 so handled, many times that carried by passengers. Furthermore, there was heavy traffic via mackinaws in 1866, a Yankton editor reported in August that the Missouri was "covered with returning miners" and he later estimated that 2,000 miners had stopped off at Yankton in October and November.

Freight was around 10c to 12c a pound delivered at Fort Benton, some higher, and steamboat passage $150 to $200—a bargain, stage fare was far higher and trips rougher, plus meals at $1 or $2, plus heavy surcharges on anything beyond a few pounds of baggage. Excess baggage was far more reasonable by boat. Another advantage, King & Gillette, with a toll road franchise, had opened a relatively good freight trail through the Little Prickly Pear canyon, a vital link on what came to be called the Benton Road and early Montana's greatest and busiest highway.

Some 51 boats started from St. Louis for the Upper Missouri in the spring of 1866, 32 arrived at Fort Benton, several more brought cargoes to Milk River or beyond, and five or six were bound only for the mouth of the Yellowstone. Overall, the best record by far of accomplishment to that date. By early June, 31 boats with 1500 passengers had started for the Mountains, average fare $150, and by mid-June the Helena Radiator, later Herald, said 14 boats had already reached Fort Benton. (By date of the paper, the total was 18.)

First at the head of navigation was the St. John, two hours ahead of the speedy Deer Lodge, with over 300 tons of freight between them on May 18. The St. John took down $100,000 gold, the other $70,000. May 29 Joe Kinney's Cora came in with 225 tons of freight—part of her cargo an owner's speculation, salt bought for $1.25 a barrel in St. Louis found ready purchasers at $45 in Helena. The Cora took down only $35,000 gold in her safe, but a note that the boat made a big profit indicates many passengers with heavy belts.

Tom Rea's Waverly carried 250 tons and 100 passengers to Fort Benton May 22; he ended up making $50,000 on the trip. Last May arrival the 31st was the sidewheeler Wm. J. Lewis, a big boat which found the water stage high enough that her power this season was an advantage in bringing the biggest cargo to then, 260 tons. $240,000 gold, about a thousand pounds, went down on the Lewis, her owners' profit between $40,000 and $60,000.

The Mollie Dozier, another sidewheeler, came in with 246 tons on June 1st;

Granville Stuart, coming up on another boat, said the Dozier came down Dauphin's Rapid's "like a whirl-wind," breaking off guards ahead of the wheel house and looking as if "a young mountain fell on her." Nevertheless, the Mollie made $50,000 for Frank Dozier. Marcella and Ontario were June 5 arrivals, next day Sanford Coulson had made his first trip as a master to the Mountains, on the Big Horn.

The Mepham Bros. of St. Louis sent off three boats to the Mountains that year, the Iron City June 9 and the Gold Finch June 15 with more than 400 tons total, but right in between, like money in the bank, their Peter Balen, a new boat, on June 12 landed the prize freight cargo of the year, 400 tons and a freight bill of 12 1/2 cents a pound, or $100,000, in gold, not greenbacks, and a profit of more than $70,000. The Mephams probably understated the $100,000 they reported making on their three boats. The approximately $35,000 gold each carried was probably only payment for freight.

Walter B. Dance, which took down $115,000 gold, came June 8 and the Amelia Poe June 11, with the Balen next day making seven steamboats along the levee at one time. More boats, Miner and Only Chance June 13, Tacony and Favorite the 15th, each with about 200 tons.

June 17, Grant Marsh brought his first command in to the levee, the Luella toting only a laughable 113 tons and no indication it would make gold rush history.

Ten days later an arrival a day, the Helena, Tom Stevens, David Watts and Lillie Martin and Agnes ended June. Only the last rates a note, $125,000 gold and 150 passengers down. July 4 in came the Huntsville, the Nellie Rogers July 12; next day the Marion, wrecked on her down trip, and Deer Lodge, on its second full trip from St. Louis, first time the feat had been accomplished. The Gallatin on July 19th was tail end Charley with 250 tons of St. Louis freight, but her down cargo included a ton of gold dust, $500,000, and doubtless plenty of passengers from that data, and with more treasure on their persons.

While at Fort Benton in early June the Peter Balen "planned to run up to the falls" according to an item in the Montana Post. A later item said the boat went up 15 miles, a distance which would be bettered by the Gallatin next year and the Tom Stevens in 1868. Way's Packet Directory says this trip was made June 18, and the distance was 38 miles, near the mouth of Highwood Creek. This source adds that receipts of the 1866 trip of the Balen amounted to $102,690, with $70,690 net profit.

The navigation season wasn't quite over. The Luella had hung around looking for odd jobs, Grant Marsh earning his $1200 a month salary. He took the Luella down to Fort Peck in June, July 11th was back at Fort Benton with North West Fur's Fort Union inventory, probably 150 tons. Then Marsh advertised a September 1st departure from Fort Benton, in the meantime going down to near the Judith to salvage what was left of the Marion, which had lost a bout with a rocky bar at Pablos Rapids. Her machinery was salvaged by the Luella crew and Marsh sold it at Fort Benton.

## Trip of Steamboat Luella

By that time it was late August and Grant Marsh organized a hunting party into the Highwood Mountains about 25 miles from Fort Benton. These mountains were then full of game which had never been disturbed by hunters other than an occasional Indian with a taste for venison, and there the party spent an enjoyable week, returning to Fort Benton on September 1st.

What happened at departure the next day can be pieced together from sources other than Marsh's biographer, Joseph Mills Hanson, who said the Luella "had on board 230 miners and $1,250,000 in gold dust, the most valuable cargo of treasure ever carried down the Missouri River." He referred to H. M. Chittenden's "History of Navigation on the Missouri River." But there are other sources.

Granville Stuart wrote: "While in Benton on August 29, 1866, a freight wagon drawn by four mules and escorted by a company of miners, arrived. The wagon was loaded with two and one-half tons of gold dust, valued at one million five hundred thousand dollars. The gold was all from Confederate Gulch and was shipped down river by steamboat. This was the first and only time I ever saw a wagon load of gold dust at one time." (Robert Vaughn, in "Then and Now," recalled: "In the summer of 1866 a party took out 2 1/2 tons worth $1 1/2 million. In early fall of same year the gold was taken by four mule team, escorted by 14 armed men to Fort Benton. Mr. Lindiman and Mr. Hiedeman owned most of the gold." This from Confederate Gulch, and probably Montana Bar, richest deposit.)

The Helena Record Herald in 1922 reviewed ancient history, saying that about $1,500,000 gold to be shipped by steamboat, left Helena August 23, 1866. The September 1, 1866, Montana Post carried an August 23 letter from a Helena correspondent, "The great sensation...has been the arrival of 2200 lbs. of dust from Montana Bar." The cleanups there about that time understandably threw miners into a frenzy. Located in Confederate Gulch, it is little wonder that Diamond City, which grew up there, boasted perhaps 5,000 population at a peak. Dan Cushman in "Gold Frontier" says $1,000 in a pan was not too unusual, record about $1400 or seven pounds in a pan. A Helena reporter a couple of years later when miners thought they had hit a continuation of Montana Bar, was invited to try a pan and keep his take—about $73. Later he reported a bit jealously that a workman had gotten over $700 in a single pan.

Most of the Confederate Gulch area was panned out in 1866, reported C. W. Cook in a 1924 letter. Cook managed 20 man day and 20 man night crews in one of the richer areas. "The most I took out in 24 hours was $16,000." Cook also wrote that C. Fredricks cleaned up more than a bushel in a summer, and had Cook clean the dust. The owner couldn't guess within $20,000 of its worth and told Cook to put about $5000 in a bag.

The steamboat Granville Stuart referred to was, of course, the Luella, the only boat left at Fort Benton, other boat owners having learned distressing things about staying past into the low water of late summer. The treasure aboard was by no means all that went down river, by steamboat and mackinaw. Accumulated notes from varied sources show virtually all others carried substantial amounts, headed by a ton on the Gallatin and half a ton on the Rubicon—and those reports may be in a number of cases simply what was in the steamboat safes, or even the pay in gold for freight delivered. There may have been another Helena shipment of only slightly less that fall. John X. Beidler memoirs tell of being one of 14 armed men who escorted two and a fourth tons of gold belonging to Mr. Fredericks (probably the man with the bushel of gold) from Helena to Fort Benton in three two-mule wagons, where it was sent down on mackinaws, "there being no steamboats" at the time. Empty 10 gallon kegs were fastened to each safe in case of accident or upset. (George Baker of the firm of I. G. Baker & Bro., of Fort Benton, told Lt. James Bradley the firm had shipped gold in this fashion for years without any loss. In case of a sunken boat the buoy made recovery easy.) Comparing the two stories, it would appear that this was another giant shipment down the "golden highway".

Not all the gold on the Luella was in any form of safe. The Luella, Marsh told Hanson, went aground at the mouth of Milk River and a miner named

McClellan fell overboard in only two feet of water. The swift current took him off his feet, and his gold belt was so heavy he was dragged down and drowned—the body never recovered. One of the few instances noted of Sioux hostility along the river in 1866, the Luella went aground a short distance into Dakota. With 230 armed miners aboard it wasn't much of a contest after the first Indian volley. The Luella arrived in St. Louis in early October, the boat's profits $24,000.

Yet another newspaper item fuels the all but incredible story: November 1, 1866, Montana Post, from the St. Joseph Herald of October 11: "The Luella, mountain boat, arrived from Fort Benton yesterday morning at noon. She had 65 cabin, and 115 deck passengers, and more treasure than any other boat has brought down from the mines during the season. It is impossible to state the value of the dust; the officers of the boat fix it at three millions of dollars, while some of the passengers are of the opinion that it will sum up over four millions. A number of the miners had very large amounts; Frederick & Campbell alone, miners in Confederate Gulch, Montana Bar, having about $475,000 of the precious ore." Further mention of a slow trip with less than a foot on some bars makes it seem possible that the Frederick gold X. Biedler launched at Fort Benton may have caught up with Luella and been transferred.

It is just a bit awesome to contemplate that at the 1985 price of gold the cargo the Luella was carrying amounted to about $25 million in hard cash at the lowest figure, more than $60 million at the highest.

After all departures, the Montana Post had a footnote on September 29, "right now with 500 people floating down the Missouri from Fort Benton there is also $1,500,000 in gold dust." There was a tremendous exodus from Montana Territory to the States that fall in mackinaws. Virginia City and Alder Gulch were far over the hump of success though. The fall before the Post had reported, "million after million; one man 400 pounds, another 200 pounds, 25 to 100 pounds has been so common, as to look like a record of our postoffice list." (100 pounds would be about $25,000, at the time, affluence in the East in those days.)

### Steamboats Help Found Camp Cooke

In addition to the Fort Benton arrivals, there was considerable navigation to the mouth of the Judith in 1866. In late June the steamboats Rubicon and Lexington arrived there, and troops of the 13th Infantry under Major William Clinton landed to build Camp Cooke, founded July 11, the first military post in Montana Territory, begun a few weeks before Fort C. F. Smith on the Big Horn, northernmost of three forts intended to protect travelers on the Bozeman Trail to the Montana mines. (Fort Phil Kearny and Fort Reno in Wyoming were the other two on this trail from the Overland and the Platte River.)

Camp Cooke was intended to protect the freight of steamboats. Neither Montana post was very successful. Fort Smith was abandoned in 1868 after hostile Sioux had made their point and forced abandonment of the Bozeman Trail. Camp Cooke lasted a while longer, was the only Montana post to withstand a direct attack by hostiles, may have been the only army post to surrender to rats. Selection of the site was an immediate subject of criticism, Montanans apparently wanted the business, the soldiers represented more than their problematical protection from Indians. It was isolated, save in the boating season, and an orderly abandonment completed in 1869-70, with a small contingent coming to Fort Benton, most to found Fort Shaw.

Companies B, D and E of the 1st Battalion of the 13th Infantry came to the Judith on the Rubicon, Co. F on the Lexington. The latter company left in late

September 1866 to protect the mail, stage coaches and freighters along the Benton Road to Helena, and one company of Camp Cooke troops wintered at Fort Benton in 1866-67, most likely to protect military shipments.

Army posts require supplies, the Big Horn after its trip to Fort Benton freighted military supplies up the Missouri, as did the Waverly in June and July. The Rubicon went up in late June, the Lexington and Amanda in July, the latter including Crow Indian annuities probably intended to influence the tribe in their attitude toward the uniformed newcomers in one of the loneliest spots the "brass" could have chosen. One further possibility with Camp Cooke supplies is the Ontario. Cargoes were perhaps about 1100 tons.

Two steamboats apparently went to the Milk River freight drop, the Montana with about 200 tons of freight and the Mary McKelon with a light 125 tons, both in July. One steamboat, Mary McDonald, came only to Fort Buford, near old Fort Union, at the Yellowstone. Jennie Brown and Jennie Lewis, both on the river in Dakota, may have had cargoes for army posts in that area.

After departure of the Luella there was one last flicker of steamboat navigation, to Fort Benton, said the Helena Radiator, while the Virginia City Montana Post claimed the Miner never reached here. The effort, though, set a precedent. The Miner was operated by North West Fur to Fort Benton, and came up to Milk River in late September, unloaded its freight, probably around 200 tons. Meanwhile, from September 1st, the Radiator had been carrying ads "LAST STEAMBOAT OF THE SEASON". A train of wagons was to meet the boat at Milk River for the cargo, and the Miner was to make the run to Fort Benton light for an October 1 departure.

The boat didn't quite make that date, but the Radiator on October 13 had an item: "The arrival of the North-Western Fur Company's steamer 'Miner' at Fort Benton last week, marks a new era in the navigation of the Missouri. Light-draught vessels, it is now demonstrated, can ascend the Missouri any month in the year that the current is not blocked by ice...Most gratifying!" The date would have been on or about October 6, and the Miner undoubtedly carried a good load of passengers down. This boat was a forerunner of steamboats which in the next dozen years pretty well mastered the Missouri River. (Next year's reports show this boosterism on the part of the Radiator, the Miner took on its passengers at Cow Island.)

The year 1865 had found the Montana Post at Virginia City publishing sly little plugs for the settlement at Ophir, designed to end Fort Benton's brief reign as working head of navigation on the Missouri and goal of the Mountain steamboats. That failed after the killing of ten by Blood Indians in May. Early in 1866 the Helena Radiator took up the cudgel in behalf of Kercheval City near the Musselshell, as saving the travail of the rocky river passage to Fort Benton. The proposed metropolis took its name from an old river captain who perhaps had been balked in the 1865 low water. Kercheval City never expanded past a cabin or two, the founding Rocky Mountain Fur Co. having woes of their own in hauling freight across the Judith Basin, and on June 2, coming up river aboard the Walter B. Dance, Granville Stuart sketched the "city" of two diminutive cabins and a three wall palisade extended to a steep cut bank at river's edge. "Played out" was his comment.

This was to be a lengthy, decade long will o' the wisp for Helena, an alternative to reliance on Fort Benton cargoes. Their merchants ultimately gave up, several put in branches at Fort Benton, including the large firm of Kleinschmidt & Bros., the latter in 1877. Fort Musselshell, the Corinne Trail to the Union Pacific in Utah, and Carroll, all failed Helena.

St. Louis records show 51 steamboats left there in 1866 for the upper Missouri with 10,385 tons. Available records show Fort Benton arrivals number 32 with four more to Camp Cooke.

1866 Summary: Arrival date, steamboat, tons, passengers up, down

| Date | Steamboat | Tons | Pass. | Down | Notes |
|---|---|---|---|---|---|
| May 18 | St. John | 190 | 19 | | $100,000 gold |
| May 18 | Deer Lodge | 200 | 15 | | $70,000 gold |
| May 20 | Cora | 225 | 30 | | $35,000 gold |
| May 23 | Waverly | 250 | 25 | | $50,000 profit to owner |
| May 28 | Wm. J. Lewis | 260 | | | $240,000 gold |
| June 1 | Mollie Dozier | 246 | 12 | | $50,000 gold |
| June 5 | Marcella | 300 | | | |
| June 5 | Ontario | 200 | 38 | | |
| June 6 | Big Horn | 293 | 35 | | |
| June 8 | Walter B. Dance | 200 | | | $115,000 gold |
| June 9 | Iron City | 270 | 19 | | $35,000 gold |
| June 9 | Peter Balen | 400 | 25 | | $100,000 gold freight bill made $70,000 for Mepham Bros. |
| June 11 | Amelia Poe | 200 | 40 | | |
| June 13 | Miner | 200 | 25 | | |
| June 13 | Only Chance | 200 | 15 | | $85,000 gold |
| June 14 | Tacony | 200 | | | $20,000 gold, cleared $16,000 |
| June 14 | Favorite | 200 | 40 | | |
| June 15 | Gold Finch | 200 | 23 | | $35,000, 7th boat at levee |
| June 17 | Luella | 180 | 26 | | $1,250,000 gold—2½ tons |
| June 27 | Helena | 120 | 6 | | |
| June 28 | Tom Stevens | 100 | | | |
| June 29 | David Watts | 150 | 6 | | |
| June 29 | Lillie Martin | 250 | 15 | | |
| June 29 | Agnes | 160 | 20 | | $125,000 gold |
| June 30 | Sunset | 150 | | | |
| July 4 | Huntsville | 225 | | | |
| July 11 | Luella | 150 | | | short 2nd trip, 230 pass. down |
| July 12 | Nellie Rogers | 250 | | | |
| July 13 | Marion | 200 | | | |
| July 13 | Deer Lodge | 225 | 58 | | 2nd full trip, 147 tons to Cooke |
| July 19 | Gallatin | 250 | 10 | | $500,000 gold |
| | 31 arrivals | 6644 | 502 | | estimate 2000 passengers up, 1000 down, 350 tons down |
| Oct. 6 c. | Miner | - | | 150 | to Cow Island only |

Stonewall (?) brought $100,000 gold "from Fort Benton"

Boat totals account for about $3 million gold, there was much more, 32 arrivals, 6644 tons, also many more up passengers, by early June 1500 had left St. Louis on boats. Also many went down by mackinaw, about 2,000 miners stopped at Yankton in October and November.

**1866 lower points, tonnages**
Rubicon, June, Camp Cooke, 200
Lexington, June, Camp Cooke, 200
Mary McDonald, June 12, Fort Buford, 200
Big Horn, June 21, Fort Buford, 200, also about 160 soldiers
Waverly, June 25, Fort William just below Buford, 200
Rubicon, June 25, Milk River, 175, bound up from Union June 25
Montana, July 3, at Buford from above, probably Milk River, 200
Ontario, July 4, Buford from Fort Sully, 200
Ben Johnson, July 10, Buford, 150, with Indian commission, up July 11 and 17
Amanda, July 15, Buford, 150, Crow annuities, probably to Milk
Waverly, July 27 at Berthold, 150, from near Judith
Mary McKelon, July 27 at Berthold from above, 125
Jennie Brown, at least to Big Bend, 250
Lexington, no date, to Judith, 200
Jennie Lewis, at least to Pierre, 200
Sept. 29 Post, 2500 men, 3000 teams, 20,000 oxen in Fort Benton freighting.
 Overall, 8944 tons est., 2000 passengers up, 1000 down.

## 1867 Made It Two Big Years In A Row

There were a few more steamboats reaching Fort Benton in the busy season of 1867, a bustling year on the river but profits generally down a bit due to increased competition. Early boats in particular were filled to capacity with passengers, a profitable sideline. This was also to be the final year that St. Louis dominated the Mountain trade. Early in the year the Helena Herald was trumpeting the great news of a Northern Overland Route from Minnesota, which eventually became Montana's only organized Pony Express. Via Fort Benton, of course, following in part the route of the previous Fisk trains. The Herald saw the route as used by speedy stagecoaches. Also the paper was beginning, a year early, to tout another "Muscleshell" (the way they spelled it then) road. May 2 the Herald said "most were predicting low water" in the Missouri and that it would be "hazardous and oftentimes very detrimental to rely on Benton as the only receiving point."

Early in 1867 Isaac G. Baker had been appointed first postmaster at Fort Benton, C. C. Huntley getting the contract to carry the mail, and by April he was planning daily trips of his stage and express line through the busy season, Helena to Fort Benton. Protecting stages and passengers, Company D of the 13th Infantry was building a stockade at the Dearborn crossing on the Benton Road. Small patrols were to accompany travelers, for the Blackfeet were restless and dangerous.

The Missouri had been low in early spring, it wasn't until May 25 that the Waverly came into the Fort Benton levee with 180 tons of freight and loaded with passengers, at least 100, even possibly double that, for the boat had previously carried considerably more freight. Waverly dropped back down to Camp Cooke and in early June came back with 250 tons more. As an early boat it took down about 200 passengers.

Meanwhile, the Miner arrived May 31st with 180 tons of freight as well as 25 cabin and a few deck passengers, the goods mostly for North West Fur. It took down as many passengers, a big cargo of buffalo robes and $35,000 in gold, probably company receipts. Next day the Only Chance whistled in with 186 tons and 52 passengers, taking down an unreported number, but as a St. Joseph paper reported later $500,000 in gold aboard, it was a goodly list.

June 5 was a big day at Benton, the Deer Lodge, possessor of the "horns" for the fastest trip, had had its troubles around Fort Pierre, but landed 207 tons of freight and 75 passengers, the 165x35 steamboat must have been cramped for space indeed. Right behind came the Walter B. Dance with 198 tons and 58 passengers, and the Cora with 210 tons and an unreported passenger list. All three boats had to double trip in Dakota but thereafter had little trouble. (One source has the Dance as the one warned off by a pistol waving Madame Mustache—this had to be the occasion if that smallpox scare episode ever occurred. The previous year Granville Stuart reported his trip on the Dance without comment about smallpox.)

The Helena Herald's Benton correspondent June 5 reported "Benton is quite lively now, and looks like a young St. Louis. About 1,000 head of oxen can be seen attached to their teams, waiting for loads. Freight to Helena is 7c and 8c per pound; but I am informed that contracts are now being made for large lots at 5c."

The writer added a neighborly message: "Can you not induce the Rev. Mr. Hough to pay us a visit? I think he would be warmly welcomed by a large number of anxious looking lovers, who are now here awaiting the arrival of their sweethearts."

The Cora took down $100,000 gold, the Gallatin, which arrived June 8, $250,000 and 160 passengers. The Gallatin had brought arms, cannon and ammunition for a projected Montana militia. No wonder the Benton resident wrote: "The entire road from Silver City is guarded by squads of from ten to twenty soldiers, and it would seem to be perfectly safe. A great deal of treasure is being shipped over this road, to be sent down the river on the steamers. Before going down, probably waiting for that gold, the Gallatin made a trip aimed at the 'Great Falls,' went 12 miles further up river than any other boat has ever gone."

Arrivals were now in rapid succession, Amelie Poe the 9th, Mountaineer and St. John the 10th, Nile June 12, Yorktown (with goods to start the T. C. Power firm at Fort Benton) and Ben Johnson the 14th, the Huntsville and Ida Stockdale the 15th—the 15th arrival.

Grant Marsh had the Stockdale, making the passage in good time with a load of mining machinery and few passengers. The previous year Marsh had made $24,000 with the treasure ship Luella, in 1867 he would all but double the profit to owners. After unloading its 250 tons, Marsh apparently had a planned rendezvous with the James H. Trover, which had run into trouble below the Musselshell. The Ida Stockdale June 29 brought the Trover's trip of 165 tons and 20 passengers into Fort Benton. The Marsh boat may also have been the trouble shooter that stripped the machinery off the Trover after its captain found he couldn't get off the bar. That would have been in mid-July. Then the Ida Stockdale headed down river, with what biographer Hanson termed a valuable load, and "Conquest of the Missouri" is chiefly the source of the following: A couple of hundred miles below the Yellowstone, the roar of a cannon, a signal known to every captain and pilot on the troubled Missouri, had Captain Marsh swinging the Ida Stockdale to the bank. The boat was being hailed by General Alfred Terry, there with five companies of infantry. Terry had been establishing posts to protect the route of that Northern Overland mail from Minnesota.

(The Helena vision of a stage route had faded, low bidders in July contemplated simply a relay of horsemen from Fort Abercrombie to Fort Benton via Milk River, thence by stage to Helena.)

Terry was anxious to get to Helena with utmost dispatch, Marsh and owner Thomas Calhoun, enjoying his excursion with Marsh fully in command, to get back to St. Louis. There was much dickering, but Terry had authority to commandeer the boat, the terms were liberal, insuring the owner against possible loss of his steamboat. The Ida Stockdale dropped on down to Fort Rice below later Bismarck to pick up army personnel and doubtless to store the private and valuable cargo before turning back Benton-bound once more, with Terry and a sizeable staff as passengers. About 125 miles into Montana the Stockdale had an odd delay of hours when buffalo swimming the Missouri resulted in a non-negotiable, mobile "bar." The remainder of the trip to Benton and return to St. Louis was rather uneventful, but owner Calhoun could later reckon that Grant Marsh had earned his $1200 a month, for the profits of the Ida Stockdale for a five months cruise were $42,594, nearly twice her rated value and claimed to be the biggest return to any of 40 or more steamboats in the Mountain trade in 1867.

The Helena Herald of August 7 added some data: "Major General Alfred Terry and staff arrived by Benton coach Wednesday morning. On July 15 Terry took passage on the Ida Stockdale to Fort Benton in 20 days, arriving Monday, August 5." General Terry's Montana business was chiefly to select the site for a permanent post for the six companies at Sun River. This became Fort Shaw, Fort Ellis near Bozeman was also established.

The Octavia came up to the levee on June 20, the Montana Post of June 26 reporting the trip as 41 days and quickest of record, later amended it to 39 days. However, Joseph LaBarge's fine new boat hadn't beaten the time of his Emilie in 1862 of 32 days in a year when the river was high all the way and there were few stops. The Octavia's trip put Joe LaBarge back on his feet financially, $45,000 profit, he reckoned, due in part to a special army contract to move 100 soldiers from Omaha to Camp Cooke. Apparently that included about 100 tons of freight, for at Benton there were 200 passengers and as many tons, but certainly the LaBarge reputation had insured a bigger trip. Bolstering that reputation, Octavia passed 26 boats, carefully listed in the Post. Tragedy marred the trip. Wilfred D. Spears, an English nobleman of great wealth, got on at Omaha. Army being army, there were armed sentries aboard the Octavia nightly, and at a late hour June 7th, Spears was shot and killed by one of the guards. There were numerous stories, the sentry was charged with willful murder, with implications this was the outgrowth of Irish hostility for the English. Inquest by passengers included names later familiar to Montanans, new governor Green Clay Smith, former delegate to Congress Sam McLean, and Washington J. McCormick. Later in Dakota court William Barry was acquitted on his claim of obedience to orders; Joseph LaBarge felt it a travesty on justice. The Octavia's down trip drew many passengers and great quantities of gold dust. "I filled the office safe and every other available receptacle with it." So the $35,000 gold must have been for freight and passenger fares, that stored for passengers not included. Profit on the trip, $45,000.

The Guidon arrived at Benton shortly after the LaBarge boat, with 225 tons of freight. General Terry's party went down on the Guidon, along with them on one of the fastest trips from Fort Benton to St. Louis, went a million dollars in Montana placer gold, to make the boat one of the great treasure carriers. June 26th the veteran Benton came in with 200 tons, 50 passengers up and as many down. Next was the Amaranth with 225 tons of freight and 113 passengers; the down voyage included 120 and "considerable" treasure, a word not used lightly in those years.

Last of the June arrivals was the G. A. Thompson on the 30th with at least 200 tons and 20 passengers; J. M. Woods' command would next day figure in one of Montana's more tragic riddles. Acting Governor Thomas Francis Meagher had come to Fort Benton—a fighting Irishman after weapons with which to fight some more. Montana Territory was experiencing one of its periodic Indian scares, and Meagher, acting governor once more until Green Clay Smith arrived, was attempting to organize a militia. (One of the captains was John Evans, to have later a spectacular career in the Fort Benton area.) Meagher had come to get those guns reportedly aboard the Gallatin, spent July 1st enjoying the hospitality of a riotous inland port, took his last meal at the home of I. G. Baker and retired that evening to a stateroom aboard the Thompson. That night passengers heard a loud splash, the Irish rebel and Civil War leader of the Irish brigade was gone. He had enemies, some thought these had done him in. Although $2,000 reward was offered for recovery of the body, it was never claimed. As to fall, pushed or suicide, Ferd Roosevelt, then Wells Fargo agent at Fort Benton, claimed in 1923 to have been an eye witness, that he saw Meagher fall overboard, no attacker and no suicide; the acting governor had been drinking heavily.

Early July 1867 was a busy time, over 2,000 tons and several hundred passengers arriving in a dozen days on 11 boats, Antelope, Abeona, Agnes, Tacony, Jennie Brown, Luella, Big Horn, Tom Stevens, Lady Grace, Lilly and Little Rock—not all unscathed, a deck hand had been killed on the Big Horn in a Sioux attack. So quickly did the boats arrive that down passenger totals were half the incoming until the Luella's reputation drew 200 for H. J. Hazlett.

The remainder of July brought only four more new arrivals, Ida Fulton, Nymph No. 2, Viola Belle and Richmond. Also the Gallatin July 17, from Camp Cooke, for those guns had been left there despite the news item. The arsenal was loaded for Helena a week after the drowning. The Richmond deserves mention, for Hans J. Wackerlin, Fort Benton pioneer, was a passenger, years later told his son-in-law, Charles N. Pray, that this boat had been hijacked in southern waters by remnants of Quantrill's guerilllas, coming to Montana to get even with an absconding member, Farmer Peel, who before the boat arrived had been killed in Helena. The later congressman and federal judge included the story in a biography of Wackerlin.

The Gallatin took down 160 passengers, all but wrecked itself near Dauphin's Rapids, after weeks on the rocks continued and staggered into Omaha in early December, having yielded its passengers and $250,000 gold to the Huntsville.

The Only Chance August 19 was the final through arrival on a rare second trip from St. Louis, took down about 200 passengers. It almost certainly came with a light load for passenger traffic. The St. Joe Herald of October 10 reported the Only Chance on arrival had 300 passengers and $3 million in gold aboard—not impossible as mackinaw passengers often abandoned their flimsy craft for a steamboat ride.

There was a low water ending to an otherwise successful year on the river. The Miner and Huntsville second trips were short of Fort Benton, the Zephyr was credited with reaching the Marias, and several boats stopped at Fort Buford, Milk River, Musselshell or Cow Island.

Over-selling is nothing new. The Imperial fiasco of 1867 is evidence. In Helena and Benton agents spread the word about the palatial, king size boat laying by Cow Island, getting so many to sign for passage that other boats such as Huntsville cut cabin fares to $100. The Imperial got the last of a reported 300 passengers on two mackinaws that left Fort Benton September 13. Imperial reportedly had $100,000 gold aboard—that of passengers would have been a large multiple. With pilots off the lower river, the Imperial's first stop was ten days on the Grand Island bar. Thereafter the boat reeled from bar to bar, aground four days below Milk River in late September, and nearly out of grub. Indignant passengers demanded that the captain hire the second pilot off the Benton, which was having no such woes. The provident master not only declined to spend the $1,000 fee but also informed them that the $100,000 gold had been sent down by another boat, so no refunds could be made if anyone wanted to hop another boat, so certainly no money to pay a pilot $1,000.

November 15 the Omaha Republican reported the Imperial was still 150 miles above Fort Rice, passengers searching the banks for edible berries, no food. Zephyr, which had been at or near Fort Benton on September 6 and left the 26th was also having difficulties, but nothing to compare with the Imperial, leaking passengers whenever they found an abandoned mackinaw. Zephyr was loaded with a couple hundred passengers and lots of gold, made it to St. Louis in late November, about the time the limping Imperial was abandoned above Omaha. So ended a very successful season with a dreary finale.

### SUMMARY 1867:

| Date | Boat | Tons up | Down | Pass. up | Down | |
|---|---|---|---|---|---|---|
| May 25 | Waverly | 180 | | 120 | | |
| May 31 | Miner | 210 | 150 | 135 | 25 | $30,000 gold |
| June 1 | Only Chance | 186 | | 52 | 100 | $500,000 gold |
| June 2 | Waverly | 250 | | | 200 | from Camp Cooke |
| June 5 | Deer Lodge | 207 | | 75 | 25 | |
| June 5 | Walter B. Dance | 198 | | 58 | 50 | |
| June 5 | Cora | 210 | | 50 | 50 | $100,000 gold |
| June 8 | Gallatin | 250 | | 25 | 50 | $250,000 gold |
| June 9 | Amelia Poe | 183 | | 50 | 25 | |
| June 10 | Mountaineer | 225 | | 200 | 30 | |
| June 10 | St. John | 129 | | 125 | 125 | passengers, troops |
| June 12 | Nile | 140 | | 30 | 25 | |
| June 14 | Yorktown | 210 | | 15 | 10 | |
| June 14 | Ben Johnson | 300 | | 11 | 25 | |
| June 15 | Huntsville | 190 | | 20 | 10 | |
| June 16 | Ida Stockdale | 250 | | 10 | 15 | est. $200,000 gold |
| June 20 | Octavia | 300 | | 200 | 40 | $75,000 gold |
| June 20 | Guidon | 225 | | 57 | 20 | $1 million |
| June 27 | Benton | 200 | | | 50 | trip of Trover |
| June 29 | Ida Stockdale | 165 | | 20 | | |
| June 29 | Amaranth | 225 | | 12 | 120 | est. $100,000 gold |
| June 30 | G. A. Thompson | 200 | | 68 | 20 | Meagher drowned |
| July 3 | Antelope | 175 | | 4 | 10 | |
| July 4 | Abeona | 230 | | 31 | 10 | |

|         | Boat             | Tons up | Down | Pass. up | Down |                     |
|---------|------------------|---------|------|----------|------|---------------------|
| July 5  | Agnes            | 160     |      | 30       | 10   |                     |
| July 5  | Tacony           | 175     |      | 15       | 10   | A. C. Meyers trip   |
| July 6  | Jennie Brown     | 125     |      | 40       | 10   |                     |
| July 8  | Luella           | 129     |      | 36       | 200  |                     |
| July 8  | Big Horn         | 213     |      | 7        | 10   |                     |
| July 10 | Tom Stevens      | 100     |      | 10       | 10   |                     |
| July 11 | Lady Grace       | 234     |      | 110      | 30   | includes 80 soldiers |
| July 12 | Lilly            | 242     | 100  | 15       | 10   |                     |
| July 14 | Little Rock      | 165     |      | 50       | 15   |                     |
| July 16 | Ida Fulton       | 175     |      |          | 15   |                     |
| July 17 | Gallatin         | 185     |      | 30       | 150  | $250,000 gold       |
| July 20 | Nymph No. 2      | 150     |      | 10       | 10   |                     |
| July 23 | Viola Belle      | 170     |      |          | 40   |                     |
| July 28 | Richmond         | 316     |      | 30       | 180  |                     |
| August 5 | Ida Stockdale   | 150     | with Gen. Terry etc. from Buford area |   |   |  |
| August 25 | Only Chance    | 57      | 110  | 6        | 300  | immense gold cargo  |
| August 8 | Tom Stevens     | 150     |      |          |      | with Sunset trip    |
|         |                  | 7934    |      | 1757     | 2035 |                     |

OTHER POINTS:

|         | Boat             | Tons up | Down | Pass. up | Down |                     |
|---------|------------------|---------|------|----------|------|---------------------|
| August 16 | Miner          | 160     | 50   | 12       | 12   | Dauphins Rapids     |
| August  | Centralia        | 100     |      |          |      | Cow Island          |
| Sept. 6 | Zephyr           | 200     |      |          | 300  | Marias              |
| Sept. 11 | Imperial        | 225     |      |          | 300  | $100,000 plus gold  |
| Sep.-Oct. | Huntsville     | 250     |      |          | 16   | Cow I, $175,000     |
| July 18 | Silver Lake No. 4 | 150  | to Camp Cooke only |   |   |           |
| May 28  | James H. Trover  | 200     | to Musselshell |    |      |                     |
|         |                  | 1285    |      |          | 628  |                     |
|         | **Overall totals** | 9219  | 600  | 2200     | 2600 |                     |

To Fort Buford only: June 28, G. W. Graham, 200 tons; July 1, Paragon, 400; July 5, City of Pekin, 295

July 23 Sunset went up from Buford, may be unknown boat mentioned as at Cow Island by several lists. August 7, Carrie, 200 tons to Buford; August 24 Deer Lodge gave up second trip from St. Louis at Fort Buford, unloaded 150 tons; Last Chance gave up August 27, 175 tons; Amaranth brought 75 tons to Buford Oct. 17, and Benton 250 tons Nov. 1.

Dora left St. Louis for Fort Benton April 18 with 150 tons, no local record. Nora sank near De Soto last of May, probably Benton bound.

Totals into Montana may have neared 11,000 tons, passengers 5,000.

## 1868 Fading Steamboating Boom

The bloom was wearing off the Montana gold rush in 1868, and a lessened demand due to a decrease in number of miners in the territory resulted in a drop in Missouri River commerce to Fort Benton. Boats carried many passengers to and from the territory, the first three steamboats brought 175. A major factor was an agreement with Red Cloud and his triumphant Sioux which resulted in three army posts on the Bozeman Trail being abandoned, and adding to the appeal of the Missouri River route to and from the territory. Another abandonment, the Northern Overland Mail from Minnesota, which had switched from the Milk River-Fort Benton route to the Missouri with a post at Fort Hawley, near the Musselshell, then via Central Montana. There Indians didn't like the idea of a mail route. Little or no mail reached its Helena destination via this Pony Express—Indians didn't usually kill the mail carriers, simply stripped the horsemen, left them afoot and tossed the mail to the bitter winter winds. Final act was a tough little Indian fight and terse comment in a March 19 letter from stageman C. C. Huntley, "the mail service between Fort Abercrombie and Helena has been discontinued."

Helena, which had backed Ophir in 1865 and Kercheval City in 1866 as an alternative port to Fort Benton, had run out of choices in 1867. In this spring of 1868 the Helena Herald and some businesses went full tilt in favor of Montana Hide & Fur and their new facilities at the mouth of the Musselshell—facilities considerably exaggerated in the releases to the Herald. The project actually never did amount to much, in part because of an excess of Sioux, but it was a forerunner of the far more ambitious Carroll Trail of the mid-70s. The April 9, 1868, Herald dutifully reported a big building program at the new town of Musselshell, work on a toll road from Diamond City and Helena eastward was begun, it was reported. (James Wells, in the Musselshell area at the time, later recalled only about 80 tons landed for freighting over the central Montana route, probably in 1868.)

Of far more importance to the commerce of the territory, the railroad reached Sioux City and patterns of steamboat supply began changing. The rise of Sioux City lopped a thousand miles from the long river route to the head of navigation, ending St. Louis dominance of the trade, Chicago the beneficiary. New steamboats of light draught and capable of solving the tough problems of low water navigation, began appearing.

The Missouri was reported remarkably low along the lower river at the end of March, in St. Louis owners were advertising "Will leave when navigation permits." April 2nd the new Northwestern Transportation Co. of Sioux City was reported about to send the Bertha, North Alabama, Fanny Barker and the well proven Miner to Montana. All were to bring freight to Fort Benton.

King & Gillette were making further improvements on their toll road through Little Prickly Pear on the Benton Road. Their rate in 1867 for a three wagon outfit had been $6.25—the rate was reduced a year or so later (the note not found). Owners of this valuable franchise on the heaviest travelled road in the territory made a fortune—eventually and without much objection by the owners, the route became a public highway.

There was an ample supply of freight wagons, the Helena Herald reported April 16. The Missouri began rising by early May, and there were enough Indians about the Judith Basin that even the Montana Hide & Fur reconsidered the matter of routes and facilities—their Helena trains were Benton bound. Freight to Helena from Benton was about half that of previous years with a low of around 2 1/2c a pound. (Eight tons on a three wagon hitch at 3c would be $480—an attractive sum to a small farmer who had an outfit and his crops in.)

May 13 the Success lived up to her name with the first arrival, but only half a cargo, 70 tons and 50 passengers, the rest left at Dauphin's Rapids—a name to become familiar through the next two seasons. (The point was about 15 river miles below Camp Cooke and may have been used in this period because of the proximity to military protection. The more often used, through the years, Cow Island, was 25 miles farther down and 127-8 river miles below Fort Benton.) Dauphin's Rapids was strewn with boulders, making passage dangerous as well as difficult. From the beginnings of steamboat navigation the point was reckoned the worst obstacle on the Upper Missouri. Through the season of 1868 a number of boats made double trips, others had cargoes moved by freighters.

Second arrival was by the Cora on May 15, likewise with a short cargo and 25 passengers, then the Deer Lodge May 19, heavily loaded for this season, 130 tons and 100 passengers. All three boats were delayed at Dauphin's for varying periods; the Deer Lodge brought up the remainder of its cargo on the 27th, a heavy 235 tons, for this boat, in all. The other two may have made similar double trips, but were unreported in the Benton news in the Herald. The Cora is the only one with down cargo indicated, 30 passengers, many hides and $97,000 gold. (During the gold rush period it was a rare boat, aside from those operated by or for a Fort Benton concern, that had anything like a good down cargo.)

Low tonnages were the rule through the season. The Nile brought 130 tons May 21, the Miner 80 and Only Chance 170 the 25th, the Miner having a slow trip of 52 1/2 days from Sioux City. The Miner probably had additional freight either freighted or by an unreported double trip for North West Fur. The Sallie with 208 tons May 25 was an exception, followed by the St. Luke (called Yellowhammer by roustabouts for its yellow trim) on the 28th with 200 tons.

River conditions were evidently improving, there were seven arrivals, all with medium sized cargoes, in the next seven days, Henry Adkins and Mountaineer May 30, Octavia, Ida Stockdale and Peninah May 31, and Antelope and Huntsville June 1. Passengers on the Mountaineer included Wm. G. and Charles E. Conrad with a silver dollar their entire estate and the golden touch. Joining I. G. Baker & Bro. at Fort Benton, they ultimately multiplied the dollar several million times.

A successful trip of 1868 was the Bertha, coming in June 2 with over 300 tons of cargo and 100 passengers, though some of the freight may have been deposited below. This boat left Sioux City April 30, so was fast for the season at 34 days. The boat bore the nickname "Scarred Wolf" for some now lost reason. Part of its cargo was a new printing plant for the Helena Herald, which reported June 18, "boats arriving report a general abandonment of woodyards between Camp Cooke and Fort Buford." In some instances woodhawks had been killed. S. V. Clevenger, manager of the brand new Thwing House at Fort Benton, built jointly by the Power and Baker firms, wrote the Herald, "Times are brisk here, and there is now no question but that we will have an excellent season." With arrival of the Bertha, there were seven boats at the levee.

Lacon and Guidon both arrived June 8, followed on the 13th by the Benton with a big trip plus 120 tons left at Fort Peck, making its total over 400 tons, and in view of the Benton's record in previous years probably all delivered in unreported extra trips. Aboard was the army paymaster with $400,000 in greenbacks and armed guard for what the June 18 Herald termed a "semi-occasional jubilee." Paydays on the frontier were sporadic, celebrated alike by soldiers, booze bosses and hungry gamblers.

The freight was moving, the same Herald showed: "From Benton, Col. Slim Grim's bull train of 15 wagons, only nine days on road, each with 8,500 to 9,300 pounds. Burd's mammoth ox train also today. Two Diamond R. trains today, at least 75 tons."

But not keeping pace. After arrival of Importer, Ida Rees, Andrew Ackley, North Alabama and Fanny Barker, June 15-20, Clevenger noted, "Levee pretty well covered with goods." Part was mining machinery from the Rees and Alabama, still visible in an 1868 picture of Front Street taken weeks later.

Not all reached here, the Amelia Poe sank May 24 a few miles below Milk River with 100 tons of freight and arriving boats reported that 1500 Indians were swarming around the wreck in a riotous salvage operation. There was some salvage by whites also. Bertha brought in the Poe passengers and Cora salvaged part of the freight. (Also see later note of this year.)

Late June arrivals, Hiram Woods the 23rd, Viola Belle 26th, Columbia 27th and Urilda 28th, with a total of 560 tons. The steamboats were keeping ahead of the hard working freighters such as Hugh Kirkendall's train of 16 new wagons from Benton, "finest we have seen," said the Herald reporter, and Valentine McCartney's large mule train from Benton in a round trip of 13 days, "by far the fastest of the season." Also noted by the paper, sale of the Diamond R Transportation Co. of John J. Roe & Co. to Edgar G. Maclay & Co. at $75,000 for 116 wagons, over 700 oxen, and with 70 men employed, "probably largest in west." Matt Carroll and George Steell of the Fort Benton firm were soon in the new Diamond R. The Hiram Woods had an 80 ton cargo of vegetables, an expensive treat in Montana, and a single passenger. The Urilda carried 130 tons of government freight. Indian annuities had been a large item in early steamboating days to the head of navigation, military freight would become increasingly important to rivermen.

The Deer Lodge celebrated July 4 at Fort Benton, unloading 160 tons of cargo and making the trip from Sioux City in 22 1/2 days, bolstering its record as the fastest boat in the Mountain trade. A letter of appreciation signed by all passengers appeared in the July 9 Helena Herald. July 7 the Tom Stevens and Silver Lake came in, each with 100 tons, July 26 the Leni Leoti with 180, and successful Success on August 4 with 100 tons, its second trip from Sioux City. Chartered by North West Fur operating from the old fort, and in part reflecting a busy and successful season for that company, the Benton correspondent for the Herald reported Success took down $307,000 gold, biggest found for the year. Quite likely this golden cargo in part came from an offshoot of Montana Bar at Diamond City reported that Sunday in the Helena Herald. Success was the 34th and last through arrival. Captain Dave Haney of the Leni Leoti on arrival at Fort Benton reported finding the bodies of seven men at a woodyard 45 miles above Fort Peck, killed by Indians, and who had been dead some time. Rather gruesomely, Haney knew several, as they had been his passengers in the spring on the Peninah.

There remained the movement of excess cargoes left below. Andrew Ackley cleaned up its load with 50 tons here July 23, the St. Luke had done the same early in July, Bertha brought its excess to Dauphin's Rapids August 2 and a couple of days later the Ackley came to Benton with this load at a charge of 1 1/4c a pound, August 16 with Lacon freight, then left the 17th with 50 passengers. The Success also went down for more cargo, returned August 6th with this and reported the Urilda at Dauphin's Rapids and Lacon expected there.

Considerable freight was left for the busy freighters. To Cow Island only came the Only Chance, freight moved by Carroll & Steell, and Fanny Barker on another pickup run. The North Alabama got to Fort Peck with part of its load. November 5 the Herald reported arrival in Helena of 150 tons of North Alabama and Fanny Barker freight via the big freight trains of Garrison, 32 wagons, and Burd of 24, a 41 day trip from the Teton and back. By then it was "waiting and preparing for spring the main occupation," said a Fort Benton correspondent.

There was one last act in the 1868 navigation season. Remember that wreck of the Amelia Poe? In December seven men on their way to the wreck got into a fight with 300 Sioux near Fort Peck, four whites killed, McGregor, Tabor, Thomas and Steve the Stutterer. Five Indians were killed and Moses Solomon of Fort Benton badly wounded but recovered. The other two were A. S. Reed, acting Indian agent for Gros Ventres, who shortly after shot and killed one of his petulant charges in Reed's office, and Tom Campbell, long time trader around Fort Benton and credited with most of the coups in the fight, a cool hand in a tight. Joe Culbertson would add that Tom was the champion Montana squawman. A final segment of the saga of Amelia Poe's freight: In early November Tom Gorman's freight train was snowbound at Dearborn with a part of the cargo on which X. Biedler as deputy U. S. marshal had filed an attachment on behalf of United States Insurance Co. Gorman had loaded the goods at the wreck, meanwhile fighting an ox-power shortage, 57 animals run off by Sioux.

Thus ended one of the more difficult, but rather successful seasons for the Mountain Steamboats.

SUMMARY 1868:

| Date | Boat Name | Tons | Pass. Up | Pass. Down | |
|---|---|---|---|---|---|
| May 13 | Success | 150 | 50 | 30 | double trip |
| May 15 | Cora | 150 | 25 | 175 | $97,000 gold |
| May 19 | Deer Lodge | 130 | 103 | | |
| May 21 | Nile | 130 | 94 | | |
| May 25 | Miner | 70 | 25 | | |
| May 25 | Only Chance | 192 | 42 | | $50,000 gold |
| May 25 | Sallie | 213 | 18 | | |
| May 27 | Deer Lodge | 105 | | | rest of freight |
| May 28 | St. Luke | 180 | 30 | | Yellowhammer |
| May 30 | Henry Adkins | 162 | 83 | | |
| May 30 | Mountaineer | 205 | 25 | 10 | |
| May 31 | Octavia | 175 | 101 | | $150,000 gold |
| May 31 | Ida Stockdale | 200 | 20 | | |
| May 31 | Peninah | 140 | 35 | 5 | |
| June 1 | Antelope | 180 | 46 | 10 | |
| June 1 | Huntsville | 200 | 10 | | |
| June 2 | Bertha | 300 | 100 | | |
| June 8 | Lacon | 150 | 25 | | |
| June 8 | Guidon | 125 | 20 | | |
| June 13 | Benton | 300 | 6 | | 150 tons down |
| June 14 | Yorktown | 125 | 50 | | |
| June 15 | Importer | 150 | 50 | | |
| June 16 | Ida Rees | 100 | 10 | | machinery |
| June 17 | Andrew Ackley | 175 | 20 | | |

*Continued on next page*

| Date | Boat Name | Tons | Pass. Up | Pass. Down | |
|------|-----------|------|----|------|---|
| June 19 | North Alabama | 150 | 20 | | machinery |
| June 20 | Fanny Barker | 200 | 20 | | |
| June 23 | Hiram Woods | 100 | 1 | | vegetables |
| June 26 | Viola Belle | 175 | 10 | | |
| June 27 | Columbia | 175 | 10 | | |
| June 28 | Urilda | 130 | 10 | | |
| July 4 | Deer Lodge | 160 | 25 | | 2nd trip |
| July 7 | Tom Stevens | 100 | 10 | 50 | |
| July 7 | Silver Lake No. 4 | 100 | 10 | | |
| July 23 | Andrew Ackley | 50 | | | trip of Lacon |
| July 26 | Leni Leoti | 180 | 10 | | |
| Aug. 3 | Success | 100 | 25 | | $307,000 gold |
| | | 5627 | 1200 | 800 | |
| Aug. 10 | Only Chance, Cow I | 89 | | | |

In above a list by Raymond Rossiter was used showing 4823 tons of freight for 1868. The writer does not believe all the double trips to lower points were included—Montana Post and Helena Herald totals varied both ways from above. The writer in addition to 4824 tons of freight believes about 800 tons should be added to the year's total. At least 150 tons of that excess was freighted from Fort Peck, the remainder from Cow Island. Thirty-five boats brought cargoes to Fort Benton.

### Tough, Bloody Year of 1869

Of all the events of the tough, bloody year of 1869, the junction of the Central Pacific and Union Pacific May 10 at Promontory Point in Utah was the most portentuous. The first transcontinental railroad, it superseded the river haul up the Columbia-Snake to old Fort Walla Walla and the Missouri route to Fort Benton with the 624 mile Mullan Road between as the quickest way to get across the continent.

The railroad completion also set Helena merchants to dreaming of yet another bypass to the Benton Road and the head of navigation, as the steamboating season of 1869 proved the tiny settlement at Musselshell good only as a secondary freight drop to Cow Island and Fort Peck. Much space in the Helena Herald in the latter part of 1869 was devoted to the manifest all year advantages of the Corinne, Utah, route, which in the end also proved visionary for Helena due primarily to the mileage. For more southerly settlements such as Virginia City, the route north from the railroad was somewhat more advantageous.

By 1869 it appeared probable, as was later proven, that most rich placers had been located and stripped of easily obtainable gold. It was the final year of the Montana gold rush as such.

There was trouble with the Blackfeet tribes all year, at times Fort Benton was virtually a beleaguered settlement in the midst of a tough little Indian war. A grand jury in the fall at Helena cited killings and horse stealing, and another source claimed 56 whites killed in Chouteau county during the year, a thousand horses stolen and freight wagons harrassed by hostile warriors. The murder of Malcolm Clarke, former chief clerk at Fort Benton, in August was the trigger for the tragedy of the Baker strike on the Marias in January 1870.

As Fort Benton emerged from a mild, open winter, the place was unusually dull, wrote a resident, but Bentonites looked for a busy season. That they got. But they already had, with little snow in the mountains, low water in the Missouri.

Then came distressing news from St. Louis: March 29 the steamboat Ben Johnson caught fire at the levee, the fire spread to Henry Adkins, Carrie V. Kountz and G. B. Allen. The Jennie Lewis, ready to start on its trip to Benton, stopped to save lives on boats in flames near the center of the Mississippi, caught fire herself and was a total loss. The Fanny Scott, also loading for Montana, was another victim. The fire specialized in Mountain boats. Only one boat of the seven burned was not Montana bound. Then the new Nick Wall, headed down from Pittsburgh, sank about May lst, although raised and repaired. There were two more casualties ahead of the first arrival at Benton, the Urilda snagged, a steam pipe burst, and that was it, fortunately no deaths; Antelope snagged, sank in shallow water, both accidents in late April. (Nearly all tonnages this season are estimated, based on previous cargoes and the river conditions. Passengers were numerous to mid-June.)

So it was with depleted ranks that the 1869 flotilla headed for Fort Benton. May 19 the trusty Deer Lodge brought in about 150 tons, and it wasn't until the 27th that Importer and Nile came in, bringing around 275 tons. The Importer was the last of the great treasure ships of the gold rush, based on available information. The June 3 Herald in a Fort Benton item of May 29 reported: "Messrs. Ingram moved their treasure from the Thwing House to take passage on the Importer." That "treasure" wasn't a word used lightly, "they also paid passage for several unfortunate miners and wives, children." The Importer was scheduled to leave June 1 "with a full load of passengers and about $500,000 plus respectable freight." Actual departure was June 2.

May 30 the Ida Rees arrived with about 150 tons of machinery, next day the Cora came with 150 tons and 50 passengers—the boat setting the season's trend by dropping down to Dauphin's Rapids for the rest of her freight. In early June Fanny Barker, North Alabama and Silver Bow arrived, officials of the latter boat reporting only 30 inches of water in Dauphin's Rapids. The Silver Bow brought up 76 passengers, took down "many."

June 8 here came a fleet, Peninah, Andrew Ackley, Only Chance and Big Horn "with about 200 passengers and upwards of 500 tons of freight." Probably not all the freight came at that time—reported tonnages 250 on Peninah, 172 Only Chance and 238 Big Horn. Another trio breezed in on the 11th, Sallie, Mountaineer and Huntsville.

When the Miner arrived June 14th that made nine boats at the landing that date, topping the seven along the levee at certain dates in 1866 and 1868. Fort Benton had been dull off and on, June 14th wasn't one of the dull spots. The joint was jumping at the upriver corner of Front where there was a "genuine squaw hurdy-house for bullwhackers, big crowds." A few days later some spoilsport in a letter to the Herald noted "the squaws promenading men to the bar after every dance, like any other hurdy would do, and of course these squaws partaking whiskey with the men." The writer called on U. S. Marshal Charles Hard to come down and abate the nuisance.

Between June 15 and 21 there were six more through arrivals, making 23 in all, Lacon, Utah, Silver Lake, Peter Balen, Colossal and Bertha. There is also a probability that the Mollie Ebert arrived, records are fragmentary.

There were further cargoes which never reached Fort Benton but were dropped at Cow Island for later freighting or carriage by other, lighter draught boats. These included the Tempest twice, the repaired Nick Wall, Flirt, Ida Stockdale twice, St. John, Arkansas, Columbia, all in July; and to Milk River, the General Sully and Admiral Farragut in August.

There were 19 double trips to Dauphin's Rapids by steamboats which had Fort Benton arrivals. Of these, the Andrew Ackley had to be the busiest boat on the Missouri with three such trips back to Benton in June and July, the Peninah, Big Horn, Only Chance and North Alabama two; single trips by Cora, Silver Bow, Fanny Barker, Viola Belle, Peninah, Huntsville, Miner, Silver Lake and Peter Balen. The Tempest on its second trip got only to Cow Island late in July.

One freighting note in July, the brand new freight train of I. G. Baker & Brother of 20 wagons just received by steamboat, had its arrival in Helena duly noted by the Herald.

Fort Benton was connected by telegraph line with the outside world in June—a newspaper item of June 8, "We are informed the telegraph line will be in to the Thwing House very soon." Actual completion date not found, but Herald items from Fort Benton with date line indicate about June 15.

In mid-July there was a report that there was "about a foot of water on Dauphin's Rapids, river falling slowly. That had to be the reason the Peter Balen, its work done for the season, was on the upriver end of Dauphin's Rapids, unable to get down. July 26 a telegram from Fort Benton advised the Herald: 'The steamer Peter Balen was burned to the water's edge about noon Thursday (22nd). A man ironing in the ladies' cabin went out for a few minutes, and on his return found the boat on fire, and the flames so far advanced that it was impossible to stay their progress.'" Thus ended the career of the steamboat which had probably made the most money on a single trip for its owners of any that ever came to the Mountains. Its 12 1/2c a pound freight bill (gold) on 400 tons of cargo in 1866 was $100,000—cost of sending such a boat to Fort Benton would be $25,000 at top, and value of the Balen the year it was destroyed about $10,000-12,000.

By mid-July, with a rather dreary steamboating season winding down, the Helena Herald had found a new love, the big railway warehouse at Corinne, Utah. However, only relatively small amounts of freight were hauled to Helena from there until late in the year. November 25 Hugh Kirkendall's fast mule train of 24 wagons made the haul in 26 days. A few weeks earlier the same train had loaded with 40 tons of Bourbon, among other Montana staples of the time, out of Benton.

1869 Summary (*initial arrival at Fort Benton):

| Date | Boat Name | Tons | Pass. Up | Pass. Down | |
|---|---|---|---|---|---|
| *May 19 | Deer Lodge | 115 | 121 | 225 | 200 soldiers down |
| *May 27 | Importer | 100 | 29 | 100 | $500,000 gold |
| *May 27 | Nile | 150 | 32 | 20 | |
| *May 30 | Ida Rees | 150 | 25 | 20 | machinery |
| *May 31 | Cora | 150 | 50 | | |
| *June 2 | Fanny Barker | 150 | | | |
| *June 4 | North Alabama | 100 | | | |
| *June 4 | Silver Bow | 100 | 76 | 75 | |
| June 4 | Cora | 75 | | | |
| *June 8 | Peninah | 250 | 30 | | |
| *June 8 | Andrew Ackley | 150 | | | |
| *June 8 | Only Chance | 172 | 19 | | |
| *June 8 | Big Horn | 238 | 50 | | |

*Continued on next page*

|          |              |      | Pass. |      |              |
|----------|--------------|------|-------|------|--------------|
| **Date** | **Boat Name** | **Tons** | **Up** | **Down** | |
| June 8 | Silver Bow | 100 | | | |
| *June 10-11 | Viola Belle | 200 | 8 | | Mountaineer frt |
| June 10 | North Alabama | 100 | | | |
| *June 11 | Sallie | 110 | 17 | | |
| *June 11 | Mountaineer | 150 | | | |
| *June 11 | Huntsville | 125 | | | |
| June 13 | Big Horn | 60 | | | |
| June 14 | Fanny Barker | 100 | | | |
| June 14 | Viola Belle | 100 | | | |
| June 14 | Only Chance | 100 | | | |
| June 14 | Peninah | 100 | | | |
| *June 14 | Miner | 130 | 27 | 130 | tons down |
| With arrival of Miner there were nine boats at the levee | | | | | |
| *June 15 | Lacon | 150 | | | |
| *June 15 | Utah | 150 | | | |
| June 15 | Andrew Ackley | 120 | | | |
| *June 16 | Silver Lake No. 4 | 75 | | | |
| *June 18 | Peter Balen | 200 | | | |
| | Balen burned at Dauphin's Rapids July 22 | | | | |
| June 19 | Huntsville | 75 | | | |
| *June 20 | Colossal | 175 | | | |
| June 20 | Big Horn | 65 | | | |
| *June 21 | Bertha | 250 | | | |
| June 21 | Miner | 70 | | | |
| June 23 | Peninah | 100 | | | |
| June 23 | Only Chance | 100 | | | Arkansas trip |
| *June 24 | Mollie Ebert | 100 | | | |
| | this date reported making 2nd trip, however not on Cooke list | | | | |
| June 24 | Silver Lake No. 4 | 75 | | | |
| June 26 | Andrew Ackley | 120 | | | |
| | above total for Ackley on this and July 2 arrival | | | | |
| July 10 | Miner | 100 | | | just below Benton |
| Totals | | 5300 | 484 | 440 | |
| Boats at points below Fort Benton (Cow Island) | | | | | |
| July 21 | Tempest | 150 | | | second trip to Cow |
| July 21 | Nick Wall | 100 | | | |
| July 21 | Flirt | 100 | | | |
| July late | Huntsville | 75 | | | |
| July 15 | Ida Stockdale | 100 | | | perhaps another trip |
| July 15 | St. John | 100 | | | |
| July 21 | Columbia | 75 | | | |
| | boat wintered near Buford wrecked next spring with loss of cargo of robes | | | | |
| Aug. 12 | Admiral Farragut | 175 | | | |
| Overall totals | | 6175 | 700 | 800 | est. 400 tons down |

Other notes: Mollie Ebert at Buford May 31, Arkansas June 1, both went up. General Sully and Admiral Farragut went to Fort Peck apparently with about 100 tons each. Deer Lodge was expected to reach Milk River by July 30. Tacony reached Fort Peck, estimate 200 tons, wintered and sank there.

# Across "The Medicine Line"

## 1870: Fort Benton Looks Northward

Fort Benton's interest in opportunities in the British Possessions, the new Dominion of Canada, had its beginnings in the winter of 1869-70 when two seasoned frontiersmen, John J. Healy and Alfred B. Hamilton, the latter a nephew of I. G. Baker of Fort Benton, built a small trading post north of the border and, according to a June Helena Herald, netted about $50,000, "not so very bad for a six months' cruise among the Lo family across the border." In view of Shirley Ashby's recollection of receiving $7,500 and a tenth interest in the Baker Co. for a very similar venture at what became Fort Conrad on the Marias and which brought a return of $40,000, Healy and Hamilton, although staked by Baker, probably made what then was considered a neat small fortune. It was enough to make anybody's eyes light up, especially with the Territory of Montana and Fort Benton in particular in the grip of a tough depression. It would be another fifteen years before Bentonites ceased to profit from international trade.

Commerce was off on the Missouri in 1870, any riverman or shipper knew that before the ice was out of the river. Interest of Montanans early in the year was on the Blackfeet War and the expedition of Major Eugene Baker against the Piegan tribe which had slain so many whites along the Benton Road during the bloody summer of 1869. The two scouts for Baker, Joe Kipp and Joe Cobell, were well known Bentonites. Cobell's Piegan wife was a sister of Mountain Chief, the intransigent chief the whites intended to punish. The soldiers located instead the smallpox stricken village of Heavy Runner, and Cobell later said he killed the chief, precipitating the slaughter to protect Mountain Chief's group. At any rate 173 Piegans, mostly women and children, were killed on the Marias January 23. White Montanans generally approved, then and later, although the affair went into history books as the Baker Massacre. The bloodletting broke the spirit of the Blackfeet, and trails were safer for the few freighters who found employment from the head of navigation in the next few years.

Montana had much snow during the winter, overall prospects for navigation were good. However, freighting north from Corinne was heavy enough to cut sharply into traffic previously pretty much monopolized by the boats. Total from Utah had amounted to only about 560 tons in 1869; in 1870 it was nearer 3500 and reached a peak of around 3750 tons the following year. Ultimately, the difference between 465 miles from Corinne to Helena, and the Fort Benton to Helena 140 miles tilted the scales in favor of the Missouri. The 325 mile differential represented 25-30 days longer on the trail northward by ox team. Working in favor of the longer wagon haul was the evident advantage of a longer shipping season via rail which in the next few seasons proved rather illusory, with snow stopping winter freighting and even the trains. Attempted fast mule express using relays of animals got the time down to 9-12 days from Corinne but quite evidently was too expensive for most goods.

The 1870 Montana Territorial census, first ever, found Fort Benton with a population of 367, tremendously large Chouteau county with 517. Sun River was the only other point of note, there was a scattering along the Missouri river of woodhawks. The 367 was a far cry from summers in the boating season when 1500 or more miners and freighters crowded the Fort Benton bottom. Of the 1870 total, 272 were white males, of those 97 were French Canadian, reflecting the long fur trade period. About 80 were part Indian, with a few blacks.

In April Wm. F. Wheeler, U. S. marshal and census enumerator for then unorganized Dawson county (about the northeastern 20% of Montana and 177 population) combined two pieces of business, the enumeration on a trip down the Missouri in a small boat and auction at Fort Peck of the steamboat Tacony, which didn't make it to Fort Benton in the 1869 season, wintered there and sank before the auctioneer arrived. A Helena man bought the hulk for $350 to scrap it.

The Helena Herald, covering both the Corinne route and citizen meetings to back Major Baker, found little space for river news in the spring of 1870. As a matter of fact, there wasn't much. Bentonites had hoped for 15 or 20 boats, got just over half the lower figure.

Despite the census count, men reminiscing later would recall a Fort Benton with a population of about 180 in 1870, with four Indian trading houses, two blacksmiths, carpenter, tailor, shoemaker, butcher shop, bakery, brewer and about a dozen saloons.

Navigation, despite snow in Montana, was delayed along the lower Missouri, and it wasn't until May 26 that the Nick Wall out of St. Louis arrived at Fort Benton with an estimated 200 tons of cargo and 36 passengers reported. Two days later came the Ida Rees, also from St. Louis, with 150 tons reported, 17 passengers up and 25 down. June 2 the Deer Lodge came with 180 tons of government freight and 65 tons private.

The early arrivals could have expected fair down cargoes, but over 200 tons of buffalo robes (18,000) in storage here were embargoed by the federal government because of smallpox the previous winter among Indians. The embargo wasn't lifted for months, it was September when I. G. Baker shipped 3,000 robes to Helena for government inspection and got them cleared, as this portion had been traded for with Assiniboines, who did not suffer from the disease. This was probably the largest rail shipment, via the UP from Corinne, that a Fort Benton firm ever made.

There was another boat besides the Tacony which hadn't made it down river in 1869. The Columbia probably reached Cow Island, then wintered near the mouth of the Yellowstone, went down that spring with robes and furs, and was wrecked in late May near Sioux City.

June 9 Fort Benton greeted the Viola Belle, which brought about 250 tons of freight and 40 passengers; another week and the Sallie came in, 16th, loaded out of St. Louis with 293 tons for Fort Benton.

The Bertha came June 19, an estimated 200 tons and 26 passengers, followed by two more boats the 20th: Peninah, 161 tons, 11 passengers, out of St. Louis, and Ida Stockdale, a good sidewheeler from St. Louis with 250 tons and 50 passengers.

That, eight boats and 1599 tons of freight and 230 passengers, was the navigation season of 1870. Total freight may vary by 200 tons, four cargoes were estimated. Fall off in passengers was in large part due to the end of the good placer mines, in part to the year round passage by rail, then stage north to Montana. However, the seasoned traveler of those days would take steamboat over stage when possible, cheaper, and more comfortable. Depending on the time of year, Fort Benton steamboats had a good passenger trade until rails replaced stages.

Four other boats were reported in the papers as Benton bound, the Silver Bow, Flirt and Carrie V. Kountz from the lower Missouri, the Sioux City clear from Pittsburgh, an almost traditional maiden voyage for a steamboat new to the Mountain trade. Lack of loads more than the river stage probably changed the minds of the owners in regard to these trips.

1870 Summary:

|  |  | Tons | Pass. | Down |
|---|---|---|---|---|
| May 26 | Nick Wall | 200 | 36 | 25 |
| May 28 | Ida Rees | 150 | 17 | 25 |
| June 2 | Deer Lodge | 245 | 25 | 20 |
| June 9 | Viola Belle | 150 | 40 | 30 |
| June 16 | Sallie | 293 | 25 | 20 |
| June 19 | Bertha | 200 | 26 | 20 |
| June 20 | Peninah | 161 | 11 | 10 |
| June 20 | Ida Stockdale | 200 | 50 | 50 |
|  |  | 1599 | 230 | 200 |

Down cargoes estimated at about 250 tons

## 1871 Another Low Point For Steamboating

Helena gave the Corinne Trail a big try in 1871 and Montana freight off the Union Pacific hit a new high point of about 3750 tons, which was slightly less than double that off the steamboats to Fort Benton and Cow Island, through a dull boating season. Considerable effort was made by Helena freighters to speed the normal seven weeks from Utah by oxen. In February the big Diamond R, which included former Bentonites Matt Carroll and George Steell, announced April plans for a "Time Freight" line from Corinne, promising delivery of goods in eight days by using relays of mules. That would be expensive, but cost wasn't indicated in Helena Herald ads. Other freighters such as Hugh Kirkendall took their cue from the ads, but the "time freight" idea died after a season or two.

There were the usual ads of departure for the Mountains in down river papers. Announcing their trips in the Missouri Democrat were Peninah, Ida Stockdale, Andrew Ackley, Carrie V. Kountz, Mollie Moore, Henry C. Yeager, May Lowry and Kate P. Kountz. Only two of the boats were able to make it, another got to Cow Island.

Of more interest to Fort Benton residents was the growing robe and fur trade in the British Possessions, and whisky forts flourished. Bill Gladstone was finishing the two year chore of building a stout Fort Whoop-Up on the Oldman. Another at the junction of Belly and Waterton rivers was Fort Standoff, built by Dutch Fred Wachter, W. McLean, Antoine Juneau, John "Liver Eating" Johnson and Joe Kipp after "standing off" U. S. Deputy Marshal Charles Hard with Winchesters on the claim the party was safely into Canada. (Wrong by a few hundred yards, right by four rifles) Fred Kanouse built another on the Elbow River, a sort of forerunner to Calgary. There were others. One who didn't make it that spring, according to a great nephew, was Fred F. Gerard. After trading with the tribes near the Yellowstone mouth for years, Gerard had his trading license revoked in 1870, loaded his goods on a steamboat and came to Fort Benton, where he bought the Carroll & Steell business. Some time during fall and winter of 1871-72, Gerard sent a small freight train into Whoop-Up country. Indians, probably Blackfeet, attacked the train, killed five men and took over the trade goods, wet and dry.

There were many robes coming into Fort Benton from the north in the early spring of 1871. A 1979 estimate by the author of 18,000 robes that year may be short of the mark, one of the Fort Benton steamboats reportedly brought down 39,000 robes, probably not all handled through Fort Benton. That's about 480 tons, and another boat unloaded enough robes and furs at Sioux City to fill 23 freight cars.

Navigation story of the year was the beginning of the Coulson Line as Northwestern Transportation Co., later Missouri River Transportation Co., at the time including E. H. Durfee, C. K. Peck, Sanford Coulson, William S. Evans; and I. G. Baker & Bro. of Fort Benton had an interest. The firm got the Indian contract for hauling annuities and other goods for 1871-June 1872, while Wm. J. Kountz had the military contract. Rate on agency freight was $3.36 per hundred to Benton. During the year government freight may well have been over half the tonnage moved to the Fort Benton area. For the Blackfeet agency alone a thousand sacks of flour and 1500 pounds of coffee were among supplies up for bids in April, along with 150 tons of various grains to the army posts providing an example of the extent.

The Herald carried a few river items in the spring. Grant Marsh, in charge of the brand new Nellie Peck, which made its maiden trip down from Pittsburgh, at Sioux City had deckhand trouble. He fired all the roustabouts and employed a gang of raw Scandinavians, reported the Sioux City paper, which added that the fired hands were threatening to drink the river dry and ground Nellie Peck. They probably settled for a more appreciated beverage.

First arrival at Fort Benton, however, was the Ida Rees on May 13th, the boat which was reported to have taken those 39,000 robes down to Sioux City (about 500 tons). On a second trip, the Rees sank near Fort Randall in Dakota with 208 tons of freight and 38 passengers for Fort Benton, on June 20. E. H. Durfee took off the cargo, but never made it to Fort Benton; other boats perhaps brought it on.

The Ida Stockdale was a May 24 arrival from St. Louis, bringing an unstated amount of cargo and many passengers. The Far West, destined to become the most famous of the Mountain Steamboats in 1876, came in just behind the Stockdale with an estimated 225 tons and 30 passengers.

June 3 Grant Marsh brought the Nellie Peck on her first trip to Benton with an impressive 328 tons and 42 passengers—about the same time the Helena paper reported an exodus to Benton to take passage on the Peck, 53 listed on departure. The boat had a bulky cargo down, filled 23 railroad freight cars with furs and robes at Sioux City.

The Peninah came up to the levee June 18 for Kountz, probably with the military supplies the owner had contracted to deliver. Forty passengers down, but down cargo wasn't mentioned for other boats except the Nellie Peck, leaving the freight tonnages to be estimated. Last boat of the season was the Flirt June 29, advertised in Helena to leave July 1st.

There were four boats to Cow Island, the Miner July 15 or 16, unable to get further due to low water, but lying there until about August 1st waiting for passengers by mackinaw from Fort Benton. Based on previous record, the Miner probably drew a good list. The Silver Lake, Andrew Ackley and Nellie Peck were also at Cow Island about that time. The Flirt advertised a down trip from Fort Benton, but on her second trip apparently only managed to get as far up as Fort Peck.

Winter 1871 set in with extreme cold and a big November storm, followed by mild weather a couple of weeks, then a three day blizzard and deep snow that promised well for the 1872 boating season. Fort Benton's new telegraph line was in trouble. There were thousands of buffalo in the Sun River area to 28 Mile Springs and "they have commenced rubbing down telegraph poles," said the Herald.

Summary for 1871:

| Date | Boat | Tons up, | down | Pass. up, | down |
|---|---|---|---|---|---|
| May 13 | Ida Rees | 200 | 500 | 40 | 55 |
| May 24 | Ida Stockdale | 250 | 100 | 30 | 40 |
| May 29 | Far West | 225 | 50 | 30 | 14 |
| June 3 | Nellie Peck | 328 | 150 | 42 | 53 |
| June 13 | Peninah | 200 | - | 20 | 40 |
| June 29 | Flirt | 200 | - | 10 | 30 |
| Totals | | 1403 | 800 | 172 | 212 |
| | To Cow Island | | | | |
| July 15-16 | Miner | 200 | 50 | - | 40 |
| July 15 | Silver Lake | 100 | 20 | - | 10 |
| | Andrew Ackley | 100 | | | |
| | Nellie Peck | 200 | | | |
| | Flirt to Fort Peck | 150 | | | |
| Totals | | 750 | 50 | | |
| | | 2150 | 850 | 200 | 300 |

### 1872—The Longest Steamboat Race

Hard times had hit Helena, mourned the Herald January, 1872, with charity fairs and other efforts to relieve the impoverished. Chiefly it was due to dwindling returns from placer gold, and few of the productive quartz lodes had yet been opened. Adding to the woes there was a prolonged blockage by snow drifts and avalanches on the Union Pacific 500 miles to the south across the Wyoming plains. Snowed in, too, were Helena freight trains on the long route from the south after chancing the winter.

Fort Benton was in similar shape, except an increasing number of local men were up in the Whoop-Up country. "Times are rather dull at present, and the merchants are carrying light stocks," wrote a Benton correspondent in February. T. C. Power, I. G. Baker and Gerard & Co., the latter successor to Carroll & Steell, were doing business; only the Overland Hotel was open, and those, with three saloons and a bakery, comprised Fort Benton's business district. Wetzel & Weatherwax, a new Indian trading firm, was probably trading north of the border.

The Union Pacific snow blockade ended in February but Montana was waiting for about five tons of precious mail up to six weeks delayed. Corinne reported arrival of six passenger trains on February 10, three of which had left Omaha three weeks before; most out of grub, passengers living on cheese and crackers. Freighting of the coming season was to indicate that the Corinne Trail had lost its glamor for Helena firms. Oddly, by late February a report came to Helena via George Baker that winter losses of work oxen were light; bull teams were "fat" he said. Also no snow around Benton and roads were dusty.

Down river Durfee & Peck and the Coulsons had bought the boats of the Northwestern Transportation Co., and also secured Indian and military freight contracts. A new generation of Upper Missouri boats had begun to appear the year before in the Nellie Peck and Far West, in 1872 the Western was added. These were spoonbill types built for the river conditions. Most were based on Sioux City.

First freight arrivals of 1872 reached Helena in early April—these the several trains which had been snowed in along the Corinne Trail.

A factor to influence Fort Benton's future, the Northern Pacific began building across Dakota to the Missouri River where The Crossing that became Bismarck would be built—the final shuttle point of the Mountain steamboats. Oddly, for ten more years the railroad would rely on steamboats to move its freight west.

Steamboats were on their way from St. Louis and Sioux City the fore part of April, first arrival here was Nellie Peck under Grant Marsh on May 18 with 300 tons of cargo, the Far West under Mart Coulson coming six days later with over 250 tons. Together they brought 40 passengers, took down 55. This season fare was $100 from Sioux City, probably lower for the quicker down trip, but with the UP to the south, the large numbers up on early boats and down on late ones had dwindled sharply. The season total was about 400 to Montana, 200 down river. The two boats probably cleaned up most of the buffalo robes at Fort Benton from the winter's trade in Montana and Canada.

June 1st the E. H. Durfee came with 200 tons, the Esperanza with about the same on the 9th and the smaller Fontenelle all the way from St. Louis with 150 on June 11, the same day the Sioux City made its first appearance at the Fort Benton levee, 200 tons of freight and three companies of the 7th Infantry, perhaps 240 men.

Another new Coulson boat, the Western, made it three arrivals in two days the 12th of June, with 300 tons. The Mary McDonald, a 200 foot sidewheeler rather large for the upper Missouri, made its only Fort Benton arrival June 15 with about 300 tons, having loaded out 150 tons in St. Louis, picked up more at other ports. The boat had a slow trip to Omaha, where it had to cut down its stacks to get under the bridge.

The last day of June saw three arrivals, the Katie P. Kountz the tailender with 200 tons from St. Louis. The others were the fastest boats of the emerging Coulson combine with record-minded captains. Grant Marsh with the Nellie Peck had kept ahead of Mart Coulson's Far West from Sioux City to Dauphin's Rapids, where the heavy load caused Marsh problems. The Far West tooted past and came into Fort Benton several hours ahead, 17 days and 20 hours from Sioux City, the Peck couldn't have been many hours more. A to become noted Montanan aboard the Far West was William Wesley Van Orsdel, better known from arrival as "Brother Van."

That wasn't the end. Neither boat could have had much down cargo, what there was went aboard with both captains pressing, the Far West getting away a few hours quicker. It wasn't until Fort Berthold, now under the waters of Garrison reservoir, that the hands and passengers on the Nellie Peck caught sight of the other boat, passed where the Indian agency stood and kept ahead to Bijou Hills reach. There John LaBarge, perhaps with more river miles on the upper river than any other helmsman, ran the Peck aground. That was it, the Far West passed before the other boat could get clear and reached Sioux City three hours ahead in 3,000 tough river miles. Each boat had beaten by several days all previous records for the round trip between Sioux City and Fort Benton.

That almost closed navigation for 1872, but not quite. The Sioux City struggled up a shrunken stream to Fort Benton July 23 with perhaps as much as 200 tons, then back to Buford to bring up the remainder in early August, as well as to take down passengers. Later the Coulsons arranged with T. C. Power to run mackinaws down to connect with steamboats delivering late Indian supplies at Fort Peck and Fort Buford.

Probably the down cargo of the Nellie Peck and Far West, the Helena Herald quoted the Chicago Tribune of August 3 to the effect that P. B. Weare & Co. there had received the largest shipment of furs ever sent to Chicago, from Thomas C. Power & Bro., 15,400 buffalo robes, 1,000 calf robes, 5,000 antelope, 1,100 deer, 1,200 elk, 1,200 beaver, 5,000 mountain wolf, 800 fox and 125 grizzly, "said to be a third of this year's crop." At a rough estimate, about 225 tons.

At year end the Northern Pacific was planning a fleet of seven steamers to ply the upper Missouri from the NP Crossing to Fort Benton. The promoter seemingly was shouldered aside in the tough business methods of the era, and arrangements ultimately made with boat owners working the stretch of the Missouri involved.

The year marked a sharp revival of Fort Benton tonnage, 12 cargoes and about 3,000 tons being nearly equal to 1870 and 1871 combined, also the down tonnage.

Summary for 1872:

| Date | Boats | Tons, up | down | Pass., up | down |
|---|---|---|---|---|---|
| May 18 | Nellie Peck | 300 | 150 | 31 | 30 |
| May 24 | Far West | 250 | 150 | 9 | 25 |
| June 1 | E.H. Durfee | 200 | - | 13 | 10 |
| June 9 | Esperanza | 200 | - | 4 | 5 |
| June 11 | Fontenelle | 150 | - | 10 | 10 |
| June 11 | Sioux City | 200 | - | 240 | 10 |
| June 12 | Western | 300 | - | 4 | 5 |
| June 15 | Mary McDonald | 300 | - | 20 | 10 |
| June 30 | Far West | 200 | 125 | 20 | 10 |
| June 30 | Nellie Peck | 300 | 125 | 20 | 10 |
| June 30 | Katie P. Kountz | 200 | - | 10 | 10 |
| July 23 | Sioux City | 200 | - | 10 | 10 |
| Aug. 7 (?) | Sioux City | 150 | - | - | 10 |
| | Totals | 2950 | 850 | 400 | 200 |

## 1873 A Dreary Year

The 1872 part of the winter had been relatively mild in northern Montana, January more than made up for it. It took Charles Rowe and three others 37 days to make the trip of 200 miles south from the Cypress Hills in deep snow and bitter cold after losing their eight horses and mules. Late in January epizootic in horses hit the Gilmer & Salisbury stage line from Corinne to Helena. The disease was enervating but not generally fatal; it did, however, cut deeply into available horsepower, and storms did the same. Such a winter of heavy snow was usually a forerunner of a good navigation season, but 1873 was different, the Territory of Montana was in deep trouble.

It was to be a season in which tonnage on the Yellowstone would rival that to Fort Benton, due to the Northern Pacific Railroad survey that aggravated the Sioux into rewewed hostility. Survey parties were escorted by a couple of thousand troops, meaning reliance on steamboats to supply these large numbers.

In part probably due to the hard winter, the robe trade was good in Canada and northern Montana. But the Helena Herald reported a side note in April, "The town of Whoop-Up...is reported to be one of the toughest camps now existing in the Rocky Mountains," and made first mention of British troops coming west "this spring." A year and a season off of coming events.

Three steamboat lines were operating on the Upper Missouri in 1873, the Missouri River Transportation Co. (Coulson) out of the new river port of Yankton with 15 boats; Durfee & Peck as the old North West Transportation Co. with 7 based on Sioux City, and the Kountz Line with 4 boats at the new settlement, now Edwinton instead of The Crossing, and soon to become Bismarck. (In this period there was a surplus of steamboats looking for work due to the rapid expansion of railroad building that cut previous markets. Despite the number Fort Benton arrivals and tonnages dropped off sharply.)

The boats which had staged the 3,000 mile race in 1872 were first at Benton, the Far West with 250 tons came all the way from St. Louis and her speedy rival Nellie Peck chased the other in to Benton levee with 292 tons. The boats took down heavy cargoes of robes and furs, probably the lion's share of the 40,000 robes indicated in a June Herald. They brought up 82 passengers and took down a few less. A brand new boat, eventually to be the oldest surviving Mountain boat, coming up from Bismarck, is reported in old lists as arriving at Fort Benton June 1st—erroneously. The Josephine went direct to the Yellowstone and worked that season on the tributary stream. All three, incidently, were Coulson boats.

Third steamboat at Fort Benton was the Peck Line E.H. Durfee with 250 tons and a whopping passenger list that included 141 recruits for the 7th infantry in Montana, along with 24 passengers who doubtless enjoyed their trip far more than the soldiers, the latter making the ride as deckers. The Esperanza from St. Louis delivered 200 tons of freight and 63 passengers, the trip requiring a few days over two months.

Joseph LaBarge seemed to alternate between great trips and bad, his 1873 perhaps in between for a change. He had just bought a brand new boat, named for his old and good friend, Father Pierre Jean DeSmet, who was able to bless the boat as a token of friendship in one of the last acts of a grand useful life in the west. The DeSmet arrived at Fort Benton June 29 with 230 tons of freight and 30 passengers. Montana streams were still running high, a picture of the boat taken here proves. There was an apparently trumped up charge of selling liquor on an Indian reservation which resulted in a federal seizure while here. It took LaBarge a trip to Helena to get the impoundment lifted, and the DeSmet went down July 15th with a pretty nice load of furs.

The Katie P. Kountz came in July 5th with a big 325 ton load, best of the season, but only three passengers. For Fort Benton the navigation season ended with arrival of the Western and 200 tons on July 13th, a later arrival than owners had hoped for, judging from ads that the Western would leave on the 5th, soon changed to the 17th.

The total tonnage here, mostly reported in the Herald, was 1747 tons, down cargoes 600 tons or more, robes weighed about 500 tons. On the Yellowstone, about 1500 tons, supplies for that big Northern Pacific survey party and military escort. Besides the Josephine, carrying cargoes were the Katie P. Kountz, Mollie Moore, Peninah, Key West and quite possibly others. The Silver Lake may have made two trips to Fort Peck, the second in August probably for freight offloaded on the first trip in June. The effort on the Yellowstone included a special Crow commission aimed at cession by the Crows of 6½ million acres along that river.

The new town of Bismarck got off to a slow start freightwise, it wasn't until June 14 that the Peninah was loaded out of the new railhead. The Northern Pacific had intended to keep building, but the panic of 1873 intervened, and the Bismarck to Fort Benton run was to be a major factor in supplying Montana and the North West Territories for another decade.

After three years of the long freight haul from Corinne, Helena merchants and the Herald were turning back to an old love, that elusive short cut from the Musselshell (they still spelled it Muscleshell), just a bit above where Kercheval City and Musselshell had their brief careers. The Herald in October picked up a story from the Bismarck Tribune of "the important announcement is made that the Northern Pacific has effected an arrangement with the famous Maclay Diamond R freight line to run in connection with the line of steamers, from the mouth of the Musselshell to Helena." Also, "Commodore Kountz has been in the city for several days looking after his interests here." The Kountz Line was to become anathema for the promoters of the Carroll Trail the next boating season. In November Story's bull team left Helena for the Musselshell to establish a depot, with Peter Koch, an old hand in that area, in charge of the work.

And at year end the Bismarck Tribune went small size, the last train left and the hopeful settlement closed up for the winter; at least the dance halls, which had been popular, noisy places with all the soldiers around.

1873 Summary:

| | | | | | |
|---|---|---|---|---|---|
| May 22 | Far West | 250 | 200 | 25 | 30 |
| May 22 | Nellie Peck | 292 | 200 | 57 | 35 |
| June 9 | E.H. Durfee | 250 | 25 | 165 | 20 |
| June 19 | Esperanza | 200 | 25 | 63 | 25 |
| June 29 | DeSmet | 230 | 100 | 30 | 10 |
| July 5 | Katie P. Kountz | 325 | - | 3 | 10 |
| July 13 | Western | 200 | 50 | 10 | 30 |
| | | 1747 | 600 | 356 | 160 |

Silver Lake to Fort Peck in August, estimate 100 tons

On Yellowstone: Josephine, Peninah, Key West, Mollie Moore, Katie P. Kountz and perhaps others.

### 1874: New Customers For Fort Benton

In 1874 Helena people and the Herald vigorously promoted their Musselshell route; the settlement there soon took the name of Carroll for Matt Carroll of the Diamond R, whom Bentonites probably regarded as a turncoat at best. It apparently drew slightly more tonnage, the writer's estimates based on very incomplete records indicate about 2000 tons here, as high as 2500 at Carroll, but by no means that tonnage delivered to Helena. The Herald was turning from the Corinne Trail, in its fifth season, rather piously pointing out that the river route had its advantages, one being that money paid for freighting would remain in Montana rather than going to Mormons, "as it largely does now."

Edgar G. Maclay of the Diamond R, one of the chief promoters of the Carroll Trail, saw no danger from hostile Indians, a good road through the Judith Basin, and reported contracts for about 4,000 tons of freight. He proved a poor prophet three ways, especially in reliance upon the steamboat owners and their promises.

For Fort Benton, the most important news of the year came in early fall when a group from the newly arrived North West Mounted Police traveled down from Three Buttes (now Sweet Grass Hills) to Benton to make arrangements for supplies. Their business, and that of a gradual influx of settlers in Canada's west, was to create one of the strangest and closest international relationships in history. Also, during the summer months a joint survey party of British and Americans was completing a survey of the boundary line with Canada. According William Lass, author of a book on the boundary determination, the British party included 257 men, 324 draft animals and 179 vehicles. The American party he estimated about the same size with the addition of troops to protect against Indians. The two parties undoubtedly meant some supplies secured out of Fort Benton.

Spring issues of the Herald were filed with plugs for their new Carroll route;

steamboat news from St. Louis, Sioux City and Bismarck of course routinely carried. By May 22 there came a sour note, the Fontenelle advertised to leave Fort Benton May 25, the Herald "very dubious about the boat getting to Benton." Then Montana skies opened, it began to rain. The paper later called it the wettest June in memory, a factor that hurt Carroll badly, along with the hostile Sioux, stirred up in several clashes with the soldiers escorting the Northern Pacific survey the year before.

Carroll got the first steamboat, the Peninah on May 8 and again the 17th, a double trip with about 300 tons, half unloaded at Buford. The Fontenelle was Fort Benton's first, with 160 tons, May 21st, in time to make an advertised departure with a bigger load down. The Western followed, bringing about 360 tons on May 29 and taking down about 150 tons, including a somewhat unusual 113 head of horses from the Beaverhead, at a guess 45 tons of horseflesh at 800 pounds each. The Nellie Peck was third, May 31st, 350 tons, 40 passengers, 150 tons down and even more passengers heading to the States.

June 1st the Josephine with about 250 tons and more left below, made its first of some three dozen arrivals at Fort Benton, and going down met the Key West which reached port June 5th with another 250 tons. Grant Marsh and the Josephine played a profitable Good Samaritan when for a $1250 tow charge the boat pulled the disabled May Lowry up to Carroll on June 6, making the Lowry the second through boat to stop there. Boats coming to Benton were chiefly Coulson and Peck Line boats—no love for Kountz Line boats serving Carroll.

The Peninah arrived at Carroll June 11 and again the 17th, this time with the trip of the disabled Ida Stockdale. There seemed to be a jinx on Wm. Kountz's Carroll-bound packets that season. The Fontenelle reached Carroll June 21, a day before the Josephine got back to Fort Benton with the rest of its first trip freight.

Another Carroll boat, the Katie P. Kountz, got there July 9th—it had been the whole season on the trip, later was reported as badly disabled. Arrivals of the Fontenelle July 17 and August 23, of the Peninah August 4 and the May Lowry September 6th, closed out the Carroll season. A list by an observer boat by boat comes to about 1700 tons, but more likely it was around 2500 in all, and 400-500 tons down.

Finally, in its August 31st issue, the Helena Herald grew critical of the Kountz Line efforts, quoting a St. Paul Press article as overflowing with praise of Kountz and Braithwaite, "which may be all well enough so far as the captain is concerned, but as for the boats, probably the less said about the excellence of most of them the better." The Herald said the town of Carroll was about 20 log cabins, permanent population about 150, with two good stores, three restaurants, one hotel and two blacksmith shops, not so many saloons "but one can generally find sufficient." Diamond R "is quite a mammoth affair, several hundred wagons, innumerable mules and oxen." Later in a resume of a disappointing season for Carroll and the Carroll Trail, the Herald had even harder words: "The Kountz Line failed miserably to do its part, that is, provide efficient transportation. The Coulson operators shipped ore by mackinaws, sent wagon trains down to Fort Peck where the Kountz boats stopped, settled claims without waiting for Kountz settlement, and incurred a heavy loss on the year." (The criticism undoubtedly read with appreciation by Bentonites.)

The Josephine was proving her mettle in late season. The boat had to make two trips from Round Butte to bring another 300 tons to Benton in late July. Then it served as relay to Cow Island three times in the latter part of August for about the same tonnage from the Fort Peck freight drop. This had been brought by the freight carrier Western, which took down the largest cargo of the year, about 230 tons, including 2300 bales of robes the Josephine had brought from Cow Island.

A Benton reader reproved the Herald for its Carroll reporting, the paper gamely printing July 21, "Benton still maintains her supremacy as 'the head of navigation' on the Missouri in the arrival of the Josephine, one of the finest boats that ever ascended the Big Muddy, for it was generally predicted that she would not be able to reach a point above Cow Island, on account of the low water."

By August 7 the Herald, in a lengthy editorial, included, "we have taken some pains to gather data bearing upon the transportation of Montana freights...at least four-fifths of all imports and exports into and from Montana should be by the river route." The paper continued to plug the Carroll Route but evidently had heard from disappointed users of the Carroll route and gleeful merchants who had stuck with the Benton steamboats. "We are aware that our merchants have been disappointed in their expectation of the advantages to be derived, owing to the tardy delivery of goods...by the new route again." The Herald also cited bad management by Kountz boats and Carroll-to-Helena difficulties "such as will never arise again. Continuous rains in April, May and June, never known in Montana before." (August 25 a brief note proved the Herald had believed its own items on the Carroll route, the paper was forced to use wood pulp paper for printing, its order had been six months on the way.)

In its October 9 issue the Herald carried an item in regard to a recent contract between the I. G. Baker & Co. and the NWMP, and "Mr. I. G. Baker...has been several days in the city purchasing groceries, hardware, clothing and other goods to fill out a complement of 40,000 pounds of supplies for the Queen's Mounted Police, ordered for duty across the border...Messrs. Baker & Co. have the supply and freighting contracts this year." The Baker firm would hold the contract until after arrival of the Canadian Pacific in Calgary in 1883.

Another facet of a coming Benton revival was reported November 14: "We can state authoritively that Messrs. T. C. Power & Co., I. G. Baker & Co., and other capitalists have ordered a light draft steamboat, first class in all its appointments, for the Upper Missouri River, and that the boat is to be ready for the spring trade of 1875." The Missouri river captains, and the Fort Benton merchants were on their way, in the next decade would rival the influx of freight from nearing railheads.

1874 Summary:

| Date | Boats | Freight up | down | Pass. up | down |
|---|---|---|---|---|---|
| May 21 | Fontenelle | 160 | 170 | 20 | 20 |
| May 29 | Western | 410 | 150 | 20 | 20 |
| May 31 | Nellie Peck | 350 | 150 | 40 | 50 |
| June 1 | Josephine | 250 | - | 50 | 40 |
| June 5 | Key West | 250 | - | - | - |
| June 22 | Josephine | - | - | - | - |
|  |  |  |  |  | (rest cargo) |
| July 20-21 | Josephine | 300 | 100 | 50 | 50 |
|  |  |  |  |  | (fr. below) |
| Aug. 7-8 | Western | - | 230 | - | * |
| *estimated |  | 1720 | 800 | *300 | *300 |

(Western transferred 240 tons to Josephine at Cow Island, left 140 tons at Fort Buford.)

Josephine brought at least 300 tons in three trips to Cow Island.
100 members Boundary Survey left Fort Benton by mackinaw Sept. 15.
Two companies 6th Infantry down by boat from Fort Peck.

CARROLL cargoes:

| | Boats | Freight up, | down | Pass. up, | down |
|---|---|---|---|---|---|
| May 8 & 17 | Peninah | 300 | | | |
| June 6 | May Lowry | 200 | | | |
| June 11 | Peninah | 150 | | | |
| June 17 | Peninah | 150 | | | |
| June 21 | Fontenelle | 150 | | | |
| July 9 | Katie P. Kountz | 200 | | | |
| July 17 | Fontenelle | 150 | | | |
| Aug. 5 | Peninah | 100 | | | |
| Aug. 23 | Fontenelle | 112 | 125 | | |
| Sept. 6 | May Lowry | 200 | 150 | | |
| | | 1712 | 400 | | |

Estimates for Carroll may be short, with a possible total of 2500 tons but wagons from Fort Benton probably moved part of tonnage. Several hundred tons of ore at Carroll Sept. 14 may have gone down by mackinaw.

| Overall estimate.... | 4100 | 1250 | 400 | 500 |
|---|---|---|---|---|

## 1875—Touchstone For Benton Boom

With the arrival of the North West Mounted Police and subsequent exodus of most of the whiskey traders, established business firms of Fort Benton rightly foresaw improved and legitimate trade north of the border. For the small traders, out for quick money, the lesser risks were on the U. S. side and many were the ruses adopted to improve the odds—Canadians had a couple of hundred Mounties, the Americans only a couple of deputy marshals.

January of 1875 was extremely cold, with heavy snow the prophet of a good navigation season. Several Blackfeet in the vicinity of the Teton agency were frozen to death while hunting, a necessary risk when game was scarce near the camps, and whites suffered also. There were three new steamboats being completed for the Upper Missouri, one of course the Benton. Another was for the Kountz Line, the third at the time unknown except that the machinery of the Miner, one of the better boats of the late gold rush and bad years following, would go into it.

Early in February the Helena Herald noted the advent of the Benton Record of W. H. Buck, who previously had published a temperance paper, the Good Templar, at Fort Shaw. While first issues were printed on the army equipment at Fort Shaw, the Record, promised the editor, would soon be printed at Fort Benton.

Mr. Buck could be rated a better than average prophet, in his first issue February 1 he wrote: "Benton is rapidly emerging from the darkness...it commands the traffic of the country, holds the key to the business homes of the Territory...in short, Benton is the transportation center of Montana."

The second issue of February 15 (the Record was twice a month until June when it became a weekly) referred to the "Utopian enterprise called the Carroll Route." Coming months would prove Buck correct in that as well. He also had a fine command of innuendo, evidenced by another comment May 1st after the hard winter, "A correspondent states that the cattle losses in the Sun River Valley were almost exclusively confined to worn out stock belonging to the Diamond R." This giant concern was, of course, the major promoter of the route from Helena through the Judith Basin to the ambitious if embryonic settlement of Carroll, slightly above the mouth of the Musselshell. And Diamond R trains had in 1874 found Montana gumbo tough.

Fort Benton had a previously little needed facility for traffic to the Judith Basin when Ed Smith launched his new ferry in April 1875. High water later hampered the operation—on June 1st the Missouri overflowed its banks slightly, just about to the gates of the old fort.

June 1st the Benton Record printed the first of hundreds of similar items in later Fort Benton papers, on a topic dear to the hearts of residents: "At 15 minutes past five the morning of the 27th, the small piece of ordnance in front of the I. G. Baker store announced the first boat of the season, also one of the large brass Napoleons. Nellie Peck. About 1 the Benton arrived, 310 tons and 45 passengers."

Quite aptly, that issue of the Record carried an account by Cavalier (Lt. James J. Bradley, Fort Benton's first historian), of the history of steamboat navigation on the Upper Missouri.

Arrival of the Benton was of special interest to Bentonites and Montanans, the first steamboat owned by Montana people, the two largest firms of Fort Benton, T. C. Power & Brother and I. G. Baker & Company. The arrival marked the appearance at the head of navigation of the Fort Benton Transportation Co., better known as the Power Line when Baker began running its own steamboats, and, for the emblem between the stacks of the boats, the "Block P." The Benton itself would make more trips to the town for which it was named, and carry more tons than any other steamboat. The line it represented would survive until the 1930s as the Benton Packet Co., although during this century in the Bismarck area.

Two days behind came another boat, oddly the Carroll for the would-be nemesis down river, and with 296 tons of freight. At Carroll, first arrivals had been considerably earlier, the Josephine on May 10 and Key West on May 15, the Helena Herald making much of these early arrivals. Unfortunately for the Carroll Route, the next four boats whistled by the hamlet of Carroll, bound for Fort Benton on a rising river with the problem not sandbars and shoals but strength of the current. That meant much wood needed for the boilers—and with hostile Sioux teeming along the river, the life of the woodhawk was again a dangerous one.

It wasn't until June 9 that yet another new boat, the C. W. Mead, blew for its landing and welcoming salute. The Mead brought another good cargo, 236 tons. This was the new Kountz boat, and the captain planned a quick turnaround, foiled by a complaint of two deckhands, probably for unpaid salary, owner Wm. Kountz was always in hot water for one cause or another. The attachment was filed June 13th, lifted a day later.

The Key West June 5 made its second trip to Carroll, arriving there a day behind the Mead, to break the string of four Benton boats, but the Carroll project was in trouble, due chiefly to muddy roads across the Judith Basin. The Fontenelle, Far West and Josephine arrived at Benton the 22nd, 24th and 26th, then after an interlude the Benton on another trip, from Bismarck, first had been from Pittsburgh, about July 4, paper files are inexact. In between its first trip to Carroll and visit here, the Josephine had made an historic trip up the Yellowstone under Captain Grant Marsh, past the Big Horn, Pompey's Pillar, and the Narrows where the struggling Josephine inched ahead—full speed but with progress amounting to about a mile in six hours. That was through "Hell Roaring Rapids," and the Josephine ended her voyage there near present Billings—the head of navigation on the Yellowstone.

Thanks to the Key West and Josephine, Carroll had almost as many cargoes in 1875 as did Fort Benton, four by Key West, five by Josephine. There were ten cargoes to Benton, not counting a double trip by the Benton from Wolf Point.

The Benton made its second arrival of July 4th ahead of that double trip, then the Katie P. Kountz the 10th, leaving some of its 300 ton cargo below; the Carroll sneaked in again July 18 with a bare 65 tons and took down a load of perhaps 100 tons in cleaning up late arriving wool, furs, robes and silver ore. Deliveries at Benton by boat were somewhat short of the 2827 tons total reported and estimated, but with some freighted from Cow Island, while down cargoes were perhaps 2000 tons, one of the better balanced years. About 1315 tons were dropped at Carroll, perhaps 600 tons went down from there.

Fort Benton based freighters had around 465 tons of freight to move from Cow Island on a July 8 arrival by the C. W. Mead, another by the same boat August 18, and a couple hundred tons offloaded from the Benton August 27th.

Down freight this year of 1875 was especially heavy due to vast numbers of buffalo robes, 60,000 to 75,000 from Benton, estimates vary, and they could have been even higher, plus other furs and hides, wool and substantial tonnages of silver high grade ore. Not all went down from Benton. The Katie P. Kountz may have taken the heaviest cargo ever out of Montana, reportedly 28,330 buffalo robes, a hundred tons of ore and a miscellany leading to an estimate of 440 tons, much here, more at Carroll and probably additional from Milk River.

In 1875 the Power firm shipped more than 23,000 robes, 5,000 calf robes, tons of deer, antelope and elk hides, a total of around 382 tons, and with their trading posts at least equal, the Baker company probably had as much. John Goewey of Sioux City shipped 12,500 robes (value that year about $4 each), many other furs, including more than three tons of beaver, in all about 194 tons. These were the major part of an immense trade in robes and furs that year; W. S. Wetzel and J. D. Weatherwax, minor in comparison, added 1,300 robes and valuable furs despite having several hundred robes confiscated in Canada on a charge of whisky trading that brought a six months sentence and $500 fine for Weatherwax.

1875 Summary:

| Date | Boats | Tons up | Tons down | Pass. up | Pass. down |
|---|---|---|---|---|---|
| May 27 | Nellie Peck | 360 | 330 | 30 | 30 |
| May 27 | Benton | 330 | 410 | 45 | 50 |
| May 28 | Carroll | 296 | - | 12 | 5 |
| June 9 | C. W. Mead | 236 | - | 20 | 10 |
| June 22 | Fontenelle | 300 | 200 | 10 | 10 |
| June 24 | Far West | 320 | 200 | 50 | 30 |
| June 26 | Josephine | 225 | 100 | 30 | 10 |
| July 4 | Benton | 245 | - | 12 | - |
| July 10 | Katie P. Kountz | 300 | 440 | 10 | - |
| July 14 | Benton | 150 | 160 | - | 20 |
| July 18 | Carroll | 65 | 100 | 10 | 5 |
| | | 2827 | 1940 | 235 | 180 |

At Cow Island:

| Date | Boats | Tons up | Tons down | Pass. up | Pass. down |
|---|---|---|---|---|---|
| July 8 | C. W. Mead | 105 | 25 | - | - |
| Aug. 27 | Benton | 210 | 100 | 20 | 10 |
| Aug. 18 | C. W. Mead | 160 | 25 | | |
| Total both | | 3302 | 2090 | 249 | 190 |

Carroll cargoes:

| Date | Boats | Tons |
|---|---|---|
| May 10 | Josephine | 200 |
| May 15 | Key West | 200 |
| June 5 | Key West | 150 |

*Continued on next page*

|  | Boats | Tons up, down | | Pass. up, down | |
|---|---|---|---|---|---|
| July 1 | Key West | 185 | | | |
| July 12 | Josephine | 140 | | | |
| July 27 | Key West | 100 | | | |
| Aug. 25 | Josephine | 100 | | | |
| Sept. 4 | Josephine | 100 | | | |
| Sept. 17 | Josephine | 140 | | | |
| 1315 tons up listed, estimated 600 down | | | | | |
| Overall | 4600 | 2690 | 300 | 250 | |

### 1876: Year Of Sioux And Custer

The Sioux problem occupied most of the territory in 1876, at Fort Benton, in a continuing boom, it was often incidental. Fort Benton residents could look back at a substantial building boom, although materials, as for another eight years, were scanty. Chief items were the new Flanagan & Turner Drug and the Overland Hotel extension. In February the legislature added to Chouteau county's size, expanded to the crest of the Rockies from part of Deer Lodge county, and eastward to include Carroll, on the Missouri above the Musselshell.

The latter settlement would offer no navigation opposition during the season, the army-Sioux hostilities were swirling westward with the greening of range grass. And Helena merchants were joining with Fort Benton firms to support a subsidy proposal for a rail line between the cities—logical by 1876 reasoning, but a proposition that never materialized in that form—to move Helena freight.

Fort Benton trade north to Fort Macleod got under way early, hampered by snows in March, rate was 6c a pound—about $900 freight on each three wagon hitch. By April T. C. Power and I. G. Baker had a special contract in support of the coming military campaign against the Sioux—to supply the Montana column from Forts Shaw and Ellis under General Gibbon—a third arm of what could have been a classic military movement. George Houk and Wheeler Dexter of Fort Benton were with the advance of the supply support down on the Yellowstone, along with scouts sent to look for hostiles.

Local interest in such sideshows abated with arrival of the Carroll May 14, followed by the Key West and Benton next day. The three brought more than 900 tons of loads for the busy wagons and about 130 passengers, but most of these were soldiers, probably recruits to reinforce garrisons. The Carroll left empty, most likely to pick up some of the 1875 leftover silver ore at its namesake settlement. The Key West had a whopping down load of nearly 260 tons, most of it doubtless robes and furs. Robe trade had been tremendous in Canada, memoirs mention stacks as high as a two story building here and there around Benton, such must have been the case this spring of 1876. The Benton left with 150 tons from Baker and Power, this would have been the most valuable portion of the winter Indian trade, probably not all of it. It wasn't until May 26 that the E. H. Durfee arrived on a rising river, fighting high water instead of low, and June 1st the Missouri overflowed its banks here slightly, heavy rains damaging adobe buildings as well.

June 5 the Western came in with a heavy load, on the 9th the Nellie Peck and Benton, the latter boat showing its heels in the best round trip time from Bismarck. Roads were impassable for days at a time but the freight was moving sporadically. June 17th nearly half a million pounds went out via Power, Baker and Diamond R wagons, five days after the second arrival of the Carroll, which was only four days slower than the Benton. Late in the month the Key West,

Yellowstone and C. W. Mead completed the June arrivals.

There was one notable absence from the parade of the packets to Fort Benton to supply Montana Territory. Grant Marsh and his Far West were off to the Indian wars on another river.

If ever an Indian campaign deserved to succeed, it was General Alfred Terry's masterpiece of 1876. General George Crook and 1000 soldiers, supply wagons, pack mules and scouts, white and 250 Indian, was to come up from Fort Fetterman (named for the officer who rode rashly into 1866 ambush near Fort Phil Kearny with death for 81). Colonel John Gibbon was to bring all available troops, about 450, eastward from Fort Shaw and Fort Ellis. The Dakota column of about 1000 under Terry, chiefly the approximately 700 man 7th Cavalry under General George A. Custer, moved west from Fort Abraham Lincoln near Bismarck. Somewhere in the valley of the Yellowstone the columns would converge on the hostile Sioux, Cheyenne and a few strays from other tribes.

Then everything came unstuck. The Indian hero was Crazy Horse, who must have instinctively known what to do about converging columns. June 17 on the upper Rosebud the Sioux and Cheyenne hit Crook with everything they could muster, killing more than 25 and wounding double that number of soldiers. Crook held the battlefield but that was all, he retired, badly mauled and out of the campaign.

Terry, by then on the Yellowstone, had no word of this, but revamped his strategy with a plan to unite his infantry with Gibbon's force, send Custer on a swing to the Rosebud and Little Big Horn and snare the hostiles between two powerful forces. Custer completed the fiasco, dividing his 700, told Reno he would support him and rode into oblivion with 260 men on June 25. Gall and Crazy Horse led their warriors to victory, nearly overwhelmed Reno before and after erasing Custer, but only postponed an inevitable defeat.

It was Fort Benton's historian, Lt. James Bradley, with a small scouting party from Gibbon's command, who found the scene of Custer's disaster.

Unfortunately, the issue of the Benton Record which would have contained the earliest report is missing. But judging from the tone of the July 14 issue of the Record, reaction in a town full of Indian fighters was that Custer had sprung an Indian-proof trap and Terry might well be driving the Sioux westward where civilians would have to cope with military blunders.

The Record pretty sourly commented on confirmation of the disaster by reference to Custer's forced marches and an attack "which resulted in his own death and the slaughter of nearly half his regiment... If Custer had not died on the field he undoubtedly would have been tried and punished for his unpardonable breach of military discipline." Later editor Buck was to tone that down in view of nationwide adulation of a fallen soldier.

Next week the Record gave a Bismarck report: "The Far West arrived from the Yellowstone about midnight July 5th with news of Custer's defeat, 43 wounded men and several officers."

The Far West, accompanying Terry's expedition, had not only made its way up the Yellowstone, but had pushed up the Big Horn, high with the spring rise, to the mouth of the Little Big Horn with supplies for the soldiers. It was there that the Crow scout Curley brought first news of the disaster, to the men on the boat. The wounded from Reno's command were taken aboard June 29, but military exigencies required that the Far West remain at the mouth of the Big Horn with supplies until July 3. Then the Far West with its cargo of wounded made a record run of 710 miles in 54 hours to Fort Abraham Lincoln at Bismarck.

The boat and Captain Marsh were in the history books and national spotlight.

The defeat triggered a westward movement of troops; the Far West didn't linger at Bismarck, returning with supplies and 60 horses to partially remount the survivors of the 7th Cavalry. The Josephine, on its way before July 5th, brought more supplies. The Carroll, which had made a July 5 arrival at Fort Benton, down river was impressed to bring up the 22nd infantry, the E. H. Durfee to carry part of the 5th.

At Fort Benton only the already loaded Benton and Key West arrived the rest of July, on the 17th and 18th, the Benton completing her trip with a short run to and from Cow Island the 2nd of August. Down trip of the Benton included 80 horses, 16 wagons and 200 tons of cargo, perhaps all the supplies that could be provided for coming military operations. By that time the good water stage was over as usual. The Western on August 3 and Peninah on the 15th completed the approximately 4000 tons of cargo delivered at Fort Benton that season.

From there on cargoes dropped at Cow Island bore out the water stage, 175 tons on the Key West and 125 on the Carroll August 31st. September 25 the Benton with 150, E. H. Durfee with 100 tons—down cargoes from Cow Island on the three boats outweighed those destined for Benton-bound wagons. October 8 the Josephine and Carroll at Cow Island made the total supplies via Benton 4791 tons on best estimates possible. Down cargoes were nearly half as great, somewhat unprecedented but in part indicating the disruptions of a military campaign. Included, an estimated 75,000 buffalo robes. Passengers numbered about 450 each way and not including soldiers ferried short distances or brought up to the Yellowstone.

The steamboat Yellowstone which arrived June 28 at Benton was a new boat, not the American Fur vessel of the 1860s. This boat was built by Bozeman interests to carry freight up the namesake river. It was diverted by military orders, stern and positive, no unauthorized civilians on a stream taken over by the army.

Troops continued pressing Sitting Bull and his warrior chiefs into a winter campaign, harrying the stricken remainder that was not killed or forced to surrender toward the Canadian line below the Cypress Hills.

Chiefly due to military demands, a mid-November freeze iced in 13 boats at Yankton, Dakota Territory, the roster reading almost like a list of Fort Benton packets: Josephine, Western, Far West, Nellie Peck, General Meade, Yellowstone, Key West, Benton, Carroll, E. H. Durfee, Dr. Burleigh, Silver Lake, Peninah.

Aside from a confused navigation season, of importance to Fort Benton citizens in the summer of 1876 from August on was that they could become legal owners of properties they had occupied under squatters' rights. The federal government had ordered a survey, and occupants or claimants paid $10 per lot plus the official probate fee of $4. Judge John W. Tattan turned the latter over to help build a brick school, the $10 went to the county.

During the fall freight season I. G. Baker & Co., which had the Canadian contract, and T. C. Power, with stores north of the line, were shipping large quantities across the border, Baker September shipments mentioned in the Record about 300 tons, probably four wagon trains.

|  | 1876 Summary: | | | | |
|---|---|---|---|---|---|
|  | Boats | Tons up, | down | Pass. up, | down |
| May 14 | Carroll | 239 | - | 111 | 15 |
| May 15 | Key West | 285 | 258 | 10 | 10 |
| May 15 | Benton | 325 | 150 | 6 | 10 |
| May 26 | E.H. Durfee | 228 | 100 | 10 | 10 |
| June 5 | Western | 278 | 100 | 10 | 10 |
| June 9 | Nellie Peck | 175 | 200 | 36 | 20 |
| June 9 | Benton | 275 | 200 | 25 | 10 |
| June 12 | Carroll | 239 | - | 26 | 10 |
| June 26 | Key West | 245 | 100 | 20 | 10 |
| June 28 | Yellowstone | 209 | - | 44 | 20 |
| June 28 | C.W. Mead | 231 | 200 | 151 | 25 |
| July 5 | Carroll | 239 | 200 | 20 | 75 |
| July 17 | Benton | 250 | 100 | 25 | 10 |
| July 18 | Key West | 192 | - | 11 | 10 |
| Aug. 2 | Benton | 100 | 225 | - | 32 |
| Aug. 3 | Western | 195 | - | 10 | 15 |
| Aug. 15 | Peninah | 175 | - | 10 | 15 |
|  |  | 3880 | 1833 | 400 | 410 |
| Cow Island: | | | | | |
| Aug. 31 | Key West | 175 | - | - | - |
| Aug. 31 | Carroll | 125 | 100 | - | - |
| Sept. 20 | Benton | 150 | 200 | - | - |
| Sept. 25 | E.H. Durfee | 100 | 150 | - | - |
| Oct. 8 | Josephine | 100 | 50 | - | - |
| Oct. 8 | Carroll | 100 | 50 | - | - |
|  | est. pass. | - | - | 25 | 50 |
| totals at Cow Island | | 750 | 550 | | |
| Overall totals | | 4630 | 2283 | 425 | 460 |

# *T*ough *T*own *C*omes of *A*ge
## Fort Benton Came Of Age In 1877

*F*ort Benton came of age in 1877, the year a bustling and tumultuous river port began taking on the trappings of civilization. (Although not so far removed from a boisterous past that the port did move to form, equip and send a contingent of experienced Indian fighters to protect steamboat cargoes at Cow Island when the Nez Perce passed.) Steamboating and freighting increased sharply in 1877, the town got its first buildings other than adobe, logs or wood, the Canadian freight boomed—every thing on the upswing, a measure of which was, finally, Helena's acceptance that Fort Benton was head of navigation on the Missouri and a vital link in the territory's supply line.

The building mentioned included another evidence of Helena's bow to the march of events, Kleinschidt & Bro. established a branch store and built a 35x140 feet concrete warehouse, largest in the territory, from which they would ship about 2,000 tons yearly for six years to their Helena stores. Snell & Co., brickmakers, moved from Sun River to become Fort Benton's first of several, and produced the material that built a brick school, another local first. L. H. Rosencrans became the first saddler, the I. G. Baker Co. remodeled to provide some banking services. That was a start of a seven year building spree in which shortage of materials, bricks, lumber, lime, hardware, was the only limiting factor.

The January 3 Benton Record set the freighting tempo—I. G. Baker's fast mule train had just pulled out for Fort Macleod with 30,000 pounds of oats to meet an urgent order from the Mounted Police. Three weeks later the paper boasted, "It is doubtful whether in any town of the territory there are now better order, a healthier morality, a greater immunity from unpleasant sights and sounds than now prevail here." The paper went on to point to the large and increasing number of families, a school well attended, and social life and amenities that probably amazed early residents. Town lots, after the federal sale in 1876, were in great demand. A going price seemed about $10 a front foot—a building of any sort was a multiplier. In February came a slightly surprising development, Chouteau county approved $80,000 in bonds, Lewis and Clark county $350,000 to assist in building a Benton to Helena narrow gauge railroad. It never materialized, but was indicative of the change in attitude of Helena merchantile firms. In a later editorial, the Helena Herald said, "We ought to have a railroad to connect us with the head of navigation on the Missouri. Then, if goods were landed in Benton on May 1, our merchants could have them on their shelves the following day."

The year brought a good navigation season, but there was a price, heavy rains delayed arrival of steamboat cargoes in Helena, chiefly in the area termed "the Lakes." (Benton Lake.) The Benton Road was still impassable late in May. One Helena wagon train had pulled out from Helena for Benton "30 days ago and has made only 30 miles in that time." A Murphy Neel train, loaded, was still 50 miles from Helena.

It was about that same time though, that the Benton Record triumphantly observed, "The merchants of Helena seem to have lost faith in the Union Pacific and 500 miles of wagon transportation." Also in the Carroll Trail from that virtually abandoned point on the Musselshell. One could scarcely fault Record editor W. H. Buck for the comment. The UP route was the old Corinne Trail from Utah, virtually abandoned by Helena shippers in favor of the route via the Judith Basin. The Utah & Northern railroad would soon eliminate Corinne and become the first to enter Montana in 1880.

The Benton Transportation Co. steamboat Benton, already "The Old Reliable," was first at the levee May 7 with a whopping 429 tons of freight, and 80 passengers, 11 days and an hour from Bismarck, beating the best previous time by 16 hours. That was some of the freight Helena merchants were waiting on. The Key West followed on May 13, C. K. Peck and Peninah the 20th. All brought more than 200 tons each; the Peninah became the first to navigate the Marias on her down trip, going up five miles to ship 325 bales (3250) of buffalo robes, over 5,000 in all aboard. Early boats also had a share in several hundred tons of silver ore on the levee waiting. The Yellowstone on May 21 was making its second "perforce" trip to Fort Benton. Built to carry Bozeman freight up the Yellowstone, it had been shunted to the Missouri in 1876 by the military after the Sioux—this year it was low water, oddly, in view of the Missouri navigation season.

Then came the Western, Kate Kinney and the Benton, the last with 250 tons, on the 31st its second May arrival. There were return trips for the Key West, Peninah, and Kate P. Kountz and Silver City on their first, over 21 June days. A June 22 arrival was something special, the Red Cloud. I. G. Baker & Co. and J. H. Conrad had bought this Tennessee River Packet Co. boat for $25,000 in April, so now in addition to the Benton, Kountz and Coulson lines, the Fort Benton trade was being served by a fourth, the Baker Line. The Red Cloud was almost the equivalent of two boats, bringing 320 tons and 22 passengers—46 down, anxious to ride the new speedster. Nevertheless, the freight carrier Benton on June 27 came in with 253 tons and a new record, 10 days 18 hours out of Bismarck.

The new General Custer of Wm. Kountz completed its maiden trip from Pittsburgh on July 1st, with 226 tons for Kleinschmidt. Next came the big Fannie Tatum, rated 900 tons on bigger waters, with 404 tons and a record or near record to July 9, the E. H. Durfee next day with 250 tons—Mountain boats were piling up the tonnage. But the water was falling—probably trying for the record 9 day 23 hour trip, the Red Cloud brought only 175 tons but the fastest time yet from Bismarck. Fontenelle, Josephine, Benton again, Red Cloud third, E. H. Durfee and finally August 25, fifth visit of the Benton. Rivermen had cause to brag out the winter months of 1877-78. Twenty-five boats, 5300 tons to Fort Benton.

The scene for some though had just shifted, and a faraway Indian war was storming eastward. First accounts of the flight of the Nez Perce had appeared in the Benton Record in July. The war came close to home in the August 17 account of General Gibbon's fight at the Big Hole in southwestern Montana. In that battle, Lt. James Bradley, stationed at Fort Benton and Fort Shaw for years, was the first killed. Friends of the area doubtless mourned with Mrs. Bradley when she arrived at Fort Benton to go down on the Benton for her Atlanta, Georgia, home. Lt. Bradley was the town's first historian. Henry Bostwick, one of the most experienced guides on the western plains, and a Fort Benton fixture from before the gold rush, was another killed at the Big Hole.

The fighting fugitives beat Howard at Camas Meadows, made their way through Yellowstone Park and licked Sturgis at Canyon Creek on the Yellowstone river approaches September 13 and headed north. By that time their evident goal was Canada, and that meant a crossing of the Missouri, fondly "ours" to Bentonites. Two steamboats had unloaded at Cow Island in August, more were coming, right where the battling Nez Perce could replenish their commissary.

There had been semi-organization at Fort Benton when Governor Potts called on the Montana militia in late July, but when the threat to steamboat freight became apparent, Bentonites acted swiftly to form what the Record termed the Fort Benton Volunteers. Probably no more experienced white warriors could have been assembled. Heading them was fire-eating John J. Donnelly, Fort Benton attorney with an impressive Civil War record, and participant as a leader of two Fenian raids across the border in the east after the war, advisor to Louis Riel in his 1869 Manitoba rising. Lieutenants were John H. Evans, a captain in an earlier Montana militia and leader of a momentous Indian fight at Cypress Hills in 1873, and John J. Healy, founder of Fort Whoop-Up and Chouteau county sheriff, as well as a veteran of the "Mormon War" of the 1850s. Most were Civil War veterans, several army scouts, or in the old whisky trade in Canada. About 30 rode out of Fort Benton, September 21st, and to head them Major Guido Ilges, who managed to muster one lone Company F enlisted man. James Wells, in charge of the T. C. Power trading post at Fort Clagett at the Judith, had appealed for help—it was the other logical crossing point.

The Fort Benton party reached Clagett the evening of the next day, where they were joined by six more volunteers and Lt. Harden and 15 soldiers with a howitzer traveling by mackinaw. The mounted group reached the south bank of the Missouri opposite Cow Island September 24 after a tough time with their supply wagon, crossed the Missouri by mackinaw, where they found "the destruction of property sad to behold."

They were at the scene of a sharp brush with the Nez Perce, where Chief Joseph's band had burned 50 tons of freight, more to the point 20 of that private. Sgt. Molchert, 11 soldiers and four civilians were in the rifle pits September 22 when Joseph and 20 warriors rode up. There was a truce of sorts for a time, the whites giving the Indians some supplies, but as Nez Perce kept arriving, firing broke out, and the men in the pits could only watch the burning of the freight after the Indians took needed supplies. The Nez Perce, battle weary, did not try to wipe out the whites, but kept them under fire, two of the civilians being wounded.

Early the morning of the 22nd, Michael Foley, in charge of the freight, had loaded out bull teams of O. G. Cooper, Frank Farmer and Fred Barker, about eight men with this small train. Going along up Cow Creek ahead of them, a flicker ahead of deadly border trouble, were four ladies in a wagon, accompanied by Dr. Brown, military surgeon, Capt. Frechette of the North West Mounted Police, and a five soldier escort. The wagon train was headed for bad trouble, but the ladies and their escort got through without seeing an Indian—although, in view of activities of the Nez Perce in their sad epic, the Indians may well have seen and identified the party.

The Ilges party of Benton volunteers, after getting this news September 25, rode up the tortuous Cow Creek canyon after the wagon train, with Lt. Harden and his men to follow. Ten miles out of the Missouri canyon, here came their scout, Murray Nicholson, in a tremendous hurry to report. The wagon train was in sight, but the scout had also eyed all the Indians anybody could want, about 200 Nez Perce. By noon the Benton volunteers were in a full scale action with the Nez Perce rear guard, with Ed Bradley, Fort Benton carpenter, hit by one of the Nez Perce sharpshooters and instantly killed. (Not uncommon out west, this was assumed, his real name Edwin B. Richardson.) The volunteers reported the Indians broke off the fight as reinforcements were coming, more likely it was out of mutual respect, there were some of the best riflemen on the frontier in that fight. John W. Tattan, an old cavalry sergeant, was one of those who could show a memento, a massive belt plate stopped a Nez Perce bullet, preserving him for a long and useful career as district judge.

Lt. Harden's party came up, reported Fred Barker of the burning wagon train had been killed, and the two white casualties were buried at the spot. The party went back and camped near the Missouri. The evening of September 26 the Benton came up and began unloading 60 tons of freight. The Silver City was just below with 100 tons of government freight for General Miles' windup campaign. Cooper and Farmer of the burned wagon train made it to camp at night, five others followed next morning, and the body of Charles Steele was found and buried the day after. The Benton volunteers made it home midday of the 29th, praised by Major Ilges for their operation.

Indicative the Nez Perce methods of war, a party of whites going down in a mackinaw was stopped by Nez Perce, took to the hills. After using the boat to cross the river, Chief Joseph hunted out the men and told them to take their boat and go on unharmed. But freighters were fair game, hauling supplies for the enemy—at least one more, James Downey, was killed in the Cow Island area.

Rather strangely, in those times when a good Indian was said to be a dead one, the Benton Record wrote about the Nez Perce, "fought as bravely as any men could have fought and conducted their warfare more like civilized people than savage Indians. During the siege they never harmed a wounded soldier, and on no occasion have they been known to take a scalp or otherwise mutilate a victim." John Healy, who had seen most everything, thought the Nez Perce "displayed remarkable skill and ingenuity in constructing their defenses. They fought so well and never scalped."

After that season of bustle, confusion and war, Fort Benton citizens could look around and see every sign of progress, buildings going up all over, wood—the Snell company wasn't turning out bricks as fast as promised, and it was late November before a ball opened the town's first brick building, the new school.

Toward year end Editor Buck of the Record had some suggestions for needed improvements: A fire marshal (John Evans later appointed); a new court house (a year or so away and which burned January 5, 1883); new church (soon to be); army post on or near Milk River to protect Montana from the Sioux in Canada (Fort Assiniboine built in 1879); a railroad to Helena (10 years away and it ended steamboating); more brick buildings (December the Record announced a three story brick, and many more would follow). The editor had some powerful suggestions! Or a good crystal ball!

### Steamboat Arrivals and Tonnages 1877

Down cargoes included 1,225 tons ore valued at $750 per ton (several 100 tons of ore waiting for shipment on Benton's first arrival), 104 tons wool, 50,512 buffalo robes, 68,530 pounds deer and other hides, 6,700 pounds beaver, 15,267 cow hides, 1,482 sheep skins, 112 head of cattle and miscellaneous peltries, amounting to about 2,000 tons. Cargoes to Fort Benton, 5760 tons, to Cow Island 390 tons, biggest year since 1869.

| Arrival | Steamboat | tons | down | pass. | down | notes |
|---|---|---|---|---|---|---|
| May 7 | Benton | 429 | 120 | 80 | 8 | |
| May 13 | Key West | 225 | 170 | 26 | 20 | |
| May 20 | C.K. Peck | 220 | - | 36 | 20 | |
| May 20 | Peninah | 218 | 140 | 8 | - | |
| May 21 | Yellowstone | 120 | - | 16 | 15 | maybe more freight |

| Arrival | Steamboat | tons | down | pass. | down | notes |
|---|---|---|---|---|---|---|
| May 27 | Western | 290 | 100 | 48 | - | |
| May 29 | Kate Kinney | 250 | 71 | 23 | 20 | |
| May 31 | Benton | 250 | 145 | 8 | 26 | |
| June 9 | Key West | 263 | 111 | 18 | - | |
| June 17 | Peninah | 220 | - | 23 | - | |
| June 20 | Katie P. Kountz | 250 | 82 | 10 | - | |
| June 21 | Silver City | 234 | - | 36 | - | down empty |
| June 22 | Red Cloud | 320 | 240 | 22 | 46 | maiden trip, Baker boat |
| June 25 | Josephine | 176 | 70 | 8 | 8 | |
| June 27 | Benton | 253 | 120 | 150 | - | 10 days 18 hour record |
| July 1 | General Custer | 226 | 45 | 13 | - | new boat |
| July 9 | Fannie Tatum | 404 | 10 | 50 | - | |
| July 10 | E.H. Durfee | 250 | | | | |
| July 11 | Red Cloud | 175 | 20 | 15 | - | 9 days 23 hrs record |
| July 17 | Fontenelle | 235 | - | 9 | 4 | |
| July 18 | Josephine | 100 | 129 | 16 | 10 | |
| July 20 | Benton | 240 | 10 | 14 | - | |
| July 28 | Red Cloud | 150 | 210 | 27 | 32 | |
| July 30 | E.H. Durfee | 150 | 140 | - | 2 | |
| Aug. 15 | Benton | 112 | 90 | 9 | 27 | 5th trip of season |
| | | 5760 | 2023 | 960 | 350 | |

Arrivals at Cow Island: General Meade Aug. 24, 37 tons; Peninah Aug. 27, 26 tons; Fontenelle Sept. 21, 69 tons; Benton Sept. 27, 52 tons; Silver City Sept. 29, 102 tons; Benton Oct. 3 and 5, govt. charter, estimated 200 tons; Big Horn Oct. 11, 104 tons. More than the 390 tons probably were carried in windup of Nez Perce campaign. About 73 tons in all lost to Indians or burned.

(Lt. Edward Maguire, in charge of river improvement, reported 25 steamboats to Benton, 5283 tons to Benton, 1500 passengers, down about 3200 tons and 500 passengers—the down tonnages 1225 gold ore and silver bullion, 200,000 pounds of wool and 50,000 buffalo robes. The New Northwest next January reported 9500 tons to the Yellowstone River, where the army was building posts following the Custer disaster. Thus 1877 was one year in which use of the Yellowstone surpassed that of the upper Missouri.)

### Great Boom Took Off In 1878, Lasted Five Seasons

Despite the Nez Perce campaign, 1877 had been an upbeat year for steamboat navigation, in 1878 the boom took off, to roll on uninterrupted for five seasons during which Fort Benton quadrupled in size, its large merchants prospered vastly and its businesses and amenities multiplied. There were four big firms, T. C. Power & Bro. about a hundred yards from the old fort and I. G. Baker & Co. operated by Wm. G. and Charles Conrad at the upper end of the block from Power. Three blocks further up was Murphy Neel & Co. All three firms were housed in rather disreputable buildings, a matter all would rectify as soon as possible. The fourth, Kleinschmidt & Bro., had the large concrete warehouse about another block above Murphy Neel, so close to river edge that steamboats could virtually run gangplanks inside. All four operated several wagon trains, one of which standing empty might represent a cost of around $25,000, an indication of the scope of their businesses. Each handled at least 2,000 tons of river freight annually. A smaller but not insignificant business entrant was W. S. Wetzel, who had his own wagon train, shipped in 530 tons in 1878.

The town had two druggists, doctors, tinsmith, two saddlers, stables, blacksmiths, bootmaker, ferry, the Benton Record and a plethora of saloons. There were the Block P and Baker steamboat lines, the Coulsons of Yankton thought enough of their business here to have George Clendenin as resident agent. Power was adding the Helena to the Block P Benton, Baker had the Red Cloud lengthened 50 feet for lighter draft and was adding an innovation, the tiny Col. McLeod to shuttle the freight from Cow Island to Fort Benton in late season. Murphy Neel relied on the Coulson line, Kleinschmidt on the Kountz boats.

Early in January 1878 residents were planning a Catholic church, which would become the town's first permanent place of worship. The general businesses were planning expansions, most had already added warehouse space, but who would have believed nearly everybody would be too busy to build! In any case, there was a shortage of artisans, as well as building material, although W. G. Conrad managed a showplace brick residence.

In February the Benton Record estimated Fort Benton's population as 500, logical enough in view of the 1870 census of 367 which had dropped off sharply in the early 70s. Population, transient of course, could swell to 1500 to 2000 during the peak of the freighting season. April 5 the paper rather proudly announced that the Benton Transportation Co. (Block P) had contracted for Montana delivery of goods at a lower rate than the great Diamond R freighting concern, backed by Northern Pacific freights rebates, could.

The first steamboat of the season, the Coulson Line Big Horn, blew for its landing April 27, to then the earliest arrival on record. It brought only 100 tons of freight, rolling toward Helena by May 1st. The boat had left 300 tons of way freight, brought 140 passengers, including 100 army recruits—Fort Benton had become an important passenger port of entry.

Coulson's Rosebud followed on May 4 and its Josephine the 9th. The two Benton lines weren't in such an all-fired hurry. May 14th, here came the spanking new Helena, built under the supervision of and captained by James McGarry, which had left Pittsburgh March 24, steamed down the Ohio to St. Louis, then begun the long 3000 mile climb to the "mountains." (Old estimate of rivermen, actually a bit over 2300 as army engineers later figured distance.) The Helena brought 245 tons and 56 passengers. The Benton, veteran of three seasons and a couple of Indian campaigns, puffed in May 15 with 245 tons and 116 passengers, had to drop back down to pick up cargo left at Dauphin's Rapids and made the round trip in what was termed a "remarkable" 42 hours.

The lengthened Red Cloud arrived for Baker with 250 tons and 120 passengers on May 17, famed Captain Bill Massie finding her buoyancy much improved. Several Coulson boats followed, Key West, Big Horn and Rosebud by May 26, the last with 240 passengers, 220 of them replacements in the 3rd Infantry. The veteran Nellie Peck brought 260 tons, few or no passengers, on June 2.

About this time the Record reported return of Wm. Rowe after having purchased horses (in Oregon) and coaches to stock the Benton Road, with John Power backing the Benton-Helena stage had become locally owned, a start toward the staging center Fort Benton would become.

There was a whiff of nostaglia June 4 in the arrival of the John M. Chambers, an independent steamboat, for Joseph LaBarge was master and John LaBarge pilot. The brothers had been on the Missouri since shortly after steamboating began. John had brought the Chippewa to Fort McKenzie in 1859 (and would die at the wheel of the Helena in 1885), Joseph had brought the first "opposition" boats here in 1862. June 9 the E. H. Durfee, another new boat clear from Pittsburgh, brought in 455 tons, largest cargo yet, 300 of that Helena bound for the Kleinschmidts. That was the 18th arrival—just a start. The same day the Red Cloud was in again, a favorite of travelers, 115. Through June cargoes had virtually all been well past 200 tons. July was as usual, a month of lower water, although on the 7th the Benton brought in 306 tons, most of the dozen boats that month.

The pace slowed in August, Eclipse and Helena early, Benton the 26th. The Baker Line unveiled a low water winner with the August 29 arrival of their new Col. McLeod, only 110 tons, but that was as planned for this small entry. The Helena sneaked in September 2nd, after which the Fort Benton levee belonged to the McLeod. The small shuttle arrived at Fort Benton September 3rd, 13th and 23rd, October 2nd, 10th and 19th, latest arrivals to then. Seven cargoes, all but the first under 100 tons, but doing the job the boat was built to do.

Much of the McLeod freight was that of other boats from Cow Island, 686 tons left by Red Cloud, Key West, Benton, Josephine, Big Horn, Rosebud. On the McLeod's final trip the boat left 56 tons of her own freight at Cow Island, but took down 80 passengers. Biggest passenger trip from there was the Big Horn's 150 troops from the outgoing 7th Infantry. There was still considerable freighting over the trail, but steamboats had brought more than 9400 tons to Fort Benton, more than 1400 passengers upbound and took down about 400, with about 100 more up and 560, mostly soldiers, down from Cow Island. In all, 51 steamboat arrivals at Fort Benton, including two or three double trips, 11 more below.

One of Fort Benton's principal exports in 1878 was buffalo robes, an estimated 75,000. Power shipped 25,000, Baker 20,000—wagon trains hauled around 30,000 robes from the Whoop-Up country and Cypress Hills in Canada. North of the border, that staple of wild Indians was nearing exhaustion, next year fewer than half that number of robes came in. Wool was a growing export, over 600,000 pounds.

At year end the Catholic Church had passed the planning stage and Fort Benton businessmen had bought a fire engine, badly needed—there were haystacks all over the bottom for the thousands of head of animals used in freighting. Also there was little knowledge of the dangers of sheet iron chimneys used by local residents, fire warden John Evans was issuing warnings right and left.

Late in 1878 Ed Smith and John Castner launched a big ferry, 75x20, which could handle two 6-mule freight teams at one time. There were a growing number of residents, mostly farmers and ranchers, south of the Missouri in Chouteau county, and also in central Montana where the livestock industry had been non-existent due to hostile Indians.

In its final 1878 issue the Benton Record announced that it had contracted for a three story, 45x50 brick building and would have a new plant, including the latest model news press, for the next year.

Steamer arrivals and tonnages 1878

| Arrival | Steamboat | tons | down | pass. | down | notes |
|---------|-----------|------|------|-------|------|-------|
| April 27 | Big Horn | 400 | 55 | 140 | 5 | earliest arrival |
| May 4 | Rosebud | 120 | 35 | 50 | 8 | |

| Arrival | Steamboat | tons | down | pass. | down | notes |
|---|---|---|---|---|---|---|
| May 5 | Josephine | 150 | 25 | 5 | 15 | |
| May 14 | Helena | 202 | 125 | 56 | 36 | maiden trip |
| May 15 | Benton | 205 | 60 | 115 | 10 | |
| May 17 | Red Cloud | 250 | 25 | 120 | 40 | rebuilt, 50' longer |
| May 18 | Key West | 245 | 5 | 14 | 5 | |
| May 20 | Benton | 80 | - | - | - | from Dauphin's r. |
| May 26 | Big Horn | 135 | - | 81 | 7 | |
| May 26 | Rosebud | 100 | - | 240 | 1 | 220 soldiers |
| June 2 | Nellie Peck | 260 | - | 8 | 10 | |
| June 4 | John M. Chambers | 250 | - | 30 | 1 | |
| June 6 | Josephine | 200 | 7 | 7 | 4 | |
| June 6 | Helena | 275 | 25 | 25 | 5 | 150 sheep to Carroll |
| June 6 | Far West | 170 | - | 16 | - | |
| June 6 | General Terry | 200 | - | 4 | 4 | |
| June 8 | Western | 175 | - | 10 | 2 | |
| June 9 | E. H. Durfee | 455 | - | 12 | 2 | |
| June 9 | Red Cloud | 281 | - | 115 | 5 | |
| June 15 | Benton | 301 | 100 | 40 | 12 | |
| June 16 | Rosebud | 195 | - | 21 | 3 | |
| June 21 | Big Horn | 202 | - | 8 | 7 | |
| June 23 | Fontenelle | 250 | 60 | 5 | - | |
| June 23 | Helena | 252 | 10 | 7 | 5 | |
| June 24 | Nellie Peck | 223 | - | 25 | 7 | |
| June 29 | Western | 218 | 60 | 17 | 3 | cattle down |
| June 29 | Josephine | 210 | 80 | 3 | - | cattle down |
| June 29 | Red Cloud | 250 | 20 | 5 | 5 | |
| July 2 | Key West | 200 | 40 | 25 | 6 | |
| July 2 | General Terry | 100 | - | - | - | |
| July 7 | Benton | 306 | 40 | 25 | 4 | |
| July 10 | Yellowstone | 190 | - | 1 | - | |
| July 10 | Big Horn | 106 | 60 | 4 | - | |
| July 11 | Helena | 237 | 43 | 4 | 2 | |
| July 11 | Nellie Peck | 167 | 45 | 4 | - | |
| July 15 | Fontenelle | 200 | - | 5 | 3 | |
| July 24 | Josephine | 190 | - | 20 | 8 | |
| July 25 | General Terry | 235 | 75 | - | - | |
| July 27 | Benton | 215 | 50 | 23 | 15 | |
| July 28 | Rosebud | 145 | 100 | 13 | 15 | |
| Aug. 1 | Eclipse | 200 | - | 12 | 2 | |
| Aug. 4 | Helena | 145 | 25 | 40 | 8 | |
| Aug. 26 | Benton | 140 | 25 | 27 | 5 | |
| Aug. 29 | Colonel McLeod | 110 | 50 | 40 | 6 | maiden trip |
| Sept. 2 | Helena | 93 | 15 | 1320 | | |
| Sept. 3 | Colonel McLeod | 65 | 50 | - | - | to Coal Banks |
| Sept. 13 | " | 65 | - | 20 | 23 | to Benton |
| Sept. 23 | " | 90 | - | 20 | 25 | |

| Arrival | Steamboat | tons | down | pass. | down | notes |
|---|---|---|---|---|---|---|
| Oct. 2 | Colonel McLeod | 70 | - | 7 | - | |
| Oct. 10 | " | 70 | - | 3 | | |
| Oct. 19 | " | 60 | - | - | - | latest arrival |
| | | 9653 | 1310 | 1475 | 364 | |
| To Cow Island: | | | | | | |
| Aug. 12 | Key West | 100 | | 55 | | |
| Aug. 22 | Red Cloud | 75 | | | 30 | |
| Aug. 27 | Josephine | 75 | | | 10 | |
| Sept. 3 | Benton | 40 | | | 20 | |
| Sept. 9 | Rosebud | 70 | | | 15 | |
| Sept. 17 | Josephine | 40 | | | 8 | |
| Sept. 27 | Red Cloud | 125 | 50 | 20 | 6 | |
| Oct. 10 | Big Horn | | | 40 | 150 | 7th Infantry |
| Oct. 19 | Colonel McLeod | 56 | 30 | | 80 | |
| Oct. 20 | Benton | 65 | | | 10 | |
| | To Cow Island | 686 | 80 | 75 | 329 | |
| | OVERALL TOTALS | 10339 | 1470 | 1625 | 693 | |

Yearend totals are given as 10180 tons up, 1833 down, as for passengers with no totals given, Rosebud is reported making trip to Cow Island empty to take down 7th Infantry soldiers who marched to that point—no numbers found.

Helena Herald article reported 9680 tons via Missouri River.

## Major Businesses Manage Buildings In 1879

Two of Fort Benton's major businesses managed to build new quarters in 1879, along with the Benton Record, but of greatest importance to steamboatmen was the building of Fort Assiniboine, resulting in much additional freighting business. The Fort Benton boom rolled along, more small businesses came into town, population increased and the freighting to Helena and other points in the territory continued great. Three new steamboats, the Block P Butte and the big Coulson Montana and Dacotah, made their first trips to the head of navigation. By year end, the tonnage in the Fort Benton trade had equalled that of the more favorable river year 1878.

Conclusion of the last major Indian war in Montana had lessened dangers on the freighting trail, but there were still hostiles, in April Lt. Loder and a patrol of 18 men killed eight Sioux in a savage small Indian fight east of Martinsdale. By that time plans were being executed for the building of a great fort in the Milk river area, the 18th Infantry was ordered to Bismarck in readiness for the first boat for Benton, with a note that the entire military and construction force for Fort Assiniboine would be in Montana before May 1st.

Also in April, Martin Maginnis, territorial delegate, proposed a Benton-Martinsdale mail route, also to Fort Logan, Highwood and Belt, into an area which would depend for some years on supplies from Fort Benton. A direct offshoot, apparently, was the cutting of a road through the bluff across the Missouri for a road to Martinsdale, in August, first use being arrival of six ox teams from Meagher county. The road would be heavily traveled into the later 80s by wool shipments.

First steamboat arrivals came a day apart from April 27, the Col. McLeod leading the way with 118 tons and 28 passengers, then the Benton with 165 and 35, the Eclipse with 75 and 28. (Files of the Record missing and so no report of troop or worker arrivals.) The Eclipse took down 40 head of cattle, setting a pattern that would continue for two years, after which cattle drives would be to Canadian Pacific or Northern Pacific railheads. (Cattle are figured at 1200 pounds in estimates of tonnages.)

Early arrivals were low in tonnage, probably brought up some government freight which was unloaded at Coal Banks. That station soon drew an army freight guard, had a postoffice Oct. 1879-81 named Ruger for the commanding officer at Fort Assiniboine, although after three postmasters in a week in 1880 it was temporarily discontinued. The freighting trail from Coal Banks to the new fort would be heavily traveled during construction extending into 1880. An early day freighter from Fort Benton, Charles Broadwater, had the construction contract. Several hundred workmen were imported from more easterly points; in October the steamboat F. Y. Batchelor took down 200 workers and the Big Horn as many.

May 5th Coulson's Key West and Josephine arrived at Fort Benton with about half usual tonnages, first important shipment to Benton the Helena on May 11 with 225 tons for Power, the Red Cloud the same day with 278 for Baker, also 150 passengers. A week later the Far West arrived with 250 tons, took down 70 cattle, as did most other Coulson boats this season. The Benton brought 274 tons the 22nd as the river stage improved, Baker's Col. McLeod made its second appearance on the 23rd with 171 tons, and a surprising 67 passengers. Two days later the C. K. Peck came in with 300 tons. It wasn't until May 28 that the Coulson line brought in the first of its great upper Missouri freight carriers. The Montana split its 550 ton cargo, biggest yet in the Fort Benton area, 260 at Coal Banks, 290 to Benton, and took down 200 head of cattle.

The boats were triplets, the Dacotah on the river in 1879, the Wyoming not completed until 1880 and with only one trip to Benton. These boats were 252 feet long, built on the same light draught spoonbill pattern as other upper Missouri boats but about 40 feet longer than average. They drew very little water, that 550 tons would have required slightly over three feet. The Dacotah in later years brought a cargo of 16,000 sacks of wheat, 900 hogs, 5,200 railroad ties and 450 tons of other freight into St. Louis from Kansas City with five feet of water on the crossings and never touched bottom, according to steamboat historian Dr. E. B. Trail. Had the triplets been in use in gold rush days each could have made $100,000 on a single trip to Fort Benton, Trail calculated. Their drawbacks became apparent in later use. They drew so little water that they slued on the crossings and went aground, and a stiff wind blew them onto bars. But in 1879-80 they were a success.

Eclipse finished May and Helena ushered in June the 2nd. Another new boat came the 9th, Power Line's freight carrier Butte, meant to bring top tonnages for its size, for example, 230 tons on three feet of water, 100 on two—this trip 300 tons. The Red Cloud, May 15 and a favorite of passengers, had 193, including 100 Mounted Police, along with 349 tons of freight that included 75 horses; going down, 167 cattle. June water was quite evidently high, Far West had 250 tons the 11th, Fontenelle 295 the 13th, then Col. McLeod which normally loaded 100 tons on the 16th with 192. Key West followed next day with another 250.

What might have been the record combined load arrived June 20, Dacotah with 550 tons and 273 passengers—of this 441 tons freight and 68 passengers at Benton, the remainder at Coal Banks, the 205 Assiniboine workers a bit behind that May 1 report in April. There followed the Peninah the 21st and Montana the 23rd, the latter left most of 600 tons at Coal Banks, brought the rest and 132 sheep (these were usually purebred rams to upgrade the flocks) to Benton. The Montana took down 175 cattle. One steamboat Fort Benton never saw, the General Sherman, came up river with telegraph poles for a Fort Assiniboine-Benton connection, completed by August 8 but no operator or instruments!

Well into July, after the slow start, the steamboats continued to deliver heavy cargoes. The Dacotah on her second trip July 13th brought over 600 tons, so the two Coulson boats had divided honors, about 1150 tons apiece. The Baker boats Red Cloud and McLeod, ended with well past 2,000 tons; Power boats, Benton, Helena and Butte more than 2500, and the other Coulson boats made the line's deliveries past 4800 tons, much of that for Assiniboine. About 1,000 cattle were taken to market via Bismarck, Montana's livestock industry was emerging from its infancy. There was probably unreported tonnage landed at Coal Banks in addition to the rather shadowy report on the necessary telegraph poles on the Sherman. At Fort Benton the boating season ended with the October 3 arrival of the F. Y. Batchelor, which also took down 200 of those Assiniboine workmen. There was the usual fall use of Cow Island as a freight drop, about 750 tons by nine steamboats. In October George Clendennin, Coulson agent, reported the road from Cow Island to Assiniboine and Benton "covered" by wagon trains. A week later the Record said 500 tons of freight were still at Cow Island.

Government engineers, finally, were improving the channel at Dauphin's Rapids and other bad spots, building four wing dams to narrow channels and increase water depth, and removing rocks, blasting boulders that had made some reaches impassable in years of low water; appreciated, the channel was 10" lower than in 1878. At Dauphin's about 5,000 rocks were removed and the wing dam deepened the channel by a foot.

During 1879 freighters and stagemen had their usual troubles. In October the 28 Mile Springs stage station was invaded by nine drunken Piegans, who made off with as many horses, returned next day by fellow tribesmen. Ed Lewis told the Record a Power wagon train was surrounded by Blackfeet near Fort Macleod, but their head chief, Crowfoot, turned up in time to prevent casualties. Metis near Lewistown petitioned the military for help against hostile Sioux, and numerous notes on cattle being killed and horses stolen appear in the Record files.

Chouteau county ranges had an influx of cattle during the year: Jessie Taylor was enroute to Teton range with 2500 cattle, Ryan & Dunphy with 1100, Howell & Jack Harris were about to purchase 1000 head, Dan Flowerree and Matt Carroll were buying large numbers in Oregon, and John Drew bought a large and well selected herd. Farming, in the immediate area begun in the early 1870s by Joe Cobell on Shonkin, was developing. Wheeler Dexter, an old timer and mechanical genius, into well drilling and sawmills, had branched out, threshing about 25,000 bushels of grain on Highwood. Agriculturists were "grangers" to the Record, whether animals or farming.

A fiasco "discovery" in the Bear Paws had all but emptied Fort Benton in 1878, in 1879 there was a more promising discovery in the Judith Basin in August, the Fort Benton ferry was kept busy hauling fiddle-footed stampeders, and Billy Rowe was thinking about a stage line to the new diggings.

Despite the handicaps of a busy year, and discouraging shortages of lumber, brick, lime and workmen, progress was made in getting Fort Benton out of frontier log and adobe buildings. The Benton Record got its three story brick up and occupied by year end—the most impressive in town, and territory, bragged owner W. H. Buck. T. C. Power & Bro. had what was to be the first half of a two story brick up, and I. G. Baker & Co. also had a slightly larger brick in use—both had been in the log and adobe buildings in which they opened business in in 1867 and 1865. The lumber situation can be judged by Paris Gibson's venture, a lumber yard opened in June was sold out of stock six weeks later. Some might have gone into the new Catholic Church, Fort Benton's first religious structure. A planning and finance committee was promptly named for what became St. Paul's Episcopal Church. A frame court house was completed on Main Street in early fall—it burned in 1883.

The Fort Benton business community had numbers of newcomers, most important George Crane's Variety Store and Hirshberg & Nathan's clothing.

Doubtless attracting local interest, Fort Benton's first legal hanging. Although the body of Patrick Farrell was not found until June, Joseph Koble and O. H. Marsh were convicted of the murder of their fellow soldier on April 21, on testimony of two accomplices, and sentenced to hang. The other two drew life sentences, one died in prison and one later pardoned. Koble and Marsh were hanged at Fort Benton jail yard October 6.

Steamer arrivals and tonnages for 1879:

| Arrival | Steamboat | tons | down | pass. | down | notes |
|---|---|---|---|---|---|---|
| April 27 | Col. McLeod | 116 | 30 | 28 | 15 | |
| April 28 | Benton | 169 | 40 | 35 | 6 | |
| April 29 | Eclipse | 75 | 28 | 28 | - | 40 cattle |
| May 5 | Key West | 125 | 42 | - | - | 60 cattle |
| May 5 | Rosebud | 150 | - | - | - | |
| May 11 | Helena | 69 | 20 | 102 | - | |
| May 15 | Red Cloud | 349 | 40 | 193 | 33 | |
| May 19 | Far West | 250 | 50 | - | - | 70 cattle |
| May 22 | Benton | 274 | 8 | 36 | 4 | |
| May 23 | Col. McLeod | 174 | - | 67 | 8 | |
| May 25 | C. K. Peck | 200 | - | 44 | - | |
| May 28 | Montana, 1st trip | 550 | 120 | 50 | - | 200 cattle |
| May 31 | Eclipse | 200 | 30 | 40 | - | 40 cattle |
| June 2 | Helena | 226 | 5 | 36 | 8 | |
| June 9 | Butte, maiden trip | 302 | 38 | 44 | 3 | |
| June 9 | Red Cloud | 379 | 120 | 160 | 21 | 167 cattle |
| June 11 | Far West | 250 | 88 | 15 | - | 60 cattle |
| June 13 | Fontenelle | 295 | - | 28 | - | |
| June 16 | Col. McLeod | 192 | 60 | 19 | 4 | |
| June 17 | Key West | 250 | 48 | - | - | 60 cattle |
| June 20 | Dacotah | 550 | 120 | 273 | - | record tonnage |
| June 21 | Peninah | 165 | - | 4 | - | |
| June 23 | Montana | 600 | 100 | 16 | - | 175 cattle |
| June — | General Sherman | 200 | - | - | - | telegraph poles |
| June 28 | Benton | 266 | 14 | 14 | 13 | |
| July 1 | Far West | 275 | 55 | - | - | 60 cattle |
| July 4 | Red Cloud | 358 | 20 | 25 | 19 | |
| July 6 | Josephine | 175 | 50 | - | - | |
| July 11 | Helena | 246 | 112 | 5 | 33 | |

| Arrival | Steamboat | tons | down | pass. | down | notes |
|---|---|---|---|---|---|---|
| July 13 | Dacotah | 600 | - | - | - | |
| July 15 | Col. McLeod | 142 | 30 | 16 | 6 | |
| July 16 | Eclipse | 175 | 30 | - | - | 40 cattle |
| July 22 | Far West | 225 | - | - | - | |
| July 24 | Red Cloud | 240 | 20 | 47 | 7 | |
| July 26 | Butte | 217 | 169 | 13 | 7 | |
| July 30 | Josephine | 150 | 30 | - | - | 40 cattle |
| Aug. 12 | Col. McLeod | 100 | 50 | 35 | 26 | |
| Aug. 14 | Big Horn | 150 | 75 | 34 | 25 | |
| Aug. 31 | Helena—Marias | 152 | 160 | 49 | 53 | |
| Sept. 8 | Rosebud—Coal Banks | 60 | - | 20 | - | |
| Sept. 20 | Col. McLeod | 110 | 40 | 15 | 14 | |
| Oct. 3 | F. Y. Batchelor | 81 | - | - | 200 | Assin. workers |
| Fort Benton, Coal Banks total | | 9932 | 1731 | 1561 | 505 | |
| Cow Island arrivals | | | | | | |
| Sept. 25 | Benton | 40 | 43 | 18 | 5 | |
| Oct. 2 | Butte | 93 | 29 | 9 | - | |
| Oct. 12 | Big Horn | 145 | - | - | 200 | lumber, workers |
| Oct. 13 | Rosebud | 70 | - | - | - | for Fort Walsh |
| Oct. 15 | Butte | 41 | 50 | - | - | |
| Oct. 19 | Gen. C. H. Thompkins | 191 | 10 | 5 | - | |
| Oct. 22 | Benton | 53 | 7 | 29 | 3 | |
| Oct. 31 | Col. McLeod | 70 | 20 | 11 | 53 | |
| Nov. 1 | Butte | 76 | 13 | - | 3 | |
| Cow Island totals | | 779 | 172 | 72 | 264 | |
| Overall totals | | 10711 | 1903 | 1633 | 769 | |

Notes: The Col. McLeod was sunk at Bismarck when the Butte slipped off stays and sank her in eight feet of water Nov. 18, ending the career of this useful small steamboat. There may have been further Cow Island arrivals, Big Horn, Josephine, Rosebud and Batchelor were reported above Fort Buford in mid-October. Down cargoes were probably higher than reported in papers. Passengers not always reported. The Benton Record reported T. C. Power boats brought 2529 tons, 443 passengers 25 horses and 184 rams, took down 637 tons and 100 passengers. At Cow Island, its November 7 issue said, there were a million pounds of freight, the Baker wagons especially busy—that 500 tons would have required 67 3-wagon outfits more than a week on the trail to Benton.

## Steamboating Increases With Territory's Population

Montana's population had increased sharply in the decade, everyone knew that and the decennial census confirmed it—almost double the 20,595 of 1870. The June count would show 39,159. Furthermore, the head count would put Fort Benton's population at 1618, which would make the river port the third largest settlement in Montana, only rising Butte and Helena, territorial capital, surpassed the total—about double. No other place had yet reached 1,000.

The growth in population meant more customers, and a greater demand in the northern area. The Utah Northern, which had been moving north by fits and starts, on March 9, 1880, drove its first spike, laid its first tie in Montana Territory, an event hardly remarked by the Benton Record. The arrival of steel rails in southwestern Montana meant little to Fort Benton, which was busier than ever through the steamboat season—it was still farther to the Helena area from railhead than from Benton. When the Northern Pacific neared Wibaux in the east late in the year it drew a bit more attention. In a yearend issue, devoid of advertising, the Record of January 2nd outlined the progress of 1879, reviewed the river business, and the town's growing list of businesses, new and old. There was comment on Fort Benton's limping building boom, due to continue another season and even further. The newspaper had its own success story, set up in the largest brick building in Fort Benton with new equipment, powerful steam engine and boiler and three steam job presses, proudly boasting the "largest paper published in Montana." Editor Buck meant in size, not circulation—the four page Record had nine columns, print size about 22 inches wide and 28 high—a startled contemporary likened it "unto a barn door" unfolded. The new Record was about as big as Fort Benton business plans.

Some early signs of a busy year: The military telegraph from Fort Assiniboine was doing a landoffice business in January. The school had 36 primary and 33 grammar students. Kitty Tonge and Alicia Stanford were planning a select day school for children and young ladies. The bumptious river port was getting society. First ore shipments from the Barker mining district were looked ahead to by freighters. The Record in February learned of 24 locations on agricultural lands within five miles. The surge of the new livestock industry was indicated by formation of the Sun River Stock Growers Association; organizers included Robert Ford, Granville Stuart and J. H. Ming. Plans were underway for building of a mammoth hotel in Benton, begun the next year. The Benton-Assiniboine stage was planning a daily instead of tri-weekly schedule. There were still vestiges of the frontier, hungry Indians had pestered Fort Benton whites through the winter.

Business activities included steps toward establishment of two banks, first formal ones in Fort Benton. There were planning announcements by T. C. Power for a doubling of space, Murphy Neel for a large brick building, brick livery stable by Harris & Strong—two brick yards would be busy. All over town residences were going up as lumber and/or brick became available. The building boom had spread beyond city limits, an early 1880 news item, "The stock grangers of Shonkin are building substantial residences," naming nine.

One news item, "With saloons, Benton is more than well supplied." Six named, "others so numerous we have not the space for extended notice of any."

The winter had been open, little mention of storms, to Montanans that meant a slow start for the boats, late April or early May arrivals depending upon lowland snow melt and showers, the bigger June rise came from rains and high mountain runoff. It was not until May 6 that the Rosebud opened the Fort Benton navigation season; credited with 149 tons and 50 passengers, this almost certainly meant 100 tons left at Coal Banks; the Butte next day can be credited with 370 tons and 100 passengers. (Newspaper accounts this season are frustrating, often cargoes were listed by packages, although the season totals appear solid enough. Passengers upbound were usually reported, down freight or passengers seldom.)

May arrivals were Far West 13th, Key West 16th, Helena 17th, Benton 25th, Nellie Peck and Rosebud 27th, an estimated 2150 tons during the month, at Coal Banks and Benton, by distributing the season's total. In anticipation of a busy season, John Hunsberger bought out his partner in the Overland Hotel and Jere Sullivan and Harry Hill were opening the former Thwing House as the Choteau House, a name with insertion of a second "u" to endure more than a century. The Benton Record apologetically noted "Our paper stock having failed to arrive, we are again compelled to issue the Record on separate sheets." The owner had picked the wrong boat line.

A matter of greater pride, Bank of Northern Montana opened in a corner of the Record building, followed by the First National Bank in the center of the first floor—the Record's new printing outfit was in the basement, editorial offices on the floor above the banks. After years without formal facilities, Fort Benton had two banks. The first was content with its housing, local owners were Timothy Collins and Charles Duer, with connections through L. H. Hershfield with a long established Helena firm. First National was strictly local, backed by the Conrads of Baker, the Powers, Ed Maclay of Murphy Neel and Scott Wetzel, Sam Hauser representing a Helena connection. This firm was pressing its contractors to get going on a brick behind the first Power store. George Anderson, photographer, arrived in Fort Benton late in May, having in mind a location but apparently did not stay. A more noted taker of historic pictures, F. Jay Haynes, probably was already registered at the Choteau House. He came up the Missouri on the Far West from Bismarck, where he had an established photography business. Haynes was so fascinated by wild Montana that he snapped his shutter often—probably his last four plates took pictures of the Choteau House, Record building, a view of Fort Benton from across the Missouri, and the Great Falls of the Missouri—at any rate those were the last surviving of his 1880 Montana trip.

From June 9 there was a well spaced procession of steamboats with heavy cargoes, judging from the package counts: Helena 9th, Red Cloud 10th, Far West 12th, Peninah 15th, General Sherman 16th (last three at the levee two days), C. K. Peck 18th, Rosebud 19th (an estimated 375 passengers includes 5 companies of Mounted Police), Butte 23rd and Minnie H(eerman) to close June. Minnie was a small trim craft chartered by a group of homeseekers—the June tonnage ran to around 2300. Experienced stampeders Cyprian Matt, Jack Little and George Farmer brought back reports discouraging to Yogo prospects, little pay except on bedrock. Other Bentonites spoke well of developing pay lodes in the Barker mining district near later Neihart. Fort Benton had two brickyards, and busy ones, that of J. R. Wilton, contractor, and Storer & Storer, back of the butte behind the town—Storer at the time making 7,000 a day and later cited by the Record for quality—but anything shaped like a brick would have been acceptable that season.

Red Cloud arrived to a Fourth of July salute with 350 tons and took down 180 cattle, hides, furs and part of the Baker Co. trade of 20,000 buffalo robes that season. Not until the 11th did the Key West arrive, 308 tons; both tonnages reported, as were 76 and 30 passengers. Then the Nellie Peck and Helena the 13th, Rosebud 18th, Red Cloud 23rd, Benton 27th, Key West and Butte 29th, C. K. Peck closing July on 31st—about 3000 tons and certainly a new record for the month. Wool was reported accumulating on the levee with many trains arriving from Meagher county, but wool was in its infancy in 1880 as an export.

Cargoes became lighter and the steamboat parade slowed, as always, in August but the Eclipse and Far West the 1st could have been a first, General Terry came only to Coal Banks with government freight the 5th, but the Helena the 6th, Rosebud 12th had good loads. Helena stopped at Coal Banks the 15th, Butte, Josephine and General Meade ended August, 21st, 26th and 29th—about 2100 tons for the month.

There were still the September arrivals, Helena, Meade and Butte to Marias, Rosebud to Coal Banks, and in October Meade, Helena and Eclipse to Coal Banks, the last taking down 120 Fort Assiniboine workers. Butte got to Cow Island October 28 with a good cargo, but a final attempt to deliver government freight found the F. Y. Batchelor caught by ice at the Musselshell November 12.

The season's total looked like 12,460 tons up, 2250 down, 1800 or more passengers up and 700 down, probably not including way pickups.

Back at Fort Benton, Storer & Storer not only made bricks but laid them, completing a fine brick pyramid roof house for Ed Dunne and Rufus Payne's mansard roof home. Wilton got the First National building up. Fort Benton's most pretentious livery, Park Stables, Murphy Neel's long brick were completed and other buildings begun, including a twin beside the Power store. It was no wonder a Benton Board of Trade was organized late in September, cashiers of the two banks heading the officers. In December the Power and Baker stores and First National were connected by telephone.

October 27 the first issue of The River Press was printed in an adobe cabin that once held Jim Nabors' "hotel" and rather sourly welcomed by the Benton Record. As was the custom of the day, the two journals differed in politics, missed no opportunity to slur the other but by 1880 newspaper standards there was room for both.

At Christmas time Fort Benton residents, almost for the first time, took note of the festive season and of appropriate religious services.

Steamboat arrivals, cargoes for 1880:

(As noted in text, tonnages of boats for most part are estimates based on year end reports. Few individual down totals were available or possible, figures are based on best data as to robe, wool and ore exports.)

| Date | Steamboat | Tons | | Pass. | Notes |
|---|---|---|---|---|---|
| May 6 | Rosebud | 249 | | 50 | |
| May 7 | Butte | 370 | | 100 | |
| May 13 | Far West | 270 | | 40 | |
| May 16 | Key West | 285 | | 60 | |
| May 17 | Helena | 270 | | 43 | |
| May 25 | Benton | 300 | | 55 | |
| May 27 | Nellie Peck | 200 | | 60 | |
| May 27 | Rosebud | 290 | | 100 | |
| June 9 | Helena | 300 | | 25 | |
| June 10 | Red Cloud | 350 | | 70 | |
| June 12 | Key West | 300 | | | |
| June 15 | Peninah | 250 | | 30 | |
| June 16 | General Sherman | 200 | | 37 | |
| June 18 | C. K. Peck | 250 | | 50 | |
| June 19 | Rosebud | 300 | | 375 | 300 Mounted Police |
| June 23 | Butte | 300 | | 30 | |
| June 29 | Minnie Heerman | 150 | | 33 | homeseeker charter |
| July 4 | Red Cloud | 350 | 100 | 76 | cattle, robes |
| July 11 | Key West | 308 | | 30 | |

| Date | Steamboat | Tons | Pass. | | Notes |
|---|---|---|---|---|---|
| July 12 | Eclipse | 250 | | | 78 tons lumber |
| July 13 | Nellie Peck | 275 | 27 | | |
| July 13 | Helena | 330 | 18 | | |
| July 18 | Rosebud | 221 | 14 | | |
| July 23 | Red Cloud | 300 | 74 | 30 | 180 cattle down |
| July 27 | Benton | 253 | | 30 | 153 tons Coal Banks |
| July 29 | Key West | 240 | 6 | | |
| July 29 | Butte | 300 | 17 | | 30 tons Coal Banks |
| July 31 | C. K. Peck | 265 | | | |
| Aug. 1 | Eclipse | 220 | 7 | | |
| Aug. 1 | Far West | 300 | | | |
| Aug. 5 | Gen. Terry, Coal Banks | 300 | | | |
| Aug. 6 | Helena | 300 | | | |
| Aug. 12 | Rosebud | 300 | | | |
| Aug. 15 | Helena, Coal Banks | 225 | | | |
| Aug. 21 | Butte | 225 | 70 | | |
| Aug. 26 | Josephine | 250 | | | |
| Aug. 29 | General Meade | 150 | | | |
| Sept. 8 | Helena, Marias | 275 | | | |
| Sept. 16 | Rosebud, Coal Banks | 200 | | | |
| Sept. 17 | Gen. Meade, Marias | 150 | | | |
| Sept. 21 | Butte, Marias | 250 | | | |
| Oct. 2 | Gen. Meade, Coal Banks | 150 | | | |
| Oct. 17 | Helena, Coal Banks | 275 | | | |
| Oct. 20 | Rosebud, Coal Banks | 150 | | | 120 Assin. workers |
| Oct. 22 | Eclipse, Coal Banks | 264 | | | |
| Oct. 28 | Butte, Cow Island | 250 | | | |
| Nov. 12 | F.Y. Batchelor | 200 | | | stopped Musselshell |
| | | 12160 | 2500 | 1800 | 700 pass. down |

```
Benton P Line private ............4250 tons
P Line government ..............4000 tons
Coulson Line ...................2840 tons
Baker Line ....................1015 tons
Benton lines to Fort Peck ..........355 tons
    Total on Missouri ...........12460 tons
Yellowstone Line ................1580 tons
    Montana river freight ........13685 tons
```

Railroad freight from the Utah Northern railhead in 1880 was slightly under 10,000 tons, from the Northern Pacific about 6700 tons, both were barely inside Montana Territory, so the Bismarck-Fort Benton steamboat run and freighting was in a favorable competitive situation. About 300 tons wool went down by boats.

## Biggest Year On Missouri In Montana

Dan Maratta, representing the Coulson Line at Bismarck, in November 1881, told the Tribune there that upbound traffic from that point to Fort Benton and places below that year totalled 17,420 tons, a figure almost identical to a report by the chief of engineers. As there were few settlements in western Dakota and those in Montana were largely tributary to Fort Benton, that added up to the biggest year ever on the upper Missouri, Montana tonnage-wise. In addition, Maratta said, Yellowstone river freight was 4200 tons. There were 21 boats on the upper river, Dacotah, 1400 ton capacity, the largest, the General Thompkins smallest at a rated 250 tons. The steamboats carried 4100 passengers, including 2400 Indians, also 1800 cattle and horses and 600 sheep. For shipment east there came to Bismarck via the boats 160,000 buffalo hides, 180 tons of wool and a large number of other hides and pelts. The buffalo hide shipments were the product of possibly 5,000 white hide hunters, as well as Indians, as extermination of the buffalo neared the final stages. Supplies for the hunters undoubtedly accounted for hundreds of tons of freight along the rivers. Tonnages were the largest ever but returns to the steamboaters far lower, Bismarck to Fort Benton a cent a pound and less.

At Fort Benton, 1881 dawned with cold weather, following a severe December. Wood was $12 and $13 a cord and that not good. Although no mention in the papers, this was probably the winter Murphy Neel burned several hundred pounds of rancid bacon to heat their business, and one resident paid $1.50 for a hod of coal, translated by the eastern press into a price of $75 a ton for coal at Fort Benton. The city's postmaster, M. A. Flanagan, ordered 100 lock boxes and 200 call boxes and planned to move the postoffice to the rear of his drug store. Late in January the River Press reported the road to Helena was almost impassable due to snow, next week reported, "recent storm the worst ever, here about 15 inches of snow, up to 7 feet in Prickly Pear canyon."

The usual chinook was early, February 3rd, and the breakup of ice in the rivers a disaster. Fort Benton got off lightly, Mike Lynch's small ferry was crushed, the big Ed Smith ferry unhurt but pushed up on the bank, along with large ice cakes lining the levee. On the Teton no casualties, but a great ice gorge near the Stocking ranch sent the Neubert, Hammond and O'Fallon families to Benton as refugees. Worst was on the Marias, "disaster" headlined a small River Press special, one man drowned, several others missing. This was a winter that old time stockmen who went through both rated worse than the more publicized winter of 1886-87. Devastation on the Missouri in Dakota was tremendous.

In March came the usual reports on the coming river season. Power's Block P Line was adding its fourth boat, the Black Hills, to leave Yankton about April 1st. The Benton was coming clear from St. Louis, the Butte and Helena from Yankton.

The frontier wasn't completely quiet, in February three men, two well known in Benton, were killed by Indians in the Belt country; April 2 Matt Duncan, herder for James Wells at Claggett at the Judith, was killed by Indians, later in the month Charles Jackson got in a fight with Piegans over a mare, killed two and died of his wounds. Cattlemen were also wrought up over hungry red men killing their beeves, Granville Stuart one of the protesters.

In early May the wooden sidewalk at the old Carroll & Steell store was torn up; alert residents panned the dirt, got two or three dollars a pan—it was near the site of the one time Wells Fargo office. Also in May, the small Fort Benton garrison was packing up to move to Fort Shaw in June. An old frontier vehicle figured in the robe trade in May, 35 Red River carts brought Power robes to Benton from Fort Belknap (later Chinook)—Metis from Canada for some years had been moving into northern and central Montana—Lewistown's beginnings dated from arrival of about 50 families in 1879 and Louis Riel, their leader, was a Power contact man.

As a preliminary to the river season, new businesses were popping up in Fort

Benton almost weekly: Dutro & Kielhauer, stone masons; Allen & Tierney, saloon; Mrs. Beckman, Cosmopolitan Hotel, more a boarding house; John Lilly, the old Lee Isabel Break of Day House; George Farmer, the "Jungle"; W. H. Burgess, first strictly grocery store; Gans & Klein, clothing, was building a new brick; Baker & DeLorimier, home furnishings, new, ready to move into brick; Neil McIntyre, boots and shoes; W. J. Minar, druggist; "Elite," Marshall & Wilson; Phoenix, Bernard Tierney. Fort Benton would continue more than well supplied with saloons. On the upper levee, George Clendennin was having a brick warehouse built for the Coulson Line.

But where were the steamboats? April 27 (Record files missing until June) the River Press noted high water down river had delayed their arrival. Local publications were short of paper by the end of May, others of the territorial press had felt the pinch earlier—even newspapers could learn the dependence on steamboat freights in face of the railroad building.

It was not until May 19 that the Far West reached Fort Benton, followed by the Helena next day, undoubtedly with cargoes about that estimated in arrival list, but for first two weeks of June no local papers survive. May 27 the C. K. Peck came in with half a 350 ton cargo, rest at Coal Banks. The June 15 Press explained, "Seven million pounds of freight are in Bismarck awaiting shipment, and the business of the Territory kept lagging therefrom, while a fleet of steamboats are carrying numerous bands of Indians on a picnic down the Yellowstone." The refugee Sioux had been starved out of Canada, were crossing the border in bands to surrender to the military at Buford and other posts, the boats would transport about 2400 to reservations down the Missouri.

Red Cloud arrived May 25 with 250 tons and 25 passengers, having left 150 tons of Canadian freight and about 100 Mounted Police recruits at Coal Banks. May 30 the Benton came to its namesake port with 300 tons of long awaited freight and 75 passengers. (Papers disagreed on arrival dates, as do other sources, these are best guesses.)

Dacotah, "Big D," was 6th arrival June 8, the boat had arrived at Coal Banks by the 1st, was delayed to repair machinery, but brought in 498 tons and 163 rams and with next day's Rosebud the new Barker smelter, so probably 600 tons in all. Rosebud had 200 plus part of smelter. Far West and Key West came in June 17.

Some well known boats were missing from Fort Benton arrivals for weeks. The Benton Record of June 30 reprinted from the Bismarck Tribune: "Five boats transferring 1700 Indians from Keogh to Standing Rock left under command of Capt. Snyder and 20 men on the Eclipse, 20 men and officers on the others, Capt. Overshine on Sherman, Capt. Ewer on Helena, Lt. Hargens on Terry and Lt. Avis on Sherman." 1680 Indians, Helena 524, Eclipse 440, Gen. Terry 320, Josephine 218, Gen. Sherman 178. About 50 Indians and 493 ponies went overland.

Late in June the pace of arrivals at Fort Benton picked up, Red Cloud 23rd, Benton 24th, Rosebud 25th and C. K. Peck 29th, about 1250 tons as the river stage was good rather late in the high water period, also 67 passengers. July 1st the Dacotah came again, with 627 tons and took down a good load of hides, robes and furs. It was the 11th before the Butte came in, bringing word of a strike of roustabouts at Bismarck, owners were stubborn about more pay, the roosters correctly figured the steamboat men in a bind to move freight, hanging up Nellie Peck, Far West, Butte, Big Horn and Batchelor for days. (During one such strike roustabouts threatened, telling the captain they would switch to water and ground Grant Marsh's steamboat; no evidence they carried out the drastic threat.)

There were six boats in the last dozen days of July, Nellie Peck, Benton, Red

Cloud, Josephine, Gen. Sherman and Josephine again with some of Dacotah's freight. Lower August water plus government freight resulted in stops below, Helena, Butte and Far West to Coal Banks, about 1st, Rosebud to Marias on 5th and apparently ran up to Benton, Red Cloud to Coal Banks the 5th, Butte to Marias 8th and Josephine 14th. Four days later the Rosebud brought government lumber to Coal Banks, two days after the Josephine there with the rest of her freight.

The late start and army requirements kept the boats busy, news reports only indicated their efforts, including the Dacotah heading for Poplar Creek the last of August, with the smaller boats busy shuttling freight from various drops. These are listed in summary with approximate high point and date.

Down around Carroll above the Musselshell, robe and hide trade was brisk. The Record in July said Joe Kipp's white buffalo robe there attracts the attention of passing pilgrims. (James Willard Schultz eventually sold the robe to one for $100, to the dismay of Kipp, who had learned from Charles Conrad it would bring at least $500.)

In September the Record noted, "Carpenters are scarce in Benton." Probably masons, stone workers, plasterers and painters, too, or any reasonable facsimile for Fort Benton was in a frenetic building boom right along with the busiest freighting season ever. Bank of Northern Montana got their brick building up, as did George Clendennin for Coulson, the new county jail, a Power dry goods store, John J. Kennedy's Centre Market (he opened with a party for 250), Davidson & Moffitt harness, Baker & DeLorimier. Residences were going up as citizens could draft services of harrassed craftsmen. No wonder construction costs at Fort Benton were twice as high as any where else in Montana Territory. So serious was the housing shortage deemed that a Benton Building Association was formed with $75,000 capital. It would construct a dozen or more homes in the next two or three years.

The improvement fad even extended out of town, residents found the Barker mining district a good customer, donated $1000 to improve the road, and at Arrow Creek John LaMott was building a toll road, probably at least as passable as in certain later day eras. To turn a profit as well as mitigate local hardship, Trevanian Hale and John Evans had cleared the Shonkin for a spring drive and down the tiny creek in high water went 2400 cords of wood. A one day conversation piece in October was the $274 telegram a London Times correspondent sent describing the Fort Macleod visit of the Marquis of Lorne, a member of the British royal family and duly noted by Canadian historians.

There had been talk for more than a year of a big hotel, seemingly one of Fort Benton's greatest needs. In August ground was broken for the big brick structure. It was barely completed in time for a November 1, 1882, formal opening and became a Fort Benton landmark—the Grand Union.

Indicative of the great slaughter of buffalo in addition to the Maratta report of 160,000 hides to Bismarck via steamboat, in August the Bismarck Tribune reported on her latest arrival from above the Black Hills brought more than 12,000 hides—more than 150 tons and bulking tremendously.

Steamboat arrivals on the Missouri in Montana in 1881:

(This year also there were few newspaper reports of down cargoes or down passengers. In about half the cases arrival tonnage was estimated, and about 4000 tons of way freight not included in totals in table.)

| Date | Steamboat | Tons | Pass. | Notes |
|---|---|---|---|---|
| May 19 | Far West | 350 | | |
| May 20 | Helena | 400 | | |
| May 25 | Red Cloud | 400 | 125 | |
| May 27 | C. K. Peck | 350 | 35 | |
| May 30 | Benton | 300 | 75 | |
| June 8 | Dacotah | 600 | | Part Barker smelter |
| June 9 | Rosebud | 300 | 9 | 163 rams |
| June 17 | Far West | 300 | 90 | cattle down |
| June 17 | Key West | 300 | | |
| June 23 | Red Cloud | 400 | 32 | |
| June 24 | Benton | 350 | 24 | |
| June 25 | Rosebud | 290 | 11 | |
| June 29 | C. K. Peck | 260 | | |
| July 4 | Dacotah | 627 | 100 | record cargo |
| July 11 | Butte | 300 | | |
| July 20 | Nellie Peck | 250 | 3 | |
| July 21 | Josephine | 170 | 8 | |
| July 22 | Benton | 350 | | |
| July 23 | General Sherman | 200 | | |
| July 24 | Red Cloud | 350 | | |
| July 31 | Josephine | 300 | 115 | freight of Dacotah |
| Aug. 1 | Helena, Coal Banks | 350 | | |
| Aug. 1 | Butte, Coal Banks | 350 | | |
| Aug. 1 | Far West, Coal Banks | 300 | | |
| Aug. 5 | Rosebud, Benton | 300 | 125 | big load of wool |
| Aug. 5 | Red Cloud, Coal Banks | 350 | | |
| Aug. 8 | Butte, Marias | 325 | | |
| Aug. 14 | Josephine, Marias | 300 | 60 | |
| Aug. 18 | Rosebud, Coal Banks | 200 | | government lumber |
| Aug. 20 | Josephine, Coal Banks | 160 | | |
| Aug. 23? | Dacotah | 400 | | Poplar or Buford |
| Aug. 24 | Rosebud, Coal Banks | 200 | | more govt. lumber |
| Aug. 25 | Black Hills, Judith | 300 | 15 | |
| Aug. 25 | Far West, Coal Banks | 250 | | |
| Sept. 9 | Josephine, Benton | 200 | | |
| Sept. 9 | Rosebud, Cow I. | 150 | 12 | |
| Sept. 13 | Butte, Cow I. | 60 | | |
| Sept. 15 | Big Horn, Judith | 286 | | 200 tons Cow I. |
| Oct. 5 | Black Hills | 250 | | |
| Oct. 8 | Rosebud | 250 | 12 | |
| Oct. 9 | Emily, Cow I. | 150 | | government boat |
| Oct. 18 | Josephine, Cow I. | 200 | | |
| Oct. 20 | Big Horn, Judith | 150 | | |
| Oct. 23 | Helena, Cow I. | 300 | | |
| | | 12,928 3000 | 1300 | 2800 pass. down |

About another 4000 tons up, most to Montana on Maratta report of 17,420 tons up, 4200 tons down. The large number of passengers down included the Sioux from Canada who were transported to Standing Rock reservation down river.

# Decline of an Inland Port

## By A Trifle, Benton's Biggest Freight Receipts

*T*he previous river season had been the busiest into Montana, by a fraction 1882 was to be Fort Benton's greatest. Fort Benton residents were intoxicated with prosperity and visions of future greatness as the New Year began. A cold spell in December had been followed by a prolonged chinook and the Missouri was wide open and ice free with both ferries busy crossing teams bound for the Barker and Judith mines, and the tri-weekly Benton & Barker Stage line was busy as well. Railroad rumbles were scarcely disturbing, for the largest settlement in northern Montana felt certain both roads would build to Benton, and in the 1880s where rails crossed, sizable cities grew. So mild was the winter that coal, often as high as $25 a ton (the previous winter a bid of $60 had been rejected), was going begging at $14.

Fort Benton's building boom had renewed energy in the opening months, work on the big hotel about half done in February, and carpenters were busy—aside from a December storm, coldest night was about -5. In February contractor J. R. Wilton got the contract to build frame houses wholesale for Benton Building Assn., one and a half story at $2,000, one story at $1600. Other residents, better fixed, went higher, W. S. Wetzel contracted for a brick home to rival that of W. G. Conrad (it later served as the Benton Sanitarium), and more modest building hinged on availability of carpenters, lumber and brick.

George Clendenin, Coulson line agent who had been at Fort Benton fresh from Civil War service, six years at the Musselshell and at Carroll in its best years, died in a rock fall in a Barker mine February 6. His funeral at Fort Benton was impressive, rating a Benton Record extra. Freighter John O'Connor, veteran of Montana trails, killed when a big Power warehouse door blew shut, was another of early burials in new Riverside Cemetery, which replaced the county cemetery of 1868, which was too near the town.

Fort Benton living costs were far below the gold rush days when any item sold for at least $1 a pound: Ham 20c, bacon 18c, apples 18-20c, rice and beans around 10c and potatoes and flour around $5 a hundred. Ranch produce was high, though, ranch eggs and butter 50c a dozen or pound and vegetables of all kinds bringing top prices.

Business as well as building notes were numerous early in 1882. I. G. Baker & Co. had just been awarded, for the 8th consecutive year, the contract to supply the North West Mounted Police, a mere $450,000. Power was moving into its new dry goods store and backing H. J. Wackerlin in building a new brick hardware store next to this. In their main building the Power firm installed the first freight elevator in Fort Benton. The device fascinated visiting half breeds from Canada, as well as locals, the lessee of Nick Welch's Occidental, once rated the toughest saloon in a tough town, changed its name to The Elevator. Miss Kitty Tonge gave up her young ladies' school in favor of a sales position in the Power dry goods store, first sales lady in Fort Benton. Responding to the new hotel, R. S. Culbertson moved his frame Centennial back to the alley in preparation for stonework foundation for a brick replacement. A new brickyard was opened by John Houston, a newcomer, the third, and all found plenty of business, in April the Record reported a big building boom in full swing.

First freighting note came in March when Ed Trainer put the brand new Baker bull team on the road, probably up the old Whoop-Up Trail to Macleod.

Initial steamboating note was in February, Power's Block P line was guaranteeing shippers against loss or non-delivery providing their freight was in Bismarck by July 1st, a first ever in shipments via the river. Low water slowed the initial arrival about a week from previous bests. The Josephine came to Benton on May 3rd with a short cargo, the day before the boat had hung up on the Shonkin bar and had to unload 75 tons to spar over, then went back for the rest. Josephine took down 40 head of cattle and a party of Canadian Pacific surveyors. Key West arrived on the 6th, 128 tons, probably making a second short but unreported trip. General Terry arrived the same day with 219 tons, next day the Butte for Power, the Black Hills the 10th—between then 450 tons. The same day the Rosebud and Big Horn for Coulson, another 500 tons. The Big Horn lost its stacks on the lower ferry cable, a couple of pilots under the influence looked for another way down river.

Helena, pride of the Block P, arrived May 14 with 300 tons, followed by the Far West the 14th with 190, most left at Coal Banks. Benton on the 22nd ushered in the high water period, 300 tons, and later cargoes reflected that. General Meade brought 250 tons and a brief smallpox quarantine, a chambermaid having died at Rocky Point. General Sherman with government freight and army recruits, Helena again, along with Josephine to close out May.

The steamboat pace quickened in June, Rosebud and Far West the 1st, Butte and Red Cloud the 3rd. The latter, Baker's only boat, had a noteworthy 450 tons, took down perhaps 200—one of the largest export cargoes. There was also an impressive passenger list, about 330, that including 205 Mounted Police to Coal Banks, and perhaps 100 immigrants from Missouri, the so-called Patrick Colony, which occasioned a stir in Fort Benton as many arrived impoverished and a local delegation took up a collection to assuage pressing needs. There were passengers on most boats arriving, although the Northern Pacific, past Billings, cut sharply into this traffic. Helena came June 6, Far West, Key West and Rosebud in the next couple of days, the Emily only to the Judith, then Big Horn and Dacotah on the 10th, the Big D with 500 tons. Black Hills and Benton returned for the Power firm on 11th and 14th. On June 25, two notable arrivals, the Red Cloud with 400 tons and the Wyoming with 600—even for Fort Benton a thousand tons was a big day. As it turned out, that was the last arrival for both steamboats, the Wyoming was sold down river by Coulsons—last of the triplets, it was by a few tons the biggest boat that ever came to the Mountains. The boat took down 316 of Samples cattle, not quite 200 tons of beef. Red Cloud sank July 12, 1882, at Eight Point above Milk River, victim of a snag. Among the cargo lost about 150 tons of flour, but no casualties. That was the end of the Baker Steamboat Line, for the remainder of the steamboating period the company leased boats.

Butte, Helena, Key West and Rosebud closed a busy June at the head of navigation. Benton opened July the 5th with 323 tons, but cargoes of later boats, Big Horn, Butte, Josephine and Rosebud indicated a lower water stage. The Rosebud, here on July 19 brought the first electric lights residents had seen, and as at Bismarck, put on an evening display appreciated by residents. Fort Benton legend has it that when the Bud's searchlight swung around, it settled on the Chouteau House balcony, providing unappreciated publicity for a well known citizen sitting there with one of the "girls" on his lap. To the tune of a roar from an amused crowd, the man dumped the girl on the floor and fled the scene. Last trips with more than 200 tons, with one exception, were by Butte July 18 and Helena next day. From that point 13 more boats made trips to Fort Benton, Coal Banks or other points. Exception as to cargo was the sturdy veteran Far West on July with a total of 280 tons, leaving part of the cargo at Shonkin bar. A side note was the Big Horn arrival August 8 with a light cargo and a small group of Bismarck lady passengers, first purely tourism note found, although the Benton Record reported some of the group had made a similar trip on the Dacotah two years before and enjoyed it very much. Navigation season closed October 18 with arrival of the Butte at Judith or Cow Island, 80 tons aboard.

The Benton papers indicated more tonnage to Fort Benton than during the previous season, which is quite possible. Estimates total 12,804 tons, about the same as a year end summary by boat lines, virtually all to Benton. Passengers up were reported at 1750, down 750, plus 1200 troops moved. Down cargoes were probably up a bit from the 2500 tons in 1881, as the Barker mines were shipping ore concentrate of considerable weight, wool shipments had increased, as did the number of cattle sent down river, although many more doubtless were trailed to the railroad in the Billings area.

Despite the big navigation year, in Fort Benton it almost took second place to city building, right up to capacity. Business buildings included a brick and also a frame building for Thomas Cummings, frame drug store for W. J. Minar, Odd Fellows hall, Gans & Klein, start on new Centennial Hotel and a two story brick for W. S. Stocking and brick Masonic hall. (To make room for the Masonic hall, the old Carroll & Steell warehouse of Fort Benton's first general business firm was torn down.) Altogether, the Record estimated three million bricks had been laid during 1882, that including numerous residences not mentioned; this was about as cheap as lumber and surer. One bit of 1881 construction carried over—the brick jail, constructed that year, was ready for customers, but the ironwork for cages was delayed in the bustle of the navigation season, when it finally arrived, no one in Benton was able to put it together. Services of a Diebold Safe & Lock expert from the east was required before the jail could be put in use. The luxurious lockup may have been the reason Sheriff John J. Healy wasn't a candidate in 1882, citizens resented coddling prisoners.

Some odd notes: By June 6, 1882, Fort Benton had four newspapers, the Record had started a daily in February 1881, doubtless to put pressure on its rival, the first edition of the Daily River Press came out in June, 1882, to be continued five days a week to the end of 1919. In September the Record thought it worthy of note that the first trial of an Indian, Antelope Shirt, was held—he was charged with taking a shot at one Omar Gregg. Both publishers had to print summer issues on manila paper due to newsprint shortages. When the Grand Union held its formal opening with grand ball and supper (tickets $3) Record Editor Buck marvelled that it was "attended by almost 100 of the fair sex." When he came from Fort Shaw in 1875 he could have counted white women in town on the fingers of one hand.

Charles Conrad, a partner in I. G. Baker & Co., assisted Sheriff Healy in making an arrest of a Blackfeet youth; a member of the party credited Conrad with saving the lives of the white posse by courage and coolness. The aftermath: "Since Chas. E. Conrad raided Black Weasel's camp and arrested his son, Piegans have been making every effort to make a treaty with the house of I. G. Baker & Co. Robes, horses, and peltries of all kinds are brought in by the friends of the prisoner for the purpose of securing the release of the prisoner, as well as a guarantee of future good behavior." It required more than simple business ability to be a successful Fort Benton merchant.

Fort Benton steamboat arrivals in 1882:

Another year in which data on down cargoes is lacking and estimated. The estimate are based on usual cargoes and stage of river. Totals are based on a published year end summary.

| Arrival | Steamboat | tons | down | pass. | notes |
|---|---|---|---|---|---|
| May 3 | Josephine | 200 | | 50 | 40 cattle down |
| May 6 | Key West | 128 | | | 88 cattle down |
| May 6 | General Terry | 219 | | | |
| May 7 | Butte | 250 | 50 | 30 | |
| May 10 | Black Hills | 200 | | 45 | cabin, livestock down |
| May 10 | Rosebud | 250 | | | |
| May 10 | Big Horn | 250 | | | |
| May 14 | Helena | 300 | | | |
| May 17 | Far West | 190 | | | only 25 tons here |
| May 22 | Benton | 300 | | | much govt. freight |
| May 24 | General Meade | 250 | | 6 | smallpox quar. |
| May 27 | General Sherman | 293 | | 50 | govt., recruits |
| May 29 | Helena | 300 | | | |
| May 29 | Josephine | 242 | | 22 | 135 sheep up |
| June 1 | Rosebud | 230 | | 4 | |
| June 1 | Far West | 231 | | 10 | |
| June 3 | Butte | 300 | | 50 | |
| June 3 | Red Cloud | 450 | 200 | 330 | 205 Mounties |
| June 6 | Helena | 300 | | 36 | |
| June 7 | Far West | 176 | | | 80 cattle down |
| June 7 | Emily, Judith | 200 | | | |
| June 7 | Rosebud | 23 | | | |
| June 8 | Key West | 330 | | 10 | |
| June 10 | Dacotah | 500 | 60 | 20 | 100 cattle down |
| June 10 | Big Horn | 200 | 10 | 8 | |
| June 11 | Black Hills | 200 | | 12 | |
| June 14 | Benton | 300 | | 21 | |
| June 14 | Gen. Sherman, Coal Bk | 207 | | | |
| June 22 | Josephine | 240 | 23 | 15 | |
| June 25 | Wyoming | 600 | | | 316 cattle down |
| June 25 | Red Cloud | 400 | | 12 | |
| June 27 | Butte | 200 | | 19 | |
| June 27 | Rosebud | 200 | | 11 | |
| June 29 | Helena | 186 | | 18 | |
| June 30 | Key West | 200 | | 3 | |
| July 5 | Benton | 323 | | | |
| July 7 | Big Horn | 209 | | | 600 sheep up |
| July 10 | Butte | 250 | | | |
| July 13 | Josephine | 247 | 65 | 20 | |
| July 18 | Butte | 250 | | | 4th trip |
| July 19 | Rosebud | 232 | 65 | 31 | electric lights |
| July 19 | Helena | 210 | 112 | 6 | |
| July 28 | Benton, Coal Banks | 112 | 18 | | |

| Arrival | Steamboat | tons | down | pass. | notes |
|---|---|---|---|---|---|
| July 29 | Butte | 130 | | | |
| July 30 | Far West | 280 | | 26 | |
| July 31 | Black Hills | 200 | | | |
| Aug. 7 | Josephine | 70 | | | |
| Aug. 8 | Butte, Coal Banks | 100 | | | |
| Aug. 8 | Big Horn | 183 | | | |
| Aug. 14 | Josephine | 50 | 60 | | |
| Aug. 21 | Butte, Coal Banks | 200 | | | |
| Sept. 10 | Butte, Cow I. | 200 | | | |
| Sept. 20 | Rosebud, Judith | 150 | | | |
| Oct. 15 | Helena, Cow I. | 100 | | | |
| Oct. 17 | Butte, Cow I. | 80 | | | |
| | Totals.......... | 12,828 | 2750 | 1750 | 750 pass. down 1200 soldiers |

Block P (Power) ......... 5425 tons Helena, Butte, Benton, Black Hills
Coulson Line ........... 3853 " Josephine, Big Horn, Rosebud, Dacotah
Baker Line ............. 1956 " Red Cloud, Wyoming, Key West
Peck Line .............. 1120 " Far West, Gen. Meade, Nellie Peck, Gen. Terry
General Sherman ........ 700 "
   Total Missouri ...... 13064 "
Yellowstone ............. 695 " Eclipse and Peck Line
   Overall Mont ....... 13759 "

**1883 Rail Building Mortal Wound, Not Instant Death To Packets**

Completion of the Northern Pacific to Helena on June 12, 1883, and of the Canadian Pacific to Calgary on August 11 was not a death blow to the Upper Missouri steamboats, but it proved to be a lingering, and mortal wound. The southern route ended the long supremacy of the Benton Road as the Territory's most important highway, the Canadian railroad even more abruptly ended the importance of the northern roads into Alberta. The Helena area had perhaps been the most important customers of the boats, Kleinschmidt & Bro. alone shipped about 2,000 tons yearly, Canadian customers probably exceeded that total. But so rapidly was northern Montana's cattle industry growing, providing numerous customers, that Fort Benton continued as a major port of entry.

Benton merchants of course knew the import of railroad building, but they felt they continued to hold certain advantages, including the Missouri River as a route always available to combat monopolistic rail practices. In fact, they felt, and were encouraged in the belief, that both rail companies would hasten to build to Fort Benton, if for no more than to end or curtail river traffic. Both Fort Benton papers eagerly published reports of arrival of surveyors seeking the best rail routes to the head of navigation, and of building plans.

In its 1883 Holiday Edition, the Record felt the space the ruins of old Fort Benton occupied far more important than this relic: "It is time it was removed. There is nothing particularly attractive or picturesque about the old ruin. A lingering affection for the spot where the earlier years of their lives were spent may be felt by some of the old employees of the American Fur Company." There had been a stampede by speculators to purchase lots in what became the Military Reservation addition to Fort Benton the year before when the reservation was turned back to local authority—that year there had been unbounded optimism about Fort Benton's future. Some reservations may be conjectured from newspaper files of 1883.

January 5 a fire starting in the "Eagle Bird" saloon had also wiped out the Chouteau county court house, although some records were salvaged. Almost immediately plans were underway for a large brick replacement, which was to be completed next year. (The owner of the saloon reopened in the appropriately named Phoenix.) Plans were also afoot for a modern school house to add to the small brick built in 1877 for much more room. However, main topic of early 1883 was the matter of incorporation of Fort Benton, both papers endorsing the proposal, and surprisingly in view of Civil War animosities reflected in politics of the day, this was accomplished by a two to one vote, and a coalition ticket elected. Wm. G. Conrad, manager of the giant I. G. Baker Co., was first mayor. After twenty years of being Benton, Benton City or occasionally Fort Benton, the River Press of April 11 advised, "You must write it Fort Benton now, as that is the name in the charter." That view drew general approval of residents who agreed, "probably every state in the Union has its Benton, town or county, there is but one Fort Benton in the whole wide world." (A look at an atlas index confirms the Press comment.) When the later Great Northern came in 1887, it tagged its station Benton, not changed until about 1922.

The one word title remained in usage. In February, aiming to end forever Fort Benton's recurring fuel shortages, the Benton Boom & Lumber company was incorporated, backed by leading merchants and both banks. Aim was to cut and float logs down the Missouri from timbered areas above, a boom aimed at shunting the logs into a bywater was constructed to steer the incoming timber into a retrieval area. The affair flopped, but evidence remains in the form of stone piers. Even the failure indicates considerable civic enterprise.

Construction in 1883 turned downward, and was mostly completion of buildings begun the previous fall such as the Stocking building and Centennial Hotel (which changed to Pacific but was long termed the Culbertson House). Starts were made on court house and school, a fire engine house and Sisters' hospital which was built by private subscription and materialized in 1886 as St. Clare Hospital, first such in northern Montana—residents were taking assumed civic duties seriously. There was even a subscription library ($5 per year) with many books.

Early issues of both papers carried the usual steamboat line ads, halved this spring, Baker and and Peck lines gone, for the Block P and Coulson lines. They were to be busy, bringing a surprising tonnage in view of the onrushing railroads. There were still frontier incidents, though the country was getting pretty civilized. In March Crees staged a raid at old Fort Conrad, gathering up Joe Kipp's horse herd and butchering six Tingley steers. Little Dog the younger led a Piegan war party which gathered two scalps, among the last such trophies for the tribe. Despite the punishment of the Crees, it was a raid to stir Joe's Indian side. Later James Grant, son of the noted Richard, was killed by an Indian on Dupuyer creek—no court case, the Piegan was found out on the prairie, shot to pieces. Fort Benton had a shooting affair that taxes credulity in September. John "Frenchy" Vizenir, out on the town, fell in with John Macauley, alias Joe Bush, in Brennan's saloon. According to the booze boss, the pair after some heated discussion stepped out on Front about midnight, turned their backs, stepped off some paces, turned and fired. Frenchy was hard hit, his life hanging in the balance next morning when he assured all and sundry that it was just a friendly little duel, and I lost. Joe Bush was quite solicitous of his shooting partner, Frenchy recovered and no charges pressed.

Steamboats were slow getting underway, Power and Coulson about this time had a working agreement and in 1883 split the private freight just about down the middle. First boat in was the Rosebud May 10, 200 tons and 23 passengers, next the Butte with 250 and 20 the 11th, Helena in the 19th bringing 40 tons for Coal Banks, along with 70 army recruits, and 250 pure blood rams along with 210 tons Power freight. Coulson lost a step and a boat when the Big Horn snagged on its trip May 8 enroute, some salvage. Benton's 365 tons May 31st signified advent of higher water, and the Coulson Line began catching up in June. This year robes came in only by trickles, save that Tom O'Hanlon had 6,000 robes at Fort Belknap, probably from the final 1882 hunts.

First of June came the Rosebud with 250 tons, took down 54 tons of bullion from Barker, at an estimate worth about $1 a pound. Next two were also Coulson boats, Josephine on the 2nd with 275 tons and next day Dacotah with 400 tons, including salvage from Big Horn, down went bullion and robes. While at Benton the two boats were attached on a shipper's damage claim; as the boats left soon, the matter was quickly settled. Power's Butte arrived the 4th, Rosebud the 7th, then Batchelor and Black Hills 10th, the latter bringing 80 passengers to Coal Banks. Others in order during June, Helena, Benton, Josephine, Butte, Black Hills, all with good sized cargoes.

July began on a quick pace, the little government Emily and fine Helena the 1st, F. Y. Batchelor, bought from the Northern Pacific after use as a transfer (ferry) at Bismarck, and Dacotah the 2nd. Rosebud came July 7, Butte and Black Hills 13th, Josephine and Benton 15th, the latter to Coal Banks with Fort Assiniboine freight. Customary wool market time being early July, the boats were carrying substantial cargoes of this export that month. First convention of the Montana Woolgrowers Association was held in Fort Benton in July 1883, shortly after the River Press boasted "Fort Benton is the best wool market in the Territory." George Patterson of Fort Benton was first president, although Paris Gibson had chaired an organization meeting in January. For several years, even to after arrival of the railroad, Fort Benton was a primary shipping point for northern and central Montana wool. Rosebud and Helena closed July arrivals.

That was the end of the boat freight clear to Benton, although numbers arrived below and the government Emily came September 11, "water very low," to work on channels and crossings in the area, including Shonkin bar.

One reason for the late summer decline in arrivals was of course the railroads. Helena merchants naturally held off on all but essential orders while awaiting arrival of steel. As for Canada, Paul Sharp is authority for the statement that last important shipments went north in July 1883. August 18 the Record bravely published the item, "Benton streets look quiet, but local firms are claiming to do more business." The same paper was cited by Sharp as later retracting, "not even a dogfight relieved the monotony." A townsite survey of later Great Falls made in 1883 was to be a decisive influence on hopes of Benton people. Kleinschmidt & Brother, one of the big Fort Benton firms, had already decided to abandon its Fort Benton branch, although the manager refuted the report. Early next year it would hold a closing out sale in Fort Benton, and others of several Helena branches, including Gans & Klein and Davidson & Moffitt, would follow suit. The last began its closing August 1883. One evidence of impending events probably was cheered by local imbibers, Peter Macdonald of the Pacific Hotel saloon, lowered drinks to one bit, 12 1/2c. Another item of import, several items about some man shooting the "last buffalo" appeared in papers. The now disappearing luxury of living in a boom town could be seen in a note about the price of beef in the markets, porterhouse and sirloin steak were a costly 25c a pound, the only beef most Bentonites would eat.

In November an old timers association was planned, with a committee of John Donnelly, T. F. Healy, George B. Parker, C. E. Conrad, John Power, W. S. Wetzel, Henry Kennerly, John H. Evans, Charles Rowe, Ed Dunne, John W. Tattan and Jacob H. Kanouse. Clark Tingley might have told all but Kennerly and James Arnoux about the time in 1862-63 when Fort Benton and Sun River had but one mail a year, via Fort Laramie on the Oregon Trail.

Steamboat arrivals in 1883:

(Pretty comprehensive summary totals are given of up and down river freight for this year, some single boat figures found, the remainder estimated. Passenger totals for individual boats were fairly frequent.)

| Date | Steamboat | tons | down | pass. | notes |
|---|---|---|---|---|---|
| May 10 | Rosebud | 200 | | 23 | |
| May 11 | Butte | 250 | | | |
| May 19 | Helena | 250 | | 100 | 70 army recruits |
| May 31 | Benton | 365 | | 30 | |
| June 1 | Rosebud | 250 | 54 | 20 | |
| June 2 | Josephine | 275 | | 5 | |
| June 3 | Dacotah | 400 | 100 | | bullion, robes |
| June 4 | Butte | 250 | | | |
| June 7 | Rosebud | 230 | | | |
| June 10 | F. Y. Batchelor | 270 | | | most Coal Banks |
| June 10 | Black Hills | 350 | | 80 | pass. Coal Banks |
| June 13 | Helena | 275 | | 10 | 60 Mitchell wagons |
| June 23 | Benton | 300 | | 15 | |
| June 24 | Josephine | 275 | | | |
| June 24 | Butte | 300 | | | |
| June 27 | Black Hills | 300 | | | 13 d 23 hr rd trip |
| July 1 | Emily | 100 | | | govt boat |
| July 1 | Helena | 300 | | | |
| July 2 | F. Y. Batchelor | 350 | | | |
| July 2 | Dacotah | 700 | | | record cargo |
| July 7 | Rosebud | 250 | | | |
| July 13 | Black Hills | 350 | 35 | | wool down |
| July 13 | Butte | 300 | 75 | | wool down |
| July 15 | Benton, Coal Banks | 300 | | | |
| July 15 | Josephine | 250 | 110 | | big load wool |
| July 25 | Rosebud | 200 | | 15 | |
| July 26 | Helena | 300 | | | |
| Aug. 6 | Black Hills, Marias | 85 | 112 | 15 | |
| Aug. 19 | Emily, Shonkin | - | | | |
| Aug. 20 | Black Hills, Marias | 118 | | | |
| Aug. 21 | Rosebud, Judith | 75 | | | |
| | Josephine | 200 | | | left Bism. 8-11 |
| | Helena, Cow I. | 200 | | | left Bism. 8-29 |
| Sept. | Rosebud, Poplar | 100 | | | with annuities |

| Date | Steamboat | tons | down | pass. | notes |
|---|---|---|---|---|---|
| Sept. 11 | Emily | - | | | govt work here |
| | Black Hills, Cow I. | 75 | | | left Bism. 9-24 |
| | Rosebud, Poplar | 50 | | | left Bism. 10-9 |
| | Black Hills, Poplar | 50 | | | left Bism. 10-12 |
| | Eclipse, Poplar | 50 | | | left Bism. 10-15 |
| | Helena, Cow I. | 100 | | | left Bism. 10-15 |

Big Horn snagged April 30, Butte burned July 31

Year end report:

| Line | Tons up | Down | Pass. |
|---|---|---|---|
| Power Block P | 5472 | 884 | 525 |
| Coulson Line | 3820 | 514 | 365 |
| Transient boats | 952 | 156 | 75 |
| Totals | 10244 | 1614 | 965 |

1686 tons government, 1545 of that upbound.
Power boats....Benton, Helena, Butte, Black Hills
Coulson.......Rosebud, Josephine, Dacotah, Big Horn
Transient......Eclipse, W. J. Behan, F. Y. Batchelor

### Portents Of Doom For A River Port

The January 2, 1884, holiday edition of the River Press included a map which summarized local dreams. From across the Dakota and Montana plains there was a rail line of the St. Paul, Minneapolis & Manitoba Railroad, along virtually the route it would follow in 1887. Joining it at the approximate location of later Havre was a Benton branch of the Canadian Pacific, coming from the Medicine Hat area. Up from Billings and skirting the west side of the Highwoods was the Benton branch of the Northern Pacific. The edition boasted that Fort Benton commerce was greater than any other place in Montana, local traffic via steamboat 8500 tons in 1883. There was more, of course, to now cut off markets in Canada and the Helena area. The map indicated a vast trade area, half way to Helena, south into Meagher county and the Judith Basin, west to the Rockies and east to the county line near Malta. Fort Benton's position as head of navigation would insure against excessive rail freight rates.

The editor had a differing omen in his ad columns. The extra pages carried a woodcut of W. Scott Wetzel's fine and large brick mansion, financed by success in the Indian trade on both sides of the border at great individual risk to him, his former partner J. D. Weatherwax, and employes. The Wetzel firm was a success story of what a man of limited financial resources could accomplish. The firm, the Press had reported previously, had an indicated business of $250,000 in 1882. That figure seems confirmed by an incomplete Wetzel invoice book of the year 1881 showing $80,000 plus in wholesale purchases from eastern manufacturers. Adding local wares and freight (like Power and Baker the firm handled literally every item desired) and freight bills, the reported $150,000 in 1881 sales may have been more. But in December 1883 the large Wetzel ad in the River Press had quietly disappeared. December 12 a "cash sale" ad appeared for until January 1st. No comment found in news columns. It was not until January 16, 1884, that another ad appeared offering Wetzel stock at close-out prices, David G. Browne, former Wetzel bookkeeper, as assignee in a re-opened Wetzel store. Creditors had closed in. At Scott Wetzel's death in 1891 W. K. Harber explained his financial disaster was due to his "faith and trust in his fellow man." Too many unpaid bills. The failure was a shocker to Bentonites. There would be more.

Paris Gibson, who came from Minnesota's Twin Cities in 1879, operated a short lived lumber yard and then turned to sheep, start in the latter probably on shares with Henry Macdonald, first viewed the Great Falls area in 1880, saw possibilities of hydroelectric power, had with H. P. Rolfe of Benton surveyed in 1883 the townsite of a city at the mouth of Sun River. Gibson made a trip to Minnesota to interest an acquaintance, James J. Hill, railroad man, in the possibilities. Townsiting could be a quick route to wealth or ruin in those days but Gibson had made a good choice. Hill was interested and backed the project. From March 1884 the new townsite was the scene of considerable activity. The pioneer group included a number of Fort Benton men and by year end Gibson reckoned the population of new Great Falls at about 200, probably mostly from the only nearby settled points, Fort Benton and Sun River. James J. Hill visited the site in June and eventually provided most of the financial backing. A big ad appeared in the July 16 River Press for the Great Falls Townsite Co. It probably paid the promoters, with a drop in long distance freighting there were many unemployed teamsters and others dependent on them around Fort Benton. The author estimates that possibly as many as 800 of the 1000 population Fort Benton lost between 1880 and 1890 moved to Great Falls. At the time, the new settlement drew the customary story in the Press and was welcomed by Benton merchants as a new customer. Until the railroad came in October 1887 the place was supplied by Fort Benton wagons.

Farming was growing in the area, chiefly in the Highwood foothills. In a report on 1883, Wheeler Dexter threshed 2200 bushels of wheat, 126 of barley and 94,211 of oats, indicating their stock growing customers. About 212,000 bushels were threshed by others. In earlier years farmers like Joe Cobell on the Shonkin side had raised potatoes, onions and other vegetables for Fort Benton markets.

There were still handy guns and frontier troubles. February 27, 1884, William Jones, rider for the Shonkin Stock Association, was killed on Arrow Creek. The story in the River Press was that Jones and William Gilham surprised Bloods butchering a steer and in the gun fight that ensued Jones was killed. It is also possible the killers were white rustlers and this was the opening gun in a rangeland war that brought death to an untotaled number of loose loop characters along the Musselshell area by gun or rope that summer. Veiled references in Shonkin Association minutes indicate the Chouteau county group was represented, but chief participants from the ranchmen were cowboys headed by Granville Stuart, the only one to publicly announce participation, so the rangeland Vigilantes go down in Montana informal history as Stuart's Stranglers. In one case, two who had avoided the informal posse added grim zest to Lewistown's first Fourth of July when Rattlesnake Jake and Long Haired Owen "took on" the infant village and when the bullets had settled Rattlesnake and Owen were dead of nine and eleven bullet holes.

Although the Fort Benton bottom had sustained mild overflows of the Missouri a couple of previous years, there was more damage when a February 24 ice gorge put water over the banks and caused about $20,000 loss in flour and similar items in warehouses along the levee. One ferry boat was swept away and wrecked.

Canadians got a steamboating urge in 1884, Galt Coal Mining Co. building or buying small boats to take their coal to Canadian Pacific at Medicine Hat. Pilots were the Todd brothers, John, Nelson and Wesley, right off the Bismarck to Benton run. The Oldman and South Saskatchewan proved to be virtually unnavigable and this navigation effort failed.

Navigation season to Fort Benton extended into August but it occasioned relatively little attention in the River Press (the Record, in financial trouble, issued only a few papers), Bentonites had probably grown blase about steamboats. First was the Helena on May 6, only 149 tons here but surely more, say 200, at points below, a dozen passengers, and 90 tons down. This year down tonnage was better reported in the paper, and surprisingly large until one notes that 400 tons of wool were shipped by river in 1884, and some cattle, there were still shipments of ore from Barker, although some of the three categories went south to the NP. Also, there was a gold stampede to the Little Rockies drawing about 2,000 miners, so Rocky Point near Cow Island had a thriving business.

Coulson boats Josephine, F. Y. Batchelor and Rosebud followed the 13th, 16th and 21st, hitting high water and bringing about 800 tons between them, 62 passengers, down judging from the Batchelor about 270 tons. It was apparent that steamboat arrivals would be down, but probably not that incoming tonnage total would be only about a third that of 1883. Benton and Helena arrived for Power May 27 and 28 and nearly 600 tons, 50 passengers. In June the Batchelor arrived the 9th and 27th, 300 tons each time, the first with 52 army recruits, one of them was left behind at a wooding place, fate unknown. The second trip the Batchelor carried down 250 tons, the heaviest down cargo ever, though far from the most valuable. Helena came June 13 and Benton 23, the Benton carrying about 120 soldiers plus 20 passengers.

July found the Helena and Batchelor arriving on the 19th carrying about the same rather large tonnages, 249 and 275, the Benton finishing the month the 27th. Batchelor on August 2 came in with a big 310 tons, that is after a double trip to Dauphin's Rapids for the rest of cargo. That made it 15 arrivals, being 3821 tons with way freight probably boosting it to 4000. The exports, which could be closely estimated from the paper, about 1500 tons. Incoming passengers around 450, down about a third as many.

There was a last flicker of steamboating in October when the Benton was sent out for Rocky Point (those miners in the Little Rockies probably hungry) with an estimated 100 tons, but the boat ran into unmentioned woes and the Helena finished the trip in late October. Engineers did some more work on the rapids below Fort Benton in 1884, there had been $125,000 appropriated for river work Sioux City-Fort Benton. One of the captains complained that high water had wrecked the job done on Dauphin's Rapids, making it a worse obstacle than ever. At any rate, there would be extensive improvement work in years to come, now that use of the Bismarck-Benton stretch was ending.

Depressing events around town: The Benton Record went broke in its 10th year; Benton Townsite Co. to include 450 acres across the river was still-born; Kleinschmidt & Bro. March 19 notice the concern was withdrawing from Fort Benton, its freighting had meant about eight more boats a year; biggest jolt, sheriff's sale in May of Grand Union, the hotel would have a number of optimists take on the challenge; W. H. Burgess, grocer, goes broke in May.

An October 1884 Sanborn insurance map bears out the Fort Benton depression on Front (Fort Benton's main street and mostly one side only): Kleinschmidt concrete vacant, log warehouse and across the street, a dwelling, Davidson & Moffitt brick and bakery beside vacant; next block only one small vacant building, but nearly every other one in the block below also vacant or about to be; the block below the old bridge, once the center of riotous night life, seven spaces vacant—Fort Benton was getting short on saloons. All this in a town of probably 2,000 or more two years before, busting at the seams, where a business space was something to negotiate for and a roof over one's head a blessed thing. The closing of saloons and small shops went virtually unnoticed, then as now newspapers tended to overlook such items.

The Piegan starvation winter of 1883-84 had gone almost unremarked in area papers, despite the fact that quite possibly 600 died and although limited steps were taken toward relief that spring. Starvation rations continued, alleviated somewhat by hunters of small game. By spring 1884 the Indians were desperate and a July 9 River Press said there was "alarm at the Piegan agency over starving Indians, growing desperate, terrible suffering." An August editorial spoke out on humanity to 3,000 starving Piegans. It wasn't altogether altruistic, hungry Indians were killing cattle near the reservation. Army surplus rations would be issued, said a September 24 Press. Evidently this was done, November 26 the paper said Piegans were starving last winter, now full of food with nothing to do but steal.

Fort Benton's school was completed during the year, quadrupling the space available, first use in December, and the Chouteau county court was also completed and accepted by the commissioners in September. A building for a Sisters' hospital was completed during the summer, although Sisters would not be assigned to it for another two years. Fort Benton merchants were still looking ahead, a flour mill was being planned, and initial steps taken to build a bridge across the Missouri which materialized in 1888 as a toll bridge, intended to tap that growing wool production to the south.

Steamboat arrivals in 1884:

| Date | Steamboat | tons | down | pass. | notes |
|---|---|---|---|---|---|
| May 6 | Helena | 200 | 90 | 12 | |
| May 13 | Josephine | 250 | 90 | 32 | |
| May 16 | F. Y. Batchelor | 300 | 100 | 4 | |
| May 21 | Rosebud | 250 | 80 | 26 | |
| May 27 | Benton | 300 | 100 | 45 | |
| May 28 | Helena | 287 | 110 | 10 | |
| June 9 | F. Y. Batchelor | 300 | 100 | 52 | army recruits |
| June 13 | Helena | 300 | 100 | 12 | |
| June 23 | Benton | 250 | 150 | 180 | 160 soldiers |
| June 27 | F. Y. Batchelor | 300 | 250 | 12 | largest down cargo |
| July 19 | Helena | 249 | 100 | 14 | |
| July 19 | F. Y. Batchelor | 275 | 138 | 17 | |
| July 27 | Benton | 250 | 50 | 7 | 12 pass. down |
| Aug. 2 | Batchelor | 310 | - | 12 | |
| Aug. 8 | " from Dauphin's | | 50 | | |
| | Totals | 3821 | 1508 | 435 | 150 down |

Oct. 15 Benton on way to Rocky Point, Helena took in her cargo there. Other way freight would bring total to about 4200 tons. 400 tons wool down.

## Fort Benton's Decline Continued In 1885

Fort Benton's decline in importance to the Territory continued in 1885, although the town showed considerable resilence in the face of adversity. The new settlement of Great Falls was growing and drawing numbers of Bentonites, the more important duly recorded in the only newspaper. The Benton Record had gone under, its fine plant to be moved to a warehouse in preparation for a sheriff's sale. The River Press was now in quite comfortable quarters on Main Street, the lower floor of the Odd Fellows hall and beside the new furniture store of F. C.

Roosevelt. Its January 14 issue noted that A. J. Samuel paid $1400 for perhaps the best printing plant in Montana, "maybe a white elephant." The buyer had a pretty quick turnover, however, the River Press being burned out in early July (along with the Roosevelt store,) and bought the plant. W. H. Buck of the Benton Record took one more whirl at Montana newspapering, salvaging the badly fire damaged news press and starting the Choteau Calumet, which succumbed in a couple of years.

Merchants, notably the Power and Baker firms, had large investments in Fort Benton and continued efforts at salvage. The city found funds to pay Sam Johnstone for digging drainage ditches—heavy rains often created problems on the bottom. By contributions a building for a Sisters hospital was completed—first opened as St. Clare in 1886, it was a first in northern Montana.

Although no longer freighting from Fort Benton, the Power and Baker firms continued to operate Canadian stores, shipping by Canadian Pacific—both eventually sold out these stores, the Baker Co. in 1891, the same year they abandoned the Fort Benton store. Up in Canada, Wm. G. Conrad, manager, recalled that a Hudson Bay director drank a gleeful toast to the end of a firm that had "scaled our stock from pounds to shillings," on completion of that sale. Area ties with Canada continued strong, in 1885 Chouteau county growers from a small part of later range area shipped 10,400 cattle east over the Canadian Pacific; at that time the Indians owned the land north of Marias and Missouri save for the Fort Assiniboine military reservation. In November the Conrad Circle outfit trailed 5000 cattle north across the line, probably with a dual purpose, to fill Canadian government contracts and to augment what became their "Canadian herd." The eastern beef market was depressingly low, slightly over $4 a hundred that fall.

Residents were still avidly reading about proposals for a railroad branch to Fort Benton, the visit of a CP chief engineer was a well heralded event. As to the upstart village of Great Falls that was draining its population, Bentonites still looked upon the new settlement as a captive client, anything not locally made or grown came either from steamboats or at greater expense via express from the Northern Pacific. However, the River Press had sharp words about failure of Fort Benton citizens to raise the money for a flour mill when Great Falls was already building one.

An event across the border which drew attention of citizens was the Riel Rebellion, first note found was in the April 1 issue, "assuming large proportions." Louis Riel, who had led an abortive uprising of the half blood Metis in Manitoba in 1869, had been teaching at St. Peter's Mission near Cascade the previous year. Riel had for several years been in employ of the T. C. Power firm at Carroll and was well known in Fort Benton. He had been naturalized as a U. S. citizen in 1883 but returned to Canada when Gabriel Dumont, Michel Dumais and two others rode in to summon Riel to lead them again. Delay in recognition of rights to the lands on which they squatted led to the rebellion. Many families of these Metis crossed the border into Montana, a large number to the site of later Lewistown, and their descendants by hundreds still live in northern Montana. Naturally, the Mounted Police were first to attempt to quell the rising. Apparently John J. Donnelly, Fort Benton attorney and one time Fenian firebrand, was advisor to Riel. After the Mounties failed, Canadian troops were called in, incidently giving the quiescent Canadian Pacific later government help in completing their line to the Pacific. Under leadership of Dumont, a first class fighting man and brilliant military strategist, the Metis, few in numbers, sadly embarrassed the military before they were crushed by overwhelming force at Batoche. Riel surrendered, was hanged for treason at Regina in November. Gabriel Dumont, Michel Dumais and others easily escaped to Montana, the object of great interest and considerable support. Dumont resided in the Bear Paw country for several years, at one time was a prime attraction in Buffalo Bill's Wild West show on a European tour. But when Cody scheduled a British appearance, Dumont made his own way home—his treason warrant still held. In 1970 Canadians issued a Louis Riel stamp, in 1985 another for Dumont.

First nautical note of 1885 was a strange one in April. Mike Lynch, ferry operator, had gathered about 50,000 Anheuser beer bottles, "a good estimate of Fort Benton capacity" noted the River Press, built two boats he named Juno and Mars to tote them and planned to float same down to St. Louis, value about $2,500, from which Mike expected to net $1,500. A June report was that one of the boats had been wrecked at Dauphin's Rapids, perhaps erroneous, as the Helena reported meeting Lynch and his boats at the Muddy—but no report found on success or failure of an interesting project.

The F. Y. Batchelor was the first boat to Fort Benton on May 7 with about 300 tons and only three passengers, although the boat left Bismarck with cabins full. Next issue of the Press brought news of the close of one of the most illustrious steamboating careers on the Missouri. John LaBarge, who brought the first boat, Chippewa, to Brule Bottom in 1859, dropped dead at the wheel of the Helena, dying as he would have doubtless preferred, enroute once more to the Mountains. Second arrival was unusual, the Josephine on May with barges in tow or scattered along the river to come later—500 tons of lumber and material for a 85x35 dredge for engineer improvement work on the Montana stretch of the Missouri. The government boat Josephine had a long and troubled trip from Sioux City, breaking a shaft near Bismarck and having to wait for repairs.

Next boat was the Helena on May 16, obviously delayed due to the sudden death of John LaBarge, with Benton and Batchelor both arriving the 24th, each about 300 tons—the Benton also dropped off 207 tons of military freight below. June arrivals included the Rosebud on 6th, Benton 17th and Helena 25th. The Rosebud, last boat of the once great Missouri River Transportation Co. (Coulson), had just been bought by the Power Block P, other boats were Benton, Helena and Batchelor. T. C. Power, through Isaac Post Baker, head of the Benton Transportation Co., now owned the final years of Upper Missouri River steamboating.

A gold strike in an area tributary to Fort Benton was bringing in a bit of gold; the Sweet Grass Hills placers were paying—the Little Rockies after an 1884 flurry were not much in the news, would be later when Pike Landusky, the Whitcombs and others located pay streaks. Meanwhile the Record building, which when demolished in 1983 would be oldest brick survivor of the steamboating boom, went at $6,000 at sheriff's sale, probably 35% of cost. In May the River Press welcomed the new Great Falls Tribune; on reflection noted "it looks very much like the former Sun River Sun." Fort Benton was making preparations for the coming wool marketing season, which would mean bulky down cargoes for river boats from early July. Murphy Maclay leased the old Kleinschmidt building, free storage pending sale of about one and a half million pounds—it was a happy reunion for sheepmen with price 20c a pound and heading up, ten years later the Press would comment on the great wool boom of '85 and prices.

Rosebud arrived July 3 and took down 50 tons of that wool and 150 tons of grain, almost as big as her upbound cargo. The Benton in June had down freight which would occupy many gatherers in the next few years, correctly termed "Bison bones."

Next day, as in bygone years, Joseph LaBarge set another bit of navigation history, bringing the tiny government boat Missouri in on the last through trip from St. Louis, fetching a Missouri survey party of 20 engineers. He too had been on the Missouri since boyhood and the LaBarge brothers probably logged more miles than did the Coulsons, Massies, Andersons or Todds. The Missouri had made a trip to Fort Benton in 1880 as the Minnie Heerman.

Boats going down were bulging with wool, the Helena came again July 18, the Batchelor the 26th and the Helena with remaining cargo from Rocky Point the 27th. The last boats had an obstacle, there had been a large slide at the Cracon du Nez bar just below Benton, about two feet of water after good depth into July—a job for the engineers and that dredge. After a couple of early August arrivals by Benton and Batchelor, the Bismarck Tribune reported 3,000 bales of wool on the last three boats, about 400 tons. Batchelor to Coal Banks September 6 and Benton to Poplar the 11th closed the 1885 season as far as commercial steamboating was concerned. The River Press mentioned one long time staple—buffalo robes had numbered in the thousands for many years, "now not 100 robes in a year." But about 4800 tons in the season and a thousand down.

Still in a single small page makeshift after its July 8 fire, the Press used much of the front page July 29 reporting the launching of the dredge, City of Fort Benton, on July 23. There was still machinery to install and test, engineers expected to get the dredge to work in September. It did some work before retiring for the winter. One piece was building a small wing dam (wiped out by ice next spring) opposite the old fort to narrow and deepen the channel across the old ford used from fur trade days on. City of Fort Benton was put up on the bank by ice the next spring; it was used two or three seasons for river improvement work. The dredge burned near Eagle Creek in August 1892, a boiler grate salvaged by Raymond Gray was embedded at front of Fort Benton's museum.

For cattlemen, the fall of 1885 brought devastating range fires, which may have been the reason for stock movements to other ranges as that of the Circle to Canada. Another River Press item of October 28 reports 6,395 head shipped on the Canadian Pacific at Maple Creek, with owners—that after the market had slumped. At year end it cost $20 for the 46 hour trip on the Benton to Billings stage. Wheeler Dexter, long Fort Benton's handy man, built a 17x69 ferry at Great Falls, and established an express line from Great Falls to Fort Benton via Sun River.

There were outcroppings of violence in a taming land. Pres. Lewis and freighting party up around the border had a shooting affray, plenty of bullets, no hits, with Bloods, who cut out the mule herd and one horse; in frustration the Bloods then fought other Indians, most likely Crees, who happened along. A week or so later Henry Neihoff had a scrap with three Indians who were eyeing his 75 horse herd, 25 shots fired, again no casualties. It was a good thing the chaps who victimized Jack Harris were not in on the fights. For Thanksgiving Harris set up a turkey shoot, lost the gobbler first shot, then a rooster also going on one shot. His loss $3.10. Harris was game, he tried it again for Christmas. Charley Rowe needed two tries at 25c each for a $3 bird.

In the last months of 1885 numbers of Metis families were slipping across the border, including Gabriel Dumont's family; not so fortunate were 137 Crees who had been in the North West Rebellion, nabbed by Fort Assiniboine soldiers and held for higher ups.

Steamboat arrivals in 1885:

| Date | Steamboat | tons | down | pass. | notes |
|---|---|---|---|---|---|
| May 7 | F. Y. Batchelor | 300 | | 20 | |
| May 12 | Josephine | 500 | | | For dredge boat |
| May 16 | Helena | 300 | | | |
| May 24 | Benton | 507 | | | 207 tons military |
| May 24 | Batchelor | 300 | | | |
| June 6 | Rosebud | 275 | | | |
| June 17 | Benton | 300 | | | bison bones down |
| June 25 | Helena | 315 | 100 | 13 | |
| July 3 | Rosebud | 250 | 200 | | |
| July 4 | Missouri | 200 | | 25 | once Minnie Heerman |
| July 6 | Josephine | 200 | | | rest of barges |
| July 18 | Helena | 200 | | | from Rocky Point |
| July 23 | City of Fort Benton | | | | govt. dredge launched |
| July 26 | Batchelor | 200 | | | much wool down |
| July 27 | Helena | 100 | | | rest of cargo |
| Aug. 1 | Benton | 256 | 135 | | |
| Aug. 8 | Batchelor | 150 | 135 | | |
| Aug. 14 | Josephine | | | | |
| Aug. 28 | Rosebud | 150 | 135 | | wool |
| Sept. 6 | Batchelor, Coal Banks | 150 | | | |
| Sept. 11 | Benton, Poplar | 150 | | | |
| | Totals............ | 4807 | 1000 | 200 | 150 pass. down |

# Final River Echoes

## "A Disagreeable Navigation Season" 1886

The year 1886 opened in Fort Benton with little cause for optimism, save that the River Press continued to publish rosy accounts of prospects as a railroad center, "Galt railroad extension assured," said one item. The town, which had lacked hotel facilities in early years, now had a surplus, Overland, Chouteau House, Pacific and Grand Union. So Lee Gee, moving into the Tom Cummings two story brick on Front wasn't blessed by hotel operators when he added the Enterprise House to his Chinese restaurant. Olden days were recalled, the 45 boats and 1200 passengers of 1878; and then the tale of Donald Fisher, who died in 1881 as merely "Drunken" Fisher in a Benton saloon. He would drink anything, was particularly fond of Jamaica ginger. Up at Fort Macleod in 1875 freighter Dick Smith tried to protect his private stock, locking the keg in a stout box, padlocked and chained it in a locked warehouse and left on his trip. Fisher armed himself with a double bitted axe and was into the booze before the Smith train dust had settled.

The Conrads of the Baker firm in January reported receipt of 185 ounces of gold worth $3,300 from their Macleod house, either could recall the days when store receipts of the yellow stuff equaled that on a slow day in autumn. The gold was from the Sweet Grass Hills placers and stood right up with the old $17-18 an ounce for Montana gold. The Baker firm was still operating the Montana part of the Benton-Macleod stage line and held the mail contract to Fort Conrad on the Marias, where an 1868 fort put the company on the high road to wealth. The Power firm's interests turned southward, it was low bidder on the mail route to Maiden. The Power steamboat line also had bought another boat, the former Northern Pacific Transfer No. 2, which had crossed thousands of freight cars before NP built a bridge at Bismarck, was renamed the Judith.

It had been a cold January, 1st to 24th, and 51 below the 21st. Naturally that meant heavy ice on the Missouri, when the chinook hit in mid-February townspeople worried about a heavy ice gorge above town, a recurring menace. This one went out quietly, but in passing the city by daylight broke loose one of the ferries, which ended a brief voyage against a barge behind the dredge City of Fort Benton, up on the bank for safety. To the relief of Mr. Hilton, in charge, the dredge wasn't damaged, although a picture shows it nearly surrounded by ice but safe. The wing dam across from the old fort went out with the ice.

Early in the year and throughout, for that matter, the local paper had much on the Montana Central Railroad. Overly optimistic, perhaps, the River Press seemed to expect that the road would be completed from Helena to Great Falls in 1886. Charles Broadwater, an early day freighter from Fort Benton, was in charge. Another freighter, Hugh Kirkendall, was a contractor. Actually, the Central was a subsidiary of James J. Hill's railroad, the St. Paul, Minneapolis & Manitoba, building west to Minot in 1886. In April the local paper noted that this effectively squelched Galt railroad plans from Canada, one more blow to Fort Benton planning. Preliminary work on the Montana Central went on through the year.

In March the Press noted that vast Chouteau county, about 150 by 300 miles, had only 12 postoffices, not nearly enough: Belknap, Belleview, Choteau, Christina, Conrad (Fort), Dupuyer, Fort Assinaboine, Fort Benton, Great Falls, Johnstown,

Judith, Piegan. Highwood was added a few weeks later, at Yank Smith's place, Joe Braithwaite P.M.

A note from the past: In May Abel Farwell died on Clark's Fork near Billings, and the River Press in an odd obit, "If deceased had any friends they are not in Fort Benton." Farwell ran a trading post in 1873, scene of the Cypress Hills massacre by wolfers of Assiniboines and credited with bringing the Mounted Police west. Farwell was a crown witness in an extradition hearing to take a number of Bentonites to Canada to stand trial. The paper said that when the papers were served on five in Fort Benton in 1875 a troop of cavalry surrounded the settlement to back up marshals Charles Hard and X. Beidler in making the arrests. Tourism note: A lengthy article extolled the grand scenery on the Missouri River below Fort Benton, a feature noted in many accounts.

Water was low and business slow on the river that spring. The Benton Line had added another boat, Eclipse, for no discernible reason. It was not until May 15 that the Rosebud came in, the Helena the 22nd and the Batchelor the 25th, about 700 tons on the three boats, said the paper. June brought only three more, Rosebud the 5th, Benton and Helena 17th with about the same total. There was a resurgence in July for a very plausible reason—wool. The Montana Woolgrowers met early in the month, headquarters the Grand Union, but all other hotels in town were full to bursting, and the wool was coming in, the roads were dusty from lofty if lightly loaded wagons from all the way down to White Sulphur Springs. By July 14 the River Press reported 3,000 tons on 11 boats.

Secretary Peck provided a list of shippers and amounts, 1,565,941 pounds in 5,461 sacks, slightly under 300 pounds each, went down on steamboats. Furthermore, wool growers were happy with prices of 22-24c per pound, a sharp contrast to the 1885 collapse of the beef market, which still stung. The differential probably turned many cattlemen to the lowly sheep, numbers of the woollies went up and up in years to come.

Incoming July boats didn't bring too much more cargo than the 750 tons to go down. Rosebud, Judith and Helena came the first week with about 600 tons, thereafter no boat approached 200 tons, but Rosebud and Benton brought in 450 in three trips, thereafter 100 tons was standard as the boats battled some of the lowest water the captains had ever seen, but successfully. In all nine July arrivals, two in August, other arrivals around the Judith, where some wool was being loaded. At season's end about 3000 tons up, 850 down and around 400 passengers both ways. The Bismarck Tribune saw it in dreary pattern for a town hit hard by loss of markets to the railroads: "Navigation is all ended after a disagreeable and discouraging season. Low water, two or three boats damaged." It had been much the same at the upper end of the boat route.

New Great Falls was drumming up recruits for its fledgling business district, in June Ben Lapeyre, Fort Benton druggist, was advertising in the Tribune as the city's first drug store—it endured for years. About the same time, Howell Harris was moving to Lethbridge—for years he would be manager of the Circle Cattle Co.'s "Canadian Herd," his brother Jack remained in Montana to manage the American side of a big livestock business.

August 4 the River Press announced the Sisters had arrived to take over the hospital which had been begun by public subscriptions in 1883. The three were Sister Mary of the Resurrection, Mary Wilfred and Anna Magnan of Sisters of Charity of Providence. They were in Fort Benton to begin a work that continued, with one complete rebuilding in 1959, until the close of 1974 when St. Clare Hospital was succeeded by a district hospital. The three Sisters of 1886 found the 86x54 brick building had been used as a granary, hence had to shovel out the debris, but with help of townspeople had the place open for patients by August 11. It might have been regarded as an omen when the first patient, Tennessean C. E. McCutcheon died, probably of tick fever. However, St. Clare drew patients from as far away as Medicine Hat, after coming of the railroad in 1887 from all across Northern Montana.

There were still touches of the frontier to be noted. A bizarre affair was an Indian raid on the nearby Marias River cabin of rancher Fred LaBarre and Matt Bruneau, the whites responded to rifle shots, then sent a squaw posthaste to Benton for 600 more rounds—in all lots of shooting, no claims of hits. Even more prodigal were the cowhands at Dupuyer who ran Julian Burd out of his own saloon. Next morning after a riotous night, 200 bullet holes were counted in the saloon and 50 more in an adjacent store. The period was the start of Jacob Harris' wild reputation, too. Regarded here as a "peaceful citizen", gambler Jew Jake emigrated to Great Falls, was in one scrape after another, got his man in one, lost a leg in a memorable shootout at the Great Falls rail station, in 1894 was using a Winchester for a crutch in his Landusky saloon when Kid Curry killed Pike Landusky. Perhaps Jake had just felt repressed in Benton. John J. Healy, one of the more noted Fort Benton freebooters, had found the place too tame and was up in Alaska, where he would figure even more prominently on another frontier.

Fast horses were a tradition on the frontier of Whoop-Up country, and old timers heartily approved the horse ranch Dan Blevins was operating out at Highwood. In November he was back home from a swing down through Butte, Helena, Belleview in Idaho, and Salt Lake—his Daniel B and Ida Glenn ran 21 times, 15 firsts, 5 seconds and one no show. There was something about a horse race—first Fort Benton sporting event, aside from pistols for two, was an 1868 match for $250 or so a side.

The late summer and fall of 1886 brought a number of bad range fires, and there may have been a premonition, an August River Press noted "much hay being put up, a hard winter anticipated by some." Wolves were a greater nuisance than ever, a natural result of the slaughter of buffalo on which they had depended for food. Winter and severe weather arrived early, by mid-December the paper felt the fuel problem "is again serious this year." It was to be even worse than that.

Fort Benton steamboat arrivals in 1886:

| Date | Steamboat | tons | down | pass. | notes |
| --- | --- | --- | --- | --- | --- |
| May 15 | Rosebud | 250 | | 15 | |
| May 22 | Helena | 260 | 70 | 22 | 3 pass down |
| May 25 | F. Y. Batchelor | 260 | | | |
| June 5 | Rosebud | 250 | | | |
| June 14 | Benton | 425 | 200 | 13 | |
| June 14 | Helena | 300 | 200 | | |
| July 2 | Rosebud | 300 | 70 | 5 | |
| July 6 | Judith | 250 | | | |
| July 8 | Helena | 300 | | | |
| July 10 | Rosebud | 150 | 105 | | wool down |
| July 14 | Benton | 250 | 150 | | |
| July 19 | Rosebud, Marias | 150 | | | |
| July 25 | F. Y. Batchelor, Marias | 100 | 70 | | 450 sacks wool |

| Date | Steamboat | tons | down | pass. | notes |
|------|-----------|------|------|-------|-------|
| July 25 | Helena, Cow I. | 100 | | | |
| Aug. — | Eclipse, Marias | 150 | | | |
| Aug. 11 | Judith, Cow I. | 100 | | | |
| Aug. 18 | Rosebud, Judith | 100 | | | |
| | Totals | 3745 | 865 | 300 | 100 pass. |

Helena, Batchelor also reported in Cow Island vicinity in August, which would increase tonnage about 200 tons. Wool down amounted to nearly 800 tons, passengers estimated. Newspaper sources short this season, most loads estimated.

### 1887—Curtain Call For The Mountain Steamboats

With a few minor exceptions, 1887 was the final year for Montana steamboating, and the end of Fort Benton's importance, although traces of the one time commerce lingered into the next century. It was curtain call for the Mountain steamboats, which played a substantial role in completion of their final nemesis, the St. Paul, Minneapolis & Manitoba Railroad, known in those early years to Montanans as the Manitoba.

There was far more than that to interest Bentonites, the breakup of a winter the like of which many had never seen, and a revival of freighting reminiscent of the palmy days of the late 1870s and early 1880s. In addition, knowledgeable Fort Benton merchants planned to cope with the changes the railroad would bring.

First there was that wild winter and tragic stock losses. January 19 the River Press reported snow two feet deep on the level and six freight outfits snowed in out south at Harwood Lake. That issue a comment summed up the local situation: "Only 100 sacks of flour in town, coal oil $6 a case, fuel short—Fort Benton is in a bad fix." Two weeks later the paper headlined a bad storm, intense cold and unprecedented wind whipping the white stuff into drifts. (A contributing factor to the memorable winter had been a December chinook which partially melted the snow over wide areas, then froze up, leaving a crust through which usually self reliant beasts could not paw to grass below.) In Fort Benton the fuel was so short that Tom Cummings had the old log jail he had bought in 1881 sawed up for firewood. Another note, $60 was offered for a ton of coal, and refused. A month before coal, $3.75 at the mine at Belt, sold for $27.50—the refusal indicated the seriousness of the situation. Matters went from bad to worse out on the snowbound ranges. February 9 the Press reported five feet of snow since November 1st, then another inch Sunday. Thermometers weren't any consolation, after checking the best in town January 26, the concensus had been "it might have been 60 below that night." Saturday, February 16, one of the worst blizzards of the season hit the area. John F. Patterson and two men stayed with their band of sheep for three days and nights, and brought their woollies through o.k. Range cattle had no human nursemaids. Reports began to drift in from the great white wastes. The Press called the range outlook "woeful—frightful losses in the Choteau area." There it was so cold the quip ran, they sold whisky by the square inch. Snowfall and temperatures from Fort Assiniboine helped establish that point's chill record before there was a Havre.

The winter broke February 26 in a whistling, chilling gust that ended the grip of ice and snow and metamorphised that into gulley washing torrents. Next Wednesday the River Press reported the chinook had been blowing since Saturday, and naturally there was flooding everywhere. The Teton and other streams went on a rampage. A tremendous Missouri ice gorge threatened, but did no damage at Fort Benton. When the breakup reached Bismarck it created havoc, but the reassuring word came up river that the steamboats were safe. Just as well—their loss might have slowed Jim Hill's epic rush westward.

Stockmen and townspeople only tardily could assess their losses. These were probably not as bad as on the bitter plains of eastern Montana, but John Lepley, one of the larger of the Shonkin range cattlemen, suffered a loss reckoned later at $100,000. John Green brought a robe to Fort Benton which had cost him $761.15, the tanned skin of the last of 11 Polled Angus bulls, all casualties of the winter. "Pilgrim," or new cattle were virtually wiped out. By the end of March for Blackfeet on the reservation, there was a silver lining, the Indians had lived well on winter killed meat after starvation years, and were skinning dead animals for 75c a hide. Naturally, beef hides were coming in to Fort Benton in quantities reminiscent of the buffalo trade. Evidence that other ranges had suffered even more, numerous great grey wolves were drifting onto local ranges, a discouraging peril to what calf crop there was. So costly was the wolf menace that cattle outfits such as the great Circle were buying staghounds, which acquitted themselves well in running down and dispatching the lobos.

One sketch on the lid of a collar box by Charles M. Russell that he titled "Waiting for a Chinook and Nothing Else," catapulted the artist into state wide fame. Probably more commonly "Last of 5,000" it was made down in the Judith Basin. A copy was on display in Fort Benton by the first of April. Another then more noted Montanan, Granville Stuart, surveying his DHS losses, said "I never wanted to own again an animal that I could not feed and shelter." Yet Stuart noted that his stock had survived an 1880-81 winter he felt was more severe. That year ranges were not overstocked as in 86-87, cattle were acclimated to winters and found shelter in creek bottoms and draws, drifting in the storms. In 1886-87 the animals were stopped by fences and died there. At any rate, it was the effective end of the open range and free grass. Of the 100,000 pilgrim cattle driven onto Montana ranges that summer, few survived. Other sheepmen besides the Pattersons managed to bring their flocks through. Henry Macdonald, a pioneer of the industry in the Arrow Creek area, reported only average sheep losses—their wool the saving factor.

First navigation note came in early April, the fast, reliable F. Y. Batchelor was to haul material for the Hill railroad—following the old American Fur Trail Alexander Culbertson had blazed in 1851, as had Isaac Stevens in 1853 and James Fisk and others. Out of Minot as the snow cleared, James J. Hill with 10,000 workmen was extending the Manitoba—past Fort Assiniboine, Fort Benton and to Great Falls to connect with the Manitoba subsidiary Montana Central, begun the previous year. Military men of Civil War and wars to come could well have studied the building of this road and the extreme success of the railroad logistics. For example, railroad ties, a necessity. Contractors were secured for 50,000 down the Dearborn, 250,000 down the Sun, 150,000 down the Teton—and just like clockwork as the steel moved westward, the ties arrived as needed. Perhaps no wonder, old time freighters took a hand (although freight outfits were short at times at Benton that season), among them Charles Broadwater and Hugh Kirkendall. As the Manitoba drove west, grade was 100 miles ahead of steel much of the way —though August 16 trackmen laid 8 miles and 60 feet near later Malta, a rail record. It was about 500 miles from Minot to Fort Benton, across former Indian country—no land grant, the Manitoba bought its right of way and bridging that gap was a source of pride to that generation of railroaders.

The Benton Transportation Co. (Block P) had five electric lighted steamboats that spring, I. P. Baker's packets were ready for a season's work and their last great effort. Some of the boats were busy on the short hauls into Montana to supply the Manitoba, but the Rosebud came to Benton April 26, by a day the earliest ever, the Helena followed April 30 and the Rosebud back again from Rocky Point with last season's late freight May 3. Despite low water following the snow runoff three more arrivals made it 1500 tons on six boats to Benton, and then the June rains began. They kept coming, June 22 there were floods everywhere in the area, the Helena coach was two days late to Benton, Fort Assiniboine mail was slow over terrible roads, Shonkin creek highest local people had ever seen, the Missouri bank full and a bit of slopover, the Marias out of its banks.

The Helena on its first arrival in place of river chanties and coonjine songs, its roosters provided a concert of good old church hymns, a repertoire repeated on later trips, making those something of an event. But Captain Joe Todd's Rosebud crew May 22nd provided an experience Bentonites would not soon forget. On the down trip the roustabouts struck at Fort Berthold, an Indian agency, thinking there was no chance of strike breakers. Instead of ceding the point and extra pay, Todd went ashore, came back with a crew of Gros Ventres, Rees and Mandans and took off up river. It was their first try at such work, and they soon reproved the mate for scolding them, saying their mothers never did, so he shouldn't. For the mate it was an experience in toting the first bale, rolling the first barrel, carrying off the first sack of wheat, to demonstrate how it was done. Then too the Indian roosters demanded the right to rest now and then, smoke the pipe with the mate. Said the River Press, "Captain Todd's novel crew...have covered themselves with bacon grease, dirt and glory on their trip...have worked remarkably well considering that this is their first experience." Then, "As the Rosebud left port last night for Bismarck, her Indian crew poured out their souls in song to which five or six of them industriously kept time on old tin cans. The immediate effect of this rare musical treat was to set all the dogs in town howling; cats flew to shelter with their back hair all out of shape; the small boys yelled with delight while their elders endured the harrowing affliction with that fortitude and resignation becoming maturer years."

The boats kept coming, in June the General Terry, Benton, Eclipse, Rosebud, Helena; in July Judith, Rosebud, Helena, even the government boats Josephine and Missouri. The River Press on occasion mentioned the freighting business, cargoes unloaded and going out as in the early 1880s. In July there was excellent reason for another flurry of action, wool. The Woolgrowers met with every hotel room in town taken, wool coming in by trains—two million pounds expected so every warehouse was full until the boats could move the thousand bulky tons of it. Fort Benton took time out for a Fourth of July celebration, 38 gun salute in the morning plus an extra for the soon to be State of Montana, parade with the 20th Infantry band playing, horse racing of course, shooting, no mention of baseball.

Sweet Grass gold was coming in well, the Power store received $5,000 worth during May, then a batch of half as much a few weeks later. As mentioned earlier, wolves were a problem for stockmen; the territory recognized this and had passed a bounty law with a financial limit. Only thing, some joker had added prairie dogs at 10c and gophers at 5c, with results not regarded as humorous. For example, a ne'er do well former guide Joe Mulligan brought in 180 prairie dog skins—that $18 with drinks a bit each probably put him in the drunk tank. It was no joke with the ranges gray with the predators, Fergus county paid out $675 one month, one wolf skin, the rest dogs and gophers. The little animals broke the bounty fund of $60,000 with 1600 wolves, 2500 coyotes and near a million midget pests.

The Manitoba steel entered Montana at Fort Buford July 6, graders were nearing later Chinook at the time. The Batchelor about the same time brought 200 tons of oats for the railroad; local men had contracts for about 2,000 tons of hay. Much of that undoubtedly was cut on the hay meadows near Big Sandy Creek, where one day soon 2500 men would suddenly appear with as many horses, graders and equipment. Northern Montana watched the progress from July on with interest. Sometimes with admiration, too, Jack Harris, Fort Benton stockman, on a visit to end of steel had supper in the railroad mess car, awoke the next morning to find the car two miles down track from his tent. D. G. Browne July 13 reported graders stretched from Belknap (Chinook) to Sandy Creek. By August 17 end of track was within 100 miles of Fort Assiniboine, at month end the long time freight camp at Coal Banks was abandoned and soldiers returned to the fort.

Manitoba track September 6 was 12 miles south of Assiniboine, while 12 pile drivers were at the Marias for a bridge. Just a minor contract, Murphy Maclay bought a million pounds of grain locally to sell to the railroad contractors. The railroad reached Fort Benton, or rather a depot two miles out on the flat on September 28, ending the reason for being of the Mountain steamboats which had so impacted the Montana supply system for three decades. So efficient was the Hill organization, that the first local freight rolled in on October 5, a stockyard was built and first major stock shipments headed eastward by rail from Benton by the first of November.

In Fort Benton the advent of Hill's railroad left two enduring legends. One had it that James J. Hill said he would make grass grow in the streets of the town. He didn't, but Paris Gibson, who went to found Great Falls, did say he "would see grass growing in the streets" after unsuccessfully trying to buy an acreage in Benton for Hill. The second concerns the July 30 visit of Hill and party to Fort Benton during which he assured local people that the rail station would, as soon as practicable, be moved to a lower point and within the city limits (done in 1900) and that the Manitoba would donate transportation of materials for a bridge across the river, and make concessions on freight for a city water plant—both done. But the accompanying story goes that Hill expected a tough reception from the people of a river town, and had sent a man ahead to arrange for horses and carriage. Fort Bentonites tied up all available transportation to force Hill to attend a public meeting before going on to Great Falls. This story appears factual from available sources and was incorporated in a 1954 local pageant. Another related story almost certainly factual is that Mrs. James J. Hill on September 28, 1887, drove the silver spike that commemorated completion of the railroad to Fort Benton, forever ending the city's importance as a transportation center. That spike, then presented to Jere Sullivan, mayor, is incorporated in a railroad display in the Fort Benton museum. Unfortunately, the October 5 issue of the paper which would have carried the account is missing from the files, hence cannot be quoted.

## Fort Benton WAS Looking To Its Future

Fort Benton merchants were not unaware of the changes the advent of the Manitoba would bring, and were planning for the future of a city most still expected to grow and prosper. Press files of 1887 contain news of their efforts. June 29 a long item reported planning for a bridge across the Missouri to help hold firm to that wool traffic—by rail instead of by boat—Wm. G. Conrad, partner in the Baker Co. heading the committee; James J. Hill had already promised to transport bridge steel free of charge. It of course was good business for the railroad in the long run, and the bridge did contribute to Fort Benton's holding a large share of the Judith Basin trade for years. By October $25,000, half the estimated cost, had been pledged and there was no doubt that the expense would be met. The city, which only in the decade had gotten into the brick building stage, had only incorporated five years before, was looking ahead to civilized conveniences. George F. Woolston of Helena was granted a 20 year franchise for a water plant in July. First sizeable shipment over the Manitoba was in mid-October, 169 tons of material for water works and mains at the depot, five cars unloading and three more on the track, and a week later Woolston had 30 men digging ditches for water mains ahead of cold weather, by November he was ready to start building the brick water works and tower. Meanwhile, he had another proposal for electric lights, a brush arc lighting system, and an afternoon of canvassing by Wm. Conrad and John Power was enough to guarantee the cost of that as well. As early as 1879 O. C. Mortson had done some experimental work with electricity, although most residents saw their first lights on the Rosebud in 1882; to residents, it was a desirable addition. At year end neither project was quite ready, the progressiveness of Fort Benton would startle the territory next year. Meanwhile, there was a beginning to a running feud that never became completely quiescent—the River Press repeatedly complained about frightful mail service, charging mail was being deliberately held up in Great Falls, presumably to give that fledgling but growing city a jump on the old river port which had supplied it in infancy.

The railroad, completed to Sun River and Great Falls in early October, connected to the Montana Central and when the last work to open the line was done a delegation of 25 Bentonites joined the special train to Helena to celebrate the capital's second rail connection. By that time the bridge fund was only about $4,000 short of the amount needed, the solicitors breezed to a quick windup, and December 14 the "town is full of bridge engineers," reported the Press. The contract was let early in January 1888 for what would be the major event in Fort Benton that year.

Steamboat cargoes in 1887:

| Date | Steamboat | tons | down | notes |
| --- | --- | --- | --- | --- |
| April 26 | Rosebud | 300 | | |
| April 30 | Helena | 200 | | Low water early season |
| May 3 | Rosebud | 200 | | Freight of '86 from Rocky Pt. |
| May 22 | Rosebud | 330 | | Trip of disabled Judith |
| May 28 | Helena | 357 | | |
| June 1 | Judith | 200 | 50 | |
| June 2 | General Terry | 230 | | |
| June 10 | Benton | 400 | | |
| June 16 | Eclipse | 300 | | 1st trip sunk, raised |
| June 16 | Rosebud | 260 | | |
| June 19 | Helena | 300 | | Missouri in flood stage |
| June 23 | General Terry | 200 | | Oats for railroad |
| July 1 | Judith | 300 | | |
| July 3 | Josephine | 150 | | Dredge timbers |
| July 6 | Rosebud | 250 | | 50 soldiers up |
| July 6 | Benton | 400 | 217 | Wool |
| July 12 | Josephine | | | |
| July 14 | F. Y. Batchelor | 300 | | Part 450 tons rr. oats |
| July 17 | General Terry | 200 | 100 | Wool down |

| Date | Steamboat | tons | down | notes |
|---|---|---|---|---|
| July 19 | Helena | 375 | 50 | |
| July 27 | General Terry | 200 | | |
| July 31 | F. Y. Batchelor | 200 | | |
| Aug. 2 | Eclipse | 100 | | With Missouri's cargo |
| Aug. 9 | Helena | 250 | | |
| Aug. 9 | Eclipse | 100 | 60 | |
| Aug. 11 | Missouri | 100 | | Shuttle, Coal Banks-FB |
| Aug. 15 | Judith | 100 | | |
| Aug. 16 | F. Y. Batchelor | 100 | | |
| Aug. 18 | Missouri | 50 | 45 | 300 sacks wool |
| Aug. 28 | Missouri | 65 | | From Rocky Point |
| | | 6517 | 1200 | Est. 200 pass. up, 100 down |

## End Of Commercial Navigation

The final years of commercial navigation on the Missouri can be briefly told. The St. Paul, Minneapolis & Manitoba Railroad would provide all year freight delivery to Fort Benton. However, the Block P line of T. C. Power was used to provide a demonstration that the alternative route by the Missouri river would protect the head of navigation from discriminatory rate schedules. Army engineers had done and would do, much to improve the river route although the real need for the work had passed.

In 1888 the Block P sent three boats, the F. Y. Batchelor arrived May 30, the Rosebud June 30 and the small Missouri September 12. Logistics indicates the last boat was sent up river to handle freight left at Cow Island in late July by the Rosebud, which twisted off the crank of wheel shaft and had to return to Bismarck. It was an extremely low water stage when the Missouri reached port, "five inches lower than the lowest" said the River Press. The trip was evidence that the final boats on the tricky Missouri were, indeed, its masters. There was also a trip up from Bismarck the last of July by the Batchelor, quite possibly with supplies for the Little Rockies area. In addition, the government steamboat Josephine was in the area during the navigation season.

Total tonnage for 1888 would have been about 600 tons up, 200, chiefly wool, down, and a scattering of passengers enjoying this form of transportation.

The Power store at Fort Benton, and probably that at Lewistown, were supplied by the boats to a degree during this period, and on return they were in position to offer favorable rates on wool, with Fort Benton a major shipping center by rail or boat. In 1889 the Josephine was first arrival on May 14, while the freight carrier Rosebud came May 23 with a large load and taking down one of the largest cargoes, 150 tons to Bismarck and considerable freight to way points. The Rosebud came again on June 23, and as mention was made of the importance of Fort Benton as a wool market the down freight was probably heavy and bulky.

Montana's first year of statehood saw the last of the Mountain Steamboats make it to Fort Benton. The F. Y. Batchelor arrived June 12 under Thomas Mariner, with Bob Wright and Ben Jewell the pilots. The captain told the River Press that the river was 100 percent better on account of work of army engineers. Loaded to the water's edge at Bismarck, the boat dropped way freight along the river and brought a heavy load, took down a big load of hides, pelts and wool, as well as general merchandise for Rocky Point, Judith, Carroll and other landings.

Thomas C. Power may have had a sentimental streak, certainly Isaac Post Baker, manager of the Benton Packet Co. did, for Power continued to finance, and Baker to operate steamboats in the vicinity of Bismarck into this century, last of the new gasoline powered boats working up to the early 1930s.

For that matter, other Bentonites noted the early times with nostaglia. May G. Flanagan, girlhood resident of the 1870s, mentioning an old timer "seeming always to be watching the river," added, "We all watched it, from Front Street until it disappeared around Steamboat Bend in the blue mist of the mountain air."

### The Last Echoes

The Josephine, first on the Missouri and Yellowstone in 1873, in 1889 was laid up just below Fort Benton, relaunched in May 1891, and made a final trip to Fort Benton in August 1894. Sold to private ownership, the boat was cut down by ice March 8, 1907, perhaps the last of the Mountain Steamboats. Boilers and machinery were salvaged and shipped to Yukon for use on that river.

The Mandan, a government snagboat, dutifully ran several times to the head of navigation, July 15, 1908, the first trip. The Mandan came again in 1912, 1913, 1915, 1916, 1918, welcomed by old timers who recalled the glamor years. June 10, 1921, Capt. W. S. Maulding brought the Mandan in for Fort Benton's last view ever of a sizable incoming craft.

The Missouri river after close of commercial navigation was useful through the years for flatboats making a one way trip with supplies for stores and homesteaders along the now isolated waterway. Also ferries were built and taken down for lower point crossings. From the flatboats' timbers were built numbers of homesteader cabins, ruins still to be seen by floaters on the present Wild and Scenic Missouri River.

An interesting episode occurred in 1894 when about 350 members of "Coxey's Army" were financed to Fort Benton by other cities after being shuttled from jail to jail. Here they built ten large flatboats, and set off down the Missouri for a planned rendezvous with the "Army" in its planned march on Washington. They arrived at Yankton, perhaps 200 remaining and disintegrated.

In 1907, more as a publicity stunt than anything else, George Stevens, new owner of the Grand Union Hotel, brought the tiny O. K. to Fort Benton August 15. He ran an excursion or two, the boat burned June 30, 1908, up on the bank at Fort Benton following a flood June 6. The O. K. was about half the length of old time steamboats, a fraction of the tonnage.

A more ambitious effort was the Baby Rose, built by Bentonite Charles Crepeau and launched May 26, 1909, though not commissioned for use until July. The boat was intended to supplant the one way flat boats, but lacked the power to pull the barges the owner intended to use, was cranky. The boat made a couple of trips to the Judith area, and by 1911 was laid up at the Fort Benton levee, where it gradually disintegrated.

Just ahead of the closing of Fort Peck dam in 1937, Fort Bentonites recalled olden days with a St. Louis-Fort Benton motor cruiser race, four 25-footers, an event that drew amazing publicity and interest. And the four had the distinction of being the final powered craft to make a continuous voyage up the Missouri to the river's head of navigation.

### Fort Benton Fights For Survival

By 1888 it had become apparent that Fort Benton aims of becoming a rail center was now a fantasy, yet the multiple efforts of a city with declining population and importance were determined and worthy of mention.

During the year a water system, electric light plant, wool warehouse and a bridge across the Missouri were all constructed and in use.

The first two were indications of enterprise and determination. First mention of a water plant was in the boom year of 1882 when local citizens donated $300 for a survey of possibilities. Several seemingly fantastic plans were advanced, including tapping of either Teton or Shonkin water, much more potable than local water tables, polluted from the refuse of freighting days. In 1887 George F. Woolston of Helena made a proposal for a water plant, and in July was granted a 20 year franchise by the city authorities. Work had gone ahead on this through fall and winter and was nearing completion.

At almost the same time Woolston requested and got a franchise for an electric light plant. Work on this also moved ahead during the remainder of 1887, after a canvas for financial backing and participation. At a time when millions had never seen an electric light, Bentonites were well acquainted with the appearance at least. The steamer Rosebud in 1882 had provided a first look with an electric searchlight; in later years numbers of the boats were so supplied. As Edison's first central power plant had opened operations only in 1882, the town was right in the forefront.

As winter turned to spring Fort Benton business men celebrated St. Patrick's day at the Chouteau House with a gala banquet, observing the completion of both water and light plants. Mayor Jere Sullivan and George Woolston were among the speakers, the latter saying the city had enough water pump capacity for a city of 10,000. The entire affair somewhat awed state papers, the Inter Mountain article reprinted in the River Press said Benton was many times ahead of Butte and other places, save only for the Woolston franchises at Helena. The electric plant at Helena was tested in April briefly, work on their water plant was to get underway soon. The Copper Camp simply couldn't be bothered with such frills of civilization. (The electric light plant was later abandoned for a year or two, while the water plant was sold to the municipality, which secured voter approval of bonds, the price being $12,500, a sixth of the $75,000 cost as estimated in 1889.)

Biggest event of 1888 was building of the bridge across the Missouri. This project was organized as Benton Bridge Co., a toll bridge. It was built almost entirely by local subscription, with generous freight concessions made by Jim Hill's Manitoba. Primary aim was to preserve Fort Benton's position as a major wool market, making freighting of that commodity from the Judith Basin and Meagher county easier and cheaper than use of the local ferries.

Contracts were let in January 1888, approaches and piers to Ryan & Henry, iron superstructure to Milwaukee Bridge Co. The total cost eventually was about $60,000, two thirds of which had been raised at contract time. Specifications were for three spans of 175 feet, one of 76 feet, and a swinging draw span of 225 feet. Construction included three big ice breakers upstream from the main piers, for Fort Benton had experience with ice gorges.

Construction was in full swing by March, in April two workers drowned when a boat overturned. By November all spans were in place, flooring was being laid and approaches completed. When it opened in mid-December John H. Green was first to drive a vehicle across; a few days later Ben Swigert's ten mule outfit was the first freighter to cross. In June 1889 bridge tolls were reduced: Two horses and wagon cost 30c, 50c for round trip; 4 horses and wagon, 40c and 75c; 6 horses and two wagons, 60c and $1; 8 horses and three wagons, $1 and $1.50. The toll company operated until 1896 when the bridge was sold to Chouteau county for $9,999—the odd price being to avoid the vote necessary for any expenditure of $10,000 or more. The draw span, so well balanced a man could swing it using a pry bar, was used only for a passage by the Josephine and two by the O.K. When the flood of June 6, 1908, wrecked the draw span, permission was secured from army engineers to build a solid span, ending the myth of the Missouri above Fort Benton being usefully navigable.

"Historic Bridges in Montana," 1982, has this: "The Fort Benton bridge is the most historically significant bridge in Montana. Besides its historical associations, it was the first vehicular bridge across the Missouri in Montana; it was the first all-iron vehicular truss bridge built in Montana; and it is the oldest remaining bridge in the state." Restoration work has been done on the structure through grant money and local funds. The second bridge, first used in 1963, was financed through a county bond issue to match federal funds, so neither bridge had state funds involved.

The Josephine, first on the Missouri and Yellowstone, was one of the last survivors of the Mountain Boats, cut down by ice at Running Water, South Dakota, March 8, 1907. Boilers and machinery were salvaged for use on the Yukon. The local paper dutifully and probably sadly reported such items as of history past. In 1888 the paper had reported the close of one of the four great trading firms of Fort Benton, as it had of Kleinschmidt Bros. in 1883. This time it was Murphy Maclay, successor to Murphy Neel. September 3, 1890, the paper noted the recent closure of Gans & Klein, and also of the third of the big four, I. G. Baker & Co., holding a closing out sale. This was the firm which at the end of 1882 could report to the founder in St. Louis, a quarter million profit.

The census of 1890 reported the black news, the head of navigation, the premier port of entry to Montana Territory, in statehood was down to 624 from the June 1880 count of 1618 (and from a probable 2000 or more in 1882).

# Lines and Combines

## Steamboat "Lines" On Upper Missouri

*H*azards encountered on the Upper Missouri led to steamboat lines, often termed combines, after the initial years of the gold rush, when boats were owned by hit or miss profit seekers. A combine of several boats by the owners was a method of self insurance, spreading the risks, with each owner or speculator owning a portion of each boat—if one was sunk, profits from the others might still make the season's ventures profitable.

First of the "lines" was of course American Fur; oddly, their first and last steamboats bore the name Yellowstone. The first of the name made it only to Fort Pierre in 1831, next year to Fort Union. American Fur then added the Assiniboine, after it burned in 1835 the company leased steamboats. They did own the Chippewa on its 1859 trip to the Fort McKenzie bottom, a voyage which opened the Missouri to the Fort Benton area. Their second Yellowstone got only to Cow Island in 1864, next year reached Fort Benton to transfer the post to North West Fur.

First indication of a steamboat line to the upper river as the gold rush opened was 1863, when John J. Roe & Co. of St. Louis advertised a new and very light draught steamer to leave April 2 for Bighorn City (at that river on the Yellowstone), and two light draught steamers to Fort Benton, John G. Copelin freight and passenger manager. Whether the attempt was pressed isn't clear, at least none made it to the Montana-Dakota line.

For 1864 what was termed the Idaho Steam Packet Co. advertised in the St. Louis Republican, departures of Benton, Welcome, Florence, Marcella and Fanny Ogden for the gold fields. The Benton was the success story that year, the Welcome got to Milk River, Benton bringing on her freight, and making yet another trip to the Marias. Fanny Ogden reached Fort Union, Marcella was impressed there for Sully's canpaign. The combine's year must have been a great one, only Florence unrecorded to Montana.

Copelin & Roe in 1865 formed the Montana & Idaho Tranportation Co., to then biggest on the Missouri. They advertised the Dr Lodge, Bertrand, Benton, Yellowstone (mentioned above, apparently chartered to American Fur) and Fanny Odgen. The boats hit the third, and in some respects worst, low water year in a row on the upper river, and only one reached Fort Benton. The Bertrand snagged on its up trip, but the company doubtless made good money that season, for in the Deer Lodge and Benton they had a pair of winners. The Benton logged 10,000 miles on the Missouri that season, never reached Benton, but transferred its cargoes to the Deer Lodge to bring into Benton.

The golden year of 1866 was when shipments of precious metal down on the boats peaked. Success of the season had to be the Mepham Brothers of St. Louis who sent the Gold Finch, Iron City and Peter Balen to Fort Benton. All three had successful trips and the St. Louis Democrat reported them as bringing down about $35,000 gold each. Evidence is that the sum represented the profit they said they made on the trips of the three craft. The Balen, a new, quickly built boat, is credited with presenting a freight bill, in gold, on 400 tons of cargo at 12 1/2 cents a pound, which figures out to $100,000. Profit of the Balen trip is mentioned in the Frederick Way directory as $70,690 on receipts of $102,690—so Mepham profit on the trio that season probably was much understated.

At the conclusion of a quite successful year in the 1867 Fort Benton trade, Joab

Lawrence began organizing the Northwest Transportation Co., incorporated in Iowa that fall, with a view to taking advantage of impending arrival of the Chicago and Northwestern Railroad at Sioux City. The new river port cut off a thousand miles of dangerous travel and further about halved previous freight rates, at 5c a pound to Benton 6c from Chicago via Sioux City. Some of the concern's first year boats were the veteran Benton and Deer Lodge, Bertha, Fanny Barker and North Alabama. The concern later became known as the Peck Line when Durfee & Peck, Indian traders, became involved. Some of the later Coulson captains were also shareholders.

The greatest of the combines got its start in the fall of 1871 when the Missouri River Transportation Co. was organized by Sanford Coulson, joined by his brothers, John, William and Martin Coulson, as well as J. C. McVay, D. H. S. Gilmore and William Evans. This line headquartered at Yankton, and although the Peck Line continued operations until 1882, Coulson Packet Co. for some years appeared dominant on the Upper Missouri.

While relations between these lines seemed low key, another entrepreneur raised Coulson hackles. He was Wm. J. Kountz, who tried to tie up the port of Bismarck business after the NP Crossing was reached in 1873. Kountz on occasion made bids on military and Indian freight his competitors regarded as outrageously low. Thus it was with considerable glee that Coulson captains witnessed the Kountz Line take a financial and performance beating in 1874-75 on Carroll, a settlement above the Musselshell aimed at supplanting Fort Benton as practical head of navigation. Only his oddly named and odd luck Peninah performed up to promises in 1874, while Coulson boats cemented Fort Benton connections.

From the beginning of the 1870s spoonbill steamboats were built for the special, tough problems of the Upper Missouri (although the Deer Lodge might be considered a prototype); the Coulsons put a succession of these successful craft on the river: Western, Far West, Key West, Big Horn, Rosebud and others. Their final effort, and a costly one, came out late in the decade when they brought out the Montana, Dacotah and Wyoming, 252 footers with about double the freight capacity of regular mountain boats. They could, and did, bring 600 tons to Fort Benton, fifty percent over the best of the others, but these boats slued on the crossings and skittered onto sandbars in wind. By the time the first of the triplets reached Fort Benton, the place had two home grown lines.

First entry was a joint Power-Baker venture, its Benton arriving in 1875. Two years later the Baker Company sold its interest and bought the Red Cloud off the Tennessee River and remodeled the boat. In 1878 the Baker Line had an innovation, the small Col. McLeod, intended to lessen dependence on the Cow Island freight drop by bringing in late season freight from Cow Island at about 100 tons a trip. The small boat made a dozen trips to Benton in two seasons, then was destroyed in an accident and not replaced. The Baker Line ended with the sinking of the Red Cloud in July 1882.

Meanwhile the Power Line added the nice, speedy packet Helena, then the Butte and finally the Black Hills. A giant P inside a square marked the boats and named it the Block P Line, as the Coulsons sold their boats, the Power Line bought most, in the final year of major navigation owned or operated 11 boats. Manager Isaac Post Baker kept the Benton Packet Co. going well into this century, the final 40 years in the Bismarck area.

During the period of heaviest freighting on the Bismarck to Fort Benton run, four lines or combines sent boats up regularly, Power, Baker, Coulson and Peck. Kountz sent steamboats on occasion, and a few independents came, the most freight came to Montana on boats owned by the first four.

# The Golden Highway

Gold is a compact item indeed, as oldsters will recall from the days when it passed for currency. A double eagle weighs an ounce although less than the size of a silver dollar. In gold rush days the troy ounce pure officially was worth $20.67, and was commonly legal tender in the camps. What greenbacks there were, while the Civil War raged, were worth considerably less, sometimes half, or even less. Steamboatmen rather naturally preferred payment in gold—the Peter Balen, arriving in Fort Benton in 1866 presented a freight bill of $100,000 gold, 12 1/2c a pound for 400 tons of cargo. Montana merchants in shipping season bid up the price of greenbacks, as eastern manufacturers priced their goods that way, and Montanans didn't want to confuse the eastern slickers with a more valuable medium of exchange.

Montana gold was on the whole surprisingly pure. Some gulches, including Bannack, produced gold purer than the gold currency hardened and diluted with about 10% copper. From there raw gold purity ranged down to perhaps $12 a troy ounce, but in relatively few areas. Hence $17 an ounce is used for an average. A troy ounce weighs not quite 1.1 of the more common avoirdupois but with only 12 ounces as against 16, a troy pound is .823 avoirdupois. This deals largely with estimates, with weight not important. One item though, is useful. Give or take a few thousand, a ton avoidupois at $17 an ounce is worth very close to $500,000. Tons and major fractions of tons are involved.

In its March 12, 1868, issue the Montana Post quoted Major C. W. Howell as saying that five sixths of the mining products reached the east by way of the Missouri River. He also estimated that 10,000 persons used this route during the 1867 season at an average charge of $150, which would make a million and a half in fares. Howell didn't expect the traffic ratio to continue, due to the westward effort of the Union Pacific. In the same paper the Post reported Wells Fargo had shipped $1,451,000 in gold in five months and the editor figured $5 million yearly went south by stage, about an equal amount to Fort Benton. The split appears dubious—in studying available data.

Two months earlier, in a history of Confederate Gulch in the Big Belts, the Post editor ran one of the reasons for doubt about that even division between stage and river. During 1866, ran an article, Montana Gulch gave up wealth "computed by the wagonload, and portions of which were actually transported to Benton in wagons carrying no other freight, and guarded by a company of armed men."

Probably only California's larger area of gold bearing gravels eclipsed the Montana placer deluge, which some historians credit with propping up the shaky Union economy to help win the Civil War. Despite the legendary dashing stage laden with gold, the lion's share of the precious metal went down the Missouri. And when Wells Fargo for a 1%, $10,000 commission contracted to deliver two tons of gold to Benton it seems they used three wagons and hired a party of dependable riflemen. Rich Alder Gulch diggings resulted in miners trying the slightly more convenient Yellowstone, the Post in late 1864 was laden with items about mackinaws down that river, but other items indicate as many tried the Missouri route from Fort Benton.

### Early Discoveries Rang No Sirens

Gold had been found in Montana streams as early as 1852, Francois (Benetsee) Finlay picking out float gold on Gold Creek in western Montana to become the original discoverer of record. The Fort Owen Journal Feb. 15, 1852 has an entry "Gold hunting found some." At that Fr. DeSmet may have been first by several years, keeping mum about the matter. In 1856 there was the visit of John Silverthorne to Fort Benton for supplies, offering Culbertson a quantity of what he said was gold as tender for supplies. The suspicious trader finally took it on his own speculation and was greatly pleased to turn a profit of more than $500 on $1,000 (fur trade prices) worth of supplies. Later it became apparent this gold was probably from California, although Silverthorne in his later years was pleased by attentions of curious and greedy.

The tale perhaps influenced Granville and James Stuart to take a whirl at prospecting in later Montana. They set up a small operation in the Gold Creek area in the spring of 1858 and found some colors, but soon went back to stock trading on the Oregon Trail. The Stuarts returned in the fall of 1860, next summer sank a shaft and got moderate encouragement near later Deer Lodge. Meanwhile paying placer deposits had been turned up across the mountains near Pierce in later Idaho.

July 28, 1862, John White and William Eades found coarse gold above what became Grasshopper Creek and Montana's gold rush exploded. Next spring some of the boys who couldn't find placer gold set out from lively Bannack for the Yellowstone, and a few of these, Bill Fairweather and friends, refugees from hostile Crows, on May 26, 1863, found Alder Gulch. From then on, for several years, discovery followed discovery, and well under a year after the Alder Gulch find there was a Territory of Montana.

Some of the first Bannack gold may have gone down the Missouri on Joseph LaBarge's Shreveport, the St. Louis Register of September 13, 1862, reported $100,000 aboard the boat. Source likely was the Deer Lodge area and a bit off the Grasshopper diggings. They were probably lucky. Just how much the Innocents of Henry Plummer garnered is lost in the shreds of history, and any hidden troves may still be buried under wickiup sites around Bannack. Merchants managed to get a portion off to Salt Lake City to replenish stocks and keep the few hundred miners from starvation.

About $8 million in placer gold came out of the Virginia City and Bannack areas in 1863, but records are scant indeed for this year. Granville Stuart reported $25,000 down from Benton by small boat that summer with 13 men, who were cut off and killed by Sioux at Burnt Creek bar in present North Dakota in August, other sources give it as $75,000. Both stories have it that the Sioux dumped the yellow dirt to salvage the buckskin bags, which were useful. Fred Gerard, trader near Fort Union for years, salvaged part, family sources indicating salvage may have been about a fourth the lower total. The Shreveport got to Cow Island in June, and almost certainly carried a substantial sum down river, and certainly from the Stateside publicity given the Burnt Creek episode, numerous parties aboard mackinaws successfully made their way down the Big Muddy with cargoes of gold.

Finds at Last Chance Gulch July 14, 1864, virtually guaranteed that Fort Benton would be the major shipping point for placer gold henceforth. Confederate Gulch, about 30 miles east and a bit south of Helena, in the Big Belts, had a slightly different start than the others. Unionists were mopping up Sterling Price's Confederates in Missouri in 1864, and rather than be bothered with prisoners suggested parole on condition they work their way up the Missouri on steamboats. Thereafter, wrote Dan Cushman in his excellent "Gold Frontier," a "very tough breed of Missourians started to show up in Montana." Late that year some found bacon and beans placer shows along what came to be known as Confederate Gulch. More finds followed, and the supply center, rather mockingly named Diamond City, grew to about 5,000 at its peak, and as a sensational gold producer Confederate Gulch and especially its Montana Bar were unrivaled.

However, figures for gold shipments in the season of 1864 are seemingly nonexistent. A few ads are suggestive, for Oliver & Co.'s tri-weekly stage line to Salt Lake was soon taken over by Ben Holladay. Many favored a less jolting passage to the States. Oct. 1, 1864, Montana Post: "In a few days, 15 boats will leave Fort Benton for the states. These boats are all made bullet proof, with double sides and pierced with port holes. Each boat will carry 15 passengers, and will be propelled by oars through holes cut in the sides. The oarsmen will be entirely out of sight, and the pilot will have a bullet proof house over the tiller." Next issue reported the "gun boat Nancy E. Wilber, left Fort Benton on the 20th ult." In September 25 men had left for the Yellowstone to build boats for a joint expedition. The items suggest a vast advantage for river travel, and a preference for the proven Missouri route, to move much of a spectacular $13 million (26 tons) of gold eastward.

On the scene estimates ran even higher for 1864. Henry Blake, for a time editor of the Montana Post, later figured Alder Gulch area gold by that year as $30 million, by two years later double that. In the 1930s then Montana Supreme Court Judge L. L. Callaway estimated about 120 tons or $60 million in 1862-65 from Montana placers, with another $40 million by the end of the major gold rush in 1869. No one can feel certain, after the road agents of Plummer had been eliminated by Vigilantes there remained a residue of toughs, so miners understandably were secretive about their stakes.

Two reports of steamboat shipments are available for 1865, a year when gold production rose to an estimated $14.5 million, or 29 tons. The St. Louis Democrat July 13, 1865, reported arrival of the St. John from Fort Benton with $200,000 gold aboard. The Yellowstone, one of the boats which managed to reach Benton that dreary navigation year, was credited by the same paper on June 20 with $250,000 (about a thousand pounds). But the Sioux City Journal three days earlier had it $400,000—both reports can be credited, perhaps, many of the miners were from the midwest and would have left the boat at Sioux City. In both cases, bills for freight and passengers brought up would have netted a substantial fraction of sums mentioned.

In June the Post had a Helena item beginning, "The pilgrims are coming." In spite of low water and few steamboats completing their trips, an estimate of 1850 up bound passengers seems conservative. News of Alder and Last Chance had spread far and wide, and many of the pilgrims would be sadly disappointed. The tide ceased in late July, although others arrived via the Overland Trail. Then came the exodus of fortunates. Judging from Post ads, in Virginia City the Missouri was favored about two to one over the Yellowstone. In August one train bound for Benton carried 75 passengers headed for mackinaws. Others arranged for mackinaw-steamboat passage down at about $75 to $100 in gold. A German Flat Boat Co. offered cheaper passage via the Yellowstone, $15 transport to the river, $15 more by boat and passengers fed themselves.

September 30 the Post in Virginia City editorialized: "Million after million of gold has left the Territory, by way of the River and the Overland route. The sums which have been sent and carried by traders, miners and others, are both large and numerous. One man that we know of, took 400 lbs. (about $100,000) in clean dust; another carried 200 lbs. with him; and from 100 lbs. to 25 lbs. has been so common, that a record of the names would look like our postoffice list." The

Post that fall duly noted Helena's Vigilante cleanup, four hangings in a week, noted 600 men down via the Yellowstone. The bloom was off Alder Gulch's great strike.

November 4, the paper surely added to another wild stampede, telling about "The Richest Gold Discovery Known!" This was by a foreigner named Brown sinking a shaft near the head of Dry Gulch, 4 miles from Helena, who ran his stope to where "Gold, in almost solid masses, glittered before his bewildered vision." Brown filled several gunnysacks with his strike before recording his claim. No aftermath found, except perhaps a brief note of the richness of "Uncle Sam" lode.

While notes on actual gold shipments by river are scanty, a few projections can be made. In the four years, 1862-65, steamboats had brought about 7900 tons of freight into Montana waters, and at an average price of 12.5c a pound, that would have been almost $2 million in freight bills, at 10c over $1.5 million, precious owners' freight in gold dust for office safes. The boats took down approximately 1600 passengers those years, another quarter million. Just how much gold these passengers possessed is sheer conjecture. From the tone of the Montana Post report of departing miners, an average of about 25 pounds, about $6000 each, might be assumed. Call it $10 million. A dead broke miner wouldn't be a passenger, for certain, and a steamboat's down trip was so easy there were no work your passage jobs. Miners leaving by mackinaw probably didn't come close to that estimated $6000, but some, who just missed a steamboat or made a lucky summer strike undoubtedly had hefty pokes. So many items sold by merchants in Montana were $1 a pound or higher that one might use that figure for the value of that 7900 tons incoming, almost $16 million dollars.

### Missouri In 1866 Had Golden Tinge

Montana placers turned out an estimated $16,500,000 in gold during 1866, by a considerable margin the largest total of any gold rush year. The southern and early camps were fading, but Last Chance and Confederate Gulches roared ahead. Some one estimated about 10,000 persons came up or went down the Missouri that single year. Passengers on boats then were far more numerous than the 2000 up and 1000 down projected by passenger lists. Quite apparently deckers who rustled their own grub were seldom counted. The influx included a large percentage of veterans of the Civil War, avid Yanks and dead broke Rebs. Before the year was out old timers and pilgrims had quite a year.

For the late comers who couldn't locate a paying claim, there were plenty of jobs. The Montana Post in September carried an estimate that 2500 men, 6000 horses and 20,000 oxen were involved in freighting, virtually all along the Benton Road to Helena. From Fort Benton there were more than 6600 tons to move. Another 2350 tons, much of this to establish Camp Cooke at the mouth of the Judith River, entered Montana.

Gold sent down by steamboat in 1866 is far better documented. Largely from Wm. Lass's fine research on Upper Missouri steamboating, but not entirely, entries can be found for around $3 million on 16 boats, including the first six arrivals: St. John $100,000, Deer Lodge $70,000, Cora $35,000, Waverly made $50,000 so add cost of trip at least, Wm. J. Lewis $240,000, Mollie Dozier $50,000. Later, Walter B. Dance $115,000, Iron City $35,000, Peter Balen had a $100,000 freight bill and made over $70,000, Only Chance $85,000, Tacony $20,000, Gold Finch $35,000, Luella $1,250,000, Agnes $125,000, Gallatin $500,000. And Stonewall, unlisted as an arrival, brought $100,000 gold "from Fort Benton." This boat doubtless picked up one or more parties off mackinaws, it apparently didn't get past Dakota.

Once again projections help clarify the figures. An average freight rate that year was at least 11c a pound, $220 per ton; freight bills at Benton around $1.5 million, fares of passengers equalled this or more. Most of the above steamboats were reporting their own gold, one or two including amounts deposited in safes by passengers. No steamboat went down from Benton that year with an IOU from freight recipients. Then merchants of the territory were doing well, some sent gold out by stage for next year's orders, but the river route was much safer despite Indian attacks on occasion.

In late summer 1866 the exodus by mackinaw began, three mackinaws a day down from Benton during August, average 15 passengers—later Sheriff Bill Hamilton said 200 mackinaws and 3500 people went down from Benton. At Helena, "'Down the river' is the cry everywhere, numbers leave daily for Benton." Files indicate about 500 down the Yellowstone from declining Virginia City, certainly not all empty handed.

Near booming Diamond City, Confederate Gulch was producing heavily that summer, and Montana Bar was cleaned up, the richest strike in the world. It wasn't extensive, a couple of very lucky partnerships got the lion's share. Record pan on Montana Bar was reported at $1400, about seven pounds, while $1000 pans of dust weren't too uncommon.

Granville Stuart was witness to one result: "While in Benton on August 29, 1866, a freight wagon drawn by four mules and escorted by a company of miners, arrived. The wagon was loaded with two and one-half tons of gold dust, valued at one million five hundred thousand dollars. The gold was all from Confederate Gulch and was shipped down the river by steamboat. This was the first and only time that I ever saw a wagon load of gold dust at one time."

X. Beidler had another story of the fabulous year, which may have involved the same gold, but for several reasons the writer believes it to be a second great gold shipment. He recalled 2 1/2 tons of gold from Confederate Gulch shipped via the Hershfield Bank in Helena for a man named Fredericks. X. and 14 other armed men guarded three 2-mule wagon outfits, the gold in three small kegs. At Benton they put the kegs of gold aboard mackinaws with a ten gallon keg securely tied to each keg of gold to help retrieval in event the boat sank.

The genesis of this shipment can be followed through two other sources. C. W. Cook, writing in 1924, recalled that after a gun fight with claim jumpers though then quite young, he was placed in charge of one of the rich claims, and over 40 hired hands, but "the most I took out in 24 hours was $16,000." Then he reported C. Fredricks asked him (Cook) to clean more than a bushel of gold and sack it: "He could not guess within $20,000 of what he had. My only instructions were to put $5,000 in a sack...I handled gold as a farmer does wheat."

The first shipment went down on the Luella, Grant Marsh's biographer, Joseph Mills Hanson, wrote in "Conquest of the Missouri," $1,250,000 worth of dust in safes and either the tallest of tall tales or the greatest gold shipment of all. Or was it?

The St. Joseph, Missouri, Herald, Oct. 11, 1866: "The Luella, mountain boat, arrived from Fort Benton yesterday morning at noon. She had 65 cabin, and 115 deck passengers, and more treasure than any boat has brought down from the mines during the season. It is impossible to state the value of the dust; the officers of the boat fix it at three millions of dollars, while some of the passengers are of the opinion that it will run up over four millions. A number of the miners had very large amounts, Frederick & Campbell alone, miners in Confederate Gulch, Montana Bar, having about $475,000 of the precious ore. Two large safes were well filled, and many of the passengers took care of their own stuff."

When the Frederick gold arrived in Helena it opened eyes. The Montana Post had an August 26 item from Last Chance: "The great sensation connected with mining has been the arrival of 2200 lbs. of dust from Montana Bar, the fame of which has reached you ere this. I saw the three fortunate possessors of this magnificent pile, and have seen more than three who have sought long and diligently in the bowels of the earth without success."

Assuming two shipments, the Frederick gold on a mackinaw caught up with the Luella, which had trouble in Montana, and the boat probably scooped up other small boat travelers, such pickups are reported by several accounts of trips. That would add up to the 6 or 8 tons of gold reported at St. Joseph.

Some small boats made it all the way. September 1 the Sioux City Register reported arrival of 17 men with 700 pounds of gold (about $200,000) from Benton. September 29 the Montana Post mentioned "500 people floating down the Missouri from Fort Benton, also $1,500,000 in gold"—whether referring to one of these or yet another group wasn't clear.

Next spring newspapers were still printing items about the fabulous year of 1866. One enthusiast thought Montana had sent out $40 million in the form of gold, the Post editor figured $30 million closer and the secretary of the treasury credited Montana with $18 million. St. Louis Board of Trade in another estimate thought the merchandise sent up river was worth $7.5 million. It was a year famous for gold and trade, and rivermen and merchants were looking ahead to 1867.

## The Waning Years

At any rate, the steamboaters were geared up for the 1867 season and trips to the Mountains, to the extent that there was bidding for cargoes, instead of begging for carriers, and naturally, freight prices dropped. It was a good year on the river, 41 boats brought almost 8000 tons of freight, another 1200 at lower points, but the average freight was 8c a pound. Still almost $1.5 million in freight charges. Down passengers for the first time outnumbered incoming, 2600 to 2200, for those down fares about a quarter million.

After 1866, papers were rather matter of fact about gold cargoes. A few were found, Miner $300,000, Only Chance had at least 100 passengers and $500,000 gold, Gallatin $250,000, Cora $100,000, Ida Stockdale $200,000. Joseph LaBarge filled the Octavia's safes and passengers carried more—$75,000 listed was just about the freight and passenger fares to Benton. Amaranth carried $100,000, Huntsville far more than the $75,000 listed—the St. Joseph Union reported $175,000 and 16 passengers, and Imperial was a special case. This big steamboat laid up at Cow Island in late season while agents drummed up trade in Helena by describing its palatial accommodations. When the final group of passengers left Benton by mackinaw for the boat, Imperial was said to have 300 passengers and $100,000 in its safe—many times that carried by passengers.

An almost overlooked gold carrier of the 1867 season was the Guidon, which followed the Octavia into port, made a fast turn around and took down General Terry's party; more importantly a Wells Fargo escorted gold shipment of about two tons of yellow placer gold worth about $1,000,000. It came from Confederate, Highland and other gold bearing gulches, and to move the stuff from Helena to Fort Benton the famed express company collected about $10,000 at 1%, helping swell Wells Fargo profits to about $4200 for their Helena-Fort Benton run that season.

Late season brought extremely low water, the so-described "palatial" Imperial limped from bar to bar, passengers ate up all its grub before the boat reached the Dakota line, and when angry passengers urged the captain to hire a licensed pilot off another boat (he wanted $1,000)—surprise, that $100,000 in Imperial's safe had been sent down on another boat and the captain anyway didn't have authority to hire a pilot. So it went, the boat leaking disgruntled and hungry fares to every abandoned mackinaw along the river. The Imperial was finally abandoned above Omaha. The Gallatin, despite prior successes and big gold cargo, fared only slightly better, but that was on account of bad luck at the bars (sand).

Success story of the year was the Only Chance, back to Fort Benton August 27 in time to collect 300 passengers for a boat that could and would go, leaving with what was described only as an immense gold cargo. The St. Joseph Herald reported the Only Chance's arrival in early October on a shriveled river, "3 million in treasure." Again, about six tons, and a great season. Much of the freight this season was government, the army was establishing Fort Shaw and Fort Ellis in Montana.

The season of 1868 emphasized the fading placer boom, freight down, cargoes lighter more for lack of demand than otherwise. A few notes on gold, first boat, Success $97,000; Only Chance a bare $50,000, Octavia at least $150,000 and finally Success again, from Sioux City and with a third of a million gold for the richest cargo indicated this year. Boats carried 1200 passengers up, 800 down on estimates, many more by mackinaw, discouraged miners were leaving in droves. Fares were about $150 up (that in currency), down perhaps $100 gold, no definite price found.

A final flicker came in the dismal season of 1869, enough die hards to bring a healthy tonnage to a struggling territory, but many boats were loaded light for lack of cargo, also a new line out of Sioux City with low tonnages to beat the Missouri. About half the boats had to make double trips to Dauphin's Rapids about 120 miles down to deliver all their loads. But the second boat of the season was the Importer, which got the last sizable gold shipment located. This arrival was May 27, a couple of days later a Bentonite wrote the Helena Herald, "Messrs. Ingram moved their treasure from the Thwing House to take passage on the Importer; they also paid passage for several unfortunate miners and wives and children." A fine sendoff for the next note, "Importer leaves with full load of passengers and about $500,000 plus respectable freight." In October about $150,000 arrived at St. Louis from Benton by small boat.

The Pacific railroad had connected at Promontory, Utah, in early May, thereafter most treasure took the 500 mile stage ride to Corinne to ride the rails to eastern banks. There was a flurry of silver concentrate, some gold, even some copper for the steamboats in years to come, but the gold rush had ended and with it much of the glamour of steamboating to the Mountains.

## Estimating The Gold Shipments

Much of this is pure guesswork based on such factors as the amount of gold carried by estimated numbers of passengers on steamboats and mackinaws. A basic factor is the item in the Montana Post indicating that most departing miners carried from 25 to 100 pounds of gold out of Virginia City, and using $17 per Troy ounce as its value. The lower figure, about $6250, is used for steamboat passengers, and a quarter that for those aboard mackinaws, on the theory that this was the poor man's way of getting back to the States. Newspaper sources seem to indicate that only in 1864 and 1865 did the Yellowstone serve as highway for many mackinaws. In the first year about 850 men went down the Yellowstone with a presumed $1.3 million gold, 600 down the Missouri with $950,000.

An assumption is made that virtually all freight was settled for in Montana gold on Montana delivery. This may be somewhat erroneous, but river lore had a $100,000 bill in gold for 400 tons of freight off the Peter Balen in 1866. Incoming freight is reduced by amount for military, surely settled for in more conventional manner.

A departing steamboat then should carry the value of its freight charge, price per pound varying over the period, and fares of departing passengers, usually $150 to $200. Reports of up to $100,000 on a steamboat would probably be from such payments.

Mackinaws were built at Fort Benton in unbelievable numbers, in 1866 the sheriff reported 200 with 3500 passengers, an earlier 1866 report three daily launched in August. Down river papers reported such items as 400 miners in one party, and 2,000 stopping off at Yankton or Omaha in a couple of fall months. Not all were broke, though some doubtless worked their passage. In 1866 James Hubbell took 30 down to Omaha in a bullet proof boat, fare $175. Two different mackinaws whose passengers were carrying about $200,000 in gold, were reported in down river papers. Hence gold carried by small craft may be underestimated.

1862 on freight and passengers, $100,000 on Shreveport....... $   525,000
1863 virtually all by mackinaws .......................... 650,000
1864 on 1660 tons, 400 passengers, $1 million by mackinaw .. 4,000,000
   plus $1.3 million via Yellowstone, not included in bottom total
1865 3700 tons, 800 passengers, $1 million by mackinaw ..... 8,000,000
   big cargoes, $400,000 on Yellowstone, $200,000 on St. John's
   about $600,000 on Yellowstone River
1866 Golden year, some of gold from 1865 carryover ........ 20,000,000
   big cargoes, Wm. J. Lewis $240,000, Agnes $125,000,
   Luella $3 or $4 million, $10.5 million by mackinaw, $6.3
   million by steamboat passengers aside from Luella etc.
1867 7,000 tons private freight, 2600 passengers, $1.5 million mack. 17,000,000
   big cargoes, $3.5 million on Only Chance in two trips,
   Cora $250,000, Ida Stockdale $250,000, Guidon $1 million,
   Gallatin $250,000, Huntsville $175,000, Imperial estimated $500,000
1868 5,000 tons, 800 passengers, by mackinaw $2 million .... 6,500,000
   big cargoes, Success $307,000, Octavia $150,000,
   Importer $500,000
1869 5,000 tons, 800 passengers, last of important gold shipments.. 3,500,000
   $500,000 on Importer in June last large shipment located
Total estimated gold shipment via Missouri River............. $60,175,000
   A more thorough search might increase total $10-$15 million.

# On the Yellowstone

John Buchanan, editor, Montana Post at Virginia City, Aug. 27, 1864: "No steamer has ever attempted to ascend the Yellowstone, though the effort will be made this year." From his diary of trip via steamer Yellowstone about June 15, 1864.

Granville Stuart, May 27, 1866, aboard the Walter B. Dance at the mouth of the Yellowstone: "The Yellowstone is by all odds the main stream; the Missouri looks like a small tributary coming into it."

Stuart's view has been advanced by geographers. However, for navigability, the Yellowstone's ultimate head of navigation was at the lower edge of Billings, the practical head below Pompey's Pillar, approximately the same distance from the junction as if the Missouri's head had been at Carroll near the Musselshell, and in the steamboating period of 1859-90 into Montana waters more than 700 boats delivered freight at a higher point and greater distance via Fort Benton than the relative handful to utilize the Yellowstone. In addition, most of the freight offloaded along the southern stream was for the military. Most boats on the Yellowstone were primarily in the Fort Benton trade.

John J. Roe, St. Louis steamboat owner, apparently entertained the first notion of navigating the Yellowstone, in 1863 advertised an unnamed boat for the Yellowstone to the Big Horn as a more advantageous route to Bannack and Alder Gulch, but low water that year prevented the attempt.

Editor Buchanan probably talked with persons at Fort Union who had heard of General Sully's planned use of steamboats on the river in making his comment about the attempted navigation. He had completed his trip to Virginia City when a small armada arrived at Fort Union July 25—or at least two thirds of it. The Island City, with a cargo of grain for the army's animals, sank 8 miles below. The Chippewa Falls and Alone spent the next several days salvaging the Island City's cargo, on August 2 went up together for Brasseau's Houses, an old trading point, about 50 miles up from the mouth. The boats came back after about two weeks, presumably their cargoes were left at a supply base for the Sully forces.

The Minnesota Sioux rising in 1862 and ensuing campaigns of General Sibley from Minnesota west across Dakota, coupled with Sully campaigns in 1863-64 provided more Sioux than new Montana Territory really wanted, driven into the area of the Yellowstone. Steamboats were still unproven as to providing supplies for Montana mining camps in 1864. John Bozeman that year gave his name to a trail, a cut-off from the Oregon or Overland Trail, spang across the new hunting grounds of the Sioux. The army in 1866 would establish three forts along that Bozeman Trail—the result bloodshed through its Wyoming-Montana length. Through the rest of the 1860s steamboats would shun the Yellowstone.

In fact, it wasn't until 1873 that the next and more successful navigation attempt was made. First came the Key West under Captain Grant Marsh, who seemed to have a flair for being on the spot for colorful events. His boat was charged with a preliminary survey of the river, entering the Yellowstone May 6 for nine days, with two companies of the 6th Infantry for escort. Marsh gave geographic features names, some still in use, noted shoals and obstacles, and the boat reached a point just below the mouth of Powder River before turning back at a shoal he rightly reckoned would be passable when the snow melt of the high Rockies came down. The Key West, Far West under Mart Coulson and Peninah under Abner Shaw had an army assignment to supply a base for a Northern Pacific Railroad survey party west from Bismarck. It was no small party, with an escort of 1451 men and 80 army officers plus a detachment of Aricaree scouts and a large wagon train. Gen. David S. Stanley was commander.

The three boats hauled cargoes up as far as present Glendive, on arrival of the advance party the supplies were moved 20 miles above Glendive Creek. Marsh and the Key West took up surveyors, took mail to troops at Powder River. The military presence wasn't ignored by the Sioux. They had their first Indian skirmish August 2nd, cavalry went after the hostiles, one result they rode up the Yellowstone to find General Custer surrounded, rescued that party, had another light skirmish near Pompey's Pillar before the surveyors had covered their assigned survey. The expedition was on the Yellowstone into September. A couple of weeks before the Key West met the brand new Josephine under John Todd coming up near Glendive, and by previous arrangement Marsh took over the lighter draught Josephine, which was to prove itself beyond the years of Montana steamboating history.

There was no record found of any boats on the Yellowstone in 1874, perhaps the military felt they had stirred up the Sioux sufficiently.

In 1875 Marsh and the Josephine had another military chore, to explore the limits of navigation. The steamboat reached Fort Buford at the mouth on May 25, took on three companies of the 6th Infantry (100 men, 7 officers), plenty of firearms, drawing only 22" of water. The Josephine passed river mouths, Powder, Tongue and Rosebud, reaching the Big Horn June 2—and went up that river 12 miles (Marsh might have had a premonition). Each mile was a new head of navigation, but June 7th captain and crew had what might be described as a helluva time passing Hell Roaring Rapids, near later Billings, and turned back. A park there was named Josephine, marking the ultimate head of navigation for the Yellowstone.

It was a prophetic reconnaisance. Next year of course, Grant Marsh, the most knowledgeable captain took the Far West up the Yellowstone as support ship for General Terry's plan to tame the Sioux. One of Terry's small armies under Crook ran into Crazy Horse and Sioux and Cheyenne on the Rosebud and was out of it, Custer damned all strategy, divided his 700 cavalrymen and rode into oblivion.

The Far West reached the Big Horn June 25 and after the disaster went up that stream to the Little Big Horn, and after necessary delays for urgent military reasons, took the wounded of Reno's command down to Bismarck in 54 hours, and boat and captain were more than a footnote in American history.

In the aftermath, with the army sending everything it could muster westward, the Yellowstone became a busy, navigable stream indeed. Steamboats were impressed to support the fall and winter campaign and subsequent building of military forts in the Yellowstone valley. August 1 the Carroll and E. H. Durfee got to the Rosebud, August 19 the Yellowstone and Carroll were up to Wolf Rapids near later Miles City, the Josephine was on the river up to the Tongue and the last of the month the Silver Lake and Benton in the Glendive vicinity.

Army posts require supplies, and in 1877 Fort Custer was built, up the Big Horn at the point the Far West began its epic trip down. June arrivals included the Florence Meyer, F. Y. Batchelor; July, Peninah, Far West, J. C. Rankin, Savannah, Western, Big Horn, Rosebud, General Sherman, Silver City and possibly Peninah again. In January 1878 the New Northwest reported Yellowstone steamboats had moved 9500 tons up the Yellowstone in 1877, only year that river drew more tonnage than came to Fort Benton. Another boat, Osceola, was sunk that year above Glendive, data indicates it was more sight seeing than useful—aboard was a preacher, hands saw a fine white stallion and managed to rope him with assistance of range ponies aboard. The combination meant disaster, old time rivermen maintained. The Osceola was wrecked and sunk that day by a cyclone!

More from the Fort Custer list of arrivals, and other sources, 1878, General Meade, General Sherman, F. Y. Batchelor twice and perhaps the Rosebud; 1879, Batchelor three times and Helena.

In 1880 the Yellowstone line is listed as handling 1580 tons, meaning probably around eight boats. In 1881 total was 4410 tons, a pretty busy river; in 1882 only 700 tons, but then the Northern Pacific was building. A few scattering arrivals are all we have for these years, last the Batchelor which appears a dozen times from 1877.

One interesting addition, the third by that name, Yellowstone. It was built in the winter of 1875-76 for Bozeman interests, headed by Achilles Lamme. The owners planned to shorten the long haul from Fort Benton and save considerable on freight by running the boat up to Pompey's Pillar. It was a 153 footer, considerably smaller than the usual upper Missouri packet. Though listed as a sidewheeler, the usually reliable Way's Directory has it the more customary sternwheel boat. Nevertheless, it could haul well over 200 tons. Lamme got one of the best pilots on the Missouri in John Massie, brother of the more flambouyant Bill and the boat left St. Louis May 3, 1876. Amount of Bozeman freight was disappointing, so at Omaha the Yellowstone took on about 200 tons of oats for I. G. Baker of Fort Benton. This was a fine small steamer and did everything an owner and pilot could ask. But at Fort Buford Lamme got a stern military warning, no civilians on "our river," to be Sioux targets. As an alternative, the Yellowstone made a good trip to Fort Benton, arriving June 24. Going down, the boat was drafted by the army, got to tour the Yellowstone river a ways and ferried some of Terry's troops across after hostiles August 27.

Next year Lamme had a big order of goods for Bozeman lined up, got his boat to Buford April 30. No snowmelt yet, and after butting at bars and grasshoppering over shoals for 50 miles he gave up, turned the boat down, then up the Missouri, delivering his cargo at Fort Benton May 21.

Perseverance paid off in 1878, the Yellowstone left St. Louis with 150 tons in late April, added another 80 tons at Bismarck, a good load, and had no trouble reaching Pompey's Pillar, the highest a boat with cargo had ever attained. The Josephine made its trip "light," little cargo. June 20 back down at Bismarck, Lamme picked up 200 tons of Coulson freight for Benton—success!

But the Yellowstone as well as the Missouri had tough tricks for scoffers. In early June 1879, the only steamboat built specially for the Yellowstone, was wrecked at Buffalo Rapids, a few miles below Miles City. No casualties, and deck cargo salvaged for the long haul to Bozeman. Bell and anchor of the boat are in the Range Riders Museum at Miles City. Salvaged timbers in 1891 went into Steamboat building in Miles City—torn down about 1940.

Following are roughly estimated tonnages by years of steamboat use of the Yellowstone, the year first, tonnage and number of steamboats: 1864, 100, 2 boats; 1873, 500, 4 boats; 1875, 50, 1 boat; 1876, 700, 6 boats; 1877, 9500, would require about 44 boats; 1878, 2230, 8 boats; 1879, 800, 4 boats; 1880, 1580, 8 boats; 1881,

4410, 20 boats; 1882, 700, 4 boats; 1883, 1200, 6 boats. In the present century a few steamboats, probably all Benton Packet Co. steamboats working out of Bismarck.

# Cow Island Trail

## Cow Island Trail Adjunct To Benton Steamboating

*A*n important adjunct to Fort Benton's freighting in steamboat days was the Cow Island Trail, the low water, late season freight drop that over the years was a transfer depot for thousands of tons of supplies badly needed in Montana Territory. It was figured at roughly 120 miles to Fort Benton, which pretty well conforms to the river distance of 126 miles on BLM maps of today. It would be about a nine day journey for a loaded ox train.

The trail left Cow Island, following Cow Creek some miles, then headed generally westward overland, across fittingly named Bullwhacker coulee, passing near later Warrick, skirting the southern portion of the Bear's Paw Mountains and the northern bend of the Missouri, after which it headed southwesterly to Fort Benton, from there in general the present route of highway 87.

### The Trail's Beginnings

One can trace the beginnings of the trail to 1863, a frustrating low water year for the steamboats which tackled Montana waters. At the outset of that year, a number of St. Louis rivermen were interested in trade to the Idaho gold fields and Bannack and Virginia City, but even they weren't prepared for the extent of the stampedes and consequent tremendous demand for supplies. Highest point any steamboat reached in 1863 was Joseph LaBarge's Shreveport, with about 250 tons of freight and swarming with argonauts, to Snake Point, near Cow Island. LaBarge had established a business at Fort Benton in 1862, in 1863 he was hauling freight for John J. Roe of St. Louis as well. To meet the urgent demands of his consignor, LaBarge's manager, Robert Lemon, at Fort Benton, contracted with King & Gillette, later builders of the toll road through Little Prickly Pear on the Benton Road, to haul the Roe company freight at a ruinous 25c a pound. Somehow the contractors hacked out a crude freight trail to the Shreveport cargo. The Nellie Rogers made it as far as Milk River with another 250 tons. Joe Slade, former Ben Holladay division boss, from Bannack followed the Mullan Road to Benton and the route of the 1862 Fisk and Holmes emigrant trains to Milk River with wagons. On the return trip his freighters had to beat off two Indian attacks and further harrassment, but made it to Bannack just ahead of winter snow and perhaps saved the infant camp from starvation.

### Gold Stampede Years, Opening The Trail

The gold stampede to Montana was on in full swing in 1864 and St. Louis boat owners responded to the opportunity for tremendous profits. This was also the year that Fort Benton began expanding beyond its three "forts," Benton, Campbell and LaBarge. It was another low water year, only six cargoes and about 900 tons of freight to Fort Benton or the Marias, and one of the boats halted by the river stage was the brand new Yellowstone of American Fur, pioneers of Montana steamboating. The boat was stopped at Cow Island by low water.

The aftermath provided an eye witness to the true beginning of the Cow Island Trail in William Gladstone, former Hudson Bay boatwright. When word reached Fort Benton, Gladstone was commissioned to build a mackinaw, went down with the party in early July. Enroute they met the Benton, the big success of 1864, with I. G. Baker aboard to replace Andrew Dawson at the American Fur post.

After moving the 400 tons of freight from Cow Island to the north bank, the next task was evident.

Gladstone wrote, "About two weeks after our arrival some of us laid out and made a road to Benton. We expected a lot of wagons from Benton any day and after the road was ready a big outfit, comprising 16 large prairie schooners, drawn by oxen, arrived. We loaded the wagons with the baggage and personal effects of the passengers who had been transferred to the steamer 'Benton,' and then with other freight." The road building quite evidently was confined to the route up Cow Creek and out onto the rolling plains. It certainly wasn't the best of roads. Further on Gladstone noted, "The road up Cow Creek was a very bad one and in ascending a very steep hill one of the wagons went over the precipice, dragging four pairs of oxen with it. The tumble of 300 feet of course killed the oxen and I had hard work getting the wagon mended."

### Freighting Problems

I. G. Baker at Fort Benton was sending transportation as rapidly as possible for that 400 tons of cargo. A hundred mules followed the first wagons, the animals loaded with 300 pounds apiece, then more wagons came as the round trip to Benton and back was completed. Right in the middle of the cargo handling, here came special treatment for some set aside wares—two teams and four Mormons from Salt Lake City with orders to load 200 barrels of whisky. Baker was showing good business sense—Mormons didn't imbibe, other freighters and Indians did. The Yellowstone had Indian annuities aboard, and a distribution was to be made to Gros Ventres at Cow Island—so get that whisky off the bottom. Indians were not very hostile that year, Gladstone recalled, but the Mormons with whisky had a hair raising adventure that didn't end literally so. About at present Warrick a war party of Blackfeet swooped down on the miniature caravan. The four whites quite wisely knocked the head off a keg, their visitors passed out "talking through their noses of what they were going to do to that whiskey when they woke up." The Mormons didn't wait to see and the booze arrived at Benton to the vast relief of non-Mormon whites. The shipment was probably short a barrel or so, the Cow Island work force had determined it to be far better than what they had been drinking at Benton. Distribution of annuities to about 2,000 Gros Ventres was a grand party, according to Gladstone's description of the event.

The third low water year in a row, 1865 was so bad that apparently the trail to Cow Island was little used, possibly the Deer Lodge and General Grant dropped around 300 tons of cargo. It was so low that three steamboat companies built a stockade fort at Milk River, complete with cannons, and divided into three compartments, which ultimately handled about 2200 tons of freight. There was evidence that the long overland route via Fort Benton was heavily traveled that season. The Montana Post reported late June or early July departure of 125 wagons from Benton for Milk River, and Hiram Upham in an August 1, 1865, letter commented on a July 31st caravan of 250 wagons, each drawn by four to eight yoke of oxen, from Benton bound for Milk River and making "a big show." Indians were hostile enough in 1865 to make for big trains with plenty of rifles. It was also a year or two before two and three wagon hitches came into general use in Montana.

### Use of Cow Island Trail Dwindles

The trail was little used during succeeding years of the gold rush. In 1866 there was a fine stage of water and steamboats arrived at Fort Benton well into

July. An empty boat, Miner, coming for passengers, advertised a trip to Benton but managed only a pickup at Cow Island, it was reported next year; that fall the Helena Herald's Benton correspondent was a trifle vague about this trip. There was other traffic to the Judith River, Camp Cooke was founded in July and several boats went only that far, and a couple more unloaded at Milk River late in the season. Near year end the Montana Post reported that 2500 men, 3000 teams and 20,000 oxen had been engaged in 1866 in Fort Benton freighting.

The years 1866, and to a lesser extent 1867, were golden years on the Missouri in a literal sense. There is evidence backing up a rough estimate that 60, probably more, tons of gold went down by steamboat or mackinaw in those two years.

Arrivals at Fort Benton in 1867 extended even into August before low water slowed the parade of the packets. Records indicate a few hundred tons of freight dropped at Cow Island and at least one boat, Silver Lake, with supplies for Camp Cooke. Cow Island had slightly more use in the low water year of 1868, when 35 arrivals can be listed for Fort Benton, but with lighter than usual cargoes. There was considerable gold sent down, but nothing like the previous three seasons.

A tough steamboating year followed, with a big jump in freighting on the Cow Island Trail to nearly a thousand tons, and a few hundred only to Milk River. At Fort Benton the steamboats came in with short cargoes, the remainder left at Dauphin's Rapids, possibly with an eye to protection of freight by soldiers from Camp Cooke. No fewer than 19 steamboats made double trips from Dauphin's Rapids. The year 1869 was a deadly one on the freighting trails, Blackfeet were sporadically hostile and at summer's end some claimed 56 whites had been killed in the territory. A sequel was the January 1870 massacre of 173 Piegan men, women and children on the Marias.

## Bad Years For Territory And Fort Benton

The bad years came to Montana and Fort Benton as the 1870s opened, in large part due to virtual exhaustion of placer gold in paying quantities. Only eight steamboats arrived in 1870. Helena was boosting the long new trail north from Corinne, Utah, on the Union Pacific and broke miners were leaving the territory in droves. There was no use indicated of the Cow Island Trail or Milk River this year. In 1871, six boats left 1400 tons at Benton and 600 more at Cow Island. Next year, a good navigation season, brought 3000 tons in 13 boats. That fell off to just over half as much in 1873, the year of a financial panic. The following season was about as dreary, but in the summer the International boundary was surveyed, meaning supplies needed by the hundreds of soldiers escorting Canadian and U. S. commissions. Then in September the North West Mounted Police arrived in Alberta, and for a decade virtually all supplies came via Fort Benton. It was the start of a tremendous boom in tonnages handled, if not in total value. With new boats, built for the Upper Missouri, and for the most part shorter trips from the Northern Pacific railhead at Bismarck, there were to be few trip failures, and a tremendous jump in use of the Cow Island Trail.

Carroll, Helena's new project to bypass dependence on Fort Benton boats, near the mouth of the Musselshell, in 1874 drained off half of Fort Benton's tonnage, about 1700 at each point, but the rival town failed miserably in 1875 due to mud, hostile Sioux and high water. It seems that hundreds of tons of Carroll freight eventually reached Helena by way of Fort Benton wagons, but a year late. The 1875 Fort Benton total was not impressive compared to gold rush totals, but was about 2800 tons plus another 500 at Cow Island. Montana's growing livestock industry also meant increasing population, demand for supplies.

The campaign against the Sioux in 1876 drew steamboats off the Fort Benton run, but over 4000 tons came to Benton, another 750 to Cow Island. The latter total would have required 100 three wagon outfits, ten or twelve trains, all moved in late summer and fall, in addition to the longer run to southerly towns. Reporting on 1876, the Benton Record figured that freight handled, including Cow Island, with live animals, passenger baggage, robes, etc., was probably 20,000 tons, but this seems about double the logical figure. Boosters were boosters in those days.

### Year of The Nez Perce

Fort Benton freighters and boats had gone off to the Sioux war, but the passage of the Nez Perce east of Fort Benton in 1877 involved loss of life and property, and much more direct participation. Freight was arriving via three steamboat lines, the Power Block P, Coulson and Baker, the latter the Red Cloud and chartered boats. By August 15 when the Benton made its last of five arrivals, 5300 tons had gone across the levee. Water was very low and remaining tonnages, including government supplies, stopped at Cow Island. By September 14 it became apparent that the fugitive Nez Perce were headed for Cow Island. The Fort Benton Volunteers, 29 handy men with rifles and veterans of the Civil and Indian wars, rode off to protect Fort Benton freight at Cow Island, arriving September 24th, meanwhile augmented by six more volunteers and 16 soldiers from the Judith, to find that Sgt. Molchert with 11 soldiers and five civilians had stood off the Nez Perce for two days. Besieged in their rifle pits, they had not been able to prevent burning of about 50 tons of freight by the Nez Perce. As the Indians had already crossed the Missouri, the volunteers rode over, up Cow Creek, to a point where the freight outfit of Farmer and Cooper had been burned and two men killed. There was a sharp fight (Nez Perce were expert riflemen, too), with a white and two Indians killed before the skirmish ended. Several other freighters in the area were killed, total not determined. Even from normally Indian hating Benton whites, the Nez Perce warriors earned respect and admiration, for their fighting abilities; also they never scalped the dead.

In 1878 for the first time, Fort Benton tonnage, up and down, topped 10,000, in a season beginning April 26 and ending October 19. The Baker Line had added the very light draught Col. McLeod this year, for the primary purpose of ending much of that freighting from Cow Island. The boat was an unqualified success, from its first arrival August 29, four trips from Bismarck, but so great was the demand for supplies in growing Montana that bigger boats were leaving more freight at Cow Island than the Col. McLeod could handle at about 100-125 tons per transfer. End result was about a thousand tons for the freighters, Cow Island to Benton.

The year 1879 was a virtual carbon copy in tonnage, but river stage was higher, cargoes heavier, with 42 cargoes of 9500 tons, plus another 800 tons left at Cow Island. Before the 1880 season began the little Baker boat was destroyed when the Butte slipped off its storage ways at Bismarck, so the busy McLeod (11 arrivals at Benton, 2 more to Cow Island in two seasons) never had its chance to clean up that Cow Island freight. The Missouri was high most of the 1880 season and only relatively insignificant amounts of the 12,500 upbound tons were left at Cow Island.

### Biggest Montana Tonnage Year

Dan Maratta of the Coulson Line, who would have known, said Bismarck-Fort Benton freight was 17,420 tons upbound in 1881, with 3700 passengers, nearly

2,000 horses and cattle, and 160,000 buffalo hides and robes. This was the next to the last year of the great buffalo slaughter. Not all this tonnage came to Fort Benton. Several thousand tons supplied the 5,000 or so hunters along the rivers, but it undoubtedly was the biggest steamboating year in Montana history. Another 4,000 tons went up the Yellowstone. There was considerable freighting from Cow Island, the last significant amount. In regard to those buffalo hides, the Black Hills brought over 12,000 down to Bismarck—a large cargo.

In 1882 although the buffalo were dwindling, Fort Benton tonnage was up a bit from the previous year, but there was not as much into Montana on the Missouri. The season was not the last for steamboating, but with completion of Northern Pacific and Canadian Pacific, Fort Benton's supply area dwindled, and tonnages dropped. There was little indicated use of the Cow Island Trail in this and later years.

# On Dusty, Muddy Trails
## Freighting

*F*reighters seem to fall into three categories, the individual, business firm and contractor. Applied particularly to freighting off steamboats in Montana, although the other two existed in initial years, the individual dominated the early years. First steamboat freight to the Fort Benton area in 1859 through 1861 was primarily freight for the fur posts, plus some sold or consigned to John Owen at Fort Owen in the Bitter Root valley, and in 1861 at least, to the Higgins & Worden store at Hell Gate.

In 1862 LaBarge & Harkness planned to do their own freighting to western Montana communities, one a recent development around Gold Creek, and brought oxen and wagons on their boats. There was, of course, both contract and individual freight north from Utah. Later that year the gold discovery at Bannack triggered the Montana gold rush, fueled the next year by rich Alder Gulch.

In 1863 long distance freighting from Milk River and Utah saved southern Montana mining camps from starvation, including Joe Slade with unnamed backers, and Alex Toponce and Jerry Mann, who ran substantial trains.

Massive emigration to the gold camps via the Oregon Trail, then north from Fort Hall actually brought a surplus of wagons and often of work oxen. Many of these beasts were slaughtered at journey's end and the meat sold across makeshift butcher counters. One side note, American Fur wintered its work animals on Sun River as early as 1863, although later years are given as the date when Montanans learned that cattle and horses could be wintered successfully in northern Montana.

That this was general knowledge and practice by 1866 is indicated by the purchase by Toponce and Mann of several hundred work cattle in the Helena area to replace stock winter killed in northern Montana.

Heading into the peak years, 1864, 1865 and 1866, it appeared to be the turn-out of individuals with small outfits that moved the bulk of the freight. The rate from Benton to Helena was around 6c a pound the latter year, meaning $300 freight for a 2 1/2 ton load, to Virginia perhaps $500—not bad for a man with a busted claim. The Montana Post in September 1866 quoted a "reliable party" as estimating 2500 men, 3000 wagons and 20,000 oxen on the Benton Road that season.

Thereafter freighting became more business-like. Trains grew larger and better equipped, freighting more specialized in operations by professionals such as King & Gillette, Garrison & Wyatt, and Hugh Kirkendall. What became the greatest of all, John J. Roe & Co.'s Diamond R, dated to those LaBarge & Harkness oxen and wagons, after a law suit begun in 1864. With reorganization and purchase in June 1868 (for $75,000, then employing 70 men, owning 116 wagons and more than 700 oxen) the Diamond R rolled out as biggest on the Montana scene, one of the biggest in the west. With Edgar Maclay, Matt Carroll and George Steell, Diamond R met competition on every Montana trail and the long haul up from Corinne, Utah, from 1869. Their drivers flaunted the emblem in tattoos. One of their wagon masters, James Brown, was known to his death as "Diamond R" Brown.

The merchants, consignors and forwarders of Fort Benton, notably T. C. Power and I. G. Baker & Co., growing wealthy, entered the freighting scene in the closing years of the 1860s, and ultimately ended Diamond R's one time dominance of Montana freighting. By the end of the 1870s most of the steamboat freight rolled from Benton in locally owned wagons, with a pair of major additions in Murphy Neel and Kleinschmidt Bros. The latter boasted that they had the wagons to move 250 tons of freight at a time. That would represent an investment of perhaps $10,000 in wagons alone, stock to move same several times that. The boast was probably well based, Kleinschmidt shipped about 2,000 tons yearly from Benton to Helena, an amount to keep those wagons moving for long months. At that, Kleinschmidt was probably smallest of the big four. A Baker partner later said his firm did 15,000 tons business in one year, also that his firm at one time owned 500 yoke of oxen and several hundred head of mules.

The small freighter had a place; there was David G. Browne, hauling for W. S. Wetzel and others, and Ed Smith, who seemed to specialize in silver ore cargoes.

By the time early freighting from the steamboats began from Fort Benton and lower points, wagons had evolved to pretty much their later form. Will Sutherlin claimed to have introduced the twin wagon hitch in 1866 in Montana, simply because he and partners lacked the money to buy animals and hire men, and the saving was enough to encourage imitation. In later gold rush years two and three wagon hitches were commonly used; some times in later years four hitch outfits with a longer string of oxen. Eight or ten outfits made up a wagon train, with 12 to 15 men the customary crew. A three wagon outfit's load would vary of course, 7 1/2 tons seems a reasonable average, with the heaviest load on the front vehicle, less on the second and least on the third or trail wagon. Number of oxen varied according to load, nine yoke or 18 animals for a heavy 3-wagon hitch.

In Montana the Joseph Murphy heavy freight wagon was favored—the make was of a successful and reputable St. Louis manufacturer, numbers came up on the decks of steamboats yearly. With red running gear, white top and blue box the Murphy wagon flaunted the national colors when new, a few miles on the trail dulled the effect. The lighter Chicago wagon was favored by farmers. Probably on price, Schlutter wagons, built by convict labor, were also frequently seen on the trails; there were numerous other makers. Montana, the remotest destination, was also a catchall for outside wagons driven in and sold on arrival.

Horses, mules and oxen were all used for motive power, but the mule was favored over his equine relative, the latter usually reserved for stages. Mules were much more expensive, three times oxen, but were favored by teamsters as far stronger. Oxen had one decisive advantage, which meant that steers by the thousand were broken to the yoke. They were slower but could week after week work on a bait of prairie grass. Horses and mules needed grain, which used valuable cargo space. Furthermore, harness for oxen was much simpler, just the yoke and chain. Despite the mere 12-15 miles per day, the others considerably faster, economics of the trail determined the matter.

Distances, Indians and weather were all major obstacles in western freighting, the first usually most important. This meant that navigable rivers, which would lessen distances of hauls by animal power, provided an important asset. These included the Mississippi to St. Paul, the Columbia with a short rail bypass, and for shorter distances, Sacramento and San Joaquin, Colorado, Rio Grande, Red and Arkansas. By far the most important to western supply was the Missouri, ultimately navigable to Fort Benton, a matter of 3,000 miles as rivermen reckoned it. (Engineer surveys, disregarding the meanders, later came up with about 2300 miles.)

First long distance hauling of substantial freight west of the Mississippi began with use of wagons from Missouri to Santa Fe in then Spanish America in 1822—for years prior some commerce existed via pack animals. To the northwest Bill Sublette took two wagons to Wind River in 1830 and two years later Capt. Benjamin Bonneville took 20 vehicles to the Rockies. Then Joe Meek and Bob Newell guided families over what became the Oregon or Overland Trail in 1840. That opened the great land route to the Northwest coast, about 1000 persons in 1843. Mormons by 1847 had opened an offshoot to Utah, and of course that was the forerunner of the California Trail to the diggings soon after.

### Freighting Beginnings In Montana

Records are scanty, but the early fur forts, Fort Union by 1830, and Fort McKenzie from about 1833 used Red River type handmade carts pulled by horses acquired from Indians to transport firewood and logs. Perhaps the even earlier Canadian trading posts in Northwest Montana did the same, as the Red River cart originated on their back trail.

First arrival of white owned animals noted were with the wagon and three carts of Fr. DeSmet's party off the Oregon Trail in 1841, when the party came into the Bitter Root valley to the site of St. Mary's Mission. This mission became the well known Fort Owen after sale to John Owen in 1850. That same year the Owen Journal shows John Jacobs as owner of a mule and three oxen in December, and that Jacobs hauled logs for Fort Owen in April 1851.

In 1843 Alexander Culbertson had told Audubon that Fort McKenzie had 30 or more horses, some likely used to cart firewood. Culbertson in December 1851 brought the first wagon from Fort Union to Fort Benton. He may have beaten the first commercial freighter to Fort Owen, Emanuel Martin bringing wagons from Salt Lake City in an unstated year, likeliest being 1852.

First arrival of wagons, aside from fur company traffic, at Fort Benton was September 1, 1853, when the Isaac Stevens expedition arrived from Fort Union. Here, due to the late season, the wagons were left, the main Stevens party going to the new Washington Territory by horseback and with pack animals. The army owned wagons in large part probably moved westward with the 300 soldiers under Major Blake who arrived on the Chippewa and Key West July 2, 1860, but arrival of Mullan's party from the west doubtless included other wagons. Whatever the source, William Cary, passenger on the Chippewa which burned above Fort Union, reported Dawson bringing a train of 21 wagons in 1861 down from Fort Benton for supplies. In the next three years there was considerable traffic both ways, on the Mullan Road between Fort Benton and old Fort Walla Walla.

### Montana's Gold Rush

While confirmation of gold discoveries in the later Deer Lodge area had been made in 1861 by the Granville Stuart party, it was not until July 28, 1862, that John White and William Eades made their rich strike in Grasshopper Gulch, the settlement became Bannack. Result of the news was explosive, and gold rush freighting dates from the find.

Fueling the rush were arrivals of the Thomas Holmes and James Liberty Fisk overland expeditions from Minnesota, grouping the emigrants for safe passage across the plains, bound for the earlier gold discoveries in what became the state of Idaho. Many members of these trains stayed for the bird in hand. About 70 of the first party arrived in Fort Benton August 9, 1862, the second September 5th. These emigrants came of course by wagon with what of their worldly goods they could transport. Such emigrant parties continued from Minnesota through 1867 with the exception of 1865, adding about 1000 population to the northwest—but steamboats carried many times that number through the decade of the 1860s. Other thousands came via the Overland Trail and Fort Hall, later by the Bozeman and Bridger cutoffs, along which hostile Indians killed many.

One reporter of considerable traffic westward on the Mullan Road in 1862 was C. P. Higgins, who in 1861 had lost a $7,000 stock of merchandise for his Hell Gate store in the burning of the steamboat Chippewa. That disaster meant considerable freighting for the salvage and new supplies from Fort Union, Andrew Dawson going to Fort Benton for vehicles and returning in six weeks with 21 wagons, meaning the moving of about 50 tons and as many passengers west.

Wm. Berkin in 1862 was one of the freighters to the new mining camps in later Montana, also noting in too scanty memoirs that next year pack trains, one of them of 60 mules, began operations from the west—this form of transportation was noted for two more years, afterwards seldom. The mules, carrying about 300 pounds apiece, brought only small weight, high value goods. Other 1862 freighters from Fort Benton included C. P. Higgins.

The next year, 1863, was one of bitter frustration for merchants at the mining camps who depended on the Missouri steamboats. Not a single one reached Fort Benton, nearest being the Shreveport to Snake Point near Cow Island, although an estimated 1250 tons of freight made it up the Missouri for Montana markets. LaBarge, Harkness & Co. had guaranteed delivery at the mines of about a fifth of that total—the ruination of the company. Robert Lemon, their Fort Benton agent, contracted with King & Gillette at 25c a pound—that, with other factors, meant a heavy loss and ultimate bankruptcy. Goods from the Nellie Rogers and Alone reached Milk and Poplar rivers, then were transported to Bannack by Joe Slade's trains, an "almost incredible" feat that involved beating off two full scale Indian attacks. The goods arrived at Bannack just ahead of winter storms and perhaps saved the miners from starvation. (Father DeSmet's saving presence with the passengers of the Nellie Rogers—he turned back hostile Sioux when recognized—helped Slade's start on that trip.) Other freight was handled by a Frank Worden outfit from the Hell Gate store, some by teams sent by Andrew Dawson 400 miles, with Matt Carroll, Bob and Jim Lemon, Joe Cobell and Jerry Potts on this desperate expedition, and King & Gillette teams apparently managed a second trip—data is missing. Mormon freighters from Salt Lake City over 400 miles south also profited from needs of miners at Bannack and new Virginia City. The cost was high, Dan Cushman in "Gold Frontier" suggests the gold dust mined went to stave off starvation. Probably the only reasonable price in the camps was for tough beef from worn out oxen which brought in the goods.

Four years of Missouri river navigation into Montana had brought alternate success and failure for owners and freighters alike. Despite two more years of trouble, the tide would begin to turn for commerce on what would be the Benton Road.

### More Freight For The Wagons

John Bozeman and John Jacobs had routed (and touted) their cutoff from the Overland Trail in 1863; in 1864 Jim Bridger laid out an alternative a bit further westward. Old Gabe was knowing about Indians and figured his route safe from attacks by Sioux, being harried westward by General Sully after an 1862 rising in Minnesota. Bozeman and Bridger figured to gain financially by guiding emigrants. Either route, barring hostiles, was the route to new Montana Territory in 1864 for emigrants off the older trail. But neither could beat the steamboats for freight in volume.

The 1864 season was the first in which rivermen of St. Louis fully realized the profits to be made by a steamboat to Fort Benton. Freight was around 12c to 15c a pound, occasionally higher—a 200 ton cargo at 15c figures to about $60,000, a couple hundred passengers up and down would add about $40,000 and it cost around $25,000 to make the trip. But if 1864 boats left St. Louis in fleets, arrivals were in dribbles, for it again was a low water year. It wasn't until early June that the Benton reached the place it was named for, it dropped down for added cargo and returned, in all about 350 tons, loads for 150 wagons; a couple more boats reached the Marias and finally the Cutter came in, making about 860 tons. At Cow Island another 400 tons, at Milk River as much. Enterprising and lucky freighters would profit greatly.

Chief 1864 chronicle available is that of Bill Gladstone, who helped handle the 400 tons left at Cow Island by the American Fur steamboat Yellowstone. That Fort Benton freighting resources were increasing is evidenced by his mention of 100 pack mules, another of 16 wagons, all after the work party had roughed out a road of sorts up Cow Creek, start of the long time low water freight route to Benton. Freighters, rivermen and merchants seem to have harvested much of the tons of gold being washed out at the mines, for prices were high. That profit came after considerable risk, for while about 30 steamboats had left St. Louis for the Upper Missouri, only nine cargoes came into the territory, four others nearly reached the Montana line. Indian attacks along the river were pretty frequent, adding another dimension.

Slowness of the steamboats in 1865, with first arrival May 28, left the Virginia City area dependent on freight from the south for needed supplies. An April item in the Montana Post reported that Western Stage Co. had sold out to Ben Holladay, Omaha to Denver, and of his intentions to run a stage line to Montana. The issue of April 29 noted the first arrival of flour in a number of months, six sacks. Next issue, "large lots of flour arriving in Virginia—market still high at $75." (per 100 lbs.) Also Oliver & Co. were planning a daily coach to Helena, in May adding coaches to Benton, and first train of 12 wagons leaving for Fort Benton, "the grass around Ophir is now very good."

Prime destination that spring was to Ophir (present Loma), about 12 miles below Fort Benton at the mouth of the Marias, where a group of Montanans were building a townsite after being granted a legislative franchise. On May 25 nine whites and one black wood cutters were killed by Bloods a short distance up the Marias valley, while cutting logs for cabins, effectively ending that proposed settlement. Naturally, the obvious possibility of an Indian war drew the alarmed attention of territorial residents. May 20 the Post had reported Indians very troublesome on the Fort Benton Road (first time noted as so termed), and that flour was down to $30 after a train arrived from Salt Lake. Subsequent issues were of course full of the Ophir tragedy, and of Gov. Sidney Edgerton's proclamation which called for activation of a Montana militia.

American Fur's Yellowstone, with Charles Chouteau aboard to turn the fur post over to North West Fur Co., arrived at Fort Benton May 28, followed by the Deer Lodge the 30th—this boat to be the success story of 1865. Despite the Indian danger, freighters were heading north in numbers in May—a June 17 Post included Helena news to the effect that freight and passenger trains were collecting on the south side of Sun River until enough had gathered to force their way through to the steamboat landing; Indians were present in large numbers on the north side of the Sun. First freight and passengers from the boats arrived in Helena June 13th. Trips were far from trouble free. Simeon Estes, driving a four horse team to Benton was chased by five Indians, raced his outfit for a mile to the edge of the plateau above Fort Benton. The hill was even steeper then, Estes stopped and his six or seven passengers got out with their firearms and the Blackfeet rode away, doubtless with bullets whistling by. Estes made it back to Helena in seven days with flour and passengers. (Usual passenger charge for such a trip varied, apparently of the nature of an ounce of gold dust, say $17.)

By July 1st the Post could report freight and passengers by way of the river arriving fast, after three trips by the Deer Lodge, bringing freight of heavier boats. One Virginia City firm received a train of 17 four mule wagons "laden with States flour, sugar, coffee and whisky." Dance & Stuart had received two small trains. By that date about 2500 tons of freight had reached either Fort Benton or the Marias—the bulk of an estimated 3700 tons to Montana points. There were around 2700 passengers, two thirds upbound, on the boats, quite possibly many hundreds unaccounted for. Also many hundreds more went down river by mackinaws, ads in the Post evidence.

At Helena and Virginia City freight by mid-July was arriving in such amounts as to be unworthy of mention beyond the July 29 comment, "Some very heavy freight trains arrived here during the week, from Benton." It is clear that the freighters, largely operating as individuals, were out in impressive numbers this season. The evidence is in a William Pfouts report on returning from Benton, to the Post editor, that on July 20 125 wagons left Benton for Milk River to freight goods left there by steamboats. At that point steamboat owners had built a three compartment fort of 100x50 yards, mounting three guns, to protect the freight.

In addition, an August 1 letter from Hi Upham at the Blackfeet agency in Fort Benton mentions that on July 31st a caravan of 250 wagons had left the place for Milk River, each drawn by four to eight yoke of oxen, making a "big show." It certainly would, and represented enough firepower to handle a mass attack by hostiles—Montana freighters had to be tough customers. The combined capacity at around two tons per wagon would have almost exactly balanced the estimated 750 tons of freight left by boats at Milk River.

First arrival of that section of the freight at Helena was reported in the September 16 Post, 11 wagons, and first to Virginia City a week later. The later train left Milk River August 4th and Benton the 26th. One of the last trains to Helena from Milk River was in early December.

A considerable exodus of miners from Montana was indicated early in the boating season; the major one, by ads on bullet proof mackinaw passage, at around $75 per person and provide own subsistence, began in August. In cooperative ventures, all working to build boats, one advertised price via the Yellowstone was $15. This year of 1865 Alder Gulch area miners split between Yellowstone and Missouri, from Helena it was by way of the Missouri—there may have been 2,000 in all going down the rivers in small boats.

The gold exodus was tremendous. September 30 Post: "Million after million of gold has left the Territory, by way of the river and by the overland route... One man that we know of, took 400 lbs. in clean dust; another carried 200 lbs. with him; and from 100 lbs. to 25 lbs. has been so common, that a record of the names would look like our postoffice list." One hundred pounds represented about $25,000 face at an intrinsic worth of $17 per Troy ounce, a fortune then. An added bonus, gold was worth about $1.50 in greenbacks. A man could have put his money out at interest and lived a life of ease, if not luxury, on the amount.

One later estimate is that five-sixths of the placer gold went down the rivers, chiefly the Missouri after 1865. A sort of evidence of the choice of routes comes from the halving of the Overland stage fare, Virginia to Salt Lake, to $75 if paid in gold dust.

## Freighting Not For The Faint Hearted

"Reminiscences of Alexander Toponce," French born early day freighter, provides evidence that Montana freighting was not for the faint hearted. He had come to Montana, arriving at Bannack May 14, 1863, then followed the stampede to Alder Gulch and had some success with a mining claim. Turning again to freighting, he brought flour, tea, shovels, picks and butter to Virginia City from Salt Lake December 24, 1863, just in time to witness the beginning of the big Vigilante cleanup of road agents. As customary then, Toponce sold his outfit and was worth $20,000 in gold, most from the sale of the train, and returned to Utah, buying a bigger train for the 1864 season. He explained it was easy to hire men anxious to get to the mines, in Utah, impossible to hire in Montana. Toponce had another successful trip in 1864, selling out again that summer.

He got his come-uppance that fall, taking a train loaded with flour north into Idaho, where he and other freighters had to winter. Cold weather and snow killed his oxen. That was the winter flour in Montana jumped to $125 a sack, and there sat that Toponce flour halfway to wealth. In March he made a deal with a packer at $20 a sack to take the flour to Virginia, hit a falling market and lost much of his stake, but bought oxen in Virginia and went down to salvage his wagons. The next trip was to the mouth of the Marias and quite profitable, and Toponce's train made two trips to Fort Union that summer.

It was a speculation on government surplus in the winter of 1865-66 that demonstrated just how tough Montana freighting could be. After selling his train following the second trip from Union, Toponce bought 40 wagons, six yoke of oxen per wagon and 25 extra, 305 in all, laying out $40,000 for the outfit. Then he headed down to Fort Union to buy that surplus, leaving Fort Benton December 1, 1865. At Union he bought nearly everything there was for sale, loaded his wagons with sugar, coffee and other items which would bring a fine price in Helena. He held up his train waiting for the Jerry Mann train, two outfits and more rifles being extra insurance through hostile country.

Forty miles out of Union the combined trains hit a storm that forced them to move down to the Missouri for shelter, where they forted up against hostiles. The weather grew so cold the freighters had to shoot their cattle, horns were freezing and exploding, and they were dismayed at having to use augers to get to the frozen whisky. Around February 1st Toponce and Jerry Mann started for Helena in 2 1/2 feet of snow aboard riding mules. The men fed the animals on their own provender, roasted buffalo meat. (A Montana Post item from Helena March 21, 1866, reported Mann in town for oxen to bring his train up from Milk River, and another April 28 from Benton that Mann and Aleck Dupont had lost 22 horses and mules at Sun River.)

At Helena, according to Toponce's memoirs, he and Mann bought 300 head of cattle each, plus horses, and two wagons. The horses were stolen by Indians near Sun River. While camped near Fort Benton, two of 20 men they had hired took off for the fleshpots, were found next day, killed and scalped. A couple more, Toponce's wagon boss Bill Sherman and Mann's wagon master tried Benton whisky, too, got into an argument and both died, one of gunshot, the other by knife. At the Marias the party lost all their grub in high water, went on, on a game straight diet. Near Wolf Point Toponce's new wagon boss went after a stray ox, ran into hostiles and was killed. In the fracas that followed the whites downed three Blackfeet and captured a wounded brave, who was turned over to the tender mercies of tribal enemies, the Assiniboines.

At the place where he had left his train, Toponce found that a spring ice gorge had swept away his wagons, leaving only a pair of front wheels, the men gone to the Mann camp six miles down the Missouri. A part of the loss was ten tons of sugar, ten of coffee, worth close to $1 a pound at Last Chance at the time. Toponce found his freighters had suffered terribly, four drowned, fifteen frozen so badly he sent them to Fort Union to go down by steamboat to Omaha. Mann's outfit got off lightly and eventually made it to Helena, accompanied by Alexander Toponce and party, rolling those front wagon wheels along. When he left Fort Benton for Union, he recalled, he had $75,000 in gold plus the wagon train. On return to Helena he sold his loose cattle and lacked $18 of being able to pay off his 45 men. Toponce bought a new wagon outfit on tick, made three more trips to Montana and when he left the territory in July 1867 figured he was worth more than $100,000.

### The Benton Road Reaches Maturity

In December 1865 the Montana Post reported arrival in Helena of a 40 horse pack train loaded with press and printing material for the Montana Radiator (which soon became the Helena Herald). A couple of years later the Herald mentioned that the disassembled press came across the mountains from Idaho, cradled between pack animals, at a cost of 60c a pound.

Issue 7 of the Radiator on January 27, 1866, carried an interesting letter that meant the coming maturity of territorial Montana's greatest highway, the Benton Road: (Excerpts) "Distance from Helena to Fort Benton is about 135 miles. With the exception of 15 miles, the road between these places is one of the best, if not the best road, in this territory. These 15 miles comprise the part between Clark's ranch and the last crossing of the Prickly Pear. This part of the road has been the great obstacle to travel from Benton to Helena and probably is the reason why other roads have been sought and attracted public attention... No doubt you will be glad to know that this difficult passage is about to be obviated by individual enterprise."

James King and W. C. Gillette had purchased the legislative franchise for a toll road from Malcolm Clarke, former trader at Fort Benton. While toll roads were in ill repute in Montana Territory; a governor once inveighed against tolls, which could cost a freighter from Utah $40 a wagon, the route that King & Gillette worked out through the Prickly Pear would make both partners rich, and contribute as well to the development of Montana. They built and often replaced numerous bridges over the years, improved the roadway of what became the busiest highway in all the territory. (A side note: Alex Toponce reported that he did much work clearing a road over mountains south of Helena to bring the first wagon train to Last Chance in 1864; on his return he found a King & Gillette toll taker and had to fork over $5 a wagon, a bit of enterprise that appealed to his French humor.) On the road north to Benton the toll was probably double at first, in 1867 it was reduced to $6.25 for a three wagon hitch, then coming into fashion, and $5 for a two wagon outfit.

### The Big Muddy Relents

For steamboat men, 1866 was the year everything fell in place: High water, 10c and up for freight and $150-$200 for passengers; incidently high wages for crews going into dangerous waters, several times Ohio river scales. Pilots were special, Bill Massie got $7500 for piloting the Cora to Benton, lost the works in a poker game the night he landed in St. Louis. Boats in proper season were full of passengers, up and down. The year was probably by far the biggest year for owners' profits, and also for gold carried—literally by the ton in some instances. The success on the river incidently ruined promoters of the Rocky Mountain Wagon Road Co. who favored an alternate port at the mouth of the Musselshell that year.

First boat arrivals at Benton were the St. John and Deer Lodge on May 18, from that time on the boats were unloading freight at Fort Benton's mile long levee far faster than the teamsters could move it. Toward the end of the boating season the Montana Post reported 2500 men, 3000 wagons and 20,000 oxen were employed in moving the freight to the camps from Fort Benton. This was the year multiple hitch wagon outfits were first used on Montana trails, according to Will Sutherlin—when his party set off for Benton, they were short on oxen, employes and cash, so experimented. In later years, three wagon hitches were commonest, four occasionally used.

As the boating season approached, territorial fears of an Indian war had not abated, acting Governor Meagher was pressing for a Montana militia to punish marauders. But Fort Benton, in the "war" area, seemed little concerned, a February Post item: "Parties from the fort go armed when securing wood across the Missouri. They also report an abundance of arms, ammunition and men." At the time, sugar and coffee were unobtainable at Benton, flour reluctantly sold at $40 in gold, tough times at the river port until boats in May.

Near opening of the freighting season, a Helena item in the May 19 Post reported, "Some twenty wagons, with over a hundred passengers, left yesterday for Fort Benton." Soon after a traveler southward bound reported he was seldom out of sight of a train, counted 290 wagons headed for Benton. So much freight was headed south that neither paper carried much about arrivals. The reported freight rate of 6c a pound brought farmers and others with wagons out in droves—a round trip from Helena would be less than three weeks, freight about $300, plus around $20 for any passenger, when freighters were risking their lives for a sixth that first figure per month.

The late season of 1866 brought the usual exodus of miners, many of whom probably had been successful. On at least two occasions, two tons or so of gold came in a single wagon shipment. Granville Stuart saw such a load, 2 1/2 tons in a wagon escorted by a company of armed miners. X. Beidler reported forming an armed party which brought a similar total to Benton in three wagons, the division probably added insurance against total loss. Will Sutherlin met Meagher's party two days out of Benton with almost a ton, $400,000. Some vast cleanups were made that summer at Diamond City, including the richest of all at Montana Bar.

In October in the Post, Bill Hamilton, sheriff at Benton, claimed that 200 mackinaws with 3500 passengers had or would go down river from there. The total sounds unbelievable, but an earlier report was that three mackinaws a day left Fort Benton during August, with about 15 passengers each—that would have been almost 1400 people. The St. Joe Herald October 11 had counted 150 mackinaws which had arrived there, with a third that many snagged, wrecked or abandoned. The September 29 Montana Post had it that with "500 miners floating down the Missouri there is also $1,500,000 in gold."

When the steamboating season ended in late July, save for a couple of strays, 31 boats had brought 6644 tons of supplies, most of which had traversed that great highway, the Benton Road. Also Camp Cooke at the Judith had been established and supplied with another thousand tons, and 1350 tons were freighted from other points on the Missouri. One item in a September Post, "the obscure landing place became Benton City."

Better by water than land, far cheaper than a lunging, bumping ride by stage. But not always. In the Helena Herald November 29 was a letter written by John Corder at Fort Union, whose party had left Fort Benton in a large skiff on September 6: "Please notice the deaths by Indians of T. A. Kent, John Ross, James Smith and Wm. Barber, after five hours hard fighting with forty Sioux. Kent killed thirteen of them, shooting ten and killing three others with his knife. When he clinched with the thirteenth, one of the cursed savages killed him with a billet of wood, striking him on the head. I received five wounds in the body from arrows, but nothing fatal, I hope." The fight occurred at the mouth of Milk River.

## Biggest Freighting Year Of Gold Rush

Biggest and easiest year of the gold rush period was 1867 when steamboats arrived from late May into August. There was little Indian trouble, despite a tragic end to Thomas F. Meagher's warlike posture. In March the St. Louis Democrat indicated the season's possibilities in a long list of steamboats loading for Fort Benton. For 1866 John G. Copelin, with steamboat connections, had estimated gold from Montana at $40 million, the Montana Post editor thought it about $30 million. There was a lessening of the golden tide in 1867, but the rather jealous Montana Post allowed an estimate by river of "over $5 million." As possessors were understandably secretive, an item from St. Joseph Union reprinted in the Post may be revealing, that Huntsville has 16 passengers and $175,000 treasure. That would be around 45 pounds of dust per passenger. Assuming half that per person, the probably 2600 down bound passengers on boats may have carried $14 million or 28 tons with them, mackinaws accounting for more millions, but probably not at the same rate per individual—mackinaws could be a poor man's way of getting home.

Some of the bloom had gone off freighting in 1867, but individuals as well as professionals turned out to move the steamboat freight south. Rates quoted by June 12 in the Helena Herald were 7c and 8c a pound, which represented $280 or more a wagon, considerably over teamster wages. In addition, C. C. Huntley, stage man, reported things quiet on the Benton Road; the infrequency of Indian problems encouraging news for farmers thinking about trying freighting. In anticipation of a good season, buildings were going up rapidly at Fort Benton.

Shippers could afford the rates, there were so many steamboats heading up the Missouri that rates had dropped from 12-15c to 8-10c. But the eager freighters had to wait while the rivers fell from flood stage. Boats to June 1st were the Waverly and Miner, then five in a week, as many the next two, with good passenger lists, though for miners already in the territory the great years were fading. One indication was the 50 ton shipment of large pipe being loaded off boats for a flume-ditch company. One reason for Indian quietude on the Benton Road, soldiers of the 13th Infantry were being stationed at 10 mile intervals, and patrols were accompanying stages.

By June 12 the Helena Herald included, "Benton is quite lively now, and looks like a young St. Louis. About one thousand head of oxen can be seen attached to their wagons, waiting for loads." Further, "King & Gillette's toll road is in fine condition, it having been fully repaired, and now teams can make trips easily and over a good grade. The entire road from Silver City is guarded by squads of from ten to twenty soldiers... A great deal of treasure is being shipped over this road, to be sent down the river on the steamers."

June 19 Herald, "A large amount of merchandise is now daily arriving here from Benton... We learn that business at Fort Benton is more brisk now than during any previous season, and that for almost a mile, the levee is covered with freight. Very soon, immense trains loaded with these stores may be expected to arrive in Helena."

A week later from St. Joseph, a report of a half million dollar gold cargo on the Only Chance. (This boat made a second trip to Benton in 1867, a rare feat.) Cargoes coming up? "Couch's ox team of 18 wagons arrived Monday, four exclusively laden with coal oil."

The Post at Virginia City carried similar items, also in early July there was mention of a Fourth of July celebration at Benton, climaxed by a squaw dance in a large hall on the levee—several fights also enlivened the 4th. July 8th seven steamboats were unloading at the levee in Fort Benton. In July Wells Fargo forced C. C. Huntley to sell his Helena-Benton stage route, also let a contract to John Kennedy to build 12 station houses and stables on the line, $1200 each, in gold.

An August 5 arrival was the Ida Stockdale, with General Alfred Terry and staff, come on a chartered boat to locate the new permanent post of Fort Shaw on Sun River and Fort Ellis near Bozeman. On the 14th the Herald reported arrival of numerous freight wagons from Benton, with several trains passing, bound for Virginia City. Navigation season ended with the second arrival from St. Louis of the Only Chance August 25th. Almost 8000 tons of merchandise and supplies had been landed at Fort Benton, another 1200 put ashore at points below, including one boat with cargo for Camp Cooke at the Judith. Fairly complete passenger reports indicate 2200 up and 2600 down. There were 41 steamboat arrivals plus some late double trips; two boats wrecked, two crippled; 46 boats had left St. Louis for Fort Benton, and another 16 started for points below. Army supplies were carried on 37 of the total steamboats.

Adding to the migration to Montana in 1867 was arrival of the Peter Davy wagon train at Fort Benton with about 70 wagons and over 220 persons (although the Herald figure was 400). Either number could be considered as balancing the down trip of the Imperial from Cow Island with around 300 passengers.

In October the influence of soldiers on the Fort Benton area roads had waned, Crows tried to corral the Diamond R wagon train of J. J. Roe & Co. on the road to Cow Island, were stood off with rifle fire. Thereafter, a letter from Matt Carroll in late November advised the Herald that Fort Benton "is now indulging in its bear-like winter snooze, from which it will only be wakened by the whistle of steamboats in the spring."

### Fading Steamboat Boom

Despite the final note on 1867, in January 1868 another resident bragged in the Helena Herald, "Benton City is growing in importance almost daily, about 30 new buildings, including Baker and Power companies building a large hotel on the levee."

Advent of soldiers in Montana Territory provided additional opportunities for merchants and freighters. For example, 1868 bids were called for 156,800 and 117,600 pounds of flour at Fort Shaw and Camp Cooke, 4 1/2 million pounds of supply freighting to be contracted, 400 horses needed, mostly for Camp Cooke.

April 25 the Montana Post reported that freighting business had been dull the past two years—the editor may have been reporting on Virginia City, the Post had just moved to Helena. The same issue the Post reported a surplus of wagons, probably due to the conditions Toponce mentioned, easy to get drivers to Montana, none wanted to leave. Heavy Murphy and Espenchial wagons were selling for $75 to $100, light wagons $80 to $125, the latter the popular Schuttler, and Helena was full of wagons, many of which would be sold for the wood and iron in them, "the fate of hundreds in the past."

That same issue had a history of Confederate Gulch (Diamond City), about 25 miles southeast of Helena. During 1866 Montana Bar gave up "wealth computed by the wagonload, and portions of which were actually transported to Benton in wagons carrying no other freight, and guarded by a company of armed men." Mention was made of $1850 panned by five men before breakfast. Another note, Fort Benton bound freighters were getting ready; and in Helena oranges were 80c each in gold dust. There was a relationship, prices would drop sharply after the first boats.

Fort Benton that spring of 1868 was anxiously awaiting those boats, encouraged by an early rise in the Missouri, and word that North West Transportation had new boats based on Sioux City saving a thousand miles and tedious days. Chicago would benefit, St. Louis lose, on the new supply base. The Chicago Post estimated 8,000 tons worth as many million would be shipped to the Upper Missouri.

Fortunate was the freighter in those days with two way income. M. H. Bird was one such, his ox train of ten wagons left Helena April 16 loaded with lumber for the building going on in Benton, then would return with mill and foundry castings and machinery for Chas. Hendric & Co. of Helena. That Hendric freight had come up on a steamboat the year before and had been sitting on the levee where it had been unloaded. Bird would still have time to head back to Benton and meet the early boats.

The head of navigation was also building, a May 1 item, "Trains loaded with lumber arriving daily, everyone building." Also, a warning of trouble, Heavy Runner of the Piegans in town, says he can't hold back his young men. One of the new buildings was open, the Thwing Hotel between Baker and Power, and a few miles down river, Coal Banks was getting out a hundred bushels of coal a day. (Probably due to grates and draft, rivermen gave up on burning this, despite their wooding problems. That was the trouble with low grade coal along the upper river; when Grant Marsh returned after twenty years he found boats using local coal.)

By date of the Post of May 22, four steamboats had already arrived at Fort Benton, headed by the Success May 13. That issue reported 750 to 800 wagons headed north, half already near Fort Benton, 300 more than the year before, with ranchers out in force, banding in trains of 10 to 20. Six woodhawks were reported killed along the river, four others missing. King & Gillette tolls through Prickly Pear, $3 for one yoke each way, $3.50 for two, $4 for four, etc. By May 29 Fort Benton was set for business, 20 saloons open, two billiard halls, despite a big horse and cattle raid there and on the Fort McKenzie bottom below that netted the Sioux a batch of remounts and fifty I. G. Baker oxen on the 27th.

Regular freighters handled most of the freight despite the others. The Herald April 16 had mentioned some of them, J. J. Roe's Diamond R with 90 wagons in three mule trains, Simms Bros., Carroll & Steell, Garrison, M. Wood, I. G. Baker, North West Fur, Coover & MacAdow, Ballard, Bird, Kirkendall and John J. Murphy.

A traveler's account in May was that he counted 725 wagons at Fort Benton or on the Benton Road, and first shipment by fast freight (usually extra charge) before June 5th, much more arriving. So many ranchers had turned out that the Benton levee was reported cleared of freight by the 6th of June—that was off 17 steamboats, almost half the season's total of 36.

The remaining freight was handled rapidly. June 19 the Post reported "immense freight from Benton, 154 wagons, over 600 tons in three days. Only 38 wagons Sunday." The paper estimated that 1500 wagon loads of freight had arrived in Helena. Late in the month heavy rains made the Benton Road temporarily impassable. Nevertheless, the freight soon moved again, on July first, Diamond R 26 wagons, J. T. Murphy six double hitches and a heavy 58,000 pounds, two other trains of nine wagons each arrived in Helena.

The rains resumed at both ends of the trail: July 3, "Benton Road in horrible condition"; July 10, 40 wagons hopelessly mired on Sun River bottom, few trains arriving. A week later some trains were trickling in, then about 150 wagons in two days. A rare mention the 24th, it took a 40 mule pack train 35 days from Wallula, the Mullan Road terrible—from 1866 few pack trains came to Montana. The last of July the Missouri was falling, and "300 tons of goverment freight yet to come up."

There had been some boosting, especially by the Helena Herald, for Montana Hide & Fur's alternate route via the Musselshell, a flat failure as it turned out, the founders soon among those freighting from Fort Benton. George Clendennin at Musselshell later mentions about 80 tons discharged from a steamboat there was the only freighting over the central Montana route, probably a Diamond R train apparently unnoted in the papers.

August 7 the Post reported a wagon train had left Helena for Benton, Dakota Territory, near the Union Pacific railhead, quite apparently because the steamboat freight was moved as fast as it was unloaded. (That Benton has not been definitely located in this century, but was near present Rawlins.)

Although in August 1868 Fort Benton's boating season traffic was nearly done and the river was low, there apparently were more boats reaching Cow Island than the papers reported; several comments on freighting from there must mean more from Cow Island than the 90 tons left by the Only Chance. Such boats would likely have been Northwest Transportation steamboats from Sioux City, which would prove their worth in the next year of very low water.

Last remnant involved the Amelia Poe, wrecked and lost in eastern Montana May 23. Crows looted what they could, fought off Sioux wanting a share of the spoils, then were shunted off and the heavier stuff salvaged. Despite the loss of 57 oxen to Sioux, Tom Gorham's train reached Dearborn in November with that salvage and was snowbound. Then X. Beidler, deputy U. S. marshal, appeared to slap an attachment on the freight in behalf of an insurance company. A further note on the lost cargo, a group of Bentonites bought the wreck, apparently in part for whisky still in the hold. In December the whites had a tough fight with Sioux near Fort Peck, four men killed. Old Tom Campbell's rifle counted most of the coups on five Sioux slain. No report on the whisky, probably destined to replenish stocks of Mose Solomon's Medicine Lodge in Fort Benton—Mose took two of his nine battle wounds in the fray.

Freight tonnage from boats for the year in excess of 5700.

### Tough, Bloody Year Of 1869

An open winter, light snow and moderate temperatures set the stage for a season of tough steamboating, not in the least helped by the March 29 burning of six Benton bound steamboats at St. Louis and snagging of a couple more during the season.

It was not until May 19, 1869, that the Deer Lodge arrived at Benton, eight days ahead of the next boat, five in all in May. From then on few brought in their original cargoes, in all 19 double trips were made to Dauphin's Rapids.

For Helena, the freighting season began with arrival of Hugh Kirkendall's train May 26 with freight off the Deer Lodge. Farm teams were again heading down the Benton Road for what freight they could contract. At Benton in June business was dull due to the low stage of the river, Diamond R and Kirkendall loading. One thing, the squaw hurdy house was full of freighters killing time. Things soon livened up with arrival of double tripping boats, and from Benton on the 11th I. G. Baker reported nine boats (a record) at the levee, and the town "full of goods."

Soldiers were busy that season trying to protect travelers on the Benton Road, without much success; near year end it was rumored that 56 whites had been killed by hostile Indians in the territory, chiefly by Blackfeet growing desperate at the continuing influx of whites, and a thousand horses had been stolen. One of Fort Benton's merchants, T. C. Power, was quite evidently looking ahead to a change from mining. In July he opened a Helena store for sale of agricultural implements.

For the head of Missouri navigation, a complicating trade factor was completion of the transcontinental railroad in Utah May 10, 1869. That was considerably closer than freighting from UP railheads in Wyoming. However, Helena to Corinne, Utah, was about 480 miles, via the Benton Road it was 340 less. Some Helena freight came from Utah, first report in the July 15 Helena Herald in 22 days at 7c a pound.

July 16 near Fort Benton two of Garrison's herders were mortally wounded by Indians, concensus was Blackfeet. In revenge, three tribesmen were killed in Fort Benton; the guilty parties turned out to be Crows, who looted and burned the wagons. The item called for soldiers to protect indicated heavy traffic on the Cow Island Trail; near the latter place several steamboats were unable to go further. In all, about 900 tons were left there by steamboats, another 400 tons at Fort Peck.

August 8 near Eagle Creek an ox team with Flirt freight was attacked, and a Diamond R train coming to help in the fight had one man killed. Whites saw the beginnings of an all out Blackfeet war; freighter Hugh Kirkendall sent eight heavily armed men from Helena to help protect his train, then near Fort Benton. Attacks weren't confined to the freight trails, stockaded Musselshell was attacked by a hundred Sioux, who charged into the small settlement, were beaten off by several shots from a mountain howitzer, according to trader Gil Norris.

Indian affairs in the Fort Benton vicinity quieted in September, the Blackfeet and Bloods moving from the vicinity as evidence they wanted nothing to do with the hostilities of the Piegans, the most southerly branch. Part of the quiet was due to efforts of Alexander Culbertson, who had returned to the town he founded and was playing his final role as peacemaker. He had influence with the Blackfeet, and by no means all of the Piegans were hostile. Had civilians and military paid more heed to Culbertson, the January 23, 1870, tragedy on the Marias in which 173 Piegans of a friendly camp were slain, might never have occurred.

## The Bitter Years

As a new decade began, the territory of Montana was in a deep depression due to plunging mineral production, and Fort Benton, a bustling river port with populations of well above a thousand in freighting season, shared in the hard times. The first territorial census in April found 367 denizens, a good third part Indians—and, ran reports of later months, a decline to perhaps 180 in all. There were four Indian trading houses, Baker, Power, Wetzel & Weatherwax, and F. F. Gerard, successor to Carroll & Steell. Others were a brewery, bakery, two blacksmiths, carpenter shop, shoemaker, butcher and a dozen saloons.

Miners had left the territory in droves, many broke, and the 6300 tons of steamboat cargoes in 1869 plummeted to 1600. Indian trading was responsible for a few bright spots. John Healy and Al Hamilton returned from a profitable trade in British North America which netted them and backers perhaps $50,000, Shirley Ashby on the Marias $40,000 for Baker. Result of the first was a stampede across the Medicine Line, as the Indians called it, the independent traders purveying chiefly whisky and firearms. Fort Benton was probably better off than the rest of the territory. Helena prices were flour at $12 a sack; bacon, ham and coffee 30c to 45c and tobacco $1, far below gold rush prices.

At Fort Benton staples of trade were buffalo robes and wolf skins. The latter came chiefly by poisoning—a baited buffalo carcass might yield 30 or more wolf skins; a fairly standard value for an almost legal tender replacing gold was around $3 a hide.

A March Helena Herald said snow in the mountains was good news for boats, miners, business. Also, the paper touted Utah freight as only slightly more than by river. Neither profited very much from the 1870 season. At Fort Benton eight boats brought an average of 200 tons each, routine business for freighters.

Despite a trade of at least 15,000 robes, more likely double that, Fort Benton merchants didn't benefit that year—smallpox among the Indians led to a government embargo on shipment of an estimated $500,000 worth of furs and robes.

Freighting notes in the Helena Herald were virtually non-existent, even from Corinne, Utah. A good share was for soldiers, some for Indian annuities, freighters on either Benton Road or Corinne Trail faced hard times.

In 1871 steamboating tonnage improved slightly, in spite of efforts by freighters out of Utah to establish premium fast freight lines. Fort Benton tonnage was 1400 on six boats, another four to Cow Island and one to Fort Peck making 2150. Despite the Herald's promotion of the Corinne route, other items indicated merchants there often intended to stick by the lower cost steamboat route. Virtually no freighting news in the paper save an occasional plug for the fast freight from Utah. There was indication in sparse paragraphs that considerable trade was going on north of the boundary with Indians.

Helena was having very hard times in 1872, charity fairs to help indigents. Also, a letter from a reader suggested that because of the distances, one train could make three trips from Benton while another from Corinne was making one. In addition, snows in Wyoming and Nebraska blocked trains for weeks early in the winter. At Benton, a killing in a saloon provided the fact that sheriff, constable, coroner and justice of peace were up at Whoop Up, trading with the Indians. "Times are rather dull at present."

In the navigation season 13 steamboats brought almost 3000 tons, a promising increase over the previous two.

In February the Herald had a report from George Baker that work oxen had wintered well at Benton and Sun River despite severe weather—Tom Power lost only a half dozen head, Baker but 9 of 180 (then a third of the Baker cattle were swept away in a buffalo stampede).

Helena in March and early April was welcoming arrival of supply trains from Corinne, but these were freighters stopped by snow in winter on the route north—that year all season delivery of freight was a bitter joke.

June 1 the paper reported mule and bull teams rolling in from the railroad and Fort Benton, laden with goods. Power and Baker trains were both on the road by then, an indication of the role Fort Benton merchants would be playing in the transportation picture. Heavy rains in late June forced detours to the old Mullan Road.

Beginings of agriculture in Northern Montana were noted, good crops at Dearborn, and Robert Vaughn similarly reported in a letter from Fort Shaw. The Northern Pacific was building across Dakota toward the Missouri where Bismarck would rise, and alter the navigation pattern on the Upper Missouri. At Chicago in August the Tribune reported the largest shipment of furs to that city from Fort Benton. T. C. Power had consigned 16,400 buffalo robes, 5000 wolf skins and enough hides and peltries to make a 225 ton shipment, about a third of Fort Benton's commerce.

Steamboating slumped again in 1873, cargoes of seven boats about 1750 tons, with a good early season river stage. Much of that was for local trade. The Herald in August reported the territory's population down, "palmy days gone." Helena was shaking off reliance on the Corinne route—shipments into Montana had been roughly equal to that of the steamboats. The paper was turning again to a route from the Musselshell. A November article reported Story's train of 30 wagons leaving to establish a freight route. Peter Koch, familiar with the area from early days, was in charge. The proposal was to blossom next season as Carroll.

### Carroll Trail Promotion

Early in 1874 the Herald had frequent articles lauding the new route across the Judith Basin from Carroll, and in March rather piously remarked that since opening of commerce via the railroad in Utah the greater part of the traffic had been diverted from the river route "though at greater expense. Since freight money has gone largely to Mormons." Protection of soldiers on the Carroll Trail was assured, the paper claimed. Promoters had made a mistake in choosing cantankerous and unreliable Wm. Kountz to provide steamboats for the river portion, Bismarck to Carroll. That doubtless helped to commit the revitalized and renamed Coulson Line to the Benton terminus.

Promoters of the Carroll Trail had laid out a wagon road for freight to Helena. Kountz had one reliable boat, the Peninah, which brought five of the 11 cargoes to Carroll in 1874. Between the two ports it was a virtual standoff, 1720 tons by six boats to Benton, a very few tons less at Carroll. There was another factor—freighting.

The Peninah brought its first load to Carroll on May 8, loaded immediately on the Diamond R mule train. Perhaps, that is; for the train was reported as only near present White Sulphur Springs by May 20th, making good time, "but recent rains may slow." Four of the wagons reached Helena June 2. On June 12 the Herald explained: "The spring of 1874 may be safely put down as the 'wettest' season ever known in Montana. Since the first of April it has rained almost incessantly." For company, the freighters had a detachment of soldiers on Big Spring Creek. They were needed, a Northern Pacific survey expedition, including many soldiers as escort, was attracting unwanted Sioux attention, and loaded wagon trains were prize bait. The larger Kountz boats were having misfortunes, the Katie P. Kountz blew a cylinder head, the May Lowry had to be towed to Carroll by a Coulson boat—$1250 towage. Late June brought a couple of Diamond R trains to Helena.

Meanwhile, the freight Helena merchants dubious of the new route had consigned via Fort Benton was arriving, as some of them must have informed the Herald, which on August 7 printed a lengthy article, including: "We are aware that our merchants have been disappointed in their expectation...owing to the tardy delivery...and that some of them have expressed with emphasis their determination never to ship by the new route again." A Benton dispatch, "Benton still alive, flourishing." Further on, "The Helena firms shipped by Benton this year, received goods early as wanted, would like others to ship via Carroll, so they can retire early, wealthy." The Herald in late August had a brief note that the paper was forced to use wood pulp paper, its order six months on the way. Bentonites doubtless enjoyed that note that indicated the Herald had believed its own articles about the superiority of the Carroll route.

Carroll may actually have received more freight than the 1712 tons reported, but many months later part was moved via Benton.

### "Supplies For The North"

So ran a headline in the Herald October 9, 1874. I. G. Baker of Fort Benton was in Helena purchasing groceries, hardware and clothing to fill out an order for 40,000 pounds for the "Queen's Mounted Police, ordered for duty across the border." The Fort Benton company had provided initial supplies for a hungry group of North West Mounted Police, and would hold the contract until after the Canadian Pacific reached Alberta in 1883. One of their wagon trains moved the goods north, and the company also provided the necessary supplies for building the first NWMP post at Fort Macleod that fall, at Calgary and Fort Walsh in 1875. In addition, the Baker company acted as paymaster for the Mounties, gave helpful information and advice freely—in effect, was godfather to the force.

The result of their arrival was the almost immediate end of the lawless whisky trading which had impoverished the Indians. The Canadian trade became legitimate, and vastly benefited Fort Benton commerce. The writer in 1982 estimated the volume of shipments from Fort Benton into Canada as in the nature of 12,000 tons, including hauls of up 600 miles, now believes it may have been nearly double that figure over the decade of its importance. Either figure means a lot of freight wagon loads at around 2 1/2 tons per wagon, and many men employed.

In November announcement was made in the Herald that T. C. Power & Bro., and I. G. Baker & Co. of Fort Benton, had ordered construction of a light draft, first class steamboat on the lines of the latest model and very successful Coulson boats. Of course this would be named the Benton, and in a ten year career, largely between Bismarck and Fort Benton, the Benton would bring in about 11,000 tons of freight and 1500 passengers, and carry down about a fifth that tonnage and a third as many passengers. The mercantile commodores of an inland port were on their way.

Another Fort Benton customer that year of 1874 was the sizable International Boundary Survey Commission, about 500 men plus troops, defining the U. S.-Canadian border. The U. S. civilian members were transported down the Missouri from Fort Benton in seven large mackinaws, some of the several hundred escorting troops by late steamboats.

There was considerable late fall freight, including military supplies, coming into Fort Benton from Cow Island. Although not mentioned in the Herald, part of this was almost certainly from hung up supplies at Carroll, not far from Cow Island. Said a November 17 Herald item from Benton: "Many who have freighted on the Carroll road prefer the Benton Road and predict freight will revert to the old road with a depot at Cow Island."

### Carroll Challenge Dies

Montana was on an upswing in 1875, reflected by the 3300 tons of Benton freight and another 1300 at Carroll. The latter place had the same woes as the year before,

Sioux and gumbo, and ultimately part of that 1300 tons traveled via Cow Island along the Benton Road, a safer way to Helena.

February 1, 1875, the first issue of the Benton Record appeared, although the first four issues were printed at Fort Shaw. W. H. Buck's initial editorial was prophetic, Benton "commands the traffic of the country... is the transportation centre of Montana." A phrase in the second, dear to Bentonites, referred to the "Utopian enterprise called the Carroll Route." As files were incomplete, some references for the year are from the Helena Herald.

April 15 the Record reported plans of Ed Smith to provide a ferry at Fort Benton, first except for small boats. For almost 30 years, the Missouri had been crossed by an ancient Indian ford. American Fur wagons went after logs and shingles in the Highwood mountains to the south, some freight wagons in the 1860s crossed by this ford to go south to Gallatin City by the Graham Wagon Road, also termed East Side Road. The ford, of course, could only be used during relatively low water. The Smith ferry would benefit from a gradually developing livestock industry.

An initial freight note of May 1: "The roads to Whoop Up are in good condition, but the water in Milk River is so high that none of the Benton trains are able to cross." These included 15 wagons of supplies for the Mounted Police.

Both the Baker and Power companies reacted quickly to opportunities in Canada, arranging for handling of goods from eastern Canada under posted bond of $100,000 as warranty against diversion to sale in Montana—which would deprive the U. S. of tariff charges. In early 1875 an immense quantity of robes and furs was coming into Fort Benton, from both sides of the line—an estimated 75,000 robes, it may have been more. Power alone shipped 28,000, Baker perhaps as many, and a relatively small shipment by a Sioux City buyer was 12,450 robes and many furs. Customs duties either side of the line at 20% added up to large sums.

Both Power and Baker freighting was extensive, Power one week over 60 tons to Helena, Baker the next 130 tons to Macleod and Cypress Hills in Canada. In September a long trip for a small train, about 50 tons to Fort Edmonton.

Navigation and freighting season at Fort Benton opened May 27 for 1875, with arrival of the Nellie Peck in early morning, the Benton at 1 p. m., "310 tons and 45 passengers." This latter arrival was of course of special interest to Bentonites, and it can be safely presumed that the boat moored equi-distant between the stores of the owners, the Bakers and Powers, one at each end of a 300 foot city block. Though the Benton came clear from Pittsburgh where it had been built during the winter, most future trips of the steamboat which provided more freight for the wagons than any other were from Bismarck.

Freighting notes from either Record or Herald were scanty that summer; from the latter chiefly reflecting difficulties on the Carroll Trail, ranging from rain and mud delays to Sioux raids on mules and horses of freighters in the Judith Basin. T. C. Power shipments to Helena were apparently very heavy, from a couple of local items. Much of Baker's trade that summer went to Canada, helping set up NWMP posts. In the fall Diamond R and other trains went via Benton to Fort Peck to handle late season freight.

October 30 the Benton Record triumphantly reported: "The levee is cleared of all outside freight, and all the transportation that can be spared is now en route to assist in hauling the Carroll goods, which have been on the road for nearly two years." End of the Carroll chimera.

There had been considerable two way freighting. For the year an estimated 2880 tons went down river on steamboats, including nearly a thousand tons of buffalo robes, plus other furs and hides, and much silver ore concentrate. That meant a more balanced freighting economy, but the total would not be surpassed in the next five years, and then only for two seasons.

## Sioux Take The Spotlight

The 1876 campaign against the Sioux thoroughly confused the steamboat and freighting scene for a Montana Territory which had been growing in an orderly manner. Fort Benton had reflected that growth, a report for the previous year indicated several new businesses and about 20 homes built.

Early freighting to North West Territory was substantial, although in late March the road to Fort Macleod was heavy with snow and several outfits were laid up en route. Benton's big two had a special contract for transport support of the Yellowstone expedition, from Forts Shaw and Ellis by April. Occasional items from participant local men appeared in the paper.

The river was so high that first boat arrivals were delayed, but Carroll, Benton and Key West brought 850 tons of freight on May 14 and 15, loads for wagons soon in action. Next week Fort Benton had an important addition, Edgar Maclay came as Diamond R representative, evidence that one of the biggest freighting firms in the west had given up on the Carroll route. Possibly a consequence, Diamond R and Benton Transportation Co. bullwhackers went on a rampage, residents had to wake up Sheriffs Billy and Charley Rowe to help quell the disturbance, next morning they contributed leftover change in Probate Judge John Tattan's court. They were temporarily immobilized anyway, a fearsome rainstorm had demolished bridges to the south and made the Benton Road nearly impassable. Despite an overflowing Missouri, up to the gates of the old fort, the boats kept bringing in heavy tonnages in June. One week's shipments by local wagons, 250 tons, the freighters were falling behind.

The previous issue missing, the July 14 Record reported the Custer debacle with an unflattering comment on Yellow Hair's strategy. There were long lists of freight forwarded to merchant consignees. But the military reaction to the disaster on the Little Big Horn began to pinch freighting and supplies for Montana civilians. Steamboats were conscripted off the Benton run as they dropped down to Bismarck, to move troops and supplies into the area of hostilities. Result was a heavy late season drop at Cow Island, in the neighborhood of 750 tons, loads for 300 wagons.

Down freight was heavy, in September Diamond R trains were still hauling quartz to Cow Island, 200 tons waiting for steamboats there, another 150 tons at Fort Benton, a pretty hefty total for a ten day period.

So severe was the disruption due to military requirements that the September 15 Record reassured, "Every pound of freight now remaining at Benton will be delivered this season, and would have been delivered a month ago, if the government had not taken possession of two thirds of the river transportation." Agriculture was coming up in the area, the Record reported about 60,000 pounds of potatoes and other vegetables; the under-generous estimate belied two weeks later when I. G. Baker wagons loaded 60,000 pounds of spuds north for the Mounted Police. Fort Benton was almost always short of fuel, chiefly firewood, October 20 the Record reported arrival in Power wagons of some tons of Whoop Up coal from deposits near later Lethbridge.

In 1876 down river freight was disrupted by the rainstorm mentioned above, none arriving until mid-July. The total was slightly under the year before but with first notation of a new export, wool—about 50 tons. The Record that summer suggested traffic on the river and thus freighting, "probably 20,000 tons, including live animals, passengers' property." Likely a booster's view, estimated figures total over 7000, plus some thousands of tons to the Yellowstone in the Custer aftermath.

### 1877 Disruption Was Slight

The 1877 navigation season was complicated by the flight of the Nez Perce Indians, which ended at the Bear's Paw Mountains with an October surrender, but disruption of freighting was slight compared with the previous year.

March 2 the Benton Record noted, "Fort Benton moves quietly ahead while stagnation and collapse prevail throughout the greater portion of the territory." They woke up when the fugitive Nez Perce traversed hundreds of miles of the territory. One Fort Benton merchant, I. G. Baker, in the spring offered 10,000 beaver traps for sale—in view of their growing business, it may have been an inventory. April 6, having sold their interest in the steamboat Benton, the same company announced start of the Baker Line; the firm had bought the Red Cloud at St. Louis. May 4 there were several hundred tons of ore on the Fort Benton levee waiting for early steamboats.

Probably some of that went down on the first boat, Benton, which arrived with 429 tons of freight. The robe trade was off a third this season, undoubtedly due to the Canadian influx of Sioux. Immediately after, the Record felt 175 tons of wagon freight outbound in three days as extremely heavy, by Baker, Power, Murphy Neel and Diamond R wagons, about 70 wagons, enough for four short trains. The outflow continued as more boats arrived, about an equal number in May, June and July. June 22 freight shipments of about 330 tons were reported. Best two way trip of the season was the Red Cloud, bringing 320 tons and taking down 240, the latter probably most of the Baker company robe trade.

This year Kleinschmidt & Bro. of Helena set up a branch in Fort Benton primarily to handle freight shipments which after the first short season of about 500 tons, ran to around 2000 tons yearly. Their first shipment was about 160 tons, with two other major freighters 234 tons in a week. During the busy season, tapering off in August, freight was going out at a similar rate.

Initial mention found on the Nez Perce outbreak was in the July 6 Record, from then on most issues contained a story on the tribe's hejira. In late July Gov. B. F. Potts proclaimed a need for militia in the Missoula area. At Fort Benton initial steps toward militia were taken, but locals were much more concerned with Sitting Bull's Sioux up north of the line. The battle of the Big Hole August 9 brought the Nez Perce war much closer, Lt. James Bradley, Fort Benton's first historian, was the first killed, and another fatality was Henry Bostwick, army scout and a Benton resident for years. Things were uneasy enough locally that one of the Baker trains was reportedly attacked and burned by Sioux, on investigation by soldiers and volunteers they found the teamsters overly terrified by friendly Indians.

But on September 21 the Record reported the Nez Perce were crossing the Missouri, with 60 tons of freight liable to capture by the hostiles. That was different, a party of about 30 volunteers, led by Major Guido Ilges and with a few soldiers rode to Cow Island. This party found about 50 tons of freight pillaged or burned, followed the Nez Perce up Cow Creek and got into a drawn fire fight, one volunteer and two warriors slain in a matchup of some of the best riflemen on the frontier. Nearby a small wagon train was attacked and burned, two freighters killed and the wagons burned. Strangely, the white participants, all veterans of the Indian wars, had high praise for the opposing Nez Perce, and sympathy for them in later years.

Despite the loss of freight at Cow Island, total for the season to Fort Benton and vicinity was about 6150 tons, possibly more. Of this 1025 tons was Canadian contract freight, hundreds of tons more went north of the border for civilian use. Indicative of a growing territory, the steamboats brought about 1160 passengers. A hundred tons of wool went down.

### Freighting Boom Takes Off

As it turned out, 1877 had been the first of a five year boom in river commerce and freighting; 1878 provided graphic evidence of a growing territory dependent in large part on freight from Fort Benton, a giant order for a town with not quite 500 population, estimated to increase to 1500 or 2000 in freighting season. The Power (Block P) Line was adding the Helena, the Baker Line the Col. McLeod, each doubling in number, each new boat to be amazingly successful. Principal competitor was the Coulson Line, there were others to account for 60 steamboat arrivals at Fort Benton and to past 10,000 tons of cargo delivered. Nearly all was from Bismarck, 800 miles down the Missouri. Nearest railroad was a bit less, the Utah & Northern gradually building north in southern Idaho, close enough to cut into the trade to southern Montana settlements. Union Pacific figures would indicate 9,000 tons north from their U&N railroad, including Idaho. On occasion, the Utah line provided freight rates aimed at breaking the hold the steamboat men had on Montana, a practice not unknown in the next century against other rivals.

The Big Horn opened the season with an April 28 arrival at Fort Benton, only 100 tons of freight, 300 left at way points, but 140 passengers, and the freight was rolling toward Helena before the month was out. From then on the wagons were busy, as the boats kept whistling in. The first six brought a third of the 1425 passengers, but cargoes were lighter than in June. May 31 the Record reported about 12 steamers and 3000 tons of freight en route on the Missouri above Bismarck. Also that the Benton Road was more of an obstacle than the river.

June 7 the paper noted, "Three arrivals in one day make things hum around the river metropolis." These were the Josephine, Helena and Far West, and at that the paper missed a fourth, General Terry dragging in after the type was set on June 6. Warehouse building was one order of business that spring, next week the comment, "Noticeable absence of freight on levee this year—all in warehouses, fortunately, as it has been wet." Some of the down freight was on the hoof, Coulson boats handled about 750 cattle bound for eastern markets during the season. Freight shipments out were so commonplace that the Record carried few freighting notes. One, July 19, "More transportation needed here. Lots of goods yet to move."

Fort Benton was also having growing pains. New businesses were opening, or trying to, almost weekly, but lumber was hard to come by; earlier, the paper had sourly commented on the matter, "not enough lumber in town to make an ax handle." Freighting across the river to mines and other southern points was evidently picking up. Smith & Castner had found the lumber to build a big ferry, 75x20, capable of handling two six mule teams. The town's sole brickmaker was busy, Wm. G. Conrad was building a large home, both Power and Baker had contracted for new buildings.

The parade of steamboats and wagon trains continued strong through July and finally into August, usually the worst month for navigation. Then the new Baker boat Col. McLeod, built to carry about 100 tons, took over to transport tonnages other boats brought to Cow Island, including two in October. That lessened by half the 700 tons dropped there, the boat easing by 120 miles the freighting problem on that tonnage.

Of the year's total about 800 tons were government freight, another 500 tons for the Canadian government. Value of exports was figured at $650,000, of imports $2,410,000, according to a Record article.

### Another Year—Another Record

In many ways, 1879 was a carbon copy of the year before; an exception that fewer boats, 42 to Fort Benton, nine to Cow Island, brought the 10,700 tons, 600 more than in 1878. The army was building its most important post on the northern plains, Fort Assiniboine, near later Havre, largely because of the continued presence of hostile Sioux in Canada. Hundreds of tons were left at the Coal Banks, 40 miles below the head of navigation. A factor in the lesser number of boats, the big Coulson twins, Montana and Dacotah, could and did bring in up to 600 tons in a trip.

Fort Benton was growing, its premier businesses, Baker and Power, managed to build brick stores during the year, the Benton Record put up a three story brick, and there were other additions. The small Col. McLeod opened the boating season April 27th, Benton and Eclipse the next two days; not much freight but still an April record and the freighters got busy.

As during the year before, the influx was so great that freighting was commonplace, very few comments found in the Record files. On June 20, "There are now 3,000 tons of freight awaiting transportation." June 27, "Shipment of cattle via the Missouri has become a prominent feature of upper river navigation. Nearly every steamer loads some for Bismarck and other markets." Cattle in the immediate area had been increasing rapidly on the Shonkin range across the Missouri, John Lepley driving in the first large herd in September 1878. Sheep were also coming, which meant wool shipments. August 29, six ox teams arrived from Meagher County by way of the new road, and September 5, Helena took down the largest load of wool ever from Benton. On the next trip the boat left with 65 tons of wool and 11 tons of fur and robes. There were several more such entries, all meaning freight teams.

It was September before busy freighters could turn their attention to around 600 tons of freight left at Cow Island and early October before the wagon trains began rolling in to complete a busy year. That month up near Fort Macleod Blackfeet surrounded a Power wagon train, but Chief Crowfoot came on the scene and prevented pillage. Indians were hungry in Canada, many cattle reported killed and gardens dug up. Presence of large bands of Sioux probably one reason.

Fort Benton's peculiar problems continued into fall. "No flooring or lath on the Benton market, not enough lime to make lime water." "Benton's population continues to increase, rents are high, space scarce. Construction costs about double any other Montana town." In November a train came in from Belt Mountains loaded with lime, all gone in a few hours. That spring Paris Gibson had started a lumber yard, in a few weeks all desirable lumber had been sold.

In 1880 for the first time, railroads entered Montana, the Utah Northern in the Dillon area, the Northern Pacific barely across the line in the east. Railroad tonnage was about 3000 more than by river, but Fort Benton business men scarcely heeded the fact. Fort Benton freight went past 12,000 tons, the Yellowstone added over 1500 more.

The year 1880 brought new businesses, including the two banks, improved quarters for the three largest mercantile firms; the river brought 46 steamboat loads to the city or Coal Banks—the road to Fort Assiniboine was a busy route as building there continued. A small station was set up at Coal Banks landing with soldiers for freight guards during the season, for a couple of years there was even a postoffice named Ruger for the commandant at Assiniboine.

There had been about 1800 incoming passengers in 1880, triple that of down listings, an indication Montana was indeed growing, after the stagnation of the 1870s. The 1880 census found 39,159 non-Indian residents, not quite double the previous count in 1870. Fort Benton was listed with 1816, third largest city in the territory after Helena and Butte, up from 367 in 1870. County population at past 3000 was up six times, many of the others in the Shonkin and Highwood areas to the south. Business that summer confirmed the continuing importance of the river port of entry. As usual, carpenters and masons had more business than they could handle. Such was the case for two brickmakers, completely unable to meet the demand in building.

Also as usual, hundreds of animals and dozens of outfits along the busy streets were too commonplace to mention, but it was worthy of note that blacksmith Rufus Payne had gone into the manufacture of spring wagons and that Frank Lepper and Louis Bradbury were new blacksmiths and wagonwrights—they were needed to keep the wagons rolling.

Wool shipments were on the increase to 300 tons by river, with many trains arriving from Meagher county in July, while high grade ore shipments had declined; in spite of development of the Barker mining district in the Belt Mountains to the south. Two routes to these mines were duly noted in the Record. The new River Press in December saw a pressing need for road work, up the Marias to the Blackfeet agency, to Fort Maginnis in the Judith Basin, and over the Belts to White Sulphur Springs.

### A Busy Missouri Highway

The year 1881 was yet another year of increased steamboat tonnage to the Fort Benton area. It was also the year of largest river freight shipments into Montana, 17,420 tons, nearly 13,000 for Fort Benton's trade, and the largest ever down river shipments from the territory, around 4200 tons. The reason for both was that several thousand buffalo hide hunters were in the triangle of the Missouri and Yellowstone, their "Big 50s" booming as they finished off the last of the great herds. About 30,000 robes went down from Fort Benton, while around 160,000 in all came to Bismarck from the upper river. Small settlements along both streams profited by supplying the hunters. At year end it was reckoned that values of cargoes handled was $18,650,000 government and $16,655,000 private.

Coming out of one of the worst winters Montana ever had (old timers reckoned that of 1880-81 worse than a later more publicized winter), the spring breakup on the Missouri created havoc on the Missouri below after causing some damage at Fort Benton and much on the Marias and Teton. It was a disaster in the Bismarck area and from there down river.

Files of the Record are missing until June 1881, the River Press more complete but again, few notes on the commonplace, freighting of immense tonnages for much of Montana and western Canada. In April there was note of some return freighting, including 150 tons of lime from the Barker area during the building season, and of coal from Belt. One oddity, 35 Red River carts from Fort Belknap for Power, doubtless robes and furs—capacity of a cart about half a ton.

On June 15 the Press had a sarcastic comment about movement of 2400 surrendered Sioux from the Yellowstone down river: "Seven million pounds of freight are in Bismarck awaiting shipment, and the business of the Territory kept lagging therefrom, while a fleet of steamboats are carrying numerous bands of Indians on a picnic down the Yellowstone." Five boats were chartered for this movement of the last of the recalcitrant Sioux returned from Canada.

In September on freight at Cow Island, the Record noted, "Plenty of transportation, goods move fast." Benton freighters had it down to a science. Another item, doubtless noted by freighters, by odometer it was 222 miles to Fort Macleod. Utah & Northern Railroad, past Dillon and headed for Butte, must have been figuring on a knockout blow to the steamboats; in November a survey party completed six weeks of work on a route to Benton.

Dan Maratta of the Coulson Line reported in the Bismarck Tribune: 1881 traffic to Fort Benton 27,560,000 pounds of private freight, 7,280,000 military freight, to Yellowstone, 8,420,000 pounds, 43,180,000 from Bismarck. There were 1300 passengers, plus 2400 Indians, 1800 horses and cattle and 600 sheep. Received for shipment east 160,000 buffalo hides, 180 tons of wool, other hides and pelts.

A December item in the Record, several trains hauled 120,000 pounds of oats to Fort Assiniboine of a Power contract for 700,000.

The 1882 tonnage record, due to the near end of the buffalo slaughter, was down from the Bismarck figure of the year before sharply, but for the Fort Benton area roughly equal to 1881, around 13,000 tons. In January Ed Lewis' train brought in 18 tons of Whoop Up coal, regarded locally as superior to that from Belt. A February local, seven six-mule teams were in Fort Benton loading with coal oil for Fort Assiniboine—kerosene was a very important item those years. In March John O'Connor, wagon boss of the Power mule train, died of injuries when a big warehouse door blew shut—fellow freighters were pallbearers and his hearse a freight wagon. Another old time freighter and wheelwright, Dixie Ward, died two weeks later. John LaMott was rated a public benefactor by improving a toll road up the Arrow Creek hill toward the Judith Basin, rated by freighters one of the toughest in the territory.

In May buffalo robes bringing $7 and $8 were coming in in numbers, most of course through small Indian trading posts—except for a trickle, the last of the once great Fort Benton robe trade. An unusual note, the Evans bull teams, 100 head, and wagons, were loaded on the Far West, taken down to Rocky Point to bring up freight left there. In June the Record reported buffalo hides coming in faster than the previous year. "Buffalo have been slaughtered unmercifully and soon will be gone." In this editor W. H. Buck again was right. South of Fort Macleod Ed Lewis' wagon train fell in with a war party of 450 Blackfeet, but wiser chiefs prevented a fight.

Despite an occasional note on several tons of coal arriving in Benton, fuel was short. Citizens saw a need for 200 to 500 tons, going price $16 to $20, in October. The same month T. C. Power received a first express shipment of goods via the Northern Pacific railhead at Billings; no doubt via the Power stage line. Some days later three freight wagons brought the rest of that order. At the same time the Record welcomed arrival of 4 1/2 tons of paper via Ben Sweigert's train from Cow Island.

### Railroads Write Period To River Trade

Arrival of the Northern Pacific at Helena and the Canadian Pacific at Calgary in 1883 effectively ended freighting over most of Fort Benton's previous routes.

However, until those arrivals, trade was substantial, 1883 tonnage of boats being down about a third from the year before, and a further drop to about half in 1884. The area served by freight wagons from Benton had dwindled, but was still substantial, and population was growing to make up part of the loss.

Growing Great Falls and Choteau, as well as needs of the Blackfeet reservation provided a market, so did the expanding livestock industry. A couple of years found steamboat tonnages around 4000; in 1887 there was a temporary spurt to supply the Montana end of the construction of the St. Paul, Minneapolis, & Manitoba Railroad of Jim Hill, about 6500 tons. With arrival of this railroad in late September, Fort Benton freighting became a strictly local affair, but "local" included the Lewistown area, 100 miles distant, into the next century.

# Stages Weren't Pullmans
## Northern Montana Stage Center

*T*he Concord stages made by Abbot & Downing of the town of that name in New Hampshire were pretty much the standard in the west. These vehicles stood about 8 1/2 feet tall with front wheels around 3 feet 10 inches and rear wheels 5 feet 1 inch. Concords were built with weight low for cornering and to prevent upsets—which they fairly often did anyway, and body weight rested on heavy leather understraps, which mitigated some of the shocks and jolts of travel. Leather or canvas curtains usually replaced glass windows. Even so the Concord was a mighty rough way to travel hundreds of miles, after which the passenger was doubtless sold on the more comfortable steamboats. The stage in Indian country had one advantage, faster; but the greater firepower of a steamboat negated that.

Furthermore, excess baggage, usually beyond a 25 pound stage-set minimum, cost much more than the toll collected by boats.

Concords were the standard, but in Montana often a late arrival. In the most isolated section left in the United States, one used what was available and bettered it later to mitigate complaints of battered passengers.

Andrew Jackson (Jack) Oliver, a former California miner, arrived on the Montana scene late in 1862 and first carried letters from Salt Lake City to Bannack at $1 each, collected from recipient. By November Oliver may have been partly in the stage business on the same route. "North To Montana" reports that he arrived in Salt Lake on November 28 with a four horse wagon, some mail and one passenger—a 16 day trip. He continued similar service, relaying teams and traveling day and night, to deliver in May 1863, 500 letters to Bannack in nine days. Finally November 2, 1863, Leonard I. Smith received the mail contract, Salt Lake to Bannack, at $1,000 a month. The contract required priority for mail to the exclusion of passengers if need be. That was the first regular mail service into what became Montana, Smith continuing until late 1864. (For more on the route from Utah see Madsen, "North To Montana.")

By early 1864 news of the great strike on Alder Gulch was widespread, and travelers were on waiting lists for their turn north, at $50 and $60—soon going higher, and of course Oliver and Smith had competition. Ben Holladay of the Overland got the news soon enough, and the Overland moved in. To drive the competition out Overland stocked the road with horses for relays, and added way stations; they also brought in better vehicles and sliced the fare to Virginia City to $25. That did it, and soon the Overland was boss of the trails north. Then the fare rose to $50 October 13, 1864, to $75 a few days later and $150 next February. What the traffic would bear was bearing well, except for luckless passengers.

Oliver moved his stage line early in 1865 to connect Helena to Virginia City, and the May 20 Montana Post announced that Oliver's "first coach will leave Helena for the landing of the steamers on the Missouri river. . .as long as steamboats arrive." While there may have been some such regular service to the head of navigation in 1864, same is lost in the dim past. Some freighters doubtless carried, for it seems an ounce of dust, pickup passengers wanting to return to the states or to check on freight orders, in those early years.

Charles C. Huntley, after Civil War service, arrived in Montana early in 1866 and immediately had an impact on the staging scene. One of his routes was announced in the May 26 Montana Post, first coach had already left Helena for Fort Benton the 16th. Soon Huntley said he would establish stage stations in the near future and make the 140 mile run in two days. Steamboat arrivals were constant that busy year and Huntley probably operated tri-weekly most of the summer; in October he ran special stages to carry passengers to Fort Benton to meet the Miner, advertised as the last boat of the season—it didn't make it all the way, passengers went on by mackinaw to Cow Island.

Late in 1866 Wells Fargo in what was termed the "Grand Consolidation" bought out Holladay, to assume effective control of the western transportation scene.

In April 1867 the Post reported that Fort Benton mail service was due to start on the 1st but C. C. Huntley had not yet returned to Montana. Isaac G. Baker had been appointed Fort Benton postmaster effective January 18, 1867. By April 13 the paper reported Helena-Benton mail was going out three times weekly. Huntley had a mail contract to October 1st, but in mid-year Wells Fargo bought him out and June 1st commenced running tri-weekly stages to Fort Benton. Later that year John Kennedy, ranching in Prickly Pear canyon, secured the contract to build 12 stage stations between Helena and Fort Benton at $1200 each in gold. Some of these stations were to provide relay horses, others meals or overnight stopovers. For the 140 miles, a later compilation shows eight: Toll gate at Little Prickly Pear, 25 miles; Kennedy's near Wolf Creek, 37; Dearborn, 53; Birdtail Rock, 68; Sun River, 84; Sun River Leavings, 92; 28 Mile Springs, 112; Bullhead Coulee, 128; Fort Benton, 140. Also in later years, from Fort Benton dinner was at 28 Mile Springs, supper at Sun River, breakfast at Wolf Creek, dinner at Mitchell's near present Sieben. Helena to Benton, dinner at Mitchell station, supper at Wolf Creek, breakfast at Sun River and dinner at 28 Mile Springs. The overnight stop on the two day run was of course at Sun River, old time pictures showing a rather substantial appearing hotel at this station. Fare was around $25, meals paid by passengers; in later years fares were slightly lower. On one occasion 27 passengers were mentioned in a newspaper item, an unusually high figure.

Wells Fargo's schedule in fall 1867 called for weekly stages to Benton in winter, in December changed this back to tri-weekly. This schedule was in effect in April 1868. This latter season the Helena Herald almost weekly published criticism of the stage service; in May a passenger claimed he had to walk nearly all the way from Dearborn to Birdtail and bull teams were used to get the stage over hills. June 28 the tune changed, "Three splendid Concord coaches and stock arrived for the Benton road." But from Fort Benton another disgruntled fare advised that Wells Fargo coaches "start out in style, next station a disgraceful bunch of stock. Walk up hill and down. You gamble if you ride on level ground." (One historian suggested that Herald editor Robert Fisk had been denied the usual complimentary pass and was making his discontent known.)

Perhaps he got his pass, a May 10, 1869 note from Benton reported the Helena stage 12 hours ahead of schedule on the 7th, the writer thought it due to restocking of the route and new vehicles. Traffic was heavy to Fort Benton that season with many miners leaving the territory. Completion of the transcontinental railroad in May across Utah was a complicating factor for stagecoach men. There may have been other reasons for what followed such as near exhaustion of rich placer deposits, the near war the Blackfeet were waging against travelers on the Benton Road. At any rate, sale of Wells Fargo Montana stage lines to Gilmer & Salisbury was announced September 2, 1869.

## New Owners Take Over

New owners were John T. Gilmer, who had worked for Holladay and Wells Fargo in Utah, and Orange J. Salisbury, also with stage line background, and later joined by a brother, Monroe Salisbury. September 23 the Herald reported a fast schedule planned of 65 hours, Corinne, Utah, to Helena. Salisbury, the source, also informed the publisher that Sunday's coach to Benton would be discontinued.

In January 1870 Gilmer & Salisbury announced tri-weekly stage to Fort Benton, apparently maintained the next few years. They bought the business ahead of two tough winters—in March 1870 Benton stage passengers reported snow 15 feet deep in places between Helena and Fort Shaw, fares had to help shovel. In November 1871, Thomas Shirlow, stage driver, was badly frozen near Birdtail station, had to abandon the coach and ride to the station on one of the horses. Nevertheless, the Herald reported Gilmer & Salisbury doing an excellent job of carrying the mail during the storm period. In February 1872 what the Herald described as "unprecedented" snow storms delayed mails. The weatherman must have held a grudge against the mail man that winter, down in Wyoming UP trains were hung up for weeks, then Corinne got six passenger-mail trains in 24 hours, half of these three full weeks out of Omaha!

In Montana the Herald credited the stage line with doing its utmost. Transport alternated, half way to Benton sled runners were used, thence to Sun River bare ground and wheeled stages, the rest of the way sleds again.

In May 1874 Gilmer & Salisbury had added a couple of new jerkies to the Benton route, a month later stages were battling mud after heavy rains. Said the Herald, travel had been slowly but steadily rising during the past three years on the Benton Road. In 1876 the stage company took federal title to half a block in the upper end of Benton where their barn, corrals and office had stood since the purchase from Wells Fargo.

## Stage Line To Local Ownership

Fort Benton business was on a substantial upbeat in February 1878 when William Rowe was awarded the contract for carrying mail between Helena and Benton after July 1. Two months later Rowe left Benton for Oregon to "buy a big herd of horses to stock the Benton Road." He returned in late May after having purchased stock and stages to open a locally owned line, backed by John W. Power. The first coach arrived in Fort Benton June 11, "Quite a nobby affair compared with the mud wagons so long in use on this road." It was evident that Gilmer & Salisbury had sold out, although no note of the sale was found in extant copies of the Benton Record. In December title abstract was received by John Power for the Benton & Helena Stage Co. About that time an item appeared, "Mail service from Helena never so good as since Rowe & Co. got the mail contract. Coaches arrive daily at noon." An 1880 note shows stage fare was $20, Benton to Helena. Trip time 7 a. m. to noon next day, either way.

First step toward making Fort Benton one of Montana's stage centers extended the long route from the southwest border another 100 miles. June 6, 1879, the Record noted arrival of Wm. Rowe on May 29 with a large band of horses to stock the mail route from Fort Benton to Fort Belknap via the new Fort Assiniboine. Work had barely begun on that large post at the time. First coach for Belknap left June 2, first from Assiniboine arrived the next day. The company had received a fine 11 seat coach named J. S. Hill for one of the company officials. The new line contributed to the T. C. and John Power business interests, they had a store at Belknap (later Chinook). And right in time for building the new military post,

205 civilian employes arrived on the Dacotah June 20. Supplies by steamboats the next two years made Coal Banks landing on the Missouri 40 miles below Fort Benton a busy point.

That summer of 1879 there were gold strikes in the Judith area and in September Mr. Rowe was thinking about a stage line to Yogo where around 400 stampeders were reported. He was still considering the matter in May 1880 and planned to start it soon, also another to deliver Martinsdale mail, a route begun and discontinued earlier. Central Montana was gradually growing, even if the Yogo Gulch strike had turned sour by June. In its place the Barker mining district was developing pay lodes, and by October that new route was described in the paper. Roads were being built into previously untouched areas to the south, but more roads were badly needed.

The winter of 1880-81 was rated the worst ever by many early day residents, a real trial for the local stagemen. The Benton & Helena stage in December killed three horses trying to get the mail through one storm. By January the route was virtually impassable, followed by yet another storm, worst yet, with 15 inches of snow at Fort Benton and up to seven feet in the Prickly Pear canyon and stages and mail delayed for days—though not weeks, as UP trains had been stalled a decade earlier in Wyoming. The winter weather broke early, February 3rd, and as a natural consequence floods all along the main route.

### The Stage Network Is Expanded

There is a bare note on one of the lines mentioned above. March 23, 1881, Al Olden, proprietor of the Martinsdale stage, visited Fort Benton. A bit more on this route calls it a new line to Barker, the old line improved. From Barker (near later Neihart) the route went over King's Hill and down into Belt Park. This general route served freighters also. The Benton to Martinsdale stage got new stock and a new manager, George Houk, a Power employe, in November, so this was an addition to locally owned stages. January 5, 1882, the Record listed the Benton & Barker stage line as tri-weekly, W. A. Olden manager.

In March John LaMott was reported as improving the road over the Arrow Creek hill, leading to Reeds Fort and a sizable Meti settlement on Spring Creek in the Judith Basin. LaMott's improvement probably meant a toll road but no mention found in papers of such. This would be the route of another stage line.

In May 1882 the River Press reported sale of the Benton and Helena Stage Co. to J. M. Powers (no relation to John and T. C. Power) with B. L. Powers, his brother, a partner. They would run the stage until after the railroad reached Fort Benton on September 28, 1887, last stage arrival in Fort Benton November 23, last departure November 25.

The Conrad brothers of I. G. Baker & Co. were not as intent as their chief business rivals in stagecoaching. Nevertheless they got their feet a trifle wet. In April 1882 the Baker company, for convenience of their best customers in Canada, began the Fort Benton & Fort Macleod Stage Line. It wasn't much, usually a simple wagon, and only tri-monthly, but it provided towns north of the line with mail and express services along the old Whoop Up Trail and beyond. The stations were Leavings of Teton, Marias, Rocky Springs, Nine Mile Butte and Fort Hamilton (Whoop Up). Usual time was six days and it probably required a determined person to become a passenger. The Benton Record noted, "where no houses a good tent is always ready." Schedule was for departures the 5th, 15th and 25th of each month. There were connections at Macleod with Calgary and Edmonton.

During the holiday season 1882 the Macleod stage had a big business in express and mail and in the week before Christmas had to send out two extras. It might be assumed this was discontinued with the building of the Canadian Pacific to Calgary in 1883, but if so it may have been revived due to the long ties between the two regions. In July 1885 the River Press had an item that the Baker company planned to operate a tri-monthly stage from Fort Conrad to Fort Macleod, this connecting with an existing tri-weekly Fort Benton to Fort Conrad stage, likely in conjunction with a mail contract route.

T. C. and John Power had sold the long established Helena line, but the former was expanding in another direction. This was the Benton & Southern, an offshoot of the Martinsdale line, eventually running between Fort Benton and Coulson, later to successor Billings. This was a direct ancestor of the Fort Benton-Lewistown stage which operated for several years into the twentieth century.

Walter Burke was superintendent for T. C. Power's long line, to Coulson, then Billings, and his memoirs give the date of start as July 1, 1882. He recalled that he had less than six weeks to stock the line and build 17 stage stations—at the start tents and rope corrals. Shortly after the stages were running, he cut off Martinsdale, the destination of a predecessor. To do that Burke had to lay out about 30 miles of new road to Lavina crossing of the Musselshell. Another hurry up chore was getting hay for all the stations on the road. In some places he paid $40 a ton, in others the more civilized going price of $10, but he got the hay.

Burke's biggest problem was horse thieves, almost every night a horse was stolen some place along the stage line. He told the station men to picket the horses and sleep on the picket ropes, but the thieves would creep up, cut the ropes and get away with those much appreciated horses. Burke named as leader of the rustlers and outlaws one Windy (for Alonzo R.) Campbell, with whom he was on better than speaking terms, one time loaned Windy some money. On repaying the debt, Campbell said, "Walter, if I can ever do you a favor. . ." To which Burke replied, "You can do me a favor right now, just quit stealing the stage line's horses." From that time the stage horses were safe.

Windy later beat the Yellowstone sheriff and Stuart's Stranglers to the Canadian line and survived the 1884 roundup of cattle and horse thieves. Walter Burke said he was told the summer toll by gunshot and rope was "43 good men who wouldn't steal no more horses." A couple were former stage line employes, Si Nickerson and Ed Owens.

The Benton-Lewistown stage line reorganization in 1894 occasioned a minor celebration at the latter place when residents saw their first Concord stages rolling in. Shortly after the stages replaced the Iron Horse as mail carriers. The Great Northern had a strike so mail from towns on the GN line went south to Lewistown for forwarding to Billings by stage. Just as that strike was settled the Northern Pacific men struck and the mail flow reversed. The Montana Central, alias "Jawbone," got to Lewistown in 1904, ending the long distance staging.

# Montana's Pony Express
## Northern Overland Mail

What isolated and overly optimistic Montanans envisioned as a soldier protected stage line overland from Minnesota to Fort Benton in 1867 turned out to be a bloodily farcical pony express. Eight large wagon trains, some protected by military escort, had made their way from Minnesota westward to Fort Benton and on to the mines in the years 1862 to 1867. So perhaps residents of the new territory of Montana could be excused for their misconceptions. Certainly the trail west had been thoroughly blazed.

The Helena Herald, which provides most of the source material, on January 17, 1867, reported on the Minnesota & Montana Overland Stage & Express Line proposal. Basis was that the postmaster general had advertised for bids on carrying mail along the northern route—to Fort Benton, naturally, and its stage connection with Helena, hence to the mining areas which contained virtually all the population of the territory. Further, on February 27 the Herald could report that General Alfred Terry had four regiments assigned to the task of building army posts in Dakota Territory, partly to protect the mail route as far as Fort Union (Buford). Tentative schedule for the mail route, as dutifully printed in the March 28 Herald was for mail to leave Fort Abercrombie on the Minnesota border each Monday and arrive in Helena 12 days after. Nor was the Herald the only booster of the route. The St. Paul Press saw it as, in a year or two, a great highway of emigration. Both editors evidently envisioned the route as one traversed by prancing stage teams.

Great was the disappointment in June when word arrived in Montana that a low bidder on the overland mail route had frustrated the plans of Burbank & Co. to use the mail contract as a backlog in opening stage service across the northern plains. The low bidder proposed to carry the mail by relays of horsemen, a Montana Pony Express. The disappointment was somewhat assuaged with arrival of Charles Ruffee in Helena in mid-July. He informed the Herald that the first overland mail from Minnesota was hourly expected; he had ridden on, leaving the first sacks of mail at Milk River. Stations were 40 to 50 miles apart, with four men and six horses at each. The route ran from Fort Abercrombie to Bear's Den on the Sheyenne, thence to Devil's Lake, Big Bend of the Mouse River, to the Mouth of Milk River and on to Fort Benton. Ruffee told the Herald he had ridden the route in 14 days and felt confident that the relay mailmen could bring the mail through in 12 days.

The army was doing its part, posts at Bear's Den, Devil's Lake. General Terry had been busy, furthermore arrived in Fort Benton in late July and went on to pick sites for what became Fort Shaw and Fort Ellis, the latter following his visit in Helena.

A further report from Terry: Posts built were Fort Ransom at Bear's Den with two companies of soldiers, Fort Totten near Devil's Lake with three, and Fort Stevenson below Fort Berthold. From that time the Northern Overland Pony Express history ranged from farce to tragedy.

September 5 the Herald had a lengthy article based on a letter from James H. Gorman, the Fort Benton station manager, on woes from there to Fort Union. Indians fired on the mail carriers and chased them many miles, stole all the horses at two stations—the entire project became a seemingly bottomless font of remounts for the thieves. Mercifully, they didn't kill the men at a raided post on Milk river, simply stripped them of supplies and they had to walk 60 miles to the next station. A rider out of Fort Benton won a ten mile race but lost his mail bag. Even at that date Gorman was weary of providing remounts for savages. They cleaned out a station on Box Elder Creek about the time Gorman's office in Fort Benton burned with loss of a valuable sporting dog and two Henry rifles, plus a batch of revolvers.

A more triumphant report, four bags of mail by way of Fort Benton September 8th—but empty on receipt in Helena—however the line was reported in good running order the far side of Fort Union.

Ten days later, Joe the Spaniard and partner had a nasty fight with hostiles, the mail destroyed and two horses killed; another post ransacked and a long walk for the station men from Milk River. Word reached the whites that the Indians were determined that the mail would not get through. While encounters were still not deadly, hostiles would grab the sacks and scatter contents to the breezes. George Clendennin, who had a trading post and woodyard near the mouth of the Musselshell, in retrospect suggested that some of the carriers burned newspapers as too weighty and used letters to light cigars. The whole affair was poorly run, he felt, although managed well enough in the Musselshell area. James Wells, another trader, indicated similar ideas of the impending fiasco. One of the more determined couriers, active through the line's history, was Henry Macdonald, later a pioneer sheepman at the east end of the Highwoods. In the same area was John "Liver Eating" Johnson, not yet possessed of his pretty nickname; Frank Grouard, later a noted army scout, and Wm. Bent, halfbreed son of Bill Bent of the Arkansas post, so they could scarcely be accused of lacking resolution or frontier savvy.

By the end of September 1867 the pony express abandoned the Benton route in favor of Fort Hawley above the Musselshell, thence hopefully across the Judith Basin to Helena. Hostiles promptly killed two men who were cutting hay for the new station. A couple of weeks later two more carriers were stripped of mail, garments and mounts near Black Butte by 25 Sioux—the three day walk to Fort Howie cured them of Indians. At this stage the warriors seemed reluctant about permanently discouraging these white riders who were supplying them with horses so consistently. However by Christmas time a report reaching Helena had three carriers much overdue, and most likely dead.

At the turn of the year Helena people were backing a new steamboat port, Musselshell, at the mouth of that river. The infant townsite had so much trouble it may have diverted the Indians from those pesky mail men. In all, about the only mail determined by the news stories to have actually reached Helena overland was eight sacks in early March 1868. Fort Hawley was nearly out of horses, so a couple of the men loaded the sacks on two mounts and started walking westward. Luckily they made it.

March 19 a curt note from C. C. Huntley appeared in the Herald: "The mail service between Fort Abercrombie and Helena has been discontinued."

It wasn't quite the end of the story. The remaining whites at Fort Hawley abandoned the station, shortly had a vicious battle with Sioux near Black Butte, fighting for about seven hours. One Fountain M. (Pomp) Dennis was wounded and separated from the others, he evaded the swarming Sioux by hiding in a small cave and made it to safety.

# Keelboats and Mackinaws

Keelboats were the mainstay of transportation of trade goods and furs in early days on the Upper Missouri, and into later Montana until the first steamboats reached Fort Benton.

Chittenden describes a keelboat as good sized, 60 to 70 feet long, built on a regular model, with a keel running from bow to stern. It was 15 to 18 feet wide with a 3 or 4 foot depth of hold, and ordinary draft 20 to 30 inches. A keelboat was generally built in Pittsburgh at a cost of $2,000 or $3,000. For carrying freight the craft was fitted with a cargo box, occupying the length of the boat except about 12 feet at each end, and with a narrow walkway on each side of the boat.

A keelboat antedated the steamboat, but resembled the powered craft, although on a small scale. Maximum cargo was 20 to 30 tons, size would be the determining factor, a limiting one the motive power.

An item in the River Press of June 23, 1886, recalled the days when fur trade goods were loaded on keelboats, about 14 tons, with a crew of 10 or 12 to cordelle the boat, with about six months required to reach Fort Benton. Crews on the Fort Benton run were double or more that total.

Motive power was almost everything except steam. Mostly used was the cordelle, with the crew going ashore with about 1,000 feet of cable to pull the boat up river. Secondly, the crew used poles—turned ashwood with ball or knob to fit in the hollow of men's shoulders. Eight or ten men to a side, would start near the bow, facing back, and on command and in unison thrust the end of the poles into the river and walked to the stern, pushing the boat up. Where water was too deep for the poles, sweeps came into play. Undoubtedly the most favored by crewmen was the sail, but as prevailing winds tended to sweep eastward, it was most often useless. With the river's bends, the sail could help part of the time. Probably a voyageur's dream came true in June 1811, when Manuel Lisa's craft sailed the 30 miles around the Great Bend with a following breeze from every point of the compass. The keelboat made 75 miles in a long day and by light of the moon, a long remembered record.

Lisa was pressing his crew of 20 creoles that year to catch up with Wm. P. Hunt's Astorians, who had a start of many days. The Lisa crew left St. Louis April 2, reached Hunt's party June 2 above the Great Bend, nearly 1200 miles in 61 days. That was more than 18 miles a day, and no sensible keelboat captain ever expected to better it.

Loads of Indian trade goods aboard keelboats supplied the stock for Fort Piegan in 1831, Fort McKenzie in 1832 and the succession of American Fur posts and opposition forts. While smaller crews are mentioned above, traders soon found the rapids, shoals and bars above Fort Union required more motive power.

When Maximilian visited Fort McKenzie in 1833, 52 were crowded aboard the Flora, most were engages whose chief job it was to cordelle the boat upstream. In 1856, when Andrew Dawson brought Edwin Hatch and Indian annuities to Fort Benton, the three boats, probably at least two mackinaws, were powered by 58 men on the ropes.

Keelboats were often wintered at the posts, taking down a portion of the spring trade. There is some evidence in the Fort Benton annals that a keelboat or two was built at the post. The down trip of course was much easier, main problem that of control to avoid shipwreck or stranding.

## One Way Mackinaws Useful

What was termed a mackinaw at the head of navigation was rather simply, any flat bottomed boat of beyond dory size, often around 50 to 60 feet long of 2 inch hand sawn cottonwood, pegged with wooden pins; at least until nails became available on the Upper Missouri, and about 12 foot beam. Gunwales were about 3 feet above water line in center, higher in bow and stern. Stringers supported bottom planks. The planks forming the side were supported by sloping "knees" (the Fort Benton Journal on occasion mentioned these as well as saw logs as the objective of trips to the Highwoods). One mackinaw built at Fort Benton in 1856 was 12 1/2 by 85 feet, largest of record.

In the Fort Benton trade mackinaws were extremely valuable, two to four built annually for the return of robes and furs traded. In gold rush days they were built by the hundreds, floating returning miners and much gold back to the States. A boatyard (chantier in French, which is credited with giving the name of Shonkin to the creek which enters the Missouri a couple of miles below the fur fort) existed in the area. Three or four wood workers fashioned boats and crude carts from lumber hand sawn from logs. Gold rush craft were probably built along the levee at Fort Benton, as no reference to site is found. The rush was in late summer and early fall, with by far the great majority built in the 1864-69 period. Only reference to such building in this period was by William Gladstone, former Hudson Bay carpenter, who in July 1864 was asked if he could build what he termed a scow. "This was right in my line, so I went to work and in four days had one finished."

One entry in the January 15, 1855, Fort Benton Journal: "Sent three men on Teton to cut knees for a large 1/2 Keel 1/2 Mack Boat we intend building."

Mackinaws carried by far the most of more than 400,000 buffalo robes shipped from the Fort Benton area prior to the first steamboats in 1860, as well as many tons of other robes and hides (elk, deer, wolf primarily). Also these oneway craft took down thousands of salted, dried and smoked buffalo tongues, a delicacy on the eastern market. Another item was pemmican—dried buffalo meat pounded and berries worked in, a provender that was also iron rations for thousands of men on western trails. St. Louis in early days had a scarcity of shortening, so buffalo tallow and even bear oil was shipped down. To handle this type of commodity a tight compartment was built into the boat, melted tallow poured into this and tightly covered for the long trip to market. From lower points, wild honey was handled in much the same fashion, no reference found to this sweet in the Fort Benton records.

At ordinary capacity a mackinaw could carry about 250 packs of robes, 30 tons; Charles Chouteau mentions bringing two boats of 45 tons capacity with him as lighters for the Chippewa on its 1859 trip to Brule Bottom.

## Gold Rush Mackinaws

Several sources make reference to a party of about 20 miners who left Fort Benton in the fall of 1863 by mackinaw and who were killed by Sioux near present Bismarck. They carried considerable gold, about $25,000 likely the best estimate; other sources say $75,000, even a half million. Fred Gerard, Indian trader, recovered some from the scene of the tragedy; a great nephew, Howard Gerard, has determined from Gerard bank accounts it was about a fifth the lower figure.

In some accounts, Sioux dumped the yellow sand from buckskin bags, keeping the useful latter.

Advent of the Montana Post at Virginia City in summer 1864 provides a better source on use of mackinaws. That year some successful and perhaps more unsuccessful miners left the territory. Alder Gulch settlements probably reached their peak that summer, as many as 10,000 by some estimates. In late September 25 men left for the Yellowstone to build mackinaws for a proposed party headed east. This could have been the one described in the Post next spring in a letter from Wm. Young: 80 left Virginia City on foot, baggage in wagons, 7 returned to Virginia, 73 turned to building boats as only two had been made by the advance party, which took a week. They were on the Yellowstone 30 days and froze in 20 miles above Fort Union. After walking there, 25 stayed the winter, 48 went on to Fort Berthold (about half way to present Bismarck from Union). All but seven gave up in that area, the last seven were stripped by a party of Indians but reached Fort Rice and from there got to Omaha.

An undetermined number left via Fort Benton, what was termed the "gun boat Nancy Wilbur" departed on September 20. Another item dated October 1: "In a few days, 15 boats will leave Fort Benton for the States. These boats are all made bullet proof, with double sides and pierced with port holes." That many could carry well over 200 passengers. In 1865 on October 14 the Post reported the "Yellowstone Fleet, carrying some 600" had made 100 miles the first day. The exodus from Alder Gulch was well underway. Perhaps as many went via the Missouri, based on ads and items in the post. In July one Virginia City concern advertised departure of their fleet of mackinaws from Fort Benton August 25th, "the bullet-proof 'fixins' are very consoling." Another freight train left with 75 Alder Gulch men bound for the states the last of August. Several other ads for Benton departures were noted. The heavily traveled freight route to Benton would have afforded greater safety. Stages were doubtless filled to capacity by the more affluent miners, but no report found as to numbers.

Mackinaw traffic from Benton peaked in 1866. In October Sheriff Bill Hamilton at Fort Benton said 200 mackinaws with 3500 passengers had gone down from Benton. Backing this up, another Bentonite in September wrote departures had been three a day during August, as fast as carpenters could tack them together, and at an average of 15 passengers that would have been nearly 1400 for that month alone. Last Chance Gulch was leaking hundreds that summer: "Down the river! is the cry; numbers leave daily for Benton." The Post in Virginia City in mid-September reported 250 down via the Yellowstone, 450 down the Missouri; a later report of more to the Yellowstone would almost equal the Missouri total. What did such a trip cost? Lowest found was $15 if the passenger helped build boats, fed self; high $120 on a bullet-proof, $75 if you brought or shot your own grub.

James Hubbell of North West Fur at Fort Benton in late fall 1866 had Wm. Gladstone build a 12x80 foot mackinaw, planning to meet a steamboat at Fort Union. The vessel had a low 50 foot cabin. He was taking down about $125,000 gold for the firm and also 30 passengers at $175 each, over $5,000. The high fare was because he waived the usual 2 1/2% fee for handling gold, though some of the men from Confederate Gulch had very large amounts. Expecting to meet a late steamboat, the party took its time in Montana, accounting for the about 30 day trip to Sioux City when the party missed the steamboat. Bradley reported mackinaws usually made 100 miles a day, about three weeks.

One mackinaw arrival at Sioux City September 1 drew notice, 17 men with

700 pounds of gold dust, value then about $210,000. Another party was less fortunate, as a letter from John Corder printed in the Helena Herald November 19 shows: "Please notice the deaths by Indians of T. A. Kent, John Ross, James Smith and Wm. Barber, after five hours hard fighting with 40 Sioux." He credited Kent with killing 13 Sioux; as for the writer, "I received five wounds in the body from arrows, but nothing fatal I hope. We left Benton on the 6th of September." The fight occurred at the mouth of Milk River.

Armored craft weren't the only unusual boats. In fall 1867 an attempt was made to provide horsepower, October 1 a Benton report said mackinaws were going down daily but "great event of yesterday was launching of horse boat by Capt. Hammil. About 100 men assembled, boat put in river with no difficulty, looks a success." It wasn't—a November 7 item from Fort Buford "turned out to be a failure...21 days from Benton, liable to be frozen in."

In 1867 there was considerable shorter traffic, mackinaws down to Cow Island where passengers boarded waiting steamboats. A couple hundred who went down to board the big Imperial regretted it, nearly starved and the boat was abandoned above Omaha.

The one way boats continued to be useful through some dreary years, and even into homestead days when the by then termed flatboats supplied settlers along the Missouri as far as Fort Peck. In gold rush days and later, the craft were sold for their lumber, $5-$10, or simply abandoned at destination. Also returning miners overtaken by steamboats heading down would often pay passage for a safer journey.

### Smaller Boats

Until better tools became available, the commonest small boat on the Missouri was the dugout, sometimes called a canoe, although it little resembled the birchbark craft of eastern waters. The dugout was usually 15 or 20 feet long, carved out by fire and axes from a three or four foot log. Vessels such as these were often used for what fur traders termed express, carrying reports of furs and robes traded, and of supplies needed for the next season, to company headquarters in St. Louis.

Used on waters such as the shallow Platte was the bullboat, made of buffalo hides, up to 30 feet long and 12 wide with framework of willow. Properly made, two men could handle it; cargo capacity up to three tons. A single bullhide was used for the bathtub shaped skin boats used by Mandans and other river Indians.

### The Last Mass Cruise

The depression of 1893 resulted in mass unemployment across the land, and in 1894 there was the final mass use of the Missouri as an artery of transportation. The loudest voice for the stricken work force was Jacob Coxey, who proposed action today reminiscent of the New Deal of the 1930s. He also called for a march of the jobless on Washington to pressure congress, and was heard by hungry workmen across the land. Answering from the northwest coast were hundreds riding the blinds and box cars into southern Montana. Officials tried to stem the tide; some 350 stole a Northern Pacific train, got as far as Billings before the train was stopped by soldiers. Returned to Butte, then Helena, they represented a costly problem. It was uniquely shuffled on, to Fort Benton, the Helena mayor assuring the small river port that lumber, fuel and other supplies would be furnished, allowing the men to build flatboats for a trip down the Missouri on their way to Washington.

The May 30, 1894, River Press reported: "The Coxeyites are coming. ...now it seems an assured fact that the Montana disciples of General Coxey will congregate at Fort Benton, and build boats here, and then float gaily down the old, historic Missouri, from the head of navigation to the mouth." The day before an advance party of about 30 had arrived in Benton, along with a Helena representative with letters of credit. Men came drifting in on every train to join them, a final group by wagon from Helena to cheers and jeers from those who had taken the easier way at the expense of Jim Hill and the Great Northern.

William Sprague, the Helena representative, had been at Fort Benton from 1864 to 1868 building the mackinaws which sent thousands of miners down the Missouri. The 300 or so men worked like Trojans under Sprague's direction; at night they slept dry in the big wool warehouse on the levee. Ten large flatboats were built, bearing among others the names Butte, Helena, Livingston, Bozeman, Great Falls, Free Silver, Hogan (a leader) and Fort Benton—the latter in particular was gaudily decorated with flags and bunting. The cook stove, 48x10, carried nearly a box car load of provisions along with a large brick oven. Fort Benton took up a collection to supply the party with well over a hundred pounds of tobacco, as well as additional supplies. There were no local complaints of misbehavior by the Coxeyites, but the vagrants who followed were another matter. A start was planned the 4th of June, but a high wind delayed departure for two days. Riverwise Bentonites shook their heads at the handling, several of the boats swung end for end in the current, and many feared wholesale drownings.

Apparently none did drown, but many of the men deserted the expedition enroute, while about 200 mighty hungry men arrived June 28 at Yankton, to beg food from door to door. There they gave it up, and went their separate ways.

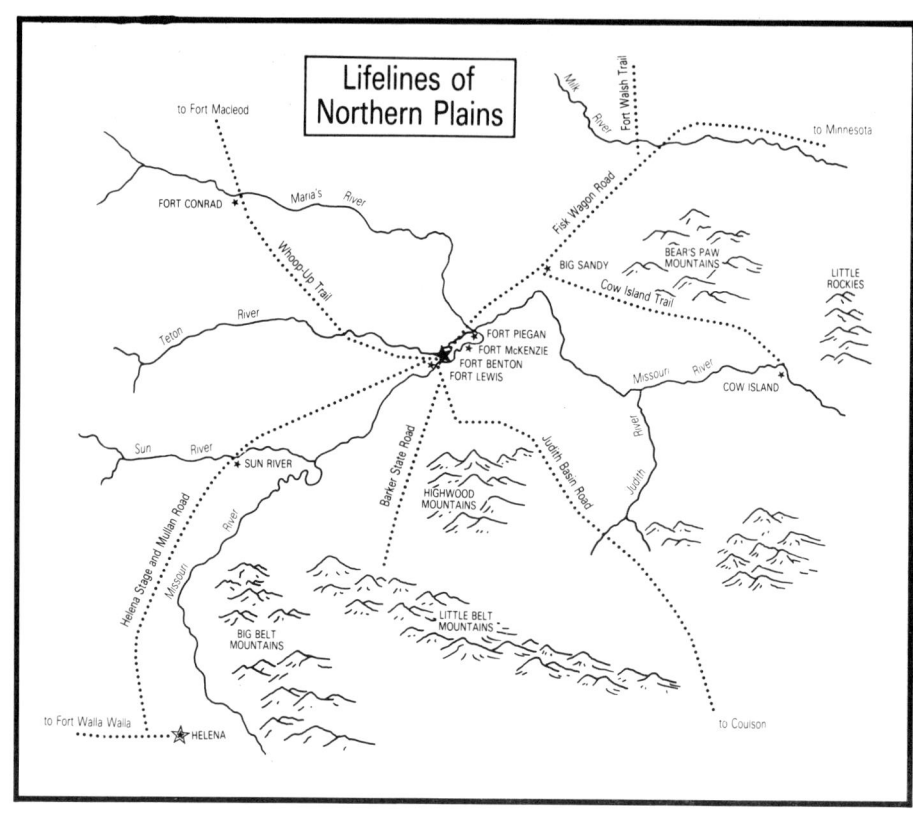

*Many pictures were secured by copying and trading half a century ago with Montana Historical Society, others even earlier by River Press from local residents, exact sources lost.*

*Steamboat Rosebud proudly struts up Drowned Man's Rapids about 1878, one of the finest Upper Missouri steamboat photos. Courtesy River Press.*

*Alexander Culbertson*

*Natawista Culbertson*

*Peacemaking Couple*
*Alexander Culbertson and Blood wife Natawista provided an effective deterrent to open warfare between races for many years. Courtesy John G. Lepley.*

*John Mix Stanley 1853 sketch shows fur post Fort Benton lower right, competitor Fort Campbell barely visible toward upper left, between are Indian tepees. From Stevens 1860 report.*

*Michael A. Flanagan secured T. C. Power and I. G. Baker backing to start one of Fort Benton's first specialized stores aside from saloons, in 1875. Courtesy Flanagan family.*

*Horse drawn freight team on Fort Benton's Main Street Near Record building and across from I. G. Baker store, about 1883. Courtesy John G. Lepley.*

*An 1886 ice gorge left government dredge, City of Fort Benton, unharmed. The dredge, built here in 1885, burned near Judith Landing in 1892. Courtesy John C. Lepley.*

*Benton-Lewistown stages pulling out in 1896, entry to the toll bridge is at mid-left. "Jawbone Railway" in 1904 ended this route. Dan Dutro photo from Frields family.*

*Earliest picture of Fort Benton in gold rush days, taken by A. S. Addy c. July 10, 1867. To left Wells Fargo office and Overland Hotel, then Carroll & Steell buildings. Below left, boat, a length, I. G. Baker, then T. C. Power Store, brand new. In old fort buildings to right North Western Fur. Steamboats, tentatively, Luella and Tom Stevens. Out of picture to left stage stables and probably Big Horn unloading on upper levee. Indian agency of 1865 below long Carroll & Steell warehouse, near left margin. Courtesy Ben Woodcock.*

*Completed in mid 1850s, the adobe brick buildings of old Fort Benton gradually crumbled in the 80s, far bastion preserved and protected early this century. Courtesy John G. Lepley.*

*Fort Benton levee late season 1868. Mining machinery on bank near foreground was freighted to Helena area the next spring. Chouteau House (then Thwing) sticks up to left of unknown steamboat. J. C. Brewster, Helena, photo.*

*Upper Front Street, Fort Benton, looking down in 1878. About the earliest part of the river side of Front had businesses, four years later the Grand Union stood below the cluster. Courtesy John G. Lepley.*

*First Fort Macleod, hurriedly built in fall 1874 for North West Mounted Police by I. G. Baker & Co. contractors. Courtesy John G. Lepley.*

*Interior view of Joseph Sullivan saddlery. One of his orders was 500 special style saddles for North West Mounted Police across border. Courtesy John G. Lepley.*

Bull train lines out across prairie above Fort Benton; note simple equipment, double yoke and chain to wagons. Courtesy John G. Lepley.

Power Block P classy Helena with sign "U. S. Mail" near spars. Only in 1881 did the line carry mail officially, from Bismarck to Fort Benton. Next year stages met advancing railhead of Northern Pacific in the Yellowstone valley. Courtesy T. T. Anderson.

*Fort Benton's first school, 1877. Before cabins and warehouses sufficed. This was the town's first brick building. Stereo, courtesy W. H. Todd family.*

*Three partners in I. G. Baker & Co. became millionaires from this store, a fourth who left in 1874 came close. The Baker firm held the Canadian government contract until after 1883. Courtesy John G. Lepley.*

*Steamboat Ida Rees, 1868-71, at Fort Benton levee, freight and passengers suggest one of first two years. Stereo, from W. S. Stocking family.*

*Brick Park Stables, Fort Benton's finest, probably financed by nearby Power and Baker stores. Young Frank Flanagan on horse. Courtesy Flanagan family.*

Warehouses on upper Fort Benton levee wouldn't hold all incoming freight either. About 1878, men believed to be W. H. Todd and George Clendenin, representing Coulson Line and Murphy, Neel. Stereo, Courtesy Todd family.

Starting from a Methodist revival tent in spring 1867, T. C. and John Power built a mercantile empire, the former becoming a first U. S. Senator from Montana. The bells went on arriving and departing jerk line mule trains. Courtesy Pioneer Mercantile Co.

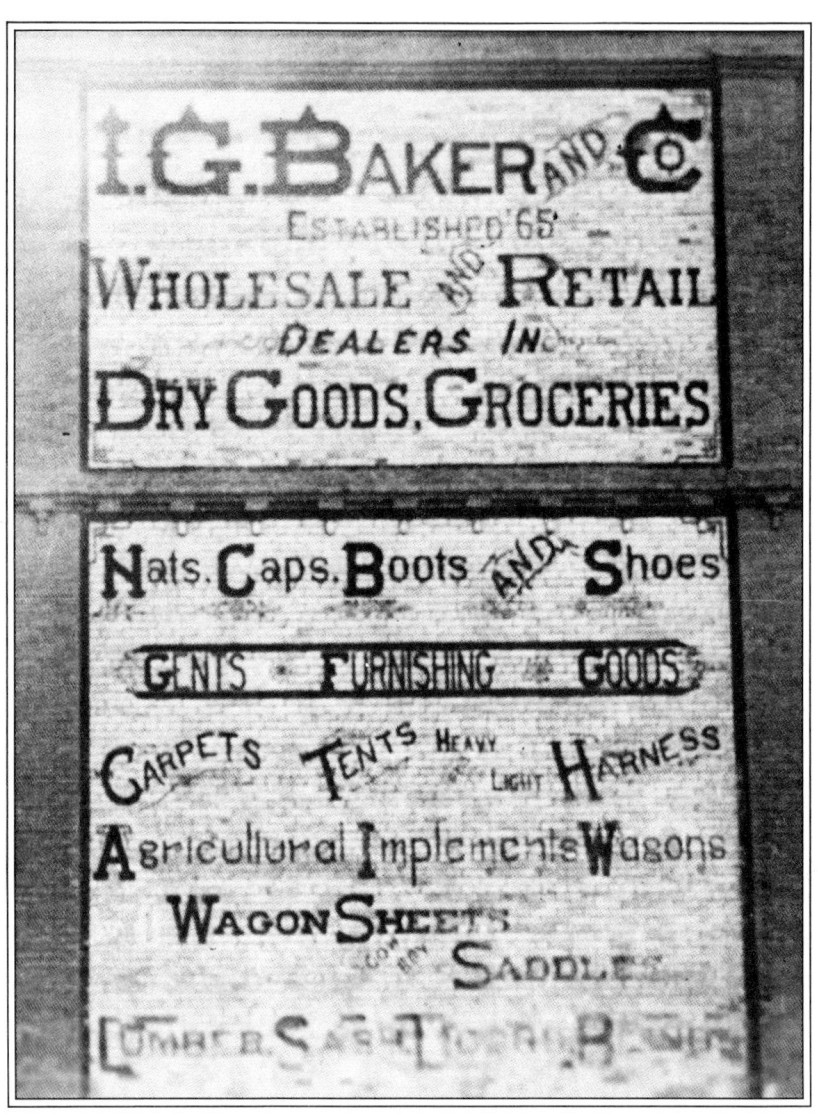

*Sold everything, I. G. Baker & Co. sign on second store; one inventory showed 10,000 beaver traps. Building demolished 1974. Photo by author.*

*Power and Baker freight crams warehouses, crowds lower levee, circa 1880. Courtesy Pioneer Mercantile Co.*

*St. Clare, first hospital in northern Montana, built 1884, occupied 1886. Courtesy John G. Lepley.*

*Fort Benton's last view of a steamboat was on June 20, 1921 when the U. S. Engineers' Mandan (snagboat) arrived at the head of navigation. Courtesy Mrs. Carl Larson (Cecile Pelley).*

*Fort Benton school built 1884, 1877 school out of picture to right. Courtesy Museum of Upper Missouri.*

*Early freighting reports mention "a thousand oxen standing hitched." Here about 50. Murphy, Neel had the animals and wagons to put 250 to 400 tons of wares on the trail at one time. Stereo, courtesy River Press.*

*Metis family party at later Lewistown—two Ouelette girls married Wells brothers. Courtesy George Wells.*

*Fort Benton was beginning conversion to brick buildings when this was taken in 1879. At left steamboat Benton, near center three story Record building, to front new I. G. Baker Co. brick and at right first part new T. C. Power building. Courtesy River Press.*

*Northwestern Transportation Co. (Coulson Combine) brought a new look, three new steamboats to the Upper Missouri in the early 1870s. Here E. H. Durfee out from bank, Nellie Peck rear and Western wait at Yankton for Fort Benton cargoes. Courtesy River Press.*

*L. T. Marshall killed desperado Dennis Hinchey in this saloon in 1872, to general approval of Fort Benton and Montana residents. Stereo, courtesy River Press.*

*Newly completed Grand Union Hotel just before formal opening November 1882. Courtesy John C. Lepley.*

*Chouteau County court house at Fort Benton, completed 1884. With additions in use 1987. Jail of 1881 off to left. Courtesy John G. Lepley.*

*Built by Jim Nabors in 1866 this adobe was Fort Benton's first hotel, in 1880 first home of River Press, being demolished in 1913. Courtesy of River Press.*

*The first steamboat, the Chippewa, July 2, 1860. The Chippewa reached Brule Bottom (old Fort McKenzie), 14 river miles below Fort Benton, July 17, 1859, to effectively open the way for later steamboats. Courtesy John G. Lepley.*

*Front Street, Fort Benton in quiet days of 1872. Fred Gerard, noted fur trader was about to or had abandoned Carroll & Steell after two years. Courtesy John G. Lepley.*

*Piegan Indians in camp on nearby Teton River. Courtesy River Press.*

# A Reluctant Civic Body

Chouteau was one of the nine original counties of Montana, created by act of the Territorial legislature February 2, 1865. At the time its boundaries were stated as the international border, 49th parallel, on the east by 108th parallel of latitude to 47th longitude on the south westerly to the Missouri River near Wolf Creek, up the Missouri to the Sun River, up the Sun to 113 latitude, thence north to Canada. In 1876 the western boundary was changed to the crest of the Rocky Mountains, on the east to include the small settlement of Carroll. Its then area comprised seven of today's counties besides Chouteau, and parts of five others.

Chouteau was named for the Chouteau family of St. Louis, prominent in the fur trade into what became Montana. At first the correct spelling of the name was used, at least in early issues of the Montana Post, but within a year or two the first "u" was dropped, a misspelling perpetuated in the county seat of Teton county. In 1903, at the suggestion of Chouteau descendants, the original and correct spelling was restored by the legislature, an action not yet comprehended by certain departments of state government.

At the time of creation the sole white residents were at Fort Benton, head of navigation on the Missouri River, except for individual traders and wood hawks, and a handful at the crossing of the Sun on the Benton Road.

Nor were residents in the least interested in any action which involved payment of taxes or licenses to prop a territorial government by that time moved from Bannack to Virginia City. No representatives were present from Chouteau county at initial sessions of the legislature, nor at a Constitutional convention in April 1866. Worse yet, no taxes coming in for a hard pressed territorial government.

In the November 10, 1866, Montana Post of Virginia City, Gov. Green Clay Smith was quoted as saying: "The county of Choteau has paid no taxes and the people refuse to organize or conform to the laws and perform their reasonable duty... Officers have been appointed, but many of them and especially the commissioners refuse to act; hence there is no county government." Smith suggested repeal of the act creating Chouteau and making it a part of Edgerton (later Lewis & Clark) where, he felt, officers "would do their duty." On December 14 a legislative act provided for appointment of an assessor by April 1, 1867. Whether they did or not, Chouteau county residents organized a citizens' party and voted on a full slate of officers September 2, 1867. These included that much desired assessor, A. B. Hamilton, and George Steell, George Baker and W. S. Stocking as commissioners. Also citizens for the first time elected a sheriff, Asa Sample—after appointees Bill Hamilton and George Croff. Aftermath, a county assessment of $438,887 but no record found of tax payments.

Fort Benton residents did find the wherewithal to build a county jail, so apparently some local taxes were levied. For the year 1869-70 after the glitter had gone off the gold rush, territorial taxes of $1829.39 were listed. For two years members of the lower house of the legislature were duly elected, but didn't bother to make the long trip to Virginia City. They were probably busy trading north of the boundary.

"The treasurer was a gambler and had depleted the treasury."

So James Lowell in 1924 wrote from Kansas, adding he was county assessor at the time in 1871 and it took Tom Power three years to get Lowell's salary for him. The comment was interesting and an inquiry to Dave Walter at Montana Historical Society brought a sheaf of interesting copies about the affair.

H. A. (Fred) Kanouse, then sheriff, Sept. 28, 1871, acknowledged receipt of a letter from the territorial auditor, including: "The Co. Clerk is in British Columbia. The Assessor is in Pa... I shall as soon as I am able go North for the winter even should I be obliged to resign the Office of Sheriff (the only one I hold) in order to get away. There is no encouragement whatever for me to do work where there is no prospect of pay. 3/4 of the work which I do is for the County and that when warrants are worth but 15c on the Dollar." He said there were no fees for making out the treasurer's warrant, "Consequently I shall not dip pen in ink again for the mere novelty of it as Honour will not buy food nor clothes."

On October 30, 1871, for the board of commissioners, George Baker: "We have arranged to have an abstract made from the tax lists given in of all the taxable property in this county, and are in hopes to be able to forward you by next mail, if not by the mail following. We have had trouble here, as our Assessor left the country, and we found he altered the lists after they were given in, and on many of the lists he did not specify the kinds of property... The County Treasurer informs me that he has recently forwarded some money to the Territorial Treasurer and will send some more soon, that the reason of his delay he was notified by the present incumbent to forward all monies to him."

Oct. 30, 1871, Treasurer S. J. Perkins wrote to the territorial treasurer: "Send you today per W. F. & Co. Eight hundred thirty five and 60/100 Dollars ($835.60) / $306.40 collected on Licenses for qr. ending July 31/71, $268.40 for Licenses collected qr. ending Oct. 31, 1871, $268.80 Taxes."

Then on Nov. 14, 1871, the former treasurer, S. J. Perkins, wrote the auditor: "On the 30th ult. my safe was robbed of all the money belonging to the Terr. and Co. I have mortgaged sufficient property to the Co. Commissioners to secure the payment of all." Henry Kennerly had been appointed treasurer on Oct. 31, the record shows. There is some doubt as to who officially was assessor. M. P. Lowry was elected, but in October 1870 James Lowell forwarded an assessment list, according to a letter, November 2, M. P. Lowry, who had been ill with Lowell acting, approved. And both men were old Pennsylvania friends. The treasurer, S. J. Perkins, is probably the Jeff Perkins who ran a restaurant in the 1860s next to Moses Solomon's Medicine Lodge. A few weeks into 1875, Perkins shot and nearly killed Solomon, rather oddly in view of mores of the day, Perkins drew a five year sentence for attempted murder.

Chouteau county's woes with non-acting officials weren't over. February 10, 1872, the Helena Herald reported one Dennis Hinchey, "a somewhat notorious character of the border," shot and killed by L. W. Marshall in the latter's saloon by four pistol shots February 4. That didn't bother Bentonites but: "This affray brought to light the strange fact that the only officers of the law present in Chouteau County are two Commissioners and the Assessor; no Sheriff, no Coroner, no Justice of the Peace, no Constable... most of them are presently out at Whoop-Up, trading with the Indians." One wonders who convened the coroner's jury which quickly exonerated and probably praised Marshall.

The county's errant sheriff quite obviously spent the winter north of the border, for the April 13 Helena Herald, citing advices from Fort Benton, carried the story of the "recent" killing of Jim Nabors, a long time resident of Chouteau county by H. A. Kanouse, who "is sheriff of Chouteau county, and has not up to present been arrested." According to later testimony, the two men had an argument over a horse at a camp 15 miles north of the Marias in a party returning from Whoop Up. Nabors was known locally as "Jim the Bluffer" with a reputation of backing down when hard pressed. The affair was kicked around Montana courts after a hiatus. Kanouse claimed that Nabors had fired first, also that he had attempted to have the affair cleared up by proper authorities but no action was taken. In July 1873 U. S. Deputy Marshal Charles Hard arrested Fred (as he was best known) Kanouse in Fort Benton and took him to Helena—a ruling soon followed that the U. S. court had no jurisdiction. As the shooting had been reported as in then Deer Lodge County, Kanouse was then taken to Deer Lodge. Various witnesses of the slaying, Lee Protsman, Dennis Halpin, George Croff, J. A. Wells and Jas. Scott, were duly reported on their way to the trial by the Herald. The hearing there August 23 brought a ruling that the homicide had been committed in Chouteau, not Deer Lodge, county and he was released. It was many months later that a Chouteau county warrant was issued; by then Kanouse was in Canada. He apparently spent years as an exile, authorities not willing to press the matter. Fred Kanouse is credited by Canadian historians as perhaps the first white semi-permanent settler in the Calgary area and one of the first stockmen of Alberta. At the time of trial he was recovering from a common frontier ailment, a battle wound. This occurred in March 1873 at Sol Abbott's saloon at Whoop-Up. A band of thirsty Blackfeet walked in, opened fire, wounding three whites in the cabin saloon. Abbott, in a back room, came out with his Navy smoking, killed three Blackfeet in as many shots. Kanouse, worst hurt, had his shoulder nearly blown away, suffered through an agonizing lengthy trip to Helena, where a Dr. Glick somewhat repaired the injury. The man was like a lightning rod for trouble. He went back to the Fort Whoop-Up vicinity, built a small trading post. In the spring of 1874 the traders had a fight with Kootenais, beat off the Indians. In celebration one of the men discharged his pistol, the shot hit a keg of powder. The trading post was demolished, but there were no white casualties. Kanouse probably grew into the job as sheriff, in 1870 he is listed by the census as deputy sheriff to J. D. Weatherwax, who like other former and later sheriffs John Healy, George Croff, Trevanian Hale, Billy Rowe and Asa Sample, moonlighted in the whisky trade.

That lightly used county jail built in 1868 had three occupants, two Diamond R bullwhackers and a wayward soldier, the Herald indicated on December 4, 1872, after they had attempted to tree the town. All three were assumed to have perished in the wee hours of Nov. 29; the logs burned fiercely. However, only remnants of two were found, and Bentonites assumed one of the prisoners had killed the other two for their money, nominee being 'whacker Frank Thompson and Chouteau county needed a new jail, built promptly by Power Bros. early in 1873. This served until 1881 when a new brick jail was constructed, and its logs served further in the ill winds of 1886-87 when the purchaser sold the logs for firewood in the fabled winter.

The territory apparently had no more trouble with its portion of taxes, at least no comments were found. In fact, in 1873 the Helena Herald seemed to marvel: "Choteau county stands well financially. Her warrants are about at par, and have been so quoted for a year past." Chouteau county had joined the rest of Montana. There were even four legal hangings, all for murder, two in territorial days, although impromptu Vigilante action would have multiplied the total. The new brick jail did accommodate some bad men with high publicity ratings, even on occasion

Indians who may have wondered about the white man's legal councils. Fort Benton tradition has it that this then fine jail was constructed through the efforts of then Sheriff John J. Healy, and residents so resented such coddling of prisoners that they voted him out of office. At any rate, Healy was not the Democratic nominee in the 1882 election.

# Fort Benton Businesses
## Carroll & Steell, The Pioneers

*M*atthew Carroll and George Steell were both chief clerks at the American Fur post of Fort Benton when the Montana gold rush exploded in 1862, both old timers by standards of the mining population though certainly not by long time employes in the fur trade. With the rich find at Alder Gulch next year opportunity was evident; the pair apparently formed their partnership that year, for the Matthew Carroll obituary reports receipt of a stock of merchandise in May 1864. William Gladstone, an 1864 arrival from Canada, recalled only one building on the Fort Benton townsite in July, spent 10 weeks at Cow Island and on return found eight or ten structures, including a large store. That was Carroll & Steell, built by Vincent Mercure and Joseph Laurion.

In old photographs the store looms importantly down river from the Wells Fargo office and Overland Hotel. Both partners were leaders in a local Vigilance committee, much needed, for Fort Benton was lawless indeed in those years. The firm quite evidently prospered in its first two years, the Montana Post by May 1866 was carrying their ad offering storage and handling freight on consignment. Furthermore, Carroll & Steell were enlarging facilities and planned to quit the lucrative but dangerous Indian trade. That December Steell was in Helena for the holidays, preparatory to leaving for the east "to buy a couple hundred thousand dollars of goods," according to the Helena Herald.

The partners evidently saw some handwriting on the wall; in 1869 they purchased an interest in the Diamond R Transportation Co., a giant on the western scene. This freighting company had its beginnings in 1863 when John J. Roe & Co. took over after legal action, oxen brought up the Missouri by LaBarge & Harkness. Nick Wall, Roe's son-in-law, was manager and young Edgar Maclay a guiding spirit. The change in ownership as the decade was ending began in mid-1868 when Maclay bought Diamond R, then employing 70 men with 116 wagons and over 700 oxen, "probably largest in the west," said the Herald. Charles Broadwater entered the firm along with the Fort Benton men, the reorganization probably providing capital for expansion.

That was needed for the long haul from Corinne, Utah, on the Union Pacific from the latter half of 1869, following abortive efforts for a steamboat terminus near the mouth of the Musselshell, primarily in 1866 and 1868. In 1870 the Corinne trail apparently handled about 5,000 tons of Montana freight. The route to Helena, however, was about three times that from Benton to Helena, and merchants there tended to favor the steamboats as a source. Heavy snows on the wagon road north from railhead often stopped the wagons altogether. Freighters made efforts to move "time" or fast freight to Montana camps, but this proved too expensive. George Steell apparently recognized the difficulties of the Corinne Trail earlier than others, for he left Diamond R in 1873 in favor of ranching at Sun River. By 1874 Helena merchants were backing a new plan for the Musselshell, a freight drop at the new settlement of Carroll and a freight trail through the Judith Basin to Helena. The project, with Diamond R backing, was put into operation in 1874. Soldiers from Fort Logan were expected to protect freighters from Indians, especially Sioux. The Carroll Trail had more troubles than hostile Indians, however. The Kountz Line of steamboats failed miserably to deliver the goods, and freighters fought the mud from what the partisan Helena

Herald termed the "wettest season" in memory. The next year was more of the same. Both seasons steamboats had few problems getting to Fort Benton.

Matthew Carroll left the Diamond R in 1879 and tried cattle like his partner—he later attributed his financial setbacks to the Corinne Trail. Edgar Maclay got out in 1881 and came to Fort Benton to join Murphy Neel. Perhaps the gradual disintegration of the great Diamond R can be attributed to Fort Benton merchants who found freighting a worthwhile sideline.

Carroll & Steell's successor in Fort Benton was Frederick F. Gerard, who lost his trading license in the Fort Union area early in 1871, loaded his wares onto a steamboat and came to Fort Benton. He bought the Carroll & Steell property and advertised in the Herald as successor, territorial licenses show the firm name for general merchants, liquor and gambling in 1872. Gerard suffered a crippling but untraceable loss when a wagon train was cut off, looted and five men killed north of the border, probably in the fall of 1871. The sole reference indicates this was in the Whoop Up country, a newspaper report may refer to the event, to the east in the Cypress Hills area. The Gerard business record ends with the 1872 licenses. T. C. Power owned the lots in 1876 when titles were sold by the federal government.

## I. G. Baker & Co., International Business

Few firms have ever had the trans-border influence that the I. G. Baker company of Fort Benton wielded. And few loom so favorably across the years as does founder Isaac Gilbert Baker. During his career he made a fortune with few detractors, certainly not the Albertans who benefited greatly while helping to build that fortune.

Consider: A rival to be, T. C. Power, to whom established Baker offered a large tent for storage while Power erected his own store at the far end of the same business block. Their two firms became vastly competitive, but the two remained friends and cooperated in numerous enterprises, some completely altruistic. Two dead-broke Virginians, Wm. G. and Charles Conrad, who went to work for Baker in 1868 and left Fort Benton millionaires. A Conrad cousin, Shirley Ashby, volunteered to take a dangerous trading post on the Marias with no discussion as to reward. Ashby made $40,000 for the company, was given $7,500 and a tenth interest in the Baker business. (He soon sold to the Conrads.)

Isaac Baker was no fledgling Indian trader when he came to Fort Benton in 1864 for Charles Chouteau of American Fur. Born in Connecticut in 1819, his family moved to the Iowa frontier in 1836. Baker from youth traded with Sac and Fox Indians. He was 45 and father of two on coming up the Missouri on the Yellowstone with 400 tons of cargo to relieve ailing Andrew Dawson. His competence was quickly tested, for the steamboat could get no further than Cow Island, 120 miles below Fort Benton. Baker went overland to the post, began sending wagons, pack mules, independent freighters, whatever available, to move that cargo, testified ubiquitous William Gladstone, who helped load the cargo and repair the wagons at Cow Island. Baker was also knowing and resourceful, he sent Mormon teamsters with two wagons to transport the most precious cargo, 200 barrels of whisky, that frontier necessity.

Baker returned that fall to Salt Lake City, San Francisco and round the Horn to New York, came again on the Yellowstone in 1865, this time clear to Fort Benton with Chouteau again aboard, this time to transfer ownership of the trading post to James B. Hubbell and Alpheus F. Hawley of the new Northwest Fur Co. Baker had declined Chouteau's offer of sale, but had seen opportunity in Fort

Benton. He did handle some business for Chouteau until June 1867.

William Gladstone reported that he built the first I. G. Baker store in 1865 for $6 a day and grub. Baker continued his practice of returning to St. Louis each fall, this time via Salt Lake and Atchison, Kansas, probably to purchase as well as visit his family.

Coming up river in the spring of 1866 he brought a large stock of goods and his brother George, making it I. G. Baker & Bro. That was the most profitable and successful steamboating year of the gold rush. George Baker, who became local manager, reported immense receipts of gold. In boating season to September or October, daily store sales were $200 or $300 to a high level of $1500 or $1800 in dust, and one could see wheelbarrows laden with gold trundled down the street. Safes were overflowing with stored metal. Shipment was of course easy by steamboat, but in late fall mackinaws were the only resort, with buoys of small kegs attached to the golden cargo, well packaged, one may be certain. George Baker told historian James Bradley that so far as he could recall, no gold so shipped was ever irretrievably lost, although some mackinaws sank.

Frances Wilson Baker accompanied Isaac and his brother to Fort Benton in the spring of 1867. By that time the Baker firm was following Northwest Fur's practice of Indian trading in outposts—near the Musselshell, on the Milk and Marias, and as Ashby's account indicates, this was profitable. Fort Benton those years could be a deadly place for Indians, so taking the trade to them was good business policy.

In the summer of 1867 Isaac Baker had built the adobe and log home near his store which is still (1986) preserved as an adjunct to the Fort Benton Museum, and oldest surviving home in the town. In the fort, their former quarters, Mrs. Baker had felt quite safe, but a home in roisterous Fort Benton was another matter. Nevertheless, their daughter Frances was born in this house December 4, 1867. The next fall mother and daughter returned via mackinaw to St. Louis, and little Frances did not see her birthplace again until 1882, although Isaac Baker continued lengthy sojourns during busy summer and fall seasons.

A rival trader, T. C. Power, arrived in June 1867 with a stock of goods unloaded on the levee near the Baker store, and Power could find no building to rent. Power never forgot Baker's loan of a "Methodist revival tent" in which to start his business. (Letter from son, Charles Power, 1926.) The first more permanent Power store was built on the down river end of the block on which Baker located. The two concerns built the Choteau House between them, later shared in first locally owned steamboat, first hardware store and first bank, among other projects.

The Baker firm continued its policy of trading posts among the Indian tribesmen; Ashby traded for them with Sioux and Assiniboine in 1869-70 near Poplar Creek with Wm. G. Conrad second in command. In view of the fact that Al Hamilton was a nephew of Isaac Baker, it is probable that the first venture north of the boundary by John Healy and Hamilton was Baker backed. The company was slightly less lucky in their Medicine Rock or Sun Fort on the Marias near the later site of Fort Conrad and the Whoop Up Trail, the same years. Medicine Rock, a mile or two away, was sacred to the Blackfeet, and when one killed a spotted white buffalo, the robe was carefully tanned and secured on Medicine Rock. Not illogically, the valuable robe found its way to the trading post, whereupon the outraged Blackfeet refused to trade there, the post was abandoned, and early in 1870 was burned. Fort Benton traders in 1870 were much distressed by a government embargo on shipment of robes due to smallpox among Indians; in late fall the Baker company managed to clear 3,000 as not contaminated (probably some of those Ashby traded for with Sitting Bull) and this shipment went by freight south to Corinne for shipment by rail. After Medicine Rock, the Baker men built Fort Conrad, longest lived of such branch outposts.

First admitted intrusion of the Baker Company into Canada was in 1871-72 at Belly River, followed by a second at the Spitzee River in 1872. These posts mark the formal beginnings of the long relationship between the Baker concern and the people of Alberta.

In the final years of the gold rush, I. G. Baker & Bro. went into freighting on a growing scale, the Helena Herald first mentioning this in April 1868. Next year in July the Herald reported arrival of 25 brand new Baker wagons, "shipped this season." Indicating gradual growth, early in 1872 the Herald reported that the Baker company had lost only nine of 180 work cattle on Sun River, and those by accident, despite a severe winter. Two weeks later though, a stranger loss, 60 head had trailed along with a buffalo herd in the Sun River valley, no sequel noted and likely most were recovered—otherwise a routine business debit. Two months later the Herald reported that Charles E. and Wm. G. Conrad had become associated with I. G. Baker & Bro., the new name, I. G. Baker, Bro. & Co. This was from purchase of the Shirley Ashby tenth—two years later the brothers bought out George Baker.

Both Power and Baker were quite successful in their branch posts, in June 1873 the Herald reported each would ship east around 17,000 robes and assorted furs. They were surviving a severe depression and in fact, flourishing.

### Canadian Connection

Word reached Fort Benton and its merchants during the summer of 1874 of an expedition westward from Winnipeg which would make millionaires of the partners in the Baker enterprises.

The October 9, 1874, Helena Herald carried an item headed "Supplies for the North." I. G. Baker, "of the extensive mercantile trading and forwarding house of I. G. Baker & Co., Benton, has been several days in the city purchasing groceries, hardware, clothing and other goods to fill out a complement of 40,000 pounds of supplies and stores for the Queen's Mounted Police, ordered for duty across the border." The Baker company not only had the supply contract for the North West Mounted Police (NWMP), but would hold it until after the building of the Canadian Pacific in 1883. If Fort Benton was "Birthplace of Montana," as residents assert, the small Baker store in Fort Benton was "Birthplace of Alberta." The firm not only filled supply contracts, it helped build posts at Fort Macleod and Calgary, handled Mounted Police payrolls, goods shipped from eastern Canada via rail to Bismarck, by steamboat to Fort Benton, and stored under $100,000 bond until the merchandise could be freighted north.

(Shirley Ashby recalled that the Canadian contract with the Baker Co. was no accident, they had contacted Robert W. Donnell of a Helena firm for a reliable trade contact, and Donnell had suggested I. G. Baker as "a very trustworthy, reliable and honest man in every respect, and could feel perfectly safe in trading with him. They could be supplied with anything that they wanted from a Jew's harp, to a threshing machine!")

In November 1874 another item reported that Power and Baker firms had ordered construction of a light draft steamboat, first to be locally owned. This boat, Benton, made its initial appearance at Fort Benton the following spring; a steamboat which would make more trips, carry more freight and perhaps passengers, than any other into Montana.

## A Vast Business Arena

In an article which appeared first in the Great Falls Tribune December 16, 1906, Wm. G. Conrad, general manager of the Fort Benton business, recalled:

At Fort Benton was located a "business metropolis that had for a radius for its active business activities, nearly a whole continent, that purchased goods from New Orleans on the south and the Great Slave lakes on the north, almost within the Arctic Circle and sold goods all over the world, in St. Louis and New York, in London and St. Petersburg, a business running up into many millions of dollars in value annually. . . .

"In one year, we have handled as high as 30,000,000 pounds of freight for the United States government, the Canadian government and the merchants of Montana, much of this freight being delivered at distant points, hauled over trackless country by our bull teams and mules. For this purpose we had at one time about 500 yoke of oxen and several hundred head of mules. . . .

"I recall once opening a letter which contained an order for $160,000 worth of provisions at one delivery." He also wrote of 30,000 buffalo robes and 25,000 wolf skins as one year's business—the lush trade in robes and hides ended with 1882.

The firm later, 1877-1882, operated its own Baker Line of steamboats, principally the Red Cloud, also the Col. McLeod and leased boats. As many as eight Canadian trading posts with the best available transport and supplies all but pushed the Hudson's Bay Co. out of the Alberta market, and Conrad recalled proudly that on the 1891 sale of Baker stores in Canada to HBC that one of their directors drank a toast "to the health of the writer as the man who had scaled the value of their stock down from pounds to shillings."

After an 1882 statement to I. G. Baker in St. Louis, the Conrad brothers received an answer to the effect that he would have thought $40,000 or $50,000 profit would have been remarkable, but "now when it is a quarter of a million I don't know what to say." Isaac Baker made a number of summer visits to Fort Benton in steamboat days, one in 1887 by rail as far as Fort Assiniboine and thence by stage, then almost each summer, spending weeks at the Highwood ranch of his son Joseph, last the year before his 1904 death.

In Fort Benton the Baker firm held a closing out sale beginning at the end of 1890, and completed next year, their bank being moved to Great Falls. Continuing into the 20th century was the Benton & St. Louis Cattle Co., better known as the Circle, at one time largest in Montana, and a major livestock company in Alberta as well.

## T. C. Power & Bro., Perhaps Largest

Thos. C. Power, born in Dubuque, Iowa, in 1839, first entered Montana in 1864 as a civil engineer with a surveying party. He returned, to Fort Benton, June 14, 1867, landing from the Yorktown with a stock of goods on credit from Joseph Field, brother of the more noted Marshall, and plans as extensive as the wide frontier. There wasn't a shack to be rented on the town's busy waterfront, but Isaac G. Baker, graciously loaned the new come competitor a large tent for the start of a firm which may have been Fort Benton's largest. For the rest of his days, wrote Power's son Charles in 1926, T. C. Power remembered that kindness. The two firms, at times bitter competitors in the outlands, cooperated thereafter in numerous local projects.

The first T. C. Power store was located at the "down river" corner of the block which also held the Baker store. Additional stock came on the Lady Grace in

July. As had been the case with Isaac Baker, a brother, John W., soon joined the firm and the name became T. C. Power & Bro. Unlike their chief rival, there were no more partners in the parent firm, although in a wide range of unattached enterprises, the Powers, and especially Thomas C., were open or silent partners.

In 1868 came the first joint enterprise, the Thwing House in mid-block, run by a woman of that name and managed by S. V. Clevenger. Remodeled in 1879, it became the noteworthy Chouteau House. The Powers soon showed a tendency to branch into diverse enterprises. First freighting began in 1868, John Power built a meat market beside the store, showing in old pictures. June 4 the Helena Herald carried an ad of receipt of farming and labor saving implements, a year later the agricultural store in Helena was thriving. The firm hedged by opening a trading post at the Musselshell in 1869 against the possibility the Fort Benton route would be bypassed. Perhaps routine sale, more likely a limited small partnership, J. D. Weatherwax appears on a sizeable 1869 invoice, about the time Wetzel & Weatherwax began their Indian trading—soon across the Canadian boundary. In the next few years, John Healy, Joe Kipp, Fred Kanouse, John Kerler and others were customers and one may assume the firm was a silent partner in the Canadian whisky trade. An intriguing entry in the Power papers dated July 30, 1874, is headed "Adventure to Belly River." A fuller picture of these wild years can be gained from the Montana Historical Society Power papers, but these help explain the growth of the Power business.

T. C. Power may have been the first Montana merchant to sense the coming growth of farming in a territory hard hit by exhaustion of extensive placer mining. He announced intent to establish farm implement agencies at Bozeman, Deer Lodge and Virginia City in March 1871, as well as that in Helena. A year later the Helena Herald reported the store there doing $1,000 business daily—300 machines ordered would not be half enough.

His freighting buildup continued, the Sun River wintering spot for work oxen had virtually no loss in the severe 1871-72 winter. There were other perils, a Power wagon train was attacked by Indians in 1872 north of Fort Benton. That had to have been a good trading season. In August the Chicago Tribune reported the biggest robe and fur shipment in city history, from T. C. Power of Fort Benton, Montana Territory, 16,400 robes and many peltries, "about a third" of the Fort Benton commerce. (This shipment may have been a result of the original backing from Joseph Field.)

The Powers were definitely in the Whoop Up whisky trade in the final years, posts on the Old Man, near Whoop Up and in the Cypress Hills. But, like Baker, the Power firm was perfectly willing to adjust to and accept the arrival of the North West Mounted Police in September 1874 as providing better opportunities in legitimate trade. There also appeared an evident working agreement between the firms. Baker could keep the Canadian government business, Power would be unopposed by Baker for a probably understood share of the lucrative U. S. military and Indian contracts. Actually, even with the Union Pacific to the south and the Utah & Northern crawling north, no merchant far from the head of navigation stood much chance of winning an important contract.

### Birth of The Block P Line

It was November 14, 1874, that the Helena Herald carried the joint announcement by the T. C. Power and I. G. Baker firms that they had ordered construction of a brand new steamboat to be built in the Pittsburgh area along the lines of the successful Nellie Peck of the Coulson Line. This would be the first locally owned steamboat, and as it turned out, start of what became the biggest and most successful of the Upper Missouri lines. By that time, steamboats chiefly shuttled between Bismarck, railhead of the Northern Pacific, and Fort Benton bringing the lion's share of all the supplies of Montana Territory.

The Benton duly made its maiden trip down the Ohio to St. Louis, up the Missouri to Fort Benton. It had to be a prideful moment for the Fort Benton firms when the little signal cannon boomed and the Benton swelled in size, up past Steamboat Point to moor, one can feel certain, midway between the stores. That was at 1 p. m. May 27, a few hours after the speed queen Nellie Peck. The Benton, two short years later the "Old Reliable," would make more arrivals at Fort Benton, carry far more freight than any other boat, and perhaps more passengers.

The Baker firm chose to sell its interest in the Benton in 1877 in favor of buying the speedy Red Cloud, and the Powers in succession brought out the classy Helena, the fine freight carrier Butte and finally the Black Hills. Over the boats of the Fort Benton Transportation Co. and between the stacks was the Block P, by which the line was better known. The company bought the Coulson boats, one by one; one season had 11 steamboats in the Fort Benton trade.

Looking back, it seems that Thomas C. Power, often the typical grasping business man of the times, had more than a touch of sentiment for the steamboats which helped build his fortune. He not only kept the Block P boats coming to Fort Benton for three seasons after arrival of the railroad in 1887, but his financing kept the Benton Packet Co. alive in the Bismarck area through a couple of reorganizations to his death in 1923. Isaac Post Baker, cousin of Isaac G., kept the final line on the upper river into the 1930s.

From the 1870s, when the Coulsons began bringing out their upper river craft, it was seldom that a boat failed to make a planned trip to Fort Benton, accident to machinery might force substitution of another boat. The steamboats built for Power possibly had better records. Use of the old late season freight drop at Cow Island was virtually discontinued, with exception for special cargo. One note of interest to collectors, only in 1881 did the Block P carry U. S. mail, as distinct from way letters.

After the beginning of recovery from the depression of 1873, Fort Benton merchants were dominant in the transportation picture. Editor W. H. Buck in the first issue of the Benton Record, February 1, 1875, put it concisely: "In the interests of transportation it commands the traffic of the country, holds the key to the business homes of the Territory. . . .in short, Benton is the transportation centre of Montana." The two major firms on the same block were those who largely made Editor Buck's words true.

That year 1875 was the last rumble for the ambitious town of Carroll, good stage of water for steamboats, mud on the Carroll Trail and intransigent Sioux contributing factors. Nearest railroad was the Utah & Northern in southern Idaho, slightly farther away, the Northern Pacific to the east.

In 1879 both Power and Baker firms built brick buildings, Baker moving back a block to Main, Power across the street on Front. Both would add space shortly. Also, where the old Power store had stood would rise a brick hardware, another shared enterprise. Still another was the First National Bank in June 1880, after a few weeks in the Record building the bank moved to yet another brick on the original block near and between the two firms.

T. C. Power moved to Helena in 1878, while John W. Power was in charge of the Fort Benton interests, where he would remain until his death in 1901. The senior member's path led him into the U. S. Senate in 1890, with Wilbur Fisk Sanders the first after statehood.

Members of the Power family maintained a sort of proprietory interest in Fort Benton, still evidenced by descendants. When the second two section Power store burned in 1916, it was promptly rebuilt. In homestead days a lumber yard and garage were added, in the 1920s several residences. It was not until the depth of the Great Depression that sale was made in 1932-33 of the various stores and properties in Fort Benton, the general store surviving as Pioneer Mercantile until 1985, the other businesses and houses went to others.

The forced retrenchment involved a surprising number of other towns, for the elder Power scattered his business shots, generally profitably—in cattle, sheep, stores, mines, stage lines. He had a store at later Lewistown by 1879, had the initial business at Chinook. The Power papers bear evidence of 95 firms which he founded or invested in, and few lines of business unrepresented.

One interesting addition, at least to the writer, occurred after T. C. Power became U. S. senator. The two parties had split evenly in the legislature, which named senators then, the republicans being seated by the U. S. senate. The then editor of the River Press, Wm. H. Todd, or perhaps his editorial writer Daniel Searles, had no liking for "gold republican" Tom Power, and became vociferous enough to draw Power's dislike. The Powers started the Fort Benton Review late in 1890, withdrew their ads from the River Press—in a town with by then only one store of consequence. After a few weeks Todd in 1891 sold his stock in the paper through an intermediary, giving Power a majority interest in the corporation. In 1923 people connected with the Press bought the stock from the estate. So far as known, T. C. Power never attempted to control editorial policy, except perhaps a general "just keep off my back." The investment, probably less than $7500, was after all inconsequential to a wealthy man juggling interests in several score companies.

## Wetzel & Weatherwax

Certainly not of the scope of the Power and Baker firms, the partnership of W. Scott Wetzel and J. D. Weatherwax was on the Fort Benton scene in wild Whoop Up days, and although both lost their considerable fortunes, they demonstrated the frontier possibilities for resolute, daring and enterprising men. Scott Wetzel came west after Civil War service, was in Fort Benton by 1868. In 1870 the partnership was formed. Weatherwax, New York native, lost a fortune in the Civil War, came out on the Agnes in 1867. Their trade was largely with Indians up north, Weatherwax tarried too long, was one of the first punished by the Mounted Police ($500 fine, six months, and confiscation of several hundred robes), friends seemingly believing him a scapegoat. At his death in 1887, the River Press obituary included "no truer or more honest man ever lived." Weatherwax withdrew from the firm twice, second time for good when he went to ranching.

After the second withdrawal David G. Browne became office manager for Wetzel and his fortunes improved. The Wetzel business was reported at $150,000 in 1881 and $250,000 the next year. An incomplete invoice book for 1881 indicates it probably was over $150,000, purchases of more than $80,000— usual markup then was double, and the book did not show transportation and local items. Further, a considerable number of invoices had been torn off. He and Browne were into freighting and other enterprises. Wetzel in 1882 built a residence which compared favorably to the showplace Wm. G. Conrad home. Later the Wetzel home was the Fort Benton Sanitarium, finally demolished. Wetzel failed in late 1883. At his death in 1891 the River Press said his extension of credit to needy was the cause. Both partners served as county commissioner, indicating standing with fellow citizens.

### Hitchhikers On Benton Boom

With the arrival of the North West Mounted Police in September 1874 Fort Benton's two largest merchants found their trade growing far beyond what had been a basic dependence on the Indian trade. Meanwhile, a strong effort was made by Helena merchants in the summer of 1874 to import goods via the Carroll Trail to a town of the name on the Musselshell, an alternate route to Fort Benton. That year failure of the Kountz steamboats to adequately master the Missouri's vagaries left most of those relying on the route short of merchandise. In 1875 the water was high, steamboats had no trouble reaching Fort Benton. Also it rained so much the wagon trains from Carroll bogged down, and Sioux were staging a sneak preview of next year's big show with Custer. So the Carroll Trail was definitely dead before the 1875 shipping season ended, with some of the delayed Carroll freight hauled via the safer route from Cow Island to Fort Benton.

Never again until the Northern Pacific arrived in 1883 did Helena firms ship much except via the Benton Road, which became Montana's busiest freight route.

### Murphy Neel & Co.

John T. Murphy was one of Montana's early merchants, from 1864, opening stores in the gold camps as opportunity offered, with Samuel Neel as partner. Murphy Neel & Co. supported the Carroll enterprise, but after its failure quickly opened a warehouse in Fort Benton, with Wm. H. Todd as agent in 1876. By 1878 the firm was solidly established in Fort Benton, in the first Wetzel & Weatherwax store. Their Fort Benton agency, like the earlier merchants, quickly expanded into what became the big four. They were already into freighting, had to build a large warehouse on the levee in 1877.

In 1880 they followed Baker and Power in erecting a large brick business building, 44x125, and costing nearly $15,000, a sizeable sum in those days, moving in at year end. By that time Murphy Neel had a large investment in freighting, with fifty freighters, more than a hundred wagons, 400 oxen and 120 mules. One of their freight trains standing empty, the River Press noted, represented an investment of $25,000. The firm required two, perhaps three, sprawling warehouses to store and protect their merchandise, largely shipped on Coulson Line steamboats. Their chief men were Wm. H. Todd, J. R. Rice and George Clendenin.

Todd withdrew in favor of other interests, including the Grand Union Hotel, in 1882, and Edgar Maclay left the Diamond R to become a partner. As a result the firm name changed to Murphy Maclay. They were among the first to establish a branch at brand new Great Falls in 1884, which perpetuated the firm name well into the 20th century. In hard times of the decade at Fort Benton, that store was closed late in 1888. The building stood empty for years, except for a brief lived beer hall in 1900, later was occupied by the Davis Grocery for more than fifty years, then converted to restaurant and offices.

### Kleinschmidt & Bro.

Reinhold and Albert Kleinschmidt came to Helena in 1867 and quickly with shrewd and often sharp business acumen became extremely successful. The firm backed the Carroll route, too, and were not as quick to set up in Fort Benton. Then they moved swiftly.

March 23, 1877, the Benton Record noted "Mr. Kleinschmidt is in town selecting a site for a new warehouse." By July plans were complete for a 35x165 foot building, and it would be unique in Fort Benton. Said the Record, "Walls will be made of concrete composed stone, coarse gravel and broken stone." The structure, first business building in Fort Benton other than adobe, log or lumber, and also the first fireproof, was done by late fall. Meanwhile, showing their operation to be far from small, they chartered the General Custer which brought their eastern orders from Pittsburgh, and the Fontenelle with a cargo from St. Louis, about 500 tons for the first season.

Kleinschmidt Bros. store and warehouse was so close to the river bank that gangplanks could be run inside and freight unloaded directly. Virtually all their business was channeled to their Helena stores. Newspaper files give evidence that their gross business was on the order of 2,000 tons a year. At the peak, Kleinschmidt & Bro. had freight outfits capable of hauling 250 tons of freight at a time, and in 1881 they carried a $150,000 stock of merchandise at all times in Fort Benton, about the same as reported for Murphy Neel. The 2000 tons yearly would have meant around 270 loads for three wagon hitches, around 30 freight trains yearly.

When the Northern Pacific reached Helena in 1883, the Kleinschmidts reacted swiftly, closing out their Fort Benton stock early in 1884. The building was a livery for years, then deserted. Shortly before World War II Charles Bovey and Kiwanis members worked to convert it to a museum, interrupted by war and never resumed. The structure was razed in 1947 for a Veterans' Memorial building, but a real estate exchange resulted in the Benton Funeral Home being built on the site in the 1950s.

### Other Helena Branches

Several other Helena firms established branches in Fort Benton as business at the head of navigation boomed.

Most notable was that of Louis Gans and Henry Klein, natives of Austria, who opened their strictly clothing store in Fort Benton in mid-May 1881. They occupied the former Wetzel-Murphy Neel frame building, but found business so good that in 1882 they contracted for a 25x100 brick adjoining, and moved in by late September. The firm proved to be innovators in advertising, their sales and sale prices quite modern in tone. Although the boom ran out in 1884, Gans & Klein continued operating until 1890 before closing. Long vacant, the building in this century was converted to a mortuary, on a trade became Vets Club in 1957.

Davidson & Moffitt, Helena harness firm, also came in 1881 to an anticipated harvest, building a 30x60 brick before opening, probably because no other quarters could be found. The business limped from the start, Fort Benton had two saddle and harness firms already and the big stores also handled such goods. The brick was completed in October 1881, the business gave up less than two years later. The River Press, following a fire, moved into it in July 1885, the paper's home since.

### Hotels And Restaurants

William T. Hamilton in memoirs told of building the first, log, hotel in Fort Benton in 1864, which may have been the one sketched by Granville Stuart on

June 9, 1866, titled Metropolitan Hotel. Hamilton's account indicates it was primarily a restaurant and butcher shop, all three prime needs in the place at the time. Hamilton, who was courier to Indian villages prior to the peace treaty of 1865 at Fort Benton, drew added profit from the trip, as he was called on to provide meals for some of the chiefs at $1 per meal, although he complained it should have been $2, one Indian ate as much as two whites. At one meal the chiefs and about a dozen warriors "had plenty to eat, but no fancy dishes."

John Healy and brother are credited in some sources as operating a saloon, restaurant and hotel of sorts in what was then termed "Council House" because of that 1865 treaty—the building had been the Indian agency and Healy's memoirs mention both his being assistant to Agent Gad Upson, and being in business in Fort Benton in 1865-66. "Council House" was later the Jos. Sullivan saddlery and can be seen at Nevada City, Montana, moved from Fort Benton in the 1940s.

## Overland Hotel

A couple of doors above Council House, beyond Carroll & Steell, was the site where Jacob W. Schmidt in 1866 built the first formal hotel in Fort Benton—from lumber hauled by bull train from Helena. That was the peak gold rush season, and the place was boiling with business the day a big freighter tugged at Schmidt's coat tail to get dining room service. "Uncle Jake" swung around, outraged, chucked an armload of dishes out the nearest window and shouted at the offender: "My name is Jacob Schmidt and I am the boss of this hotel, and I want you to know I don't allow any tam man to pull my coattail." Then he grabbed dishes off other tables and fired them out the window, turned to the patrons and said, "Gentlemen, this hotel is closed." It was, until friends persuaded the explosive German to reopen for the benefit of a hungry horde.

He may not even have named the place, and left soon for other points, Ben Stafford taking over and operating it the season of 1867 as the Stafford House. Next year Ferdinand C. Roosevelt took over—why not? It was right next the Wells Fargo stage station Roosevelt had managed the year before—he could handle both with ease. Naturally it became the Overland Hotel, a name it bore until destroyed by fire June 6, 1949—the name continuing in a saloon nearby.

A succession of owners followed, John W. Tattan and John Healy, John Hunsberger, Charles and William Rowe. John Sneath rebuilt it in 1897 as a large three story frame structure, the one which burned in 1949. During demolition, in 1897 alert townsmen collected and panned the dirt, profitably, which had lain below the Wells Fargo office, where in 1867, a $10,000 fee was collected for handling a shipment of about two tons of gold.

The year 1868 brought another small hotel, Jim Nabors built an adobe cabin and operated it as restaurant and hotel for a time, soon disposing of it to W. S. Stocking, he and wife ran it several years as Benton Hotel.

## Choteau (now Chouteau) House

A prime addition to the Fort Benton business district and one of the first and most pleasant sights a steamboat passenger saw along the levee, was the 1868 hotel T. C. Power and I. G. Baker built between their stores, a block and a half above the old fort. Tom Clary, later sheriff, hauled the lumber from the Holter sawmill at Montana City, a problem freighting the stringers over twisting Lyon's Hill. So the two story frame lined with adobe, Fort Benton's only readily available building material, went up. It opened in the spring of 1868 with a Mrs. Thwing in charge and bore the name of Thwing House. S. V. Clevenger was manager for the owners.

The depression of the 1870s caused its closing, but Power and Baker, with extensive U. S. and Canadian government contracts, rented it as officers' quarters for the Fort Benton army garrison, and for visiting VIPs. In the spring of 1879 Jere Sullivan decided to move from Sun River, and with H. B. Hill as partner reopened the hotel as the Choteau House (changed to Chouteau after 1903). This hotel looms prominently and comfortably in pictures of the period. Hill sold out in 1882, but Jere Sullivan continued as "mine host" in an establishment well regarded from frontier years to his death in 1919. From the turn of the century to 1910 the structure was rebuilt in brick by stages.

### Culbertson House

Robert Mills appears on the 1870 census as hotelman, quite possibly in the Overland, for it was as Rowe & Mills that a hotel license was issued in 1871. By 1874 Bob Mills was running what a Helena visitor called a popular restaurant on or near the corner by the 1888 bridge, and probably with James Douglass, for he married the latter's daughter Mattie in 1877. Most likely in recognition of Alexander Graham Bell's recent achievement, he named it the "Eataphone." The same year John Hunsberger dissolved partnership in the hotel portion. Robert S. Culbertson left clerking in a store to join Mills in what was by then the Centennial Hotel. The partnership was dissolved in April 1881, Culbertson becoming full owner.

In 1882-83, joining the local building fever, Culbertson had the Centennial rebuilt of brick, the old frame moved back to the alley so the hotel could continue operating, according to his daughter, Mollie C. Sedgwick. His son, Frank, informed the writer that R. S. Culbertson inspected the material, literally brick by brick, to insure best construction. It was opened in 1883 as the Pacific, but over the years became better known as the Culbertson House. In 1985 the structure housed two small businesses.

### "A Mammoth Hotel"—Grand Union

Most imposing structure in Fort Benton, and one that draws the eyes of visitors, is the Grand Union Hotel, a substantial three story brick. Completed and opened in 1882, it was several years too late to reap the benefits of a Fort Benton boom that swelled yearly until the year it was completed.

Plans for "a mammoth hotel" underway, said an 1880 Benton Record. From that inception the Grand Union was the brain child of promotional minded Wm. H. Todd. John Ellingsen made it his master's thesis in 1971, a detailed and excellent account of the building which Fort Bentonites labelled "the finest between the Twin Cities and Seattle."

Ground was broken in August 1881 and work pushed on the structure late into the winter, by February 1882 more than half the brickwork was done. First mention of the name it has borne more than a century was found in the October 12, 1882, Benton Record. The project had been incorporated as Benton Hotel Co., financed by subscription and estimated to have cost $50,000, several times that much to finish and furnish. And it was said to have been largely designed as workers laid more than a half million locally fired bricks.

The Grand Union was formally opened November 2nd with a banquet and ball, attended, noted Record editor W. H. Buck, "by almost 100 of the fair sex." Resident from 1875, Buck could recall when white women could be numbered on the fingers of a hand. The lessors had more than a bit of trouble in preparing rooms in the still unfinished portion.

The hotel flourished for a season, into summer and fall 1883, but shocking evidence of the end of Fort Benton's boom came in May 1884 when the Benton Hotel Co. assets went at sheriff's sale to a local banking firm. The structure was so impressive and prestigious that virtually every hotel man in Fort Benton took up the challenge of making it pay. There were numbers of changes, a major remodeling around 1900. Mr. and Mrs. Charles Lepley bought the building in 1917, Harold Thomas in 1951—he undertaking a tremendous one man restoration that probably preserved the structure. By then one of several Fort Benton buildings on the National Register, Mr. and Mrs. Thomas sold it to Levee Restorations in 1979.

Restaurants, as any traveler knows, are here today, gone tomorrow. Fort Benton had too many to attempt a list. Best recommended, and best bets for transients, were those in the various hotels, which had to serve decent grub—traveler accounts of stage station fare are disconcerting. It may have been one such who gave Charles Rowe points for the hash he served at the Overland. But that was in the gold rush period when anything edible was great food. In later years, a succession of experienced travelers commented favorably on the fare at Overland, Centennial, Chouteau House and Grand Union.

## Doctors And Drug Stores

From 1866 through territorial days the presence of nearby military posts tended to insure doctors' services in Fort Benton, a blessing many a mining camp lacked. Frontier doctors varied widely in competence, were often self taught or self proclaimed, while the contract provisions for army service probably meant at least minimal qualifications.

First doctor at Fort Benton, barring a fur post visitor, was George Suckley with the Isaac I. Stevens expedition September 1-21, 1853. One item noted: Stevens planned to send down the Missouri several discharged soldiers and most of the dragoons, to his surprise several wanted to see the expedition through and Dr. Suckley was asked to certify those fit to continue.

Other earlies were Dr. James A. Mullan, who accompanied his brother to Fort Benton when Lt. John Mullan's party opened the military road from Washington. Dr. William D. Gibb came with the Fisk expedition in 1862 and treated some patients at Fort Benton. Visiting doctors were Monroe Atkinson from the gold camps, year unstated, and Roswell Tibbitts, mentioned in Phillips' "Medicine In the Making of Montana," as first to be in actual practice in Fort Benton, in 1867—a daughter was born May 27, one of the first white children in Benton.

Dr. H. M. Lehman had been surgeon at Camp Cooke, moved to Fort Benton in 1868 and ran a professional card in the Helena Herald that year. He was elected coroner and was first to suggest the need for a hospital. Lehman was shot by a drunken soldier and died of the wound December 17, 1868. In the 1870s three army doctors were in the town briefly, A. B. Campbell, Philip Chapman Davis and William Eugene Brandt.

Dr. Will E. Turner was the first with a lengthy period of practice, coming to Fort Benton in 1874. As the army garrison was small, there was plenty of time for other patients, and he was rated highly by the Benton papers for surgical skills. Turner was partner with M. A. Flanagan in opening Fort Benton's first drug store next year, was joined by his father, also a doctor, in 1877, and the Turners were in practice into the 1880s.

Another army doctor was Francis Atkisson from 1881 until his death in 1914 a Fort Benton character for his formal attire and air of mystery. Dr. James Wheelock, in Fort Benton 1878-85, was both physician and educator. Locally remembered for long years in practice were C. D. Crutcher and John V. Carroll. The latter began as hospital steward at Fort Assiniboine in 1878, soon was recommended as fully qualified by Dr. Atkisson, and after informally working as doctor went to medical college to secure a degree.

## Druggists

Firms such as Baker and Power in early years sold literally everything, including the various drugs and patent medicines of the period. Michael A. Flanagan came to Fort Benton from Virginia City in 1868 to work for his brother-in-law, T. C. Power. In 1875 he entered partnership with Dr. Will E. Turner in the pioneer drug store of the city. The drug stock of Power and probably Baker was bought, and the store constructed of adobe and log a block down from the later 1888 bridge. The partnership was dissolved in 1877 when Dr. Turner's father, William, joined him in practice and a second drug further up the block, until 1884. Flanagan continued his business, and also became postmaster in 1878 and after an interval, 1888-1896, in and later to the rear of the drug store. He died in 1906; two years later the adobe store crumbled in a June flood. Dexter G. Lockwood, a former employe, started his own store in 1900, continued to 1985 under various owners.

Walter J. Minar, another druggist, opened in 1881, with an interval continuing until the early homestead years across from the Grand Union. In 1912 he sold to what became the Benton Drug, which continued under various owners until a 1958 fire.

Ben LaPeyre worked for Flanagan for a time from 1882, opened his own store which he continued until 1886 when he joined a brother in operating the first drug store in Great Falls. T. B. Shoebotham was another druggist in Fort Benton before statehood, working for Minar, later operating his own store.

## Fort Benton's Newspapers

Fort Benton did not have a newspaper during the gold rush, a matter to be regretted by historians. However, microfilms of the territory's first paper, the Montana Post of Virginia City, were used, as well as Helena Radiator, then successor Herald. Surprisingly, Post files are complete in those early years, 1864-67, those of the Helena papers less so. The space given to Fort Benton and river news provides evidence of the importance of the head of navigation to the mining camps in the south.

Unfortunately, files of the Fort Benton papers of territorial days have many missing issues, in particular the Benton Record. However, these do provide much basic source material.

William H. Buck, who had previously published a temperance paper for the soldiers at Fort Shaw, brought out the first issue of the Benton Record February 1, 1875, bi-monthly at the time, and printed on equipment of the 7th Infantry at the post. His April 15 issue was printed at Fort Benton. Editor Buck's enterprise was begun at the right time, and his lead editorial started, "Benton is rapidly emerging from the darkness" and concluded with a flat "Benton is the transportation centre of Montana." The latter was soon to be very apparent. The Record was newsy, readable and evidences a fine command of English by Buck.

At some period in the next two years, John J. Healy became a partner in the enterprise. In the final issue of 1878 the Record announced it had contracted for a three story, 45x50 brick building—the lower two stories preserved as Fraternity hall by lodges from 1929, the building demolished for a church in 1984. The Record moved into its building in late 1879, proudly proclaimed it had the finest plant in Montana and proceeded to produce a nine column paper a jealous contemporary likened "unto a barn door."

Probably in an effort to overwhelm opposition, the Daily Benton Record was begun on February 2, 1881. In June 1881, two local attorneys, Horace R. Buck and W. H. Hunt, took over the Record—W. H. Buck repossessed it a year later. The Record appeared spasmodically in 1884 and was sold at sheriff's sale in February 1885, victim of the hard times that hit Fort Benton in that period.

First issue of the River Press, by the later 1900s fourth oldest paper in Montana, was October 27, 1880. So far as known, the title is unique. James E. Stevens, who had worked for Buck and the Record, disliked his boss, and when H. C. Williams and Thomas D. Wright suggested going in with them in a new paper Stevens was receptive. The three got backing from republicans at Fort Benton and Helena, and the River Press was on its way. Leading citizens took a turn at the hand crank of the cylinder press for that first issue in the old adobe cabin that had been built as a "hotel" by Jim Nabors. In issue No. 1, the founding trio bragged a bit: "We present to our readers this week a paper which in typographical execution and general appearance is the equal of any in the west." A perusal of early files bears them out; they were masters of their craft.

Eight months later Williams sold his interest to new arrival Jeremiah Collins, just off a June steamboat. In August 1882 the Press was incorporated. One of the early stockholders was W. J. Harber, who in February 1884 yielded his place and stock to brother William K. Harber, fresh from England, and who was editor and manager from 1891 to his death in 1922. Collins went off to start the Great Falls Tribune in 1887, Wm. H. Todd buying his shares.

Going into statehood, Todd or his editor Dan Searles took after new U. S. Senator T. C. Power. Upshot was that the Powers started the Fort Benton Review in late 1890, took their ads out of the River Press. Early in 1891 Todd gave up, sold his majority interest to T. C. Power, and the Review was promptly suspended. It was not until after T. C. Power's death in 1923 that ownership became local once more.

Back in 1882 the River Press had responded to the Daily Record by bringing out the first Daily River Press on June 6. Hence until the Record quit a town of perhaps 2000 had two daily papers, although small format, four page affairs appearing five times weekly. The Daily River Press ceased publication at the end of 1919—at the time, according to a one time employe, press run was only about 150.

Only other newspaper in Fort Benton came in homestead days, The Chouteau County Independent, 1910-1925, discontinued the last of July 1925.

## Fort Benton's Banks

Fort Benton got along without formal banking through gold rush and depression of the early 1870s. However, I. G. Baker & Co. provided some banking services, in conjunction with Helena banks, from as early as 1866, including deposit and forwarding of tons of gold. Company sales meant large amounts of cash in the form of gold dust, and both Baker and Conrad brothers apparently made small loans, as well as the necessary extension of credit to Mounted Police, Montana merchants and federal agencies and troops. T. C. Power & Bro. would of necessity have done much the same.

It was not until steamboating was reaching its highest peak that the first banks opened, within a few days of each other. The First National Bank was chartered

May 14, 1880, with principal stockholders A. J. Davis, S. T. Hauser, Wm. G. and Charles E. Conrad, T. C. Power and Jos. S. Hill. Bank of Northern Montana was first to open by a few days, established June 1, 1880, by T. E. Collins, Chas. E. Duer and L. H. Hershfield & Bro., the latter representing a Helena bank. Both were first quartered in the Record building. First National soon completed a brick structure between the Baker and Power stores, representing continuing cooperation between the two big firms. Bank of Northern Montana moved into its own building in October 1881, midway in the block across from the Grand Union, a building still standing.

First National moved to Great Falls in 1891 and became the Northwestern National Bank. The Conrads, by then owners, sold the bank later; it was run into receivership in a short time. Reaction of the Conrads was exemplary; while not owners, they personally guaranteed depositors against loss and paid all claims. Later the brothers opened the Conrad Banking Co. in Great Falls; ads bore capitalization and the further defiant, "Individual responsibility $2,000,000!"

Bank of Northern Montana changed its name to Stockmen's National Bank in 1890; in pre-homesteading days carried accounts from all over northern Montana. After it closed in 1924 the Stockmen's eventually paid off 96.46%, indicative of its actual financial solvency.

The Stockmen's National Bank figured in an odd occurrence at the turn of the century when Loney and Bob Curry (Logan), operating a Harlem bar, sent in banknotes of a Portland bank. Someone noted the bills were mutilated in the area where bank officials signed to validate them, and forwarded the notes to the parent bank. Investigation showed them part of the loot from a Wyoming train robbery. Word got out, the Curry boys blew Harlem between dusk and dawn just ahead of the Pinkertons, selling the bar for what a party had in his wallet.

By contrast to the Stockmen's 1924 closure, a 1910 Benton State Bank failed in 1922, paid out only 38.78% of obligations after 11 years.

Chouteau county had all but five banks of 23 close in the desperate 1920s, two later liquidated. The Square Butte State Bank was moved to Fort Benton in 1924 after the Stockmen's closing, later became First Bank.

## A Miscellany Of Business
### Saddlers and Harness Stores

Lucus H. Rosencrans later proudly termed his store Pioneer Harness Shop; the Record's first 1877 issue noted he was coming, and February 2 reported L. H. Rosencrans, saddler, was open for business next the Record office, diagonally opposite where the later Grand Union would stand. At any rate he was the town's first saddlemaker, although the larger stores handled saddles and harness, as evidenced by their earlier ads. In June 1883 Rosencrans sold to William Glassman, from Helena, who operated the business until about September 1885.

August Beckman, who may have arrived some months earlier, was reported in business in a tall narrow frame structure below the later bridge by June 1878, making him the second saddler and harness maker in Fort Benton. In 1881 he built a 35x40 brick two blocks back, his wife Louisa running a boarding house and restaurant on the upper floor. Beckman later returned to Front Street— information lacking after 1882, except they were ranchers near town in 1898. Peter Burnett, shoemaker, occupied the Front Street quarters for years in the 20th century.

Mention is made elsewhere of Davidson & Moffitt harness store, a short lived branch firm from Helena in 1881-83.

Longest in business and best known of Fort Benton saddlers was Joseph Sullivan, who with partner V. K. Goss moved in 1881 from Deer Lodge at insistence of John Healy. Goss soon returned to Deer Lodge. The well remembered sign, "Jos. Sullivan, Saddler", hung for years over the door of the 1865 building that had housed the Blackfeet Agency and treaty of that year. One of Sullivan's orders was for 500 lightweight saddles for the North West Mounted Police—at times he had up to a dozen employes. Jos. Sullivan was a crusty old timer; a friend recalled that cowboys would hock their outfits to him to prolong a spree, get a tongue lashing later and be sent back to work with saddle and gear—they usually paid up next time. Before homesteaders the shop was a gathering place for old timers, among them good friend Charley Russell. Joseph Sullivan died in 1940 and the shop eventually wound up in Nevada City, Montana, one of Montana's historic buildings. A one time employe, Arnold Westfall, operated his own shop for a quarter century, to 1931, a few yards down street.

### Tinsmith To Hardware

Hans J. Wackerlin first came to Fort Benton in 1867 aboard the steamboat Richmond, worked in Fort Benton and at other points for several years, probably at his trade of tinsmith. That was an occupation important on the frontier; for instance you did not ship an item such as stovepipe, readily crushed, instead fashioned sheet metal on the spot.

He returned to St. Louis about 1871, two years later coming back with a wife. In 1878 he opened his own tinsmith shop, gradually expanding into hardware. With the backing of two local firms, Baker and Power, he built a brick business between the two stores, which opened in 1882 as H. J. Wackerlin & Co. It became the Benton Hardware after T. C. Power & Bro. bought his interest in 1895. The business was sold to local people in 1931, continued into the 1970s.

### Multi-Talented Cash Lanning

A century later it can be disclosed that Fort Benton's one time gunsmith, silversmith, jeweler and printer-by-hobby actually was christened Cassius M. Lanning. No wonder it was Cash for a quarter century! First note found, in November 1879 he was "returning" from Fort Macleod and his talents with gun and silver would be welcome. His store was first on St. John's (old bridge) street, then on Front diagonally across and down from the later Grand Union. Cash Lanning was in Fort Benton until 1897, then had a store in Dupuyer a couple of years. While here he served as alderman, mayor and county commissioner.

A task which would make any old time printer shudder! The River Press October 16, 1881, reported C. M. Lanning had developed an interest in the Blackfeet language during his five years at Fort Macleod. (In compiling his "A Grammar and Vocabulary of the Blackfoot Language" he had the assistance of Joe Kipp and Wm. Gladstone.) This he proposed to print on a hand lever Novelty press and a few fonts of type. (Slightly more than a kid's toy outfit.) That involved picking one character at a time from a small type case, putting in a printer's "stick" and justifying, locking up in a tiny chase. "With the meagre facilities he has at hand he will find it slow work and may yet be compelled to call in the assistance of the River Press book and job department." After putting in a sheet, the hand lever was pulled, the form reinked, 200 times for the press run, each of 150 pages. Then redistribute each letter in the case and start on the next page. Cash Lanning surely fooled the Press. The book was completed in February 1882. Ask any older printer how much work that was! A very few copies, perhaps two or three, still exist. Fort Benton museum files include a copy of a copy.

## Biggest And Best Meat Market

In 1864 with hundreds of hungry miners along the levee, "Old Bill" Hamilton set up the first meat market—two whisky barrels on end topped by three slabs, and soon was selling one to five beeves daily to boats and transients. Business was so good he had to hire a butcher and herder.

W. S. Stocking a couple of years later put a wooden frame around such a market, John Power apparently added another in 1868. There were several more, including Sample Bros. and the Tingleys, that came and went in the next years.

John J. Kennedy, in partnership in cattle with Ed Kelly—both had worked for the Benton-Helena stage line—had a market by 1879 in the former "Council House" but saw need for expansion of from on the hoof on the range to retail counter, and June 1881 let a contract to build a two story brick market on Main Street. This Centre Market was completed by November, and on the 10th Kennedy held a grand opening in western style, a supper and probably other refreshments for 250 friends, the Benton band playing for the house warming. It was Fort Benton's biggest hall and certainly its best meat market. Too big, too costly, creditors soon moved in.

In 1883 W. W. Higgins and Charles Ayres rented the facility, added Centre Produce Market to the title. The partner left the scene soon, Ayres moved once, then after the Baker store quit in 1891 to that building. With departure of the Baker store, commented the River Press, Ayres grocery and bakery had become the second largest firm in Fort Benton.

Kennedy's building remained a meat market under various operators into the next century, then was converted in turn to motion picture theatre and auto body repair shop.

Things don't change much, about 1880 the Benton Record had a note that because Bentonites wouldn't eat anything but steak, that item was mighty high at 25c a pound, but butchers couldn't sell the lower priced meat.

## First In Home Furnishings

A son of George Baker, W. S., and A. O. DeLorimier went into partnership in 1881, getting their home furnishings store completed early in the year, right next the Kennedy market. Baker & DeLorimier planned their grand opening for May 21, but it was a miserable low water year and steamboats were delayed. So after two postponements it was mid-June before they could get their store open. For a couple of seasons business was very good, the firm branched out with a store in White Sulphur Springs about 1883. In 1886 the partners split, DeLorimier taking the Fort Benton store, which he finally closed in 1890 and went back to work at the T. C. Power store.

## W. H. Burgess Specializes

W. H. Burgess came to Fort Benton in 1881, in May prepared to open the first strictly grocery store. This was in familiar quarters to old timers, the "old stand" of Wetzel & Weatherwax, from which Murphy Neel had just moved to their new brick building 100 feet up the street. Burgess found business pretty good, as all did in the early 80s, and in 1883 moved to the lower floor of the new Masonic Hall a stone's toss from the later bridge. There he went broke, in June 1884 turning his stock over to Collins, Duer & Co., bankers, for liquidation.

## First Furniture Store

Ferdinand C. Roosevelt, who had seen Fort Benton life in the rough when he was Wells Fargo agent in 1867—he claimed to have been an eye-witness to the drowning of acting Governor Thomas F. Meagher that July lst (substance, he didn't fall, wasn't pushed, staggered in), somehow lingered in Benton. He operated the Overland Hotel for a time, then was bookkeeper for W. S. Wetzel until 1881. That year Roosevelt had a frame building erected on Main Street for Fort Benton's first furniture store, buying part of his stock from the Power store, and opened in June 1881. It too did well for a time, but went out of business in a fire July 8, 1885, that burned the Odd Fellows Hall which housed the River Press as well. He never rebuilt. Roosevelt had a residence on an island just above Fort Benton, later in 1885 resigned as mayor on finding his home was beyond the city limits. His name appears on the city plat for an addition toward that home.

## Some Clothing Stores

Joseph Hirshberg and Arge Nathan joined the Fort Benton boom in May 1879, renting quarters for a clothing store on the site of the later Grand Union. Later they were located across the street and down a few doors. The firm kept going through some of the worst times, in 1886 partners may have fallen out, for soon each had his own store, Nathan near the I. G. Baker building. Hirshberg closed out his store and moved to Choteau at the turn of the year. Nathan moved to Great Falls in 1887.

Mose Kaufman first came to Fort Benton in 1880, where he leased a large warehouse, divided the structure in three, leased two parts to other businesses, and conducted a candy store for himself in the third. Soon he turned the venture into a $1500 profit by selling and went back to New York. He married Celia Nathan there in 1881 and came back to Montana shortly after. Mose was manager of his brother-in-law's store in Benton prior to the 1887 move to Great Falls. The store he later founded in Great Falls is still run by descendants.

## A Variety of Ventures

George W. Crane came to Montana after Civil War service, for several years ran a store at Clancy. He came to Fort Benton in the spring of 1879 to open a variety store; John H. Green was a partner for a time from 1881. His stationery, tobacco and oddments store was first in the middle of the block across from the Grand Union, later in several other locations, longest on the site of the later Benton State Bank, then in rear of that building.

John Schwartz in 1881 had a somewhat similar business near the Flanagan Drug, Sam Kohlberg kept his Bee Hive next to Wetzel's open to 1888.

Wm. Joyce and Neil McIntyre opened shoe stores in the same general area in 1878 and 1881, none very long lasting.

Bakers were a frontier luxury appreciated by residents—much more so than would be the case today. Fort Benton had numbers. H. E. Bond may have operated the first bakery noted in 1868, probably continued for a number of years when he had a saloon. Leon Rocron in 1881 operated a bakery in the rear of L. T. Marshall's Elite on the corner below Murphy Neel. The same year J. C. Guthrie had a bakery next the present River Press, burned early this century but date not found. John Gamble about 1880 operated the Star Bakery in his saloon.

## Fort Benton's Saloons

At the beginning of Montana's gold rush in 1862 Fort Benton consisted of the American Fur trading post and that year's Fort LaBarge which existed as such only about a year. There were many arrivals by steamboat in 1862, next year no boat made it to Fort Benton but many passengers, probably several hundred, came overland from four steamboats reaching lower Montana points. At the fort they could buy provisions and liquor, but at ruinous prices. One would guess that in brush wickiup or clumsy tent, some entrepreneur had himself a saloon for a season on the Fort Benton bottom.

For the year 1864 Wm. Gladstone provides some references to that crutch of frontier relaxation, the saloon.

On his arrival about the first of May he found a great crowd of miners, steadily growing in numbers, the fort the only accommodation. They had to pay $4 a day, supply their own blankets, and got corn bread, bad bacon and coffee. Gladstone, English, found tea was unobtainable; only two drinks popular in Benton, coffee and bug juice.

Looking for friends in the fort, in one room he found four eager eyed gamblers at work, a bag of gold dust and pistol in front of each, and two buckets of whisky in the small room. "Shooting and stabbing and rows of all kinds were a daily occurrence." It was a wonder to Gladstone that only two men were killed during that brief first stay—in early July he went down to Cow Island to help handle 400 tons of freight off the Yellowstone. That included 200 barrels of whiskey, forwarded to Fort Benton via Mormon teamsters to mitigate leakage. The precious cargo arrived safely except a barrel broached to assuage a Blackfeet war party. When Gladstone returned to Fort Benton about the first of September 1864 he found Benton had grown, instead of only one building there was a large store, blacksmith shop and six saloons—the cargo of the Yellowstone certainly had an effect.

Just who ran same is uncertain. One nominee is Moses Solomon, who later advertised that his Medicine Lodge was the first saloon in Fort Benton and is mentioned as here by 1865 at least. Another mention appears in the June 29, 1867, Montana Post mentioning a street brawl in Fort Benton which got two men arrested (one wonders who by); after release one still wanted to fight and new arrival, Governor Green Clay Smith had to subdue him with a club; the report concluded, "the affair started in Moses' Saloon." After side trips for Moses to Fort Peck for whisky salvaged from the sunken Amelia Poe in 1869, where Mose took two of his nine battle wounds in a fight with Indians, he was running a trading post in the Cypress Hills in May 1873. Al Wilkins recalled the Medicine Lodge and owner also: "He sold an Indian whiskey once and after the brave got his spirits up he came back and tried to take the contents of the saloon by storm, but only succeeded in losing his scalp. Solomon's medicine was the strongest with an army needle gun in his hands... A few days later he sold too much booze to an Irishman and relieved him of some money at poker... Tom left the saloon with the remark, 'will be back and get you.' True to his word he returned with a six gun and fired one shot at Mose. The shot went wild, but when Mose came up with his old needle gun we had a dead man to carry out. Solomon was arrested and had a jury trial. After a deliberation of about fifteen minutes and a snort of bourbon the jury told the defendant to get the h—- out of there and tend to his business." It wasn't much later that the Feb. 15, 1875, Benton Record carried an account of Jeff Perkins shooting Moses, right next door to the Perkins restaurant. Oddly, Jews were out of season, Perkins drew 5 years for attempted murder. Mose later moved to the Marias where he ranched, ferried, and of course ran a saloon. He died at Kendall in 1906, in bed.

Saloons, of course, proliferated in the later years of the gold rush. The writer can't be certain, but speculates that by 1867 "The Jungle" was aroar with night life in all its hues, and that it was from the second story of the flimsy frame that Madame Mustache (Eleanor Dumont) left her blackjack game, sprinted down to the riverbank fifty feet away, flourishing two pistols to warn off the pilot of the Walter B. Dance, reported to have smallpox aboard. (The Dance is listed as landing 198 tons of cargo, however.) In the waning years of the gold rush Dena Murray acquired the business, died in 1884 as "a woman who had accumulated considerable wealth."

The saloons had customers in freighting season, May-September, after which Fort Benton settled down for a sort of winter siesta. In 1866 one paper estimated 2500 men were involved in freighting. Three-wagon hitches later reduced the overall number, but a hundred 'whackers might well hit town in a bunch to recover from the dust of the trail and real peril from Blackfeet. Some entertainment genius in June 1869 really packed them in, a genuine squaw hurdy gurdy made the night lively around where Bentonites would later build a bridge. A week later some spoilsport carped in a letter, "with the squaws promenading men to the bar after every dance, like any other hurdy would do, and of course these squaws partaking of whiskey with the men as any hurdy would do."

The gold rush ended and Fort Benton's population dropped to about 180 in the fall of 1870, with a dozen saloons and one brewery. From there it was survival of the fittest, and in mid-1870s Al Wilkins recalled only four saloons. There was John Lilly in that dance hall; the Exchange, "where J. C. Bourassa and Phil Deschamps dispensed cards and whiskey to French clientel." There was L. T. Marshall in the Elite, where in 1872 with four well directed bullets he killed Dennis Hinchey, "a notorious character of the border" who "wouldn't be missed," as a coroner's jury also ruled by acclamation. Wilkins gave a nod of approval to the Extradition Saloon of John Evans and Jeff Devereux, as "no one was ever rolled in their place."

One of the odder names was the Extradition Saloon of John Evans and Jeff Devereux. This resulted from the 1875 court hearing in Helena on whether to honor Canada's request to extradite five Fort Benton men for trial in Canadian courts on a charge of slaughter of a number of Assiniboines in May or early June 1873 in the Cypress Hills. The request was dismissed, the partners, two of the five, returned triumphantly to Fort Benton and named their business from the trial. Another unusual name resulted from installation of the first freight elevator in Fort Benton in the new Power store building in 1882. Frank Hughes leased the Occidental Saloon from ailing Nick Welsh and renamed the place Elevator.

About the same time an English visitor commented on a saloon which stood on the site of the present Pastime: "Fort Benton in the seventies was the toughest joint in the west. An armed robbery, a lynching or a gunfight was not only expected daily, but it is on record that, when Nick Welsh, a local saloon keeper, opened his joint one morning without finding the usual 'stiff' sprawled outside with a bullet in his brain, he said: 'I'm hitting the trail further west. This dump is getting civilized.' Nick ran a keno game, and as all the tinhorn cheats gathered round like hungry wolves, every man jack played with guns on the table." This was the Occidental, which Welsh opened before 1876, as he is listed as deeded owner that year. Nick didn't leave despite above, he rebuilt in 1878 when things were getting civilized, and died in Fort Benton of consumption in September 1882.

In the late 1870s and early years of the next decade, names included Cosmopolitan, Gem, Benton Brewery, Eureka, Marshall & Gray and numerous others. Visitors in the period reported playing cards swept out of saloons blanketed Front Street. At one time there was a Chinese saloon. The 1880 census lists about

30 blacks, consequently saloons. Wm. Foster, barber, sought an easier way to make a living, opened the flambouyantly named Eagle Bird. When fire destroyed the Eagle Bird early in 1883, Foster found other quarters nearby and reopened in an appropriately entitled Phoenix. Not long after he skipped town, leaving long faced creditors, and a little over a year later was killed at End of Track on the Canadian Pacific north of the border. Another place in the black, and red light district, was the Break o' Day House of Lee Isabel, listed as mulatto in 1880.

As late as 1883 there was a rather outre duel, fueled by the wares of Dick Brennan's place, when John "Frenchy" Vizenir and John Macauley, alias Joe Bush, had strangely quiet words, then walked outside. The pair apparently stepped off their paces, turned and fired at each other. Frenchy was hard hit, but able to explain later it was just a friendly contest, and he the loser. Frenchy finally recovered, his shooting partner solicitous, and the matter dropped.

One of the most elusive connections, alongside or with saloons, were the houses of ill repute, and frontier editors generally refrained from mention of prostitution. The census taker at Fort Benton seemingly referred to the matter as women "keeping house" in 1870, three such named. In 1880 the "soiled doves" were variously actress, dance hall woman, perhaps also seamstress and laundress. By 1900 the census taker in Big Sandy used "prostitute" for occupation without challenge. In wards 1 and 2 Fort Benton the Anglo-Saxon whore and whore house keeper were duly written down in some instances; as duly his superior had neatly lined out the words and beside wrote NG or NA, which it can be assumed meant "not given" or "not available." In ward three "variety performer" was acceptable for four. The last case was at a location well documented by oral tradition.

The squaw hurdy gurdy is mentioned above. Best direct evidence of existence of prostitution occurs in the Benton Record of June 27, 1879: "It is said that one of the leading saloon keepers of Benton is negotiating for an invoice of hurdy-gurdys, to be shipped from Bismarck via the river. We are not sure that this enterprise will be any detriment to Benton. Dancing damsels of questionable repute may not improve the morals of a community, but they are several shades better than negro prostitutes, and it is thought they will have the effect of driving out the latter. If social evils are an indispensable feature of Benton, by all means let us have the hurdys." It might be mentioned that a certain sector of Fort Benton into the 20th century had the oral repute of being or having been the red light district, and this was the same sector in which the negro population of Fort Benton existed at the time of the 1880 census. There were very few blacks listed in the 1900 census.

No outcome was noted in regard to the 1879 item about the hurdys, but the Benton Record of May 13, 1882, reported the arrival by steamboat of four girls, very young, who claimed to be servant girls. The Record carried a sympathetic piece about their destination, the "notorious hurdy house of Jo Brooks," and cited the villain as one Jack Lahey or Lame Jack. A week later an item in the Record noted the four girls were at work in the Brooks establishment.

Existence of what was often regarded as a necessary evil draws further confirmation from the River Press: April 8, 1891: "Madame Anna Green, who lived without the pale of society many years here, died April 3." Dec. 31, 1902: Georgia Bryant, "landlady of one of the resorts of our city," fined for selling liquor without a license. July 8, 1903: Mention of "Corinne" one of the "soiled doves of the red light district" in some fuss; a week later occupants ordered to vacate premises. August 26, 1903: Georgia Bryant, Blanch Brandt, Ellen Clyde cited in vagrancy charges against inmates of houses of infamy. "Georgie, noted character of red light district, has left town."

## Barbers Came And Went

Earliest barber noted in newspaper records was Charles Bryer, by 1878 somewhere on Front Street, and that is about all. Barbers came and went largely unnoted, until one felt festive and in need of shave and haircut.

Two black barbers do crop up out of the unnoted, one for his background, one for pure flamboyance. The latter was named William Foster, and is called to mind for his saloon which he first named the Eagle Bird, and after that burned in 1883 the new location was christened the Phoenix.

Duke Dutrieuille, to give the full French spelling, made his way under twin handicaps, a mulatto and in addition a dwarf. He quite apparently overcame prejudice, for the Benton Record several times had a word or two of praise for him and his shop. First time was in May 1879 when with one Rosier he came from Helena to open a second barber shop, across from the later Grand Union. Duke apparently liked a change, for he left, returned in 1882 and perhaps a third time, each time back to Helena and finally to Belt where he and wife lived for years. He met his wife, Maria Adams, on that first visit; they were married in 1880 in Helena. John Lambert Dutrieuille was born in 1837 to a Jamaican mother and French colonial father on a ship in the harbor of Philadelphia; he was in the Civil War as an aide or personal servant to General Joe Hooker on the Union side. As to the "Duke," what else would one call a congenial character who didn't reach to a grown man's armpits?

## Blacksmiths Did Well, But Went Unnoted

Relatively little information seems available about the men performing vital operations to improve and augment motive power in Fort Benton's early days—the blacksmiths. They shod the horses and mules and often, not always, the oxen; repaired broken iron work on wagons and tightened or replaced the iron tires on wooden wheels. Judging from the estate notes and their residences, they did well in relative obscurity. There had to be numbers from the gold rush years when several thousand wagons might be employed in a single season.

One of the earliest may have been the Johnson whom Robert Vaughn in "Then and Now" mentions as buried at Vaughn. A descendant says Frank Day came in 1869 to be farrier for the Fort Benton army garrison. Another would be Joseph Hamlin, who sold his shop to the Mee brothers in the early 1870s. These were Isaac, Richard and William, the latter obscure but the others mentioned a number of times. Their shop was first near a livery on Main, from 1881 opposite the Kleinschmidt store and Murphy Neel warehouses on Front on the site of the city hall of the 1980s. Ike in particular was successful, leaving a Montana estate of about $100,000 and a matching total in Ohio where he died. The brothers left Fort Benton in the dull years of the latter 1880s.

Al Wilkins, in 1874 a youth helping his father at a trading post on the Marias, winters worked for the Mees. The work was chiefly repairing freight wagons and forging out horse and mule shoes from bar iron. A lesser task was making horseshoe nails as factory mades were not always available. The smithy was busy the year round, Wilkins recalled.

Frank Lepper was a later arrival, apparently in 1879, and for a time was associated with Lewis Bradbury, a wagon repair specialist in a shop on lower Main. Lepper bought out his partner in 1881 and the two went their separate ways. Lepper continued in the trade at least until 1900. Bradbury rented the Mee Bros. smithy in 1883 but soon disappeared from local records.

Best documented was Rufus Payne, who moved his family to Santa Fe about 1859, a year or so later moved to Denver, then on to the Virginia City gold fields in time to take a hand in the Vigilante cleanup at year end 1863-64. The northward course of the Payne family continued to the Helena area not long after.

A wagon builder as well as a blacksmith, Rufus Payne brought his family to Fort Benton in 1879, finding all the work a smith, wagonwright and assistants could handle. The next year he had built a square mansard roofed brick building across from the later court house—a structure which still catches the eye although rear additions have altered the original appearance. When the Benton boom ended Rufus Payne made yet another move northward, to Lethbridge. He died in California in 1897.

There were numerous blacksmiths to follow, but most in the statehood and homestead periods. The few remaining iron craftsmen exist on nostalgia for the past and as the much more specialized farriers serving horse fanciers.

### Fort Benton's Brickmakers

First brickmakers on the Fort Benton bottom of course were employes of the fur posts, Fort Campbell under the driving energy of Alexander Harvey leading the way. These were adobe, made from the clay and grass of the neighborhood, sun dried with mud as mortar. Building and protective walls were thus very thick, the bricks about 6x4x15 inches. A double course the long way would certainly stay any projectile of the day except a cannon ball. Fort Campbell in 1847 was largely constructed in this manner.

Alexander Culbertson at Fort Benton soon followed suit, although saying he learned use of adobe while at Fort Laramie. His fort's first building was completed toward Christmas 1850, with a consequent feast and party that day at which Culbertson announced the change in name, from Fort Lewis to Fort Benton. Conversion to adobe continued through the next decade and completion as the post appears in old prints and photos coincided with the first steamboats of 1860.

With the gold rush quite a number of business buildings were made of readily available adobe bricks, although much more costly lumber was freighted in or whip-sawed locally, and some businesses combined the two materials.

During the gold rush of 1862-69 any kind of room with a roof served, and during the letdown of the early 1870s there was a surplus of business space. (Rev. George McDougall visiting from Canada for supplies, gives an 1873 description: "There are probably about 200 houses. In its palmy days 2/3s of these were liquor saloons. At present this fountain of iniquity is nearly dried up.") After the Benton Record began in February 1875 there were a few mentions of the advantages of kiln fired brick for building.

The situation changed in 1877. January 5 the paper reported that H. B. Snell of Sun River was in Fort Benton negotiating for bricks and brick work, needing contracts for at least 100,000 to make the move. In March he leased a house and with equipment arrived about the end of the month.

Snell & Co. in early May expected to have 150,000 bricks ready the next month. They had the contract for the first brick building in Fort Benton, a relatively small school house. Ground was broken and the foundation well along by the end of July, but it was two more months before Snell could report much more progress. Paralleling the school in time, Kleinschmidt & Bro. went to cheaper construction, a concrete and stone warehouse-store near the levee, into which they moved about December 1st. After the school walls went up in late October, progress was rapid, and a grand ball in late November formally opened the building. The new school was in use in January 1878.

No further mention was noted of Snell & Co., although A. B. Snell appears as a brick mason in the 1880 census. Best assumption seems to be that they continued making bricks with John R. Wilton, who contracted more building in Fort Benton than any other, buying their product. In 1878 Wm. G. Conrad and Joseph Baker had brick residences completed, both later demolished.

The April 11, 1879, Benton Record reported that John Wilton had begun making brick, probably marking the end of Snell & Co. as brickmakers, and Wilton brick went into new buildings for the Record, T. C. Power and I. G. Baker stores.

There is another possibility. James D. Wolff claimed he "conducted the first brickyard in Fort Benton." Perhaps he took over from the Snells. At any rate Wolff turned out bricks to meet demand through 1900 when he burned his last batch for the new Stockmen's Bank building. According to notes he supplied bricks for the Murphy Neel, Masonic Hall, Stocking, and Centennial and Grand Union hotels.

There was other competition—probably 8 million locally made bricks were used in buildings in the 1880s. C. T. and D. G. formed Storer & Storer, whose source of clay and kiln lay back of the butte on the bottom. They arrived in 1880 and filled contracts for 725,000 bricks that year; several homes, including the Rufus Payne residence across from the court house, the imposing W. S. Wetzel home, and also the second half of the Power store. T. G. Storer left the firm in April, W. H. Wilson replacing him. Poor investment. In late June 1881 the company had an oversupply, advertising 350,000 bricks for sale. The senior partner may have sold some of these, for the July 27, 1881, River Press had an interesting headline, "Storer Has Skipped!" He had sent his wife down river on the steamboat Benton, and leaving sad creditors, hid out on the Josephine a few days later until the boat pulled away from the levee.

Last of the brickmakers found was John Houston, another contractor, later with Dan McKay a partner, running a kiln near the old fort, in the early 80s, making three in a type of local business scarcely heard of today.

Fort Benton's millions of bricks were fired in the open area in the lower part of town, the kilns not housed in buildings. The clay was taken from promising spots after the overlay was removed. Quality varied, but about 25 structures of locally made brick already have a good start on a second century.

### The Major Builders

Early building in Fort Benton was largely by former employes of the fur companies, with Clement Corneille (Cornoyer) credited with putting up the first cabin outside the forts circa 1863. Vincent Mercure and Joseph Laurion erected the first store building for Carroll & Steell in 1864, and William Gladstone the first I. G. Baker store next year. Such carpentry was probably a sideline, one of the major industries of the gold rush was tacking together flat bottomed mackinaws that carried miners returning to the States with or without full pokes. One season's report was 200 such boats and about 3500 passengers.

There was a lengthy hiatus in any type of building from 1870, Fort Benton business revival dating from 1875. By the time John R. Wilton, architect and the city's foremost builder, turned up in Fort Benton in 1878, supply of bricks, finish lumber and other materials was vital and almost to the end of the boom builders had more work than they could handle.

Wilton's 1878 season included the showplace Wm. G. Conrad mansion. Early the next year he was into brick making, 10 to 14 thousand a day in April with 200,000 ready for burning May 1st. His product went into the first portion of new Power and Baker stores and the three story Record building.

From there the list of his contracts becomes impressive, the Episcopal Church, John J. Kennedy's market on Main street, the hospital, fire house and long time city hall on the river bank, a second brick for Baker, W. S. Stocking business block, and finally the 1884 school, a three story affair. Wilton perhaps returned occasionally from budding Great Falls where he moved in 1885 to view his buildings, several still in existence today.

That amount of construction required financing, a September 23, 1884, First National Bank summary indicated John Wilton's account was an active one indeed, over $3,000 owed in two notes at 15% interest, $7,000 on the hospital; five added notes amounted to about $7,000; security, builder's contracts.

Another active construction man was Frank Coombs, who built the brick warehouse and office George Clendenin had erected for the Coulson steamboat line, teamed with Gus Senieur; a residence long occupied by the Harber family, and the IOOF building that housed the River Press until a fire in July 1885. But Frank Coombs' true monument is still impressive, the Grand Union Hotel, Thomas Tweedy sharing in handling the brick work.

Gus Senieur, a Helena builder in the 1870s, moved his family to Fort Benton in 1879 to share in building the second half of the Power store and also of the Clendenin building, a number of frame residences, and also left a still enduring and attractive brick, the Chouteau county court house, which reached its centennial in September 1984. Senieur also constructed numbers of frame buildings in this century.

### Lawyers, Varied And Versatile

Fort Benton's early day lawyers were colorful, and certainly versatile. Nowadays the legal profession has grown in power and financial standing. In the last century, often self taught attorneys needed another financial crutch. A couple were surveyors, others school teachers, and most held county offices.

Perhaps the first professional to practice in Fort Benton was James H. Lowell, wide ranging traveler and unsuccessful miner at Diamond City, who came to Fort Benton from the latter camp in August 1869 with intent to return east, instead lingered for two years. Lowell had been wounded at Antietam in 1862. Some of his letters to the girl he met in a Harrisburg, Pa., hospital while recovering are in museum files. He came west in 1866 after discharge, traveled in a number of later states of the Rocky Mountain west.

Lowell was deputy district attorney and county assessor, as well as lawyer in Fort Benton, for kicks and cash traded with Indians for T. C. Power near Cow Island. He returned to the States in fall 1871 with the family of retiring Governor J. M. Ashley by mackinaw, after serving on a commission of new Governor B. F. Potts to organize Dawson county, then about a fifth of Montana. Lowell for half a century after was lawyer and local judge in Holton, Kansas.

Jacob A. Kanouse came to Fort Benton in 1872 as attorney and also helped organize and teach in an 1873 school. Later in more prosperous years he built a brick home that once housed the Benton Brewery, in which he had an interest. He was U. S. commissioner in the sale of Fort Benton lots after the townsite was surveyed in 1875, dying here in 1884. Death was attributed to Bright's disease, but one local historian felt it was of a broken heart over the misadventures of son Fred, a noted figure in the Whoop Up whisky trade.

A book could be written about another 1872 arrival of this profession. John J. Donnelly served with more than distinction in the Civil War, rising to lieutenant colonel of volunteers with a Wisconsin regiment and taking two battle wounds. As Irish as his name, despite a Rhode Island birth, he answered the call of Sinn Fein to make Canada a part of the U. S. He was a leader of the thousand Fenians who in June 1866 crossed the Niagara into Ontario and captured Fort Erie before being forced to withdraw by U. S. authorities. Not content, in 1869 Donnelly commanded 200 men in a raid from St. Albans, Vermont, into a battle at Pigeon Hill in Canada. Against superior force the Donnelly command held their position all day, with 12 of the raiders killed and 17 wounded, including the leader. Drifting west, Donnelly took part in the first Riel rebellion in the Red River valley in 1869-70, and was leader of the Fenian expedition that took the Hudson's Bay post just across the border from Pembina.

In Fort Benton by 1872, John Donnelly was spokesman for the Irish of Fort Benton still aiming at making John Bull pay for past sins by bringing western Canada into the U. S. Donnelly was defender of five Fort Benton wolfers in Helena in 1875, an extradition hearing stemming from a white-Assiniboine fight in the Cypress Hills of Canada in 1873. By that time John Donnelly was county clerk and also served as probate judge. He heard his last bullets whistle in 1877 as leader of the Fort Benton Volunteers in a fight with the Nez Perce north of Cow Island.

Donnelly also served one term in the Montana legislature; it seems a tribute that he was elected speaker of that house. A later years law partner in Fort Benton was Charles N. Pray, who would serve three terms as Montana's sole congressman and secure passage of the bill creating Glacier Park, and as federal judge become the most distinguished legal light of and from Fort Benton. Donnelly's final years were troubled, one would suspect cancer from repeated suicide attempts and heavy drinking reported by friend R. S. Culbertson. In 1899 Donnelly was a "determined suicide," the Press reported.

John W. Tattan was born in County Cork, Ireland, landed in New York just as the Civil War was ending. With an excellent education in that specialty, he went to civil engineering in the iron mining area of Minnesota. He soon found that too tame, in 1870 signed up for a five year hitch with the 7th Infantry and sent to Fort Shaw, then Fort Benton, where he took his discharge in June 1875. He occasionally recalled his army career, including a July 4, 1873, risky celebration involving a Sioux war party on the Musselshell.

John Tattan had been studying law while in service, set up his shingle and in August 1875 was elected probate judge. That position assumed added responsibilities next year, when through the probate office U. S. title was granted to lots and buildings on the townsite where for 30 years all had been squatters. The young attorney married Alice Siefred in April 1876; probably as a natural consequence he donated his title fees toward building Fort Benton's first brick school house.

In September 1877 Tattan was one of thirty ex-soldiers and Indian fighters going off with the Fort Benton Volunteers to battle the Nez Perce for steamboat freight at Cow Island. The luck of the Irish held, his belt buckle stopped a Nez Perce bullet. Years later General Howard gave him the rifle Chief Joseph surrendered at the Bear's Paw Battle. Tattan served several terms as county attorney, in 1900 he was appointed district judge, served by election to his death in 1926. The Irish born democrat changed his party oddly. In 1920 Non-partisan Leaguers "stole" the primary ticket, John Tattan the loser, but 400 republicans had written in his name, enough for nomination. He was easily re-elected in November, and in 1924 filed and was elected as a republican.

Herbert P. Rolfe came to Helena in 1876 after marrying Martha Edgerton, daughter of Montana's first territorial governor. At Helena he was school principal for three years, bringing his family to Fort Benton in 1879 as an attorney, with useful Helena legal connections. An innovator, he became agent for the Bell company, and had Fort Benton's first telephone installed between his office and the telegraph office. For Paris Gibson he surveyed the Great Falls townsite in 1883, moved to that place shortly after. Between fusses and fights with Gibson's son Phil, Rolfe founded the Great Falls Leader, and his untimely death in 1895 resulted in his wife becoming Montana's first lady editor.

Two young attorneys from the east, Horace H. Buck and William Hunt, opened a hopeful partnership in Fort Benton in 1880. Law business lagged, it was a stroke of fortune that Hunt was named U. S. collector of customs next year and they built a small brick office, perhaps in celebration. Also, in June 1881 they took over the Benton Record, but lawyers aren't always successful publishers, and they had to turn it back a year later. Both moved to Helena in the mid-1880s, both became justices of the Montana supreme court. Buck died soon after election in an accident, Hunt had a lengthy and honorable career as judge.

Max Waterman was another Civil War veteran, twice wounded, and with a lively legal and judicial career in then wild Kansas before coming to Montana in 1877, next year to Fort Benton. One note in his memoirs, he twice successfully defended Kid Royal against horse stealing charges, sent the Kid to prison next time as county attorney.

There were, of course, many more attorneys over the years, these seemed the most interesting. Though past the territorial period, the predecessor to John Tattan as resident district judge was a newsworthy character.

Prior to 1880, court was held in Helena; after a decade judges from Helena would preside at Fort Benton. In March 1891 the 10th district, Chouteau and Fergus counties, was created. First judge, appointed, was Dudley DuBose, 27, a grandson of Robert Toombs, Southern fire-eater who led Georgia into the Confederacy and became secretary of state of CSA. The grandson acquired some of his traits. One day while passing a Fort Benton saloon, his honor heard a cowhand roundly cussing out the judge for a decision on rustling. Judge DuBose walked into the saloon, grabbed the speaker and tossed him through the saloon window. DuBose was elected twice with little voter problem but walked off his job in 1900, heading for the Alaskan gold fields, a more lucrative career. John Tattan was appointed after the seat was declared vacant. DuBose was held in contempt of court after a Nome mining deal, drew a six months jail sentence, "served under comparatively comfortable circumstances," reported the River Press.

### Fort Benton's Photographers

Photography began coming into its own only the second half of the 19th century, Karl Bodmer's 1833 sketches of the Fort McKenzie area and Fr. Nicholas Point's of Fort Lewis in 1846-47 the earliest pictorial records of the Fort Benton area. John Mix Stanley in 1853 with the Isaac Stevens expedition was first to bring photographic equipment—the report says he took some daguerreotypes of Indian chiefs at Fort Benton, which unfortunately were reportedly buried with recipients. Only Stanley Fort Benton relic is a sketch of the two fur forts. Granville Stuart on visits to Fort Benton in 1865 and 1866 made pencil sketches—it is to be regretted he was not an early victim of the photography bug. Carl Wimar, western artist, is reputed to have brought a box camera with him on an 1858 visit to Fort Benton, no indication of any surviving pictures.

The earliest existing picture found is an excellent photographic view of the Fort Benton levee from across the river, noted as dating to 1867 and verified by existing buildings shown. This was unearthed by Ben Woodcock about 1981, the finest of the gold rush period. During the gold rush a visit to Fort Benton in the boating season was a source of revenue for photographers, so there is a possibility of others turning up. A poorer but still interesting 1868 picture, probably taken by John Douglas of Helena, also exists.

Scattered photographs from the earlier 1870s exist, one or two possibly unidentified products of Stanley J. Morrow, an 1873 visitor, and a panoramic view of Fort Benton in 1879 is timely, just as the city was turning to brick buildings. F. Jay Haynes, perhaps Montana's most noted early photographer, visited the upper Missouri and Fort Benton in summer 1880. Unfortunately, after fairly numerous pictures of lower points, Haynes apparently ran low on supplies, in Fort Benton taking Choteau House and Benton Record pictures and a from the bluff panorama.

It was not until 1881 that the city first had a resident photographer in Justus Fey, although Wm. Culver may have visited a few weeks in 1880 before moving to Fort Assiniboine. Either Fey or R. M. Duffin taught stonecutter Dan Dutro the art, and Dutro was the chief and usually only, photographer in Fort Benton for 20 years. Unfortunately when the Record building was converted into lodge quarters in 1929, the Dutro glass negatives, stored there, were discarded. A fairly good number of positives exist in various places.

### Stables And Liveries

Earliest mention of a stable at Fort Benton was found in the Helena Radiator of February 17, 1866, when a youthful Indian scored a coup by lifting George Steell's prized mount from the Carroll & Steell barn. Joe Kipp, part Mandan guide and trouble shooter, earned the owner's gratitude and a generous reward by thefting the horse right back from the Indian camp, one of several times Joe would perform the service. The stable, the writer suspects, was right behind the store where Joseph Spearson operated a small livery about 1870.

The private stable would have been of little use for the swarming teamsters in that boating season. C. C. Huntley doubtless added a stable or corral of sorts when he started stage service to Fort Benton in June 1866, for those stage horses would have been far too valuable to risk, even close herded, out on the flat at Benton night times. The Huntley runs, semi-weekly, continued to October. Next year Wells Fargo forced Huntley off the profitable routes with three times a week overnight service to Benton, and their successors, Gilmer & Salisbury, stabled stock in barn and corral on the then edge of town. None of this would have provided service for transients.

First mention of livery service came in the May 21, 1868, Helena Herald in a letter from Benton: "Remarkably low rates for stabling and herding stock. $3 currency per head singly, in bands of 10 to 50 $5 per week." Currency was meaningful, gold was worth about $1.75 to $1 at the time. The project was probably that of John Morgan, who built a long adobe stable and corral across the street and a block up from the Carroll & Steell barn. Morgan had come to Benton in 1865-66 as head of a group of militia.

Some of Morgan's animals may have been among the 15 mules and horses pastured across the Missouri and driven off by Indians in broad daylight while Bentonites raged at lack of boats and most of all a dearth of long range Sharps to "fetch" some of the pesky redskins. Not only that, but after securing their remounts in a safe place, the Sioux returned to drive off 50 Baker work oxen.

While the latest loss was being assessed loudly and profanely, here came a messenger from down river, Brule Bottom, with word a detachment of warriors was raiding the Diamond R herd. A white war party dusted north, returned with a coup stick from, they hoped, a wounded Sioux in late evening. Things like that were a good ad for stables and corrals.

Morgan's livery was terminated by his death November 14, 1868. The stable passed to James Cassidy and Tom Hardwick, the latter also in news of the day as an Indian hater and fighter and known as the "Green River Renegade." Al Wilkins, in Fort Benton about 1874, recalled it as the only feed stable in town, but that was at a Fort Benton nadir. Hardwick soon went off to Indian fighting and wolfing and James McDevitt, later sheriff, became Cassidy's partner. Possibly from early years this was known as Benton Stables, certainly it was by 1875. After more owners, it was acquired by George and Ed Lewis in 1883, rebuilt in 1895, burned eight years later and moved to Front Street under the same name.

Most pretentious of such businesses was the Park Stables, behind the Record building, probably in existence a couple of years earlier; in 1880 a large brick stable was completed for Howell Harris and Frank Strong. This was quite handy for the I. G. Baker firm, which had a vast freighting business, and the Power firm was within a block, so perhaps Park Stables was another joint venture. Howell Harris left the business about the time he became foreman for the Canadian Herd of the Benton & St. Louis (Circle) Cattle Co. up north in 1883. William Rowe was owner in April 1890 when the big Park Stables burned, killing ten horses and a cow.

Another stable was the Montana on upper Main Street started by C. W. Thrailkill and Charles Crawford in 1879. There were several smaller stables in territorial days through the homestead period. One worth mentioning for its construction was the Buck & Kennon stable built on a quarter block about 1910, reminiscent in size and form to the old fur fort, enclosed except for entrance gates, making large stall space. The writer's father recalled that around 1914 a farmer had to arrive by early afternoon to secure a place for teams. For most a trip to town was a two day affair then.

### Two Flat Failures

Fort Benton business people in the 1880s as their own boom was ending tried yet another kind of boom. The place seemed to breed odd ideas for projects, a surprising number being pushed through to a more or less successful conclusion.

The Fort Benton Boom & Lumber Co. was incorporated early in 1883, the Benton Record duly noted, with a capital stock of $10,000. The idea was to end the city's recurring fuel and lumber shortage by cutting logs on the Sun or other waterways, and construct a boom above town to catch same when they were floated down the Missouri. Something akin to this was done about 1865, according to John Neubert's memoirs, when a small crew cut firewood at Highwood creek and two small steamboats went up there to transport it. Boats and woodhawks split the $15 a cord chilled residents were glad to pay next winter.

The 1883 boom company was organized with W. G. Conrad, Edgar Maclay, John Power, W. S. Wetzel, T. E. Collins, J. H. Rice and F. C. Roosevelt—four merchants, two bankers and a furniture dealer—the directors. At least enough of the stock was subscribed to put a crew of men at work building piers (which remained as mementos in this century) to back the catch boom in the small side channel that creates Roosevelt Island. Another boom stretched into the main channel of the Missouri above the island which formed the small side channel, to shunt the logs into the detour. Work started promptly, but there were doubters. The October 13, 1883, Benton Record noted the boom company had been a "laughing stock" for months, but the operation had been taken over by Ed Maclay, and in a later paper felt there would be no fuel shortage "this winter" with Castner (Belt) coal and Maclay logs.

The fall run of logs down the Missouri hung up due to low water, and the 1884 effort found the logs sailing grandly past the boom on their way to New Orleans, using a change in channel to evade the boom. End of project.

As early as 1881 Wheeler O. Dexter, pioneer in threshing area grain, proposed a flour mill to end dependence on outside sources for the flour. The proposal hung fire, Dexter lacking the necessary financing. Revived in December 1884, C. E. Conrad and John Power headed a committee to sound out potential investors, but nothing came of that either.

March 1889, yet another effort, contacts made with reputedly experienced millers. Funds were raised, the River Press noting that with a market, wheat would become a more important crop. April 24 the paper reported start of work on the Benton Roller Flour Mill, J. H. Kenney arriving from Illinois to supervise and manage same after building. On the Fourth of July the first sack of flour was ground with ceremony. The mill quickly developed problems. September 4 the Press said the mill was again in operation with new cleaners. On November 27 an old Murphy Neel warehouse was crammed with 20,000 bushels of wheat, the "mill can't keep up." Nor did it. References in the Press were notably lacking in later months. December 10, 1890, the paper did in an item refer to J. H. Kenney, who "built mill, left this city under a cloud." No further explanation found.

In January 1892 one item said the Power firm hoped to restart the mill; in October, after a visit by a Wisconsin miller, the Press was informed the mill had been leased by eastern parties. A week later the paper was informed machinery had been ordered for the mill, more likely a getaway story for the easterners. The structure stood empty until it burned in July 1909.

## Life and Services
### Fort Benton Schools

*C*hildren of the fur post personnel had one opportunity for schooling, in St. Louis convent schools. Charles Frush in an 1856 visit to Fort Benton from Fort Owen mentions "Miss Champaigne just returned from school in St. Louis, and dressed in latest style." Available material indicates a fairly substantial number of part Indian children received such schooling.

During most of the gold rush period there was such an overwhelming preponderance of males in the area that local schooling received no attention. It was 1868 before a short term school was opened in a log and adobe cabin on Main street. An 1881 River Press recalled first teachers as Misses Power, Culbertson and Clevenger, and Mr. Lowell. These would have been Sarah Power, sister of John and T. C.; Maria Culbertson, later Mrs. Joe Kipp, daughter of Alexander and his first Indian wife, and a daughter of the S. V. Clevengers who ran what became the Chouteau House. James Lowell was a young attorney and disappointed miner. This school operated for three years, an 1869 Helena Herald reporting a Benton meeting to keep the school going.

With the drop in population in the early 1870s, the school disappeared. School was revived in 1873, according to that 1881 resume, with J. A. Kanouse, Fort Benton attorney, having about 25 pupils. Permanent residents were increasing in the next few years, there were soon plans for a regular school house. In July, 1875, a site still occupied by elementary schools was selected on a block set aside for same. Raising the money for a building was helped along by survey of the Fort Benton townsite and in 1876 the federal government issued title to the land on which residents had in effect squatted for years. Probate Judge John W. Tattan, handling the matter and U. S. fees of $10 per lot, received a legal fee of $4, and, perhaps because he was a spring bridegroom, donated the second set of fees to the building fund. First brickmaker in Fort Benton had just moved from Sun River, and the first bricks made went into a small brick school. One of the 1875 teachers was Helen Clarke, daughter of Malcolm of the fur trade, and Mrs. M. A. Flanagan taught for a time prior to arrival of Miss Clarke from Helena. The school building was completed in late 1877 and was in use early the next year.

By 1879 there were 72 pupils enrolled in eight classes and the small building was crowded. A 34x46 addition in 1880 eased that problem. Another arose two years later when trustees voted to admit colored children of good character and there were immediate repercussions, some children apparently withdrawn from school. In 1882 there were about 30 blacks in Fort Benton, and only two seemingly of school age. The squabble then edged into obscurity, although the republican River Press defended the action of the trustees on 14th Amendment grounds.

As early as 1880 there were newspaper suggestions about the need for larger school facilities. At the time population had passed 1600 and assessed values rose sharply on an influx of cattle. A 17 mill levy in 1883 provided substantial funds for a two story brick building with stone basement and part of a third story. At the time school enrollment was 176, using both the first brick and two log cabins. The year 1884 saw completion of the new $30,000 building. With declining population in Fort Benton, it was 1916 before a near twin to the bigger school, in cost and size, was built. All three brick buildings burned August 2, 1937.

Fort Benton did not provide a high school course until 1901; at the time it was one of 8 or 9 in the state. Starting enrollment was 17.

One problem school trustees had far beyond territorial days was general throughout the west—men far outnumbered women. School teachers were fair game for men with matrimonial inclinations, creating a constant turnover. In one case in 1888, Marie Healy was hired as teacher about January 2nd. She resigned the 18th, and on February 6 married O. W. Jackson, who had just opened a branch of a Helena music store. The couple moved to Helena; the town lost both teacher and store.

First schools outside Fort Benton in the county were Highwood, Old Agency (Choteau), Belt, two in the Shonkin area and one on the Teton River, the list for 1883. Great Falls and Sand Coulee first had schools in 1885.

## Early Libraries

Anyone ever in the armed services will recall the importance of books and reading to lull one through idle hours. So it was on the frontier, even men not far beyond their ABCs would find a touch of contentment from a book, even the nearly illiterate would puzzle out words on tins and packaged goods.

For the more literate the lack of books on the frontier was an unmixed evil. Granville Stuart recalled the late winter of 1861 when he and brother James learned that a white man in the Bitter Root had brought a trunkful of books. The Stuarts promptly saddled their horses and set forth on a 150 mile ride which included three dangerous river crossings. The man they sought had gone, but left his precious trunk in care of another. After much pleading the Stuarts secured five of the books and joyfully rode off on their 150 mile return trip.

James H. Lowell at Fort Benton in November 1869 as gleefully wrote to his future bride: "There is one institution which does credit to the place and that is a fine library and reading room—this has been accessible to the public about two weeks and bids fair to become a permancy." (The writer suspects that books and months old state-side papers were the property of George Baker.)

Nothing more about libraries was found until February 1883 when the Benton Record reported that a subscription library of 500 books had been ordered, Eugene Clingan, school superintendent, a chief promoter. The books arrived in June on an early steamboat, a modest fee of $5 a year was charged. Photographer R. M. Duffin promptly offered space for the library, virtually on the site of the present county facility. This subscription library's further history is lost in the mists of time, but doubtless some of the books survive in area homes, some possibly in the present library.

Fort Benton, which seems to have had an amazing number of firsts in Montana, largely through the efforts of Mrs. A. E. McLeish, in 1915 benefited from creation of the first county library in Montana under a legislative act of that year. It was opened in 1916 and shortly after that secured a Carnegie Foundation grant for the present building, in use by the final years of the decade. Long gone pioneers would have wondered and approved.

## Early Postal Services

An early day area resident, Clark Tingley, 20 years later recalled that in 1862-63 the nearest postoffice was Fort Laramie on the Oregon Trail, from there to Sun River once a year. This may have been a private express, the carrier charging a dollar or whatever the traffic would bear upon delivery (and forever after a friend of the recipient), and the possibility exists of survival of such letters bearing envelope markings to or from Fort Benton before regular U. S. mail service via stage coach began. The writer, as well as collectors, would certainly appreciate information on any such.

North from Utah a few enterprising men as early as 1862 were carrying letters to Bannack and next year to Virginia City as well, usual price seemed to be $1 per letter, and at least three such carriers were killed by Indians en route to the mines. Jack Oliver was one of the lucky who made money as well as lived, in May 1863 carried 500 letters to Bannack in the fast time of 9 days. Later that year he began a stage line. First official mail carrier was Leonard L. Smith, for $1,000 a month to Bannack by postal contract in 1864; so the postal service was trying to move mail, one of the most desired items, always, on the frontier. As the contract indicates, postoffice contracts could be lucrative, and took into consideration the very real risks involved. (Data from Madsen, "North To Montana.")

December 16, 1864, Montana Territorial Governor Sidney Edgerton asked for establishment of several mail routes, including one from Virginia City to Fort Benton via Prickly Pear.

C. C. Huntley stages had a short term mail contract in the summer of 1866, carried some mail on the Fort Benton run, probably distributed by one of the Fort Benton merchants, a likely prospect I. G. Baker, who was later named first postmaster effective January 18, 1867, with offices in his store. Regular tri-weekly mail service from Helena to Fort Benton began in April that year.

There was also mention about that time of a Northern Overland mail from Minnesota via Fort Benton to Helena. The Helena Herald dreamed of a regular stage route overland as well as mail, instead the successful contractors planned a sort of pony express delivery. First sacks, apparently empty, arrived at Helena in July. Late that year the attempt was fizzling out, the route changed to via the Musselshell and Judith Basin. In March 1868 the overland mail contract was abruptly discontinued. Any piece of mail existent which could be verified as sent by this route would be valuable.

Fort Benton's postmasters after Isaac Baker were George Baker from 1869, John W. Power from 1874, Michael A. Flanagan from 1878 and Charles W. Price from 1888, in the territorial period. From October 1887 most mail arrived by train.

More interesting was the Canadian mail service via Fort Benton. After the arrival of the North West Mounted Police in September 1874 in later Alberta, official mail was probably largely handled through the I. G. Baker Co., their contractor for supplies and payrolls well into the 1880s. A Fort Macleod note on mail in the September 9, 1875, Helena Herald: "Our official mail carrier, D. Leveille, makes the trip punctually once a fortnight." Mail also was undoubtedly carried by Baker wagon trains loaded with supplies.

As to outgoing Canadian mail, G. M. MacInnes in "In The Shadow of The Rockies" said "that mail was made up in Mounted Police barracks and the letters stamped with American stamps and carried by messenger under contract with the Police to Fort Benton." When the Macleod Gazette began publication July 1, 1882, it entered for a second class mail permit at Fort Benton to reach eastern Canadian subscribers.

It appears that the Baker store at various Police posts and Alberta settlements carried U. S. postage stamps for convenience of their customers. Envelopes of the period 1874-1883 which can be identified as carried by such service, either way through Fort Benton or Sun River would again be very interesting to students of postal history.

Western Alberta in April 1882 got stage service, tri-monthly, from Fort Benton when I. G. Baker began a line to Fort Macleod, about 225 miles away. It wasn't very impressive, scattered data indicates a four horse light wagon. It had stations at the Leavings of the Teton, at the Marias crossing near old Fort Conrad, and at Rocky Springs near the border. In Canada at Nine Mile Butte, then Fort Whoop Up—so a six day trip. Where the station didn't include a house a "good tent is always ready." Bull trains took about 14-18 days, Benton to Macleod. In December 1882 the Benton Record reported the line doing a big business in freight, mail, and possibly passengers, carrying 10 to 15 sacks of mail each trip, and said it had been necessary to send out two extras the week before Christmas. One could bet those "stages" were welcomed by Canadians. Regular schedule included departures from the Overland Hotel the 5th, 15th and 25th of each month. The stage's usefulness for mail ended when the Canadian Pacific reached Calgary.

## Early Religious Services
### The Catholic Fathers

First religious service in the Fort Benton area was September 27, 1846, when Fr. Jean Pierre DeSmet celebrated Mass at Fort Lewis, a couple of miles above and across from Fort Benton. With Fr. Nicholas Point, the famed peacemaker had arrived from Flathead country three days before. Fr. DeSmet went down the Missouri the 28th with the American Fur men taking furs and robes to St. Louis, his companion wintering at Fort Lewis. A large proportion of the engages at Fort Lewis were of French descent, from Canada or St. Louis, so the Catholic faith ministrations were welcomed. Fr. Point reported 33 persons baptized his first day at the fort, 21 children on the 29th. There were a number of marriages solemnized, in some cases perhaps with their children as witnesses.

The Catholic Fathers had been at St. Mary's Mission in the Bitter Root, established by Fr. DeSmet and others in 1841. Fr. Point went down river to St. Louis in a keelboat next spring, the voyage starting March 19, 1847, the day the fur post was moved to new quarters, in 1850 renamed Fort Benton. There were visits by Catholic priests at Fort Benton in 1855 and 1858. August 1, 1859, Fr. DeSmet celebrated Mass, married Clement Corneille and Mary Champaigne, and baptized eight children.

Thereafter Catholic services in Fort Benton became dependent upon visits of priests from St. Peter's Mission—at first near present Choteau, then Fort Shaw and in 1865 near present Cascade. Fr. DeSmet, one of the great men of western history and a tremendous traveler, made three more visits to Fort Benton, in 1862, 1863 and 1866. His final years were spent in peacemaking efforts among the Sioux, and one of the final acts of a long and useful life was to bless on May 13, 1873, at St. Louis, the boat his long time friend, Joseph LaBarge, had named the DeSmet. By the time the LaBarge boat lined to the bank at Fort Benton, "Black Robe" had died.

(It might be noted that the American Fur Co., which owned Fort Benton, was very generous to missionaries of various faiths, providing free transportation, free shipment of supplies and a welcome as guests at their trading posts.)

It was not until 1878 that Fr. C. Imoda, assigned to Fort Benton, built the first church in the city—making the Catholic denomination the first and longest lived of the Christian faiths, although the church itself burned in 1905.

### Presbyterian Effort Fails

First Protestant services at Fort Benton were August 17, 1856, when Rev. Elkanah

Mackey, Presbyterian minister, held services attended by whites of the post and by many Indians. The latter at the time had their first glimpse of a "white squaw," Mrs. Mackey, who had accompanied her husband on the arduous river and mackinaw trip to Fort Benton. It was her illness that caused the Mackeys to return by mackinaw on the long trip back to the States a few weeks later.

### Episcopal Church Founded

It was Bishop Daniel Tuttle, pioneer Episcopal clergyman in Montana from 1867, who was responsible for the establishment of the denomination in Fort Benton with the appointment of Rev. S. C. Blackiston to visit Fort Benton monthly from November 1877. The bishop also visited the city to secure a committee to build a church. More than $3,000 was quickly subscribed, soon another thousand, and work began on a brick church in August 1880. First services in the new structure were August 10, 1881, Rev. Blackiston officiating. The building is the oldest surviving Episcopal church in Montana and Fort Benton's oldest church building.

### Methodist Beginnings

June 30, 1872, was a Sunday and the day of the first Methodist services in Fort Benton. William Wesley Van Orsdel, a young Pennsylvanian, had just landed from the steamboat Far West. Possessed of a fine voice, he had almost literally sung for his passage aboard the boat. Undying Fort Benton legend has it that "Brother Van," as he was quickly entitled that day, held his first prayer meeting in the Four Deuces Saloon with the bar temporarily closed. By the name, it has never been located, but whatever, there was an inspiring touch of tolerance when Catholic Father L. Van Gorp helped the young missionary find a place for a more formal religious observance in an old warehouse, probably one of the buildings in decaying Fort Campbell.

Brother Van was not to be the founder of a Methodist church in Fort Benton, that honor was reserved for Rev. Jacob Mills ten years later, but the former who became a Montana legend in his own right, always regarded Fort Benton as his "mother church." For years the local congregation observed Brother Van's birthday in March—the guest of honor again attended in 1918, next to last birthday of a long and useful life. His original intentions were to be a missionary to Montana Indians, and one, learning of his death in December 1919, replied, "So Great Heart is gone. Well then the red man has one friend in heaven."

Rough, tough Fort Benton was not unmindful of the solaces of religion. In June 1875 a news item reported that $359 had been raised, and much more was available, to build a church which would be available to all denominations. However, there was no followup on that occasion.

### First Hospital In Northern Montana

Fort Benton's medical services in gold rush days were probably better than most mining camps, but facilities even after 1869 were limited to an army hospital, likely more a dispensary with a few crude cots. With Fort Benton growing to more than 1600 by 1880, citizens noted the need for a hospital, doubtless sparked by the 1881 withdrawal of the small freight guard stationed in town.

Both local newspapers noted the need in articles late in 1882, then listed pledges to build what they termed a Sisters' hospital, amounting to about $5,500 by year end. Construction actually began in early September 1883, masons at work building, and well along when shortage of funds and weather halted work in late fall. From there work dragged for occasional shortage of money, but completion was noted in August 1884, and "waiting for Sisters." Bishop Brondel in Helena contacted the Sisters of Charity of Providence in Montreal, but it was not until July 27, 1886, that three Sisters arrived. They found the building had been used for grain storage, so their first task was to clean it up. The building was described as of brick, 86x44, two stories of 20 apartments.

The hospital was named for St. Clare of Montefalco, whose canonization in Rome Bishop Brondel had attended, and the property was deeded to the order. First patient was admitted August 11, 1886. At the time it was one of three Catholic operated hospitals in Montana. St. Clare patients were from a wide area of northern Montana, even from Canada. Several Sisters in 1892 went to Great Falls to help in the founding of Columbus Hospital there. Several additions to the Fort Benton structure were made in the first half of the twentieth century. The building was determined unsafe by an inspector in 1957, and in 1959 was replaced by a new fireproof building, helped by local contributions of about twenty times the $12,000 the original building cost.

After December 31, 1974, St. Clare Hospital was turned over to a tax supported hospital district after more than 88 years of operation by the Sisters.

### Ferries Replaced River Ford After 1875

At Fort Benton there was an ancient Indian river ford, beginning near the fur post and running diagonally upstream to emerge just above the site of an 1888 bridge. Employes of both Fort Benton and Fort Campbell used the ford to cross the river and travel about 20 miles to the Highwood Mountains to cut and transport logs for lumber used in building, for shingles and "knees" to support the sides of mackinaws—vital in the fur trade to transport furs and robes down river, and built by the hundreds for returning miners in the 1860s. Probably some lumber, and certainly firewood was secured from nearby Shonkin, Teton and Marias valleys.

About 1863 in the early stage of the gold rush, the existence of a ford at Fort Benton also permitted limited freighting using the old American Fur route as far as Highwood creek, and on to Gallatin City. A January 1, 1865, DeLacy map shows this route as the "Graham Wagon Road" although little information has turned up about this route beyond an alternative "East Side" title. The Military (Mullan) Road out of Fort Benton drew by far the most freighting usage, as steamboats arrived during the high water season when the ford was either dangerous or impossible to use. Possible boat landings on the other side were few, often nonexistent.

The Highwood Mountains had been termed by one old timer as productive only of Indians and grizzlies before the time James Arnoux located a ranch near the old fur trail, in 1872, soon joined by then small rancher John Harris, and on the Shonkin side by farmer-rancher Joe Cobell.

What was later termed the Gallatin Road was quite evidently the same as the Graham Wagon Road, two or three mentions found so termed, and there was a considerable revival when wool was "coming up in the territory" in the early 1870s.

On the Benton Road, or Mullan Trail, toll ferries were in existence, in 1867 the Helena Herald mentions two at Sun River crossing of that stream, one "built by Mullan." The narrower Dearborn was evidently bridged by then, teamsters paying toll when water was high, fording otherwise.

There had been no ferry at Fort Benton, other than small boats for passengers, until Ed Smith in June 1875 launched a much needed, by then, ferry; size unspecified but presumably big enough for a wagon and enough animals to pull same aboard. Smith had been hunter and woodhawk at Musselshell for four years before seeing his future as a freighter from Benton in 1872. Until he sold it in 1883 the ferry was his chief interest, despite success moving freight. The original ferry was replaced in August 1878 by one 75x20, big enough to cross two 6-mule teams and wagons at a time.

By the end of the Indian wars, settlers were coming in numbers into Meagher county and to the east in the Judith Basin. It was scarcely remarkable that the Benton Record in September 1880 commented that a second ferry was an established fact. This materialized in the 1881 season, Lynch & Flynn operating it a block above the Smith ferry. The next season Mike Lynch moved it down river to Baker Street, issuing ferry tokens under that name, 25c and 50c denominations for one way and round trip crossings perhaps, or more likely for foot or horse fare. (In later years these tokens became quite rare, in the 1960s the Fort Benton museum created something of a furore among transportation token collectors by restriking about 2500 from original dies owned by a grandson of Mike Lynch.)

Both ferries did a good business, D. G. Browne once recalling he made a quick $15,000 by getting a ferry monopoly after buying the Smith ferry in 1882 and the opposition next year. The monopoly might also have spurred building of the Fort Benton bridge in 1888. The permanent crossing effectively ended the ferry business after the 1888 season, although two or three times in the 20th century, temporary ferries have been in use during bridge repairs.

Owners in 1889 however found ferries were virtually legal tender along the Missouri in a Montana expanding in population, Indian cessions of much of northern Montana also made ferries helpful in moving livestock by the thousand north of the Missouri. The Judith ferry in the late 1880s moved thousands of sheep and hundreds of cattle to new ranges north of the Missouri, lower ferries also found it a profitable period.

Moses Solomon operated a ferry across the Marias about 12 miles from Fort Benton in the 1880s on the trail to Fort Assiniboine and Fort Walsh, more profitable in high water—even though one traveller risked his life by swimming his horse across when Mose raised the price to $10.

An early one of importance to Benton freighters was at old Fort Conrad on the upper Marias. Rev. John McDougall of Canada recalled crossing there on a "scow type" ferry in the early 1870s.

## Railroads Influenced, Finally Destroyed Missouri Steamboating

Steamboating on the Missouri River speeded the opening and settling of the Northern plains east of the Rockies, and the railroads followed, benefiting from the markets and populations created by cargoes of the boats. Eventually, the rails ended the era of steamboating, save for lower Missouri barge traffic.

The outcome was understandable, the railroads had the capacity for moving needed supplies the year around, the Missouri steamboats were limited by river stage and winter.

In early years of steam navigation on the river, St. Louis was dominant. First indication of the iron nemesis was demonstrated when the Chicago & North Western reached Sioux City March 9, 1868. The latter place, first settled in 1855, had grown to about 1,000 population when the first train arrived. From that time Sioux City hurt St. Louis markets badly, supplied through Chicago and other eastern points—so from Sioux City came most of the Montana cargoes for a time.

Linkage of the rails in Utah May 10, 1869, coupled with the virtual end of the Montana gold rush, meant a bleak depression at Fort Benton, arriving tonnages dropping about 75 percent. Helena merchants turned enthusiastically to freighting from Corinne, then gradually learned the logistics of rail transport and of freighting three times the distance, rather than the 140 miles from Fort Benton. For the most southerly camps, the time-distance factor was not overwhelming.

Then the Mormon backed Utah & Northern started inching northward, and when it neared the Montana line, then crossed it in 1880, steamboat supply of the southern camps was a dead issue, although by then the Benton Road was dominant in supply of the camps in the Helena area.

On the Missouri, major changes in the traffic pattern on the river began in 1873 when the Dakota Southern reached Yankton and the Northern Pacific got to Bismarck. From then for a decade the Upper Missouri steamboats largely shuttled between Bismarck or Yankton and Fort Benton with constantly increasing tonnages.

After several years in receivership the Northern Pacific resumed building late in 1878, reached Wibaux in November 1880 and June 12, 1883, Helena, with a later junction that year at Gold Creek with another extension building eastward. The same year the Canadian Pacific reached Calgary, and the Fort Benton trade area shriveled to an area from about Cascade to the Canadian line.

The St. Paul, Minneapolis and Manitoba Railroad reached Fort Benton September 28, 1887, effectively ending steamboat navigation, although the Block P Line sent a few more boats in the next three years.

Arrival of the Montana, alias Jawbone, Railway at Lewistown in 1904, ended the last long distance stage out of Fort Benton—at one time there were five lines, and even more freight roads.

### Fur Post To Emerging Town

After the evident failure of Fort Lewis (it also was Cotton, Honore and Picotte) due to its location on the wrong side of the Missouri for the Blackfeet trade, Alexander Culbertson planned a replacement.

Fort Benton residents date its founding at an undecided point in 1846. More proper historians can point to a source on the spot, Fr. Nicholas Point, who March 19, 1847, went down river the day the transfer was completed.

Alexander Culbertson, family and relatives give the year as 1846. Best reconcilement is that during the last months of 1846, Culbertson had a party of workmen at the site, only a short distance down and across the river, so regarded its start as the year of founding. The reader can decide for himself.

March 22, 1847, Fr. Point with fur post employes started on from Fort Clay (soon to be called instead Fort Lewis in new location) on a trip to St. Louis by small boat. A graphic and reasonably good artist, he sketched points of interest, Fort Campbell, the one other white settlement in hundreds of miles, meaning Alexander Harvey had not yet relocated above what became Fort Benton. Then Fort McKenzie, burned in 1844; Fort Piegan, abandoned and burned in 1832; Fort Fox & Livingston, short lived 1843 opposition, near the mouth of Shonkin Creek; Fort Chardon at the Judith, burned 1845. There was also a sketch of "La Maison Hamel," Hamell's House, in the area of the Musselshell.

Harvey moved Fort Campbell later in 1847 from about eight river miles down, building it largely of adobe with log palisade. There was hard feeling between the posts in the early years, largely because of Harvey's fiery temperament and American Fur's intolerance of any opposition. After the death of Harvey in July 1854 and advent of Andrew Dawson at Fort Benton, and Joseph Picotte and Malcolm Clarke at Campbell, relationships bettered. In February 1856 the Fort Benton Journal noted: "Traded in all 435 robes, but from appearances we think the opposition must have doubled this," without rancor. Then April 13, "Mr Picotte of the opposition left with his 'Returns' in three Boats—Gave him a passing Salute from our Cannon being we suppose the first time an opposition Bourgeois had such an honor paid him by this Fort, but both houses have been on the most amicable terms this winter both have done a most satisfactory business."

About three years after Harvey's death Malcolm Clarke, formerly at Fort Benton, was in charge of Fort Campbell for a time. The post was bought by American Fur in the spring of 1860, ending opposition, and Catholic missionaries for a time utilized the buildings. Although all the buildings of Fort Campbell had disappeared before first existent pictures of the area, occasional beads indicate its location. Fort Campbell had been built of adobe brick in 1847-48, followed shortly by Culbertson, first large building at Fort Benton completed in 1850. Vincent Mercure, almost constantly at Fort Benton in the period, said the bastions were built after the mid-1850s and the final large buildings facing the river at the south corner erected in 1860.

Next sizeable addition to the Fort Benton townsite came with the first steamboats other than American Fur boats. The Emilie LaBarge and Shreveport of LaBarge, Harkness & Co. landed large cargoes about two blocks above Fort Campbell on June 17, 1862, and workmen proceeded to build Fort LaBarge. This was not palisaded, although occupants of buildings during later Indian scares doubtless wished it had been. Builders must have been busy; when the fort property, which included the first sawmill in Montana, was sold under attachment in 1866 by Sheriff Wm. Hamilton for creditors, John J. Roe & Co., after court action, the site included an adobe dining room, blacksmith shop, log store room, carpenter shop, dwelling room, carpenter shop, saw and grist mill attached, office, ice house and 11 log cabins, more or less.

First building aside from the forts is reported to have been a log cabin built by Clement Corneille (Cornoyer) in 1863, tentatively located as on Main Street about 150 feet above the 1975 postoffice building.

First business building on the townsite, aside from saloon shacks, was the Carroll & Steell store, built by Vincent Mercure and Joseph Laurion, in the summer of 1864. Matthew Carroll and George Steell were Fort Benton's first businessmen aside from those in the forts. They had been chief clerks for American Fur and apparently operated the first few months from the fort. In 1869 they left Fort Benton to become partners in the giant Diamond R. Transportation Co.

Wm. Gladstone, former Hudson Bay boat carpenter, came south early in 1864 and witnessed the birth of the town of Fort Benton. He wrote that in July 1864 when he went down to handle freight of the Yellowstone, which could go no further, there was but one house outside the forts. On return at the end of September there were six saloons, a large store and a blacksmith shop. Gladstone built the first I. G. Baker store near the river in 1865.

Bill Hamilton was 42 when he arrived at Fort Benton in 1864 and had started his apprenticeship as a Mountain Man under Old Bill Williams in 1842, hence was no tenderfoot on the western scene. He added to that initial spurt described by Gladstone. On arrival Hamilton found it was almost impossible to get anything to eat, and "I determined that I would start a hotel. I built a log house, hired a cook and a Negro for a waiter, gave $50 for an old stove, bought and borrowed all the cups, knives, forks and tin plates that I could get from the Fur Company employes, and opened my hotel at $1 per meal." Then he bought some beef steers, "two whiskey barrels on end, with three slabs on them, set up by the hotel, formed the counter of a butcher shop, the first one opened in Chouteau County." He sold beef at 20c and 25c per pound, selling one to five beeves daily to boats and freighters, soon had to hire a butcher and a herder. (His description of that meat counter would have served as well as bars for those first six saloons.)

### Tough Start For A Tough Town

Fort Benton's off-on relationships with Blackfeet came to bloodshed in early May 1865 when a small group of Blackfeet, probably come to visit the agency in Council Hall (later the Jos. Sullivan Saddlery), began boasting of the white scalps they had taken. Two "old mountaineers" sitting next the building, wrote Hi Upham second hand, cut loose with their firearms, killed four and threw the dead Indians into the Missouri a few steps away. Two escaped, a minor matter that confused a later event. The whites were identified in another source as Henry Bostwick and Joe Spearson, each to die by the weapons of hostiles.

All spring long the Montana Post at Virginia City had been touting Ophir at the junction of the Marias and Missouri as true head of navigation. Post owners may even have had stock in the ambitious venture with a much longer name for the townsite, in those years a favored means to wealth.

At any rate a group of whites, the steamboat Cutter (which had wintered at the Marias) and its captain, Frank Moore, were working toward the townsite, evidently had completed two or three cabins. The morning of May 25 a party of ten, including prominent Montanans, went up the Marias to cut logs for buildings. About 100 Bloods under Calf Shirt wiped out the party. First reports cited the cause as the Fort Benton affair, later it turned out that the war party was getting revenge for retribution Charley Carson and two friends visited on three Bloods who had stolen their horses a few weeks earlier. At any rate, Ophir was as dead as the woodcutters—steamboats used the cabins for firewood.

The Ophir affair triggered consternation and demands for retaliation in the mining camps, and acting Governor Thomas F. Meagher, a Civil War hero, willingly joined the chorus of demand for a Montana militia to punish the red men. Little came of that activity, but a few months later Gad Upson, Blackfeet agent from 1863, got busy arranging for a general Indian peace treaty to be held at Fort Benton.

By then sheriff, Bill Hamilton was asked to contact Gros Ventres and Crows. The latter wisely skipped the appointment; the Gros Ventres, then at odds with the Blackfeet nation, were drawn by the lure of presents from the whites. Hamilton and his Piegan scout had to kill five bronco Blackfeet, according to his account, and they sided the Crows in a battle with the Sioux—otherwise a pretty routine trip for a courier in Indian country.

The peace council was held as Upson planned, in Council Hall November 16th, 1865, 43 chiefs of Blackfeet, Piegans, Bloods and Gros Ventres agreeing to peace with whites and each other in a building decorated with red, white and blue flannel and the weapons of whites and redmen symbolically hanging from pillars. It provided for $50,000 in annuities annually for 20 years, according to the Montana Post, which earlier had quoted B. A. Melton of a Fort Benton consignment firm to the effect that 10,000 to 15,000 Indians had gathered at Fort Benton for the proceedings. The treaty was never ratified by congress, and failure of annuities to arrive probably resulted in more white and red deaths than if the council had never been held. There was a distribution of gifts after the signing.

Melton's estimate may make Bill Hamilton's account of the sequel more believable, for his figure was 3,500 to 4,000 Indians camped in the Fort Benton valley. The three tribes of Blackfeet were at the upper end of the bottom, the Gros Ventres on the lower end near the fur post. After the formal signing and gifts, the commissioners, including Meagher, hastily left for Helena and missed the "fun."

An hour later, Hamilton recalled, Little Dog of the Piegans, friend of the whites, warned that others of his nation had gotten whisky and were planning an attack on the Gros Ventres camp. A dozen North West Fur men (American Fur had turned the post over to them in spring 1865) wisely buttoned up, locking the gates of the fort. That left about 45 whites in rifle pits and adobes. The agent's office had a 12 pound cannon that the whites loaded with six pounds of powder and 20 pounds of one ounce balls. (Hamilton seemed convinced that firing the cannon would have been deadly for all concerned, but at least there would be company heading for the hereafter.)

The Gros Ventres too dug rifle pits, moved their lodges into a tight circle, ponies corralled. Little Dog issued every warning he could, then brought his own warriors to fight with the whites if need be. Young men of the other Blackfeet bands rode round and round the lower camp, daring Gros Ventre warriors to come out and fight—wiser older men restraining them from folly. Eventually the affair blew over without bloodshed, but it was a tight couple of hours.

### Early Courts And The Law

Law was slow making its appearance in Fort Benton, even more slowly than in the mining camps, although a system of courts was set up soon after the creation of Montana Territory May 26, 1864. Chief Justice Hezekiah Hosmer and Justice Alonzo Williston arrived that fall. Justices were to travel to county seats for court cases, a somewhat disagreeable chore for the judges in view of crude travel facilities. A later justice, Decius Wade, recalled holding his first Chouteau county court in an adobe building in the fur post at Fort Benton.

Justice was as yet often as abrupt as Vigilante action in many cases, Fort Benton Vigilantes hanged Bill Hynson in August 1868.

Although Chouteau county had an appointed resident sheriff with the appointment of Wm. T. Hamilton in late spring 1865, the first noted legal proceeding at Fort Benton antedated him. This was the suit and May 13, 1865, sale with Wm. Berkin special officer, of 2525 buffalo robes and assorted furs and steam sawmill belonging to LaBarge & Harkness, on the attachment suit of J. J. Roe & Co. The suit stemmed from 1863 non-delivery of freight at Bannack as agreed on by the defendant steamboaters. About a year later Fort LaBarge on the Fort Benton bottom was also sold on attachment, comprising a number of small buildings.

In those years it seemed the most important duty of a sheriff was handling such matters, rather than law enforcement, which it might be noted was at a minimum. Personal disagreements were apt to be settled by physical confrontation.

While judges were only rarely in Fort Benton, the county had a procession of sheriffs; after old trapper and trader Bill Hamilton, about 1867 George Croff by appointment, in September 1867 Asa Sample became the county's first elected sheriff but he may have tossed up the job, as John R. Morgan was sheriff at Morgan's death in November 1868, John Buckmaster appointed to succeed him. J. D. Weatherwax was sheriff in 1870, and may have been elected in 1869, no data turns up. All the foregoing except Hamilton, and the next five, were involved in some manner in the whisky trade in Canada. H. A. (Fred) Kanouse rates added comment. In 1871, wrote James Lowell in 1924, "the county treasurer was a gambler who exhausted the treasury," and Lowell was three years getting his pay for serving as county assessor. Dave Walter of Montana Historical Society supplied material on this odd case, including a letter from Sheriff Kanouse dated Sept. 28, 1871, explaining to the territorial auditor his complete disinterest in assuming added duties as county "warrants are worth but 15c on the dollar." Kanouse also planned to go to British America, and did for that winter. Coming back from Whoop Up country in the spring Kanouse got into a violent disagreement over a horse, and shot and killed Jim Nabors, a member of the party. Nobody in Fort Benton was even interested in accepting Kanouse's resignation. As to the derelict treasurer, he mortgaged some property, repaid the $835 due and resigned office.

Kanouse spent the next winter too up at Whoop Up, had his shoulder nearly blown away by a Blackfeet bullet, with an agonizing trip to Helena for remedial surgery. Then a murder charge was brought in 1873 in the Nabors killing—the U. S. court threw it out, so did Deer Lodge county, and by the time Chouteau county possibly acted, Kanouse was across the border once more.

His replacement was probably Trevanian Hale, who resigned as sheriff with Wm. Rowe appointed—the latter was elected for a term but resigned in June 1877 to run a stage line instead. John Healy, pioneer of the Whoop Up fort and trail, got the nod, twice was elected, each time telling voters in effect "don't vote for me if you plan on stealing any horses" followed by a hanging threat. For the times, most of these men performed their duties honestly, comments of peers indicate. Healy secured the building of a brick jail in 1881, legend has it he was voted out for coddling inmates. Not so, he wasn't a candidate in 1882.

Justice and law enforcement by court and sheriff became stricter with a gradual change in local attitudes beginning around 1875 and getting more backing as the number of white women in Fort Benton grew. On April 16, 1875, two Gros Ventres Indians in jail for attempted murder, were taken from the county jail and lynched. The May 1 Record had harsh words about "this fearful deed...Benton is cursed with a floating population of as hard a set of desperadoes as perhaps exist on earth." For whites there was some measure of law, Jeff Perkins in February 1875 went into Mose Solomon's Medicine Lodge, locked the door and shot the proprietor. At his trial Perkins called it self defense, said Solomon was armed but dropped his gun. Perkins, incidently the county treasurer who made unwise investments across the green cloth, drew five years for attempted murder but apparently was out in a year. Mose was no mollycoddle, Al Wilkins recalled him the victor over a Piegan brave and an Irishman disputing results of a poker game—in each case a coroner's jury told Mose to get back to his booze counter.

But tame as Fort Benton supposedly had become, June 21, 1875, when U. S. marshals Charles Hard and X. Beidler came to serve a bit of paper on Trevanian Hale, John Evans, Tom Hardwick, Charles Harper and Jeff Devereux, they took the precaution of bringing along a troop of cavalry to surround the town. The warrants were to appear in Helena, the Canadian government wanted to extradite the five for killing of Assiniboine Indians in the Cypress Hills in 1873. Two unnamed arrestees got away, the others turned loose when extradition was denied.

Finally October 6, 1879, Fort Benton residents witnessed a double, and legal, hanging, Joseph K. Koble and Orlando H. Marsh for the murder of a fellow Company F, 3rd Infantry, private, Patrick Farrell. The executions took place in the jail yard of the county jail. There were to be two more hangings in 1894 and 1895.

### Port Of Entry And Exit

Location of an office of U. S. collector of customs for Montana and Idaho at Fort Benton for years, hinged on the place's position on the northern frontier; port of entry for Canadian freight via steamboats, and port of exit through which robes, furs and later other commodities from Canada were handled.

N. P. Langford of Virginia City was customs collector in 1866, a year later X. Beidler of Helena filled the post. Tom Cummings was appointed in 1873 while a Helena resident, soon moved the office to Fort Benton.

Earliest note found on actual customs charges dates to 1872, certifying that I. G. Baker & Bro. had paid to the collector of customs at Fort Benton, 20% of the inventory valuation on robes shipped from Canada to Montana Territory during the winter of 1870-71, Charles E. Conrad and John Healy and Alfred Hamilton so testifying. Canadians collected a similar tariff through the Mounted Police on American merchandise, one unattributed note indicates 1874-75 the Baker Co. paid more than $13,000 at port of Fort Macleod.

The 1872 note indicates a collector, unnamed and unfound, at Fort Benton at the time. Around 1874-75 Cummings moved his office to Fort Benton, the Record files indicate. By the latter year both the Baker and Power firms had posted bond in Washington in order to handle supplies originating in eastern Canada and bound for North West Territories. Robes from Canada bound for eastern Canadian markets were similarly covered, the bonds protecting the U. S. from loss of customs through diversion.

Tom Cummings was the collector of customs at Fort Benton until 1881, when Wm. H. Hunt was named. After Hunt's term it was Cummings again, then Jere Sullivan, and finally David G. Browne, appointments were political in nature. In 1892 a safe expert was two days trying to pick the lock on the local customs safe. The office by then was no big thing, the collector was allowed four mounted police for the long Montana-Idaho border. The office was moved to Great Falls in July 1896, after more than 20 years in Fort Benton and ten after the town had lost its one time importance.

### Messages By Wire

First telegraph into Montana Territory was a Western Union line to Virginia City in 1866, a 470 mile jump from Salt Lake City. Next year the wires reached Helena, citizens raising about $12,500 to encourage the builders. It was not until May 1869 that work started on an extension to the head of navigation. Work went swiftly as by early June "a line into the Thwing House very soon." Helena Herald news item datelines seem to indicate June 15 as the date Fort Benton had telegraph service. The government, with army posts at Fort Shaw and Fort Benton, may have had a part in the extension. The military later contributed to upkeep, and seems to have taken the line over.

Out on the plains in buffalo country, the shaggies often wrecked communications by rubbing down the poles. One genius who tried spikes in the poles misfired, the big bulls just loved the nails as something that controlled that itch. Another hazard was freighters—an open prairie campfire fueled by segments of telegraph poles heated coffee and seared bacon much faster than buffalo chips or green cottonwood.

Telephones, invented later, naturally appeared after the singing telegraph wires. H. P. Rolfe, Fort Benton attorney, in February 1880 set up a line from his home to the telegraph office, and it worked, a surprised Benton Record noted. Two years later Power and Baker stores and First National Bank were connected by telephone. There was some talk of a local exchange, but it wasn't until August 1902 that Rocky Mountain Bell set up a 55 subscriber exchange.

### Fort Benton's Near Demise

Thursday evening, November 2, 1882, Fort Benton celebrated the formal opening of the new Grand Union Hotel with a grand ball, attended, said the Benton Record somewhat wonderingly, "by almost a hundred of the fair sex." Editor W. H. Buck doubtless recalled his start in 1875 when white ladies of the city might have been counted on the fingers of a hand. The newer River Press (from Oct. 1880) called the Grand Union the "finest hostelry in the Northwest." Jerry Collins wasn't far wrong. Both papers were publishing five times a week dailies as well as weekly editions.

Fort Benton had 367 residents in 1870, and had grown to 1618 in 1880, and it was the third largest in the territory, topped only by Helena and Butte, and no other settlement as much as one thousand. In the two years prior to the ball, the business district had been largely rebuilt to brick structures. The 1882 brick construction had included the H. J. Wackerlin Hardware, Gans & Klein, second halves of Power and Baker stores, Masonic and Odd Fellows halls, Grand Union, and a start on the Pacific Hotel of R. S. Culbertson, as well as a number of brick homes.

The year's building cost was about $200,000, and three million locally made bricks went into it. Week by week notes from the papers of small businesses opening and of new residents indicate the city's claimed population of 2,000 may have been understated—it may have reached 2500 in freighting season.

Fort Benton's trade area in 1882 stretched from Helena and the Judith Basin north of the border to Edmonton, and east from the Rockies. Fort Benton stages ran to Fort Macleod, Fort Assiniboine, Helena, Billings, Barker and way points. There had been 49 steamboat arrivals in a year of low water, moving 14,000 tons of freight and 3700 passengers. Hundreds of men and thousands of animals were employed in freighting out of Fort Benton.

### Merchants Foresaw Changes

To wide-awake Fort Benton merchants the impending construction of the Canadian Pacific to Calgary and linkage of the two lines of the Northern Pacific railroads represented changing conditions, but also a challenge and opportunity for the city to prosper and grow. Not unreasonably, they expected the Canadian railroad would build south to Fort Benton, and the Northern Pacific north to meet at the crossroads of the northern plains. In those years, where rails crossed, sizable cities grew. There was also the Missouri, to provide a brake on rail rates.

North of the Marias and the Missouri was Indian reservation, the opening of which would provide a great, rich range that would more than replace the lost trading area. And the falls of the Missouri would provide power for a growing Fort Benton. Local people had seen a demonstration of electric lights by the steamboat Rosebud that summer, they were more conversant with its possibilities than were most easterners.

### The Dreams Fade Away

Yet in less than eight years from that ball in the Grand Union, Fort Benton was a basket case, its population down to 624, most gone to boost the as of 1882 unborn village of Great Falls. The 1890 population probably dropped another hundred or so down toward the 1870 level before the worst was over. If Paris Gibson made the attributed comment of local legend about "making the grass grow in the streets of Fort Benton," he doubtless felt he came close to being correct.

The Canadian Pacific reached Calgary August 11, 1883, and traffic north on the Whoop Up Trail faded away. Mourned the Benton Record soon after, "Not even a dog fight relieved the monotony." The Northern Pacific reached Helena in June, completed its line at Gold Creek in September. Davidson & Moffitt, Helena harness firm which had built a fine brick business in 1881 (River Press from 1885), promptly held a closing out sale. Kleinschmidt & Brother, Helena merchants who had built a concrete warehouse at Benton in 1877 and yearly shipped about 2,000 tons of merchandise from the steamboats, closed their business within months.

## Fort Benton Fights Decline

What Fort Benton citizens, with stout backing from its leading merchants, did in those years after 1882 to make their dreams come true is impressive.

The city was incorporated early in 1883, Wm. G. Conrad first mayor. Bids were taken to build a big county court house to replace the one burned January 5, 1883. To relieve overcrowded schools, from 1877 in a two room brick, an imposing $30,000 structure was approved. Residents passed the hat for a Sister's hospital, started that year and finished next at a cost of $12,000, although it was not until 1886 that St. Clare Hospital was opened.

The season of 1883 found steamboat arrivals down to 35, and freight down a seventh at 12,000 tons. Down freight included 50,000 hides and robes, some the carryover from the final buffalo slaughter, a third of a million pounds of bullion and more than a million pounds of wool. A seer might have augured regarding the survey of a new townsite by H. P. Rolfe for Paris Gibson, but only one man occupied the Great Falls townsite that winter and he was stripped of grub and supplies by wandering Indians.

The year 1884 opened with a shocker, Scott Wetzel turned his assets over to creditors a year after he'd built a finer home than any of the Conrads, two years after his $250,000 business of 1882, one of the oldest general mercantile firms in Fort Benton; too generous with credit to all did him in.

River traffic was down this year, 15 boats bringing 4,000 tons of freight, although the summer was enlivened by gold strikes in Little Rockies and Sweet Grass Hills so close together that it provided stampeders with an enviable choice on which way to ride. Gold dust flowing in via outlying branches of local firms did help. Also upbeat, completion of new court house, school and hospital, and the town was getting its first sidewalks, required of owners by the city.

Paris Gibson, who had gone broke on a lumber yard in 1879, since recuperated on sheep, in June had James J. Hill out from the Twin Cities to look over his new townsite of Great Falls. Hill provided the bulk of the financing of what became a successful townsite operation.

Fort Benton's pride, the Grand Union, went up at sheriff's sale in mid-1884, local people relaxed a bit when Benton bankers bid it in. W. H. Burgess, first strictly grocery business, went broke in the first floor of the new Masonic hall, and the Benton Record was staving off the end, so the year ended gloomily, even though a bridge at Fort Benton drew promises of support.

There was that matter of being a rail instead of a steamboat center, the River Press heralded each evidence of interest in a line to Fort Benton by the Galts of Canada or the Northern Pacific. Residents pledged $75,000 toward the first. Somebody bought the plant of the now defunct Benton Record, and the fine brick Record building went at sheriff's sale in mid-1885. Fort Benton was leaking residents to Great Falls at a fearful rate. A couple of losses, J. R. Wilton, who had put up many of the city's finest buildings, and Wheeler O. Dexter, handiest man in town, gone to build a ferry there and run an express to Sun River and Fort Benton. Curiously, the head of navigation found new Great Falls their best customers, the Electric City to be would depend on steamboats for a while yet. When the Record printing plant was sold, the Press thought it might be a white elephant.

The writer was wrong, July 8, 1885, the F. C. Roosevelt new furniture store, Odd Fellows building, which also housed the River Press, was destroyed by fire. The paper bought the Record plant, moved to the former Davidson-Moffitt building.

## Slight Pickup In 1886

There were 15 steamboats in 1886, a slight increase over the year before in number and tonnages, and three Sisters of Charity of Providence arrived to open the hospital, which for several years drew patients from all over northern Montana. One bright spot for local merchants continued to be Fort Benton's position as a wool market, the steamboats offered favorable rates. The Montana Wool Growers had organized at Fort Benton in 1883 and for some years held their convention in the city around July 1st, about the time the big wool shipments were coming for shipment down river, so in mid-summer the town was busy. In 1886 shipments were 1.5 million pounds. There were railroad notes that summer, too, work was being done on the Montana Central, Helena to Great Falls, to connect next year with Jim Hill's St. Paul, Minneapolis & Manitoba. Toward fall the River Press noted, "much hay being put up, a hard winter expected." The writer must have been a prophet.

Stockmen in the Fort Benton area came through the hard winter of 1886-87 in better shape than elsewhere, although John Lepley later was said to have lost $100,000 and Benton & St. Louis (Circle) and Montana Cattle Co. were hard hit. Bentonites gladly bought cordwood sawed from the old log jail. After a bad breakup from melting snow, the city was ready for business in what proved to be the curtain call for the Missouri River packets. Jim Hill had big plans for his Manitoba, and the steamboats ironically helped make many of them possible. They carried much of the line's supplies that season, and at Fort Benton with about 35 arrivals, it looked at times like olden days on the Missouri.

The Manitoba reached the Fort Benton depot (though two miles out on the flat, and it was "Benton" until the 1920s when the Great Northern added "Fort") September 28. First local freight followed October 5, a carload of groceries for I. G. Baker and a carload of whisky for Gans & Klein.

## Benton Bridge Built

While the railroad was coming, Fort Benton plans for a steel bridge roared ahead, Jim Hill's road later giving freight concessions for the steel—Fort Benton's wool market would be coddled by the later Great Northern as so much the NP didn't get. Not content, Bentonites approved the franchise of George F. Woolston of Helena for a water plant, another for electric lights.

A toll bridge built by private capital at a cost of about $65,000 was event of the year at Fort Benton in 1888. Yet not the only effort.

At a March banquet local businessmen were enthusiastic at the completion of a municipal water plant, and electric lights, beating the capital city of Helena by a few weeks on both. And now that they had a sure supply of fuel and water, long time bugaboos, a city park was laid out, and residents were beautifying their city. In olden years almost anything looking like a tree was apt to be cut down in a cold wave.

Building of the bridge took all summer, into fall and early winter. It operated as a toll bridge for some years, eventually was sold to the county for $9,999 and was in use until 1963. Refurbished by grant money, the bridge is the oldest steel vehicular bridge in Montana, hence regarded as most historic.

In 1888 Fort Benton had lost another of its giant businesses when Murphy Maclay moved to Great Falls to become a purely hardware store. As Murphy Neel it had moved to Fort Benton in the 1870s ran a tremendous freighting business exceeded only slightly by Baker and Power.

In 1889 Fort Benton raised enough to build a flour mill, aimed at providing a market for locally grown grain. There was more wheat than capacity, a few barrels of flour were milled, the man in charge committed an unspecified tort, and the mill was soon abandoned. But once again in wool season all local hotels were full of growers and buyers, the wagons came rumbling in from the south, and 70,000 sheep were shipped.

Next year in April found that 624 population mentioned. There was more grief to come. Fred Bucksen, a minor but long time merchant, gave up in June, Gans & Klein in September. Then I. G. Baker late in 1890 announced its closing out sale, completed in early 1891, with a residue sold to Strain Brothers of Great Falls. In February the firm had sold its far flung Canadian stores to Hudson Bay Co., ending an era in which, as one HBC director put it, the Baker firm "had scaled the value of our stock from pounds to shillings." The exodus of the Conrads, then in full charge of the Baker operations, was a final, almost deadly blow to Fort Benton. The Charles Conrads went to build Kalispell, the Wm. G. Conrads to Great Falls, the latter to innovate a large irrigation project in later years.

# Cooperation Was Keynote

*I*n the days of the fur trade the bourgeois, head of the fur post, was definitely in charge and responsible for the well being of the people in the small forts. That changed with the gold strikes to the south in 1862-63, and the boating season brought hundreds of miners and freighters to Fort Benton, William Gladstone estimated 1500 as early as July 4, 1864.

The throngs were not necessarily criminals, indeed, the Vigilantes to the south had eliminated, abruptly, many of the worst. But the visitors were certainly lawless, and aggravating the situation were the animosities of the Civil War. Little value was set on human life, as Gladstone recalled. A drunk insulted perhaps the only woman on the Fort Benton bottom, and her aged husband appealed to bystanders to take the fellow away. Instead, one man walked up to the drunk and shot him dead. "That's the way to fix that sort." Nothing was said or done.

Matt Carroll and George Steell, former Fort Benton post chief clerks, in 1865 were in business for themselves. Joseph Culbertson, part blood son of the founder, Alexander, credits Carroll and Steell with being heads of the too shadowy Fort Benton Vigilance committee. Certainly Isaac G. Baker, starting his own business after two years in charge of the fort, approved, as did Sheriff Bill Hamilton, who certainly needed the help. They were surprisingly often joined by X. Beidler, a deputy U. S. marshal, on visits to Fort Benton. Three actions by local Vigilantes survive: An 1866 whipping of a thief of steamboat freight, recalled by Grant Marsh, captain of the steamboat Luella; the 1868 hanging of Bill Hynson for repeated rolling of drunks, and an impromtu 1871 duel in which the murderer known only as "Bowlegs" was taken from jail and killed by the father of the slain small girl, Baptiste Racine. There were doubtless others. Occasional poster warnings that the Vigilantes were watching perhaps were a deterrent, although a fight or shootout concerned only the principals.

So much for law and order. An 1867 act of kindness by a rival merchant began a collaboration in community affairs which persisted for years, still seems in evidence well over a century later among residents.

Charles B. Power wrote the River Press in 1926: "Father (T. C. Power) brought his first stock of goods up in 1867, and found when he got there that there was no building that he could rent. Mr. I. G. Baker was an old time Methodist who was very partial to revivals, and amongst the things that he had brought up to then was a revival tent. When he knew that father was without any place to store his goods, and notwithstanding that they would be in competition, he loaned father this tent, and in it was started the first T. C. Power business." Power never forgot.

Rivals they would be, and occasionally there were dirty tricks in the outlands, but T. C. Power & Bro. and I. G. Baker & Co. repeatedly joined forces and finances in ventures that turned out well for Fort Benton. Some were for financial gain, true, but there were others in which no reasonable man could have expected to gain a penny.

Certainly there were profits for both in that great steamboating season of 1867, one of the best in years, profit-wise, on the Upper Missouri. First cooperative followed swiftly. The only sizable hotel was the Overland, built in 1866, a couple of small cabins. Other housing included a small adobe cabin, and floors of saloons.

January 9, 1868, a Bentonite wrote the Helena Herald: "Power and Baker are shaping out the framework of one of the largest hotels in the territory." It was opened in mid-June, just in time for the peak of the boating season, as the Thwing House. After a couple of seasons the owners closed the 90 foot frame, due to the collapse of gold rush freighting, later used it as army officers' quarters and as housing for business visitors on occasion. Reopened in 1879 by Jere Sullivan as the Choteau (in this century Chouteau) House, it looms attractively in early day pictures and became a Fort Benton landmark; buildings of an early 1900 reconstruction are still in use, although no longer as a hotel.

Fort Benton business suffered in 1870, the year there was a rush north into British possessions to join in the lucrative whisky trade there. Both Baker and Power backed traders who risked their lives during the wild days up north. Sadly hurting both firms as well as independents was a U. S. embargo of the 1869-70 winter trade. A June Herald item said "little less than a half million locked up." A smallpox epidemic among Indians was the cause. Baker managed to get 3,000 robes which the firm traded for from a non-affected tribe, cleared for shipment. These were freighted over 600 miles south to Corinne, Utah, to be shipped via Union Pacific east, only sizable use of that route from Fort Benton.

By that time only mercantile houses doing business were the two, and Fred Gerard, who came up from Fort Union and bought the Carroll & Steell firm. Gerard's efforts to profit in a Canadian venture ended with a looted and burned wagon train and five men killed. He gave up and went down river in 1872. Wetzel & Weatherwax, in existence by then, were probably trading at an Indian outpost.

The Power and Baker firms toughed it out much more successfully despite a dwindling dependent territory, a sharp loss of local population and partial loss of freighting business to the railroad in Utah. Eventually the outflow of population from the camps reversed and settlers began coming in to agricultural areas in the south. There was an indicated revival for 1874, the year Helena papers and merchants began boosting a new settlement at Carroll, above the mouth of the Musselshell, as a bypass to Fort Benton steamboating. During that season the rival heads of navigation broke about even on steamboat tonnages unloaded, but freight trains out of Carroll ran into mud and hostile Sioux, and deliveries to Helena disappointed supporters of the Carroll Trail.

Wm. G. and Charles Conrad by that year had bought into the Baker business, but it was the founder of the firm who had the connections to draw the business that would make millionnaires of all three. In late September a party from the just-arrived North West Mounted Police came to Fort Benton looking for Isaac Baker, who wasn't hard to find. Two weeks later Baker was in Helena purchasing about 20 tons of odds and ends the Baker store couldn't supply—a Canadian government contract backing the purchases. The Mounties had come to stop that whisky peddling.

### Beginning of the Block P Line

Both Power and Baker actually welcomed their coming, although it dismayed the men who had bet their hair for a small share of the profits. There would be settlers and legitimate business in Canada. Furthermore, it was time to wipe out that Carroll challenge. The announcement came less than two months after arrival of the NWMP, in the Helena Herald: "T. C. Power & Bro., I. G. Baker & Co., and other capitalists have ordered a light draft steamboat, first class in all its appointments, for the Upper Missouri River, and the boat is to be ready for the spring trade of '75."

The second major cooperation would put Fort Benton in the driver's seat in transportation for almost a decade.

Both the Power and Baker firms controlled such vast business in the mid-1870s that they apparently welcomed and even financed offshoots. For example when M. A. Flanagan and Dr. Wm. Turner started the city's first drug store in 1875, there were small item announcements in the Benton Record that the druggists had purchased the stocks of such items from the two major stores. Virtually the same procedure was followed when Hans J. Wackerlin began a hardware business in 1878. In this case surviving letterheads of the firm show that both Baker and Power had a financial interest in the new venture, at least by the time the Wackerlin Hardware brick was completed in 1881.

Again, both the major stores shared in the opening of the First National Bank in June 1880—the Bank of Northern Montana, backed by Helena interests, began at the same time. Both banks for a time did business in the Benton Record building. The First National was the first to move, into a brand new brick building located near Main Street across from the Power store. Had there been space open in the center of the block, it is apparent it would have been located there, midway between the sponsoring firms. In March 1882 the first telephone linkage found in Fort Benton put phones in the two stores and their bank.

Another approach was a bit unusual, formation of the Benton Building Association in 1881. Fort Benton had for six years been suffering from constriction of living quarters, the census of 1880 providing graphic evidence of overcrowding of hotels in the busy season—and there were shortages of building material, lumber, lime, brick and stone, as well as of skilled workmen. Both Record and River Press often referred to the building needs; one said construction costs were double those of any other town in the territory.

The Benton Building Association was just what its name implies. The aim was to build residential properties at as reasonable cost as possible and sell or rent same. While original capitalization was $75,000, only a fraction of that was ever involved. In November 1882 assets totaled $20,400, against capital stock paid in of $8,240. The company had four houses, two brick and two frame, on hand already, and was renting these; pending possible sale of course. The association apparently built a dozen or more houses. When liquidated in 1895, it sold 39 lots and two brick houses to a savings and loan company.

In several of the above enterprises, participating firms and individuals undoubtedly hoped to turn a profit. An 1883 venture was certainly more profit orientated, the Fort Benton Boom Co. This was intended to end Fort Benton's recurring fuel problems. The basic idea was to cut wood in the Sun River area, float same down to Fort Benton, where a catch boom in the Missouri would shunt the wood into a side channel. As it turned out, nothing worked as planned, and the boom was a flat failure. (Another failure was a flour mill, first proposed in 1884, eventually built in time to turn out a sack of flour on July 4, 1889, but thereafter idle and eventually abandoned due to faulty construction.)

One project that didn't fail was what became St. Clare Hospital. Proposals for what was termed a Sisters' Hospital were aired several years prior to an actual campaign for funds. Late in 1882 pledges were secured for $5,500, actual cash contributions less of course, but forthcoming when work started in summer 1883. The construction went ahead as long as funds lasted and suspended over winter. More money was raised and the building was completed by August 20, 1884. However, it was July 1886 when the first Sisters of St. Clare arrived and they opened the hospital in August, first hospital of any size in northern Montana.

Six years later a group from St. Clare went to Great Falls to start Columbus Hospital. The Sisters operated St. Clare until the end of 1974, turning it over to a tax financed hospital district.

### Fort Benton Incorporates

Fort Benton's first municipal election was held on April 2, 1883, voters also approving incorporation of the place as City of Fort Benton by a vote of 58 for, 28 against. At the time there were probably several hundred more residents than the 1618 counted in the census of 1880, judging from numbers of new businesses and arrivals. Local habits of cooperation extended even to politics, democrats and republicans dividing the offices on a fusion ticket. William G. Conrad was first mayor; Charles Crawford, liveryman, marshal; Charles L. Spencer, T. C. Power employe, police magistrate; Samuel L. Kelly, druggist, treasurer and assessor, and clerk and city attorney, H. R. Buck. Aldermen: Solomon Ginsberger, manager of Gans & Klein, a clothing store; Frank Coombs, builder of the Grand Union; Ed Dunne, Power department head; Jere Sullivan, owner of the Chouteau House; Thomas A. Cummings, insurance; Howell Harris, liveryman; Ferdinand C. Roosevelt, former Wells Fargo agent and furniture store owner; Timothy E. Collins, banker.

Why Fort Benton, when it had been so often Benton City or simply Benton? The River Press explained: "You must write it Fort Benton now, as that is the name in the charter." The writer, probably Jerry Collins, noted that almost every state had a place called Benton, while there "is but one Fort Benton in the whole wide world." Four years later Collins would become owner of the Great Falls Tribune. At the time Paris Gibson was merely dreaming of a townsite which would become Great Falls, it was not until next spring that Gibson would get the financial backing of James J. Hill and ruin the hopes of many Fort Benton residents.

The leading merchants, and Fort Benton boosters, were not unaware of the meaning of the Northern Pacific, stretching steel toward long time best customer Helena, and the Canadian Pacific, heading toward Calgary. The early residents knew well enough, the railroads had changed the pattern of Missouri River steamboat traffic, cargoes until 1868 coming from St. Louis, after which Sioux City, and Yankton, then Bismarck were successors as lower centers of the river trade into Montana.

Fort Benton seemed secure, solid in the center of a large trading area. Furthermore, there was little doubt that the vast Indian reservation north of the Marias and Missouri would soon be open to white settlement. The largest place in northern Montana would certainly be a target point for branch lines south from Canada and north from the Yellowstone. In those years, when rails crossed, good sized cities grew. And in their own special case, the Missouri River steamboats offered an alternative route, to curb the monopolistic practices of railroads of those days. The falls of the Missouri would provide power for such a prosperous town. Yet all their calculations went astray, though few could fault Fort Benton people for the efforts they would make.

### Fort Benton's Growing Problems

The Northern Pacific rails met in a golden spike ceremony at Gold Creek September 9, 1883, having effectively cut off Fort Benton's Helena trade earlier, the Canadian Pacific brought its first train into Calgary August 10, and suddenly the Fort Macleod distribution point at the far end of the Whoop Up Trail had lost its importance. In 1883 Fort Benton freighting was down a bit but the total plummeted the next year to about 40%, and there were unemployed freighters and saloons headed for bankruptcy at the head of navigation. Paris Gibson's new townsite benefited greatly in population, probably a majority of the couple hundred the fall of 1884 were former Bentonites. The big Kleinschmidt & Bro. store and Davidson & Moffitt's harness store promptly shut down. Fort Benton's first full time grocer, W. H. Burgess, gave up.

Thursday evening, November 2, 1882, Fort Bentonites had celebrated the opening of "the finest hostelry in the Northwest," the Grand Union, with a grand ball, attended, wrote W. H. Buck in the Benton Record, "by almost one hundred of the fair sex." The editor doubtless recalled his start in 1875 when white ladies of the city might have been counted on the fingers of a hand. The three story hotel, which still impresses visitors, was first to feel the pinch. May 20, 1884, the Grand Union went up at sheriff's sale; Chas. H. Duer, representing the Bank of Northern Montana, took it over. Further, the Benton Record was on its last legs.

At Fort Benton work went ahead on a big new brick courthouse to replace the one which burned January 5, 1883, and a large new brick school was constructed, but little other construction was done. A Sanborn insurance map of October 1884 shows the woeful result of loss of much of the transient trade, a dozen vacant business buildings along three blocks of Front Street. Year end 1883 had brought Bentonites another shocker—Scott Wetzel, though not among the big four a major merchant for 15 years, turned his assets over to creditors only a year after he had completed a finer home than any of the Conrads—his own easy way with credit the cause.

About the time in June 1885 that the River Press ran an article on Fort Benton's depression, the Record was dead and the fine five year old brick building sold at sheriff's sale. Earlier the Record printing plant, finest in the territory, had gone at $1200. Probably a "white elephant," felt its rival, but two weeks into July bought the plant, after being burned out of the Odd Fellows building along with Ferd. Roosevelt's furniture store. (There were all kinds of empty buildings, the Press moved into the Davidson & Moffitt brick building.)

The Press had dutifully chronicled the occasional railroad survey parties in the area, from either north or south, more than a dozen steamboats were bringing cargoes annually, and perhaps the bosses of the iron horse wanted to knock that river alternative in the head, once and for all, but nothing materialized. By the summer of 1886, however, work on the Montana Central, actually an extension of next summer's Manitoba, St. Paul & Minneapolis, was underway in the Helena area.

Factors to keep some life in the old river port were the growth of cattle and sheep growing, and beginnings of agriculture in the area. Fort Benton had been the birthplace of the Montana Wool Growers Association in 1883, and for years the town was a major wool market, well past the steamboat period. Cattle, too, meant trade, dozens of cowboys on occasion.

The August 18, 1886, River Press carried a brief item: "Much hay is being put up, a hard winter anticipated." The writer was either prophet or hoodoo. Cattlemen never forgot the tragic sequel. It's only a matter of proportion, but the area came through 1886-87 winter in better shape than areas out along the old cattle trail up from Texas. Still, the losses were huge. John Lepley later was reported to have lost $100,000 and the Montana Cattle Co., running 30,000 head, hard hit. Sheep got off more lightly, although sheep pelts of victims of the winter came into Fort Benton by the hundreds next July, also with a million and a half pounds of wool. But most local eyes were focused on Jim Hill's new railroad, sweeping westward from Minot across Indian country. The rails reached Fort Benton September 28, 1887, and an era had ended, although T. C. Power ran steamboats to Benton for three years more, probably as a warning to railroaders.

### A Final, Stout Hearted Effort

In the face of five years of continuous bad news and adversity, efforts of Fort Benton people in 1887-88 merit attention. For several years citizens had been suggesting a bridge across the Missouri, in view of the increasing trade from the Shonkin and Highwood sections. Benton Bridge Co. was incorporated in 1884 by a group of leading citizens and pledges made, but the 1885 legislature refused to grant a charter. Wm. G. Conrad was apparently the instigator of a more successful attempt, announcing in late June 1887, that the Manitoba Railroad would haul the material for the bridge free. That probably came from a meeting with Jim Hill at Fort Benton a few days before. By October 19, $25,000 had been pledged, a month later the total needed was down to under $5,000.

December 14, the Press reported the town "full of bridge engineers," and the big project was on its way. The free freight was no small item, Hill undoubtedly saw Fort Benton as a readymade wool market, and liked prospects of draining business from rival Northern Pacific to the south. The bridge cost about $65,000 in all, the major contract let February 1 was $40,000, work begun promptly. It was opened in December, a feature the 225 foot swing span, the corps of engineers regarded the Missouri past Fort Benton as navigable. There were three 175 foot, one 75 foot spans in addition. The swing span, so well balanced the engineer once demonstrated that he could turn it by hand pry bar, went out in a June 1908 flood, replaced by a permanent span. The bridge was taken out of use in 1963, but preserved through grant funds. A National Parks Service survey calls it "The most historically significant bridge in Montana." After some years as a toll bridge, it was sold to Chouteau County for $9,999, the odd figure because any amount over $10,000 required a voter referendum.

Despite the evident loss to the bridge company, for Fort Benton as a whole the bridge was a vital factor in survival. For more than a generation it was the only vehicular bridge across the Missouri in Montana below Great Falls, and helped Fort Benton trade and freighting into the Judith Basin into the next century. Across it came a good share of the million or more pounds of wool a year, the cattle and grain grown south of the Missouri.

Bentonites watched the building with interest that summer, an interest that grew keener as the structure approached completion. William Morrow, Shonkin cattleman, proudly reported to the River Press that he was first to cross as a "passenger" in early November, scrambling over the planks between piers of an uncompleted section. A week or so later Mrs. Dan Searles, wife of the paper's editor, became the first lady to walk the planks. It was completed in early December and John H. Green, another cattleman, was head of the line with a light rig; freighter Ben Sweigert drove the first outfit over.

Mollie Culbertson, born 1885, had sweeter recollections about the bridge; her grandparents, Mr. and Mrs. John R. Smith, were toll collectors at a little station beside it, and after accompanying one to the Power store to turn in the day's receipts, the man there gave her a lollypop. After, Mollie was nearly always present for the two block walk down Front Street. Tolls in June 1889, one way, 30c for wagon and two horses, 75c for three wagons and six horses. Two way passage was somewhat under double, and tickets in advance saved 10%.

## Fort Benton Shows The Doubters

For a municipality apparently doomed by events beyond its control, Fort Benton had already, that year of 1888, added a couple of firsts in Montana to its long list of such occurrences. Like the bridge, roots were in the previous year, but remaining residents could strut a bit.

Saturday evening, March 17, 1888, at a banquet in the Chouteau House attended by the leaders in Fort Benton business, the city celebrated the beginning of an electric light system and opening of its brand new waterworks. Mayor Jere Sullivan and Joseph Baker were among the speakers, and George Woolston of Helena, who had secured the franchises for both, told his audience that the city had enough water pump capacity for a population of 10,000.

The projects somewhat awed state papers, the New Northwest saying that Fort Benton was many times ahead of Butte and the rest of Montana, save only for the Woolston scheme for Helena. The electric plant at Helena was tested briefly in April, beginning on their municipal waterworks would get underway soon. The Copper Camp simply couldn't be bothered with such frills of civilization.

The lighting franchise would terminate and after an interval be replaced by a locally financed plant. Woolston eventually sold the water plant to the city and with gradual improvements it became the nucleus of the system of today.

Electricity was far more familiar to Bentonites than to residents of many eastern towns and cities. First witnessed in the form of a searchlight on the Rosebud in 1882, five of the last boats to come to Fort Benton were so equipped.

The water plant was a much more pressing need. The refuse of more than 20 years of freight trains had contaminated ground water, residents had proposed numerous plans for supplying the city, including tapping both nearby Shonkin and Teton streams for same. Another matter was fire, the townsite was dotted with flammable haystacks and barns, a hook and ladder and pumper were already on hand, and one of the first tests of George Woolston's water works was by the volunteer firemen, Tom Todd loudly directing as they poured a stream of water onto the roof of the Grand Union Hotel, tallest building in town. Another result, residents turned in earnest that summer to hauling in and planting cottonwoods and shrubbery of all kinds from Teton and Shonkin valleys—at last there was water available to make trees and gardens grow. Pictures of early 1880s show an almost treeless Fort Benton—recurring fuel shortages had doomed anything big enough to burn in the hard winters. Waterfront parks were laid out and gradually beautified, too.

Wool Growers Association members gathered as usual at Fort Benton in March, 1888, and looking to the wool freighting season, high on the agenda of sheepmen and city alike, was a big, new wool warehouse. The Board of Trade by April 11 was planning, in June the contract was let for a 100x108x15 structure in the lower part of town near the river, completed by early July. In all, by three Power boats and the Manitoba railroad, 1.5 million pounds were shipped. One of the shipments, Pres. Lewis with three teams and 12 wagons from the Judith Basin with 130 big wool sacks, the 25,000 pounds only a fifth of the Severance & Co. clip.

It seemed only a sort of anticlimax that the second of the Big Four Fort Benton merchants, by now Murphy Maclay, was holding a closing out sale as a preliminary to a move of all operations to Great Falls.

There would be more hard knocks, Gans & Klein were closing out their clothing store about the time the census taker in 1890 was finding only 624 population in Fort Benton, down almost a thousand from 1880, while Great Falls was looking for a count of way over five thousand, the census taker came up 20% short of that. Then the pioneer survivor, the I. G. Baker Co. in September announced a closing out sale, the Conrads were leaving, though several millions richer than the silver dollar they'd arrived with in 1868.

Actually, for Fort Benton, the worst was over, but its future would take an entirely different course, and never again would the head of navigation be of such import to the rest of Montana.

# **M**inorities **S**hare **S**tory

## Majority Became Minority

*B*ecause St. Louis was founded by the French when that nation was in possession of Louisiana, and French and Spaniards were among the early fur traders looking westward, it was natural that these would turn to countrymen for the workmen they hired, usually on contract to serve one or more years. Of about 50 men taking a keelboat to Fort McKenzie in 1833, French far outnumbered English speakers.

Although the bourgeois and clerks of the Fort Benton area were chiefly English speakers with a high proportion of Scotch-Irish, it was years before these caught up in overall numbers. As late as 1862-63 a list of Fort Benton residents shows 20 of 37 with French names, plus one Spaniard, and some of the others may have had French origins.

The 1870 Fort Benton census lists 97 French speaking males and four females, in a population of 367, so the minority was a sizable one. Indians and part Indians numbered about the same. The 1880 census of 1618 persons shows 85 males and 22 females from Canada. Only about half of these had names appearing to be French.

Most of these lonely French speaking whites in early years took Indian wives, and ultimately a sizable number, and many of the other whites, gravitated into the Blackfeet reservation area. Today's white names in the area include dozens very familiar in Fort Benton more than a century before. The gradual increase in numbers of white women was undoubtedly a major factor in this movement; the story of the squawmen and their families could be turned into an interesting treatise.

The French contributions to Montana place names is considerable. Some early ones: Cracon du nez (bridge of the nose) for the narrow neck of land between the Teton and Missouri rivers is one example. Bec d'otard (Goosebill) for a prominent butte, and Genou (The Knee) for another, further examples. Chouteau county is named for the long time head of American Fur Co., Pierre. Teton (breast) and Gros Ventres (big bellies) are names of a county and Indian tribe. A square dance club and woman's club adopting the names reportedly retreated in confusion when the words were interpreted. Pondera (county) is a corruption of Pend d'Oreille, and another corruption is chantier (boatyard) in Shonkin for the small stream.

The French voyageur, like his counterpart in the Hudson Bay Co. area, was a superior boatman, industrious, if too often thoughtless workman on the portages and cordelle, and compared to today's workers, much abused by his superiors. Working for a pittance annually he usually ended in debt to the company or at least had little to show for the dangers, sweat and toil in Indian country.

But as in any such society, a few loom as men in their own right. One of those who gravitated south to the employ of Kenneth McKenzie is among the first to emerge as far superior to the ordinary mangers du lard (lard eaters), the ordinary workmen. In 1830 Jacob Berger (Jacques Bercier) agreed to lead a party of Dacoteau, Morceau and one other to the Marias country, to negotiate with the Blackfeet to open a trading post in their territory. With the Blackfeet reputation, the trip required courage and diplomacy, especially in leading 100 suspicious tribesmen east to confer with McKenzie at Fort Union. Several times on that trip Berger had to pledge his life that his intentions were honorable. By the time of Fr. Nicholas Point's visit to Fort Lewis in 1846 Berger had become a trader, dealing directly with Indians, for several times the approximately $120 a year common workmen received. In an 1846 sketch he appears as a white headed man.

Augustin Hamell (also Armell, a creek in the Musselshell area bears this name) was in 1853 called "an intelligent voyageur" by Isaac Stevens, as well as interpreter and trader. Fr. Point's journal seemed to indicate that in 1845 he operated a small trading post near Armell's creek; later he was on the Marias near what became Fort Conrad.

Baptiste and Michel Champaigne, probably brothers, were long in the service of American Fur at Fort Benton. Baptiste was an occasional trader, oftener pilot of boats sent down river with robes and furs of the trade. Michel, when married by Fr. Point in 1846, had been with the company 27 years. Besides piloting boats, he was a trusted trader. Charles Frush, in 1858 a visitor at Fort Benton from Fort Owen, was surprised to meet "Miss Champaigne, back from school in St. Louis, dressed in latest style." There is evidence that many of the squawmen attempted to provide education and a better life for their children.

Charles Mercier's connection with the Blackfeet Post was probably the longest. He was born in 1803 near St. Louis, as a boy learned the boat building trade, and in his lifetime doubtless fashioned hundreds. His contract with American Fur began in 1830, and next fall he was with James Kipp's party of 75 which built Fort Piegan at the mouth of the Marias. Mercier was a member of the David Mitchell party which constructed Fort McKenzie in 1832, then served at Fort Chardon, Fort Lewis above Fort Benton and the final post. Being a woodworker, meaning double the wage of an ordinary voyageur, he helped build all the forts. By the time American Fur sold the fort to North West Fur in 1865 he was Old Man Rondin (for round shoulders), and it was for the nickname that Rondin Street (now 10th) was named. He died December 1891 after 60 years in the Fort Benton area that spanned the entire fur trade period. Two other streets, Laurion and Arnoux, bore the names of voyageurs.

Other French residents worthy of note: Vincent Mercure, who built a comfortable competency from boat building and saloon, lost his money in a coal mine venture and killed himself in 1877. Joseph Laurion, partner of Mercure, helped build the first Fort Benton store, Carroll & Steell, in 1864, and died in 1879. James Arnoux, also miner, businessman, county clerk and county commissioner, was the first to homestead on Highwood Creek in 1872, and was another who moved to the Browning area. He died in 1913.

A discontented voyageur was Antoine Juneau, who came to later Montana in 1859 aboard the Chippewa, left American Fur in six months on account of a diet of buffalo jerky straight or soup made from same. For the opposition next year Juneau and companions completed a winter trip to Fort Benton on dog meat. Juneau later trapped on his own, built the first cabin on the Teton River. He died in 1914 at age 81. Part of his 1864 cabin is in the Fort Benton museum.

### White Women A Definite Minority

White women were a definite rarity throughout the early west and certainly in the Fort Benton area. It was not until the later 1870s that appreciable numbers began arriving.

There is the possibility that an employe of one of the fur posts brought a white wife up river, but the first documented appearance of a white woman at Fort Benton was in 1856. Sarah Armstrong Mackey, wife of Rev. Elkanah Mackey,

Presbyterian clergyman, had accompanied her husband to Fort Benton, where he planned a mission to the Blackfeet. Sunday, August 17, there were services in Alexander Culbertson's quarters for whites, and in the Indian room as well. For the Blackfeet this was their first glimpse of a "white squaw." Both the Fort Benton Journal and Edwin Hatch mention the services. Mrs. Mackey, however, became seriously ill the next day, and when the Culbertsons left for the States on September 15 the Mackeys accompanied them.

Culbertson's Blackfeet wife Natawista was probably the most important woman in Fort Benton's history, her influence with the Indians vital to his several successful efforts at peacemaking, especially at Fort McKenzie and at the 1845 council after that fort's destruction, at which peaceful relations were restored.

There were a few white women with the Holmes and Fisk wagon trains of 1862 who visited briefly in Fort Benton. Other visitors that year are certain, from the James Harkness diary, his daughter Margaret and Mrs. Joseph (Pelagie) LaBarge were passengers on the Emilie and on July 1st were the first white women to see the Great Falls of the Missouri. Four steamboats arriving June 17 and 20 were crammed with passengers, some of them women.

First white woman to actually reside in Fort Benton was most likely Mary F. Healy. John Healy went back to the States in 1863 and married her in New York, where their first child was born. Healy returned alone on the Yellowstone in 1864, later brought his wife out, probably in 1865 when he was employed by the Indian agency in Fort Benton, later operated a small hotel in the building.

First white child born in Fort Benton is a matter of conjecture. When Frances Baker, born Dec. 4, 1867, revisited Fort Benton in 1882, the Benton Record credited her with being the first white child. A reader told the paper that the first was a child of the John Healys, over a year old when the Baker child was born, the second the son of Mrs. James Knight who afterwards died at old Fort Campbell. The informant may have confused the birthplace of Marie Healy, listed in the 1870 census as New York born, or the Healys had another child who died before the 1870 census. Nothing is available regarding the Knight child, but another antedates Frances Baker. Dr. Roswell Tibbits and wife Mary Jane had a daughter, Hattie Jane, born in Fort Benton May 27, 1867, while he was in practice in the river city.

The dearth of white women in the area is well indicated by the census of 1870 when 272 white males were counted in Fort Benton, and only 13 white females. Of the latter, four were wives and one a child of the military garrison, and there were four other young girls in the place, cutting the number of other adult females to 4, with one of those a member of an ancient profession.

Five years earlier, a Helena item in the Montana Post carried the comment: "Batchelors, take courage—we notice in our daily perambulation members of the fair sex, just arrived from Benton. Let them come. Our cup of happiness sweetens. They are welcome."

The number in the mining camps at least would soon be augmented, that year of 1865. Captain Bill Massie, who had brought the Twilight up the Missouri, recalled being met just above the mouth of the Yellowstone by a flatboat loaded with men, many of whom had been away from home for years, possibly to Colorado, Idaho and finally Montana. The scene when the men boarded the Twilight he said was undescribable, many of the men were meeting wives with children they had never seen or only as babies. But not all, a minister accompanied the men, and in brief but touching rites, 16 couples were married aboard the steamboat that evening. Massie's Twilight, he said, brought the passengers of half a dozen other boats to Fort Benton from the Marias, where low water had stalled the boats, but in the shallowest spots the throngs had to get off and walk a few hundred yards.

It would really be unfair to leave the gold rush period without mention of Eleanor Dumont, better known as Madame Mustache, who, according to an enduring Fort Benton legend left her gambling hall on Front Street brandishing a pair of pistols to warn the pilot of a steamboat (possibly the Walter B. Dance) that if he didn't sheer off from landing he'd be packing more lead than was healthy. The writer is inclined to favor another steamboat and later year than 1867, for in February 1870 this placid damsel opened the "Golden Gate" in Helena near enough the Herald office that the boys on the paper could learn the new fangled vingt et un, at a price, from Miss Dumont. Later in Fort Benton Dena Murray operated the well named "Jungle" in the building the Madame had left. Dena died in 1884 as a woman "who had accumulated considerable wealth."

William Wesley Van Orsdel stepped down the gangplank of the Far West at Fort Benton June 30, 1872, and a few hours later held a Methodist prayer service, attended he recalled, by the only white woman in Fort Benton. She was Mrs. George Baker—the place probably had a population of around 160, and there was another white woman, Margaret Stocking, wife of W. S., but they had gone to ranching on the Teton River about four miles from town, near what became the stage and horse freighter outfits Whoop Up Crossing. Most everything in Montana Territory was standing still in 1872, population dwindling as survivors were killed in bar room brawls or out on the trails by hostiles.

Fort Benton was still almost completely a man's town when W. H. Buck began the Benton Record on February 1, 1875, writing in part: Fort Benton "commands the traffic of the country...is the transportation centre of Montana." Almost as an afterthought he ended: "To conclude without paying a tribute of respect to the ladies, would be an unpardonable error; yet, fearful of being accused of flattery, we shall merely state that the ladies of Benton are good, they are kind." Yet there is virtually no mention of white women, good or bad, as legitimate trade into Canada is opened and swells tremendously; as the Benton Road to Helena becomes Montana's great thoroughfare.

Steamboat passenger lists of those first Record years record an occasional Mr. and Mrs., fewer families, with a few others, usually female relatives of men in business, gradually increasing past the midyears of the decade of the 1870s. A few notations would indicate it almost customary for an expectant mother to return to her family home before childbirth, for example Mrs. M. A. Flanagan in 1875.

For most of the single ladies who did venture west marriage often came swiftly, Kate Babbage to Wm. Rowe and Emma Brinkman to Charles Rowe three weeks apart in February 1876, Alice Seifred to John W. Tattan in April.

Short school terms had been held during the gold rush boom of the 1860s for about three years, resumed in 1873 with a partly male staff, the latter fact a blessing on the frontier. Teacher turnover was terrific with the "marms." By 1877 there were enough children that a small brick school house was begun, certainly a sign of changing times.

Once rowdy Fort Benton by 1877 had quieted so much that Record Editor W. H. Buck could scarcely believe it, although to newcomers the street scenes were probably a bit chaotic. The year marked the end of the Indian wars, and ever growing prosperity for the head of navigation, by then certainly as Buck first envisioned it, commanding the traffic of the country. Hundreds of men were employed in freighting to almost every settlement in the territory, to every point in later Alberta and parts of the two adjoining provinces. Whether man hunting or not, northern Montana was a land of opportunity for the gradually increasing female influx.

For two 18 year old girls aboard the Montana, which tied up at Fort Benton June 23, 1879, the trip from Bismarck had been the event of a lifetime. There was the scenery, especially the stunning White Cliffs area. Further there was the unremitting attention of every unattached male aboard the biggest and that year the finest steamboat on the upper Missouri. Alicia Stanford was traveling with her mother and two brothers, Kitty Tonge with her older sister, Mrs. George (Frances) Clendenin. Friendship between the two girls continued well past the steamboat trip. Neither was in a hurry to pick and choose among the eligible males of Fort Benton. Instead they teamed to open a select day school—both were well educated, and the project as a team event lasted two terms. It took perhaps the town's most eligible bachelor, Charles E. Conrad, a year and a half to convince Alicia to name the day, which came January 4, 1881. Kitty continued operation of her school. In February 1882 her sister's husband, an old timer of Musselshell adventure, Coulson steamboat representative at Fort Benton and into mining, was killed in a mine cavein at Barker. Not too long later Kitty created something of a sensation by becoming Fort Benton's first saleslady back of the dry goods counter at the Power store. "One of Benton's most popular young ladies," to quote the River Press, continued there for a time, but in September 1884 she was listed as a primary teacher. That did it. July 8, 1885, Miss Kate B. Tonge and William J. Hinckley were married; the husband was bookkeeper at the Bank of Northern Montana. Just when they left Fort Benton, unknown.

By the 1880 census the disparity between the sexes had dwindled sharply, approximately 1200 males and 400 females.

Which helps explain W. H. Buck's somewhat bemused comment in the Benton Record on occasion of the grand ball which formally opened the Grand Union Hotel November 1882, attended, he noted, "by almost 100 of the fair sex." When the Record began in 1875 he could have counted on the fingers of one hand.

The steady improvement in the sex ratio can be credited with taming what at one time may have been the toughest town on the frontier. Schools, churches and hospital, dealt with elsewhere, were another phase of that growing influence.

### Blacks On The Frontier

Blacks were in evidence on the frontier from earliest times, as witness York, Captain Clark's servant, with the Lewis & Clark expedition, who was freed by his owner after return. There were a few among the Mountain Men, for example Jim Beckwourth, actually a mulatto.

First known in the Fort Benton area was Tom Reese, killed near Fort McKenzie in 1844, his slaying by Blackfeet a cause of Harvey and Chardon turning a cannon on a trading party that year. Another early arrival was Henry Mills, who may have been owned by Kenneth McKenzie, and a resident of Fort Benton from about 1850. Phillip Barnes is listed among Fort Benton residents the winter of 1862-63. James Price was one of ten men killed on the Marias in May 1865, Bloods later reporting him the toughest fighter of the group.

Following the end of the Civil War and emancipation, Blacks began showing up in numbers in the Fort Benton area; indeed, over the frontier. The 1870 Chouteau county census shows 16 males, nearly all in Fort Benton, and four females in Benton, 11 more males along the Missouri River in Dawson county. Most were laborers or servants, several were cooks; barber and teamster were the other occupations found. Wm. Bond was the only Black noted in the whisky trade in Canada; he was arrested by Mounted Police, escaped from jail but was drowned in flight.

By the 1880 count there were nearly 50 Blacks found on the census list in Fort Benton. Most were clustered in a small area on Main Street. Occupations were much as in 1870, but one operated a saloon; another, at the time a barber, soon would.

Fort Benton at the time included numbers of men who had fought for the South, and prejudice flared in 1881 when a couple of Black children were to be admitted to the Fort Benton school. The Benton Record, democratic, didn't approve, later published a petition to force a separate school for Black children, a move trustees had voted against on account of expense, though such schools were set up in other Montana settlements. The republican River Press in an editorial wrote, "The time has certainly come when the old prejudice on account of color should be rooted out." A couple of subscribers stopped their papers, no outcome found in files.

Two Black sisters, Maria and Mary Adams, came to Fort Benton from Bismarck in 1878 on the Nellie Peck. Mary died some time before May 13, 1879, as a probate notice so dated in the Benton Record named Maria as administratrix of Mary's estate. The latter, a servant of the Custer family, played a part in the later controversy over the Little Big Horn battle. She made affidavit that she had overheard General Terry's final instructions to Custer, telling the latter to "use his own judgement," in effect a free hand in combat decisions.

Maria married John Lambert "Duke" Dutriueille, Fort Benton barber. Duke was a curious mixture, born of a Jamaican mother and French colonial father in a U. S. port aboard a ship. He served General Joe Hooker in the Civil War before coming west. Furthermore, pictures show him a dwarf. Duke came to Fort Benton in 1879, moved back to Helena, returned at least once more before settling in Belt where he and his wife died in this century.

A more flambouyant barber was Wm. Foster, in Fort Benton by or before 1877, who in 1880 decided to better himself by opening or leasing a saloon, which he named the Eagle Bird. A surviving picture shows the structure leaning precariously toward a frame court house on Main Street. January 5, 1883, fire started in the Eagle Bird, taking the court house as well. Foster, not in the least daunted, found another location and opened the appropriately named Phoenix shortly. It didn't last long; the June 2, 1883, Benton Record reported that Foster had skipped town, and creditors would like to know his whereabouts. Foster was murdered at end of track on the Canadian Pacific September 21, 1884.

One other Black business man in early day Fort Benton was Lee Isabel, who had the Break of Day House in 1878 and for a year was associated with John H. Gamble, English born, in the Star bakery about the same period. Isabel died of consumption in March 1881. Gamble, who may have financed him, took over the business.

While numbers of Chinese increased in the late years of the century in the area, few Blacks were in evidence on the 1900 census, and in the first half of the century for years shoemaker Peter Burnett and wife were the only members of the race in Fort Benton.

## Fort Benton's Chinese

Chinese, brought in by the thousands by Charles Crocker to build the Central Pacific to its meeting with the Union Pacific at Promontory, Utah, in 1869, were a strange and persecuted minority in the west, especially regarded as a threat by white workers. Fort Benton, possibly more cosmopolitan in outlook, seemingly didn't give a damn one way or other. A June 1883 Benton Record duly reported arrival of five who came by boat to start a Chinese store, adding mention of an earlier Celestial who bought a squaw in Benton for two sacks of flour.

Only three, Sam Loy, Chang Haw and Lee Wang were listed in the 1870 census, all as washermen, and in 1872 two Chinese paid $15 a quarter as license for laundries. The 1880 census shows nine Chinese as cooks or in laundries, while that of 1900 lists nearly 30. By that time some of the younger men were houseboys and cooks in local homes; several ranches list them as well. Interestingly, in Fort Benton Mrs. John Smith taught classes of two to four, bright pupils in learning to read, write and speak English, reported her granddaughter, Mollie Culbertson Sedgwick.

The earliest Chinese clustered on Fort Benton's Main Street, site of a laundry for years. By 1880 they centered on a block or so above the Grand Union Hotel, the uppermost sector long known as the Chinaman's gardens. One sold imported silk, a couple operated their own restaurants—their business distressing to white owners in depression years toward statehood.

Bentonites in general regarded them with more curiosity than wrath, an 1881 funeral for Quong Chong drawing a lengthy account in the Benton Record.

One Chinese custom did draw lengthy disapproval in the River Press, after a January 1881 visit by a reporter to an opium den. "Demonical Dens" went on for most of two columns. The effect of an opium pipe was described as producing "a pleasant effect of dreamy insensibility." The reporter found another den on Main Street, was enough under the influence that he did not stay long. The next week the Press was informed that the sheriff had his eye on the matter. It was, however, June before the Benton Record reported a raid on an opium den.

New Great Falls in mid-1887 had proclaimed its own Chinese exclusion act, their early legends including a brutal enforcement, by putting any Chinese into an oarless boat, shoved into the Missouri with ultimate passage over the series of falls likely.

Bentonites couldn't see what the fuss was about, even if there was a fracas in the Chinese saloon and Hong posted $500 bail for assault with two beer bottles and a tack hammer on Wong Woo and Tong Fong. After all, no whites were involved. Three months later throngs turned out for Chinese New Year's treats at Lee Gee's restaurant, Sam Lee's wash house and Sing Lee's saloon.

The influx of Orientals into Chouteau county late in the century was partially explained August 1891 when Gus Brede was killed by lightning in a terrific storm the 5th. First report was that he was sitting between two Chinese, who were unhurt, adding a bit to Fort Benton legend, for the hill beyond the Teton since has been Chinaman hill. The coroner's report found he was alone on the wagon seat, nine Chinese being smuggled from Fort Macleod concealed in the wagon. Eight were marked for deportation, the ninth, Lee Sing, proved himself a legal U. S. resident— he was doubtless along to locate spots for his countrymen. Brede previously had been fined $1,000 by the Mounted Police for smuggling whisky into Canada, and his outfit previously confiscated by the customs collector in Fort Benton for smuggling Chinese.

There was a new law in 1891 requiring all Chinese to be photographed; Dan Dutro mugged 21 in Fort Benton, 18 at Fort Assiniboine, 14 at Havre and 9 at Chinook. The last Chinese in Fort Benton operated the Quan Cafe until February 1923 when a cook hung himself, and manager Tom Mum and staff closed the cafe the same day and left for Butte.

## And A Scattering Of Hispanics

There were even a few Hispanics in the Fort Benton area in early days. Not too surprisingly, actually, as Spain ruled Louisiana Territory for a number of years prior to the U. S. purchase. One of the most adventurous was Spaniard Manuel Lisa, though in trade on the Yellowstone, who built the first white structure in later Montana near the mouth of the Big Horn in 1807. Some historians believe he was dissuaded from trying the Missouri by John Colter.

There were three from Mexico with Indian wives and four children listed on the 1870 census and two or three more working at woodyards along the Missouri in Dawson county.

First account involving Hispanics was in an 1864 Montana Post, an unsigned account with no year shown, of a party of six getting out saw logs (probably at Highwood or Sun River) for the fur company at Fort Benton. They were under siege by Indians for five days in a crude cabin near the Missouri. "One of the six was a brave Spaniard." The Spaniard made several efforts to get water, unsuccessfully— next day he shot one Indian and also managed to get a bucket of water, the day after made an effort to break out but was run back to the cabin. The wooders cut off the soles of their raw bull hide moccasins, soaked them in the water and ate them, beat off several more attacks by the Indians. Between fights they polished off the moccasins, and in a rain after five days managed to get to the river, took two logs per man in twilight, floated down the Missouri, reaching Fort Benton by sunrise.

Antoine Grames Amei of Taos was working for Mose Solomon in the Cypress Hills in 1873 when Fort Benton wolfers killed a number of Assiniboines, and was a crown witness in an 1875 extradition hearing. About the same time Jose Pablo Trojie (Mexican Joe) was killed by Sioux on the Stillwater. Another, "Spanish Joe" Hill, whisky trader, was arrested in 1873, then turned to freighting. He was killed by the kick of a freight horse near Choteau in 1884.

Toward the end of the territorial period, Spaniards proper and Basques were chiefly sheep shearers and herders.

## The Interracial Minority

Marriages by Indian custom, began with the first intrusion of whites into Blackfeet country, when Fort Piegan was abandoned at the end of the 1831-32 trading season, a very few of the employes at the post remained with the tribesmen over the winter, to be with newfound wives. In 1833 when Maximilian of Wied and artist Karl Bodmer came up river to Fort McKenzie, an August 27 note was of the marriage of Alexander Culbertson to a daughter of White Buffalo. "According to the local custom, he had paid to the value of 100 dollars for her and his Piegan wife had brought him a rifle. A horse was to follow." By Indian custom, divorce was about as simple.

However, many such marriages were as permanent as those blessed by Fr. Point in 1846-47 at first Fort Lewis. In some cases of the eight or nine marriages so sanctified, there doubtless were children of the couples as attendants.

The children of white and red worlds faced an uncertain and precarious future, too much for some. Whether termed half breeds or mixed bloods, it was no easy path in life. Some held to one way of life, some to the other.

While first generation of mixed marriages usually showed the fact, and were often mistrusted by both races, those of quarter blood either way tended toward the three quarter side in appearance and adaptation, and seemed to be accepted. Many Montana white families have been surprised to find great grandmother was pure Blackfeet, and doubtless the latter have been startled in similar manner.

With a gradual increase in the number of whites after influx of miners, feelings between races grew beyond distrust to hatred. Indians knew they had been robbed of their heritage, whites reckoned what the hostility of the stricken remainder meant to lives and property. Truly, to the whites, "the only good Indian was a dead one" had the ring of truth; the all but helpless Blackfeet by the early 1870s could do little but nurse their hatreds.

The two way animosity was crossed by a few of the white squawmen, a very few reds. Among these was Little Dog of the Piegans, who in the bitter winter of 1865-66 saved lives of dozens of miners around Sun River. Little Dog in 1866 was killed by fellow tribesmen, perhaps a loss to both races. Whites adopted a few Indian children, notably John Healy after a raid at Sun River when a Blackfeet warrior was mortally wounded by raiders in protecting his young son. "Die easy, father," Healy told the Indian, "I will care for your son." The boy was long known on the border as Joe Healy.

Fort Benton as agency and trading post, had a greater number of mixed bloods than other points in Montana. The 1870 Fort Benton census shows 36 males and 62 females listed as half Indian, 15 female Indians, most wives of whites, and 16 quarter blood. Virtually all were of Blackfeet derivation. Numbers had dwindled a bit by 1880, with 65 of Indian blood and all the adults female, with 40 or 50 half breed children. In the next two decades influx of white females was doubtless reason for the all but complete disappearance of mixed blood families from Fort Benton. In some cases the white husband cut the marriage ties, occasionally the Indian wife, but in a surprising number of instances white husbands refused to disown their families and moved northward with them.

W. S. Stocking, Fort Benton resident from 1866, echoed the usual white view. "There was never any such thing as a Noble Red Man...nor a handsome squaw." Yet he noted another fact, "a squaw wife was nearly always faithful to her white husband, and would tell him everything she found out from the men or women of her tribe." For that reason, whites could usually find out which Indians had stolen horses, robbed a camp or killed a white settler, Stocking said.

## Despite Mixed Heritage, Some Stood Out

Most successful adaptation to both white and red heritage was Jerry Potts, born about 1840 to the Blood woman Namo-Pisi (Crooked Back) and Andrew R. Potts, Scot trader at Fort McKenzie. Jerry's father was killed at a trading wicket by a Blackfeet when the boy was a few months old. Jerry's godfathers were first Alexander Harvey, then Andrew Dawson, and he was tutored by kinsmen who were great warriors among Bloods as well. By manhood he was war chief, tracker, hunter and interpreter for whites, a dead shot and great scout. By the mid-1860s he was such a familiar character around Fort Benton that Virginia City and Helena papers carried items simply referring to "Jerry" as if everyone in the territory knew him. On one hunt out of Fort Benton he carelessly ran into seven Crows, killed four and led a raid on the Crow camp on Shonkin creek, the ensuing scalp dance resulted in what W. S. Stocking termed Fort Benton's "wildest night." Jerry and George Star, fellow breed, were principals in a great fight near Lethbridge between Blackfeet, and Crees and Assiniboines in 1870, 300 of the latter killed. Said Jerry, "you could shut your eyes and kill a Cree." Between times he and Star enlivened Fort Benton night life by shooting hairs off each other's mustache for the next round. Jerry hunted and interpreted at the whisky forts in the Whoop Up country in the early 1870s. When the North West Mounted Police came west in 1874, Jerry Potts became their chief scout, advisor, interpreter and trainer of scouts and all but a patron saint of the NWMP.

### Part Blood Business Man

Joe Kipp was born November 29, 1849, at Heart River to James Kipp and Earth Woman, daughter of a Mandan chief. The father in 1831 built the first Blackfeet post, Fort Piegan, at the mouth of the Marias. Kipp also built a comfortable fortune from American Fur dividends and retired to a farm in Missouri about 1860, returning to Fort Benton occasionally to learn of the latest adventures of son Joe. Raven Quiver, to the Blackfeet, Joe earned his schooling—a year in St. Louis—when he restole George Steell's speedy black buffalo runner in 1867 from Indian thieves.

Joe returned to become a scout for the 13th Infantry at Fort Shaw, and in January 1870 tried in vain to prevent troops under Major Eugene Baker from attacking Heavy Runner's peaceful camp on the Marias. Baker put Kipp under guard and threat of his life if he tried to warn the friendlies, and 173 Piegans died. Joe's first wife, Double Strike Woman, was a surviving child of the attack in which her father, Heavy Runner, died.

Kipp was soon up to his ears in the Whoop Up whisky trade, in 1871 on Milk river ridge stood off U. S. Marshal Charles Hard, claiming his party was across the Canadian border. He was wrong by a few hundred yards, right by four rifles to one, and the Canadian post became Fort Stand Off. In December 1873 Kipp was credited with killing the ferocious Blood chief Calf Shirt at Fort Kipp on Oldman River, but had to share the coup after drawing first blood—it took 16 bullets from half a dozen whites to bring down the chief. With the coming of the North West Mounted Police in 1874, Joe Kipp was among traders going legitimate. In 1878 he bought Fort Conrad on the Marias and operated it for several years. James Willard Schultz, later a noted writer, was clerk for Kipp at Fort Conrad as well as Carroll, where in the early 1880s they took in the last of the buffalo robes.

Joe Kipp sold Fort Conrad in 1886 and operated trading posts on Birch Creek, at forgotten Robare and ran a hotel, general store and sawmill in Browning. Despite his part in the Baker Massacre and a mixed blood of another tribe, Kipp gradually rewon trust of the Blackfeet. He was friend and advisor to his adopted tribe in his final years, dying in 1913.

### Another Fur Trader's Active Son

Joseph Culbertson, son of distinguished parents, Alexander Culbertson, peacemaker and founder of Fort Benton, and Natawista Iksana, daughter of Blood chief Father of All Children, was born January 31, 1859, in Peoria, Illinois. He was reared in the lap of luxury; his father Alexander had retired from the fur trade with an at the time large fortune, $300,000. Poor investments and high living dissipated the fortune, and Joe came back up the Missouri as a sprout of 9 in 1868 with his parents. An old timer in the 1920s recalled the day Joe loaded a chief's pipe with gunpowder. The result blew the prized pipe to pieces and it was only by the width of a buffalo hair that the white peacemakers at Fort Hawley escaped with their own hair and a very shaky treaty.

Joe accompanied his father into the then wild Whoop Up trade on Belly River, where Alexander's long acquaintance with the Blackfeet was again turned into successful trade. Still two years short of his teens, he had a second brush with death while with a guide two miles ahead of the Culbertson wagons full of traded robes and furs. The two fell in with a war party of Crees, the companion guide killed. Joe, a small boy aboard a fast buffalo runner, got away with Cree bullets whistling by.

The Culbertsons wintered at Fort Benton and returned north to Fort Whoop Up in the spring of 1871. Next year they switched operations to old Fort Browning on the Milk River, then to Fort Peck, where the father was employed by the Indian service. Alexander was interpreter for the first delegation of Sioux to visit Washington, where 14 year old Joe saw them welcomed by President Grant.

Adventurous Joe Culbertson saw much of tribal warfare, and after the Little Big Horn was scout for General Miles and the army until 1895. After his scouting years Joe for years was peace officer on the reservation at Poplar. He had witnessed the extermination of the buffalo and the final Indian campaigns. Sitting Bull, a personal friend for years, he regarded as the greatest of the Sioux. Joe died in 1923.

## Malcolm Clarke's Descendants Were Gifted

Malcolm Clarke (e is often dropped), 1817-69, was a tempestuous character whose role in early Fort Benton history was exceeded only by its founder. At age 19 after expulsion from West Point for horsewhipping a fellow cadet, he was a lieutenant anyway, under Sam Houston in Texas. At age 24 he joined the American Fur and for years was understudy to Alexander Culbertson, in charge during the latter's frequent absences. He traded on his own in the 1850s, was also in charge of Fort Campbell, in 1861 began a ranch at present Sieben. In early trading years he had gained the Blackfeet name meaning Four Bears after killing that many grizzlies before breakfast one morning, a feat that awed the fierce Blackfeet. His killing at his ranch August 19, 1869, in a tribal feud was the trigger for the Baker Massacre on the Marias the next January.

Two of his daughters were remarkable women, especially in view of the status of their sex at the time and the added handicap of mixed blood. Helen was the older by some years, was a Montana historian, school teacher in Helena and Fort Benton, and very evidently a champion of the Indians. She was employed by the Indian service as educator and in other capacities. A two page picture in "The Women," Time-Life Old West, shows her on the Otoe agency in Oklahoma in the 1890s.

Isabel Clarke was born in 1861 at the Sieben ranch. She witnessed the murder of her father at age 8, and nearly fatal wounding of her brother Horace. Later she was sent east for schooling in St. Paul, with emphasis on music. She returned to Fort Benton in 1879, spending the winter at the Horace Clarke ranch on Highwood Creek. Isabel was first employed as governess to the family of the Flathead Indian agent, then as matron and teacher of the Blackfeet at Old Agency and promptly earned the name Singing Woman among her charges. Her piano had been brought up the Missouri and taken to the Clarke ranch. About 1884 Joe Kipp freighted the piano to the Old Agency school. (The piano, one of the first in Montana Territory, was given the Fort Benton museum in 1972.)

In 1891 Isabel Clarke and Tom Dawson, son of Andrew Dawson, were married at St. Peter's Mission near Birdtail Rock, union of families of early day figures in Fort Benton history. Dawson was born in 1859 within the adobe walls of old Fort Benton; the two had been introduced by Helen Clarke after Isabel's return to Montana. In the early 1890s the Dawson homestead near East Glacier was the place Indians and homesteaders held church services, the piano serving as an altar.

Of a third Clarke daughter, Judith, educated with Isabel, nothing found except that a daughter of Judith was adopted by the Dawsons.

It was a nephew, terribly handicapped, who was to surpass his aunts.

John Clarke, son of Horace and his Indian wife, was born at the ranch on Highwood in 1881. At the age of two an attack of scarlet fever left him permanently deaf and mute. He was taught to read and write at the Fort Shaw Indian school and sent to schools for the deaf in North Dakota, Montana and Milwaukee, Wisconsin. It was at the latter school that he was introduced to wood carving.

John Clarke had a natural talent for the art and received almost immediate and widespread attention in his life work at a studio in East Glacier. He worked chiefly with cottonwood, a difficult material because of its soft, spongy texture, by him used as an asset for wildlife carvings with realistically shaggy animal fur. He also did some stone carving, painted landscapes and sketched Indian and wildlife subjects. By his death in 1970 "The Man Who Speaks Not" was recognized as an outstanding expert in his chief medium.

### Lone Wolf Returns To Montana

James Willard Schultz, New York born, came west as a boy of 17, most likely in 1877, possibly May 7 but more probably July 20, aboard the steamboat Benton to Fort Benton. The later noted writer and champion of the Blackfeet gave various versions of his steamboat trip, none definitely proven. He promptly made friends with Sol Abbott, squawman, who lived among the Blackfeet as Sorrel Horse. Later Schultz worked for Joe Kipp (referred to usually as Berry or Raven Quiver). Schultz lived among the Blackfeet when their world was falling apart, took part in their raids and tribal warfare. In 1879 he married Natahki of the Piegans, a survivor of the Baker Massacre of 1870. Their son, Hart Merriam Schultz, was born in 1882.

The son, who preferred Lone Wolf, the name given him by his Blackfeet grandfather, grew up at the Schultz ranch on the Marias and Two Medicine, among the Indians of the reservation. The year his mother died in 1903, the father had to leave Montana after acting as guide for game killing Ralph Pullitzer, son of the noted publisher, and went to California where his reputation as an author of Indian days and ways grew.

Lone Wolf by that time had begun painting, earned his way as a cowhand and due to poor health seasonally drifted southward to Arizona, a migration that continued for him until about 1955; the southland in the cold months, to the Blackfeet in the summer. It was not until 1909 that father and son met again. The same year at the Grand Canyon Lone Wolf met the noted artist Thomas Moran, who encouraged him in a full time career as an artist, first attending schools in Los Angeles and Chicago. Working with oil and as sculptor, Lone Wolf's reputation peaked in the 1920s, when the Indian artist's paintings were a sensation. The next decade found him far more than dabbling in sculpture; his popularity gradually dwindling in the 1930s. His final 25 years were plagued by arthritis aggravated by the early bronc busting years.

Lone Wolf or Hart Merriam Schultz died February 9, 1970, in Tucson, one of the last of the real west's artists. The next spring his wife of 54 years brought Lone Wolf's ashes back to Montana for burial on the land of his childhood. Lone Wolf had returned to Montana.

# The Original Montanans
## Blackfeet Bloodlock

*A*nyone checking the indexes of books on the Mountain Men can note that there are more entries under Blackfeet than for any other Indian tribe. One example, Arthur Clark's series of biographies of these adventurous men. Almost two thirds of a page in fact, and Blood, Atsina and Gros Ventres entries swell the total.

Looking at the maps based on early explorations of the west, there are large, chiefly blank spaces in the northern half of present Montana east of the Rockies. Of course the Mountain Men knew the valley of the Yellowstone, where the Crows, at times hostile in early years of the fur trade, grew friendlier, and the whites also knew the area of the Flatheads and Shoshones to the west and south.

There was reason for the discrepancies. If the Mountain Men were the most independent, cantankerous breed of men who ever existed, the Blackfeet and associated Gros Ventres could well qualify as the most recalcitrant, toughest fighters of the Indian nations—certainly if rivals existed in frontier days they were the Apaches of the Southwest and just possibly Cheyennes or Comanches in between.

White knowledge of the Blackfeet country was hard and bloodily learned. Lewis and Clark heard much of the tribe at the Mandan villages from traders out of Canada. First encounter of the "Big Knives," as Blackfeet soon termed Americans, was near Cut Bank creek July 27, 1806, when two Piegans were killed by the knife of Reuben Field and the pistol of Meriwether Lewis after tribesmen attempted to grab rifles and run off horses. For a quarter century there was more hair than beaver collected in Blackfeet country.

The Blackfeet were the reason for existence of the series of trading posts ending with Fort Benton, and the posts were part of a cultural evolution of the tribe; in the end, the fact of their existence all but destroyed the Blackfeet.

There were three tribes, Siksika or Blackfeet proper, Kainah or Bloods, Pikuni or Piegans, roughly in order south from the Saskatchewan, and the associated Gros Ventres.

Ethnologists generally seem to believe the Blackfeet were among the first Algonkian speaking peoples to move west onto the great plains in prehistory. Around 1750 first white contacts with Blackfeet were made by traders from eastern Canada.

At the time the northern tribes were in an early period of cultural evolution involving their staff of life, the buffalo. Indians in the southwest around 1600 obtained horses from Spanish settlers. In a surprisingly few decades, the horse reached the northern Indians. The Blackfeet had been sadly shocked by mounted enemies, the Shoshones, around 1730—a couple of decades later were making up the lack. Alexander Culbertson told historian Bradley that "even as late as 1833 they were poorly mounted." Guns, even the crude North West muskets, in the hands of northern enemies, were another shock. Need for firearms to cope with enemies doubtless did much to make Canadian traders welcome in Blackfeet country. The traders also brought in metal in the form of knives, arrowheads (which effectively ended flint knapping) and kettles, a boon to squaws.

With the horse, the northern tribes found buffalo could be killed as needed, replacing the wasteful piskun, where hundreds of animals might be driven to death. The horse also made the moves of the necessarily nomadic tribes far easier than in the pre-horse days when dogs with small travois and squaws with back packs had to move camp.

## First Canadian Posts

Hudson's Bay traders had a post on the lower Saskatchewan by 1774, at the turn of the century were competing with Nor'Westers in Blackfeet country on the Bow River. Traders from the north were in the Mandan villages when Lewis and Clark arrived. Canadian traders "Northern White Men" to Indians, brought in two products that proved to be immensely in demand—tobacco, the worst of the white man's weed was far better than herbs, grass and bark, and alcohol. The latter in particular would have an effect on Blackfeet home life.

## Big Knives In False Start

First Americans, of record at least, to reach Blackfeet country were Lewis & Clark in 1805, who were happy to have no encounters on that passage. Next year of course Lewis and party had the encounter on Cut Bank drainage. This was the first contact and set a pattern. John Colter, siding with a Crow party a couple of years later in a fight with Blackfeet, helped establish the "Big Knives" as enemies. Colter's boss, Manuel Lisa, who built a trading post at the Big Horn in 1807, had compounded this by trading with the enemy, Crows. Lisa's party were just forerunners of the invasion of Mountain Men, who swarmed westward in small and occasionally large parties after brown gold—beaver pelts.

The Northern Blackfeet, meanwhile, were in good trading position in Canada, the Bloods also able to trade at Rocky Mountain House, which left the most numerous group, Piegans, isolated. This tribe provided most of the beaver pelts, and were the most pitiless toward poaching white trappers. The Blackfeet by 1830 had nearly exterminated the northern bands of Shoshones, driving the remnants south and west of the Three Forks area, and forced Selish tribes on the eastern flank of the Rockies westward.

Piegans and Gros Ventres chiefly, then met the Mountain Men head on along the streams and trails of the northern Rockies. Blackfeet turned back Andrew Henry and Pierre Menard in 1810 at the Three Forks with a loss of more than twenty white trappers. It was about a decade before the whites tried that in force again. But smaller parties did. George Catlin, portrayer of Indians, in 1832 talked with one trapper who had tried Blackfeet country seven times. In five of those trips, he had lost his entire outfit, regarded tribal domains as "bad medicine" for certain. But during 1811-1820 Mountain Men generally skirted Blackfeet country. Next year Robert Jones and Michael Immell tried the Three Forks, found warning signs and were high tailing it out when they ran into ambush, the two leaders and five others killed, four wounded. In all 23 survived, but all their equipment had been looted. In 1823 Andrew Henry sent a party to the Missouri, near the mouth of Smith River had another battle, four dead, others wounded. By 1837 Alfred Jacob Miller, artist, believed 40 or 50 white beaver trappers were killed each season. Mountain Men, no bargains as fighters, with better arms probably killed more Blackfeet.

It was little wonder that the tribe became the "Terrible Blackfeet." The Mountain Men usually termed them "Bug's Boys," vernacular for Satan's imps.

Jim Bridger, perhaps greatest of the Mountain Men, was a lightning rod for Blackfeet. From his fight in 1823 at Smith River he could scarcely set foot in Montana without drawing an attack. In fall 1832 Henry Vanderburgh, trailing

Bridger and "Broken Hand" Fitzpatrick, ran into ambush and was killed. Perhaps in gratitude for tolling the other party into ambush, Blackfeet parked two arrows in Bridger, and then young Mountain Chief counted two great coups, hitting Bridger with his coupstick and wresting away his rifle—the greater as Bridger survived to have one of the arrows dug out of him by Marcus Whitman on the Oregon Trail. Charles Chouquette of Fort Benton, always recalled the April 1849 fight at the Great Falls of the Missouri when three from the fort joined Bridger and 80 men. They had a long tough fight with 400 Blackfeet near the site of the later city.

The Blackfeet slogan for the raid and counter raid raging was quite definitely, "Trappers never!" They were soon to revise that a bit.

### The First Blackfeet Post

American Fur Co. in 1827 bought out rival Missouri Fur and acquired the services of Kenneth McKenzie, one of the canniest of Scot fur traders. He built Fort Union in 1828 just outside later Montana near the mouth of the Yellowstone. He soon sent Jacob Berger and three men up the Missouri to treat with the Blackfeet, definitely a courageous group. They flew an American flag as a symbol of peaceful intentions and made contact with a band of Piegans, and wintered with them. Next year Berger led a suspicious band of 50 or more on the long trip to Fort Union, where McKenzie made a personal treaty permitting establishment of a trading post of Long Knives in Blackfeet country.

Quite apparently that slogan had become, "Traders yes, trappers never!"

James Kipp and 44 men built the first Blackfeet Post at the mouth of the Marias in the fall of 1831. Almost as work started here came a large band of Piegans to trade. It took all Kipp's persuasive powers to get them to leave for 75 days while Fort Piegan was built. It is logical to believe no workman dallied during the grace period. The Piegans on return were amazed to find a completed post with stockades 25 feet high.

Kipp opened trade in grandiose manner. He had converted a barrel of alcohol into 200 gallons of what Hudson's Bay traders termed "Blackfoot rum." Natives had it as "white man's water," to be a staple of trade and ultimately a white men's secret (and profitable) weapon of destruction. That winter Bloods tried to destroy Fort Piegan, besieged it for 11 days. Kipp ultimately loaded a four pound cannon with grapeshot, its discharge brought a big cottonwood crashing down, and Bloods called off the siege. Two chiefs came in to parley, and told Kipp that Hudson's Bay employes had urged them to attack the post, confirming long held opinions of American Fur traders. The Britishers in off moments admitted buying pillaged furs, denied of course anything more. (American traders on occasion did the same.)

Kipp reminded the Blood chiefs that Fort Piegan had never fired back during the siege, and the tribe brought in 3,000 buffalo robes to trade.

### Emphasis On Buffalo Robes

Buffalo robes? Suddenly the Blackfeet were wealthy in white men's trade goods. Hudson's Bay traders could not take any great number of robes, no matter the quality, over the river and portage and lake system back to Montreal or Quebec. With the Missouri flowing by the string of fur posts along its banks, the Americans could take any number and profit tremendously. Further, beaver, the staple of the Rocky Mountain chain, was no longer in such demand, price dropping as white dandies turned from felt (beaver) hats to silk.

Another and tribal effect, the hard working women of the Blackfeet could tan only so many robes in a season. Logistics therefore said that the more wives and horses a warrior had, the wealthier he might be reckoned among his tribal peers. The incessant tribal raids and on occasion full scale warfare meant a surplus of women. Result was an increase in plural marriages prairie style.

Whites often misunderstood the apparent indolence of the Indian braves, who required their women to do work white husbands did not ask of their wives. But looking back in history, primitive white societies operated in the same manner. The man was the hunter, provider of the basic food, he was also the warrior, required by his society to be ready at any instant to defend the tribe or clan. It would never do to be caught by an enemy raid, unarmed and hands greasy from butchering or the like tasks.

Another difference in the cultures, the cause of much future trouble, although not a serious matter in the fur trade days, was an attitude toward property. To the Indian theft or robbery of an enemy or stranger was a coup, something to boast about, and anyway strangers were usually enemies. To the Blackfeet at the time, there were two types of whites, the trader, known and generally regarded in a friendly light or at least as a provider through barter of very desirable things; and the trapper, an interloper and stranger. In later years it was the intruding miners, and finally the settler who took root on land the Indian regarded as his by historic right.

Finally, raiding and open war was a far more serious matter to white man than to red.

Piegans brought in most of the nearly 6500 beaver pelts traded at Fort Piegan that 1831-32 season. The post was abandoned in the spring, Kipp found most of his employes unwilling to stay when the returns went down river. Including those buffalo robes, weight of the trade was about 43 tons, probably requiring the building of a mackinaw in addition to the keelboat. The more valuable equipment and unsold wares went down as well, and wandering tribesmen burned stockade and buildings. Fr. Point's 1847 sketch shows little left; Granville Stuart in 1865 could only indicate its site on a sketch of the area.

### A More Permanent Post

Returns from the first Blackfeet post were sufficient to encourage continuance of the trade. David Mitchell was sent with 60 men and keel boat from Fort Union to relocate the post. Just below Milk River a bad storm hit, sending the keel boat reeling down stream. Four miles below the boat hit a snag, two engages and a Piegan passenger drowned. Mitchell sent two employes down to Union, 150 miles, made in two days and nights, while the rest of the party built a midget fort to protect the valuable trade goods salvaged, and on arrival of another boat and supplies Mitchell sent pack horses up river with token merchandise to reassure the Piegans the traders would return.

On arrival of the replacement boat Mitchell built on a bottom about 14 river miles below later Fort Benton, 200 foot square Fort McKenzie with two bastions on opposite corners to command approaches. The site was fairly near a ridge between Missouri and Teton that Blackfeet termed a "straight or narrow place" on the river. French voyageurs called it "bridge of the nose" (cracon du nez), a name long familiar and greatly garbled by non-French whites.

Pierre Chouteau's project, the steamboat Yellowstone, reached Fort Union in June of 1832, bringing the head of navigation on the Missouri within a city block of later Montana. The "fireboat" added to the prestige of the Big Knife traders, Hudson's Bay men couldn't show their Indian patrons anything approaching this. Steamboats also greatly shortened the long, dangerous trip by keelboat or mackinaw with furs and robes.

Mitchell took the returns down in the spring of 1833 to Union. Accompanying him back was Alexander Culbertson, soon to be in charge of Fort McKenzie and for 40 years to be one of the best friends the Blackfeet ever had. Among the 52 with them on the keelboat Flora were Prince Maximilian of Wied, surprisingly a noted European scientist, an extremely competent artist, Swiss Karl Bodmer, and Maximilian's man David Dreipoppel. The trip lasted from July 6 to August 9. Paintings and sketches by Bodmer and field journals of Maximilian survived, providing valuable historical material on that summer of Fort McKenzie's youth.

August 27 Maximilian recorded the marriage of Culbertson to an Indian woman the evening before. "According to the local custom, he had paid to the value of 100 dollars for her and his Piegan wife had brought him a rifle. A horse was to follow. She was of the family of the White Buffalo." This was one of the first of numerous such weddings to follow, as dozens of white names on Blackfeet tribal rolls today testify.

It had to be a short honeymoon, at break of day, August 28, prince and artist were aroused by an engage crying in French, "Get up, there is a battle." The Europeans were to be among a small number of whites ever to witness a full-scale Indian battle. Chief Lame Bull and 30 lodges of Piegans had camped near the post and had just been attacked by a much bigger war party of Assiniboines. Whites at first opened fire, then realized the attack was not on them and stopped shooting. Culbertson later recalled that the Piegans, anxious to save their possessions, had blocked the gate to refuge with saddles, parfleches, etc., adding to their casualties. The main camp of Piegans was about four miles up river and warriors came streaming down to about equalize the numbers. Mitchell and Culbertson joined the party of avengers as they forced an Assiniboine retreat to the Marias.

Maximilian described the Blackfeet reinforcements: "They came galloping in groups, from three to twenty together, their horses covered with foam, and they themselves in their finest apparel, with all kinds of ornaments and arms, bow and quivers on their backs, guns in their hands, furnished with their medicines, with feathers on their heads; some had splendid crowns of black and white eagle feathers, and a large hood of feathers hanging down behind, sitting on fine panther skins lined with red, the upper part of their bodies partly naked, with a long strip of wolf's skin thrown across the shoulder, and carrying shields adorned with feathers and pieces of colored cloth."

Considering the surprise attack and numbers engaged, casualties were not high, Maximilian listed the Blackfeet dead at 14, seven men, five women and two children, and many more wounded. Other sources give Assiniboine casualties at about six dead and 20 or more seriously wounded.

This Assiniboine band, according to Culbertson, next fall virtually exterminated a Gros Ventres camp, killing 400, at Snow Mountain 75 miles from Benton.

In 1834 a party of three Blood warriors and sister of one arrived at Fort McKenzie for the usual few rounds of ammunition, courtesy of the traders, and told Culbertson they were going after Crow horses. Culbertson tried unsuccessfully to talk them out of a foolhardy trip. A few miles from the fort, some Crows swooped down, killed two Bloods, wounded the other and took the woman prisoner. The wounded warrior managed to unseat one of the mounted Crows, jumped on his horse and made it to McKenzie. Several days later his sister, having escaped the Crows, came to warn of an impending attack by a big Crow war party.

Sure enough, in early June a big Crow camp set up a quarter mile from Fort McKenzie. It was a more or less friendly siege, no shots fired by either side, but whites understandably weren't leaving the post. They dug a well, ate what food there was, then the dogs, then hides and moccasins. With everyone in the fort near starvation, Culbertson warned the Crows of thunder and lightning, the besiegers sneered. Then from the cannon he trundled a solid shot through their camp, and the Crows called it off. Giving up a siege he hadn't wanted, Rotten Belly, Crow chief, headed a war party up toward the Goosebill, where they ran into a dozen Gros Ventres. The Crows wiped them out, not without casualties, including a dead war chief, Rotten Belly.

Indian warfare was all out in those years. Culbertson recalled a raid by 40 Crows in spring 1835 on a Gros Ventres village. The Crows' string ran out on the bluffs of the Marias near Fort McKenzie. In retaliation, in the fall a camp of Gros Ventres was surprised by Crees and Assiniboines near the Sweet Grass Hills, and only one Gros Ventre survived.

In summer 1836 Piegans and Crows had a peace treaty which lasted for a few months, when a small party of Crows killed a couple of Piegans. They packed away the scalps, went on to visit their friends the Piegans. In camp the latter just happened to find the scalps. End of the peace treaty. End of the Crows.

Familiarity helped to generate more confidence between the races. And there was a growing dependence on white wares. Iron arrow and lance heads, for example, useful in hunt and warfare, were a relatively cheap item of commerce.

The growing confidence was strained in 1837. St. Peters, annual steamboat to Union, brought smallpox into the Northwest. The trade boat to McKenzie left Union hurriedly in charge of Alexander Harvey, but when the disease broke out enroute the trader wisely stopped and sent a messenger to Culbertson. On the latter's account of the danger of the disease (about 1780 it had killed many of the tribe) the Blackfeet scoffed. Culbertson repeatedly warned of the danger, finally opened trade. Meanwhile he attempted to inoculate the fort personnel, and Antoine Dauphin was the only white to die, although 28 Indian wives and part Indian children died. After the initial round of trade, no Blackfeet appeared at Fort McKenzie. In the fall, Culbertson remembered, he went to visit the Piegans at the Three Forks; of a camp of 60 lodges, nearly 500 persons normally, only two old squaws were found alive, the others dead or fled, the latter probably to die elsewhere in the valley. About 6000 Blackfeet, nearly two thirds of the nation's total, died.

Alexander Harvey was an efficient second in command to Culbertson, but had a vicious streak that ultimately meant the end of Fort McKenzie. In spring 1838 he had an encounter with a Blood, Big Road, an equally quarrelsome Indian, while bringing up the supply boat. When Big Road attacked Culbertson in the fort one evening, Harvey and Isadore Sandoval heard the commotion and hustled the Blood outside, killing him at the gate. After much discussion the Bloods decided the dead man had brought it on himself. Most killings in the vicinity of the fort were the result of private feuds, and so regarded by both races.

On the whole Blackfeet and white traders and their employes got along fairly well in a climate of armed men, ready to use their weapons. But when peacemaker Culbertson was sent to Fort Laramie in 1843, the upper Missouri forts had lost their balance wheel. Francis Chardon, though an experienced trader from the lower Missouri, at McKenzie tended to rely too much on Alexander Harvey.

In January 1844 a war party of Blackfeet stopping at the fort were denied the usual courtesies, and petulantly killed or drove off a cow, or perhaps shot a pig, accounts varied. Harvey followed with a party to punish the marauders, they were ambushed in the nearby Teton valley, and Tom Reese, Negro, was killed. Hair trigger Harvey wanted vengeance, and apparently convinced Chardon of the need to equalize the score. February 19, 1844, a small party of North Blackfeet came to trade at Fort McKenzie, and Harvey turned a cannon on the party. At least six died; two chiefs who had been admitted to the trading room escaped by climbing the palisade. Harvey reputedly killed some of the wounded, and the Blackfeet Post was again on the move. The whites went down river to build Fort F. A. Chardon (or Fort F. A. C.) on the north bank of the Missouri at the Judith. Blackfeet came only to harass the traders. American Fur felt the dividend loss, Pierre Chouteau summoned Alexander Culbertson to a New York meeting and gave him a free hand to restore peace.

On his trip up river from Fort Union Culbertson fired Harvey (and burned Fort Chardon on his down trip). On the next bottom above later Fort Benton, and on the southeast side of the river, Culbertson took over Fort Cotton, rebuilt it into a standard trading post, palisades and all. Then he sent a messenger with gifts of tobacco to invite Blackfeet tribal heads to a peace council at the new post. About fifty came at the appointed time, Culbertson assuring them that the perpetuators of the cannon outrage had been exiled from Blackfeet country. Big Swan, a leading chief, replied "that the ground has been made good again by Major Culbertson's return, and the Blackfeet must not be the first to stain it with blood."

The winter trade brought complaints from Blackfeet that it was difficult to cross a river clogged with ice, and Culbertson quickly planned a move. Work parties started building a new post on the north side of the river, with the actual move dating March 19, 1947, although Culbertson's year date of 1846 leads the writer to the belief that considerable work was done by the end of the earlier year.

For a few days the new post was termed Fort Clay, then Fort Lewis. It became Fort Benton on American Fur books in St. Louis by 1848, and Christmas night 1850 Culbertson made the name change official.

Peak year of the robe trade prior to the move had been 21,000 robes in 1841, nearly matched in 1847 and surpassed all but one year thereafter in the pre-steamboat period. Strangely, Blackfeet forgiveness apparently extended to Harvey—insurance, he took a Piegan wife, for he came back up the Missouri in 1846 to build Fort Campbell in opposition, and traded for between 5,000 and 8,000 robes a year to his death in 1854. It may have been that Harvey's tigerish ferocity appealed to a nation of warriors. On one occasion at Fort Campbell, a great Blackfeet warrior, Mountain Chief, climbed atop a building to boast of the white scalps he had taken. Harvey scaled the wall too, to knock Mountain Chief off the roof with a billet of wood.

In September 1846 Blackfeet had their first direct contact with a noted peacemaker, Fr. Pierre Jean DeSmet, when he came to the Judith area in an attempt to bring about peace between Flatheads and Blackfeet. The latter were probably aware of the Black Robe from his efforts at St. Mary's Mission in the Bitter Root, for the Blackfeet raided the Flatheads unmercifully. The effort in 1846 probably hinged on desire of the less warlike Flatheads to have a peaceful yearly trip to the buffalo hunting grounds.

DeSmet and Culbertson teamed to contact and secure delegates from Montana area tribes to a great peace council at Fort Laramie in late summer 1851. They traveled to the Fort Union area together to contact the tribes, and Culbertson represented the Blackfeet at Laramie, although he lacked time to secure a delegation from tribes above Fort Union.

In 1853 chiefs of the Blackfeet had much to do with another type of white men, the scientists and soldiers of the Isaac I. Stevens northern railroad survey expedition.

Most of this party came overland from Fort Union, accompanied by Alexander Culbertson, who had been named acting Indian agent for area tribes. Another task for Stevens was a general Indian peace treaty. The party arrived in Fort Benton on September 1st and remained until the 21st, a few members staying for months. As Stevens brought a small wagon train with tons of presents for sweeteners, he was well received. John Mix Stanley, photographer, while in Fort Benton took the first daguerreotypes of the Blackfeet, the procedure making Stanley an important "medicine man." Unfortunately, none of these first photos taken in Montana have survived.

Stevens men explored far and wide, chiefs answered numerous questions; by the time he left Stevens knew more about the Marias Pass below later Glacier Park than whites would know again for almost 40 years. Had the Blackfeet known the implications of another survey, that of John Mullan for a military road from Fort Benton to old Fort Walla Walla, the lieutenant might well have acquired a close haircut, for 130 miles of this route was to be the greatest white man's highway in territorial Montana.

Stevens left Fort Benton to become governor of Washington territory, planning to return for a great peace council the next summer. An Indian war in the Northwest intervened to delay the council a year. James Doty of the expedition remained in Fort Benton, visited Blackfeet camps and estimated their number at about 6,000, a third of them warriors.

## The White Presence

Isaac Stevens returned to Fort Benton from Washington Territory in 1855, met Alfred Cumming, the other peace commissioner. All was set for the great council, except that the annuity and supply boats were vastly delayed by low water coming up from Fort Union, and the council instead of being held in Fort Benton in September, opened October 16 on the north bank of the Missouri at the Judith. Present besides about 2500 Blackfeet were delegations from the Flathead, Pend d'Oreille and Nez Perce, with a single Cree chief. Stevens had already held council among Flatheads and other tribes of western Montana. A main provision declared a common hunting ground south of a line from Hell Gate east to the Musselshell. Tribal boundaries were roughly defined. Whites were to be permitted to live in the area and to be unmolested in travel, the United States to protect Indians from whites, Indians consented to roads, telegraph lines, military posts and buildings for agencies. The Blackfeet were to receive $20,000 in useful goods for ten years, plus $15,000 for schools. Blackfeet called it Lame Bull's treaty, he being a principal chief. This was the only treaty with Blackfeet made in or near Fort Benton (others 1865 and 1868) to be ratified by congress.

Another provision was for a Blackfeet farm to help the tribe through a transition period that some tribesmen may have foreseen. It turned out to be more of a trouble spot.

In accordance with treaty provisions, the annuities began coming. Edwin A. C. Hatch was first agent, established his agency at Fort Benton and distributed the first 1856 annuities at the Judith September 22 and 23. (Those distributed at the 1855 council were presents.) There were three boats, heavily loaded, Hatch reported in an 1856 diary, distributed to "about 8,000 Indians present. One small row."

While at Fort Benton in August Hatch reported arrival of Mr. and Mrs. Culbertson, and Rev. and Mrs. Elkanah Mackey—the fourth member might have been considered later as an evil omen for the tribe. As it was, those attending the Protestant service viewed their first "white squaw."

What did those heavily loaded boats contain? An 1858 list shows about 7,500 Piegans receiving 10,000 lbs. flour, 57,000 lbs. rice, 7,600 sugar (they loved it), 7,400 pilot bread (hardtack), 2,500 coffee. Also 401 pairs blankets, 2280 yards calico, 2967 yards fancy cloth, 500 yards flannel cloth, 128 pounds black and white, and 84 pounds red and blue beads. Very useful items, 119 pounds brass kettles, 26 dozen 2-quart pans, 36 dozen butcher knives, 138 dozen frying pans, 8 dozen files, 7 dozen axes, 108 North West guns ($6.50 value), 1300 gun flints, 16 kegs powder (perhaps 10, possibly 25 pounds), 29 bags bullets, 400 pounds hoop iron for arrowheads, 2660 pounds tobacco. Least useful, fish hooks and fish lines, Blackfeet those days did not eat fish.

Viewers of annuity distributions mention the waste, flour dumped for the sacks, items traded to whites for trinkets. But in view of Indian protests at the nonarrival of annuities one year, the tribesmen saw these occasions much as white kids view Christmas.

## A Friendly Chief, Little Dog

There was that bare mention of a farm. Alfred Vaughan, Indian agent in 1858, decided the Sun River valley provided a fine test plot. A long drouth in 1859 ruined the crops, but next year it rained and Vaughan was enthusiastic over wheat "as fine as ever was raised in any state," Indian corn and vegetables. The agent also asked for money to irrigate the farm and for some cattle. He regarded the valley, as did later whites, as excellent for grazing. But about the only Blackfeet interested was Little Dog, who also took the terms of the treaty to heart by paying a friendly visit to the Flatheads and made a truce of sorts with Crows and Crees. The chief probably also welcomed an 1859 effort by Jesuits to establish a mission among Blackfeet.

This friendly chief had been a raider along the Oregon Trail in his youth, one time burying a cache of "yellow buttons without eyes" on the Snake. The buried gold coins the chief refused to retrieve in later years when he learned their worth. Stevens in 1853 called him "a man of character and probity." Charles Frush on an 1858 visit from Fort Owen acknowledged "courtesy and favors shown us by the head chief of the Blackfeet, Little Dog." He was a special favorite of Andrew Dawson at Fort Benton. During the ill fated Sun River stampede of 1865-66 Little Dog hunted for and sheltered numbers of white victims of cold weather and starvation, including X. Beidler. He and son Fringe were killed May 27, 1866, by tribal enemies very near to where present highway 87 goes down into the Teton valley just north of Fort Benton. Both were buried in the old cemetery just west of old Fort Benton. Thus it is probable their bones lie under the pavement of Main street in that block.

## Changing Pressures

Lt. John Mullan, who drew the assignment for a military road from Fort Benton westward, had the project delayed by an Indian war in Washington and by lack of appropriation, roughed out his road in 1860 in time to escort 300 soldiers westward off the initial steamboats to Fort Benton and completed it in 1862. It was evil timing for the Blackfeet, although provided for in the 1855 treaty. First major gold discovery at Bannack in 1862 was followed by a bigger find at Alder Gulch next year, and Montana's gold rush exploded. Thousands of travelers were soon dusting their way to the new bonanzas via Bozeman and Bridger trails off the Overland. When steamboats opened the Missouri in the next years, and travel increased overland from Minnesota, the Blackfeet were quick to feel the threat of the influx of whites. The Mullan road was crowded summers with freighters and other travelers, and tribesmen who had felt the whites must be few in numbers, as the same ones had been coming up the Missouri to trade for years, saw danger signs.

### The Blackfeet "War"

Moreover, they had reasons for hitting the war trail. Charley Carson and friends early in 1865 wiped out a party of horse thieves, and at Fort Benton in May Henry Bostwick and Joe Spearson, hearing Blood brags about taking white scalps, came up off the ground in front of Gad Upson's Indian agency to kill three or four, tossing the bodies into the nearby Missouri.

At the mouth of the Marias white townsiters were building a village, Ophir, that they felt would make them rich as an alternative port to Fort Benton. May 25, 1865, a party of about 100 Bloods under Calf Shirt wiped out 10 woodcutters about a mile up the Marias, the dead including several well known in Montana Territory. In aftermath, Gov. Sidney Edgerton proclaimed organization of a 500 man Montana militia to protect anticipated immigration and freight coming into Montana.

(Calf Shirt was a big, truculent Blood who after the Ophir affair stayed north of the boundary until 1869 when he came to the I. G. Baker post on the upper Marias to trade, took a shot at visiting Fr. Imoda, Bill Conrad saving the priest by knocking up the weapon. Calf Shirt's death at Fort Kipp at the mouth of the Oldman in Canada in the early 1870s belongs in western legend. James Willard Schultz had it from Joe Kipp: Calf Shirt came in to demand whisky, he was a terror in his cups and had killed several members of his own tribe. Kipp refused him and the big Indian said he'd just kill the trader and take it, firing a shot at Kipp. The latter didn't miss, Calf Shirt turned and started toward the stockade gate. The shots broke up a poker game, Charlie Thomas, Diamond R. Brown, Dick Berry, Sol Abbott, Henry Powell and Jeff Devereux contributing to a fusillade, 16 bullets hitting the chief before he fell. Calf Shirt's wives wanted a tribal medicine man to pray over the corpse for three days to restore him to life. Other Bloods warned the medicine man not to make the attempt.)

(According to a letter by Wm. Hubbard, his father Charles was with the Pikuni in 1865 in a tribal gathering at Cow Creek. The council "almost but not quite" declared war on the whites.) Total soldiers in the territory about that time were a few "Galvanized Yanks" from Fort Rice via the Deer Lodge to guard freight.

Affairs at Fort Benton were apparently peaceful the rest of 1865, the Montana Post items indicating more whites were killed by whites than by Indians the rest of the year, with Vigilante ropes especially deadly in the Helena area.

There was an idiotic stampede of possibly 500 would be miners to the Sun River valley that winter, some of the whites dying of cold or starvation. Little Dog of the Piegans played good Samaritan, hunting for starving stampeders along with his family members, and his band's lodges sheltering a number of whites. One item in the Post, however, claimed that Indians had killed numbers. Acting Gov. Meagher promptly issued another call for 500 militia to punish the Blackfeet, who were probably shivering in their lodges instead. John Morgan and Fort Benton friends provided a white actrocity, at Sun River shooting one Indian and hanging three others—the four had come to the whites to beg food. Not surprisingly, a war party, probably North Piegans, attacked the Sun River government farm in April, burned buildings and killed one of two attendants, ending that experiment in teaching the Blackfeet white men's ways. The same party killed a herder at St. Peter's Mission on the Sun and forced its abandonment.

Meagher's call for militia got little response, his February general order No. 1 calling for the first 50 men to go garrison Fort Benton, the next 100 to go to the Piegan camp, demand stolen goods and horses and hang murderers, the next group to go against the Bloods. Fort Benton wasn't as perturbed as Meagher, an item in the Montana Post said parties from the fort "go armed" (as always!) but also "report an abundance of arms, ammunition and men." This may have been the time that John Morgan's militia irked Bentonites with wholesale requisitions resented even more than the occasional horse stolen by reds.

Near Benton in April 1866 though, Jerry Mann and Alex Toponce lost two freighters to Indians one night, next night their wagonmasters killed each other in Benton. A visiting Blood was killed and shoved through the ice, his feet sticking up several days, while a week later Blackfeet collected Charley Carson's scalp up on the Dearborn (he was a nephew of Kit).

But despite all the news accounts of the Blackfeet war on the Benton Road, freighters grouped up and had no reported problems getting through the war zone. Indians were too busy hunting and whites with freighting for such frills in spring. By late October, though, there was time for other recreation. A Piegan was killed and scalped (Indian scalps were legal tender at bars across the frontier), next day on the Teton nearby eight whites fought 11 Indians and claimed 7 or 8 more scalps. Bill Hamilton, sheriff at Benton, didn't think much of the location of new Camp Cooke at the Judith, figured the best solution to the Indian problem was to offer $25 per scalp. The rest of 1866 the Sioux along the Missouri took over, reported score at least nine white travelers.

There seems to have been a tacit truce in 1867, even the Montana Post in January reported the Indians quiet. The editor also wanted the Camp Cooke soldiers moved to near civilization where merchants would have a shot at soldier cash if and when the boys in uniform were paid. A few exceptions, two lone travelers in early months; John Bozeman in southern Montana April 20, reportedly victim of Mountain Chief, one of the greatest warriors of the Blackfeet. Despite the early start, whites soon achieved a much larger total just among us boys. There was little evidence that Blackfeet were among the Indians harassing the Northern Overland Mail pony express from Minnesota. Blackfeet may have secured a few remounts from raided stations—the tribesmen seem to have regarded the calibre of horses too good to discourage the mail riders by killing them, just strip and turn loose.

The "war" began heating up a bit in 1868, with horse raids and a traveler killed near Dearborn, but the Post noted there were enough Blackfeet near the Benton Road to make traveling in numbers sensible life insurance. The road was being patrolled by soldiers from Fort Shaw, helping quell attacks. May 1st Heavy Runner visited Fort Benton, complained that he couldn't hold his young warriors in check, which was the crux of the matter. The young men may have killed Nate Crabtree at Camp Cooke on April 24, and they impudently warned Bill Hamilton and John Neubert they were next. Still Sioux on the Missouri below were a greater danger than Blackfeet who could count the handy rifles of tough freighters.

A cooling off period was ushered in by early summer 1868, with news of another great peace council and subsequent presents. Also, Alexander and Natawista Culbertson were back in Fort Benton after spending their fortune in Illinois, a great influence for peace between the races. Probably promoting the era of good feeling, at Sun River in August, John Largent and Al Hamilton and 13 other whites captured 21 Indians and simply turned them over to the Fort Shaw military.

The treaty was made September 1st on the Teton near Fort Benton, with the Culbertsons interpreting and explaining matters. The change from Fort Benton was at the request of the Piegans, who felt they had suffered too many killings, abuse and insults at the agency. Calf Shirt, one of the grimmest of the Bloods, underlined a general good feeling: "We will force our young men to keep this treaty and keep them from stealing... The past is buried."

(Not all was. After signing the treaty, Mountain Chief was abused by Fort Bentonites, probably because of the killing of John Bozeman. The chief was to have ample other reasons to hate whites, a brother killed in Fort Benton in July 1869, a son in March 1871. Yet after hearing of the brother's death, Mountain Chief simply ordered all white traders out of his camp instead of killing them, possibly remembering "making his mark" on three treaties, 1855, 1865 and 1868. He and four others died in a Piegan camp fight in March 1872 near Old Agency.)

September 1868 Indians were numerous near the Crow and Gros Ventres agency on Many People's Creek, drawn by large herds of buffalo along Milk River. They seemed to echo the treaty euphoria with a message, "wolfers keep out, we won't kill, but will take all they have." Wolfers were generally whisky peddlers, but unwelcome because their baits killed many Indian dogs.

## Climactic Year of 1869

There were troubles in plenty along the Benton Road and area in 1869, but the writer in recent years has concluded that the scope of the Blackfeet "war" 1865-70 was much overdrawn in newspapers and by early historians. A figure of 56 whites killed by Indians is given in 1885 Leeson. A grand jury in Helena Oct. 9, 1869, found "great loss of lives and property from predatory bands of Indians." Also, "we believe that within six months fully 1000 horses have been stolen." The report also mentions having the names of 9 or 10 citizens murdered by Indians. Leeson mentions citizens having to carry arms on the Benton road, actually customary, but a bit different than reports that almost every wagon train was attacked.

In "Strike Them Hard," Bob Ege expresses belief that chiefs, partly due to alcohol, had lost control and respect of their young men. The latter were out to win their "letters" in coups on whites and horses, chiefly the latter. There doubtless were a number of unreported white dead in that year on lonely trails, and some mysterious disappearances of whisky traders in red camps.

Files of the Helena Herald, which certainly did not underplay Indian actrocities, seem to confirm army over reaction in the bitter climax. First war note of 1869, Jan. 14, a small party of hunters near Dearborn stripped by Blackfeet war party recently. In April a Diamond R wagonmaster was wounded near Fort Benton, which had its "young men" too. Assuming that Blackfeet were to blame, that same night two of the tribe were killed in Fort Benton. In mid-July two freighters were mortally wounded near Fort Benton—the Indians only later were identified by Isaac Baker as River Crows, the Blackfeet again blamed and three killed in Fort Benton. The Herald correspondent mentions Mountain Chief (his brother among those killed) riding into town "and did not come alone. It would seem the Indian war has begun in earnest." (This may have been the occasion of an Indian fight in Fort Benton that W. S. Stocking mentions.) Only reported attack on a wagon train by Blackfeet to August was on a freight outfit on the Cow Island Trail, one man killed trying to talk to attackers.

The murder of Malcolm Clarke August 17 at his ranch near present Seiben by Blackfeet ignited white rage throughout the territory. Clarke was one of the most prominent citizens, a long time trader at Fort Benton and the man who after the 1865 Ophir killings by Bloods, visited the Piegans and found them fearful and anxious for peace. Clarke's killing was in what amounted to a family feud not unknown among whites. Shortly after this came an item that Hugh Kirkendall had sent 8 armed men to meet his freight train near Benton. Eight! There followed several raids on stage stations on the Benton Road, and the stage manager took along plenty of guns and ammunition on a trip to Benton.

In its September 23 issue the Helena Herald reported things quiet on the Benton Road, few Indians seen and Bloods and Blackfeet moving north to avoid the more belligerent Piegans. Late in the month a lone miner was killed near Silver City. (Along the Missouri the Sioux were collecting several times the scalps indicated for the tribe on which terrible retribution would be visited.)

Montana newspapers and citizens were demanding revenge, probably partially on account of those occasional but fat army payrolls, which sweetened business receipts. Repeated demands were made on army officials for punitive strikes.

A few voices for moderation appear, notably old Montana hand Alexander Culbertson, who had talked with the chiefs of the Piegans. He attributed the cited actrocities and horse thievery as the work of "a portion of the young rabble, over whom the chiefs have no control." Culbertson also suggested that a moderate amount of food would help induce the hot heads to remain close to grub, and pointed out that the decrease in buffalo would soon reduce the Piegans to "wholly dependent on the government for support." Some attention to his letter to Gen. Alfred Sully, Montana Indian affairs superintendent by 1869, might have averted two tragedies, one at hand and the other some years in the future.

Culbertson's stance was one of few on the side of moderation, repeated demands were made on the military for protection of whites, and the army made tentative plans for organizing a striking force, meanwhile conferring with the chiefs, who reiterated their helplessness to control their dissident young men. One of the bands singled out for possible retaliation was that of Mountain Chief; one of the Indian bands known to be friendly that of Heavy Runner. Citizen reports and demands were of course passed up the chain of command, to Lt. Gen. Phil Sheridan, and on to Gen. W. T. Sherman, who approved a possible punitive strike, and back to Sheridan, who answered Gen. Philip DeTrobriand at Fort Shaw: "If the lives and property of citizens of Montana can best be protected by striking Mountain Chief's band, I want them struck. Tell Baker to strike them hard."

That latter was Major Eugene M. Baker, who headed the troops drawn from Fort Ellis near Bozeman, and Fort Shaw. The detachments camped near Fort Shaw Jan. 16, 1870, in 35 below zero weather. The soldiers then marched to the Marias, with Joe Kipp and Joe Cobell as guides, on January 23 surprised a village about 20 miles below Willow Rounds. Kipp tried to tell Baker it was the camp of Heavy Runner, the major put him under guard and threat of death for any outbursts that might warn the village. Kipp was right, and the first shot generated a general attack, at the end 173 Piegans had died. Joe Cobell, whose wife was a sister of Mountain Chief, is said to have fired that first shot at Heavy Runner, his death preventing the chief from showing papers proving his peaceful record. Lt. Doane's count was 120 men and 53 women and children among the dead. About 140 were prisoners, many of the living and dead had smallpox. Kipp, son of fur trader James Kipp and a Mandan woman, was under suspicion by the Blackfeet for years, but ended a respected figure on the reservation. Joe Cobell became one of the first farmers in the Highwoods, eventually moved to the reservation also.

While Montanans generally approved the slaughter, many easterners were dismayed, and the whole affair became the Baker Massacre. As for the Blackfeet, never again did their young men take the war trails in groups. Through the 1870s and until the final buffalo were gone in the early 1880s, the tribe lived much as before, save that food was scarcer and many were the hungry days and nights.

An item in the December 29, 1870, Helena Herald: Several lodges of Piegans have come to the Blackfeet agency with intention of farming in the spring.

Many more went to Canada for the time being, there are occasional items in the papers through the whisky fort days. Whisky was often a final solace, 88 tribal members were killed in drunken brawls in 1871; in 1873, 33 of the Piegans only. On this side of the border, the Indian agency did a bit, not enough, at one time bringing in cattle to make them stockgrowers. Expanding herds of white ranchers resulted in demands for more free ranges at expense of the tribe. In 1887 a great cession of land was forced on northern Montana tribes, to slightly greater size than present day reservations. White ranchers wanted even that, and a standard story in the bitter years was of Indians killing cattle—they were hungry.

The second great tragedy of the tribe had occurred with the virtual end of the buffalo in 1882. A Blackfeet elder had seen the end in 1878 when he told the Indian agent at Badger Creek: "The time is close when the tail of the last buffalo will be seen disappearing from the prairie." By the end of 1882 more and more families were dependent on government food rations to survive. Agent John Young could distribute 1 1/2 pounds of meat and 2 1/2 pounds of flour per week per person. In May 1883 hunters went to former buffalo ranges once more, but returned empty handed. The tribe subsisted on berries and wild vegetables but had to kill many of the small cattle herd they had built up from 1881.

Agent Young is still blamed by later generations for the 1883-84 starving time, although Indian service records show clearly he tried to warn Washington of coming starvation. When rations came, they were far from sufficient, and some rotten, no unusual occurrence in those days. Rations were cut to a quarter just as cold weather began. By February about a sixth of 600 cattle were left.

Blackfeet were living on roots and inner bark of cottonwood and dying daily. Almost A Dog counted 555 who died of starvation that winter, about a fifth of the tribe. There were probably more.

While they were starving to death, white Montana went virtually uninformed about the growing catastrophe near Badger Creek, 20 miles from Dupuyer, the then agency.

The River Press on February 20, 1884, did run a letter signed Muros on its front page, saying the condition of these 1500 or 2000 Indians is deplorable and a little flour would be a godsend. The agency had only 80 cattle and 45 sacks of flour left, and last year's potatoes were badly stored, frozen and many rotten. (The last 23 head of cattle were stolen, butchered secretly and doled out to the desperate survivors.)

Far larger headlines were given March 5 when William Jones, employed by the Shonkin Stock Association, was killed near Arrow Creek when he and companion came onto Indians killing cattle. (The possibility also exists that the rustlers were whites.)

Agent Young appealed to T. C. Power in Helena in February, the best he could do was to order the Fort Benton store to have 400 sacks of flour freighted and 50 head of cattle sent by drover to the reservation, Power taking his chances on having the shipment paid for later by the Indian service, but deep snow and cold weather slowed the movement. Fort Shaw was asked to send what supplies they could, to be replaced from the Power sending which was stalled en route.

March 12 the Press reported that T. C. Power had been awarded a special contract to supply food to the Blackfeet agency and the agency at Fort Belknap (Chinook). The bureaucratic mills were moving slowly.

April 30 a report appeared from a River Press reporter who had interviewed new Blackfeet Agent Reuben Allen, probably on a Fort Benton visit. He had taken over from Young on March 15, said that the week before a sixth rations were issued, a pound of flour and one and a half of bacon per person a week, that he had already received 30,000 pounds of flour and 14,000 of bacon. He was very critical of Young's administration, with an implication Young had deliberately tried to make his successor look bad. Potatoes were badly stored, only 75 acres land broken but 850 reported, 6000 Indians reported but only 2100 on ration rolls March 15. (Of course padded rosters should have meant rations for more.)

June 25 the River Press reprinted an item from the Sun River Sun, L. E. Pembrin, scout and interpreter at Fort Shaw, reporting terrible conditions at the agency, Indians actually dying of starvation with a ration of only half a pound of beef and of bacon per week, a quarter pound of flour.

As noted, little was found on the starvation winter, the big news that spring was a congressional bill to open the vast Indian reservation in northern Montana. The bill died in June, the whites had to wait two more years before they could take most of the land they wanted from the northern tribes.

### Associated Gros Ventres

Gros Ventres were long associated with the Blackfeet, and Mountain Men characterized them as the most warlike of the confederacy, and some of the preceding chapter pertains to them as well. But in 1861 there was a falling out and Ewers describes full scale warfare in the Cypress Hills area between Piegans and Gros Ventres—who had allied themselves with Crows, Piegans killing more than 300. (For that matter, Piegans and Bloods were on shoot first terms at times.)

Although relations were strained, a large party of Gros Ventres attended the 1865 peace treaty and council held in Fort Benton that fall. The lure of accompanying presents was probably irresistible. Wm. T. Hamilton in Forest and Stream in 1907 described the council and its climactic near war. After the signing, and departure of the white commissioners, the Blackfeet got hold of whisky and became drunk and dangerous. Little Dog of the Piegans told Fort Benton whites there would be an attack on the Gros Ventres village at the lower end of the bottom. Soon about 500 Blackfeet in war regalia began circling the Gros Ventres village, whose chiefs had a difficult time restraining their young men from answering the taunts with bullets. Little Dog's intervention with Blackfeet chiefs was probably the determining factor in the affair ending without bloodshed. Sensibly, the Gros Ventres broke camp in the night and left.

About half the Gros Ventres tribe perished in the 1869-70 smallpox epidemic.

When the northern reservation, Rockies to the Canadian border, was condensed in 1887 to about present limits, the Gros Ventres and their nearest enemies, the Assiniboines, were placed in the same area south of present Chinook.

### The Sioux Moved West

Every one it seems thinks first of the Sioux and the Little Big Horn. This confederation was largest and most powerful of the plains tribes. Minnesota virtually dates its history from the 1862 Sioux uprising in which several hundred white settlers were slain. Montana and Dakota inherited many of the tribesmen and the Sioux problem as well. (The well known name means "enemy," their own name, Dakota or variations, "the people.")

John Healy, for a time editor and feature writer for the Benton Record in tamer years, recalled the first Sioux invasion of northern Montana as 1862, when he was a member of a party of about 30 miners headed down in August by mackinaw to meet the steamboat Shreveport. The party met the boat at a Gros Ventre camp near Milk River. Just as the steamboat came in view a war party of strange Indians armed with shields and spears, swooped down from the hills, captured the Gros Ventre horse herd and raced out of sight. The Gros Ventre reacted by getting ready to follow or fight. Their chief waved his warriors up the bluffs, several hundred of them, but the strangers kept coming. Healy and other whites had felt 700 armed Gros Ventres enough to cope with anything, but he and the latter tribe were overawed as the migrating Sioux continued to show up, shouting defiance. Healy estimated 2,000 in the band on the north side of the Missouri, but later in the day more Sioux swarmed down from the hills on the south side "until the bottom land seemed a forest of lances, as far as the bluffs." (Healy may have been off a year, the Shreveport was in the area both 1862 and 1863, Fr. DeSmet having a somewhat similar experience in 1863, saving about 70 landed passengers when the Black Robe was recognized by a chief of the Sioux.)

Certainly the 1862 Sioux rising quickly impacted Missouri river steamboating. Sully used unsuitable boats in the 1863 Dakota campaign, got better performance in 1864. The effect was to determine thoroughly navigation usefulness of the Yellowstone, from 1864 to the final Sioux campaign of 1876-77 and the building of post-Custer forts. Steamboats even carried the last of the Sioux from the scene of their great triumph. In June 1881 five steamboats carried 1700 surrendered Sioux from Fort Keogh on the Yellowstone to Standing Rock Agency, "on a picnic," commented the River Press sourly, "and the business of the territory kept lagging therefrom."

Sioux along the Missouri had been troublesome from the days of Lewis and Clark; with the outbreak of the Civil War rivermen on the Mississippi soon learned boiler plate would turn guerrilla bullets—the mode soon spread to the Mountain Steamboats; rivermen were killed every season by Indian missiles.

Sioux and other Indians were lethal to woodhawks, possibly if the Sioux had known of the necessity of fuel they could have immobilized the steamboats. Part of the Sioux activities put greater pressure on the steamboats to deliver freight. Down in Wyoming and southern Montana the army in 1866 was building Forts Reno, Phil Kearny and C. F. Smith to protect the Bozeman Trail, which the Sioux, led by Red Cloud, were determined to block, and did.

Along the Missouri in the general area of the Musselshell those years the Sioux created chaos, frequently wiping out small parties of miners traveling down the Missouri and Yellowstone in small boats; tragedies often unreported.

One was: Helena Radiator Nov. 29, 1866, John Corder in a letter from Fort Union advised of the deaths of "T. A. Kent, John Ross, James Smith and Wm. Barber, after five hours hard fighting with forty Sioux." Kent killed 13, Corder wrote, adding, "I received five wounds in the body from arrows, but nothing fatal, I hope."

The touchy Blackfeet were probably best able to go one on one with the Sioux, so Fort Benton's direct experience with the tribe was limited. One came in May 1868. While locals raged impotently for lack of long range Sharps, Sioux snatched 15 horses and mules from in plain view just across the Missouri, then returned an hour later to snaffle 40 head of fat I. G. Baker cattle. While still seething, a courier arrived from Brule Bottom, eight miles down the Missouri, with word that more Sioux had nabbed 14 horses and mules belonging to J. J. Roe (Diamond R). Thirty-five armed Bentonites headed to the rescue, but the pilfered stock had been swum across the Missouri and all they managed was a long range fire fight, one raider killed or badly wounded, and a single coup stick taken.

A tiny settlement at the Musselshell in the 1860s was repeatedly harrassed and under siege in the years from 1866 until it got satisfying revenge May 9, 1869. Woodhawks were staying close that spring, wolfers were back and there were about 60 whites against 100 Sioux when the ball opened. Then a heavy rain commenced, and bowstrings were useless, flintlocks as well. Henry Macdonald and several others armed with newfangled Henry repeaters found a ford across the Musselshell, trapped the nearly defenseless Sioux against the opposite bank and killed about a third of them. Liver Eating Johnson got his name when he killed the final available warrior with his knife, a bit of liver stuck to the tip. He offered same to a pilgrim, then had to make good the jest by downing it himself. Passengers on the next steamboat saw a baker's dozen of grinning skulls on posts at the landing.

Sioux at various times killed or scared off the woodhawks between the Judith and Fort Benton, but farther below was their happy hunting ground. One small raid occurred as late as 1874 at the mouth of the Marias. A pair of Sioux had cased the camp and when two wood cutters left for a post two miles away made their move. One cutter was out ricking wood, a pistol in his pocket but rifle leaning against cut wood. One of the raiders got the rifle about the time the other white came out to dump his dishwater and took a derringer ball in the back of his head from the other Sioux. Then it was fun and games for the Indians with the apparently unarmed survivor white. In sign language they made him bark, eat grass while he was fishing that pesky handgun out. With it he downed one Sioux with the short gun, grabbed the rifle and shot the other Sioux as he raced for the river bank, with the reclaimed rifle. It turned out the other woodhawk just had a terrible headache, the Sioux load, as often the case, light for want of gunpowder.

By 1874 Sioux down around the Musselshell were giving steamboating to Benton an assist by keeping the proposed Carroll Trail under siege. Rain, high water and Sioux in 1875 ended the Carroll project for good. In the campaign that finished the Custer command, a number of Benton freighters and handy men were with the freight train that supplied the Gibbons Montana column from Forts Shaw and Ellis. Fort Benton through its freighting was deeply involved in the efforts of U. S. army and Canadian Mounted Police to get the fugitive Sioux problem settled—most of the action at the far end of the Fort Walsh Trail, Benton to Cypress Hills.

### The Fugitive Nez Perce

Chief Joseph's rifle and blanket are displayed in the museum at Fort Benton, and the final battle of the Nez Perce was fought and most surrendered on Snake Creek near the Bear's Paw mountains October 5, 1877. The site was then in Chouteau county. The role of Fort Benton in the campaign was diverse, two well known former residents killed at the Big Hole battle, and about 36 volunteers rode to protect the freight steamboats left at Cow Island, while several freighters were killed by the Indians.

Sitting Bull and fugitive Sioux were of far more interest to Bentonites in the early months of 1877. To the west greed of white men for lands of the normally friendly Nez Perce, and the usual hot headed young warriors who killed several whites triggered hostilities. After sharp but inconclusive small scale battles between soldiers and Nez Perce, in which the Indians had all the better of it, the tribe headed eastward to hunt buffalo, hoping their troubles would blow over. They made a mockery of an attempt to stop them on the Lolo trail into Montana near Missoula, then met and assured settlers in the Bitter Root that they would pass peaceably, paying for supplies for their coming hunt on Montana plains.

General Otis Howard and his troops were well behind by then, but Col. John Gibbon moved a force south from Fort Shaw, picked up a contingent of Bitter Root volunteers, of the Montana militia, including such diverse characters as later copper king W. A. Clark, militia captain, and as scout for Beaverhead volunteers Methodist minister William Wesley Van Orsdel.

At the Big Hole in southern Montana Gibbon achieved complete surprise in early morning of August 9, killing a number of warriors, but also women and children. The bitter Nez Perce rallied, drove the soldiers from their camp with crippling losses. One of the first to die in the initial attack was Fort Benton's historian, Lt. James H. Bradley, stationed at Fort Benton long enough to transcribe valuable early history. The Benton Record of August 15 sadly noted arrival of Mrs. Bradley to take the steamboat Benton down river bound for her Atlanta home. One of the last deaths in the battle was scout Henry Bostwick, who started his plains career as guide for Sir George Gore's legendary hunting trip in 1854-55. Both men had served with the Montana Column in the Sioux campaign of 1876, Bradley's advance party first whites to reach the scene of Custer's debacle.

After the slaughter of their women and children, and recognition of some of the Bitter Root volunteers in the lines against them, Nez Perce understandably were much less friendly toward whites after the Big Hole. They killed numbers of prospectors and ranchers in a sweep through southern Idaho and into Yellowstone Park. (In Yellowstone they narrowly missed General of Army Wm. T. Sherman, who had a rabbit's foot that year. Down in the southwest Satanka and his Kiowas let an army ambulance carrying Sherman go unmolested in favor of looting a following wagon train. Some of Sherman's veterans of the 1864 March to the Sea rehashed that campaign with the general August 25 in Fort Benton.)

Nez Perce, despite their woes, were considerate enough to let women of a tourist party in the new park go unharmed, though young braves shot a male companion, who survived.

Coming out of the park, the tribe's miniscule warrior contingent shrugged off a September interception attempt by 300 of the 7th Cavalry under Col. Sturgis northwest of later Billings. Fort Benton people had the message with that news—the Nez Perce were headed straight for a Cow Island crossing, and a batch of steamboat freight ticketed for Fort Benton.

There had been discussion about volunteers to protect that freight earlier, the Benton Record shows, plus appeals for troops. Now, they felt, it was up to local talent. So Fort Benton's mounted volunteers were quickly organized, but too late, it turned out, by two days. September 21 the volunteers rode out, north across the Marias, then east. With them rode the army, Major Guido Ilges and one lone soldier. Next day at the Judith, six more volunteers joined, plus Lt. Harden, 15 soldiers and a mountain howitzer—traveling by mackinaw. The civilians ran into rough country south of the Missouri but got their supply wagon past jumbled cliffs and canyons, reached the south shore of the Missouri at Cow Island September 24, finding "the destruction of property sad to behold."

For the Nez Perce had crossed September 22-23, pinning Sgt. Molchert and his eight soldiers and four civilians to their rifle pits. At first encounter, Molchert and civilian Mike Foley sensibly respected a truce offer, tendered some food to hungry warriors. But as the rest of the tribe came up, firing broke out. Two of the civilians were wounded. It was apparent that the Indians could have wiped out the baker's dozen whites, were more intent on seizing food and crossing, than in killing.

In all there were strange touches to this campaign. Nez Perce pointed rifles at men in a passing mackinaw, whites came ashore as ordered and took to the brush thankful for their scalps. After using the boat for women and children, Chief Joseph looked up the whites to tell them the Indians were all through with the boat, so come get it, and go on down.

Just before the first Indians arrived, Foley had loaded and flagged out bull team outfits of O. G. Cooper, Frank Farmer and Ed Barker. Just ahead of the wagons went a light vehicle with four ladies, an army surgeon, Captain Frechette of the North West Mounted Police and a five soldier escort. The wagon train was headed for trouble, but the ladies and others never saw an Indian, though in view of the Nez Perce trail record it seems certain the Indians had seen and identified these travelers.

After this briefing the volunteers decided here was something they could do, and rode up Cow Creek on the long used trail. Ten miles up the winding road, here came their scout, Murray Nicholson, to report he had sighted the wagon train, also all the Indians anybody wanted. By noon the two groups were in a full scale fire fight, the Indians holding the high ground of bluffs. Ed Bradley (real name Edwin Richardson), was instantly killed early in the fight. Louis Cobell's buddies figured he killed that sniper. Later, ran a note in the Record, a Nez Perce told a volunteer two Indians were killed—a casualty ratio the army never attained in this campaign, even counting women and children.

While some of the best riflemen on the frontier, red and white, were disputing that trail, other Nez Perce burned the wagon train and in the area killed three freighters, Ed Barker, Charles Steele and James Downey—others in the general area missing and probably killed.

For their long ride on a dangerous mission recompense was $6 to $10, the 1885 history reports, 44 being named. A couple of attorneys, John J. Donnelly and John W. Tattan, and ex-wolfer John Evans, officered the group, all having long army experience. Personnel included several former sheriffs, town barber, ferryman, former scouts, several merchants, plus a couple of Indian fathers in law. Virtually all were veterans of Civil or Indian wars or both.

The white warriors showed amazing empathy on return to Benton toward their red enemies. John Healy was probably the Record editor who decided previous criticism of General Howard was unjustified "in view of the remarkable fighting qualities displayed in the contest with Miles... At all events these Indians traveled and fought as no Indians ever traveled and fought before, and Howard has the consolation of knowing that he was foiled by no ordinary foe." Healy also wrote his own version of the fight at Snake Creek, "Indians displayed remarkable skill and ingenuity in constructing their defenses. Fought so well and never scalped."

Chief Joseph, who made the surrender, was by no means the only chief of note in the sad hejira of the Nez Perce. He was the survivor, when White Bird refused to quit and took the final tatters of a tribe of fighters into Canada from the field north of the Bear's Paw. Nez Perce were hunters, excellent shots and courageous almost beyond belief; adept in use of cover, natural forts and improvised rifle pits.

General Miles had made an extraordinary forced march from Fort Keogh to catch the Nez Perce on Snake Creek. He immediately ordered a general engagement and had the great good fortune to capture 700 or 800 ponies, in effect immobilizing the fugitives—but the assault was bloodily repulsed. Almost shot to pieces were units of the reconstituted 7th Cavalry. Captain Moylan, participant in all the 7th campaigns, reported 53 dead and wounded out of 115 engaged that bloody first day, and bars or stripes virtually insured a Nez Perce bullet. It was no wonder that Miles thereafter was content to tighten siege lines. The Nez Perce, too, suffered sadly prior to the surrender. Looking Glass, Poker Joe, Too-hool-hool-sote and Ollocut (Joseph's brother) died in that battle.

In the negotiation stage, Joseph was held an overnight prisoner in Miles' camp in disregard of a flag of truce, was released when warriors captured a lieutenant to force an exchange.

General Howard, who had pursued the Nez Perce hundreds of miles, arrived in time to be present at Chief Joseph's surrender October 5th: "Hear me, my chiefs! I am tired; my heart is sick and sad. From where the sun now stands, I will fight no more forever."

He surrendered 87 warriors, 40 of these wounded, and 254 noncombatants. White Bird and about 100 made their way to Canada. Numbers of separated fugitives were killed by Indians of other tribes. There were fugitives in the Fort Benton area after the campaign, and May Flanagan, a small girl then, seems to imply some Nez Perce prisoners were brought to Fort Benton, "here walked the sorrowful Nez Perce under guard after their defeat."

Miles, who had forced the surrender, was outraged at later treatment of the Nez Perce; he had promised they would be returned to their homeland. Instead, Miles worked seven years to get the tribe returned from Oklahoma.

### The Assiniboines

The Assiniboines, and spelling is the writer's choice, occupied territory along the boundary line toward the eastern end of Montana, and few direct contacts were noted.

One of course was the well documented Assiniboine attack on Blackfeet at Fort McKenzie August 28, 1833, more fully covered in the general fur trade period. Several hundred Assiniboines and some Crees killed 14 men, women and children, with smaller losses of their own. Maximilian's account and Karl Bodmer's drawing of this Indian battle are perhaps unique, as white witnesses of an inter-tribal battle. Although eventually several hundred Blackfeet took part, in 1833 guns available were more notable for noise than killing power—the bow probably more lethal, although at closer quarters.

But some tribal warfare was pretty grim. Alexander Culbertson told James Bradley that in 1838-39 about sixty lodges of Gros Ventres were destroyed by Cree and Assiniboine, a few years later an equal number of Gros Ventres were exterminated near the Cypress Hills in Canada. Eight seems an average per lodge—the two fights mean several hundred slain. The Gros Ventres territory largely adjoined that of the Assiniboines.

The Assiniboine figured in another event that helped shape border history. This was in the spring of 1873 when a party of Fort Benton wolfers had their horses lifted by raiders a few miles from town. The whites got remounts and reinforcements and trailed the raiders, who turned out to be Crees, up to Battle Creek in the Cypress Hills near two small trading posts. The feisty Assiniboine warriors told the wolfers that they had seen the horses with a Cree band that had gone on, but if the white men just wanted a fight, Assiniboines would oblige. After a night of carousing by white and red, the fight broke out; one wolfer dead, somewhere between 20 and 30 Indians, including their chief, Little Soldier.

The tribe in gold rush days was relatively peaceful, but not above assessing white travelers by mackinaw for grub and guns. In the 1880s they were accused of raiding woodyards and killing the choppers, but there is some evidence the murderers were white rustlers and outlaws along the Missouri.

Rather ironically, the reservation south of Chinook houses descendants of ancient tribal enemies, Assiniboines and Gros Ventres.

### Crows Were Occasional Visitors

The Crows, whose home area was in the valley of the Yellowstone, seldom threatened either trade or traders in the Fort Benton area. One occasion was summer 1834 when young Alexander Culbertson was left in charge of Fort McKenzie. Into Blackfeet country along the Missouri came a strong war party of Crows, who killed two of three Bloods near the fort and captured a squaw. A wounded Blood jerked a Crow off his horse and made it to the fort. The Crows made tracks out, the Blood squaw escaping them after several days, and made her way back to the fort, to warn of an impending attack by a bigger Crow party.

These duly appeared, but Culbertson's account to Bradley showed it a unique siege, after running off the McKenzie horse herd. Crows set up camp a few hundred yards from the post, to prevent trade with their enemies the Blackfeet. At Culbertson's demand, no armed Crow came near the fort, no shots were fired. The small garrison dug a well for water; food ran out quickly, then it was the dogs' turn. After the whites started on boiled raw buffalo hide, parfleche skins. About the time the whites were down to their moccasins, the Crow chief, Rotten Belly, was warned if the Crows didn't drop the siege the fort would open fire. After Fort McKenzie's tiny cannon sent a couple of cannon balls rolling through the camp, they left.

Head Chief Rotten Belly's hurt pride caused his death. He led a party of eager young braves north of the fort, and not too far away on the east toes of the Goosebill the Crows ran into a dozen Gros Ventres, and wiped them out, but their chief took a mortal wound. Tribal tradition had it that his last words were to tell his people "to keep peace with the whites." Traditionally, they did.

Crows made an intrusion in force to nearby Shonkin some time in the later 1860s. Jerry Potts, half Blackfeet, riding out across the Missouri, ran into an ambush by seven Crows, who demanded he ride with them to their village. Four with rifles rode behind. Soon one said, "Why not just kill him here?" Jerry understood Crow and at the click of a rifle bolt rolled off his horse and back up with six gun blazing. He killed the four riflemen in as many shots, the bow and arrow braves raced to safety. Hurrying back to Benton, Jerry collected a war party of Blackfeet, and they hit the Crow camp before it could get away. With scalps and plunder, the return of the braves touched off what W. S. Stocking termed "the wildest night" he ever spent in Fort Benton.

A season or two later a Crow war party killed a number of Blackfeet by remote control. Forgetting their usual friendship with the whites, in July 1869 they mortally wounded two Garrison & Wyatt herders near Benton and looted a couple of wagons. Fort Benton whites just naturally blamed the Blackfeet, at Bill Gladstone's house taking a brother of Mountain Chief out and killing him, then the freighters found two more. A day or so later three more were killed in the town. W. S. Stocking in memoirs recalled that soon a war party of Blackfeet came clattering into Fort Benton, that 25 armed men fought the Indians all over town, and found 15 dead after the battle. (A July 22 Helena Herald has a line, "Old Mountain Chief came into town today and did not come from the Sweet Grass Hills alone." No Bentonite was apt to air any disadvantages in boating season.)

## The Western Tribes

Fort Benton trade contacts with tribes in western Montana were limited, although as early as 1833 David Mitchell sent a small trading party to open barter with the Kutenais. Flatheads and Kutenais were on the east side of the Rockies in early historic years, but acquisition of firearms and horses by the Blackfeet drove them back west of the mountains, the Blackfeet also nearly exterminating the northern bands of Shoshones in the Three Forks area. The Flatheads near St. Mary's Mission in the Bitter Root valley suffered many raids.

There seemed to be a fragile truce in the buffalo range of central Montana summers, often broken. Fr. Pierre DeSmet negotiated one such agreement in 1846 near the Judith before leaving Fort Lewis with Amer Fur boats.

## Other Northern Tribes

Crees and often associated Metis (Chippewa-Cree-white) lived chiefly north of the boundary, and as for the Crees, their presence as horse raiders, and in the late 1870s when buffalo were nearly exterminated in Canada, as hunters of the dwindling herds in Montana. Andrew Garcia's "Tough Trip Through Paradise" gives an 1878 look at these almost chaotic hunting grounds.

Many of the Metis remained in Montana, a chief colony in the later Lewistown area, where about fifty families settled in 1879. Their names are common across northern Montana.

The most tragic in many respects was a small band of Chippewa-Cree, landless when reservations were fixed and hapless wanderers for another generation. It was 1916 before a miniscule reservation was set aside, named Rocky Boy, between Havre and Fort Benton near the Bear's Paw Mountains. The name, a white translation of another translation, of their chief, Stone Child.

# Grass Replaces Gold

## Free Grass Draws Cattlemen

*F*irst cattle in what became Montana came with the fur traders, to Fort Union about 1832, most likely a milk cow or two on that first trip of the steamboat Yellowstone. It was probably two or three years before Fort McKenzie acquired a cow for milk and butter; Maximilian makes no mention of such on his 1833 visit. He does refer to numerous horses at the fort, undoubtedly acquired through trade with the horse rich Blackfeet.

First specific reference, in fall 1843 a war party of Blackfeet, angered when refused the customary ammunition at Fort McKenzie, drove off cattle belonging to the fort which had been driven up from Fort Union, one source says the Indians killed two of the animals, which were charged to the head trader and chief clerk at $100 per head. Tom Reese, Negro employe, started after the war party to recover the cattle and was shot and killed. This led to the tragic incident of February 19, 1844, when a cannon was turned on a party of Blackfeet come to trade and resulted in the abandonment of Fort McKenzie.

By that time St. Mary's Mission in the Bitter Root had various kinds of livestock, including cattle, and in the next few years a cattle trade developed along the Oregon Trail in the Fort Hall vicinity, the traders giving a wintered animal for two trail-worn oxen, and by 1850 John Owen, and Dick, John and James Grant were trailing cattle up to the Bitter Root to winter, the first commercial ranchers.

The Fort Benton inventory for May 4, 1851, shows only two oxen, but lists seven cows and calves, three bulls, eight horses, five mules and 19 hogs. Interestingly, a cat at $5 had the same value as a large hog. Maximilian had given the reason in 1833, Fort McKenzie "swarmed with mice." The cat thus was a valued employe. There were several sets of harness and eight ox yokes. The Fort Benton Journal of 1854 and later indicates substantial use of wagons and carts, some in trade with goods sent to Indian camps, and a continual movement to and from the Highwood Mountains for logs, to and from the Teton for firewood. In 1855, Malcolm Clarke, former employe, arrived with 13 carts of goods to provide opposition at Teton in mid-November; about the same time six wagons were sent from Fort Benton to Fort Union, probably loaded with furs and robes. The carts were undoubtedly similar to the Red River cart made of wood throughout, which a man or two could put together in a few hours—capacity about a thousand pounds.

The Isaac Stevens expedition of 1853 brought a number of wagons to Fort Benton, which were left when the main party moved on by pack train westward. John Mullan's road building 1859-62 also brought in wagons. It should be evident that these would also be utilized by the fur company through rental or some other arrangement. Transportation was growing at Fort Benton ahead of the Montana gold rush. Granville Stuart recalled about 200 head of animals in and near Fort Benton in those early years. By January 1863, James Fergus reported American Fur had a large grazing range on Sun River where cattle and horses were sent to fatten, both winter and summer.

In 1862 Conrad Kohrs and John Bielenberg trailed the first cattle into the Deer Lodge valley, presumably from Oregon. Then there was the influx of steers from the freight trains, one unattributed note has it that at Alder Gulch in winter 1863-64 a steer would bring $100, next year 400 head were offered at $40, and another thousand later broke the price to $12.

First sizable trail herd was brought from Missouri by D. A. G. Flowerree in 1865.

## Nelson Story's Cattle Drive From Texas

Nelson Story came to the Alder Gulch diggings in 1863, ran a store and worked an abandoned claim which yielded $30,000 in gold dust, converted to $40,000 in greenbacks, according to his son Byron, chief source of the almost incredible 1866 drive of Texas cattle to Montana. (Various accounts give the number a range of 600 to 1,000, even several times the latter total. The son says his father sewed $10,000 greenbacks into his clothes and went down to Fort Worth where he found the going price $10, mostly cows with calves thrown in.)

Story hired 26 footloose Texans for the drive, armed them with new-fangled Remington breech loaders and the drive headed north. They had no trouble, few losses to the Kansas line, where former Jayhawkers had set up a rifle backed deadline against the feared Texas tick fever in cattle. Avoiding the rifles, the route was westward, and if Story had another destination in mind, same had been changed. After flanking the quarantine line the thousand cattle and party of 27 made their monotonous way north across Kansas and Nebraska and on to Fort Laramie. From there the trail led northwest on the Bozeman Trail to the Montana diggings.

Along the trail the U. S. army was building a chain of military posts, to Fort Reno and on to Fort Phil Kearny in Wyoming and Fort C. F. Smith in southern Montana. The Sioux, reinforced by tribes that had been harried out of Minnesota, in 1866 felt they had been very badly treated by whites, and repeatedly had warned that travel on the Bozeman Trail would be as perilous as thousands of warriors could make it, and that building of military posts was certainly an act of war. They were led in their most earnest endeavors by Red Cloud, one of the great Sioux war chiefs.

At the time Story's trail herd reached Fort Laramie, Fort Reno had been completed and Fort Kearney was under construction. The country north of Laramie was alive with Indians, there were signs of bitter fighting in burned wagons and dead stock. It wasn't until within ten miles of Fort Reno on the edge of bad lands that Sioux attacked the Story train, whooping warriors and flights of arrows. Those level lines of bullets from most of the 27 Remingtons turned the fight; the Sioux had some knowledge of breech loaders, but the border-wise Texans could pump out several times as many shots a minute as the old type. They retreated, driving a small bunch of Story cattle into the bad lands. Story and his Texans were outraged at the larceny and rode after the cattle. They surprised the Indians in camp and recovered the stock, every head, including three wounded animals they butchered for trail beef, and drove on to Fort Reno where two men wounded by arrows were left to recover.

In 1912 John Catlin, who joined the party at Laramie, added a sequel. The trail herd lingered near Fort Reno for a few days, had a herder killed by hostiles one night, then tramped on to Fort Phil Kearney, where buildings were still going up. There soldiers came out with orders from Col. Henry Carrington to go no farther, as the army could provide no escort; additionally, don't camp any closer than three miles of the fort, trooper mounts needed the grass.

That was too far away for help from soldiers in event of Sioux attack. After two weeks, Story put it up to his Texans. Recalled Catlin, he "proposed that we move ahead without Carrington's permission....if we started in the night we could get so far from the post before morning that none of the soldiers would dare come after us.... There were 27 men in our party. There were about 300 troopers at the fort. But the Sioux were more afraid of us than they were of the soldiers. We were armed with Remington breech loaders and the troopers had only the old Springfield rifles. The little brush we had with the Indians below Reno had taught them the effectiveness of our fire."

The Story outfit moved out the night of October 22 after the post was asleep. The night drive was so successful that from then on the herd traveled nights and rested days. The outfit was attacked only two or three more times during days, and the Sioux easily beaten off. Catlin felt that had they followed Carrington's orders the Story party would have been near Kearny December 21st when Capt. Wm. Fetterman rode out of Kearny with 80 men into the same oblivion Custer found later. On the other hand, two dozen Texans with those breech loaders might have rescued Fetterman's command and assassinated the Sioux.

The Story outfit rolled on, into Montana by night marches to Fort Smith on the Big Horn, by then relatively safe in Crow country, though they buried their fourth man, a hunter, killed by stray Sioux.

The thousand head went onto range December 4 at the site of present Livingston. Two dozen Texas cowhands, first of their breed in Montana, could whoop it up in Bozeman saloons, and would be followed in years to come by many more. Appropriately, "their brand" was the Ox Yoke on left ribs.

(In later years numerous Texas trail herds made the long trek to Montana ranges. One of the hands, Teddy Blue Abbott, said in 1883 "all the cattle in the world seemed to be coming up from Texas." From a hilltop near the North Platte he saw seven herds behind his, knew there were eight ahead, and saw the dust from 13 more rising far to the north of the Platte.)

The range situation in Montana in the late 1860s: Bulk of settlers in the mining camps. Fort Ellis near Bozeman provided protection of a sort for a few farmers and ranchers, Fort Shaw on the Sun did the same. The Yellowstone valley, Judith Basin and all of northern Montana was Indian country.

Aside from work oxen, most of the cattle came into Montana from Utah and the Oregon country these early years, although one small herd from Colorado and possibly a second Texas drive by Story in 1867 added to the total.

### Into Northern Montana

There were American Fur Co. work oxen as well as horses in the Fort Benton vicinity by 1861, artist William Cary, who came into Montana on the Chippewa, makes clear. After the boat burned, a number of wagons salvaged part of the goods. By 1863 American Fur was wintering stock at Sun River and the following year Fort Benton's resources, oxen and horses, were strained to move a big cargo from Cow Island. Wm. Gladstone may have been the first to try the Highwood Mountain area, contracting to winter a hundred head of horses there. He lost 60 to Piegan and Crow raiders. In winter 1867-68 American Fur and Carroll & Steell wintered work oxen in the Highwoods.

Earliest range, as distinguished from work, cattle in northern Montana probably were a small herd driven from Utah to Sun River in 1869 by old man Burd and sons, Samuel and Julian. They started a small ranch 12 miles above Fort Shaw, moved to the Teton a few years later.

A larger effort and deserving of mention as first sizable cattle ranch in northern Montana was stocked by the herd of 700 Texas longhorns Robert Ford and Tom

Dunn drove in from Colorado to the later Great Falls townsite in 1870. These were followed by a thousand head all the way from the Lone Star State that fall belonging to Dan Flowerree and John Cox, who set up below the Burd ranch. (An area legend is of the time "Uncle Dan" slept with a dead man, whose corpse had been placed on the only bed available. Said Flowerree, "Never scared of him alive; nor dead either.")

James Arnoux of Fort Benton in 1871-72 located a ranch near the mouth of Highwood creek, first permanent settler in that area. Roland Buckland a few months later in 1872 left the dangerous Whoop Up trade to locate nearby, followed next year by John Harris, who drove in a small bunch of cattle. Horace Clarke, son of Malcolm, was another early settler on Highwood.

Winfield S. Stocking, in a hotel and meat market in Fort Benton from 1867, located on the Teton River four miles from Fort Benton in 1872, possibly even earlier. Son John Stocking once recalled that the ranch house had a stockade, and also an escape tunnel, due to the ever present possibility of an Indian raid. On one occasion he and his mother, Margaret, had to parley with a war party of Bloods until the affair ended peacefully. Rev. George McDougall in an 1873 account, mentions what has to be the new Stocking spread as three miles from Fort Benton, 400 head of horned cattle and a herd of horses.

In 1874 Joe Cobell located on the Shonkin side of the Highwoods. He probably had a few cattle, but the Italian native turned chiefly to truck gardening, raising thousands of pounds of potatoes, onions, turnips and other vegetables for an eager Fort Benton market. That same year General John Gibbon of Fort Shaw won the territorial fair prize for best exhibits from benchland. He informed the Helena Herald reporter that 30 acres were under cultivation, enough to provide welcome vegetables for the entire garrison. An added note, "in portions cultivation develops alkali," a problem current more than a century later.

For the gradually developing livestock industry of northern Montana 1874 was a turnabout year, the September 23 Herald reporting organization of the "Sun River Rangers, a citizen company, organized to protect the homes and property of the settlers of the northern part of the country against Indian marauders." The Rangers engaged in an undisclosed number of minor engagements with rustlers and cattle killers, red and white, and the group was a forerunner of the various livestock associations.

### The Lure Of Free Grass

The Sioux War of 1876 and the flight of the Nez Perce the following year were deterrents to expansion onto the free grass of northern ranges, but 1878 was marked by formation of noted cattle outfits of northern Montana. That year the Harris brothers were expanding, C. W. Price went into cattle with in-laws Joe Baker and the Conrads, and John Lepley, former miner and a minor rancher near the Sun, drove a large herd into Benton to cross the Missouri in late summer and onto the Shonkin range where a few buffalo continued an increasingly hazardous existence. The Price outfit merged with the Harris in 1881 and became the Benton & St. Louis. Under this name and as Conrad Circle or just Circle it became at one period the largest in Montana with 25,000 head on the tax rolls.

Also in 1878 Malcolm Morrow Sr. and sons, Malcolm Jr., Dave and William T. entered the cattle business in the area of the lower Shonkin.

Untypical Fort Benton arrivals in 1879 were two young men from Chicago, Milton E. Milner and John Boardman, the second left five years later for the Miles City area.

By the June 1880 census there were 61 persons enumerated on the Highwood or western side, 170 on the Shonkin end of the range. Most were listed as farmers or family members, numbers doubtless ran a few head of cattle. By contrast few resided along the Marias and Teton rivers, the Marias then marking the southern boundary of the Indian reservation extending across northern Montana.

Four of Chouteau county's larger cattle outfits are more fully dealt with below, largely because of data available and as typical otherwise of the days of the open range. Several others are as worthy of more research.

### A Very Unusual Cattleman

Milton E. Milner has been painstakingly researched by Ben Woodcock of Fort Benton, and he is the source for below:

Born in Illinois in 1847, Milton Everett Miller ran away to Chicago in late 1861 to enlist in the Union army. Mustered in October 28, his papers show a mustered out date of October 31—it seems certain his parents had located the 14 year old. He changed his last name to Milner in Cook county court a year before coming to Montana. By that time Milner had received a thorough education, including Williams College in Massachusetts, and had become a very successful business man. He and John M. Boardman came to Fort Benton in 1879, got their start in the cattle business with native animals they bought, the herd soon upgraded by purebred bulls shipped in by steamboat. Boardman left the firm a few years later, moved to the Miles City area.

Milner's career in the cattle business was similar to many other enterprising men of those days, but in other respects he was a most unusual stockman. He was one of the leading spirits in formation of the Shonkin Stock Association in 1881, for years was its secretary, and after the large scale move north of the Missouri in the latter 1880s was an organizer of the North Montana Roundup—in July 1890 4,000 Milner cattle were crossed at Fort Benton enroute to the Malta area.

One of the most interesting facets: Milner originated the idea of the first Wild West Show of "Buffalo Bill" Cody, with a Milner stockholder, Nate Salsbury, helping to carry it out, travelling with and acting as business manager for the show. Salsbury is mentioned as a visitor at the Grand Union in 1890 in the interests of the Cody show and "recent" tour. One of Salsbury's contributions was doubtless securing participation of Gabriel Dumont, then a Bear Paws resident, who had been Louis Riel's lieutenant in the 1885 North West Rebellion of Metis in Canada. Dumont was a star on a European tour, left Cody when the show was scheduled in England—a treason warrant was still valid.

The Milner operation was incorporated about the time Boardman left for Miles City, as Milner Livestock Company. Investors included $7,000 by James O'Neill, actor and father of noted playwright Eugene O'Neill, who found it the most profitable investment he ever made. Mr. Woodcock, noting Milner's fondness for writing—evidence includes a classic will—nurses a belief that papers left on Milner's death in 1913 may have been the basis for some of the O'Neill plays.

Milton Milner built a showcase story-and-a-half mansion of mountain logs on the home ranch, all the inside materials imported. The home included seven fireplaces built of Vermont stone, floors of hardwood, picture window, the finest viands, beverages and chinaware. The library was most beautiful of all, finished with South American hardwoods, and included several Charles M. Russell paintings and one Frederick Remington of Milner and an employe, Judge Kennon.

Milner quite evidently lived in luxury unusual to many of the cattle kings. He was also an active humanist, a close friend said his first concern was for the people who worked for him, and next for those who invested in his company. This was evidenced after his foreman, Bill Mudgett, drowned in the Missouri at Fort Benton July 2, 1890, while swimming a herd of cattle across. Milner provided a pension for Mudgett's mother. He also sent a number of young cowboys who showed promise to college at his expense. At his death in 1913 provision was made in his will for continued college expense of some, and for Mudgett relatives. The bulk of the Milner fortune was left to faithful employes, and in accordance with his directions his body was cremated and the ashes strewn in the Missouri at the old Fort Benton ford where Bill Mudgett had been swept to his death.

Shonkin Stock Association records of calves branded indicate growth of the Milner operation, in 1883 206 calves were branded, in 1885 711, and in 1887 after the hard winter, 944.

## Miner To Cattle Baron

John Lepley was born in Stuttgart, Germany, about 1835, coming to the United States at age 16. After working in the midwest, he came to the Pike's Peak area in 1861, and a year later to Montana. After some frustrations in mining, he and a partner, Chris Keyes, headed north from the Alder Gulch diggings, in 1864 crossing some of the rich placer ground around Last Chance Gulch.

They made a small strike on Silver Creek, good for, Lepley told a River Press reporter in 1884, six or seven dollars a day. Nothing to shout about, but a fair living, except it might have been far better; Lepley had wanted to prospect Last Chance where the big strike was made later in 1864.

Keyes (the first name varies according to source, as does the last as Kies, even Keyser, but his partner should have known it) got restless. He had picked up three small nuggets in the Bear Paw area while hunting for the fur company at Benton, and wanted to go back. Lepley wasn't anxious for Indians, the north country was swarming with hostiles. In February 1865 the partners agreed to split the Silver Creek gold and whatever Keyes found, and off he went to Fort Benton. Lepley kept on at the claim, by then doing a bit better.

At Fort Benton Keyes bought an outfit, apparently went off to the north alone. Several months later Lepley received an electrifying message from Chris Keyes, back at Fort Benton again: "Drop everything and come on. You don't want any horses or money; we can get all of the latter that we can carry. Come quick."

John Lepley almost went, he recalled, reconsidered on news of Indian raids and the views of several miners at Silver Creek. Keyes at Benton waited a few days, then got itchy feet and left Benton again with a small party in August, Lepley reckoned it probably three men and two squaws. Somewhere south of the Little Rockies, the party was rubbed out, probably by Blackfeet, except that one of the squaws got away and reported the affair much later.

The "lost Keyes diggings" joined the legendary lost mines of the west, although Frank Aldrich, member of an 1884 party that triggered a Little Rockies boom, felt they had located the Keyes claim. Bill Hamilton and party in 1868 had found some gold in the Little Rockies and evidence of previous work, but decided their hair more precious than the beans and bacon diggings they had located.

John Lepley several times in later years grub staked prospectors in the general area. He regarded his dead partner as truthful and reliable, and denied the possibility that the gold Keyes showed at Benton was from robbed and murdered miners returning to the States by small boats.

Proceeds from the Silver Creek claim were sufficient to launch Lepley into the cattle business at Rocky Gap, about 20 miles from Fort Shaw, in 1871-72 with another partner, C. H. Austin. The men ran a few head, gradually expanded, and had some dairy cattle, selling milk at Fort Shaw.

The gradually increasing stock business on the Shonkin range drew the partners. September 4, 1878, a large herd of Lepley-Austin cattle crossed the Missouri at Fort Benton, bound for Arrow Creek, said the Record. Actually the home ranch was at Big Sag. Austin later sold out to Lepley.

The JL brand was quite familiar to cowhands of the Shonkin Roundup, generally the second biggest in the Shonkin Stock Association, eventually was surpassed by Milton Milner's Carpenter Square.

Calves branded JL totaled 803 in 1883 and 903 in 1885, in 1887 following the winter all stockmen remembered to the end of their days, Lepley brandings were only 366. On a visit to Helena in January 1891, the Herald remarked that John Lepley had suffered a $100,000 loss that memorable winter, since had recouped.

In August 1899 John Lepley foresaw the end of the old range system but didn't have time to adjust, dying at his Fort Benton home January 20, 1900. The estate appraisal was about $270,000, most going to nephews and nieces.

"Lepley's Bear" was one of C. M. Russell's yarns, briefly a horse hitched to an old cottonwood stump while the rider put a bullet in a big silvertip. The shot resulted in a charge on the hunter, who sprinted for his mount, which took off when he hit the saddle. At the end of the tether everything came unstuck, the horse somersaulted, ditching the rider. The bear, hit by some of the falling limbs, changed directions, and, Lepley told the author, "for months he has to walk that old hoss a hundred yards before he can spur him into a lope, and that you could stake him on a hairpin and he'd stay." The mishap was apparently in early April 1882, Benton Record and River Press giving slightly different versions, both with Lepley up a small tree at the windup.

### The Malcolm Morrow Family

The Malcolm Morrows came to this country from Canada, first to the Midwest, then Denver, and in 1864 needed 60 days to reach Alder Gulch, the two older boys, Malcolm Jr. and William T., driving 41 head of cattle along. The senior Morrows in all had 13 children, an incomplete genealogy shows, not all surviving childhood. It also shows six generations in at least one of the lines of descendants, still in Chouteau county.

They didn't have much success at mining and after paying $150 for a sack of flour the family diet became largely meat and milk. The Morrows moved to Last Chance in 1865, where dairying proved more profitable than mining. Father and oldest boys tried freighting from Benton in 1866. Early in the year freight was 40c a pound to Helena, one son recalled, which helps explain that $150 flour, but with a big turnout of farmers, freight dropped when steamboats began to arrive, to $1.50 or $2 a hundred, and the men went back to cattle.

First influx of the family into the Fort Benton area appears to have been when Malcolm Sr. and daughter Agnes arrived in early October 1878 with 1500 head of cattle for the Shonkin range. Father, and sons Malcolm, William T. and David settled along Shonkin Creek soon after; one note shows Dave had built a house by the first of 1880. The Wm. T. Morrow ranch for years was a stage stop on the way from Fort Benton into the Judith Basin.

Wm. T. also was one of the organizers of the Shonkin Stock Association in 1881, the others soon becoming members. A branding record of the association shows that 179 calves were branded for him in 1886—the next year, following the losses of a hard winter, the total was an even 100.

Several of the Morrow girls married cattlemen, including Laura Belle to J. C. Adams of Sun River, and Mary to Robert Coburn, prominent pioneer cattlemen.

Morrow family members were in business in Fort Benton also, in a ferry, meat market, and this century in the Fort Benton Drug & Jewelry.

## Conrad Circle Became Noted Montana Brand

Whether by its original Benton & St. Louis Cattle Co., or Conrad Cattle Co. of later years, the Circle was one of the west's noted brands, to rank with Montana's Square & Compass, DHS, 79, Two Dot and Circle C, or "foreign" brands which operated in Montana, such as the Matador, XIT and Turkey Track.

The brand gave its name to the Circle bridge on the road to Chester. (Circle, Montana, was named for another outfit.) The Conrad Circle operated in Montana and Canada—the writer has old checks to prove it, and paid cash dividends of $1,500,000 during its forty years of existence.

The outfit had its beginnings in the Fort Benton area in 1878 as C. W. Price & Co., with Jos. A. Baker, C. E. and Wm. G. Conrad as his partners. In May 1882 Price disposed of his interests to the partners and they with Harris & Co. reorganized as Benton & St. Louis, with $500,000 paid up capital. The Benton Record of January 1, 1883, called it the largest cattle concern in Montana, with plans to improve the quality of cattle by imported white face bulls.

In those years the big trail drives from Texas were underway. In early summer of 1883 a trail herd of 4,000 from El Paso swam the Missouri at Fort Benton bound for Pincher Creek, Canada, the property of Cochrane Land & Ranche Co. Forty men accompanied the herd, headed by Lords Walrond and Cochrane, imperturbable Britishers who to the delight of impious onlookers wore fore and aft caps, knee pants, gaiters, rolled stockings, monocles and sideburns. Expected drives that summer and fall were about 150,000 new cattle, an influx that paved the way to the disaster of 1886-87.

By 1884 the Benton & St. Louis owned about 25,000 head of cattle. A couple of years later Howell Harris moved a herd of Circle cattle north of the boundary onto leased land in later Alberta. By the time the outfit was reincorporated in 1902 as the Conrad Circle Cattle Co., Howell was signing checks as manager of the "Canadian Herd" and brother John Harris as manager of the "American Herd."

It was only a few years later that the great homestead rush forever ended the days of free grass. In the Circle area the beginnings were earlier, of course, with settlers locating near water wherever possible. Numbers of cattlemen recognized the growing problem as the end of the open range. However, homesteaders were coming into Montana in numbers by 1908, and congress gradually liberalized the rules to keep the influx mounting. By 1921 the Circle, which had been losing money for several years, was finished. The directors April 13 that year voted to dissolve the corporation, accomplished in mid-1926 with a small final dividend.

## Shonkin Stock Association

The Shonkin District Stock Association (district soon dropped) was organized July 24, 1881, at a meeting at the Milner & Boardman ranch, and was modeled on a similar group at Sun River. Pro tem officers were John Harris president and M. E. Milner secretary. Original members were Harris, Milner, John Boardman, A. W. (Ike) Kingsbury, Thos. H. Martin, Wm. T. Morrow, John Lepley and Greenleaf & Co.

During its existence the association conducted roundups, regulated the vast open range south of the Missouri to the Highwoods and Arrow Creek breaks, organized roundups, set fees for branding calves, bought high grade bulls, built corrals, set penalties for branding for non-members and for nonpayment of assessments; offered rewards for conviction for rustling, setting range fires, for selling liquor to Indians and offered bounties on wolves and other predators. Expenses were met through per animal assessments.

The association came into being following the bad winter of 1880-81, regarded by many members as worse than the more publicized die-out of 1886-87. At that first meeting it was noted that "More cattle were lost on this range the past winter from depredations of Indians than from the severity of the weather."

Journal entries were often guarded, but it is an easy speculation that some members or employes participated in the large scale range vigilante activities in 1884 in the area of the Musselshell; in view of a May 2, 1883, resolution citing "repeated offenses and depredations committed by stock thieves," and that the Shonkin Association "give and extend to the Judith Cattle Association all help and assistance that may be required of us jointly to bring to speedy justice each and all such offenders." At an April 1884 meeting the secretary was directed to write the Judith group regarding a representative to the Musselshell. Granville Stuart, leader of the "cleanup" of white rustlers, never named any other participant, nor did he provide any definite number of rustlers shot or hanged. One Helena paper in August 1884 carried an account of killing of nine horse thieves 40 miles above Cottonwood, and Walter Burke, stage man, mentioned a tree near Lavina where local people said five men were hanged. Estimates vary widely; Oscar Mueller, historian, estimated 15 to 18 shot or hanged in Stuart's DHS area. Walter Burke, who for T. C. Power set up the Benton-Billings stage line in 1882 and had trouble with horse thieves, heard it as "43 good men who would steal no more horses," but may have added a total in the Yellowstone area.

The Shonkin Association set rules for roundups, in 1881 one man and three saddle horses to participate for each 200 head of calves or fraction, low limit a man and horses for 25 or more, those with few cattle were assessed a fee, in those years $3 for branding.

In 1881 over 3700 calves were branded, assessments $2780; in 1883 the tally was 3733 spring and 1437 fall. The total branded in 1886 was 6562. After a winter in which hundreds of cattle died on the Shonkin range, the calf branding dropped sharply, a total of 4128.

In September 1883, the association members decided to employ Thos. Martin and Wm. Jones to remain on Arrow Creek from November 1st until spring to protect stock on that section of the range, at $40 per month and provisions furnished. Such jobs were very desirable to cowhands, ranchers customarily cut numbers of hands sharply through the winter, unhired hands might "ride grub line," most ranches would feed lone riders in exchange for work at chores. In the case of this employment the outcome was tragic. Bill Jones and Bill Gilham (who took the job instead of Martin) were out riding near the old stage road February 27, 1884, when they came upon a party butchering a beef and in the ensuing fight Jones was killed. Indians were blamed, in which case he would have been the last to die in the lengthy antagonism; some notes seems to indicate the rustlers were white.

A moral note in April 1884: "The Association views card-playing, gambling in any form and the drinking of intoxicating liquors with great disfavor because all such are demoralizing in their tendencies and interfere with effective work." Another, financial: "Resolved that it is the sense of this meeting that $40 per month is the proper wage for hired men upon the roundup this year."

Upgrading of range herds was a major concern of Association members, an action taken in July 1884 was purchase of 100 head of high grade bulls for the Shonkin range, members to share a proportionate cost. Other action was provision for separate herding of range bulls during off season. It was not until December 1885 that further action was taken, and the animals were driven from the railroad at Billings to the range in summer 1886.

Assessments against owners included the July 1884 40c for each calf branded for members. The bull purchase was more costly, $2.10 per calf to raise approximately $10,250.

The Shonkin Stock Association was on top of problems, minutes indicate. In December 1886 emphasis was placed on putting the roundup in shape by handling cattle "with a view of moving cattle to a better range." This came a few weeks ahead of opening most of northern Montana following an Indian cession.

Several minutes deal with the wolf problem. In July 1887 purchase of eight dogs for use against predators was approved. In December there had evidently been progress, the executive committee was to keep the wolf outfit working. Another problem was all that free beef on the hoof, in April 1888 the Association addressed the problem of meat rustlers, as usual turned over any action to the executive committee.

Although cattle had streamed north across the Missouri after the vast Indian reservation was reduced in 1887, three years later a journal entry noted, "some determined to move," and outlined the roundup in accordance with that fact.

Two additional problems occurred in 1894; the first minor, Great Northern trains were the cause of numbers of range fires—the danger abated by contacting the railroad. The second pinpointed a more serious one, growing strictures on range water, brought up by John Lepley's acquisition of Clear Lake. He was willing, if other Association members could and would contribute water access, to waive what he considered a fair settlement, 10% yearly on his cost of $1500, a $100 temporary payment was authorized.

A new group, the Northern Montana Roundup Association, was formed to cover the area north of the Missouri from Havre to Malta, where members of the older group were by 1894 running stock. First mention of employment of range detectives, not named of course, appeared a year later.

April 1895 members saw, "at the present time the end of the industry seems near." That was a reference to the influx of settlers who tended to settle near water and fenced off watering places of the range cattle. In December mention was made of a plan to buy water rights.

The Shonkin Stock Association was ended about 1910.

### Woolies Bring Wealth

Fort Benton's love affair with wool was a lengthy, mutually profitable arrangement between merchants and wool growers that for years supplied the only transportation route for that bulky commodity and that lasted into the railroad years.

In fact, Fort Benton, and its Grand Union Hotel, became the birthplace of the Montana Wool Growers Association.

As with other firsts hidden in the mists of the past, beginnings of the sheep industry in Montana are obscure. One note credits Father Ravalli with trailing a few sheep into the Bitter Roots in 1847, while James Drummond in "Montana Sheep Trails" cites the first as Thomas Harris with a dozen woolies in 1857.

Whatever, there is virtually undeniable evidence for a third. In the May 6, 1865, Montana Post at Virginia City: "On Friday evening a large drove of sheep, some 3500 in number, belonging to Mr. Geo. W. Forbes, astonished our citizens by their evolutions on the hills around Harper's Corral. They are to be shorn and the wool sent down the river." If the owner had the shears, herders were busy; at six pounds a head, the clip would have amounted to 21,000 pounds. Another if, Fort Benton's prolonged relationship with the wool industry had probably begun.

No further note on wool turns up before the August 28, 1875, Benton Record mentioning a T. C. Power shipment of 1127 pounds of sheep skins and 19,000 pounds of wool. The product may have been from the herd of A. W. (Ike) Kingsbury, generally credited with bringing the first sheep into Chouteau county around 1874.

The Record the next three years indicates the upward trend in sheep: 104,000 pounds in 1876, 208,000 in 1877 and 830,000 in 1878—wool shipped out by steamboat. Shipments apparently held firm the next two years, although in 1879 the paper commented, "Wool is coming up in the territory." In 1881, incomplete reports reached only 360,000, there was probably more, but the tough winter of 1880-81 may have been responsible for a decline. Next year, with Meagher county sheep growers sending their bulky clips north, the total listed in the Record was 1,122,756 pounds. By that time the Northern Pacific was building into southern Montana, reducing the area dependent on the Missouri River for wool transport.

There were by then a number of sheepmen in the Fort Benton area, among them Henry Macdonald, adventurer, Indian fighter, scout and pony express rider in the Musselshell area in the 1860s, who was partner with the Smith Bros. on Smith River earlier, and trailed 2,000 Cotswold and Merino sheep to a home ranch on Cottonwood Creek at the east end of the Highwoods about 1878. He found his first wool clip surprisingly heavy. A neighbor George D. Patterson, "has secured ranch on Shonkin, to arrive soon with 4,000 sheep purchased from Gov. Potts." That according to the September 20, 1878, Benton Record. And of course, Kingsbury in the Big Sag area. Another just before 1880 was Paris Gibson farther west in the Highwood area, an early Record note of Gibson & Macdonald seems to indicate the former took a band of Macdonald sheep "on shares" for his start.

Henry Macdonald, born in Scotland, arrived in the United States in time for service in the Civil War, came west after service and had a very colorful career on the Musselshell before going into sheep. He was successful in the industry, after reporting in the spring of 1887 his losses in the hard winter were only average, sold to Libby & Merrill that year. In 1882 he had hired a young Norwegian just off the Far West, the "hardest worker and thriftiest" he ever had, wrote daughter Eleanor Banks in "Wandersong." Louie Osnes later bought the former Macdonald ranch. Far from a success was dreamer Louis Riel, later to head the North West Rebellion of 1885 in Canada—Riel was discharged after losing his flock.

The sheep kept arriving in Meagher county and the Judith Basin, as well as in Chouteau county, then a fifth of Montana. They came onto the ranges along with the cattle off the long trail from Texas and by the shorter route from the Oregon country. Wool proved so profitable in those early years that numbers of the cattle outfits ran sheep as well, the result being that Montana was spared the bitter range wars of some other western states.

One could scarcely argue with success. A July 19, 1882, River Press reported wool selling at 22c to 25 3/4c per pound, pelts at 17c, the price being a good 2c higher than in Helena. The Press added that about 25 prominent wool growers were in town dickering with wool buyers, others had sold their clips and headed back to home ranges. That season about 1.2 million pounds were shipped down by steamboat.

## Montana Wool Growers Association

The next year was special. January 12, 1883, a group of area sheep ranchers met in the brand new Grand Union Hotel in Fort Benton to organize the Montana Wool Growers Association with Paris Gibson as president and his neighbor rancher L. W. Peck as secretary. A followup meeting January 31st drew more growers. The first convention was held in the hotel in July, George Patterson elected the next president.

"Fort Benton is the best wool market in the Territory," proclaimed the River Press just before that convention, reporting that at least five buyers were already in the city. Price of wool the preceding five years bore out the claim, plus a note that the Block P Steamboat Line offered better freight rates than did the Northern Pacific Railroad. This year Hays Bros. of Stanford tried an innovation, drifting their flocks by stages 70 miles or so to be shorn on the south (far) bank of the Missouri, perhaps 20,000 in several herds. The animals ate their way coming and going and beat freighters out of a hauling job. Needless to say, the July convention got good space in the paper.

Despite building of the Northern Pacific the rest of the way across Montana in 1883, the Benton wool market handled almost the exact amount of the previous summer. In 1884, though the River Press again proclaimed that Fort Benton was the best wool market, shipments dropped off a third to 800,000 pounds by river, possibly in part due to troubled affairs along the Musselshell, where cow ranch Vigilantes conducted a roundup of rustlers—freighters might have been a bit gunshy—also perhaps owners may have wanted to try rails for the novelty of it.

For the clip of 1885 Fort Benton made every effort to regain its lost wool business. Murphy Neel leased the vacant large Kleinschmidt building to offer free storage of wool pending sale, others added inducements, and shipments by river went past a million pounds. The local paper was burned out just as wool began coming in, a couple of weeks later gleefully reprinted an item from the Billings Gazette to the effect that one wool buyer there could find no wool for sale, went to Fort Benton and in a day bought a million pounds. Other major market then was Big Timber on the Northern Pacific, Billings virtually none that season. The 1885 price was around 20c a pound, a profitable level.

By late June 1886 Fort Benton was filling with sheepmen for yet another convention. It was a year wool growers would remember for some time, 1.5 million pounds going at an average price of 23c, despite some dirty low value clips, the paper carrying detailed lists of shipments by grower and sacks on August 11.

Depite the vast loss of Montana cattle in the "big die off" after the 1886-87 winter, sheep came through surprisingly well. In February John F. Patterson and two men stayed with their flock through a three day blizzard, no loss, and in March when the snow was gone Henry Macdonald reported only average losses. In June the wool began arriving in Fort Benton, warehouses were full. "Wool everywhere" noted the Press. Wool growers again met in the Grand Union, the roads from the south were busy, and ultimate shipments topped the previous year by a fraction, though the price was down at 20c. Shipments via river steamboats were far higher than by Jim Hill's railroad, which reached Benton late in September.

The first season of rail transport for wool (although three boats of the Block P Line carried some of the product in 1888) was marked by two events, first the building of a 100x108x15 wool warehouse on the levee, second by construction of the Fort Benton toll bridge, still in existence as oldest steel vehicular bridge in Montana. The bridge was not in use during the season, of course, but would be crossed by millions of pounds of wool in the future. James J. Hill gave very favorable terms for rail shipment of steel for the bridge—his was the only railroad across Northern Montana, and he saw it as cutting into shipments by Northern Pacific, only other east-west rail route.

By July 4 a wool compress had arrived and the wool warehouse was virtually completed. The compress of course was major factor in shipments by rail cars. Next week the town was crowded with wool buyers and the big warehouse was filling; much of the wool was arriving from the Judith Basin where too "wool was coming up," and making up for wool in southern Meagher county diverted to Big Timber and the NP.

In this busy season, growers again thronged the Grand Union for their convention. All was good for Fort Benton trade, the wool wagons made their return trip loaded with ranch supplies for the winter. Expansion of the wool industry had a predictable result, the price was going down, just over 17c in 1888. By the end of July 600,000 pounds of wool had been delivered in Fort Benton and much more coming in, ultimately reaching 1.5 million pounds. Old time freighter Pres Lewis came in with an outfit of three teams and 12 wagons with 130 sacks (about 36,000 pounds), which was a fifth of the Severance & Co. clip, the whole worth past $30,000. That year Chouteau county had 165,000 sheep sheared for a million pounds of wool, about six pounds per animal. By contrast 80,000 cattle—the ratio would change radically.

The year 1889 was first use of the new bridge (in prior years by large ferries). The season was similar to the previous one but the price better. Early sales were a satisfying 21c and over, and July 3 the wool warehouse was circled by wagons waiting to unload, a week later a third of a million pounds had been freighted to the depot. Another quarter million had gone by July 24 and the price was up to 24c. By this time the former Indian reservation across Montana north of the Marias and Missouri was open and livestock heading north onto ranges cleared of buffalo in the early years of the decade. (About 75 part bloods were collecting and freighting the buffalo bones to the railroad along the Milk River.) Big Sandy, new town in the center of an expanding industry, shipped out a half million bushels of wool in the season.

Result of the expansion of course was a gradual decline in the price of wool, while the poundage rose. Fort Benton continued as the wool shipping point for the Judith Basin, part of Meagher county and southern Chouteau through the 1890s, so the Benton shipments hovered around that 1.5 million pound figure. The price decline was a calamnity for many growers. There were few buyers in 1893, a panic year, next year the price was around 10c. In 1895 the minimum and often maximum was 8c; at Chinook one exasperated buyer told producers he would pay 6c, all the clip or none, or else pay 4c advance and the seller would take his chance on the eastern market. It was then that sheepmen and townspeople looked back on the palmy days of 1886.

Recovery came in 1897, the important Fort Benton market leading the way. Late in July John Patterson sold at 14 3/8c, top price to then in the state. By 1900 the price range reached 20c to 23c, but proliferation in numbers of woolies inevitably sent prices tumbling once more. Chouteau county assessed a half million head of sheep in 1897, continuing to a peak of nearly 800,000 by 1903. Two years before the Fort Benton market had handled nearly two million pounds.

Expanded demand hiked wool prices to a 20-26c range in 1905, just before the influx of homesteaders took over vast acreages of former range. The sheep men had a last hurrah in World War I, and the Benton Sheep Co. sold its clip too early at 57 1/2c—the price in late season reached 62c.

Sheep hung on in Chouteau county well into the new century, flocks herded to any available graze, but three decades after World War II numbers were laughable. The old wool warehouse, which had housed so many millions of pounds, was demolished in 1930. With it, regrettably, went the stored local records of the old I. G. Baker company, and probably of other early day businesses.

## Mobility On The Western Plains

The first Indian who traded or stole a horse in the Santa Fe area about 1600 certainly never realized the cultural shock that would ensue. Until the four legged carrier became common to the tribes, their hunting success was limited to small game, stalking deer etc., and the occasional and dangerous buffalo "surround" or the pishkun or cliff over which the big shaggies were driven. Not that they were inefficient hunters—their forebears had quite apparently exterminated the mammoth. But the small bands, they had to be few in number to survive, ranged from plenty to starvation.

With the advent of the horse, a hunter's range was vastly increased, the necessary movement of the tribe facilitated by horse travois and the tanned robe shelters could be larger. Also the Indian would base his economy chiefly on the great herds of buffalo—for food, shelter, clothing, tools and weapons. The periods of starvation were far fewer.

It took about 125 years for the horse to reach the Blackfeet, their first contact probably mounted war parties of enemy Shoshones and Flatheads, and a bloody surprise at the hands of their enemies. A tribe learned swiftly or dwindled and disappeared. The Blackfeet were fast learners.

First American contact with the tribe was probably June 26, 1806, when Meriwether Lewis and three companions encountered eight Piegans with about 30 horses on the headwaters of the Marias, a hunting or raiding party, and had to kill two. The fight undoubtedly solidified Blackfeet hostility, evident for years to come, but the explorers' contacts with traders from Canada had already given the Blackfeet a fearsome reputation as most warlike of the Indians along the border.

It was a quarter century before Kenneth McKenzie negotiated permission for an American Fur post in Blackfeet country, and the latter had repeatedly fought the redoubtable Mountain Men to a bloody deadlock, earning a grudging nickname of Bug's Boys or more politely the "Terrible Blackfeet."

The trader-tribal truce was generally observed thereafter, despite an occasional burnt fort or slain voyageur. Alexander Culbertson later reckoned the Blackfeet as poorly mounted as late as 1830, but the figure he gave for the Piegans of ten horses per lodge was in keeping with later counts of slightly more than one horse per person. For Bloods and North Blackfeet the ratio was about half that for the Piegans, a proportion soon to be adjusted by raid, trade and increase.

So there were horses available through trade for white use around the trading posts, and for every traveler on that wild frontier the best life insurance was a speedy mount with plenty of stamina. More horses were traded for than needed, Maximilian in 1833 reported 20 being sent to Fort Union as graze was scanty near Fort McKenzie. This became an annual event.

The explosive Montana gold rush from 1862 brought thousands of white men into Blackfeet country—their claimed tribal range ran to the Three Forks, and between races the theft of horses, more or less regarded as sport with a touch of war among the tribes, was an unending source of friction with deadly consequences.

There was another factor, a surprisingly early mention in the November 5, 1864, Montana Post: "Extensive whisky trading has been going on at Sun River with some Indians. The redskins first traded all their furs for whisky, and being drunk, all their horses afterwards. When they got sober, they found themselves without horses, consequently they had to steal some to get their winter's meat. If the whites would keep whisky from these children of the mountains, we would hear of very few Indian depredations in this part of the country." Some whites couldn't resist large profits, other whites paid for these in blood.

Sir Sam Steele, Canadian, once put a price on such transactions, a robe for "a cup of the poisonous decoction; a quart of the stuff bought a fine pony." He was referring to a trade a decade later north of the border, but the price seems probable and whisky was to be the ruination of the Blackfeet.

In the gold rush for the first time horses from the eastern part of the nation were coming into Montana in numbers. The mix didn't harm the species, both red and white had learned a bit about genetics, though not the word itself, and inferior stallions were usually gelded by both.

John Healy, most prominent of the Whoop Up traders, had a tip for buyers. He always bought Indian ponies "as they run," firmly believing the most active and intelligent would be first out of any corral.

Fort Benton's first horse hostels were crude affairs, in 1862-64 consisting of night herding of valued mounts on the town bottom. Next year Bill Hamilton had a stable of sorts, and Bill Gladstone that winter tried a variant. He contracted to herd and care for a hundred head of Fort Benton horses on Highwood Creek at $3 a head—his endeavor wasn't a smashing success, between Crows and Piegans he lost 60 head and understandably had a dissatisfied customer.

Even a stable was no guarantee. George Steell of the well known firm housed his fine black speedster in a stable back of the store. The son of Heavy Runner, said the Montana Radiator February 2, 1866, lifted the steed right out of the stable in broad daylight, and, say other sources, was boasting in camp that he had the finest buffalo runner on the Montana plains. Joe Kipp, half Mandan, stole the black back—grateful Steell sent Kipp off to St. Louis to school for a year as reward. Jerry Potts, Scotch and Blood, performed a simular service for W. S. Stocking in a Piegan camp to establish a sound credit line in event of future thirst.

How highly did the whites prize their horses? An 1869 Helena Herald reported a mile match race on the Benton race track for $200 a side, between Sam Debow's sorrel horse Bob and John Arner's bay mare Kate, the mare winning in 3:03, Besides the match bet, $3,000 more changed hands.

Dozens of the bloody little Indian-white fights were triggered by horse thieves, it wasn't always the red men at fault. And there also grew quite a thriving international business. In the Whoop Up years and later, it was often easy to trail stolen horses north and sell to either race with no embarrassing questions; perhaps making a return trip with remounts of another brand. Red faced soldiers or Mounties on occasion doubtless negotiated for return of their mounts at a price. The celebrated Cypress Hills "Massacre" of 1873 was triggered by a nocturnal change in ownership of horses, wolfers to Indians.

The horse stealing business thrived into the 1880s when rangeland Vigilantes under Granville Stuart and others possibly slew more whites than white Montanans ever had reds over the controversial matter of ownership of horses. At any rate, Walter Burke of the Fort Benton-Billings stage line repeated a count he had heard of "43 good men who wouldn't steal no more horses."

The harsh punishment of gun or rope of course stemmed from the fact that a man afoot out yonder had his chances of survival dimmed appreciably by the fact.

In later, tamer years, the matter of horse stealing reached ludicrous heights when Antelope, Blood Shot and Hind Shot, Piegans, arrested for horse stealing and brought to trial in Fort Benton in 1885, not only refused to plead innocent, but wanted the white world to know that they were the very best horse thieves thereabouts.

The final years of the century and into this found a two way traffic in the Fort Benton area, horses or whisky smuggled into Canada, Chinamen back. One Gus Brede, in 1891 killed by lightning atop a hill later named for his cargo—8 or 9 Chinese survived the strike on the wagon, was unluckier than most. He had already been fined $1,000 by Mounties for smuggling whisky, and had his outfit confiscated at Fort Benton for smuggling Chinese a few months earlier.

Horse numbers in northern Montana reached their peak in homesteading days—half broke range animals, some actually wild, went for $100 a head for farming!

## Beginnings Of Agriculture

Indians of the plains had a limited knowledge of agriculture, largely derived from contacts with sedentary tribes along the Missouri such as the Mandans. However, raising of beans, potatoes and corn proved a last resort. Blackfeet and other area tribes did use native wild roots and berries to a considerable degree. It remained for the Catholic Fathers at St. Mary's Mission in the Bitter Root to begin through the Flatheads, a rudimentary agriculture among some Indians. After John Owen purchased the mission and renamed it Fort Owen in 1850 he continued some farming.

Although one author suggests gardens were usual around fur posts, a search turned up no direct reference to Fort Benton area forts. First approach to agriculture in the Upper Missouri area may be assumed to have been limited haying for the few bovines and some favored horses.

The idea of Indian farming emerged in northern Montana when Alfred J. Vaughan, agent to the Blackfeet, started a government farm in 1859. It was a dry year, next was more successful, especially with wheat. From the scattered sources it seems likely the whites were demonstrating the approach, while the Blackfeet were content to watch, although agriculture did intrigue chief Little Dog to some degree.

Isaac Stevens, on an 1855 revisit to Fort Benton, may have encouraged the government farm project, writing that vegetables of all kinds, as well as cereal grains would thrive in northern Montana. He also noted the grazing was good. Later, at Sun River near the Indian farm, Robert Vaughn, William Sparks and others went into limited farming or gardening as the 1870s began. The Helena Herald in May 1869 had reported new farms being started on the Benton side of Sun River, bearing this out.

With the gold rush, down south, genuine farming developed as farmers turned miners viewed the high prices and demand for grain and vegetables of any kind and went back to their former livelihood in the mid 1860s.

At Fort Benton, a newspaper item about 1866 said a new farm was being fenced in on the flat just across the river and early vegetables were in great demand, but nothing else located in this period. T. C. Power of Fort Benton about the end of the decade was advertising agricultural implements in territorial papers, one of the first. **But at the** time, oats and wheat were being freighted to Fort Benton from the Gallatin valley where farming started shortly after the gold rush did.

Opening of the first army post in Montana, Camp Cooke at the Judith, in May 1866 undoubtedly meant considerable haying in the area for military transportation, spreading to Fort Shaw on the Sun a year later.

First direct note on sale of fresh vegetables at Fort Benton came about six years later. James Arnoux, who settled on Highwood Creek in 1872 after eyeing the dangers for a decade, by September 1875 was selling large amounts of vegetables to a ready market. The year before General John Gibbon at Fort Shaw won the territorial fair prize for vegetables grown on bench land, and said that 30 acres provided plenty of vegetables for the entire Fort Shaw garrison.

Joe Cobell picked the Shonkin side of the Highwoods for his farm-ranch venture, and became one of the first in Chouteau county to grow onions, beans, potatoes and the like. A few years later he was selling in such amounts as nine tons of onions, eight of potatoes.

Grain farming on any scale in the area got a slower start. It was 1882 before W. S. Evans and Julius Stewart became the first to try farming on bench land near Fort Benton. First threshing report found was in December 1880; Wheeler O. Dexter's threshing season was fairly good, almost 27,000 bushels of grain, virtually all of that oats for feed.

Advent of farming grangers produced good returns, in area tales as well as edibles. One reported that pumpkins grew so fast on Highwood farms that the pumpkins were worn out by being dragged. Potatoes grew so large overnight on Shonkin and Highwood that farmers had men employed to cover the spuds to protect them from sunburn. McLeish Brothers after haying had to move their first cutting of alfalfa across the road—the second cutting grew so fast there was no room for the mown hay. Jimmy Shaw in 1877 had two acres of heavy oats, the total weight up to 210 bushels. That was less the buckets full he fed to his 200 chickens. These fowl choked to death because the oat kernels were so huge. Hence Jimmy was inviting his neighbors and passing strangers to chicken stew for all comers.

# The Military Presence

## The Army And Fort Benton

The first soldiers to visit Fort Benton bottom were of course members of the Lewis & Clark expedition in 1805. Another group came September 1, 1853, with the Isaac I. Stevens party. Of this party, Lt. John Mullan was the most frequent visitor in the next few years, while exploring and then building a military road from Fort Walla Walla. Summer 1860 Mullan met Major George Blake at Fort Benton. Major Blake had brought 300 soldiers bound for the Pacific Coast up the Missouri River on two steamboats. The same year Captain W. F. Raynolds and party kept a rendezvous with the Blake party on return from a lengthy exploration of the northwest, and followed the Missouri down to Fort Union and out of Montana.

First soldiers to be stationed at Fort Benton, although only for a brief time, were oddly ex-Confederates, in the west called "Galvanized Yankees." These were men captured by Union forces who chose to enlist for frontier service rather than go to prisoner of war camps. May 12, 1865, Lt. Cyrus Hutchins of Co. H, 1st U. S. Volunteers, and 10 men, embarked on the steamboat Deer Lodge, under orders from Col. Charles Dimon, for Fort Benton "to control the trade with Indians between that point and Fort Union." The Deer Lodge arrived at Fort Benton on May 30. The soldiers may have returned to Fort Rice (in later North Dakota) in June, more likely on a later boat.

### Tragedy At Ophir

The small detachment off the Deer Lodge would have arrived at just the time Indian troubles around Fort Benton had reached an explosive stage. Lone travelers on the Benton Road were being stopped by Blackfeet and robbed or killed—the Indians regarded the tremendous influx of whites as interlopers to be discouraged, though in first stages the Indians stopped at robbery.

That spring of 1865 the Montana Post was commenting approvingly on the project of Ophir, a proposed townsite at the mouth of the Marias, about a dozen miles below Fort Benton. One of those involved was Frank Moore, captain of the steamboat Cutter, which reached Fort Benton July 14, 1864, so late that Moore decided to winter his boat in the vicinity of the river port. He went off to the mines and readily joined in the project of Ophir. At that point in May 1865 a crew of men were busy building cabins—the start of an anticipated metropolis, for which the promoters had a legislative charter.

No mention was found in the Post of the affair in which Henry Bostwick and Joseph Spearson killed several Indians in Fort Benton in early May in front of the Blackfeet agency and threw the bodies into the Missouri until a later issue. But the perhaps related tragedy at Ophir was entirely different, it involved whites. On May 25, 1865, a party of Bloods estimated at 100 and led by war chief Calf Shirt killed ten white woodcutters. The dead included several well known Montanans. In the next century a son of one of the victims erected a memorial near the site, later moved to Highway 87 just south of present Loma. The names on the memorial were Franklin and George W. Friend, Abraham Lotts, John Alley, John Andrews, N. W. Burris, Frank Angeline, Henry Martin, Henry Lyons and James Berry. There was variance in the names, Angeline was certainly Angevine, a deputy collector of U. S. customs. And James Perie, colored, whom the Indians reported the stoutest fighter of the ten, was the James Berry listed.

Accounts of the bloody event at Ophir drew much space in the Post June 3, misspellings of the names of victims adding to the later confusion. June 10 another article was headlined, "THE INDIAN WAR," followed a week later by word that teamsters on the Benton road were grouping to fight their way through to the freight at Ophir, a substantial amount due to low water which prevented a number of boats from reaching port at Fort Benton. By July 8 the Post had an account of the killing of three Indians at Benton; one had slapped a white man, so the "savages got no more than they deserved." Next week the probable real cause of the tragedy was reported, Charley Carson during the winter had followed three Blood horse thieves and killed them.

Gov. Sidney Edgerton was leaving the territory, which made his secretary, Thomas Francis Meagher, acting governor, the Post reported. There was, of course, clamor for military protection of whites. Furthermore, ran an editorial, "Million after million of gold has left the territory, by way of the river and by the overland route."

July 11, 1866, Major William Clinton and four companies of the 13th Infantry landed at the mouth of the Judith River from steamboats Rubicon and Lexington to found Camp Cooke, by a few weeks the first military post in what became Montana. Purpose was to protect steamboat freight on the Missouri River. Fort C. F. Smith, near the Wyoming border and one of a string of three posts intended to protect emigrants on the Bozeman Trail into the Yellowstone valley and on to Virginia City, was founded that autumn. Neither army post fulfilled its purpose, but where the steamboats kept coming up the Missouri, Red Cloud's Sioux so harassed travelers on the Bozeman Trail that an uneasy truce was only attained by abandoning the three forts in 1868.

Camp Cooke was definitely not the spot for a garrison to protect settlers, especially those miners inveigled into a bizarre and futile winter stampede to the Sun River. Although Chief Little Dog of the Piegans proved a true friend of whites, saving dozens from starvation by supplying them with wild game, Indians were blamed for almost everything that went wrong with the stampede. Some argonauts were robbed by Indians or whites, a few killed, more were frozen to death.

Next step came in February, when the acting governor, a Civil War hero, tried to organize a state militia, which he presumably planned to lead to more glory. A call was issued for 500 men to war against the Blackfeet in the Fort Benton area.

Meagher ordered militia Col. Neil Howie to organize volunteers to relieve and garrison Fort Benton with 50 men; when another 100 appear to march to the Piegan camp to demand stolen goods. Murderers to be hanged; next the force was to go against the Bloods.

The Piegans actually had pretty well broken with the Bloods, partly for their own safety, and a brief item in the Post in conjunction with a long story about the militia put the whole matter in ludicrous focus on how Bentonites in the "war zone" regarded matters: "Parties from the fort go armed when securing wood from across the Missouri. They also report an abundance of arms, ammunition and men." Perhaps helping allay any fears at the head of navigation was a company from Camp Cooke stationed there during the winter. Some sources indicate Fort Benton residents far more discontented with the perhaps 50 volunteers who did show up under John Morgan than they were fearful of Indians. The volunteer militia requisitioned freely and, a side effect, also stirred up the Indians.

Actual establishment of Camp Cooke had gone unnoted by the Post for weeks. First found criticism of the location at the Judith appeared August 11, as a "sad mistake." The editor favored the Marias or Sun River, with which most citizens at Fort Benton apparently agreed. Sheriff Bill Hamilton said the soldiers might as well be in New York as where they were. Later he suggested $25 per scalp would bring the Indians to terms.

One brief Post item in March 1867 was a portent of things to come: "This year the U. S. government will send an enormous amount of freight." Meagher was still planning war in May, Sherman wrote the alarm was overstated (the general referred to Meagher as a "stampeder") but that citizens might organize in self defense; troops and arms were coming by steamboat. (April 27 the upbound Jennie Lewis arrived at Omaha with 1000 soldiers.) By May 25 the Post editor wrote "understand three companies to be at Sun River." Later that month detachments of soldiers were patrolling the Benton Road near Dearborn and Sun River.

Nevertheless the militia effort continued, the acting governor rode down to Fort Benton to take charge of arms being sent on the steamboat Gallatin. He arrived July 1, fell from a steamboat that evening and drowned. Meagher's body was never found, although rewards amounting to $2,000 were offered for recovery.

With establishment of Fort Shaw above the tiny settlement of Sun River, and of Fort Ellis near Bozeman that summer, any need for militia had quite apparently disappeared, and in September the militia was ordered mustered out, leaving an extravagant bill of nearly a million dollars—congress finally paid about half in 1873. About 2500 rifles and six cannon, Civil War surplus, had been sent to Montana. Three later Bentonites, John Morgan, Joseph Cobell and John Evans, had been captains of militia at some time during three rather chaotic years.

The Helena Herald of July 31 first mentioned Sun River as a post, next week reported arrival of Major Gen. Alfred Terry and staff by steamboat, and by stagecoach to Helena. On return Terry was to inspect the six companies at Sun River and decide on the permanent location of the units, Sun or Gallatin valley. He chose both. Fort Shaw was formally established August 1, 1867, Fort Ellis August 27.

Terry, after leaving Fort Abercrombie near the Minnesota line in Dakota, had been establishing posts across Dakota to provide protection for one of the weirder postal enterprises of the era. This was what the Herald proudly saw as a stage and mail route via Fort Benton. Low bidders who got the contract instead planned what could be termed the Northern Overland Pony Express from the Twin Cities to Fort Union, Fort Benton, and by stage to Helena. After an amazing fiasco so far as delivery of mail was concerned, the contractors threw up the contract early in 1868. Little if any mail ever reached Helena via this route. To protect it, General Terry had established Fort Ransom at Bear's Den, two companies; Fort Totten near Devil's Lake, three companies; Fort Stevenson below Fort Berthold, two companies.

In 1868 the soldiers from Fort Shaw were involved chiefly in protecting south bound freighters on the Benton Road. The protection was probably needed, Blackfeet were still restless. The traffic was heavy, one May traveler counted 725 wagons at Fort Benton or on the road and a large tonnage still enroute by boat. There were also many departing miners that fall. Heavy rains in late June and early July mired hundreds of wagons for days at a time. Woodhawks were killed in numbers along the Missouri, doubtless resulting in patrols from Camp Cooke. In July Dave Haney, captain of the Leni Leoti, reported finding the bodies of seven woodcutters at a camp above Fort Peck, several he recognized as having been passengers on the Peninah when Haney commanded that boat in early spring. So many woodhawks abandoned their dangerous woodyards that steamboats often had to rustle their own fuel.

## Camp Cooke Beats Indians, Surrenders To Rats

May 17, 1868, Camp Cooke became the only palisaded military post ever attacked in force by Indians. In this case the commandant estimated 2500 Sioux were beaten off without a military fatality.

One reason merchants of Montana Territory had welcomed stationing of troops: June 13 the steamboat Benton arrived with an army paymaster, guard and $400,000 in greenbacks for a "semi-occasional jubilee." One duty, unappreciated by Fort Benton merchants, was described in a December 10 Helena Herald, "a company of cavalry made a great whisky raid on the town, confiscating intoxicants found on the premises of North West Fur, T. C. Power, Carroll & Steell, I. G. Baker and the saloons. The soldiers were provident in the matter of the saloons, after duty hours they looked up what they had missed and from appearances later in the day, they found some few." The captured contraband (Fort Benton was still the Blackfeet agency and theoretically at least on Indian land) was shipped to Fort Shaw, nothing further noted. There was a freight guard at Fort Benton that late in 1868. In mid-month, Dr. H. M. Lehman, army contract physician, was shot in the leg, "fearfully wounded," by a drunken soldier. He died a few days later; two soldiers held, outcome unknown.

The impending end of Camp Cooke was indicated by the Herald April 1, 1869, headed, "Vermin of the Bad Lands, A Ruined Fort." This said occupation of the place "is rendered absolutely impossible by the countless river rats." Quite cheerfully the paper said it was in the worst place for a fort anyway. The pests ate cavalry forage, ruined blankets, also devoured a pet female terrier and three pups. December 9 the Herald had another item, emphasis on rats. "They have taken possession of everything and every place of importance, the whole site undermined by them... Becoming insolent and overbearing toward whites. 1400 killed in a four day engagement. Government fed them on oats, corn, flour and bacon." Abandonment apparently became official about when an order was issued establishing a military reservation at Fort Benton July 5, 1869, and completed in the next few months. One company was ordered to permanent station at Benton. The other companies went to Fort Shaw.

## Militarily, Fort Benton

The order, issued by Gen. Winfield Hancock at Fort Benton July 5, set the initial point of the reservation in the southwest corner of the fort, due north to the Marias, thence to mouth, etc., excluding the county cemetery. So Fort Benton became military Fort Benton, continuing as such until June 4, 1881, when the soldiers left for Fort Shaw. The local garrison was never numerous, probably near a peak at the time of the 1870 census when 67 were listed, including six women—a wife and child, servant and three laundresses.

Routine patrols were made for attempted recovery of stolen horses, after whisky runners and for an occasional deserter from the Fort Benton garrison, but it was primarily a freight guard. One of the soldiers in the 1870s was Lt. James Bradley, who became interested in the history of the head of navigation and whose manuscripts form a very important reference source. Lt. Bradley was killed at the Battle of the Big Hole August 9, 1877.

Later in that campaign to force surrender of the Nez Perce, Major Guido Ilges headed a small detachment of soldiers which accompanied a troop of about 30 Fort Benton Volunteers to Cow Island in an attempt to save steamboat freight from the Indians. In an engagement on Cow Creek one of the volunteers, Edmund Bradley (true name Richardson), was killed in late September.

After the Sioux and Nez Perce wars in 1876 and 1877, the army decided to establish a large post in northern Montana, which became Fort Assiniboine near later Havre, built to accommodate 16 companies. Both soldiers and supplies to build the post began coming up the Missouri from Bismarck in May 1879, first troops being the 18th Infantry. Also sent up river were more than 200 civilian employes to construct the buildings at the new fort. During two years thousands of tons of supplies and materials for Fort Assiniboine were shipped by steamboat, the military stationing a garrison at Coal Banks Landing below Fort Benton to protect freight. This outpost was abandoned only in 1887 when the Manitoba, later Great Northern Railroad, reached Fort Assiniboine.

The final group of soldiers left Fort Benton for Fort Shaw on June 4, 1881, end of the place as a military post.

# Firewater On Frontier

*In* many a year of looking the writer has determined only one example of a Montana whisky famine, at Bannack, and that alleviated amply in due course. One may assume that often a freighter dusted over the hills like a hero, just when the last drop was poured.

James Kipp's grand opening of Fort Piegan at the mouth of the Marias in 1831 included transmutation of a 35 gallon barrel of alcohol into 200 gallons of "Injun whiskey" ample to provide a three day whingding for a thousand Piegans, was apparently legal and was also the first taste of white man's firewater for those Indians who had never made the long journey north to Hudson Bay posts. Lest Canadians berate the later traffic from Fort Benton, a reading of the journals of Alexander Henry and David Thompson is advised; first request of customers always seemed to involve "high wine." Then there was the testimony of Bill Gladstone years later, "I have seen as many Indians drunk at Edmonton and Rocky Mountain House as ever I seen anywhere else."

One basic recipe ran: to muddy Missouri water add 1 quart of alcohol, 1 pound of rank black chewing tobacco, 1 handful of red peppers, 1 bottle of Jamaica ginger, 1 quart black molasses, mix well and boil until all the strength is drawn from tobacco and peppers. From there the entrepreneur was on his own. Strychnine, lye, rattlesnake heads to give it the bite demanded by customers, red or white, were not unheard of. In other climes such melanges carried other names, Valley tan in the Salt Lake area, Taos lightning in the southwest; otherwise red-eye, bug juice, mountain dew, tanglefoot, Jersey lightning, forty-rod (for the distance an imbiber could travel after). Nor was the whisky of prohibition days much better despite the tales of old timers.

Whatever the hangover, survivors were back for more. Sir Sam Steele described the Whoop Up traffic of later years: "The trader stood at the wicket, a tub full of whisky beside him and when an Indian pushed a buffalo robe to him through the hole, he handed out a tin cup full of the poisonous decoction. A quart of the stuff bought a fine pony."

That was the point. When it came to firewater, Indians had the thirst for but lacked the resistance to influence that whites valiantly demonstrated. First the red man traded all his furs, then his horses or other possessions. The Montana Post in 1864 pointed out that the Indian then had to steal horses to get his winter meat—if whites would keep whisky from the Indians, there would be fewer depredations to secure the necessary remounts. Furthermore, in their cups all restraints were off— Charles MacInnes in "In The Shadow of the Rockies" stated that 88 Blackfeet were murdered in whisky inspired brawls in 1871 alone.

## Whisky At The Fur Posts

A United States law of 1832 prohibited sale of liquor to Indians (so James Kipp's 1831 party was likely legal), generally disregarded for a decade. American Fur and other larger companies had a tendency to hold down a bit on the traffic, after all the trader would get about the same furs and robes anyway; but smaller traders out for fast returns forced their hand. The Indians wanted firewater. Dodges to get intoxicants past federal inspectors were numerous; Kenneth McKenzie even operated his own still at Fort Union, and nearly lost American Fur Co.

its license by bragging about it. Allowances for boatmen, who presumably couldn't or more likely wouldn't navigate without a load on, were outrageous; one overland party got a generous permit for its non-existent navy.

That there was considerable pressure even during the 1832-42 period is evidenced by an unsigned letter from Fort Union to Alexander Culbertson at Fort McKenzie dated May 5, 1835: "Liquor cannot be obtained without risking forcible expulsion. I send two barrels of alcohol and six of wine. Make the most of it and do not sell a single drop of it to the men." If the wine was the "high wine" Hudson Bay men referred to, it was high proof alcohol, the total would have been sufficient for a handsome trade—for Kipp had prepared 200 gallons from one barrel of perhaps 35 gallons.

There is little enough data for the traffic at area forts, but growing robe receipts at McKenzie, Lewis, Benton and opposition posts in pre-steamboat days give evidence there was a supply of liquor. Otherwise the trade would have gone to Hudson Bay posts. There was doubtless an interval of drouth following destruction of Fort McKenzie early in 1844, after which discharged Alexander Harvey brought charges of selling liquor to Indians against Francis A. Chardon.

### Firewater For Miners

In the early 1860s trading emphasis shifted to incoming miners with discoveries of gold in Montana to be, coinciding closely with first steamboats to Fort Benton. Miners clamored for booze almost ahead of groceries. One bit of evidence, again Bill Gladstone, about 200 barrels of decent whisky, "better than we had been drinking," off the Yellowstone at Cow Island in 1864. Blackfeet got a bit of that when they intercepted four Mormon freighters with the two wagons loaded with the kegs. The freighters wisely knocked the head off a keg, the warriors got drunk, passed out, and the outfit slipped away. Gladstone found Benton's saloons had multiplied by the time he got back from Cow Island. Other steamboats that year assuaged thirst at Alder and Last Chance as well.

Freighters added bits of lore in regard to whisky, for they generally were a hearty bunch. "Leakage" was common, via a slipped metal stave and a bit-hole plugged and stave replaced. One merchant tried a shindy, labeled the elixir "kerosene" alongside barrels of sure enough coal oil. Surprise, on arrival the keg contained kerosene, with some evaporation from barrels of the real fuel oil.

By 1860 Canada had a liquor law to protect Indians, too; four years later began negotiations with Hudson Bay Co. to relinquish their long held royal grant rights (from 1670) to the western lands. In 1869 Prince Rupert's Land was bought from HBC. There was no immediate federal possession, simply a change in status, and suddenly Hudson Bay had no legal voice against American intruders.

Montana Territory had come into being in 1864, gradually acquired officials, including a U. S. marshal and deputies, who were soon harrying the bootleggers who had been reported in the Montana Post as active near Sun River. Active hostilities between white and Blackfeet soon intervened—their hair for a pint wasn't good business to most of these whites. But late in 1867 the hit and run traders were at it again despite the danger, and a soldier escort brought six prisoners to Helena on liquor sale charges.

The law of no liquor on Indian land applied to whites as well. Bentonites got a jolt November 23, 1868, said a letter in the Helena Herald of Dec. 10, "by the appearance in our streets at an early hour of a company of cavalry. . .whisky and such was what they wanted, and you can rest assured they made a tolerable clean sweep of those articles." The correspondent wrote that Northwest Fur suffered very little, they had disposed of a large stock except "four cases of Hostetter's celebrated bitters...for employees troubled with the dispepsia." T. C. Power and Carroll & Steell "done better, giving the boys considerable. But it remained for I. G. Baker & Bro. to do the real handsome. They turned out enough liquor to run a first-class gin-mill a year." The article went on to say that saloons suffered lightly—then it may have been the cavalrymen were provident, for one bit read: "The captured liquor stored, the gay soldiers started to look up what few bottles they missed on trip No. 1. Judging from appearances later in the day, they found some few."

Bentonites would remember the great whisky raid darkly. Also, despite a publicly expressed aversion to the liquor trade, a chink appears in the Baker and Conrad cloak of righteousness. However, the traffic was far from disreputable by the mores of the time. E. G. Maclay's train was to haul the contraband to Fort Shaw—no further record unearthed, but there was doubtless substantial "leakage." It was April 1, 1869 that another item appeared, "One thing disturbs Benton people, recent seizure of liquors on the road between Helena and this place." Again no followup found, but early in 1870, another item reported December seizure of $8,000 or $10,000 worth of Montana Hide & Fur goods at Musselshell on unspecified charges, and a note that cord wood and wolf skins were legal tender at the whisky "shebang."

## The Road To Whoop Up

By the time the last item appeared, A. B. Hamilton and J. J. Healy had wangled a strange permit from General Alfred Sully on posting bonds and security to the amount of $10,000. This was to insure that the two did not trade with any person in Montana Territory "after they leave Sun River Settlement." This did allow them to cross the boundary in the vicinity of St. Mary's Lake. "They are also privileged to take with them a party of from 20 to 30 men and six wagons loaded with supplies provided there is no spirituous liquors in the wagons except a small quantity which may be taken safely for medicinal purposes." (This permit was unearthed by Georgia Fooks for her 1983 history of Fort Whoop Up.)

The "medicinal" liquor was probably sufficient to provide alcohol rubdowns for all the men of the expedition. So despite the permit, which should have been sufficient for the military, Healy's recollections were that the soldiers at Fort Shaw were all set to stop him, he openly rode to Fort Benton to send a telegram he knew would be intercepted by the military. This told his partner Hamilton to meet him at a place 75 miles east of the route actually taken.

Then Healy galloped back to Sun River and the wagon train set out almost due north, poles tied behind dragging to simulate travois tracks in case soldiers cut the trail. The result was Fort Hamilton, which rebuilt next year became far better known as Fort Whoop Up. There were several versions of the origin of the rowdy moniker, the one favored by the writer was that a whisky runner loaded up with wet goods, left Benton or Sun River between dusk and dawn and whooped it up for the border. James "Diamond R" Brown, one of the pioneers of that trade, provided that version to Martha Plassman about 1920.

The nature of the trade was primarily "Injun whisky" but the vendors carried stocks of beads, calico and other items to delight the squaws, knives and cooking pots which had become necessities. Also guns. Healy rather piously claimed to have sold only muskets or fusees (fukes); but there is also evidence that more modern repeaters, the "many shots" so ardently desired by warriors, Blackfeet or other, were sold as well. A few years later, before the Little Big Horn battle, the military in effect accused Baker and Power of arming the Sioux by selling repeaters to Cree and Blackfeet, who resold to Sioux. This seems far-fetched, Sioux would scarcely be able to afford the second markup—the Indian, save for whisky, was a canny customer and trader.

As to the main item of the Whoop Up trade—virtually all was doubtless high proof alcohol in flat cans to load on fast pack animals, rather than cumbersome barrels on slow wagons. Up north the chef would mix his own recipe.

### Another Kind of Stampede

An item in the June 15, 1870, Helena Herald helps document a profitable winter at the pioneer whisky fort: "It will be remembered that last winter, Messrs. Al Hamilton and John Healy, two of Sun River's enterprising citizens, having received authorization to go beyond the border to trade for robes, departed with their outfit of Indian goods into the British Possessions. These gentlemen recently returned from their expedition, bringing with them a large number of robes and peltries of various kinds. We judge, from all we could learn, that this venture will net Messrs. Hamilton and Healy upwards of $50,000—not so very bad for a six months' cruise among the Lo Family across the border."

It is no wonder that the restless residue of a faded boom stampeded in another type of gold rush. "Historic Sites of Alberta" by Hugh Dempsey, lists many more than mentioned below:

Fort Hamilton, or Whoop Up, at St. Mary and Oldman rivers, built 1869 and partially burned next spring, rebuilt by Wm. S. Gladstone, a stockaded post with bastions.

Fort Kipp, by Joe Kipp and Charles Thomas about 1870, near junction of Belly and Oldman.

Fort Standoff, built 1871 at junction of Belly and Waterton rivers, by a party that included "Dutch Fred" Wachter, W. McLean, A. Juneau and John "Liver Eating" Johnson. (This party was led by Kipp and Thomas, may have been in two sections, for Joe Kipp is the main source of the story about standing off U. S. Marshal Charles Hard north of Milk River. The party claimed it was in Canada, hence Hard had no jurisdiction, backing their argument with rifles. So the name from "standing off" the marshal.)

Elbow River Post on that river in present Calgary, 1871, under H. A. "Fred" Kanouse for Healy and Hamilton.

Conrad's Post in 1871 for I. G. Baker & Co. 3 miles from Fort Kipp.

There were numerous others, many no more than a strong cabin for safety against drunken customers. (Canadian historians in 1984 felt they had located or identified 43 such whisky posts.) For example, there were two posts operated by Moses Solomon and Abel Farwell at the scene of an 1873 fight between wolfers and Assiniboines in the Cypress Hills.

A few posts were looted by Indians, numbers of whites were killed in Whoop Up country, but many more of the customers of whisky posts died in drunken brawls.

One of the more interesting ends to a whisky fort was that for Kootenai Post of Fred Kanouse near later Fort Macleod. In the spring of 1874 Kootenais attacked the fort and the traders finally beat them off. Men at Fort Whoop Up heard about the battle and rode to help, only to find it was all over. But while one "Jack" was describing the fight he accidently fired his gun into a keg of powder. There went the neighborhood, the cabin demolished, the whites lucky, no fatalities.

The April 8, 1873, Herald, referring to the "town of Whoop-Up," said it "is reported as one of the toughest camps now existing in the Rocky Mountains." Also, "At this place congregate some of the worst characters from every source, many of whom engage in the traffic of whisky to Indians, and rows which result in death are of frequent occurrence." The article also reported a fight in (Sol) Abbott's saloon when a band of Blackfeet walked in, shot down Fred Kanouse, Latleur and Horness. Abbott, in the back room at the time, opened the door and with his Navy killed three Blackfeet in as many shots. Kanouse had his shoulder nearly blown away, the other two less seriously hurt.

John Healy saw his confreres much differently than later historians. In April 1874 he told Parson John (McDougall) at Whoop Up that everything was under control. "The three who came to run things and more are under sod. We did not let any really bad men stay in this Whoop-Up Region." Healy also reminisced on arrival of the North West Mounted Police: "Instead of cut-throats they found the best band of prairie men the west ever produced more like brothers doing a legitimate business, scattered all through the different posts. They were the men who taught the Indians how to behave and made the country safe for white people to travel through in search of life and health."

Healy's comments were probably closest to the white viewpoint of the times. The latter viewed wild Indians as best removed or tamed, as Montanans had seen the slaughter on the Marias in January 1870. There might have been a few with differing views, but few of those were among persons who laid their lives on the scales in the travel and business of those times.

### Wood, Wolves And Whisky

The woodhawk's life could be a brief but riotous one, the wolves a secondary resource for winter months, and the whisky both a relaxation and source of profit if handed out from a strong log hut to a brave with a passel of ponies. It was also apt to be as brief as it was at times, merry. At Musselshell, an ambitious but strikingly unsuccessful attempt to supplant Fort Benton as head of navigation, cordwood and wolf hides ranked as legal tender with gold in the later 1860s.

By that time army campaigns had so populated Dakota Territory with hostile Sioux that steamboats had to land, cut and move their own wood—a stack of driftwood against a bank was a Godsend indeed. Inland, deckhands and bored passengers were on their own ashore—ten passengers in 1868 at Round Butte had a fire fight, fortunately for them at long range and no casualties, the exception. Whole logs were dragged aboard, sawed into firebox lengths en route.

Newspaper files yield numbers, more than 50 woodhawks killed in a decade, probably double and possibly three times as many unreported were slain by Indians. A tough life. Dave Haney brought in the Peninah in early season 1868, above Fort Peck landed seven passengers who craved to get rich selling cordwood to steamboats; on his second trip with the oddly named Leni Leoti he buried seven mutilated bodies at the site 45 miles above the present Fort Peck dam.

Cordwood in those days went for $5 and $6 per cord for cottonwood, pine and cedar for $8 to $20, depending on how desperate the captain was for fuel. Woodyard operators with finances to buy grub hired men to do piece work, so much a cord, or $50-$60 a month plus a bonus per cord for over 1 1/2 units per day. A cord was 128 cubic feet, but what pilot would quibble when Injun sign had been noted? In the winter when times were dull the woodhawk might venture out on the plains above the river to slay stray buffalo or other game and lace the carcass with strychnine; such a set might yield 30 to a high of 100 wolves, or a whole mortally indignant village whose dogs had been poisoned. For dog hides nothing, except perhaps scalps in a tepee, but standard price for wolf skins was in the neighborhood of $3 per hide.

Two of the woodyards abandoned in the bitter season of 1868 were on the Missouri below the Little Rockies. W. N. Faber and George Horn, the two owners, dragged into Fort Benton in late October expressing fears for the safety of other woodhawks who had made a try for Camp Cooke or Musselshell, fatalities concealed by the web of time. As for their thankful selves, they claimed to have hot footed it 270 miles in five days. During that time they had managed only three meals, and had a fight with stray Indians for every repast. Neither turns up on the 1870 census, probably still soaking their aching feet.

It was at the tiny town of Musselshell in May 1869 that woodhawks, wolfers and whisky traders garnered a measure of satisfaction for the death and destruction dealt them by the fugitive Sioux. They trapped a war party in a ravine of the stream nearby in a driving rain that dampened the priming of the North West flint lock fukes, and sapped the spring of bowstrings; furthermore, some of the whites had recently come by Henry repeaters, and the ensuing slaughter perhaps evened up the season's score. The 40-odd who were gathered at Musselshell approved a member who prepared some trophies.

When the next steamboat, Huntsville, tooted in, passengers saw a dozen or more skulls on stakes lining the levee on both sides of the landing in front of the palisade that was the best Indian preventative frontiersmen had yet found. Standing proudly beside exhibit A was a king size male whom Henry Macdonald described as "a hairy, lubberly creature whose summer wardrobe consisted simply of a filthy red flannel shirt" and Mac was convinced from look and smell that he had been born in it. The critter was "Liver Eatin' " Johnson for the rest of his years. He had earned the title when he dispatched the last wounded Sioux with his bowie, a bit of the Indian's liver came out with the knife tip. After inviting a horrified pilgrim wooder to partake, Johnson of course had to round out the jest and prove the superior staying power of his own stomach. Benton booze bosses scarcely appreciated his boisterous visits, but in Whoop Up country later he was welcome enough, his size and ferocious appearance impressed even the fierce Blackfeet, so to easterners in particular this 6-6 specimen became a legend.

That year 1869 was to become the last hurrah of the woodhawks for several seasons. Peter Koch testified that due to the drop in numbers of steamboats from 40 to 8 in 1870, wood was a drug on the market—of several hundred cords of wood he and partner cut they sold less than 25, and before the summer was over Indians had burned the remainder.

The April 1870 census provides testimony as to the numbers involved in the risky business. There were at least 15 listed in Fort Benton, probably the lucky and successful who were making night life rugged at the head of navigation. On the Missouri below Fort Benton to the Musselshell, 33 of 38 men listed were woodhawks, plus four miners and a cook at Coal Banks where entrepreneurs were aiming at a safer way of fueling the boats. In Dawson county 73 of the 147 white males were woodchoppers or woodyard operators and several of the 11 blacks cooked for cutters. The 148th white was one Jane Smith with an unprintable in those days occupation who had been scalped by Indians the year before; for some reason Jenny hated Indians.

As Koch indicated, woodhawks were facing a bleak future. Nor did the harvest of scalps by hostiles cease. Several more of the dwindling remainder died, and quite evidently survivors along the river shared, for a price, their precious cargoes of the cup that cheers. In May 1871 a small camp at Eagle Creek was attacked and a woodhawk killed, perhaps by dissatisfied red customers. Each year thereafter men died at isolated wood camps; in 1874 that unlucky Eagle Creek site found George Meffort killed by George Owens in a drunken brawl.

Perhaps typical, but with a lucky ending for whites, a raid occurred in the winter of 1874-75 at the mouth of the Marias. A brace of trophy hunting Sioux cased the camp, and after two of four men rode off to the Wilkins trading post two miles up river, the two Sioux made their move. Ed Ladd was out in front of the cabin ricking up cordwood, his Winchester leaning against the pile precious steps away but a Colt in his pocket. His partner Billy Osten stepped out to dump his dishwater; one of the Sioux came up behind and fired a derringer into the back of Osten's head. The other had grabbed Ladd's rifle. Believing him unarmed and helpless, the Sioux had some Indian sport, making him bark like a dog and howl like a coyote, then by further signs to get down on his knees and eat grass. Ladd was working his way closer, then came up shooting, killed the one with the Winchester and grabbed it to down the other Sioux, by then racing for the river bank. Al Wilkins and the two other woodhawks came back with supplies a few minutes later, to find Ladd working over a prostrate Ostren. As it turned out the derringer bullet had flattened on Ostren's skull, and when he came to all he had was a bad headache. The two dead Sioux were buried, through a hole cut in river ice with ten feet of water below. Then the quartet moved up to the Wilkins post to wait for the first steamboat.

For three seasons more wood for the steamboats would be costly in lives, but with the end of the Nez Perce campaign in fall 1877 most of the peril disappeared, although Assiniboines killed several in 1880-81. White outlaws took a turn around 1883 and 1884, working the badland wood camps; for a steamboat fueling up could mean $100 cash in hand for the woodhawk. And white desperadoes were as apt to kill to prevent their victims later testifying as Indians were for scalps.

In the slow period of the early 1870s many of the woodcutters turned to the whisky trade both north and south of the border; some of the names in the Whoop Up country are familiar as survivors of the desperate days along the Missouri bottoms.

### Wolfing Tough, Dangerous But Often Profitable

Total wolf skin returns from the three posts of the Upper Missouri Outfit in 1855 to St. Louis headquarters of American Fur were only 1561, with 1240 entered as worth $1 each, the remainder listed as small wolf skins probably coyotes and at 50c. It is evident that these were taken in trade at Indian insistence along with more valuable robes and furs. A skin would have been traded for a few beads or a cup of sugar.

Granville Stuart wrote that about 1866-67 wolf skins became valuable, and wolfing an important factor of commerce; but called wolfing a dangerous life, with all Indians hostile to wolfers. Reason, the poison sets killed Indian dogs as well as lobos.

Nevertheless, wolfing became a rather usual, if tough and dangerous, way of life out on the frozen winter plains of Montana. Reason, it offered quick money. By the later 1860s wolf skins passed for currency at Musselshell and doubtless hundreds yearly passed across the bar planks of Fort Benton saloons.

Perhaps the price change was more gradual than Stuart knew. There is an anonymous, undated as to year item in an 1864 Montana Post. The writer said that the morning before Christmas, several part time wolfers found seven wolves and five foxes in their traps a half mile from Fort Benton. The largest wolf showed fight and the narrator ran back to the fort for a flint lock trade gun, charged out at $10, a first rate gun at close range and nearly worthless at a distance. On his return the big wolf had broken the trap chain. He tracked the wolf to a clump of willows on the Missouri, missed his shot, broke the gun over the wolf's head, the wolf chewed the stock while the trapper beat it to death with the barrel. He was 5-4, and shouldering the wolf, its feet dragged on the ground. He got $2.50 for the hide, but had to pay $10 for the gun. Not very profitable.

That $2.50 in cash or trade is important. Herman Brinkman in 1891, recalling an event of a few years later, said he once made a poison set and skinned out 33 wolves worth $100 in Fort Benton. A good big hide brought $3.50 to $4.

If a man could keep his hair, returns were excellent.

The large wolves of the plains of course followed the buffalo herds, Lewis and Clark were amazed at their numbers. The predators provided an ecological balance, killing the aged, crippled and stragglers, which strengthened the herd instincts of the buffalo, and made protection of calves vital to continuance of the species.

Peter Koch, one of the Musselshell country pioneers, described wolfing in the 1896 Montana Historical Society contributions: "Wolfing will soon be one of the lost arts, because no wolves will be left to poison." He was wrong by two or three decades. He was reviewing the late 1860s.

"It was necessary to go to the buffalo country, because the wolves followed the buffalo herd... The first thing to do was to put out baits in convenient places; where buffalo were killed. These were partly skinned and three or four bottles of strychnine, containing one-eighth ounce each, were sprinkled over the carcass, gashing it well with the knife, and the strychnine was rubbed into the flesh and the blood with the hands and then left... frequently thirty or forty baits were put out, generally forming a circle."

Wolfers in mild weather generally kept up to date with skinning, in cold piled the dead wolves. After the spring cleanup the hides were taken to the nearest trading post, skins worth about three dollars. In hostile Indian country the wolfers might put out baits, then return to a safe place and went back in spring when hopefully buffalo, wolves and hostiles had moved on. Thus Koch explained the life. He said as many as 100 dead wolves might be found at a single set.

Wolfers usually went out in small parties, easy if dangerous scalps for a few hostiles, so many unaccountably vanished from white ken, with blizzards also deadly at times. To be set afoot by a lone horse thief could kill a small group as surely as a big war party. Extreme misadventures went unreported, of course, but a couple of examples appeared in the Helena Herald in 1869. An October note from Benton said a party of 30 wolfers out for several weeks on Milk River were back, unhurt but stripped of everything. Among them were two former sheriffs, George Croff and Asa Sample, and Indian agent Hi Upham; this was probably horse thieves, but the group may have been warned off by a large band of Assiniboines or Gros Ventres, yielding their portable property to avoid a close haircut. A second note, wolf hunters had tolerable success, but there were "several cases where lost horses cost more than winter catch would pay for."

Wolfers and Indians certainly didn't mix. April 5, 1872, there was a full scale fight between wolfers and Bloods near the Sweet Grass Hills when the tribesmen warned them off. Tom Hardwick despised all Indians and opened the ball with his Winchester. Paul Sharp in "Whoop Up Country" has so thoroughly covered next year's battle or massacre in the Cypress Hills there is no point in reviewing it, save Hardwick was there too, and it involved Indians, horses and wolfers at the Teton, and culminated in a fight that helped bring the Mounted Police west in 1874. By that year buffalo had nearly disappeared from near Fort Benton and were being thinned out north of the border. So wolves were getting hungrier and more susceptible to poison baits. Between 1875 and 1877 about 30,000 wolf skins were shipped annually out of Fort Benton. The total may have topped that figure, years later Wm. G. Conrad recalled that the Baker firm alone in one year shipped 30,000 buffalo robes and 25,000 wolf skins down river. Many of these were traded for in what became Alberta and Saskatchewan.

Buffalo were nearly exterminated in Canada in the later 1870s, and in Montana by the end of 1882. Cattlemen moved animals en masse onto the one time buffalo range, and the wolves turned to cattle, sheep and horses for provender. It was to the interest of stockmen to encourage wolfers, they inclined to hired hunters, bounties, even packs of hunting dogs.

The horrible winter of 1886-87 had an odd local aftermath. By November 1887 the River Press was reporting that stock losses to wolves were the greatest ever, the predators were moving in from ranges where the winter kill of cattle was even greater.

Bowing to increasing demands of stockmen, the 1887 legislature provided a rather scanty bounty on predators, and also set a dollar limit on bounties, but some one, perhaps prodded by an outraged gardening wife, slipped in a joker. This provided 10c on each prairie dog skin, 5c for gophers. State papers correctly assessed this as meaning bankruptcy of the bounty fund. Near year end, 164 mountain lion, 204 bear, 1581 wolf and 2587 coyote hides had been submitted—an insignificant number—Chouteau county in future years repeatedly surpassed the state total on wolves. But 709,942 gophers and 165,276 prairie dogs had paid their full debt to Montana gardeners and the bounty fund was broke.

June 1st of 1887 the River Press quietly noted that Joseph Mulligan had brought in 180 prairie dog skins for the bounty, the $18 undoubtedly financed a lively night on the town. It may have been Mulligan's jape at the law, he had been wolfer, guide and trapper, as well as scorning shoes as things for sissies.

It was not until 1889 that the legislature tried bounties again, no gophers this time, $2 for bear or puma, $1 for wolf or coyote, and county clerks had the duty of punching ears so they couldn't be reused. County Clerk Sayre did refuse to punch the ears of a live pet coyote. There were complaints by stockmen about bounty hunters who went out in spring to spot denning females, raided same dens later to get the pups for bounty while leaving the adults as "seed" for next year's crop.

Stockmen added to the bounties, in the late 1890s $3 plus the same from the state. One wolfer in 1905 made money at $10 a head plus board, but the predators continued as a menace to profits into the homestead years. This influx of settlers proved the downfall of wolves, the last gray surviving descendant of the buffalo lobos killed by a Stanford rancher in 1930.

# Canadian Connections

First white world event which would impact on Fort Benton's future history was in 1668 when what became Hudson's Bay Co. was organized in England; in 1670 a royal charter was granted by Charles II giving tenure of all land in the Hudson Bay drainage to "The Governor and Company of Adventurers of England trading into Hudson's Bay." The grant comprised about 1.5 million square miles, including some intrusion into later Montana. It became known as Rupert's Land, for a royal sponsor. The company in later years became known by its initials, often translated by irreverent as "Here Before Christ."

Anthony Henday of HBC in 1754 may have been the first white to contact Blackfeet, in 1772-73 Matthew Cocking wintered with the tribe. When Lewis & Clark reached the Mandan villages in 1804 the Louisiana Purchase had been completed, but the northern boundary had not been determined. This was fixed by treaty in 1818 setting the 49th parallel to the Rockies; from there both sides of the border it was Oregon Territory under joint British-American occupation until another treaty in 1846 extended the boundary westward along the 49th parallel. Thus several North West Co. and Hudson's Bay Co. trading posts in the Flathead country were legitimate. Both had posts near later Edmonton in 1795 and in 1799 west of Red Deer on the North Saskatchewan.

While among the Mandans, Lewis & Clark were in contact with representatives of both the Canadian concerns. At least Francoise Antoine LaRocque wanted to accompany the American explorers west; he was refused. On return in July 1806 Meriwether Lewis's party had the first American contact with the Blackfeet, one in which two tribesmen were killed. That and John Colter's encounters left the Blackfeet confederacy hostile to the "Big Knives" as they called the Americans, the Canadians were "Northern White Men," a distinction between warfare and tolerance.

Hudson's Bay merged with North West Co. in 1821, ending the competition. Further, successor Hudson's Bay in its posts on the northern side of the warlike Blackfeet, was satisfied to sit tight and occasionally trade for the furs and horses of defunct Mountain Men. It was not until 1831 that Kenneth McKenzie sent James Kipp up the Missouri into Blackfeet country to build a trading post following what amounted to a private peace treaty. The Piegans appeared satisfied to have a new source of whisky, tobacco, blankets, knives and iron arrowpoints (that relegated the ancient art of flint knapping points to the discard). Bloods and Blackfeet were less satisfied.

One fact became apparent, the tribesmen had no reason to learn to fancy whisky. They had already acquired the taste before Kipp keyed his grand opening on the conversion of a barrel of alcohol into a three day whingding. Two years later at Fort McKenzie, Maximilian repeatedly commented on the thirst of Indian visitors. The source of the taste was unquestionable. In fact, David Mitchell of McKenzie implied in a long talk with Maximilian that American Fur would be content to drop the trade in intoxicants, as he claimed the company had in the Mandan area. But he noted that the fort's customers would trade at HBC forts if the Americans offered no whisky. Neither Canadian nor American traders seemed reluctant to trade for furs acquired by warpath or pillage from whites on the other side of the line.

Nevertheless, there was an uneasy truce between the rivals, indicated by the lack of encroachment across the border. Indians generally wanted the goods the posts offered and tolerated the whites in trading posts. There was one exception, most apparent on the American side, white trappers were free prey, as dozens of Mountain Men found in their final moments. The "Big Knives" held one advantage, the annual arrival from 1832 of steamboats at Fort Union. To the Indians, those fireboats were big medicine. The Missouri provided an easy route for shipment of the heavy buffalo robes, a by-product of the high plains way of life for its inhabitants. Hudson's Bay had a long overland river and portage route that prevented the Canadians from taking in trade any but the very best robes.

So the truce held for decades. Fr. DeSmet did travel into Canada to a Fort Edmonton in 1845, next year returning south to attempt a peace between Flatheads and Blackfeet, and on to Fort Benton to go down the Missouri, but missionaries scarcely counted. There were a few small parties sent out to invite trade, a normal course for such a business, and an explorer or two slipped across the boundary by accident or intent, but the truce held.

One of the early intrusions into Canada by Americans was told to Bradley by Alexander Culbertson, and continues to be somewhat mysterious: In the summer of 1862 Andrew Dawson at Fort Benton received a package of sand from one Larue (this was probably imposter priest Jean L'Heureux) with word it was gold bearing sand from a gulch up north, and he would guide a party to it. Washed at the fort, it was rich in gold. Almost instantly a prospecting party was formed including well known Bentonites Matt Carroll, James Arnoux, Henry Bostwick and eight others. They couldn't find the writer, but understandably worked every creek from the Marias to Willows 25 miles south of Edmonton—colors but not enough to pay—such as found over wide areas north of Fort Benton. The Fort Benton party came back raging about the wild goose chase. Arnoux thought it an outright if expensive hoax, I. G. Baker thought L'Hereux had made a find, backed off after hearing of the madness down in southern Montana.

The Montana gold rush did little to disturb trade relations, some prospectors drifted north of the boundary, didn't locate enough gold to make it worth while. Wm. Gladstone's recollections were of John Healy making an 1863 trip to Fort Garry, probably after hearing of the previous group, then returning north with a party of 28, wintering and returning in the spring. They brought Gladstone with them, met a party drifting north to get away from Vigilantes in Montana, and recruited part to return south. Doubtless several more parties tried it with no attention except from Indians.

Then in 1869 the new Dominion of Canada threw the gates ajar. That was the year Hudson's Bay sold the Dominion almost half the future nation, for a hefty but still bargain price of 300,000 pounds, HBC retaining a few million acres, and a few thousand around their posts.

Suddenly, that year of 1869, there was no legal authority in Canada's own wild west, HBC legal rights were extinct and the two year old Dominion utterly unable to exercise authority. Instead Canada acquired a painful little rebellion of mixed blood Metis far eastward in Manitoba.

The Metis might be differentiated from the half breeds who figured prominently in northern Montana history by their tendency to group into settlements of their own kind, and had existed from the early years of New France. Another term for them was Bois Brule (burnt wood). In 1869 their numbers in the Red River country reached several thousand. Proportions of Indian blood varied, Louis Riel, their leader, was an eighth Chippewa. The Metis were part farmers, part hunters, and claimed land for the former in long narrow strips leading from rivers or streams, which ran athwart of the Canadian surveys. The 1869 trouble began from a survey party near Fort Garry, when the Metis sought to maintain their squatters' rights.

Under Riel they set up a provisional government. Execution of Thomas Scott speeded action in Ottawa in making promises to right Metis wrongs, but also provided a military force and in effect exiled Louis Riel into the United States. He spent the final years of that exile in northern Montana before returning in 1884 to lead a second rising, the Northwest Rebellion of 1885 (Patriotic War, insist Metis descendants). Riel ended on the gallows at Regina late in 1885.

The troubles in Manitoba were nothing to what hit the North West Territories, later Alberta and Saskatchewan. Down on the Benton Road Sun River partners John J. Healy and Alfred B. Hamilton were alertest of all. Money could be bet on Hamilton's middle initial standing for Baker—he was the son of Isaac Baker's sister Grace, and the record is easily interpreted to a trail blazing adventure backed by Isaac and George Baker.

Somehow Healy and Hamilton in November 1869 wangled a rather strange permit from Gen. Alfred Sully, superintendent by then of Indian affairs for Montana. It stated that the partners had posted bond of $10,000 that they would trade with no inhabitant of the territory after leaving Sun River and were permitted to cross the Blackfeet country and cross the boundary near St. Mary's lake. They could take a party of 20-30 men and six wagons. Sully, no lover of booze in Indian tonsils, added a provision of no spirituous liquors in the wagons "except a small quantity which may be taken safely for medicinal purposes." Despite the permit, Healy played it safe, sending a fake telegram from Fort Benton he knew the Fort Shaw officers would intercept, to Hamilton giving an easterly rendezvous. Then in December the party headed north from Sun River, Healy said with poles trailing the wagons to simulate the trace made by an Indian village on the move. As to the "medicinal," a Canadian later said Healy told him the party had taken 50 gallons of alcohol—for rubdowns, no doubt. (On the usual recipe, several hundred gallons of "Injun whisky.")

The adventurers built a post near the junction of St. Mary's and Oldman they called Fort Hamilton, a crude collection of huts and palisade. It was probably after that first trading season of 1869-70 that the fort was burned. In the spring the party trundled wagons loaded with furs and robes to Fort Benton for the split with their backers.

The Helena Herald of June 15, 1870, had just as well have rung the fire bell as to print its modest headline, "SUCCESSFUL VENTURE," telling of the return from British Possessions, "from all we could learn, that this venture will net Messrs. Hamilton and Healy upwards of $50,000—not so very bad for a six months cruise among the Lo Family across the border."

They were back across the border summer or early fall with Bill Gladstone to build a new trading post near the old. (The Herald story guaranteed they would have company.) The new post quickly drew the title Fort Whoop Up and gave its name to the region of American incursions. Several explanations are given for the rowdy sobriquet; the writer prefers Diamond R. Brown's version that the whisky trader loaded his flat tins of alcohol on pack horses and between dusk and dawn "whooped it up" for the border—more in line with moonshiner parlance for one thing.

No one has yet fully recorded and probably never will, all the traders who risked their lives in the Whoop Up country in this period, or the number of posts, but

Barney Reeves and assistant, Margaret Kennedy, in 1985 believed they had located, by evidence or tentatively, more than forty trading posts. These ranged from the solid second Whoop Up to a mere bullet tight cabin to which the traders could retire while their customers imbibed and engaged in drunken brawls that cost uncounted lives—a Blackfeet in his cups was apt to kill his best friend over who got that last swallow. Careless whites, too, were fair game, numbers died in the trade.

Among the first comers were Joe Kipp and Charley Thomas, who set up Fort Kipp in 1870, then switched to Fort Standoff at Belly and Waterton rivers, along with Dutch Fred Wachter, W. McLean, Antoine Juneau and John "Liver Eating" Johnson. The post name came after members including Kipp maintained to U. S. Marshal Charles Hard that they had crossed the Canadian border on Milk River ridge, backed up by Winchesters, which "stood off" the marshal. Dave Akers and the Liver Eater teamed in Spitzee Post just after or just before Fort Kipp. Fred Kanouse, a stormy petrel of the trade, put up a post at later Calgary on Elbow River in 1871, and I. G. Baker & Co. made a more or less formal entry into the Canadian trade at Conrad's Post, 1871, on the Belly and Oldman. T. C. Power undoubtedly was deeply into the trade, but apparently by proxy.

An appalled Hudson's Bay Co., which had complied with a Canadian edict of no more booze in its trade, saw its business beset by the influx of Americans and dispatched a continuing string of reports to Ottawa, nothing lost in transmittal, about 500 outlaws debauching the northern Indians with whisky and arming them with the latest in firearms.

Occasionally the whites fell out, the hazy episode of the Spitzee Cavalry would indicate a plot by I. G. Baker men (Healy had switched to Power backing) to drive the latter concern out of the Whoop Up country. The Spitzee Cavalry supposedly represented wolfers outraged that the white traders were selling the redskins fine new repeating rifles. Wolfers used poisoned buffalo carcasses, which also killed Indian dogs, leading the latter to kill wolfers whenever possible. Healy on his part maintained in memoirs that his post at least sold only North West fukes, and when an Indian bought a repeater, he was given an order on the Power store in Fort Benton and had to pick it up there.

The Helena Herald April 17, 1874, referred to a heavy tax levied on robes and furs at a Baker trading post near Whoop Up by a party of wolfers, next day said it was a Power post so victimized. Perhaps the Spitzee Cavalry made a second ride? Or more possibly Healy was using his imagination as to how he stood off those Spitzees. But by 1874 wolfers had already been in the news and supplied the topper to Hudson's Bay's stories about American lawlessness.

The June 11, 1873, Herald had headlined the story: "INDIANS ON THE HORSE STEAL. WHITES ON THE WAR PATH. Forty Lodges Wiped Out By Sixteen Kit Carsons; Ed Grace Shot through Heart and Buried at Cypress Mountains." The story ran that a party of wolfers returning from the Whoop Up camped on the Teton near Benton, during the night Indians stole their horses. They walked into Benton, re-outfitted and ten left in pursuit of the thieves, each man with a Henry rifle and two Smith & Wesson revolvers. The wolfers trailed the thieves to Abel Farwell's trading post at Cypress Mountains, found forty lodges of North Assiniboines who met them with arms in case the whites wanted a fight and told them that Crees had stolen the horses and gone on, but if the whites wanted a fight the Assiniboines would oblige. One thing led to another, the wolfers doubtless sampled the liquid wares of Farwell and nearby Mose Solomon, next morning attacked the Assiniboine camp and nearly wiped it out. One white, Ed Grace, was killed.

The number of Indians killed is problematical, best estimate probably the 22 passed on by Lt. Gov. Alexander Morris of Manitoba, and there was many another similar fight between truculent red men and determined whites. In Ottawa, the tale lost nothing in the telling—500 desperadoes bent on getting the last robe and weapon off the last dead Indian. The tales speeded the training and preparation of the North West Mounted Police. As to the number of whites involved in the whisky trade in Whoop Up country, careful Canadian historians have estimated about forty percent of that 500 was near the maximum across the border.

There is no question as to the harm the traffic did the Indians. Dozens died yearly in drunken brawls, the red lack of tolerance for alcohol a heavy contributor. White traders on their part took their lives in their hands in the north country trade. Yet it should be remembered that the Blackfeet had well developed thirsts when the Americans first came in trading contact with them at Fort Piegan and Fort McKenzie. Hudson's Bay was far from guiltless in this trade, read the journals of their traders. That Hudson's Bay Co. on prodding from Ottawa had a few years before discontinued trade in intoxicants may have been a cause for regret at lost opportunities.

Nor were the whites always the aggressors. Two items from Whoop Up days: Helena Herald, April 8, 1873, reported "the town of Whoop-Up...one of the toughest camps now existing in the Rocky Mountains...Ten days ago Kanouse, Latleur and Horness were in Abbott saloon, when a band of Blackfeet walked in, shot them down and helped themselves to liquor. Abbott, in back room at the time, opened the door and with his Navy killed three in as many shots." Fred Kanouse had his shoulder virtually blown away, had an agonizing trip to Helena where a doctor saved some use of that side. The other whites had lesser wounds.

Calf Shirt, the chief who led Bloods in wiping out ten whites at Ophir on the Marias in 1865, was one tough Blood. In 1869 he brought 5,000 Blackfeet south to trade at the Baker post on the later Whoop Up Trail; Shirley Ashby was well advised to make the chief his "soldier" with a fancy gift uniform, before trade commenced. At that the militant giant took a shot at Father Imoda, Bill Conrad knocking up Calf Shirt's gun. According to James Willard Schultz, Calf Shirt was never tougher than in the hour of his death. Having traded away his women's robes, he walked up to the trading wicket at Fort Kipp, demanded whisky and pulled a gun. Joe Kipp got in the first shot, the chief staggered and turned away. Hearing the shots, white poker players cut short the game to pump another 15 bullets into the big Indian, most of them mortal wounds.

Although the 1874 boundary survey was mentioned in the Helena Herald, not a word was found of what Indians and whites in Whoop Up country thought of the passing of the large groups along the "Medicine Line" of the Indians. Canadians sent a party of about 250 men, including a "corps" of mounted scouts. The American party was approximately the same size, plus additional troops, two companies from Fort Shaw and part of the 7th Cavalry under Major Marcus Reno. Bulk of American party supplies were dropped by steamboat at Milk River, moved in Diamond R wagons, later some supplies were purchased in Fort Benton. Work was completed about September 1st, meanwhile seven or eight large mackinaws were built at Fort Benton to transport the surveyors and other civilians. Late in September the steamboat Josephine picked up part of the military.

## Coming of the Mounties

There was warning of the coming of a measure of law and order to Canada's wild west in the April 17, 1874, Helena Herald, although the report was premature and a bit inaccurate. Gist: "The British government has ordered construction of a military post at Whoop-Up...the post is to be completed the present season, and is to be garrisoned by the troops at present doing duty as escort to the surveying corps engaged in locating the line between our own and their country." On the U. S. side the Herald several times mentioned arrest of whisky traders near the Blackfeet reservation, and a couple of times deaths of more prominent Blackfeet in drunken brawls, also a two-on-two of bootleggers and Indians, the whites the victors in hostilities but one in the Fort Shaw stockade, the other Whoop Up bound.

October 9, the day the North West Mounted Police were pleasantly surprised to be welcomed at Fort Whoop Up by a good dinner instead of a battle with 500 desperados, the Herald reported I. G. Baker of the Benton firm had been in Helena several days to order 20 tons of supplies for "the Queen's Mounted Police, ordered for duty across the border."

Hudson's Bay people were doubtless gratified to see the probable end of the whisky trade, but were to have a succession of unpleasant surprises.

Near the end of their trip across the plains the party of 300 NWMP was lost and nearly starving only a few miles from the heavily traveled Whoop Up Trail and less than 75 miles from Fort Whoop Up. Snow fell on September 9, so the party turned south to Three Buttes or Sweet Grass Hills. A party of seven, headed by Commissioner George Arthur French and assistant James F. Macleod headed for Fort Benton. There on September 24 they found a pleasantly warm welcome. Bentonites had followed their trek through Indian eyes, the northern tribes were a bit more than curious about the expedition.

The NWMP immediate contact and contract with I. G. Baker & Co. was by no means fortuitous, Shirley Ashby, former Baker employe, later wrote. Canadian authorities had communicated with former Montanan Robert W. Donnell in New York about a supply source, who told them "there was not a finer man in the United States than I. G. Baker" and that his company could supply the North West Mounted Police with "anything that they wanted from a Jew's harp to a threshing machine." The Baker firm held that contract until after the Canadian Pacific reached Calgary, were as well paymaster, builder, banker, even postman. Probably no state or province was ever so completely dependent for a decade, on one firm, as later Alberta was on the I. G. Baker Company of Fort Benton.

At Fort Benton the police picked up a guide, Jerry Potts, who became virtually a patron saint to the NWMP, although others in Fort Benton at the time could have filled the spot as competently. But in half Blackfeet Jerry they acquired a legend.

Charles Conrad, a junior member of the Baker firm at the time, was placed in charge of relief of the Mounties—an initial light outfit of John Glenn was already at their camp with some high priced goodies, Conrad would follow with fast horse and wagon outfits, behind him more supplies by slow oxen.

When Conrad reached the Three Buttes camp, there were the red coated Mounties with odd pillbox hats; ringing hungry men and animals were Blackfeet bursting with curiosity about these strangers. With proper introductions some of the Indians went out to hunt for meat for their new friends, Potts advised on herded grazing for the NWMP mounts, and the way was open into Whoop Up country.

When the Police reached Whoop Up, they still weren't convinced of what Baker had told their leaders in Fort Benton, that the whisky trade north of the line was dead or dying, and the white residents at least would be friendly.

These mostly green policemen had completed what they regarded as a terribly trying trip across the plains from Fort Dufferin near Winnipeg, and here they saw James Macleod, sided by diminutive Jerry Potts, riding unconcerned up to the open gate of Fort Whoop, where many had expected to fight the climactic battle of a war against armed marauders. Dave Akers and a couple of others, plus some squaws greeted the newcomers, explaining Don Davis, the head man, wasn't there, but how about some grub?

There had been limited migration overland from Manitoba to Fort Edmonton via what was termed the Canadian Trail—missionaries, gold seekers and such. Even before 1874 the supplies available at Fort Benton had drawn such pioneers as the McDougalls of Morleyville and Sam Livingstone, first settler at Calgary, so the future supply routes from the south were pretty well known.

## The NWMP Contract With I. G. Baker

One would suspect Isaac Gilbert Baker (family members used the middle name) was a poor penman. His early ads in Montana papers turn up as J. G. Baker, and the Canadian documents showing monies paid also are to "J. G. Baker of Fort Benton." In longhand a J for an I is an easy error. Amounts and items following are from Canadian Sessional Papers (No. 188) May 13, 1879.

The first accounting on expenses shows $333,583.90 for 1874-75, $369,518.39 for 1875-76 and $352,749.05 for 1876-77 for the North West Mounted Police. This included literally everything, from the initial $17,471.40 for clothing, provisions, forage and general supplies to $200 gold to Col. G. A. French for medical services, $142.17 for payment of a bill to a Helena merchant, to various individuals employed by the Mounted Police, and even an item of $7.77 for stamping letters with U. S. postage; Canada had no postal service, mail was received and sent via Fort Benton. Statements often were shown in American currency with a due discount for payment in gold by draft on the bank of Montreal, such as a March 22, 1875, statement for $3,969.93 in American currency, in gold $3,609.03.

Where the Police incurred bills with other firms the statements were sent to the Baker concern with instructions to pay the account. Individuals selling horses, providing wood or hay, or acting as guide similarly received their pay through the Baker firm. In other words the company was the ultimate in business manager for the force—an arrangement that existed to the end of the Fort Benton contracts, even after arrival of the Canadian Pacific in Calgary. Until then, the Missouri river steamboats were the only logical source of supplies for Canada's North West Territories.

The initial accounting included Major Walsh's Helena hotel bill, plus $1 for washing his clothes, a grocery bill of more than $10,000, plus thousands of other items, freighting $2238.97 and short range hauling of $475 included—on conversion a $19,065.57 bill dwindled to the initial $17,471.10 gold. Lowest priced item found was $6 for 60 papers of Sharp's needles at 10c each, lowest single entries 50c for a paper of zinc nails and 35c for a pound of candles. The Fort Benton to Fort Macleod freight rate was 2 1/2 cents a pound. Another item, probably fast freight and premium price, 4c per pound for hauling 7,000 pounds of oats (price of oats 4 1/2 cents) in winter.

Mounties paid 5c a pound to H. S. Baker for 120 pounds of buffalo meat, another time a probably hungrier bunch 40c a pound for 96 pounds of meat, each duly paid the hunter by order on the Baker company. An interesting 1874 item, payment to Lewis Wallace of $14.50 for one pair of tailor's shears bought from him, James F. Macleod adding an explanation: "These scissors were required to cut out the cow skins for the men's trousers; it was a favor to get them even at this price."

There were a few disagreements, one arose after Fort Macleod was nearly completed by Baker workmen in 1876, $2,476 for building a barrack and $1,000 extra expense for locating post further from timber than by agreement with Col. Macleod. He reduced the first amount on measuring amount completed, no argument; but felt there was no extra expense to building fort more than a mile away from timber. "They reserve the right to make good their claim for the balance."

Another Baker job was building Fort Calgary, and March 1876 there was a cent a pound charge for moving 13,404 pounds of police stores from Macleod to Calgary, $134.04. By territorial standards, the prices indicate the Fort Benton firm was dealing fairly with the Canadian government.

An expensive item was a sawmill ordered in St. Louis in April 1875, engine $1300 and sawmill $775, with parts $2652 in St. Louis. In July James F. Macleod approved a freight bill of 5 1/2 cents a pound, St. Louis to Fort Macleod, $1100. Another charge was $2500 for legal services of Merritt C. Page in Canadian attempts to extradite Thomas Hardwick, John Evans, Jeff Devereux, Charles Harper and Trevanian Hale to face charges of murder of Assiniboine Indians at Cypress Mountain in North West Territories in 1873—duly paid to Page by the Baker Co.

### An Unusual Connection

That item about "stamping letters" is another point in the unusual and intimate relationship between the North West Territories and Fort Benton's I. G. Baker & Co. The area had no postal service at the time, and what mail there was moved via Fort Benton. The firm's wagons and perhaps others carried mail to and from the Mounty posts as a convenience for a very good customer—it is probable the same applied to individuals on the road, simply a no cost but greatly appreciated service. An early purchase for NWMP, two mail sacks and locks.

If the mail originated in eastern Canada it of course bore Canadian stamps, probably carried by rail to Bismarck, Dakota Territory, hence by steamboat to Fort Benton, from there north by ox team, I. G. Baker stage or individuals heading north, eventually reaching its destination. U. S. stamps were evidently available in Baker stores in Canada, and probably in Power, for convenience of customers and doubtless affixed before being sent south, following the same course in reverse. At Fort Benton the mail would be dropped at the postoffice to receive a Fort Benton cancel. On occasion some might end at Sun River or Helena and receive the cancel of that town.

The author has not seen the cover, but has a copy of it, in 1976 possessed by a Calgary collector, dated Oc 10, 82, Carluke, Ont and addressed to Major James Walker, Bow River, N. W. Territories, via Fort Benton, Montana, U. S. Walker was a former member of the NWMP, at the time manager of the Cochrane Ranche Co.

The reverse flow, to Fort Benton or other points, is proven in the Dr. R. B. Nevitt letters, more than 100 from Fort Macleod, addressed to Ontario. These are postpaid with U. S. stamps, postmarked Fort Benton or Fort Shaw usually. The correspondence is in the Glenbow museum at Calgary, Hugh Dempsey, associate director, reported in 1987.

Some notes turn up regarding this informal mail service:

Helena Herald of Sept. 9, 1875, in a letter from Fort Macleod: "Our official mail carrier, D. Leveille, makes the trip punctually once a fortnight." Benton Record, July 14, 1876, "J. J. Everson, Cypress Hills mail carrier, who left Fort Benton on the 8th, was chased by Sioux war party from Lonesome Prairie to within a few miles of the Marias." (about 25-30 miles) Benton Record, July 14, 1879: "Saskatchewan Herald of Battleford said Pierre Leveille had received contract to carry mail from Fort Benton to Battleford by way of Fort Walsh."

In "In the Shadow of the Rockies," C. M. MacInnes said that mail was made up in Mounted Police barracks and the letters stamped with American stamps and carried by messenger under contract with the Police to Fort Benton. That for official mail?

Finally, when the Fort Macleod Gazette began publication July 1, 1882, the paper applied for second class mail permit from Fort Benton to reach subscribers in eastern Canada. That of course ended when the Canadian Pacific arrived in 1883.

## NWMP Seizes The Reins of Power

The North West Mounted Police rode into their new domain with dignity and pride, and were not long in seizing the reins of power. A bit unique in North America, the Police were not only enforcers of the law. They also acted as magistrates—assessing sentences, fines and release or suspension, and jailors should a prison sentence be assessed. But as the Bentonites had told the Police correctly, their arrival had ended the whisky trade, save for an unbelieving few.

First caught, legend has it and seems accurate, was one Harry "Kamoose" Taylor, the nickname meaning squaw thief, at Bond's Fort near present Nanton, Alberta. Mounties on a tip raided and arrested Wm. Bond and Taylor and confiscated a wagon load of robes in February 1875. Harry Taylor later conducted a hotel at Fort Macleod which had an oft quoted and intriguing set of rules for guests. Bond, described both as Negro and Mexican breed, escaped the crude jail, but drowned. A grandson of Taylor in letters seemed more pleased than not at his ancestor's notoriety.

Most important catch was J. D. Weatherwax, partner of W. S. Wetzel and of an important Fort Benton firm, who drew in March 1875, a $500 fine and six months in jail from policeman, judge, jury and jailor rolled into one, for possession of several hundred robes allegedly traded for with whisky. Evidence seems a bit shaky, primarily the testimony of an Indian complaining he didn't get enough booze for his ponies. Weatherwax maintained he sold Dick Berry supplies but no whisky—the reason he had possession of the robes. The supreme court (same commissioner) overruled the appeal, the sentence stood. Wetzel & Weatherwax at the time were conducting a legitimate, no whisky trade elsewhere. The convict had been Chouteau county sheriff and later was elected county commissioner.

No other case figured so prominently in the first months of the Mounties' regime.

The "salutary effect" of the coming of the NWMP might have been best noted in a letter a Helena Herald contributor said he found in Fort Benton, and dated Old Man's River, September 30, 1874: "Tell you what, boys, Guessingburg is in the middle of a financial crisis. All guessed wrong this time. I think I have all the goods I want and will not want the bill filled I sent to town for. My reasons for thinking so are that the d——d police wont give us any show to do anything, and a fellow may as well give up first as last while he has a chance. T. D."

This was typical, the bulk of Whoop Up country whites simply pulled stakes. Many worked as freighters and even as legitimate traders later. For confirmed lawbreakers, the odds as reckoned by gamblers were simple—300 Mounties or a nearly helpless few deputy U. S. marshals on the American side of the border.

The NWMP when they came to Fort Whoop Up in October 1874, offered to buy the fort, but John Healy asked an unrealistic $25,000 for what actually was a dead horse for him. Instead, the I. G. Baker Co. built Fort Macleod on the Oldman for the Police, getting it done ahead of dead winter—in 1875 the Mounties expanded to Fort Calgary and Fort Walsh—the latter in the Cypress Hills where there was already a settlement of about 80 Metis homes. Baker of course supplied the food, workmen, material, whatever, for both. It was not until 1885, after the coming of the Canadian Pacific and a considerable number of settlers, that the Canadians began dividing their government contracts. Until then, every need of the force was supplied or contracted through the Baker concern.

In the January 5, 1875, in the Helena Herald, Major Walsh of the Mounted Police felt the Indians were in better circumstances than for years, telling the reporter the whisky traders had been "entirely expelled." Indians were resupplying themselves with horses and buying ammunition with which to hunt for grub and clothing. He said, "It is well known that $500 worth of whisky will get from the Indians as many robes as would $5,000 worth of other merchandise, hence it may readily be seen the change is for the better." His viewpoint may have been too roseate.

In the year 1875 the Herald was much more apt to run stories critical of the methods and work of the NWMP than was the new Benton Record (first issue Feb. 1). Fort Benton was on the upbeat with the new business and reaping benefits from the presence of 300 new customers across the border, soon many times that figure.

## An Extradition Attempt

June 26, 1875, the Record had an important story: "On the 21st instant, Messrs. Hale, Hardwick, Evans, Harper and Devereux were arrested by Deputy Marshals Hard and Beidler, assisted by the military, for the killing of Assinaboin Indians at Cypress Mountains, British America, some two years ago." This was the beginning of the celebrated extradition case, mention made above of the Canadian legal fee of $2500. Extradition was denied after a several day court hearing, the five men released, and eventually all charges were dropped. (In Canada Philander Vogle, George M. Bell and James Hughes, picked up in connection with the Cypress Hills affair, were acquitted in June 1876—the entire matter dropped in 1882.) The five charged were applauded in Helena, got a roaring welcome on their return to to Fort Benton. John Evans and Jeff Devereux, partners in a Fort Benton saloon, took the occasion to relabel their business the Extradition Saloon. The June arrest marked the last time a "company of military" surrounded the town to carry out an unpopular duty. Fort Benton wasn't very big, the Record thought about 500, but its merchants were thinking impossibly big. And before the final nemesis, steel rails, arrived, they succeeded surprisingly.

## Alberta Begins To Grow

As the forts across the border were established, Alberta's first settlements of any size beyond the occasional Metis villages, were growing around them. Before the first boat in spring 1875 Baker sent 15 big wagons loaded with contract supplies. As the summer progressed, various stocks of merchandise, large and small, were accompanying the trains as Fort Macleod sprang into being. The same thing happened at the newer 1875 posts. One week in August Baker wagons started with 144,000 pounds of supplies for the new fort in Cypress Mountains, 118,000 pounds to Macleod. Until the Baker and Power companies agreed to split the sites, each had a store at each post, in 1881 Baker took Macleod and Calgary, Power kept Fort Walsh and Maple Creek. There were others of course—a business man might try Benton for a spell, then move his shop north, or reverse the movement.

Record Editor W. H. Buck in an August 1875 editorial, viewing the growing traffic north of the boundary and perhaps hearing of the job the Mounties were doing collecting customs, had a thoughtful suggestion; bonding of freight bound for Canada when it originated in the east of the new dominion but had to traverse U. S. routes to get to the Canadian North West Territories. Three weeks later, September 18, Buck wrote "Fort Benton has a bonded line, has had one for some time past, not made public." T. C. Power had posted $100,000 bond in Washington to insure that no Canadian-origin goods would be diverted to U. S. use without payment of customs. I. G. Baker & Co. soon followed suit.

Robes and furs in volume to surpass the whisky trading days were coming down out of Canada in Power and Baker wagon trains. (U. S. customs had been collecting, probably 20% of invoice value, at Fort Benton for several years and the Montana-Idaho customs collector had moved his office to the river city about this time.) John P. Turner estimated Baker traded for 15,000 robes the first season of 1874-75, next year from Fort Bow 12,000, and in all about 40,000 with about as many wolf skins.

September 25, 1875, the Record had a Macleod item: "Building the rage here. Trading posts are being erected as if by magic hands. Messrs. Conrad (of Baker) building at Bow river, near the site of new Police post, Power at Macleod and will build on Bow river." Later in the month as both firms continued shipments to British North America a new name appeared, Fort Edmonton—a mighty long trip for only 50 tons of merchandise.

With the new year of 1876 Bentonites could see the bright future Buck had envisioned in his first issue of the Record almost a year earlier. The Carroll Trail after two years had failed in delivery of supplies because of mud and Sioux— in fact some hundreds of tons of Carroll freight were moved in wagons of the Benton trade. First wagons north to Macleod were held up in March by snow en route, but more kept pulling out of Benton. Baker and Power also teamed to contract the freighting for the Yellowstone expedition against the Sioux of soldiers from Fort Shaw and Fort Ellis.

The robe trade was reported in February as very large in the Cypress Hills, perhaps 25,000, and also heavy in the Macleod area. During the year relatively few freight shipments were reported in the Record, apparently becoming commonplace; one large one, Baker wagons and 338,000 pounds to Fort Macleod. But the supplies were going out. Sept. 15, 1876, Benton Record: From Cypress Mountains and new Fort Walsh: "I. G. Baker & Co. and T. C. Power & Bro. have the inside track of all the Northwest traders and are selling immense quantities of bonded goods. It is expected that Col. Macleod will shortly arrive and will take command of the entire force of Mounted Police." The force was keeping a sharp lookout for refugee Sioux who were being harried northward after the Custer debacle. And a partial reason for lack of freighting reports, the U. S. military had requisitioned two thirds of the steamboats to move and supply more troops. One order sent north, 60,000 pounds of Highwood potatoes for the Mounties.

The October 13 Record had high praise for the Redcoats: "The Mounted Police don't scare worth a cent. Parties of two and three men are scouting along the line looking for Sitting Bull." General Terry on this side was doing the same, but with far more company. Canada had inherited another woe, which lasted more than four years, from the Americans.

### Major Walsh's Sioux Problem

Correct name of the tribe of course is Dakota, but Sioux (so termed by tribal enemies, and meaning "Enemy") is much better known, and they were Major James Walsh's legacy—all the bitter, frustrated nonsurrendered warriors, survivors of the Little Big Horn and later battles with U. S. army troops.

The news of the June 25, 1876, military disaster in southern Montana reached easterners as they were celebrating their nation's centennial. It perhaps came into Fort Benton by "moccasin telegraph" as it did to other Montana points, but the next issue of the Benton Record, July 7, is missing (no word in the June 30 paper). But July 14 Editor Buck had a hard word for the lead character, Custer, who if he had not died on the field "undoubtedly would have been tried and punished for his unpardonable breach of military discipline." Buck was an ex-ranker, later recanted in part.

What had occurred stung the U. S. army as did no other disaster in the Indian wars. Steamboats were requisitioned off the Fort Benton trade in job lots, an early sign was the Benton taking down 40 horses August 4, doubtless all the remounts the area could spare for survivors of the 7th Cavalry, and other steamboats were soon bringing regiments instead of cargo up river, to the arena along the Yellowstone. In mid-September the Record mentioned the impact on shipping, hundreds of tons of down freight still on hand as well as slow arrival of merchandise.

Ready to take the field against the Sioux had been Terry's remnants, the commands of Crook and Miles, about 3600 men, though the fall campaign was not impressive. Miles did better in a winter campaign with the 5th Infantry, reinforced by six companies of the 22nd—a bad winter for both sides. Irreconcilable Sioux were gradually drifting northward—they had exhausted their ammunition. Sitting Bull was reported within 10 miles of the border in late September, about 80 from Fort Walsh, probably erroneously. But the last of November the Record noted that nonsurrender Sioux were coming in at Fort Walsh. (In "Whoop-Up Country" Paul Sharp found indications of 3,000 Sioux in that influx, more later.)

Sitting Bull was a late comer. The June 15, 1877, Benton Record printed a report from Fort Walsh that Sitting Bull and 1,000 warriors crossed the line April 7, and that Major Walsh and a small party had interviewed him near there, as well as sleeping overnight in the Sioux camp!

Sioux spokesmen had been telling the Mounted Police of tribal legends that the Sioux had once been the White Queen's children, and so informed Major Walsh that they were simply returning home. The major in effect offered temporary sanctuary along with stern warnings that they were simply guests and their Redcoat friends would never permit them to make war across the border. Further, they were not Canadian Indians, but American.

What followed was a great example of white-red diplomacy. Walsh had about 300 Mounties in all to make it good, but treated the bitter Sioux with all the pomp and ceremony that was any Indian's delight; along with a firm, steely manner, warning and on occasion reprimanding their greatest chiefs, including Sitting Bull, bitterest of all.

There were still buffalo in Canada, but the influx of thousands of hungry Sioux helped to speed their end. Canadian Indians of course resented the Sioux presence, hunting was more difficult, less rewarding, and above all, Sioux were ancient enemies of many of the Canadian tribes.

Some of the top level diplomacy was between the two governments, but neither Ottawa or Washington knew just what could or should be done; in the end the top level hopes were Canada wanting to be quit of their unwelcome guests, and the U. S. hoping they'd seen the last of them. Through the lengthy tangle, the personal touch of Major James Walsh seems a shining light.

While the dickering was underway in 1877 the Nez Perce were moving, across Idaho into Montana, through Yellowstone Park and up to Cow Island, near safety in Canada a halt north of the Bear's Paw forced their surrender to Generals Miles and Howard. White Bird with a small remnant, reached Canada and contacted Sitting Bull to urge a joint campaign. The chief and his Sioux had seen enough soldiers.

Major Walsh in fall 1877 even arranged a meeting between General Terry and Sitting Bull near Fort Walsh, supposedly on terms under which the Sioux might return. NWMP Commissioner James Macleod was host; the meeting was completely inconclusive, but it did give Macleod the opportunity to warn the Sioux chiefs that they were American Indians, and that if they raided across the border American soldiers might be permitted to cross in pursuit. John Healy, by then with the Benton Record, reported on the council, was not impressed by Sitting Bull.

Perhaps the solution to the puzzle was the building of Fort Assiniboine beginning in 1878 near later Havre. It became the most strongly garrisoned post on the northern plains, certainly a deterrent to Sioux raids and even to sneak buffalo hunting. More likely it was gnawing hunger, for by then the buffalo were virtually gone in Canada, and dwindling south of the line. By 1880 some of the Sioux began drifting south to surrender themselves. Sitting Bull surrendered at Fort Buford (Union) July 19, 1881, among the last of the Sioux in Canada.

The NWMP, from commissioner to the lowest imperturbable, outwardly at least, trooper, deserve a vast amount of credit for preventing a frontier blood bath.

(After initial sour comments in regard to the Weatherwax case, the Benton Record grew mellow. April 13, 1877, in a story about the NWMP was the comment, "They fetched their man every time." This was perhaps the source of the famous comment about always "getting their man.")

## Freighting North From Fort Benton

While all this was going on, freighters out of Fort Benton were churning dust on the 150 mile trail to Fort Walsh as well as the 225 miles to Macleod. Not always of easy mind. In early September 1877 a Baker Co. wagonmaster arrived in town, reporting he had been told a wagon train had been attacked and captured by a large party of Blackfeet, two teamsters killed and the train burned. An armed party rode to investigate, found the men had just scared themselves. Major Ilges termed it "a disgraceful abandonment and cowardly fright on the part of six men who never heard a shot fired."

On the other hand, bullwhackers could handily restart the Sioux war if they followed their instincts. At Fort Walsh Mike Connelly saw his first scalp dangling from the belt of an Indian, and told his granddaughter, Helena Pannell, years later "when the drivers saw that it was the hair of a white woman, the wagon boss had difficulty in restraining them from taking a shot at the 'Red Devils'." Mike bought his first buffalo robe for $5 from the Baker warehouse at Walsh, said he had his pick of 30,000 robes.

Mike Connelly's reminiscences included that a train had eight bullwhackers, wagon boss and night herder. Each driver had a team of eight yoke of oxen which pulled three big Murphy wagons loaded with five or six tons of freight. 'Whackers were paid $50 a month and board, took turns cooking. An average day's journey was ten miles. Bullwhacking was a literal term, walking beside their oxen with a long rawhide whip as sole persuader and guide. Flour, sugar, coffee, ham and bacon made up the greater part of the loads hauled to Canada. Mike recalled his loads were protected by canvas, but still sure to get wet. He remembered unloading sugar with great tunnels hollowed in the sugar by water leakage.

The Baker Company business with the Mounted Police can be estimated at about

70 tons of supplies the fall of 1874, but reached about 450 tons the next year and kept growing. A summary of 1877 steamboat business provides more definite figures, 595 tons to Fort Macleod and 350 to Cypress Hills (Fort Walsh), valued at $303,000 and $180,000—Canadian contract freight in all 1025 tons with a value of $310,000. The contract freight value would have been a major part of Baker's business with the NWMP. To handle it, the firm sold its interest in the steamboat Benton and bought the Red Cloud, start of the Baker Line.

As 1878 dawned both Power and Baker concerns were looking to arrival of brand new steamboats, the Helena second in the Block P Line, the Col. McLeod named for the Mounted Police commissioner the second in the Baker Line. The Col. McLeod was a small boat, built primarily to shuttle about 100 tons of freight from the Cow Island freight drop to Benton in late season. The Record also heralded an appropriation of $150,000 for a new Milk River army post, Fort Assiniboine, and local ownership of the Benton-Helena stage line by Wm. Rowe with Power backing. In June with start of its volume IV, the paper called "The past year one of uninterrupted prosperity." Freighting north and south had become too commonplace for items on outgoing shipments, although steamboat arrivals were dutifully reported. It was a local news item in July when the Record announced the first marriage at Whoop Up, of Joseph McFarland and Marcella Sheran. It was also worthy of mention October 11 that Col. Macleod was a house guest of Wm. G. Conrad of the Baker firm, and would take passage down river on his namesake steamboat, just in port on her fifth arrival. The Col. McLeod undoubtedly handled much of the Canadian freight, and had been an unqualified success its first season.

About 400 tons of steamboat freight went north in Baker wagons in 1878, their contract probably included as much or more Montana milled flour, oats and produce, and stock for their Canadian stores. Coming back down were about 30,000 robes from Canada's dwindling herds, and an unreported number of wolf skins—available data indicates about as many as the robes. Wolf pelts were worth about $3 at a shipping point on the Missouri.

The year 1879 found another increase in Fort Benton's Canadian business, primarily due to more white settlers and also efforts by the Dominion to feed its hungry Northwest Indians. About 14,000 buffalo robes brought south represented the virtual end of the robe trade from the north. Probably a result of the Sioux problem, as was Fort Assiniboine, 100 Mounties were passengers on the Baker Line Red Cloud on a June trip—another boat, Coulson's Dacotah, brought 205 workers to help build Fort Assiniboine, and hundreds of tons of freight were landed at a Coal Banks drop below Fort Benton for that fort. Whoop Up coal from the Sheran mine near later Lethbridge, was also freighted south (first mention of this in 1875). The coal was always welcome, Fort Benton had recurring fuel shortages in almost any winter colder than normal, prices ranging from $20 to $30 per ton delivered. Teamsters apparently didn't want to shovel the stuff, only a time or two did a warmer winter result in a surplus.

One item for 1880 says for its Canadian trade the Baker Co. employed 80 men, almost 600 oxen, 100 mules and more than 100 wagons. Wagons were generally hitched in threes. A train could be of any length, usually 8 or 10 wagon outfits, some times almost double. A single train represented an investment of $25,000 or more, giving an idea of the scope and necessary investment. The ten year freighting period may have meant as much as 25,000 tons of freight hauled northward.

Railroads were barely into Montana east and southwest by the end of 1880, but railheads were busy—a summary shows about 6700 tons east side (Northern Pacific near Wibaux), and 9700 tons west side (Utah & Northern near Dillon) while Fort Benton commerce was 12,200 tons, Yellowstone river about 1580. The Baker Line brought in about 1,000 tons by Red Cloud, a good share destined for the north, but no firm figures available. Also another 1,500 tons on Coulson boats, the Baker Line's Col. McLeod was destroyed following the 1879 season. This year the runaway Sioux were finding even rabbits and other small game scanty, and were drifting back over the line and going to army posts to surrender for food and transportation back to the agencies. There were still numerous buffalo in the area along the Missouri, chiefly on the south side, but with many hunters from Montana tribes, in 1881 joined by large numbers of white hunters.

June 15, 1881, there was an editorial in the River Press about Fort Benton as a business center. In the same issue an acrimonious comment: "Seven millions of pounds of freight are in Bismarck awaiting shipment, and the business of the territory kept lagging therefrom, while a fleet of steamboats are carrying numerous bands of Indians on a picnic down the Yellowstone." The fleet was of five steamboats off the Fort Benton trade, from Fort Keogh taking 1700 surrendered Sioux to Standing Rock Agency. The Sioux in Canada were giving up.

In July Sitting Bull surrendered at Fort Buford, Fort Benton papers noted this and his later movements with interest. In August the Record reported a rumor that 3,000 Sioux were headed down from Canada, and that troops were being sent from Fort Assiniboine to safeguard the passage.

Canadians in September greeted the Marquis of Lorne on his visit to Fort Macleod, the Record made a special note of a $274 message sent by a London Times correspondent from Fort Benton or Fort Shaw, regarded as especially newsworthy.

An 1881 summary of river business into Montana by Dan Maratta of the Coulson Line at Bismarck put it at the all time peak, 21,600 tons into Montana, 4,200 of that on the Yellowstone. In the Fort Benton trade about 14,000 tons, the remainder at lower points to supply buffalo hunters. Going down were 160,000 buffalo hides, white hunters were in competition with hungry Indians in killing the last of the great herds. On the Upper Missouri 21 steamboats were in use.

Fort Benton was much too busy building in 1881 for either paper to pay much attention to the freighting and commerce scene, although one paper did mention the Red Cloud bringing 105 recruits for the Mounted Police in May. But there was another note indicating that the North West Territories was emerging from swaddling clothes, Major James Walker of Cochrane Ranch Co. in May bought 6,000 head of Poindexter & Orr cattle from southern Montana. This became a common occurrence, most of the Canadians bought their cattle in Montana, although for 1883 there is a note that Cochrane and Waldron trailed several thousand Texas cattle across the Missouri at Fort Benton northward. Some Americans also leased land in Canada, notably the Conrad Circle outfit, which for years had Howell Harris as manager of their Canadian herd, while his brother Jack Harris was manager of the American herd. At one time this outfit, originally the Benton & St. Louis, was largest in Montana, about 25,000 head.

An evil omen for a prosperous Fort Benton was the November 16, 1882, Record that reported the Canadian Pacific was 20 miles east of Medicine Hat, and hoped to build on to Maple Creek that fall. To the south of Fort Benton, the Northern Pacific, which had stopped at Bismarck in 1873 and resumed building after several years, got to Wibaux in 1880, Miles City in 1881, Billings and Livingston next year, and there went most of Fort Benton's trade area.

With the arrival of the Canadian Pacific in Calgary in 1883 Fort Benton's close ties with Fort Macleod, Calgary, Edmonton, Medicine Hat, Maple Creek and other cities ceased almost like cutting a skein with scissors. The last important shipments went north in mid-summer of 1883. The Benton Record, mentioning the drop in business, August 12 added, "Not even a dog fight relieved the monotony."

The Baker and Power Canadian businesses continued for a time, eventually were sold. Most important sale of all, at least to Hudson's Bay Company, which had been virtually exiled to the northern lands by the Americans, was the sale of the Baker Canadian stores in 1891. William G. Conrad in 1906 recalled the dinner in Winnipeg when the formalities were completed, and an HBC director "proposed the health of the writer as the man who had scaled the value of their stock down from pounds to shillings." Conrad was quick to add, "the compliment would have been more justly applied to the hardy and adventurous men who did the trading, pushing forward always into new territories, my part being only planning and directing operations from Fort Benton."

One of the men he referred to was his brother Charles Conrad, another was Donald W. Davis, Vermont Yankee, former whisky trader and first member of the Canadian parliament from the North West Territories. There were many more.

Alberta residents in particular are far more familiar with that history and century ago relationship than are Montanans, even than many Bentonites.

# Peacemaker Culbertson

Alexander Culbertson, founder of Fort Benton, first permanently occupied site in Montana, was a top trader for the American Fur Company, amassed the greatest fortune of any of its field operatives, was a trail blazer of the Upper Missouri west, and was a special agent for the government in making peace treaties with Indians.

Yet he somehow is disregarded in his premiere role, that of peacemaker, in which Culbertson certainly deserves recognition. He exercised much the same sort of influence on the Blackfeet tribes as did his distinguished and much better known friend and occasional associate, Fr. Pierre Jean DeSmet, did with the Sioux, these being the two most warlike tribes of the northern plains. Their trails crossed a number of times. Culbertson's career as peacemaker with the Blackfeet outspanned that of the Catholic missionary with the Sioux.

Alexander Culbertson was once characterized by Fr. DeSmet as "a distinguished man, endowed with a mild, benevolent and charitable temperament, though if need be intrepid and courageous. He has always given me the marks of kindness and friendship."

Culbertson was born in Chambersburg, Pennsylvania, May 16, 1809, son of Joseph Culbertson and first wife Mary Finley Culbertson. By 1830-31 he was in the Indian trade on St. Peter's River in Minnesota for American Fur and was transferred to the Upper Missouri Outfit in 1833, his first trip up the Missouri on the Assiniboine to Fort Union. Kenneth McKenzie promptly sent the neophyte trader on the keelboat Flora on to year old Fort McKenzie where he was to understudy David Mitchell, the bourgeois.

Before he was many weeks older he had married by Indian custom a daughter of Blackfeet chief White Buffalo, had taken part in an historic battle between Assiniboines and a band of Piegans come to trade at Fort McKenzie, helped entertain Prince Maximilian of Wied and accompanied Karl Bodmer and the prince on some of their field trips. When Mitchell went down the Missouri River next spring with the furs and robes traded for, Culbertson was in charge of the trading post.

He was also in charge next June in absence of James Kipp when Crows, desirous of preventing trade of white goods and weapons to enemy Blackfeet, besieged Fort McKenzie. While the Crows weren't actually firing on the traders, their blockade killed trade, and Culbertson tried to negotiate a truce. After the whites had almost literally eaten their moccasins, Culbertson warned the Crows of white men's "medicine" and finally loaded a cannon and sent a ball trundling through the Crow camp. That display ended the siege. The Crow chief Rotten Belly, heading a war party to salvage prestige, ran into too many Blackfeet a few miles away and went to his happy hunting grounds. But Culbertson's peaceful solution of the siege had worked.

A May 5, 1835, letter from Fort Union, probably written by Kenneth McKenzie, shows recipient Alexander Culbertson fully in charge at McKenzie, advising "a very valuable outfit is selected for you amounting at St. Louis prices to $11,200 and upwards," and that the company wished to push the robe trade to hold the trade of the Blackfeet. The letter also recommended "renewing" Fort McKenzie (archaeological evidence suggests Culbertson rebuilt it on the site).

What happened to Culbertson's Blackfeet wife hasn't been found, but at least a daughter, Maria, and perhaps Janie, were born to the couple. Such unions were at times very casually dissolved. There may have been another marriage before Natawista.

In 1839 Culbertson was made a partner in the Upper Missouri Outfit—the Pratte, Chouteau owners returned a third of company profits to their chief men in the field, and from his shares Alexander Culbertson ultimately retired with a then sizable fortune of $300,000. It was in 1840 that he married Natawista, daughter of Blood chief Father of All Children, and gained a wife who would aid him tremendously in his future career, an exceptional, intelligent woman with influential relatives.

That year 1840 Culbertson was placed in charge of pivotal Fort Union, succeeding Kenneth McKenzie. By 1843 his overall success in trading and in peaceful negotiations with tribesmen were so evident that when the company post at Fort Laramie on the Platte suffered trade losses, Culbertson was ordered to go there to remedy matters as the best trouble shooter on the frontier of the fur trade.

He went under some protest, for the trade in buffalo robes during his stay at Fort McKenzie had risen five times, to 10,000 his final year at Fort McKenzie in 1839. Pierre Chouteau perhaps sweetened the deal, but his stay at Laramie was brief. February 19, 1844, Francis Chardon and Alexander Harvey, in charge at Fort McKenzie, turned a cannon on a peaceful trading party following an incident in which petulant warriors killed or drove off cattle and killed a Negro, Tom Reese, one of a party which followed the braves. Six Blackfeet died, and the whites wisely abandoned McKenzie, slipped down river to the Judith and built a new post they called Fort Francis A. Chardon. Trade was scanty there, Blackfeet harassed the new post, and American Fur owners were much distressed at the drop in profits.

It took two tries to get Alexander Culbertson to return to the Missouri and try to make peace with an outraged Blackfeet nation. According to what Culbertson told historian Lt. James Bradley, he informed Honore Picotte, one of the American Fur heads, at Fort Pierre that they had ignored his warnings about the change at McKenzie when he was transferred. Then Pierre Chouteau sent a letter to Culbertson directing him to a June meeting in New York. There Chouteau in effect gave Culbertson a free hand in remedying affairs on the Upper Missouri.

The latter overtook the 1845 supply keel boat at Poplar, later met and sent Alexander Harvey down river for his discharge in St. Louis, and abandoned Fort Chardon as completely unsuitable for trade with the Blackfeet. Instead Culbertson and party went about two miles above later Fort Benton to the south side of the river and took over a small post of Union Fur (Fox & Livingston), a company American Fur had bought out earlier that year. The Culbertson account to Bradley indicates complete construction of what became Fort Lewis. Naturally, the whites did not wish to be discovered by the Blackfeet until safely behind log palisades, so they subsisted on dog meat for a time to avoid hunting. Thereafter the 70 men felt safer. With a chance contact, Culbertson sent gifts of tobacco to the Blackfeet then on Belly River, asking a peace conference.

The chiefs quite evidently trusted Beaver Child (or Little Beaver, their name for Culbertson) and a band of about 50 Blackfeet appeared at the appointed time.

Culbertson carefully informed them of the anger with which the white chiefs heard of the outrage at Fort McKenzie, and that all perpetrators had been sent out of the country, and the peace pipe was passed. Big Swan, then a leading chief, in reply said "that the ground had been made good again by Major Culbertson's return, and the Blackfeet must not be first to stain it with blood." Trade was brisk at new Fort Lewis, and on his way down river Culbertson burned Fort Chardon to help wipe the slate clean.

The winter of 1845-46 brought complaints from the Blackfeet. Fort Lewis was on the wrong bank for the tribe, ice clogged the river in winter and the Indians could not cross freely. Culbertson, back to the post in late fall 1845, readily agreed to move. Members of his family always gave 1846 as the year of founding of what became Fort Benton, which makes it appear that workmen from the upper fort began building the new fort in winter 1846-47. It was March 19, 1847, Fr. Point's Journal authenticating the date, that the last logs from the upstream post were floated two miles down and across the river. At first called Fort Clay, the name quickly became Fort Lewis, and a change of name formally made to Fort Benton Christmas night 1850.

Trade in robes had been very good in the 1846 season, probably because most of the tribesmen had no outlet for these during the Fort Chardon interval, but in 1847 20,000 robes were bartered, four times 1845 and up 3,000 from 1846. Culbertson informed Bradley that "bedding, wearing apparel, everything that could be spared from the post was bartered for the incessant flow of peltries."

The private treaty of 1845 was probably Culbertson's finest hour as peacemaker, but he was to receive further recognition and honors for his role in improving relations between tribes and between Indians and whites. In this he was greatly aided by his wife Natawista.

There was opposition in the Fort Benton area; in 1846 Alexander Harvey secured backing from Robert Campbell of St. Louis, and as Harvey, Primeau & Co. came back up river in a vengeful mood for his firing—first Fort Campbell was a few miles below Fort Lewis, on the south side of the river on a bottom below the Cracon du Nez, a narrow ridge between Teton and Missouri. In 1847 Fort Campbell was moved to a half mile above the post that would be renamed Fort Benton. Further, Harvey began building of adobe before Culbertson so reconstructed Fort Benton. Although many Blackfeet considered Harvey the "worst white man," he made peace of sorts by taking a Piegan wife, and his post traded for a fourth to nearly half the robe trade of American Fur. With Harvey's death in 1854 the drive went out of the opposition, which a few years later was absorbed by American Fur.

Culbertson's success in re-establishing the Blackfeet post soon brought promotion to in charge of the Upper Missouri Outfit at a salary more than double any predecessor, and his trader's share in profits helped build his fortune.

The year 1851 was eventful for Culbertson. Coming up on the St. Ange in the spring he and old friend Fr. DeSmet survived a cholera epidemic that killed more than 30 persons. Alexander Culbertson left the steamboat at Bellevue to go overland to Fort Pierre. Enroute he was met by a messenger with a letter from the superintendent of Indian affairs, requesting him to secure a delegation of Upper Missouri tribes and conduct them to a grand council to be held at Fort Laramie in August. The great westward migrations to Oregon and California had disturbed the plains Indians, and purpose of the Laramie council was to make secure a peaceful passage on the Oregon Trail.

At Fort Union in July, Culbertson's young daughters, Nancy and Frances, were baptized by Fr. DeSmet. Then the two peacemakers set about contacting the Indian tribes in the vicinity of Fort Union to have them represented at Laramie. They decided it was too late to contact tribes higher up the Missouri, so Culbertson represented Blackfeet interests at the Laramie council.

Culbertson's final effort of 1851 provided a first for the northernmost plains. With five men and a wagon he set out from Fort Union overland for Fort Benton, arriving around December 1st with the first wheeled vehicle to penetrate the country north of the Missouri in Montana. It became the American Fur overland route, and was followed by the Stevens expedition in 1853, and by emigrants from Minnesota in the 1860's. The route is largely the same as present highway 2 from North Dakota to Havre, and by highway 87 from there to Fort Benton.

In the spring of 1852 the head trader floated the annual shipment of robes and furs down river, in September returned overland from Union with two more vehicles. It was a quiet between busy years, for in 1853 Culbertson was called upon to help the Isaac I. Stevens northern railroad survey party, regarded as a high point in early history of Montana. Stevens was also newly appointed governor of the brand new territory of Washington. He named Culbertson as special agent to the Blackfeet, and the latter accompanied part of the Stevens expedition from St. Louis to Fort Union, where the group awaited arrival of Stevens from St. Paul with the rest of the party.

The entire group with a number of wagons carrying presents for Indian tribes as well as supplies, went overland to Fort Benton. Along the way Stevens distributed substantial gifts to Blackfeet and Gros Ventres met enroute.

From September 1st to 21st the Stevens party headquartered at Fort Benton, Culbertson and Natawista the contacts, advisors and mentors with tribesmen on trails and routes. Stevens planned a great 1854 council to bring peace between the Montana tribes. He also sent his lieutenants on lengthy exploration trips, accompanied by selected guides and interpreters from the personnel at Fort Benton. A few men of the Stevens party remained at Fort Benton over the winter, wagons and supplies were left at the fort. But not Alexander Culbertson.

He had reluctantly agreed to a special Stevens assignment, to spend the winter in Washington D.C., lobbying for funds to finance the treaty Stevens proposed to make. Also for more funds for the expedition itself—at Fort Benton Isaac Stevens in effect had thrown the expedition's budget over the palisade on finding he was low on funding, high in ideas.

One was the assignment given Lt. John Mullan, who traveled a thousand miles of wilderness looking ahead to building the Stevens brainstorm, a 624 mile military road between Fort Benton and old Fort Walla Walla in Washington. Culbertson would put in a good word in Washington for that plan, too. The trader in the nation's capital proved an effective lobbyist, meeting influential congressmen and President Franklin Pierce in the interest of treaty and road. But it was, he felt, the most distasteful task of his life—a frontiersman just wasn't cut out for such chores.

In spring 1854 Culbertson returned by steamboat to Fort Union, thence overland to Fort Benton, bringing along Andrew Dawson, who for the next ten years would be in charge of the uppermost American Fur post in the absence of Culbertson. Probably due to the year lapse in the proposed 1854 treaty, due to an Indian outbreak west of the mountains, Stevens sent instructions to Culbertson to buy a thousand dollars worth of food for distribution to Piegans and Gros Ventres to keep them in mind to attend to council in 1855. Sugar, coffee, rice, flour, and tobacco made up the trader's selection for that distribution. Piegans received theirs at Fort Benton, with squaws well instructed on how to prepare white man's food. The well intentioned distribution to Gros Ventres at Milk River was a disaster. They had no knowledge whatever of preparation, didn't listen to Culbertson. The result, half-done, indigestible messes which the Indians bolted like buffalo. Several died, and only Culbertson's reputation averted violence.

The head trader passed the 1854-55 winter at Fort Union, made another lengthy mackinaw trip in the spring to St. Louis to meet and accompany a treaty commissioner, Alfred Cumming. Congress had appropriated $80,000 for this treaty, so a large quantity of goods for presents went along to Fort Union on the steamboat St. Mary, along with Indian Agents Alfred Vaughan and Edwin Hatch. At the Yellowstone the Indian goods were transferred to two large mackinaws in charge of Andrew Dawson, bound for Fort Benton.

Cumming, Culbertson and party took the overland route and at the crossing of the Milk River met Isaac Stevens and a small party from Washington Territory, he being the other commissioner. The two didn't get along, Cumming insisting on precedence as head of Indian affairs, Stevens feeling he was most experienced in the field and the man who called the council, as well as having already concluded a treaty between Flatheads and other tribes. After the fuss, the whole party went on to Fort Benton to await the boats. It was a low water year, Dawson's men were having a terrible time. Culbertson and two other men went down in September, found the boats still below the Judith. On return of the three, it was decided to hold the council at the mouth of the Judith, couriers going out to inform the tribes.

About 2500 Blackfeet and a few others attended the October council at the Judith, a treaty signed somewhat more lasting in its effects than most such. Isaac Stevens was appreciative of the role both Culbertson and wife Natawista had played in placating for years the Blackfeet. The Fort Benton Journal of October 21 reported: "Several Indians came from treaty laden with presents and highly pleased." So they must have been satisfied. Oft repeated comments that the treaty goods delivery was held up to benefit American Fur trade can be discounted, Fort Benton trade stock boats arrived well after the council.

As for the Culbertsons, they were off down river on an icy trip and would return the next spring—these almost annual journeys meant 5,000 or more miles. Doubtless the couple were beginning to plan their retirement at Peoria, Illinois, where they had bought a farm in 1854. Four years later they built a beautiful home, where they lived in grand style with an estimated fortune of $300,000, the equivalent of millions today. The children were mostly in boarding schools during their long absences. On occasion Natawista was known to set up a Blackfeet lodge on their lawn. The couple were married in Catholic ceremony September 9, 1859, at Peoria, 18 or 19 years after their Indian ceremony.

Alexander Culbertson was back up to Fort Union on the St. Mary, escorting General Warren, who was making a topographic survey, and Professor Hayden of the Smithsonian Institute, the visitors making a trip up the Yellowstone as part of their mission. In October Culbertson went on to Fort Benton. While there he traded from his own account, $1000 worth of goods for yellow metal that turned out to be gold worth $1525, first of a golden torrent that would pour across Fort Benton counters and go down the river in the 1860s. The trader was identified later as John Silverthorne, and the gold was sent by John Owen of the fort that had been St. Mary's Mission—gold that almost certainly came from Owen's dealings on the Oregon Trail, and not Montana gold.

Culbertson's account to Bradley leaves vacant the remainder of the decade; he probably made a trip or more, and did in 1860 come to Fort Benton and returned via the Chippewa. In 1861 he withdrew from American Fur completely to reside full time at Peoria, however making an 1862 trip to Benton on the Spread Eagle and spent the summer on Sun River, his account has it with Rev. A.S. Reed. (That name appears as an Indian trader on the Missouri in the 1870 census.) The last of August Culbertson joined a party of Missourians in purchase of a 50 foot mackinaw from Andrew Dawson. The group left down river in early September; the party was stopped by Assiniboines at Milk River, but Culbertson's presence was a free passport.

The Culbertsons were living high at Peoria, their summer trips an opportunity for Natawista to visit with kinfolk while he gadded about. A niece, Anna Culbertson, was in charge of the home during lengthy absences, the daughters being educated either in a St. Louis convent or a Moravian seminary in Pennsylvania, extras in schooling and cost no object. On the frontier most of their expenses were paid, so no need to dip into salary and share money. In Illinois all was outgo. Culbertson also invested heavily in schemes of his friend, Senator Thomas Hart Benton of Missouri, most costly. Also friends and relatives were helping dissipate the fortune.

By 1866 the money was running out, by 1868 creditors were anxious, next year 33 creditors filed claims. But the Culbertsons had gone back to Montana the year before, his name appears as witness to Blackfeet, Gros Ventres and Crow treaties of 1868, made near Fort Benton.

After the winter, the Culbertsons got together a small stock of trade goods and went north to Belly River in Canada, trading with old friends and customers.

### Last Role As Peacemaker

Frontier trouble between Blackfeet and the incoming miners had been bitter but spasmodic, from the 1865 killing of ten whites at Ophir, off and on hostilities in the next years, reaching a peak in 1869. A flash point at Fort Benton was July 15 when two Garrison train herders were mortally wounded by raiding redskins. Though it turned out the killers were Crows, everybody in Fort Benton, for that matter in northern Montana, blamed the Blackfeet. Several Indians were killed in Fort Benton and the general impression seemed to be that a full scale Indian war was about to erupt.

What set the whites on the war trail was the killing of Malcolm Clarke at his Prickly Pear ranch near Helena on August 17. Clarke had been in the fur trade, a former head at Fort Benton, from 1839, so was a genuine pioneer. His killers were Pete Owl Child and Eagle's Rib, in what actually was a family feud, but white Montanans did not so regard the slaying. From that time a train of events led inexorably to a bloody climax.

Alexander Culbertson, in his final major role as peacemaker, tried to avert what he could plainly see was coming. He wrote General Sully September 2, 1869, pointing out that he had wintered with Blackfeet and Bloods in 1868-69, finding them perfectly peaceful and surprised to learn of reports of frequent Piegan raids. Culbertson put the latter in perspective, too: "My knowledge of their (Piegans) character for a great many years will not permit me to think that there exists a general hostile feeling among them; on the contrary, these depredations have been committed by a portion of the younger rabble."

Even Culbertson couldn't suggest a manner in which the young hoodlums of the Blackfeet could be restrained by their chiefs, a situation peace officers still find insoluble many years later. He did indicate to officials that part of the Blackfeet problem lay in 1865 and 1868 treaties unratified by congress, consequently promised annuities were never delivered. All the Blackfeet were in a white enforced and painful transition period.

But whites were screaming for action, the problem was passed up and back down the chain of command, and in January 1870 U.S. troops moved to punish the Piegans in bitter winter weather. The expedition headed by Major Eugene Baker was under orders to "strike them hard," really meaning the hostile group of Mountain Chief. Instead, Baker attacked a village of 37 lodges on the Marias in blizzard conditions at daybreak January 23, 1870, killing 173 Piegans. However it was the village of Heavy Runner, virtually certified as friendly even by the military. For once, army mastery of Indian drew a derogatory title, the Baker Massacre.

The Culbertsons went north again to trade with the Blackfeet in the fall of 1869, In the spring Alexander and son Joe returned to Fort Benton; Natawista had left him, and Joe wrote half a century later, "that was the downfall of my dear old father."

Culbertson traded for a time at Fort Browning near Poplar River and at Fort Peck in 1872 and 1873 near the new federal agency to distribute rations to stricken Gros Ventres, Assiniboine and Sioux. The latter year he went again to Washington D.C., as interpreter for the first Sioux delegation. From 1877 at Poplar, first permanent location for the agency, he continued as interpreter.

In early 1879, old and worn out, he went to live with his daughter Julia (Mrs. George H. Roberts) and died August 27, 1879, in Orleans, Nebraska.

The inscription on his tombstone there includes: "An important figure in the development of the Western Frontier, associated with the fur trade, entered service with American Fur Co. 1829. Began career on Upper Missouri, 1833, In charge of Fort McKenzie until 1840, then Fort Union, and Fort Laramie, a special assignment to reestablish fur trade and save from abandonment. Superintendent of Upper Missouri Outfit, which included all forts on the Yellowstone and Upper Missouri rivers, 1847. Established Fort Benton, the first permanent settlement in Montana. Married Na-Ta-Wis-Ta-Cha, a Blackfoot maiden, about 1840. Acted as interpreter and special agent of the U.S. government in making treaties with the Indians, such as the one with Blackfeet and Gros Ventres in 1855 permitting the survey through their territory for a Pacific railroad. Blazed trails on his trips from Fort to Fort and to Indian camps which were later followed by settlers and today are the routes of highways. For nearly half a century his high character and ability enabled him to make major contributions to the development of the Missouri Basin."

### The Culbertson Family

Alexander Culbertson married Blackfeet twice at least, in 1833 a daughter of White Buffalo, dated by Maximilian's visit; about 1840 Natawista, daughter of Blood chief Father of All Children. The two marriages in Indian mode doubtless cemented his influence with the Blackfeet. Data on several of the children scanty or lacking, and there may have been others. Fr. DeSmet baptized at least three.

Maria was probably born at Fort McKenzie by his first wife, and was 11 when baptized by Fr. DeSmet at Fort Union Nov. 5, 1846.

Janie, who died in 1860, was married to Wm. Hunt in 1858 or 1859, and had been educated in a Moravian seminary in Pennsylvania. She probably was a child of his first wife.

John Alexander (Jack) was born about 1843 to Natawista, and according to Joe's memoirs, went to California when the Culbertsons returned to Montana, later was at the Poplar agency as an employe. He was killed October 13, 1888, in Williston, North Dakota, by a man named Gibson.

Julia was born about 1845 and married George H. Roberts May 9, 1865, in Peoria, Illinois. They later lived in Nebraska and moved to Idaho in 1883 where he was first attorney general in 1890. He died in 1922, Julia in 1929.

Nancy was born in 1848 at Fort Union. She was baptized July 20, 1851, at Fort Union by Fr. DeSmet, and drowned some months later there.

Fannie (Frances), according to her obituary born February 14, 1858, at Fort Benton. She was best educated of the Culbertson daughters, married Louis S. Irvine about 1880. He was an attorney for the Blackfeet at Browning and died in 1918. Fannie was the last surviving child of Culbertson, and died in Great Falls February 5, 1939. She last visited Fort Benton in 1936 when her cousin, R. A. Culbertson, brought her to meet the River Press editor.

Joseph was born in Peoria, Illinois, January 31, 1859. He returned with his parents to Fort Benton in 1868, accompanied them in trading, later had an adventurous two decades as scout for the army, later was a peace officer at the Poplar agency, died in 1923.

A letter from Mollie Culbertson Sedgwick written in 1979 gives a last child as Margt. (Margaret?) who married a man named Bartlett, but nothing further found. (She may have been daughter of Julia and George Roberts, Jack Holterman's history of the Culbertson family indicates.)

# Fort Benton Legends

*F*ort Benton's varied history contributed to the number of local legends and traditions surpassing many another famed western town.

### Naming A Fur Post

Alexander Culbertson, who returned to the Missouri River from Fort Laramie in 1845 to make peace with the Blackfeet nation after the February 19, 1844, episode in which a cannon was fired at Fort McKenzie on a peaceful trading party, told historian Lt. James Bradley that he learned the worth of adobe construction there. Culbertson first built a post above Fort Benton which tentatively bore several names, Fort Lewis the last. March 19, 1847, logs and other materials were floated down the Missouri to complete the final American Fur Blackfeet post. It was apparently a year or two later that time permitted the start on rebuilding using sun dried adobe bricks made of local clay and hay.

The first large adobe building was completed late in 1850. At a Christmas party that December 25, Bradley wrote of the scene as Culbertson described it:

"Until a late hour the light-headed voyageurs and their squaw wives, sweethearts and friends, danced and whirled to the music of several fiddles. In the midst of the festivities Major Culbertson proposed that in consideration of the warm friendship of Thomas H. Benton for the partners of the American Fur Company, ....that the post should be renamed in his honor. The proposition was received with acclamation by the joyous assembly and thus upon Christmas night, 1850, the post was first called by the name it still bears and that will probably ever distinguish the locality—Fort Benton."

Missouri Senator Benton had been more than a friend, his intervention had saved the vital Indian trading license of American Fur after a charge of illicit selling of liquor to Indians was filed. The name Fort Benton had appeared upon company records two years earlier, and it did endure. A great nephew, also Thomas Hart Benton, distinguished artist, heard the story again in the summer of 1966 on a visit to Fort Benton.

### A Wild Fourth of July

William Gladstone, former Hudson Bay Company carpenter, in a diary published in the Rocky Mountain Echo of Pincher Creek, December 8, 1903, recalled one of Fort Benton's first, and possibly wildest, celebrations of the then only national holiday, in 1864:

"I shall never forget the Fourth of July in Benton. Most of the men were from the Southern army and their hatred of the North expressed itself in an unmistakable way.

"There were 1,500 men in Benton at that time and I saw such desperate characters as the James brothers among them. You can imagine the fights and rows that went on that day. With feelings of mutual hate, inflamed by bad whisky, the men of the North and South were only too eager to come to blows. It was hell upon earth for a time."

Some future Fourths were wild enough, but scarcely up to 1864.

## The Mule Was A Loser

Gad Upson, Indian agent to the Blackfeet, in November 1865 at Fort Benton arranged a peace treaty with the tribe. The Montana Post carried a report from B. A. Melton, Fort Benton consignor, that ten to fifteen thousand Indians had assembled for the ceremony. The figure is perhaps three times too high, but the assemblage may have been the largest ever on the bottom. Half a dozen differing accounts are available of one spectacular event; the following summary is taken from an 1884 River Press:

"A large Diamond R freight train was also camped on the flats, with a four pound howitzer they had transported on the back of a mule from Cow Island. The howitzer had been left to protect freight and came with the last of the supplies.

"The men in charge of the 'little gun' conceived the idea of showing the Indians its strength by discharging it from the back of the mule. The howitzer, loaded with grapeshot, was securely fastened upon the back of a large, sleepy looking train mule, and the muzzle pointed toward the tail, and the patient, unsuspecting animal was led to the bank of the river near the present site of T. C. Power & Bro.'s store, and arranged in a semi-circle around the mule were train men, officers and wondering Indians... A chief of ceremonies having been appointed, he advanced, and when all was in readiness, inserted a time fuse in the touch hole of the howitzer. In a short time the quiet, unruffled mule heard a fizzing just back of his ears, which made him uneasy, and he immediately began to turn his head to investigate. As he did so his body turned and the howitzer began to take in other points of the compass. The mule became more excited as his curiosity became more and more intense, and in a few seconds he either had his four feet in a bunch, making more revolutions a minute than the bystanders dared to count, with the howitzer threatening destruction to everybody within a radius of a quarter of a mile, or he suddenly would try standing on his head with his heels and howitzer at a remarkable angle in the air. The train men and Indians scattered pell mell over the flat toward the bluffs, running as if they thought that in flight lay their only safety, and that, too, at a rate of speed much greater than grapeshot. Judging from the alacrity with which Col. Broadwater, H. A. Kennerly, Jos. Healy and Mose Solomon slid over the bank of the river, they were not opposed to immersion; Matt Carroll, George Steell and James Arnoux sprinted toward the store; Hi Upham, J. J. Healy and Bill Hamilton began to throw up breastworks with their sheath knives, while I. G. Baker and one or two of the peace commissioners were turning back-springs toward the fort.

"While the mule, with his heels in mid-air, was shaken with the most violent agitation, there was a puff of smoke, a thud, and the mule—oh, where was he? Ask of the winds, for not a soul saw him, and they will tell you a lonely, forlorn mule might have been seen turning over and over until he tumbled over the bank with the howitzer and cast anchor in the river, while the shot went toward the fort, striking the figure of a buffalo that was used as an advertisement at the fort, and which hung there until the last two or three years, and which many of the citizens of Fort Benton will remember was well perforated with balls. Future investigation and development have brought to light the fact that X. Beidler was the commander in chief elected, and that it was his first buffalo."

(Most other accounts have the Indian guests sitting stoically in their circle, wondering about the antics of the white men.)

## War Games Follow Peace Council

That 1865 peace treaty had a war games windup. Bill Hamilton, at the time Chouteau county's first sheriff, was an eye witness, and described the aftermath.

He was also the man the white peace commissioners got to contact Crows and Gros Ventres. In this the old Indian fighter broke fifty-fifty. With a Piegan named Eagle Eye he followed the Crow trail to the Big Snowies, enroute sending five bronco Blackfeet to the happy hunting ground, Bill blessing the efficiency of the new fangled many shots; then helped Crows fight a couple hundred Sioux, after which the sensible Crows declined to visit Fort Benton while a few thousand Blackfeet were around. Hamilton and Eagle Eye found the Gros Ventres at the Little Rockies, and they did come. Bill Hamilton at Benton doubled as restaurant man, feeding the chiefs at $1 a meal but complained later it should have been $2, each ate twice as much as white customers.

He figured the Blackfeet numbered about four thousand and growing as word about eats and presents got out. The Gros Ventres about that time numbered around 1200, not all present. They had been at war with the Blackfeet tribes for four years, although previously a sort of protectorate.

The treaty signed ceded land south of the Teton and Missouri, though never ratified by Congress, in exchange for annuities. After signing there followed distribution of the first installment, which was what the tribesmen had been waiting for. Bill said it would take the pen of Mark Twain to describe the two day scene. Thereupon the commissioners, including acting Gov. Thomas F. Meagher and agent Gad Upson headed for Helena to quiet their nerves.

The dozen knowing whites at the by then North West Fur post buttoned up tight, the other 45 cleared for action by digging rifle pits at vantage points, and Bill Hamilton recalled seating a 12 pound cannon in a 12 inch loophole in an adobe warehouse, loaded with six pounds of powder and 20 pounds of one ounce balls and miscellaneous hardware, which surely would have wrought execution upon both white and red. Then came Little Dog, friendly head chief of the Piegans, to warn that Bloods and Blackfeet had gotten hold of whisky and were talking war on Gros Ventres and whites.

An hour later 500 warriors of Bloods and Blackfeet mounted, rode down to the Gros Ventres camp, whose tepees were set in tight circles against such trouble, the Blackfeet yelling insults and war cries. Smart Gros Ventres chiefs had all they could handle to keep their eager young braves from doing what came naturally and riding out to combat. Meanwhile, the whites, backed by their cannon and rifles and by Little Dog's warriors, were warning chiefs of the aggressive factions of woes to come if they hit that tight Gros Ventres camp.

One of the circle had a colorful idea, the hostiles rode back to their lodges and stripped their squaws of recently issued calico. With five to 20 yards of calico tied to their ponies, and with the loudest warwhoop of all the 1200 yelling warriors began racing pony display all over the flat, and there went all that excess energy. In the dark the Gros Ventres quietly moved out, and the great Fort Benton peace council was ended. So reported Bill Hamilton in a 1907 series in Forest and Stream.

### Pistols For The Pilot

One of the phantom legends of the old west is of the day at Fort Benton that Eleanor Dumont, a vingt et un specialist far better known as Madame Mustache, left her blackjack game brandishing pistols to sprint to the levee 50 feet away and warn the pilot of a smallpox stricken steamboat to land his boat at Fort Benton only if he felt himself bullet proof. Louis Rosche, riverman and vendor of tall tales, has it that she did all the talking: "You get the hell out of here with that boat and you do it pronto. I ain't going to let no smallpox spoil my business."

The story pops up in enough places to lend credence, and obviously in the roaring days of the gold rush. The writer, after finding backing for other tales, credits it with having a basis in truth.

Rosche wrote he was on the Lecon, and the boat which was turned away was the Omaha. Lacon brought cargoes to Benton in 1868 and 1869; there was no Omaha listed as in Montana any year. There were nine steamboats along the levee the day before, three quickly followed the Lacon, and there were several steamboats based on Omaha-Sioux City about then. Furthermore, 1869 was a smallpox year, a terrifying disease then for Indian and white. Then, too, in the winter of 1869-70 Eleanor Dumont opened the "Golden Gate" in Helena. All of which suggests the episode occurred in 1869 if it ever did.

Yet another unascribed source identifies the boat as the Walter B. Dance; the Dance came to Benton only in 1866 and 1867. Granville Stuart was aboard this boat in 1866 and left a good trip account—no suggestion of smallpox. Hence, if the Dance, in 1867, only other year in Montana waters.

On more a hunch of proof, Madame Mustache sold her gambling hell three doors down from the old bridge to Dena Murray at the end of 1869, getting the wherewithal to open the Golden Gate. Dena operated the "Jungle" in the ramshackle frame, garnering a comfortable competence by the time of her death in Fort Benton in 1884.

The by then fat and blowsy Madame Mustache died by poison at Bodie, California's rough, tough mining camp, in 1879, dead broke.

## The Strangest Voyage

Source of the strange voyage of the Richmond can be termed unimpeachable: Charles N. Pray, three times Montana's sole congressman, 1907-13 and who got the Glacier Park bill through the House, while a Fort Benton resident, then a U.S. district judge for 33 years while a resident of Great Falls. The story was told him by his father-in-law, Hans J. Wackerlin, pioneer merchant of Fort Benton, in the long ago.

After the Civil War, some one time members of Quantrill's guerrillas went south of the border to fight for Maximilian, then emperor of Mexico, headed by Langford (Farmer) Peale, but arrived about the time Maximilian was shot by Mexican patriots. After brutal depredations in Mexico and Texas, Peale absconded with most of the proceeds, leaving a dead broke band of outlaws to the tender mercies of outraged authorities. Survivors of the band soon learned that Farmer Peale was blowing their loot up the Missouri in Helena, and planned revenge.

On the Red River in 1867 they liberated a large light draft steamboat, renaming it the Richmond. They went down the Red and up the Mississippi with an impressed crew, handling freight to meet expenses, and doing well. At St. Louis in early May they got a large cargo of freight for Fort Benton and the mines. (Richmond was listed as landing over 300 tons, freight bill about $65,000, plus 30 passengers about $4000, and another $18,000 for 180 down, probably better business than robbery.) One of the passengers from St. Joseph at $130 was Hans Wackerlin, 17, the rate after dickering with the captain, who gave his name as Miller. Young Wackerlin's rifle marksmanship even impressed the tough hijackers of the Richmond, who made something of a pet of him. Generally, he told his son-in-law years later, treatment of the paying passengers was tolerable—no boat trip to Benton was a joyride those years. But at each stop on the lower river the guerrillas went ashore to blast their tonsils with whatever refreshments were available, and they were tough and brutal in their cups. After one such stop they drove the Negro deckhands overboard.

At the next stop there was a band of traveling minstrels giving a performance, and Captain Miller inveigled the minstrels into taking passage for the next town up river. After the Richmond cast off the luckless newcomers found themselves impressed as deckhands, no self respecting desperado would roll that barrel or tote that bale. Evenings they found themselves doing command concerts.

The Quantrill men hadn't forgotten their chief aim, repossession of the considerable amount Farmer Peale had taken, and their planned termination of his earthly span, preferably slowly. So when the Richmond reached the mouth of the Judith the boat was tied up while a messenger was sent on to Fort Benton to get news of Peale. A week later he returned with word that the Farmer had been slow on the draw in lawless Helena a few days before. Johnny Bull and Peale had words, the former quite sensibly shot him as he came out the door of a saloon. Said X. Beidler, Montana's chief exterminator, "Peale was such a rattler I didn't think he would be killed. He was quick as lightning and could hit a silver dollar at ten paces every time." Also sensible, Bull's method was identical to a couple of Peale's notches.

The Richmond came on to Fort Benton July 28 with a big 316 tons of cargo, and some of the Quantrill men went on to Helena to make sure Farmer Peale was firmly planted; the others, in Wackerlin's recollection, cut loose with the wildest debauch he had ever seen, terrorizing Fort Benton for several days. The boat hijackers got the Richmond back down to Sioux City to find the feds were after them, abandoned the boat and hit out overland for Idaho, Cheyenne and other points west. Several of them were later killed in unsuccessful stage and bank holdups.

"Treeing" Fort Benton for several days may be taken with a grain of salt, perhaps a shaker full, there was no tougher town in the west. Fort Benton had already seen the incoming governor of Montana grab a club to subdue a drunk who had gotten a skinful in Mose Solomon's Medicine Lodge, a drunk who had luckily escaped intact from that deadfall; and the acting governor had just flunked the drunk test by falling off a steamboat while it was moored at the bank.

Helena visitors were also much more impressed than Bentonites at the way the river town celebrated the 4th—that from a mining camp where "that same old tree" in Dry Gulch seemed to bear fruit of Vigilante cultivation about semi-weekly.

### Thomas Francis Meagher Drowns

Few men ever made as much impression on minds of Montanans as did Thomas Francis Meagher, who drowned July 1, 1867, in the Missouri at Fort Benton. Although $2000 reward was offered for recovery of his body, it was never claimed.

He was an Irish rebel against English rule, sentenced to be hanged, drawn and quartered in 1848, the brutal sentence commuted to transportation to Tasmania. He escaped and made his way to New York by 1852. In the Civil War Meagher had a gallant record after recruiting an Irish brigade, shot to pieces in the first two years. After Montana territory was created in 1864 he came west as secretary to first governor Sidney Edgerton, the position roughly equivalent to secretary of state. Edgerton soon left and Meagher became acting governor, first of two occasions. His terms were turbulent; and perhaps recalling the glory days of yore Meagher pushed hard for a territorial militia and war against the Indians. At one stage General Sherman termed him a "stampeder," it seems to fit. Meagher's trip to Fort Benton in June 1867 was to secure rifles and cannon being sent the territory by steamboat.

It is Helena tradition that one of the first men ever convicted in regular court there, named Daniels, was pardoned by Meagher, after which Daniels died on a Vigilante tree with that pardon in his pocket. That gave rise to stories about Vigilante justice on "the acting one." Strictly speaking, Meagher was no longer acting governor when he rode into Benton July 1st, Green Clay Smith had arrived a few days before on the Octavia as appointed territorial governor, and had sown seeds of friendship by his ready use of a club on the drunk mentioned above.

Meagher found a plethora of tosspot friends in Benton, recollections of Granville Stuart indicate, probably far too many. Stuart also recalled that Meagher had his final meal in the log and adobe house Isaac G. Baker had just completed for Mrs. Baker. Local friends then found an empty stateroom on the G. A. Thompson and persuaded Meagher to go aboard. The cry "man overboard" came in the darkening evening hours.

Shirley Ashby, clerk for I. G. Baker, recalled handing Meagher his final mail, and felt no need to comment beyond, "who about two hours after that stepped off the boat, and was seen no more afterwards." Ferd Roosevelt, then Wells Fargo agent, later was more explicit, he had seen Meagher fall from the boat. W. S. Stocking also called it a mis-step.

Local evidence seems to negate rumors of vengeful Vigilantes.

### The Hanging of Hynson

Only lethal proceeding of the original Vigilantes known against whites which occurred in Fort Benton was the morning of August 18, 1868, when one Bill Hynson (also Hinson, Henson, etc.) was summarily hanged. Lynch parties later on occasion assumed the title. Grant Marsh testified to the existence of a Vigilante committee—when a box of patent medicine (for its alcohol) was stolen off the Luella in 1866 the unhappy culprit was located, tried and whipped near to death. Marsh was later told that the committee had come within three votes of a hanging. And the June 9, 1866, Montana Post mentioned a Fort Benton poster: "Beware—The Vigilance Committee is in session."

All accounts of the Hynson hanging available, and there are about a dozen in files, provide slightly differing versions, and several spellings, but on one point all are agreed, the chief character was informed citizens were going to hang a man, and the victim provided the rope; in a case or two, the rude gallows. The latter varies from a reinforced squaw travois to two posts and cross bar. The exact location is also dubious, variously within a block or two.

Hynson was an emigre from Helena by request after rolling a few drunks and killing a Chinese woman in brutal fashion. At Fort Benton he was first employed in Wm. Rowe's livery stable, soon promoted himself to unofficial night marshal. There was an epidemic of rolled drunks, and X. Beidler reported Bentonites jobbed Hynson.

One night a pretended drunk displayed a small pouch of dust in several saloons, got knocked down and robbed shortly after and reported to fellow Vigilantes. Next day Hynson was told, "We've got the fellow who has been doing these robberies, and we're going to hang him in half an hour, but we need a rope." Hynson, all eager beaver, volunteered to get the rope from Power's store and brought it back. "Where is he?" Beidler took the rope, clapped him on the shoulder and said "here he is, right here." X., an expert at such affairs, slipped the noose around Hynson's neck, hustled him to the gallows, wherever and whatever, and the small crowd finished the job with dispatch. The body was left hanging two days as a warning to others. "Nigger Henry," wrote both Beidler and Joe Culbertson, dug the grave. That would be Henry Mills, an old time American Fur employe.

## Slight Misunderstanding

July 15, 1869, two Garrison & Wyatt herders were mortally wounded by unidentified Indians about three miles north of Fort Benton, part of their freight train looted and burned. I. G. Baker later identified the Indians as drunken Crows, but the damage was done. Whites attributed the atrocity to Blackfeet, and found and hung one they found in Bill Gladstone's home, and killed at least one other.

W. S. Stocking's recollection of the almost immediate sequel: "A large war party of Blackfeet Indians came clattering and yelling into town. There were only twenty-five white men in Benton, but they armed themselves, turned out, and fought the Blackfeet all over town. The whites had the best of it, and fifteen dead Indians were found." About the only pertinent item in Helena papers is a brief mention of John Morgan and armed men driving Indians out of Fort Benton.

Both Stocking and Joe Culbertson well remembered another pretty gruesome tale about the time bullwhackers found, killed and threw into Morgan's well the body of a son of Mountain Chief, an understandably irreconcilable Blackfeet chief. His brother, son and probably other relatives were killed in Fort Benton.

The year of 1869 was a bloody one, for both Indians and whites.

## Jerry Potts A Legend Before Mounties Came

Jerry Potts was considerable of a legend around Fort Benton years before he became virtually a patron saint to the North West Mounted Police from 1874. In Helena papers he was often casually referred to as Jerry, just as if everyone in Montana Territory knew the last name. He was leader of the numerous half breeds of Fort Benton, incidently the best defense whites had against Indians of any tribe. W. S. Stocking, no lover of Indians or breeds, referred to Jerry as "about the most decent specimen of that combination I ever met with."

Jerry was born in old Fort McKenzie in 1840, son of trader Andrew Potts and Namo-pisi (Crooked Back) of the Bloods. His father was killed that year at a trading wicket by White Eye, the latter executed by his own band. Jerry was raised by tough and brutal Alexander Harvey, then by Andrew Dawson. He lived with Blackfeet and whites almost alternately, and grew up a very salty customer indeed, with all the Indian love of firewater. He and a sidekick, George Star (a prominent figure in hostile camps before the Marias Massacre of 1870) played a little game while in their cups, at 25 feet popping pistol shots to trim the other's mustache with the stakes another round.

Small, round shouldered, Jerry didn't look like much, but garnered a lion's share of coups and scalps and was a major participant in a great 1870 battle between Blackfeet and Crees near present Lethbridge. Said Jerry after the Crees were on the run and swimming the Oldman, "You could shoot with your eyes shut and kill a Cree."

One day in the 1860s Jerry rode out alone across the Missouri toward Shonkin Creek and into one of his most remarkable adventures. Carelessly he ran into seven Crows, four with rifles, who got the drop. After parley they told him he must come to their camp on Shonkin and see the Crow chief. Jerry perforce consented, rode along, the four riflemen behind him. Pretty soon he heard one of the followers say in Crow, "Why not kill him right here."

With the click of a rifle being cocked, Jerry rolled off his horse and came up with his revolver smoking. A dead shot, he put all four down, the bow and arrow braves escaping. With four fresh Crow scalps, Jerry raced back to town for reinforcements to take on the rest of that Crow camp, leading a war party of Piegans to nearly wipe out the enemies.

Pioneer W. S. Stocking termed the sequel "the wildest night I ever knew on the frontier... That night there was an orgy that baffles description—drunken carousal, scalp dances, war dances, discharge of firearms, hootings, yellings, howlings, cursings, personal encounters, threats against the whites, and 'hell broke loose' all around...I tried to get my family down to I. G. Baker's store, which had thick walls, but I had to give it up. There was a dense crowd of Piegans and Blackfeet in the streets, and they all had knives and tomahawks in their hands... Any white man who got too far into that crowd would have been butchered as sure as fate, and then the whole town would have been cleaned up. So I put my family down in the cellar that was under my house, and I stood guard all night with a loaded and cocked rifle and revolver, and when the sun rose the next morning I thanked God for the blessed daylight."

### Times Were Dull In Benton

In 1871 times were dull in Fort Benton, "merchants are carrying light stocks." Besides, in mid-1870 merchants had been sitting on a half million worth of robes and furs, embargoed by U. S. authorities on account of smallpox, which greatly slowed export of the products of the Indian trade. A year later Whoop Up trade was booming but Benton wasn't, so in April 1871 a rather strange case provided conversation.

A French halfbreed, referred to only as "Bowlegs," and a vicious character, sneaked up behind a squaw carrying a papoose strapped to her back and blew the child's brains out with a pistol shot. The intermittent Fort Benton law lodged the murderer in jail, with a long wait for justice out of Helena. An April 5 Benton letter in the Helena Herald contained a brief item: "Bowlegs, who was in jail for murdering a little girl, was taken from jail by a crowd, and has not been heard of since." The writer should have had one ear open.

W. S. Stocking remembered: "The father of the child—another French halfbreed of huge stature, one Baptiste Racine by name—had become almost a maniac in his desire to wreak vengeance on the murderous Bowlegs. After much consulting the citizens agreed to this plan, to wit: it was now night and Bowlegs and Baptiste were to be placed one hundred yards apart, each fully armed, and at a given signal a footrace would begin, Bowlegs to get away, if he could, and Baptiste to overtake him and kill him, if he could. This was done, and the two men started. In about a half a minute there was a shot and a yell, but nobody knew what had happened. In two or three minutes, however, big Baptiste strode down the street, and diappeared in the darkness. Everybody knew then what had happened, and in the morning the corpse of Bowlegs was picked up and buried."

The same letter in the Herald noted that the body of Joseph Spearson had been brought in from Whoop Up, he dead of mortification from a wound by an Indian; next night, the son of Mountain Chief was killed in Fort Benton. "The boys" leaving for Whoop Up expected Indian trouble.

### A Lighter, Splendid Touch

June 30, 1872, the steamboat Far West barely out paced the Nellie Peck into Fort Benton, and down the gangplank stepped a sturdy 24 year old in somber garb. His name was William Wesley Van Orsdel, and he became a Montana legend, one tied closely to Fort Benton; to the end of his years the "mother church" for the young Methodist evangelist. He had sung for his half-rate passage from Sioux City by courtesy of the Far West master, Mart Coulson.

Undying Fort Benton legend has it that his first service that afternoon was in the Four Deuces Saloon; no matter that the saloon by name has never turned up. Over years to come, he brought his message and a fine singing voice to dozens of saloons, in many settlements the only spot with room for a small congregation.

The given name was far too much for the frontier, from the day of arrival he was "Brother Van" to saint and sinner alike. Certainly in his recollection he held Fort Benton services in an old warehouse, probably one of the old Fort Campbell buildings, this session for steamboat men, freighters, settlers and a single white woman, Mrs. George Baker. One song, certainly, was "Diamonds In The Rough," a favorite of his rough hewn audiences—his own, and the "Brother Van Song," was "Harvest Time." In a heart warming display of religious tolerance, a Catholic priest, Fr. L. Van Gorp, helped the young Methodist find space for that first service.

Not yet an ordained minister, William Wesley Van Orsdel's goal was to be a missionary to the Montana Indians, who came to know him as "Great Heart." He soon found even more sinners among white than red, traveled as many as 4,000 miles a year, usually by horseback, organizing and building for his church. A hundred churches, fifty parsonages, six hospitals and two schools were credited to him. Nor was he any psalm singing sissy. Brother Van served with a company of volunteers during the 1877 Nez Perce War. The Blackfeet were a special charge, and when he joined them in a buffalo hunt they took pains to make it possible for him to bring down the first buffalo.

In his later years Fort Benton friends annually in late March held a Brother Van birthday party, the largest for his 70th birthday in 1918, and the final one next year. He died December 19, 1919, and an Indian friend sadly remarked, "So Great Heart is gone. Well then the red man has one friend in heaven."

For the whites Charlie Russell said it best in a letter written for that March, 1918, birthday party in Fort Benton. Referring to his first meeting with Brother Van, Russell wrote: "I have met you many times since then, Brother Van—sometimes in lonely places. But you never were lonesome or alone, for a Man with scarred hands and feet stood beside you; and near Him there is no hate, so all you met loved you."

## "Assisted By The Military"

In late spring 1873, date indefinite but probably June 1, a party of wolfers from Fort Benton trailing horse thieves who had set them afoot in early May near Fort Benton, had a memorable fight with North Assiniboines. The fight occurred in the Cypress Mountains in Canada. It touched off an international incident and hastened the organization and westward march of the North West Mounted Police to the then North West Territory of Canada.

At the time of the Indian fight, there was no law whatever north of the boundary. Superior weapons of the whites resulted in the death of about 30 Indians; one white, Ed Grace, was killed. Messages rattled between Washington and Ottawa over the affair, eventually the massacre (neither side was blameless) accepted for what it was, one of the numerous and inevitable fights between red and white. But meanwhile, there was an addition to Fort Benton's legends.

As the River Press reviewed an 1875 incident ten years after, a troop of cavalry surrounded Fort Benton to back up U. S. marshals while a number of citizens were arrested for an extradition hearing in Helena.

An on the spot report in the June 26, 1875, Benton Record, with first names added in parenthesis: "On the 21st instant Messrs. (Trevanian) Hale, (Thomas)

Hardwick, (John) Evans, (Charles) Harper and (Jeff) Devereux were arrested by Deputy Marshals (Charles) Hard and (X.) Beidler, assisted by military, for the killing of Assinaboin Indians at Cypress Mountains, British America, some two years ago." Two other men were arrested, but quickly eluded the marshals.

The Helena hearings, in compliance with the request of Canadian authorities, resulted in dismissal of the extradition effort. The five returned to a roaring welcome in Fort Benton; Evans and Devereux renamed their saloon below the old bridge the "Extradition" in gloating reminder.

Fort Benton, savage often in its relations with Indians, two months earlier had a brutal incident when on April 16 two Gros Ventres Indians, imprisoned for an attempted murder of whites at Highwood, were taken from the county jail and shot by parties unknown. One of the principals was later identified as Tom Hardwick in an 1884 River Press. Attitudes in 1875 were changing slightly, the Benton Record in reporting the lynching felt that most citizens were law abiding, but "Benton is cursed with a floating population of as hard a set of desperados as perhaps exist on earth."

### They "Fought So Well"

When the Nez Perce campaign of 1877 swirled eastward out of Washington, Fort Benton through the Record seemed to have a detached viewpoint, unlike in the Sioux campaign the year before when the local attitude appeared to be wait and see if the Sioux spring the trap and get driven by the military toward Fort Benton.

But when in September 1877 the Nez Perce surged northward out of Yellowstone Park, every Bentonite knew that their crossing of the Missouri would be at Cow Island, or less likely, the Judith. So Cow Island freight would be in danger, and the Fort Benton Volunteers, about 30 strong, rode off September 21st to protect that freight, picking up six more civilian volunteers and a scattering of soldiers at the Judith. They reached Cow Island the 24th to find about 50 tons of freight had been burned by Nez Perce, by the time across the Missouri. Sgt. William Molchert with 11 soldiers and five civilians were the white heroes of a desperate two day stand against several hundred warriors. In view of the Nez Perce record, it appears certain that the warriors could easily have wiped out the small band, abstained in view of the probable cost.

The Nez Perce, hunters back home, were by far the best riflemen of the northwest Indian tribes, the Montanans as good. In a chase up Cow Creek, the Fort Benton party caught up enough to engage in a sharp but long range fire fight in which one white and two Nez Perce were killed—the whites could display numbers of bullet holes in their garb.

They brought back a strange pride and strong respect for their opposition, John Healy, one of the most daring men on the frontier, praised Nez Perce for "remarkable skill and ingenuity in constructing their defenses. They fought so well and never scalped."

### Grand Union Incident

One Fort Benton legend the writer for years has tried to authenticate has been recalled over the years by older residents, second hand. This is the tale of the cowhand who got a skinfull in the hotel bar and bet his remaining wad that he could ride his horse up the wide stairway of the Grand Union to his room on the second floor. All accounts were that he failed on account of a volley of pistol shots from an embattled night clerk. Fourteen .44 missiles later the sobering cowboy retreated, the clerk victorious.

In one of his books, Lucius Beebe reproduced an undated woodcut from Leslie's Illustrated about the episode, entitled "Fort Benton, Montana Territory, was a town with hair on."

That "Montana Territory" was a limiting factor, dating it within an eight year span, late 1882 to statehood in late 1889. That provided impetus for another search, again without result.

### "I'll See the Grass Growing In the Streets"

Ancient Fort Benton legend has it that Jim Hill, Great Northern owner, once said, "I'll make the grass grow in the streets of Fort Benton." Not so, wrote Virgil Proctor of Great Falls in the late 1970s, it was Paris Gibson, one time Fort Benton resident and founder of Great Falls, which celebrated its centennial in 1984. Mr. Proctor's source was Dr. Enoch Porter, who in turn heard the story from W. J. Minar, early day Fort Benton pharmacist.

Gibson was delegated by Hill to acquire the right of way into Fort Benton, at the time one of the most important towns in northern Montana. Gaspar Deletraz, French born, was almost certainly owner of the 80 acres involved, having homesteaded 80 acres on the outskirts of the settlement, and finally secured a patent in 1881, fortuitously in the proper place for Hill's plans. Deletraz had left handling of the deal to T. C. Power, and when Gibson approached Power with an offer of forty or fifty thousand dollars, a tremendous sum then, Power was certain that Hill had to have that land and held out.

According to Proctor's account, dickering went on for weeks, and finally Paris Gibson made a final offer for the 80 acres, $75,000. Power said, "No, we want $80,000." Gibson, "I won't pay it, and I'll see the grass growing in the streets here."

### Jim Hill's Banquet Breakfast

The St. Paul, Minneapolis & Manitoba Railroad in the summer of 1887 drove west from Minot, North Dakota, in a tremendous jump across the Montana plains. In October it connected at Great Falls with a subsidiary, the Montana Central from Helena, the lines becoming the Great Northern a few years later. James J. Hill was president and guiding spirit. Grading was scores of miles ahead of ties and steel rails in the westward drive of what all called the Manitoba; at Fort Benton the line swept in a great curve on the flat 270 feet above Fort Benton with a depot indicated two miles from town. Quite naturally residents were upset, having anticipated the largest settlement in northern Montana would be an important point on the railroad.

John Farrell, one of the determined young men Jim Hill gathered for an epic rail building project, later a prominent transportation superintendent on the coast, a half century or more ago recalled the July 30, 1887, day Jim Hill visited Fort Benton:

"I was in charge of a construction gang and train that was 'dressing' the roadbed and laying rails from Havre to Helena. We had reached a point near Fort Benton when we learned that Mr. Hill and party of officials were to arrive within the next two days. These men were making a general inspection trip of the work and were going on to Helena...

"I gave out the news and immediately the people of Fort Benton arranged a big 'banquet-breakfast,' I suppose you would call it. The arrangements for this big party were going along finely and Mr. Hill was informed that he would be royally entertained in Fort Benton. He wired me confidentially that he would not stop in Fort Benton at all and would expect me to have outfits ready to start in the morning as soon as he arrived.

"We who were on the job knew that the 'banquet-breakfast' might not be altogether a love feast, because, as you people from Montana know, Fort Benton did not relish the idea of the railroad being built so far from the main part of the town. Mr. Hill must have gotten wind of this and the result—his decision to go right through to Helena.

"I had nothing to do but obey orders. When I received Mr. Hill's wire I began making arrangements for his trip to Helena without the Fort Benton stopover.

"I went to the largest livery stable in town and asked for teams and drivers for a trip to Helena, the outfits to be ready at 8 o'clock next morning, the time scheduled for the arrival of Mr. Hill and party. To my dismay I was told that all the outfits had been engaged and my order could not be taken or filled. I went to another stable. I got the same answer.

"All day I went from place to place trying to get those teams. I went to the farmers near the city. Same answer. Nowhere, for love or money—I had increased the price offered generally charged in my now almost frantic efforts to carry out Mr. Hill's orders—but I couldn't get the teams....

"When Mr. Hill arrived the whole town was at the little shack station platform to meet him. He asked for his outfit to go on to Helena—then he asked for me. I explained as best as I could. After some discussion, very distasteful discussion to me, Mr. Hill laughed and proved himself a 'good sport.' He took his party to the 'banquet-breakfast' and immediately after the Fort Benton people had finished with him, he found better outfits awaiting him at the door than I could have hired. He and his party were then set down in Helena in what was record time for the distance in those days."

The trick was not mentioned in the River Press news account of this Fort Benton-Jim Hill conference that morning, perhaps the editor didn't know of it, more likely felt it better left out. One thing mentioned was Jim Hill's promise to bring the rails within the city limits of Fort Benton as soon as practicable. That promise was kept by the Great Northern in a major rebuilding job in 1900.

### "He'll Not See His Mother"

So ran an old cowboy ballad, the couplet concluding with "When the work's all done this fall."

The Fort Benton museum has the originals of a letter written by a young employe of the Shonkin Stock Association May 19, 1899, and a telegram received by his father in Colorado September 13, 1900, which provides a poignant reminder of the ballad.

Excerpts from the letter written in Fort Benton to father and family: "I am getting redy to start on the roundup...I am gathering up my string of saddle horses. I will be glad when we are ready to start out...I will be with you all this next winter for a while long about Christmas and New Years. I might come sooner but the roundup wont be dun be for that time. There was quite a time in Benton last night there were about 75 cow Boys in there they were having a hot time I tell you."

Edwin H. Dale may have made his visit that fall, but any plans for the next were ended by a telegram from Deputy Sheriff Cyrus W. Buck at Fort Benton September 13, 1900, addressed to Joseph Dale, Willow Creek, via Spencer, Colo.: "Edward Dale died four A. M. Wire instructions."

There was more to it. The September 19 River Press reported: "Ed Dale, a cowboy employed on the Shonkin roundup, was shot dead at about 5 o'clock this (Thursday) morning by Wm. Howell, a well known resident of this vicinity. The shooting took place in McCauley & Colgate's saloon, on Front street." This followed a dispute in a card game, friends of Howell claiming Dale had become abusive and threatening. The coroner's jury that morning returned an open verdict indicating a belief Howell's shooting of Dale was self defense. The item on the verdict concluded "friends of Dale are much incensed over the killing, expressing the belief that it was a brutal and unjustifiable murder."

The executive committee of the Shonkin Stock Association, M. E. Milner, Charles Lepley, Malcolm Morrow and Thos. A. Cummings, October 2 in a letter to the River Press praised the young man, said he was unarmed save for a pocket knife, and blasted "the class of harpies who never perform honest work, but live by demoralizing poor working men." And considerable more. Their influence must have counted, for the coroner's jury verdict was set aside and in November Wm. Howell was sentenced to life imprisonment for second degree murder.

But somehow, the lines of the ballad seem to apply.

# Bibliography

Montana Historical Society Contributions, Vols. I-X, includes James H. Bradley manuscripts on fur trade and early Fort Benton business. Vol. X includes Fort Benton Journal with notes on individuals.

Berry, Gerald L., "The Whoop-Up Trail."

Coleman, Louis C., and Rieman, Leo, "The Mullan Road."

Chittenden, Hiram M., "The History of the American Fur Trade of the Far West" and "Early Steamboat Navigation on the Missouri River."

Cushman, Dan, "The Great North Trail" and "Gold Frontier."

Denig, Edwin Thompson, "Five Indian Tribes of the Upper Missouri."

Ege, Robert J., "Strike Them Hard."

Ewers, John G., "The Blackfeet" and "The Horse in Blackfeet Indian Culture."

Hanson, Joseph Mills, "Conquest of the Missouri."

Hunter, Louis C., "Steamboats on the Western Rivers."

Jackson, Donald, "Voyages of the Steamboat Yellow Stone."

Johnson, Dorothy, "The Bloody Bozeman."

Larpenteur, Charles, "Forty Years A Fur Trader on the Upper Missouri."

Lass, William E., "A History of Steamboating On The Upper Missouri."

Madsen, Betty M., and Brigham D., "North to Montana."

Murphy, James Willard, "Half Interest In A Silver Dollar."

Petesche, Jerome E., "The Steamboat Bertrand."

Schultz, James Willard, "Blackfeet and Buffalo."

Sharp, Paul, "Whoop-Up Country."

Stevens, Isaac L., 1860 report on 1853-55 expedition.

Sunder, John E., "The Fur Trade of the Upper Missouri, 1840-1865."

Thomas, David, and Ronnefeldt, Karen, "People of The First Man," based on journals of Maximilian of Wied, 1833 visitor at Fort McKenzie.

Time-Life, "The Rivermen."

Toponce, "Reminiscences of Alexander Toponce."

Walker, Henry P., "The Wagonmasters."

White, Helen McCann, "Ho! For The Gold Fields."

"Wilderness Kingdom," journals of Fr. Nicholas Point.

Wishart, David, "Upper Missouri Fur Trade" to 1840.

## NEWSPAPER SOURCES HEAVILY UTILIZED

Montana Post, Virginia City 1864-67, Helena 1867-68

Helena Herald, 1866-75

The Benton Record, 1875-84

The River Press, Fort Benton, from Oct. 17, 1880

## MANUSCRIPTS AND CORRESPONDENCE
*These are only a small fraction of help supplied about or by.*

ASHLEY, SHIRLEY C., from MHS archives, went to work for Isaac C. Baker of Fort Benton, traded with Indians and made a start on a fortune.

BAKER, ISAAC G., biographical sketch via MHS, probably for Charles B. Power. Also letters from Baker relations, from a relative, Phillip Smith.

COLTER, JOHN, Lewis & Clark of course, also sendings by Dr. E.B. Trail on Colter's exploits and final years.

CONNELLY (Connolly) FAMILY, family history by Helena Sullivan Pannell Blend about her grandfather, Mike Connelly.

CONRAD BROTHERS, chief sources Wm. Conrad 1906 account of Baker Co. business and James E. Murphy, Kalispell, on Charles Conrad.

CULBERTSON, ALEXANDER, family members including son Joe's recollections and letters from Mollie Culbertson Sedgwick, a niece.

GERARD, FREDERICK F., a great nephew, Howard Gerard of Bellingham, WA, provided information on an almost overlooked important early businessman.

GLADSTONE, WILLIAM, recollections from Rocky Mountain Echo of Pincher Creek in 1903, of his 1864-65 stay in Fort Benton, most quoted of all.

HEALY, JOHN J., recollections, MHS.

KENNERLY, HENRY, recollections of the 1855 Stevens treaty.

LOWELL, JAMES, letters from Fort Benton in 1869, also letter to him from C. W. Cook on Confederate Gulch gold, written in 1924.

MULLENS, JAMES R., 1940 letters regarding first Yellowstone.

McDOUGALL, REV. GEORGE, diary of an 1873 trip from Canada to Fort Benton, provided by Frank Tester of Calgary.

STOCKING, WINFIELD SCOTT, "Fort Benton Memories," MHS.

# Index

—AAA—
Abbott, E. C. "Teddy Blue," 323
Abbott, Sol, "Old Sorrel Horse," 227, 298, 308, 348, 359
Adams, Maria and Mary, 251, 292
Adobe Buildings, 27
Agriculture, 103, 106, 178, 181, 234, 336-37
Akers, David, 358, 361
Alberta, passim
Alder Gulch, 42, 54, 57, 146, 163, 321
Aldrich, Frank, 326
Allen and Tierney, 111
Allen, Reuben, 313
Alley, John, 51
Almost A Dog, 312
Amei, Antoine Grames, 294
American Fur Co., also Pratte, Chouteau, passim
Anderson, George, 107
Andrews, John, 51
Angeline, Frank, 339
Angevine, Frank, 51, 339
Antelope, Blackfeet, 336
Antelope Shirt, 117
Armell, see Hammell, Augustin
Army, see Military
Arner, John, 335
Arnoux, James M., 122, 266, 288, 324, 337, 356, 380
Arrow Creek, 122, 186, 312
Ashby, Shirley Carter, 75, 177, 230-2, 359-60, 384
Assiniboines, 10, 272, 303, 313, 318-19, 358, 362, 377
Astor, John Jacob, 6
Astorians, 34
Athabaska, Lake, 1
Atkins, Carol J., 50
Atkinson, Dr. Monroe, 241
Atkisson, Dr. Francis, 241-42
Austin, C. H., 326
Ayres, Charles, 246
Ayres Grocery, 246

—BBB—
Babbage, Kate, 290
Badger Creek, 7
Bailey, Bob, 41
Baker & DeLorimer, 111-12, 246
Baker Maj. Eugene, 75, 296, 311, 376
Baker, Frances, 231, 289
Baker, Frances Wilson, 231, 289
Baker, George, 56, 177, 225-6, 231, 262-3, 357; wife, 290, 387

Baker, H. S., 361
Baker, I. G. (& Bro., & Co.), passim, 72-9, 230-3, 358-70
Baker, Isaac Gilbert, passim, 230-3, 356-57
Baker, Isaac Post, 128, 140
Baker, Joseph A., 233, 324, 328
Baker Massacre, 70, 75, 176, 296-98, 312, 377
Baker Steamboat Line, 94, 98, 99, 109, 116, 119, 144, 182, 233
Baker, W. S., 246
Bakers and Bakeries, 247
Bank of Northern Montana, (see Stockmen's National), 107, 112, 244, 281
Banks and Banking, 106-7, 243-44
Bannack, 28, 42, 146, 157, 163-65
Barber, Wm., 172
Barbers, 251
Barker, 106-7, 115, 121, 125, 185, 192
Barker, Ed, 317
Barker, Fred, 95-96
Barnes, Philip, 291
Barry, Wm., 62
Bear Chief, 9-10, 24
Bears Paw Mountains, 49, 103, 157, 367
Beaver, 7, 8, 11, 12, 300
Beaver Child (Alex. Culbertson), 372
Beaverhead, 3
Beckman, August, 244
Beckman, Louisa, 111
Beckworth, James P., 291
Bee Hive, 247
Beidler, John Xelpho, "X", 56, 69, 132, 149, 171, 175, 272-3, 384-5
Bell, George M., 364
Bella Coola River, 1
Belly River, 358
Belt, 101, 262
Benetsee, see Francoise Finlay
Bent, William, 196
Benton & St. Louis Cattle Co., 233, 258, 276, 324, 328
Benton Boom Co., 120, 281
Benton Brewery Saloon, 249
Benton Bridge Co., 126
Benton Building Assn., 281
Benton Drug Co., 242
Benton Hotel, 239
Benton Hotel Co., 240
Benton Lake, 27, 93
Benton Packet Co., 140, 156

Benton Record, 86, 97, 99, 103, 106-7, 117, 125-6, 128, 235, 242-3, 275, 283, 364
Benton Road, passim, 177-79
Benton State Bank, 244
Benton Townsite Co., 125
Benton Transportation Co., see Block P
Benton, Thomas Hart, 16, 19, 375, 379
Berger, Jacob (Jacques Bercier), 7, 10, 14-16, 27, 287, 301
Berkin, Wm., 166, 271
Berry, see Joe Kipp
Berry, Dick, 303, 363
Berry, James, 51, 339
Biedler, see Beidler
Big Hole Battle, 94
Big Horn River, Mountains, 5, 6, 57, 154
Big Road, Blackfeet, 13, 304
Big Sag, 327
Big Sandy, 137, 333
Big Swan, 15, 305, 373
Billings, 87, 154
Bird, James Jr. & Sr., 27
Bird, M. H., 174
Bird Tail Rock, 26, 27
Bismarck, 79-82
Bitter Root Valley, 3, 20, 22-3, 163-65
Black Weasel, 117
Blacks, Fort Benton, 291-2
Blackfeet, passim, 299-313; starving, 270-1
Blackfoot Grammar, 243
Blacksmiths, 251-2
Blackiston, Rev. S. C., 265
Blake, Maj. George, 26, 165, 339
Blake, Henry, 147
Blevins, Dan, 133
Block P Line, passim, 119-21
Blood Shot, 336
Boardman, John M., 324, 328
Bodmer, Karl, 9, 256, 303
Bond, H. E., 247
Bond, Wm., 292; fort, 363
Bostwick, Henry, 51, 94, 182, 270, 308, 316, 356
Bouis, Anthony, 16
Boundary Survey 1874, 83, 85, 179, 359
Bounty, Montana, 136, 353
Bourassa & DeChamp, 249
Bourassa, Charles A., 249
Bovey, Charles 238
"Bowlegs", 279, 386
Bozeman, John, 166, 309

**395**

Bozeman Trail, 57, 66, 166, 314, 322, 340
Bradbury, Lewis, 185, 251
Bradley, Edmund (Richardson), 95, 317
Bradley, Lt. James H., 8, 9, 13, 15, 19, 90, 94, 95, 182, 199, 231, 316, 356, 379
Brandt, Blanch, 250
Brandt, Dr. William Eugene, 241
Braithwaite, Joseph, 132
Break o' Day House, 111, 250, 292
Brede, Gus, 293, 336
Brennan, Richard, 120, 250
Breweries, see Saloons 247-31
Brickmakers, 107, 117, 252-53
Bridge, Fort Benton, 137-8, 141-2, 276-7, 284
Bridger, James, 8, 12, 166, 300-1
Brinkman, Emma, 290
Brinkman, Herman, 351
British, 1, 6, 7, 8
Broadwater, Charles, 102, 131, 380
Brooks, Jo, 250
Broadwater, D. K., 29
Brother Van, see W. W. Van Orsdel
Brown, Dr., 95
Brown, James "Diamond R", 163, 308, 357
Browne, David G., 123, 137, 163, 236, 267, 273
Bryant, Georgia, 250
Bruneau, Matt, 133
Bryer, Charles, 251
Buchanan, John, 46-47, 153
Buck & Hunt, Lawyers, 242
Buck & Kennon Stables, 258
Buck, Cyrus, 390
Buck, Horace R., 242, 256, 282
Buck, W. H., 93, 96, 103, 127, 235, 240, 242-43, 274, 290, 364
Buckland, Rowland, 324
Buckmaster, John, 271
Bucksen, Fred, 277
Buffalo (robes, bones), passim; see 30-32, 88-9, 161-77; embargo, 280
Buffalo Bill's Wild West Show, 127-28, 325
Buildings, brick, 93-96 and passim
Builders, 253
Bull, Johnny, 383
Bullwhackers, 157-61, passim
Burd, Julian, 133, 323
Burd, "Old Man", 323
Burd, Samuel, 323
Burgess, W. H., grocer, 111, 125, 246, 275
Burke, Walter, 193, 329, 335
Burnett, Peter, 244, 292
Burris, N. W., 51

—CCC—
Cadotte's Pass, 21-2
Calf Shirt, 51, 270, 296, 308, 359
Calgary, 360
Calhoun, Thomas, 61
Callaway, L, L, 147
Camas Meadows, 94
Camp Cooke, 57-8, 62-3, 159, 172-3, 309, 340-1
Campbell, Dr. E. B., 241
Campbell, Robert, 16-7, 36
Campbell, Thomas, 69, 175
Campbell, Windy, 193
Canada and Trade, passim
Canadian Connection, 355-70
Canadian Customs, 256, 272-3
Canadian Pacific Railroad, 119, 123-4, 127-29, 274, 360, 369-70
Canadian Postal, see Postal, Canada
Canadian Sessional Papers, NWMP, 361-2
Cannon, 271
Cantonment Stevens, 22-3
Canyon Creek, 94
Carrington, Col. Henry, 322
Carroll and Trail, passim, 82-9, 178-80
Carroll & Steell, 46, 49, 77, 110-17, 174, 229-30, 269
Carroll, Dr. J. V., 242
Carroll, Matthew, 46, 68, 83, 103, 166, 173, 229-30, 279, 356, 380
Carson, Charles, 270, 308-9
Cary, William de la Montague, 40, 165, 323
Cassidy & McDevitt, (Benton Stables), 258
Cassidy, James, 258
Castner, John, 99, 259
Catholics, 14-5, 28, 97, 99, 104, 264
Catlin, George, 5, 7, 8, 34, 300
Catlin, John, 322
Cattle, 102-3, 116-7, 119, 127, 129, 135, 183-4, 276, 321-30
Cemeteries, 115
Census 1870, 75
Census 1880, 105-6, 185
Centennial Hotel, 115-17, 120, 240
Centre Market, 246
Champagne (Champaigne) Francoise Baptiste, 15, 21, 24, 27, 288
Champagne, Marie and Josette, 15, 264
Champagne, Miss, 261, 288
Champagne, Michel, 15, 16, 27, 288
Chang Haw, 293
Charbonneau, Toussaint, 2, 4
Chardon, Francis A., 13-14, 304
Cheyennes, 154
Chicago wagon, 164
Chief Joseph, 95, 315-18
Chinese, 292-3

Chinese Saloon, 249
Chinook, 110
Chittenden, Hiram M., 56, 197
Choteau, 29
Choteau Calumet, 127
Chouquette, Charles, 301
Chouteau County, 89, 225-28
Chouteau County Independent, 243
Chouteau, Charles, 28, 37-8, 48, 51-52, 167, 198, 230
Chouteau, Pierre Jr., 13-4, 16, 28-9, 34, 225, 302, 305, 372
Chouteau House, 107, 116, 231, 234, 239-40, 279-80
Civil War, 46, 51
Clark Fork, 26
Clark, Capt. William, 5
Clark, William A., 316
Clarke, Horace, 297, 324
Clarke, Helen, 261, 297
Clarke, Isabel, 297
Clarke, John, 298
Clarke, Judith, 297
Clarke, Malcolm, 14-17, 28, 70, 170, 268, 297-8, 310, 321, 375
Clary, Thomas, 239
Clendenin, Mrs. Frances, 291
Clendenin, George, 98, 103, 111-2, 115, 175, 196, 237, 254, 291
Clevenger, Miss, 261
Clevenger, S. V., 67-8, 234, 239
Clingan, Eugene R., 262
Clinton, Major Wm., 57, 340
Clyde, Ellen, 250
Coal and Coal Banks, 102, 108, 111-6, 121, 137, 174, 184-5, 186, 192
Coastal Range, 1
Cobell, Joseph, 75, 103, 124, 166, 266, 311, 324, 337, 341
Cobell, Louis, 317
Cochrane Ranche Co., 328, 362, 369
Cocking, Andrew, 355
Collins, Jeremiah, 243, 274, 282
Collins, Timothy E., 107, 244, 258, 282
Colter, John, 3, 4-6, 300
Columbia (ship), 1
Columbia Fur Co., 7
Columbia River, 3, 20, 22
Commerce, Fur, 30
Commerce, Steamboats, 31-2
Confederate Gulch, 49, 50, 54, 56, 145-6, 174
Connelly, Mike, 367
Conrad Banking Co., 244
Conrad Circle Cattle Co., 127, 233, 324, 327, 369
Conrad, Charles E., 67, 97, 107, 112, 117, 122, 230-3, 244, 259, 273, 277, 291, 328, 360, 370

Conrad, William G., 67, 97-8, 107, 115, 120, 127, 137, 183, 230-3, 244, 258, 274, 277, 282, 328, 353, 359, 370
Conrad's Post, 348, 358
Cook, C. W., 56, 149
Coombs, Frank, 254, 282
Cooper, O. G., 95-6, 317
Copelin & Roe, 143
Copelin, John G., 172
Corder, John, 172, 200
"Corinne", 250
Corinne Trail, 58, 70, 75, 77, 79, 177
Corneille, Clement, 46, 253, 264, 269
Cosmopolitan Hotel, 111
Cosmopolitan Saloon, 249
Cotton Bottom, 14
Couer d'Alene, 36
Coues, Elliott, 4
Coulson, Mart, 80, 154
Coulson Packet Co., 79-81, 98, 103, 109, 111-2, 119, 120-1, 123, 178
Coulson, Sanford, 55, 78
Council Bluffs, 33
Council House, 239, 270
Court House I, 104, 120
Court House II, 120, 126, 283; courts, 271-2
Cow Island Trail, 42, 47-8, 63, 67, 93-96, 103, 108, 157-61, 167, 175, 316
Cox, John, 324
Coxey's Army, 140
Crabtree, Nate, 309
Cracon (Croquant) du Nez, 15, 129, 287, 302
Crane, George, 104, 247
Crawford, Charles, 258, 282
Crazy Horse, 90
Crees, 10, 120, 129, 296, 306, 320, 358, 385
Crepeau, Charles, 140
Croff, George, 225, 227, 271, 352
Crook, Gen. George, 90, 154
Crowfoot, 103, 184
Crows, 4-6, 11, 13, 40, 82, 146, 175-6, 270, 295, 299, 303-4, 310, 319, 371, 380, 385-6
Crutcher, Dr. C. D., 242
Cruzette, Peter, 3
Culbertson House, 120, 240
Culbertson, Alexander, 9, passim, 371-78
Culbertson, Anna, 375
Culbertson, First wife, 10, 294, 371, 377
Culbertson, Frances (Fanny), 373, 378
Culbertson, Frank, 240
Culbertson, Janie, 372, 377
Culbertson, John A. (Jack), 377
Culbertson, Joseph, 69, 279, 296, 377, 384-5

Culbertson, Julia, 377-8
Culbertson, Maria, 261, 372, 377
Culbertson, Mollie, 284
Culbertson, Nancy, 373, 378
Culbertson, Natawista, 10, 21, 42, 289, 372-8
Culbertson, Robert A., 378
Culbertson, Robert S., 115, 240, 274
Culbertson, Thaddeus, 76
Culver, Wm., 257
Cumming, Alfred, 24, 306, 375
Cummings, Thomas A., 117, 134, 273, 282, 391
Curley, Crow, 90
Curry, Kid (Harvey Logan), 133
Curry, Loney and Bob, 244
Cushman, Dan, 56, 146, 166
Custer, George A., 90, 154, 181, 315, 366
Customs Collector, 256, 272-3, 365
Cut Bank Creek, 4
Cypress Hills, 21, 81, 91, 99, 180, 230, 272, 358, 362-5

—DDD—

Dale, Ed, 390-1
Dacoteau,——, 7, 287
Dance & Stuart, 168
Dauphin, Antoine, 12, 304
Dauphin's Rapids, 12, 38, 53, 55, 63, 67-8, 71-2, 98, 125, 159
Davidson & Moffitt, 112, 121, 238, 274, 276
Davis, A. J., 244
Davis, Donald W., 361, 370
Davis Grocery, 237
Davis, Dr. Philip Chapman, 241
Dawson, Andrew, 12, 23-4, 27, 29, 40, 48, 157, 165-6, 197, 268, 295, 356, 375, 376
Dawson County, 76
Dawson, Thomas, 297
Davy's Wagon Train, 173
Day, Frank, 251
Dearborn River, 4, 21, 23, 26, 27, 266
Debow, Sam, 335
DeChamp, see Deschamps
Deer Lodge and County, 27-8, 41, 146, 165, 227
Deletraz, Gaspar Frank, 389
DeLorimier, Alfred O., 246
Dempsey, Hugh A., 362
Dennis, Mountain M. (Pomp), 196
Deschamps, Philip, 249
DeSmet, Fr. Pierre Jean, 15, 20, 82, 165-6, 264, 305, 314, 356, 371, 377
DeTrobriand, Gen. Philip, 311
Devereux, E. Jeff, 249, 272, 308, 362
Dexter, Wheeler O., 89, 103, 124, 129, 259, 275, 337
Diamond City, 50, 56, 147, 171

Diamond R (freighters), 42, 68, 77, 98, 163, 174-6, 178, 180, 229-30, 315, 359, 380
Dibbs, Dr. William, 46
Dickson, Joseph, 5
Dimon, Col. Charles, 51
Dixon, Joseph, 20
Doctors, 241-2
Donelson, Lt. A. J., 20, 22
Donnell, Robert W., 232, 360
Donnelly, John J., 95, 122, 255, 317
Doty, James, 22, 23, 24, 306
Doucett, ——, 10
Douglass, James, 240
Downey, James, 96, 317
Dreidoppel, David, 9, 303
Drew, John, 103
Drips, Andrew, 8
Drouillard, George, 4-6
Drowned Man's Rapids, 12
Druggists, 241-2
DuBose, Dudley, 256
Duer, Charles E., 107, 244
Duffin, R. M., 257, 262
Dugouts, see Mackinaws
Dumais, Michel, 127
Dumont, Eleanor (Madame Mustache), 241, 290
Dumont, Gabriel, 127-8, 129, 325
Duncan, Matt, 110
Dunn, Tom, 323-4
Dunn, Edward, 108, 122, 282
Durfee & Peck, 29, 79-81
Durfee, E. H., 78
Dutriueille, John Lambert (Duke), 251, 292
Dutro & Kielhauer, 111
Dutro, Dan, 257

—EEE—

Eades, William, 146, 165
Eagle Bird Saloon, 126, 250-1
Eagle Eye, 380
Eagle Rib, 8, 376
East Side Road, 180, 266
Eastman, F. H., 29
Eataphone Restaurant, 240
Edgerton, Sidney, 167, 263, 308, 340
Ege, Robert, 310
Elbow River Post, 77, 348, 358
Elections, 225
Electricity, 116, 135, 138-41, 276, 285
Elevator Saloon, 115, 249
Elite Saloon, 111, 247, 249
Ellingsen, John, 240
Enterprise House, 131
Episcopal Church, 265
Estes, Simeon, 168
Eureka Saloon, 249
Evans, John, 63, 95-6, 112, 122, 249, 272, 317, 341, 362

Evans, W. S., 78, 337
Everson, J. J., 362
Exchange Saloon, 249
Extradition Case, 364
Extradition Saloon, 249, 364

—FFF—
Faber, W. N., 350
Fairweather, Bill, 146
Fallon, Charles, 124
Farmer, Frank, 95-6, 317
Farmer, George, 107, 111
Farming, see Agriculture
Farrell, John, 389-90
Farrell, Patrick, 104, 272
Farwell, Abel, 132, 348, 358
Fergus, James, 321
Ferries, 26, 87, 99, 110, 180, 266-7
Fetterman, Capt. Wm. J., 323
Fey, Justus, 257
Fields, Joseph, Reuben, 3, 4
Finlay, Francois, 145
Fire engine, 99, 120
First National Bank, 107-8, 235, 243-4, 281
Fisher, Donald "Drunken", 131
Fisk, James Liberty, 26, 46, 165
Fisk, Robert, 190
Fisk Trail, 26
Fitch, John, 33
Fitzgerald, —, 46
Fitzpatrick, —, 301
Flanagan Drug Store, 89, 242
Flanagan, Elizabeth, 261, 290
Flanagan, May G., 140, 318
Flanagan, Michael A., 110, 241-2, 263, 281
Flatboats, 140
Flatheads, 5, 22, 306, 320, 375
Flora keelboat 9, 371
Flour Mill, 126, 277, 281
Flowerree, Daniel A. G., 103, 322, 324
Foley, Michael, 95, 316-7
Forbes, George W., 331
Ford, Robert, 323
Fort Assiniboine, 91, 101-3, 129, 134, 184, 367-8
Fort Belknap, 110, 121, 191
Fort Benton, early buildings, 269; incorporates, 120, 282; near demise, 273-7; survival, 140-2
Fort Benton Stages:
    to Assiniboine, 190-2;
    to Barker, 192;
    to Billings, 193, 335;
    to Helena, 90-2, 368;
    to Lewistown, 193;
    to Fort Macleod, 192, 264
Fort Benton, Volunteers, 94-5, 160, 316-7
Fort Benton, Legends, 379-90
Fort Benton Board of Trade, 108
Fort Benton Boom Co., 258
Fort Benton Building Assn., 112

Fort Benton Review, 236, 243
Fort Benton Sanitarium, 115, 237
Fort Bouis, 17
Fort Browning, 377
Fort Buford, 58, 63, 367
Fort Calgary, 362-3
Fort Campbell I, 15, 16, 36, 268
Fort Campbell II, 16-18, 23, 28, 36, 41, 269
Fort Chipewyan, 1
Fort Claggett, 95, 305
Fort Clay (Benton), 19, 305
Fort Conrad, 75, 120, 296
Fort Copelin, 52
Fort Custer, 154
Fort Edmonton, 15, 356, 361-5
Fort Ellis, 62, 173
Fort Floyd, 7
Fort Fox & Livingston, 14-5, 268
Fort Francis A. Chardon, 14, 16, 268, 305
Fort Gary, 356-7
Fort Hamilton (Whoop Up), 348, 357
Fort Hawley, 66, 196
Fort Jacobs, 52
Fort Keiser, 52
Fort Keogh, 111
Fort LaBarge, 41-42
Fort Laramie, 13-4, 20, 262, 372-3
Fort Lewis I, 14, 15, 264
Fort Lewis II (Benton), 16, 19, 305, 373
Fort Logan, 101
Fort Macleod, 131, 180, 263, 362-5
Fort Macleod Gazette, 363
Fort Manuel Lisa, 6
Fort McKenzie, 9-14, 34, 38, 164, 268, 302, 371
Fort Owen, 22, 145, 165, 375
Fort Peck, 67, 74, 76, 297, 377
Fort Piegan, 3, 8, 9, 34, 268, 301
Fort Shaw, 57, 62, 173, 341, 359
Fort Standoff, 77, 296, 348, 358
Fort Union, passim
Fort Walsh, 297, 363-7
Fort Whoop Up, 77, 347-8, 361, 363
Fort William, 17, 21
Foster, Wm., 250-1, 292
Fox & Livingston, 36
Fraser River, 1
Frechette, George Arthur, 95
Fredericks, C., 56, 149-50
Freighting, passim, 157-61, 163-87, 367-9
French, 1-2
French, George Arthur, 360-61
French-Canadian, 287-8
Friend, Franklin and George, 51
Frost, Todd & Co., 17, 28
Frush, Charles W., 261, 288
Fulton, Robert, 33
Fur post locations, 30-31
Fur trade, passim

—GGG—
Gallatin, Albert 3
Gallatin City, 266
Gallatin Road, 266
Galt, Alexander T., 131, 275
Gamble, John H., 247, 292
Gans & Klein, 111, 117, 121, 238, 274, 276-7, 285
Gans, Louis, 238
Garrison & Wyatt, 163, 319
Garrison, A. G., 69, 174, 176
Gass, Patrick, 3
Gem Saloon, 249
"Georgie", 251
Gerard, Frederick F., 77-9, 146, 176, 198, 230, 280
Gibb, Dr. William, 241
Gibbon, Col. John, 89, 90, 94, 315, 324, 337
Gibson, Paris, 104, 121, 124, 137, 184, 256, 274-5, 331, 389
Gilham, William, 124, 329
Gillette, W. C., 170
Gilmer & Salisbury, 81, 190-1, 257
Gilmer, John T., 190
Ginsberger, Solomon, 282
Gladstone, William, 46-7, 77, 157-8, 167, 198-9, 245, 248, 253, 269, 279, 323, 335, 348, 356-7
Glassman, William, 244
Glendive Creek, 49
Glenn, John, 360
Gold, 41, 45, 54, 56, 63, 145-52, 168-9, 171-2, 375
Gold Creek, 27, 41, 274
Gorman, James H., 195-6
Gorman, Tom, 69, 175
Grace, Ed, 358
Graham Wagon Road, 180, 266
Graham, William M., 20
Grand Union Hotel, 112, 117, 125, 140, 237, 240-1, 274-5, 283, 388-9
Grant, Dick, 120, 321
Grant, James, 120
Grant, John, 321
Grasshopper Creek, 146, 165
Gray, Raymond, 129-31
Gray, Robert, 1
Great Falls, 3, 4, 121, 124, 126, 129, 237, 262, 275
Great Northern RR, 21, 131, 193, 276
Great Slave Lake, 1
Green, John H., 135, 247, 284
Green, Madame Anna, 250
Greenleaf & Co., 328
Greg, Omar, 117
Grim, Slim, 68
Gros Ventres, 8-9, 11, 21, 23, 49, 158, 270-2, 299, 304, 310, 313-14, 374-5, 377, 381
Grouard, Frank, 196
Grover, Lt. Cuvier, 22

Gunsolis, Jim, 50
Guthrie, J. C., 247

—HHH—

Hale, Trevanian, 112, 227, 272, 362
Half Breeds, see Interracial
Halpin, Dennis, 227
Hamell, Augustin, 15-6, 21-2, 268, 288
Hamilton, Alfred B., 75, 177, 225, 231, 273, 309, 348, 357
Hamilton, William T., 171, 199, 225, 238-9, 246, 269-71, 309, 311, 326, 335, 340, 380
Hancock, Forrest, 5
Hancock, Julia, 2
Haney, Dave, 349
Hanson, Joseph Mills, 55, 149
Harber, W. J., 243
Harber, Wm. K., 123, 243
Hard, Charles, 71, 77, 132, 227, 272, 296, 358
Harden, Lt., 95, 316
Hardin, Martin, 39
Hardwick, Tom, 258, 272, 352, 362
Harkness, James, 42
Harkness, Margaret, 42, 289
Harper, Charles, 272, 362
Harris & Strong Stables, 106
Harris, Howell, 103, 258, 282, 328, 369
Harris, Jacob "Jew Jake", 133
Harris, John, 103, 129, 132, 137, 266, 324, 328, 369
Harvey, Alexander, 12-8, 36, 252, 268, 295, 304-5, 372-3
Harvey, Primeau & Co., 16-7, 21, 36
Hatch, Edwin C., 13, 37, 197, 289, 306, 375
Hauser, Sam T., 107, 244
Hawley, Alpheus, 29, 49, 51, 230
Hayden, Prof., 375
Haynes, F. Jay, 107, 257
Hazlett, H. J., 63
Healy & Co., 75
Healy, John J., 75, 95, 117, 133, 177, 227-8, 231, 234, 239, 242, 272-3, 289, 314, 317, 335, 348-9, 356-8, 363, 367, 380
Healy, Joe, 295, 380
Healy, Marie, 262, 289
Healy, Mary, 289
Healy, Thomas F., 122
Heavy Runner, 75, 174, 296, 309, 311, 377
Helena, passim
Helena Herald, 54, 61, 66, 67, 75, 87, 170, 227, 242
Hell Gate, 23, 26, 166
Hell Roaring Rapids, 87, 154
Henday, Anthony, 355
Henric, Chas., 174
Henry, Andrew, 6, 300

Hershfield, L. H., 107, 244
Highwood, 27, 55, 101, 124, 132, 233, 262, 266, 323-4, 335
Hiedman, —, 56
Higgins & Worden, 163
Higgins, C. P., 166
Higgins, W. W., 19, 28, 246
Hill, Harry, 107
Hill, H. B., 240
Hill, James J., 124, 275, 389-90
Hill, J. S., 191
Hill, Spanish Joe, 294
Hinchey, Dennis, 226
Hind Shot, 336
Hinkley, Wm. J., 291
Hirshberg & Nathan, 104, 247
Hirshberg, Joseph, 247
Hispanics, 294
Holladay, Ben, 147, 167, 189-90
Holmes, Thomas, 46, 165
Holterman, Jack, 378
Hong, 293
Horn, George, 350
Horness, —, 359
Horses, 133, 164-5, 299-300, 334-6
Hosmer, Hezekiah, 271
Hotels, 238-41
Houk, George W., 89, 192
Houston, John, 115, 253
Howard, Gen. Otis, 94, 316-8
Howard, Wm., 50
Howell, Major C. W., 145
Howell, Wm., 391
Howie, Neil, 340
Hubbard, Charles Price, 308
Hubbell, Hawley & Co. (NW Fur), 49, 51
Hubbell, James B., 29, 49, 51, 199, 230
Hudson's Bay Co., 1, 6-8, 12, 233, 300-1, 355-6, 358-60, 370
Hughes, Frank, 249
Hughes, James, 364
Humphreys, Bill, 39
Hunsberger, John, 107, 239
Hunt, W. H., 243, 256, 273
Hunt, Wm. P., 197; wife, 377
Hunt, Wilson, 34
Huntley, Charles C., 60, 66, 172-3, 189, 196, 257, 263
Hurdy gurdy, 249
Hutchins, Lt. Cyrus, 51, 339
Hutchinson, Abe, 47
Hynson, Bill, 271, 279, 384-5

—III—

Idaho, 20
Idaho Steam Packet Co., 47, 143
Ilges, Major Guido, 95, 182, 316, 367
Immel, Michael, 6, 300
Imoda, Fr. Camillus, 264, 359
Indians, passim; annuities, 20-27, 40, 47, 58, 78; agency, 27, 51

Ingram, Messrs., 71, 151
IOOF, 117, 126, 247, 274, 276
Interracial, 294-98
Irvine, Fannie Culbertson, 378
Isabel, Lee, 111, 250, 292
Ismert, Cornelius, 33

—JJJ—

Jackson, Charles, 110
Jackson, O. W., 262
Jacobs, John, 165-6
Jail, county, 112, 225, 227, 276
James Bros., 46
Jawbone, see Montana Central Rr.
Jefferson River, 5-6
Jefferson, Pres. Thomas, 2-3, 20
Jewell, Ben, 139
J. G. for I. G. Baker, 361
Joe the Spaniard, 196
Johnson, John "Liver Eating", 77, 196, 315, 348, 350, 358
Jones, Robert, 6, 300
Jones, William M., 124, 312
Joyce, William, 247, 329
Judith Basin, 58, 103, 196
Judith Council, 23-25, 306, 375
Judith River, 2, 12, 22, 57, 95, 132,375
Juneau, Antoine A., 77, 288, 348, 358
"Jungle", 248, 382

—KKK—

Kanouse, H. A. (Fred), 77, 225-7, 234, 254, 271-2, 348-9, 358-9
Kanouse, Jacob A., 122, 254, 261
Kaufman, Mose, 247
Keelboats, passim, 196-7
Keiser, John P., 46
Kelly, Ed, 246
Kelly, Samuel L., 282
Kennedy, John J., 112, 190, 246
Kennedy, Margaret, 358
Kennerly, Henry A., 24, 122, 226, 380
Kenney, J. H., 259
Kennon, Judge, 325
Kent, T. A., 172
Kercheval City, 58
Kerler, John, 234
Keyes, Chris, 326
King & Gillette, 42-3, 66, 157, 163-6, 170, 172, 174
King, James, 170
Kingsbury, A. W. (Ike), 328, 331
Kinney, Joe, 54
Kipp, James, 7-8, 11, 29, 288, 296, 301
Kipp, Joe, 75, 77, 112, 120, 234, 245, 255, 296-8, 311, 335, 348, 358-9
Kirkendall, Hugh, 68, 72, 77, 131, 163, 176, 311
Klein, Henry, 238

Kleinschmidt & Bro., 58, 93-4, 97, 99, 119, 121, 125, 163, 182, 237-8, 252, 275
Knight, Mrs. James, 289
Koble, Joseph K., 104, 272
Koch, Peter, 83, 178, 350-1
Kohlberg, Sam, 247
Kohrs, Conrad, 321
Kootenai Post, 6, 227, 348
Kountz Line, 144
Kountz, Wm. J., 78, 83-4, 98, 144, 178

—LLL—

LaBarge & Harkness, 40, 42, 45, 163-6, 271
LaBarge, John, 36-7, 40, 42, 47, 80, 99, 128
LaBarge, Mrs. John, 42
LaBarge, Joseph, 35, 40, 42-3, 45, 47-8, 62, 99, 128-9, 264
LaBarge, Pelagie (Mrs. Jos.), 289
Ladd, Ed, 351
LaBarre, Fred, 133
Lahey, "Lame Jack", 350
Lambert, John, 20
Lame Bull, 24, 303, 306
Lamme, Achilles, 155
LaMott, John, 112, 186, 192
Landusky, Pike, 133
Langford, N. P., 273
Lanning, Cash (Cassius), 245
Lapeyre, Benjamin E., 132, 242
Largent, John, 309
LaRocque, Francoise Antoine, 355
Larue, see L'Heureux
Lass, William, 83
Last Chance Gulch, 146
Latleur, —, 359
Latress, Jean, 9
Laurion, Joseph, 46, 253, 269, 288
Law enforcement 271-2
Lawyers, 254-6
Lee, Jim, 14, 16
Lee Gee, 293
Lee Sing, 293
Lee Wang, 293
Lemon, Bob and Jim, 42, 157, 166
Lehman, Dr. H. M., 241
Lepley, Mr. and Mrs. Charles, 241, 391
Lepley, John, 135, 276, 324, 326-8, 330
Lepper, Frank, 185, 251
Leveille, D., 263, 362
Leveille, Pierre, 362
Lewis & Clark, 1-3, 300, 339
Lewis, Ed, 186, 258
Lewis, George F., 258
Lewis, Pres(ton), 129, 333
L'Heureux, Jean (Larue), 356
Libby & Merrill, 331
Library, 120, 262
Lilly, John C., 111, 249
Lilly's Hall, 249

Lindiman, —, 56
Lisa, Manuel, 5-6, 34, 197, 294
Little Beaver, Alex. Culbertson
Little Dog, 21, 24, 120, 271, 295, 307-8, 311, 336, 381
Little, Jack, 107
Little Prickly Pear, 23, 66
Little Rockies, 125, 128, 381
Livestock, see cattle, horses, wool
Livingstone, Samuel H., 361
Lockwood, Dexter G., 242
Loder, Lt. Samuel H., 101
Lorne, Marquis of, 369
Lotts, Abraham, 51
Louisiana, 1, 2, 4
Lowell, James H., 226, 254, 261-2, 271
Lowry, M. P., 225
Lynch & Flynn, 267
Lynch, Mike, 110, 128, 267
Lyons, Henry, 51

—MMM—

Macauley, John, 120, 250
Macdonald, Henry, 124, 135, 196, 315, 331-2, 350
MacDonald, Peter, 121
MacInnes, Charles, 263, 345, 363
MacKenzie, Alexander, 1
Mackey, Rev. Elkanah, 264-5, 288
Mackey, Sarah Armstrong, 265, 288
Mackinaws, 35, 57, 147-52, 171, 198-201, 359
Maclay, Edgar Glenn, 68, 83, 107, 163, 181, 230, 237, 259, 347
Macleod, see Fort Macleod
Macleod Gazette, 263
Macleod, James F., 360-1, 367-8
Madame Mustache, see Eleanor Dumont
Madison, James, 3
Maguire, Lt. Edw., 97
Mahood, James, 51
Mandans, 2-5
Manitoba RR, see St. Paul, etc. or Great Northern
Mann, Jerry, 163, 169-70, 309
Maple Creek, 364
Maratta, Dan, 109, 186, 369
Marias River, passim
Marias Pass, 3, 21, 23
Mariner, Thomas, 139
Marsh, Grant, 55, 61, 78, 80, 84, 87, 90, 153-6, 384
Marsh, Orlando, 104, 272
Marshall & Gray, 249
Marshall & Wilson Elite, 111
Marshall, Louis T., 226, 247, 249
Martin, —, 10
Martin, Emanuel, 165
Martin, Henry, 51
Martin, Thomas H., 328-9
Martinsdale, 101, 192
Masonic Hall, 117, 246, 274-5

Massie, William, 45, 48, 52, 98, 171
Matt, Cyprian, 107
Maulding, W. S., 140
Maximilian of Wied, 9-11, 197, 303
Meagher County, 331
Meagher, Thomas F., 63, 171-2, 270, 308, 340, 381, 383-4
Medicine Line, 177, 359
Medicine Lodge Saloon, 175, 248, 272
Medicine Rock, 26, 27, 231
Mee, Isaac, Richard, Wm., 251
Meek, Joe, 165
Meffort, George, 351
Melton, B. A., 270, 380
Menard, Pierre, 6, 300
Mepham Bros., 55, 143
Mercier, Charles (Old Man Rondin), 288
Mercure & Laurion, 46
Merrick, George, 52
Methodist Church, 265, 386-7
Metis, 110, 129, 192, 320, 356, 364
Metropolitan Hotel, 239
Miles, Gen. Nelson, 317-8
Military, 20, 52, 57-8, 60-3, 67, 78, 81, 84-5, 89-91, 98, 110, 172, 339-43, 366
Milk River, 16, 21, 36, 52, 56, 58, 63, 64, 157-8, 167-8, 359
Miller, Alfred Jacob, 7, 300
Mills, Henry, 291, 384-5
Mills, Rev. Jacob, 265
Mills, Robert, 240
Milner Cattle Co., 325-6
Milner, Milton E., 324-6, 328, 391
Minar, Walter J., 111-7, 242, 389
Minnesota & Mont. Stage, see Northern Overland Pony Express
Missouri, 4, 6, 8
Missouri Fur Co., 6
Missouri River, passim
Missouri River Trans. Co. (Coulson), 78, 144
Mitchell, David D., 9-11, 288, 302, 371
Molchert, Sgt. Wm., 95, 316-7
Monroe, Hugh (Munro), 27
Montana & Idaho Trans. Co., 143
Montana Bar (gold), 56, 145
Montana Cattle Co., 276
Montana Central Rr., 131, 193, 266, 268, 276
Montana Hide & Fur Co., 66, 175
Montana Militia, 340
Montana Post, passim
Montana Wool Growers Assn., 121, 132, 136, 276, 330-4
Moore, Frank, 47, 51-52, 339
Morceau, —, 7, 287
Morgan, John R., 257, 271, 308, 340, 385
Mormons, 158, 268
Morrow, David, 324, 327-8

*400*

Morrow, Malcolm Sr., 324, 327-8
Morrow, Malcolm Jr., 324, 327-8, 391
Morrow, Stanley J., 257
Morrow, William, 284, 324, 328
Mortson, O. C., 138
Mountain Chief, 16-7, 75, 301, 305, 309-11, 377, 385
Mountain Men, 5, 6, 9, 12, 299, 301
Mudgett, Bill, 326
Mules, 164, 166-8, 175
Mullan (Military) Road, 22-28, 70, 165-6, 175, 266, 306, 374
Mullan, Dr. James A., 241
Mullan, Capt. John, 20, 22, 27, 28, 339, 374
Mulligan, Joseph, 136, 353
Murphy, Joseph, 164
Murphy, John, 174-5
Murphy Maclay & Co., 128, 237, 276-7, 285
Murphy Neel & Co., 97, 106, 108, 110, 164, 237
Murray, Mrs. Dena, 249, 290, 382
Musselshell Post, 58, 60, 66, 70, 115, 176, 196, 314-5, 349-53
Musselshell River, 2, 38, 50, 58, 63, 108, 314

—McMc—

McCartney, Valentine, 68
McCauley & Colgate Saloon, 391
McClellan, —, 57
McClellan, George, 20
McCormick, Washington J., 62
McDevitt, James, 257
McDonald, Finnan, 6
McDougall, Rev. George, 252, 324, 361
McDougall, Rev. John, 266, 349, 361
McFarland, Joseph, 368
McGregor, —, 69
McGregor River, 1
McIntyre, Neil, 111, 247
McKay, Dan, 253
McKenzie, Kenneth, 7, 9, 11, 34, 287, 301, 371
McLean, Sam, 62
McLean, W., 77, 348, 358

—NNN—

Nabors, James, 226-7, 239, 272
Natahki (Mrs. J. W. Schultz), 298
Natawista, see Culbertson
Nathan, Arge, 247
Neihoff, Henry, 129
Neubert, John, 258, 309
Nevitt, Dr. R. B., 362
New Orleans, 33
Newell, Bob, 165
Nez Perce, 93-96, 160, 182, 306, 315-18, 366-7, 388

Nicholson, Murray, 95, 317
Nickerson, Si, 193
Norris, Gilman R., 176
North Dakota, 2, 7
North West Co., 1, 6, 7, 300, 355
North West Fur Co., 28-9, 51-2, 58, 61, 67-8, 167, 174, 230, 271, 381
North West Mounted Police, 83-4, 102, 107-8, 111, 115-6, 159, 179-80, 232-3, 236, 280, 296, 359-70; always getting man, 367
Northern Montana Roundup Assn., 325, 330
Northern Overland Pony Express, 60-2, 66, 195-6, 263, 309, 341
Northern Pacific Railroad, 79-81, 98, 116, 119, 123, 154, 178, 184, 193, 235, 268, 274, 369-70
Northwest Passage, 1
Northwest Transportation Co. (Coulson), 78, 143-4, 174-5

—OOO—

Occidental Saloon 249
O'Connor, John, 115, 186
Odd Fellows, see IOOF
O'Hanlon, Thomas, 12
Ohlman, Lawrence, 46
Old Agency, 226
Old Man River, 358
Old Sorrel Horse, see Sol Abbott
Oliver, A. J. & Co., Stage, 147, 167
Oliver, Andrew Jackson 189, 263
Omaha, 24, 33, 63-4
One Eye, 13
O'Neill, James, 325
Ophir, 49-52, 58, 167, 270, 339
Ordway, John, 3-4
Oregon, trail & terr., 1, 6, 8, 19, 28, 57, 153, 163, 165-6
Osnes, Louie, 331
Osten, Billy, 351
Overland Hotel (Stafford), 79, 89, 107, 239, 247, 279
Overland Stage, 189
Owen, Charles (Longhaired), 124
Owen, John, 19, 22, 28, 163-5, 321, 336, 375
Owens, Ed, 193
Owens, George, 351
Oxen, passim

—PPP—

Pacific Hotel, 120-1, 240, 274
Page, Merrill C., 362
Park Stables, 108, 258
Parker, George B., 122
Patrick Colony, 116
Patterson, George, 121, 332
Patterson, John F., 134, 332-3
Payne, Rufus, 108, 185, 252-3
Peace River, 1

Pearson, W. H., 24-5
Pease, David Fellows, 29
Peck, C. K., 78
Peck, L. W., 332
Peck Line, 119
Peel, Langford, 63, 382-3
Pembrin, L. E., 313
Perie, James, 339-40
Perkins, S. Jeff, 226, 272
Pete Owl Child, 376
Pfouts, William, 168
Phoenix Saloon, 111, 250-1
Photographers, 256-7
Picotte & Co., J., 17
Picotte, Honore, 14, 17, 19, 372
Picotte, Joseph, 16-7, 268-9
Pioneer Harness Shop, 244
Point, Fr. Nicholas, 14-6, 19, 256, 264
Pomp's (Pompey's) Pillar, 3, 153
Pony Express, see Northern Overland
Poplar River, 35
Population, see Census
Postal, Benton, 60, 110, 131, 138, 190, 195-6, 262-3
Postal, Canadian, 263-4, 361-3
Potts, Andrew R., 13, 295, 385
Potts, Gov. Benj. F, 182
Potts, Jerry, 13, 166, 295-6, 319, 335, 360-1, 385-6
Potts, John, 5
Powell, Henry, 308
Power & Bro., T. C., 61, 79, 80-87, 95, 97, 103-4, 106, 108, 112, 115, 127-8, 163, 176, 178-9, 191, 233-6, 243, 273-4, 312, 358
Power, Charles B., 279
Power, John W., 98, 122, 191, 227, 233-6, 258-9, 263
Power, Sarah, 261
Power, Thomas C., 61, 79, 80, 140, 177, 193, 225, 227, 231, 233-6, 243, 279, 379
Powers, B. L., 192
Powers, J. M., 192
Pray, Charles N., 63, 255, 382
Presbyterian, 264-5
Price, Charles, 263, 324, 328
Price, James, 291
Prickly Pear, 26, 49, 54
Primeau, Charles, 16
Proctor, Virgil, 389
Promontory, Utah, 25, 70
Prostitution, 250-1
Protsman, Lee, 227
Pullitzer, Ralph, 298

—QQQ—

Quan Cafe, 293
Quantrill, William, 63, 382-3
Quong Chong, 293

*401*

## —RRR—

Racine, Baptiste, 279, 386
Radiator, Helena, 242
Railroads, general, 267-8, 282-3; proposal, 93; see by name
Ram, Jack, 9
Rattlesnake Jake (Charles Fallon), 124
Ravalli, Fr. Anthony, 330
Raven Quiver, see Joe Kipp
Raynolds, Capt. W. F., 37, 339
Rea, Tom W., 46, 50, 54
Record, see Benton Record
Red Cloud, 66
Red River Carts, 110, 165, 185, 321
Reed, A. S., 69, 375
Reeds Fort, 192
Reese, Tom, 13, 291, 304
Reeves, Barney, 358
Reno, Major Marcus, 90, 154, 359
Restaurants, 241
Rice, J. H., 258
Rice, J. R., 237
Riel, Louis, 95, 110, 127, 325, 331, 356
Riel Rebellions, 95, 127, 255, 357
Riplinger, John, 29
Riplinger Trail, 29
River Press, 108, 117, 126-7, 236, 238, 243, 274, 276
Riverside Cemetery, 115
Rivet, Louis, 23, 27
Robare, 296
Roberts, Mrs. George, 377-8
Rocky Boy Indians, 320
Rocky Mountain Fur, 6, 58
Rocky Mountain House, 300
Rocky Mountain Wagon Road Co., 171
Rocky Point, 125
Rocky River, 33, 38
Rocron, Leon P., 247
Roe & Co., 163, 271
Roe & Wall, 43
Roe, John J., 42, 68, 143, 153, 157, 173-4
Rolfe, Herbert P., 124, 256, 273, 275
Roosevelt, Ferdinand C., 63, 126-7, 239, 246-7, 258, 276, 282, 384
Rosche, Louis, 381-2
Rose, Alexander, 24
Rosebud River, 90
Rosencrans, Lucus H., 93, 244
Ross, John, 172
Rossiter, Raymond, 70
Rotten Belly, 11, 319, 371
Rowe Stage, Wm. & Co., 98, 191, 368
Rowe, Charles, 81, 122, 129, 181, 239, 290
Rowe, William, 103, 181, 191, 227, 239, 258, 272, 290, 384
Ruffee, Charles, 195
Russell, Charles M., 135, 327, 387
Rupert's Land, 355

Ryan & Dunphy, 103

## —SSS—

Sacagawea, 2-4
Saddle Makers, 244-5
St. Clare Hospital, 120, 126, 132-3, 265-6, 275-6, 281-2
St. Louis, passim
St. Mary's Mission, 19, 22, 165, 264, 321, 336
St. Paul, Minneapolis & Manitoba, 123, 131, 134-5, 137-8, 187, 268, 276, 389-90; also see Great Northern
St. Paul's Episcopal Church, 104, 265
St. Peter's Mission, 264, 309
Salisbury, Monroe, 191
Salisbury, Orange, 191
Salish House, 6; Indians 300
Saloons, 106, 247-51
Salsbury, Nate, 325
Sam Lee, 293
Sam Loy, 293
Sample, Asa, 225, 227, 271, 352
Sample Bros., 246
Sand Coulee, 262
Sandoval, Isadore, 9, 12-3, 304
Santa Fe Trail, 165
Saxton, Lt. Rufus, 20, 22
Sayre, E. Frank, 353
Schools, 93, 106, 126, 261-2, 283
Schlutter Wagon, 164
Schmidt, Jacob W., 239
Schultz, Hart Merriam (Lone Wolf), 298
Schultz, James Willard, 112, 296, 298, 359
Schwartz, John, 247
Scott, James, 227
Scott, Thomas, 357
Searles, Daniel, 236, 243
Searles, Mrs. Daniel, 284
Sedgwick, Mollie Culbertson, 240, 293, 378
Seifred, Alice, 255, 290
Senieur, Gustavus, 254
Severance & Co., 333
Seventh Cavalry, 317-8, 359, 366
Shannon, George, 3
Sharp, Paul, 352, 366
Shaw, Abner, 154
Shaw, Jimmy, 337
Sheep, see Wool
Sheran, Marcella, 368
Sheran, Nicholas, 368
Sheridan, Gen. Philip, 311
Sherman, Bill, 169
Sherman, Gen. W. T., 311, 316
Shirlow, Thomas, 191
Shoebotham, Thomas B., 242
Shonkin, 15, 112, 262, 324, 385
Shonkin Stock Assn., 124, 312, 324, 328-30, 390-1
Shoshones, 2, 3, 300

Silver City, 172
Silverthorne, John, 146, 375
Simms Bros., 174
Sing Lee, 293
Sinn Fein, 255
Sioux, passim, 172-5, 178-82, 313-15; in Canada, 365-9
Sitting Bull, 297, 366-7
Slade, Joseph, 43, 157, 166
Slave River, 1
Smallpox, 12-13, 36
Smith, Dick, 131
Smith, Ed, 87, 99, 110, 163, 266
Smith, Gov. Green Clay, 62-3, 225
Smith, J. S., 29
Smith, James, 172
Smith, Jane, 350
Smith, John R., 284, 293
Smith, Leonard L., 263; Bannack mail, 189
Smith, Yank, 132
Smithsonian Inst., 375
Snake Point, 42, 157
Snake River, 3
Sneath, John, 239
Snell & Co., 93, 96, 252-3
Snell, A. B., 252-3
Snell, H. B., 252-3
Solomon, Moses, 69, 175, 226, 248, 267, 272, 294, 348, 358, 380
Sorrel Horse, see Sol Abbott
Spain, 2
Spears, Wilfred D., 62
Sparks, William, 336
Spearson, Joseph, 51, 257, 270, 308, 386
Spencer, Charles, 282
Spitzee Cavalry, 358
Spitzee Post, 358
Squaw Hurdy Gurdy, 71
Stafford, Ben, 239
Stafford House, 239
Stables, 257-8
Stages, 98, 106, 115, 168, 189-93
Stanford, Alicia, 291
Stanley, David S., 154
Stanley, John Mix, 20, 21, 256
Star (or Starr), George, 295, 385
Steamboat - indexed separately following this index
Steele, Charles, 96, 317
Steele, Sir Sam, 345
Steell, see Carroll & Steell
Steell, George, 46, 69, 163, 229-30, 279, 296, 335, 380
Steve the Stutterer, 69
Stevens Expedition, 20-27, 36, 165, 374-5
Stevens, George, 140, 257
Stevens, Isaac I., 11, 20-27, 165, 305, 336, 339, 374-5
Stevens, James E., 243
Stevens, John F., 21
Stewart, Julius, 337
Stocking, John, 324

Stocking, Margaret, 239, 290, 324
Stocking, Winfield S., 117, 120, 225, 239, 246, 295, 310, 319, 324, 335, 385-6
Stockmen's National Bank, 244
Stone Child, 320
Storer & Storer, 107-8, 253
Storer, C. T., 253
Storer, G. D., 253
Story, Nelson, 322-3
Strachan, John, 26
Strong, Frank, 258
Stuart, Granville, 28, 56, 61, 110, 124, 135, 146, 149, 153, 165, 171, 238, 256, 262, 321, 351
Stuart, James, 28, 146, 262
Sturgis, Col: Samuel, 94, 316
Suckley, Dr. George, 20, 22, 241
Sullivan & Goss, 244-5
Sullivan, Jere, 107, 137, 240, 273, 282
Sullivan, Joseph, 239, 244-5
Sullivan Saddlery, 239
Sully, Gen. Alfred, 42, 45-9, 153, 166, 311, 314, 357, 376
Sun River, 4, 21-3, 26-7, 62, 167, 175, 190
Sun River Rangers, 324
Sun River Stampede, 308
Sunder, John, 17, 39
Sutherlin, Will, 164, 171
Sweet Grass Hills, 24, 83, 128, 131, 136, 360
Sweigert, Ben, 186, 284

—TTT—

Tabor, —, 69
Tattan, John W., 91, 95, 122, 239, 255, 261, 290, 317
Taylor, Harry "Kamoose", 363
Telegraph, 72, 103, 106, 273
Telephone, 108, 256, 273
Terry, Gen. Alfred, 61-2, 90, 154, 173, 195-6, 341, 367
Teton River, 4, 27-9, 262
Thomas, —, 69
Thomas, Charles, 308, 348, 358
Thomas, Mr. and Mrs. Harold, 241
Thompson, David, 6
Thompson, Frank, 227
Thrailkill, C. W., 258
Three Forks, 3, 5-6, 12, 300
Thwing House, 67-71, 174, 234, 239, 279-80
Thwing, Mrs., 239
Tibbitts, Dr. Roswell, 241, 289
Tibbitts, Hattie Jane, 289
Tibbitts, Mary Jane, 289
Tierney, Bernard, 111
Tingley, Clark, 122, 246, 262
Tinkham, A. W., 23
Todd, Joe, 136
Todd, John, 124, 154
Todd, Nelson, 124

Todd, Thomas, 285
Todd, Wesley, 124
Todd, William H., 236-7, 240, 243
Tom Mum, 293
Tong Fong, 293
Tonge, Kate B., 115, 291
Toponce, Alex., 163, 169-70, 309
Tough Town, 247-51, passim
Townsend, Thomas, 46
Trade goods, 29
Trails, see Benton Road, Cow Island, Fisk, Fort Walsh, Graham, Mullan, Whoop Up
Trainer, Ed, 115
Trojie, Jose Pablo, 294
Turner, John P., 365
Turner, Dr. W. C., 241
Turner, Dr. Will E., 241-2, 281
Tuttle, Rev. Daniel, 265
Tweedy, Thomas, 254
Two Medicine, 4

—UUU—

Union Fur (Fox & Livingston), 36
Union Pacific Railroad, 70, 79, 183, 191, 234
Upham, Hiram D., 51-2, 158, 168, 270, 352, 380
Upper Missouri Outfit (UMO), 7, 371-3
Upson, Gad E., 239, 270, 381
Utah & Northern Railroad, 94, 183-4, 234-5, 268

—VVV—

Van Gorp, Fr. L., 265, 387
Van Orsdel, William Wesley, 80, 265, 290, 316, 386-7
Vancouver Island, 2, 6
Vanderburgh, Henry, 8, 300-1
Vaughan, Alfred J., 24, 37, 307, 336, 375
Vaughn, Robert, 56, 178, 336
Vigilance Committee, 279
Vigilantes, 45, 124, 279, 308, 329, 335
Virginia City, 42, 50, 52, 57
Vizenir, John "Frenchy", 120, 250
Vogle, Philander, 364

—WWW—

Wachter, Dutch Fred, 77, 348, 358
Wackerlin, Hans J., 63, 115, 245, 274, 281, 382-3
Wade, Judge Decius, 271
Wagons, 174, passim
Walker, Major James, 361-2, 369
Wall, Nick, 42
Walter, Dave, 225, 271
War of 1812, 6
Ward, Dixie, 186
Warren, Gen. 375
Washington, 20, 22

Water Works, 138, 141, 276, 285
Waterman, Max, 256
Weatherwax, John D., 88, 123, 227, 234, 271, 363, 367
Weippert, George, 13
Wells Fargo Stage, 63, 110, 145, 150, 173, 190, 239, 247
Wells, James, 66, 95, 110, 196, 227
Welsh, Nicholas, 249
Westfall, Arnold, 245
Wetzel & Weatherwax, 79, 88, 234, 236-7, 280
Wetzel, W. Scott, 98, 107, 115, 122-3, 163, 247, 258, 275
Wheelock, Dr. James W., 242
Whisky, 8, 48, 75, 86, 158, 247-51, 345-53, 355; raid, 346-7
White Bird, 367
White Buffalo, 10
White, John, 146, 165
White Rocks, 3, 41, 48
Whitman, Marcus, 8, 301
Whoop Up, 81, 99, 180, 357, 359-60
Whoop Up Trail, 29, passim
Wilkins, Al, 249, 251, 272
Wilkins Trading Post, 251
Williams, H. C., 243
Williston, Judge Alonzo, 271
Willow Rounds, 16
Wilson, W. H., 253
Wilton, John R., 107-8, 115, 253-4, 275
Wimar, Carl, 256
Winters, 1871-2, 79; 1880-1, 110; 1886-7, 133-4, 283
Wiser, Peter, 5
Wolf Point, 37
Wolfers and Wolves, 133, 135-6, 177, 349-53
Wolff, James D., 253
Women, 1st white, 288-91
Wong Woo, 293
Wood, M., 174
Woodcutters, 67-8, 174, 314, 349-53
Woods, J. M., 63
Wool and Sheep, 99-107, 109, 121, 125, 128-9, 132, 134, 136, 139, 184, 276-7, 283, 285, 330-34
Woolston, George, 138, 276, 285
Worden, Frank, 28, 40, 166
Wray, J. F., 25
Wright, Bob, 39, 139
Wright, Thomas D., 243

—XYZ—

Yellowstone navigation, 153-6
Yellowstone river, 3, 6-7, 47, 81-2, 97, 109, 153, 375
Yogo Gulch, 107, 192
York, 3, 291
Young, John, 312

*403*

## STEAMBOAT INDEX

(Active boats are shown with page grouping, but are not necessarily named on every page of sequence, but major operation is. Some Yellowstone River boats are listed.)

### —AAA—
Abeona, 63, 64
Admiral Farragut, 71, 73, 74
Agnes, 55, 59, 63, 65
Alone, 42-3, 47, 49, 153, 166
Amanda, 58, 60
Amaranth, 62, 64, 65, 150
Amelia Poe, 55, 59, 64-9, 175
Andrew Ackley, 68-79
Antelope I, 36
Antelope II, 63-4, 67, 69, 71
Arkansas, 71, 74
Assinaboine, 34-5

### —BBB—
Baby Rose, 140
Belle of Peoria, 47, 49
Ben Johnson, 60-1, 64, 71
Benton I, 46-69, 157
Benton (Block P), 85-138, 154, 157
Bertha, "Scarred Wolf", 66-77
Bertrand I, 17
Bertrand II, 40
Big Horn I, 54-73
Big Horn II, 93-123, 154
Black Hills, 110-23
Butte, 101-23

### —CCC—
Carrie, 65
Carrie V. Kountz, 71, 76-7
Carroll, 87-92, 154
Centralia, 65
Chippewa, 17, 25-6, 37-40
Chippewa Falls, 47, 49, 153
City of Fort Benton, 129-31
City of Pekin, 65
C. J. Rankin, 154
C. K. Peck 94, 96, 102-13
Clermont, 16, 33, 36
Col. McLeod, 98-105, 160, 233
Colossal, 71, 73
Columbia No. 2, 68-76
Converse, 53
Cora, 54, 59-72, 148
Cutter, 47-53, 167

### —DDD—
Dacotah, 101-23
David Watts, 53, 55, 59
Deer Lodge, 50-77, 148, 158, 167
DeSmet, 82-3, 264
Dora, 65
Dr. Burleigh, 91

### —EEE—
Eclipse, 99-139
Effie Deans, 47-9, 52-3
E. H. Durfee, 78-100, 154
El Paso, 36
Emilie LaBarge, 41-2, 62
Emily, 113-23
Esperanza, 80-83

### —FFF—
Fannie Ogden, 46, 49, 52-3
Fanny Scott, 71
Fannie Tatem, 94, 97
Fanny Barker, 66-73
Far West, 78-119, 153-4
Favorite, 55, 59
Flirt, 73, 76, 78-9, 176
Florence, 17, 42, 46
Florence Meyer, 154
Fontenelle, 80-104
F. Y. Batcheler, 102-39, 154-5

### —GGG—
G. A. Thompson, 63, 64
Gallatin, 55-65, 148-50
G. B. Allen, 71
General Brooks, 36
General C. H. Thompkins, 105, 110
General Custer, 94, 97
General Grant, 47-54, 154
General C. W. Meade, 87-119, 155
General Sherman, 103-19, 154-5
General Sully, 71, 74
General Terry, 65, 100-19, 136-9
Gold Finch, 55, 59, 148
Guidon, 62, 64, 67, 69, 150
G. W. Graham, 54, 65

### —HHH—
Hattie May, 53
Helena I, 55, 59
Helena (Block P), 98-139, 155
Henry Adkins, 67, 69, 71
Henry C. Yeager, 77
Hiram Woods, 68, 70
Huntsville, 55-73, 150

### —III—
Ida Fulton, 63, 65
Ida Rees, 68-79
Ida Stockdale, 61-84, 150
Imperial, 63, 65, 150-1
Importer, 68, 69, 71, 72, 151
Independence, 33
Iron City, 55, 59, 148
Island City, 47, 49, 153

### —JJJ—
James H. Trover, 61, 65

Jennie Brown, 58, 60, 63, 65
Jennie Lewis, 58, 60, 71
John M. Chambers, 98-100
Josephine, 82-140, 154-5
Judith, 131-4, 38

### —KKK—
Kate Kearny, 52-3
Kate Kinney, 94, 97
Katy P. Kountz, 77-97
Key West I, 26, 39, 41-2
Key West II, 82-119, 153

### —LLL—
Lacon, 67-9, 71, 73
Lady Grace, 63, 65, 233
Last Chance, 65
Leni Leoti, 68, 70
Lexington, 57-8, 60
Lillie Martin, 52-3, 55, 59
Lilly, 63, 65
Little Rock, 63, 65
Luella, 55-6, 59, 63, 65, 148-9

### —MMM—
Malta, 36
Mandan, 140
Marcella, 46, 55, 59
Marion, 55, 59
Mary McDonald, 58, 60, 80-1
Mary McKelon, 58, 60
May Lowry, 77, 84, 86
Miner, 55-79, 150, 159
Minnie Heerman, 107-8
Missouri, 129-30, 136, 139
Mollie Dozier, 54-5, 59, 148
Mollie Ebert, 71, 73, 74
Mollie Moore, 77, 82-3
Montana I, 58, 60
Montana II, 101-2-3-4
Mountaineer, 61, 64, 67, 69, 71, 73

### —NNN—
Nellie Peck, 78-119
Nellie Rogers, 43, 55, 59, 157, 166
New Orleans, 33
Nick Wall, 71, 73, 76-7
Nile, 61-72
Nimrod, 36
Nora, 65
North Alabama, 66-73
Nymph No. 2, 63, 65

### —OOO—
Octavia, 62-9, 150-1
O.K., 140
Only Chance, 55-73, 148, 151
Ontario, 55, 58, 59, 60
Osceola, 155

## —PPP—
Paragon, 65
Peninah, 67-108, 153-5
Peter Balen, 55, 59, 71-3, 148
Platte, 36
Prairie State, 53

## —RRR—
Red Cloud, 94-119
Richmond, 63, 65, 382-3
Roanoke, 53
Robert Campbell I, 20
Robert Campbell II, 42-3, 50
Rosebud, 98-139, 154-5
Rubicon, 56-8, 60

## —SSS—
St. Ange, 19, 36
St. John, 52-73, 147-8
St. Luke, 67, 68, 69
St. Mary, 24, 37
St. Peter, 12, 36
Sallie, 67-77
Sam Gaty, 52-3
Savanna, 154
Shreveport, 40-3, 146, 157
Silver Bow, 71-3, 76
Silver City, 94, 97, 154
Silver Lake, 65-91, 154
Sioux City, 76, 80-1, 96
Spread Eagle, 37, 39, 41
Stonewall, 59, 148
Success, 67-70, 151
Sunset, 59, 65

## —TTT—
Tacony, 55-65, 74, 76, 148
Tamerlane, 36
Tempest, 71-2-3
Thomas Stevens, 55-70
Trapper, 36
Twilight, 17, 37, 52-3

## —UUU—
Unknown boat 1867, 65
Urilda, 68, 70, 71
Utah, 71, 73

## —VVV—
Viola Belle, 63-77

## —WWW—
Walter B. Dance, 55-64, 153, 249
Waverly, 54-64, 148
Welcome, 46, 47, 49
West Wind, 42
Western, 79-100, 154
Western Engineer, 33
W. J. Behan, 123

Wm. J. Lewis, 54, 59, 148
Wyoming, 102, 116, 118-9

## —YYY—
Yellowstone I, 28-33
Yellowstone II, 45-53, 147, 153, 157-8
Yellowstone III, 90-100, 154-5
Yorktown, 61, 64, 69, 233

## —ZZZ—
Zephyr, 63, 65